The Global Challenge

The Global Challenge

International Human Resource Management

Second Edition

By Paul Evans
INSEAD

Vladimir Pucik
IMD

Ingmar Björkman
Hanken School of Economics

McGraw-Hill Irwin

McGraw-Hill
Irwin

THE GLOBAL CHALLENGE, SECOND EDITION

Published by McGraw-Hill, a business unit of The McGraw-Hill Companies, Inc., 1221 Avenue of the Americas, New York, NY 10020. Copyright © 2011 by The McGraw-Hill Companies, Inc. All rights reserved. Previous edition © 2002. No part of this publication may be reproduced or distributed in any form or by any means, or stored in a database or retrieval system, without the prior written consent of The McGraw-Hill Companies, Inc., including, but not limited to, in any network or other electronic storage or transmission, or broadcast for distance learning.

Some ancillaries, including electronic and print components, may not be available to customers outside the United States.

This book is printed on recycled acid-free paper containing 10% post consumer waste.

1 2 3 4 5 6 7 8 9 0 DOC/DOC 1 0 9 8 7 6 5 4 3 2 1 0

ISBN 978-0-07-353037-6
MHID 0-07-353037-9

Vice President & Editor-in-Chief: *Brent Gordon*
VP EDP/Central Publishing Services: *Kimberly Meriwether David*
Publisher: *Paul Ducham*
Managing Developmental Editor: *Laura Hurst Spell*
Associate Marketing Manager: *Jaime Halteman*
Senior Project Manager: *Lisa A. Bruflodt*
Design Coordinator: *Brenda A. Rolwes*
Cover Designer: *Studio Montage, St. Louis, Missouri*
USE Cover Image Credit: *Chad Baker/Getty Images RF*
Production Supervisor: *Nicole Baumgartner*
Media Project Manager: *Suresh Babu*
Compositor: *S4Carlisle Publishing Services*
Typeface: *Palatino 10/12*
Printer: *R.R. Donnelley*

All credits appearing on page or at the end of the book are considered to be an extension of the copyright page.

Library of Congress Cataloging-in-Publication Data

Evans, Paul, 1946-
The global challenge : international human resource management / by Paul Evans, Vladimir Pucik, Ingmar Björkman.—2nd ed.
   p. cm.
   Includes bibliographical references.
   ISBN 978-0-07-353037-6 (alk. paper)
   1. International business enterprises—Personnel management. I. Pucik, Vladimir. II. Björkman, Ingmar III. Title.
HF5549.5.E45E93 2010
658.3—dc22
                                        2009040820

www.mhhe.com

Contents

PREFACE   xv

ACKNOWLEDGMENTS   xvii

ABOUT THE AUTHORS   xix

1   The Challenges of International Human Resource Management   1

Overview   3

Defying Borders: What's New?   4

International Operations in the Pre-industrial Era   4

The Impact of Industrialization   5

Prelude to the Modern Era   7

The Modern Multinational   11

Staffing for International Growth   12

Organizing for International Growth   12

HRM Goes International   17

Enter Globalization   21

The Roadmap for Managing Globalization   24

The Transnational Solution   26

Capabilities and Knowledge as Sources of Competitiveness   28

Toward a Flat World?   29

v

The Evolution Of International HRM   31

Outline Of This Book   34

2   Human Resource Management in the International Firm: The Framework   42

Overview   43

Business Strategy And Organizational Capabilities   44

Organizational Capabilities   45

Organizational Capabilities in Multinational Firms   48

The HR Wheel   49

Setting the Guiding Principles   50

Designing Core HR Practices   56

Defining the HR Function Roles   59

Focusing on Organizational Outcomes   62

Three Stages Of HRM In Multinational Firms   64

Building HRM: Focus on Foundations   66

Realigning HRM: Focus on Strategic Change   67

Steering with HRM: Focus on Dualities   71

3   Becoming Locally Responsive   81

Overview   83

Roots Of Responsiveness   83

Business Advantages of Local Responsiveness   85

People Challenges of Local Responsiveness   87

Implementing Localization   88

Overcoming Barriers to Management Localization   90

Localization Starts at the Head Office   93

Understanding Diversity   96

Know Yourself and Others: The Cultural Perspective   96

Know Where You Are: The Institutional Perspective   104

Know Whom You Talk To: The Network Perspective   112

What Shapes Local Responsiveness?   115

The Limits Of Responsiveness   117

Local Responsiveness Does Not Necessarily Mean Playing by Local Rules   117

4   Achieving Global Integration   123

Overview   124

The Logic Of Global Integration   125

The Business Advantages of Global Integration   126

The Tools for Global Integration   128

Global Integration and the Use of Expatriates   130

Global Standardization   131

Mastering Expatriation   137

The Evolution of Expatriate Management   137

Understanding the Expatriate Phenomenon   138

Managing International Transfers   142

Beyond The Traditional Expatriate Model   152

The Tensions in the Expatriate Cycle   152

Changing Demographics of the Expatriate Population   154

The Changing Nature of International Assignments   157

Alternatives to Expatriation   158

The Limits Of Global Integration   161

5   Structuring Global Coordination   170

Overview   171

From Vertical Control To Horizontal Coordination   172

Emergence of Coordination   173

Horizontal Coordination Mechanisms   176

Multidimensional Structures   179

Emerging Forms of Global Multidimensional Structures   180

Lateral Steering Tools   187

The Benefits of Lateral Steering   187

Lateral Leadership Roles   188

Lateral Steering Groups   192

People Strategies Supporting Lateral Steering   196

Building Cross-Border Teams   197

Mapping Cross-border Teams   198

Foundations for Global Teamwork   199

Working in Cross-Border Teams   204

Implementing Global Teamwork   208

Matrix Everything . . . Except the structure   211

6   Building Social Architecture   217

Overview   218

Leveraging Social Capital   219

What Is Social Capital and Why Do We Care About It?   220

How to Build and Manage Social Capital   224

Managing the Darker Side of Social Capital   228

Sharing Values Globally   230

Shared Values, Beliefs, and Norms   231

Building Shared Values   233

Challenges in Managing Organizational Culture   239

Leveraging Global Mindsets   240

What Is Global Mindset?   242

How to Develop Global Mindset   245

Rethinking the Global Mindset Paradigm   249

7   Managing Global Talent: Recruitment, Selection, and Retention   255

Overview   256

What Is Talent Management And Why Is It So Important?   257

What Do We Mean by Talent?   258

Why Is Talent Management so Important?   259

Key Challenges In Talent Management   263

The Talent Management Mindset   264

The Balancing Acts in Talent Management   265

Managing Recruitment   269

Forecasting the Need for Recruitment   269

Reaching out to Attract Talent   269

Global Employer Branding   272

Building a Differentiated Employee Value Proposition   273

Managing Selection And Assessment   275

    Selection Methods: The Importance of Context   276

    Selection and Diversity Management   278

    Competencies: Frameworks for Selection and Talent Management   280

    The Challenges of Internal Selection (Assessment of Potential)   285

Managing Retention   289

    Why Do People Leave and What Can be Done About It?   290

Balancing Short And Long Term In Talent Management   294

8   Developing Global Leaders   301

Overview   302

Global Leadership   303

    How Does Leadership Relate to National Culture?   304

    Global Leadership Competencies   307

    Leadership Passages: Intransitivity   309

The Principles Of Global Leadership Development   311

    Challenge is the Starting Point   312

    People Risk Management   316

Managing Leadership Development Top-Down   320

    Identifying and Assessing Potential   322

    Dilemmas in Identifying and Assessing Potential   324

    Challenges in Developing Potential   328

Managing Development Bottom-Up: Open Job Markets   332

    Making Self-Management Work   334

How Leadership Development Supports Global Coordination   338

9   Global Performance Management   346

Overview   348

The Global Performance Management Cycle   348

    What Is Global Performance Management?   349

    The "Upstream" Side of Performance Management   351

    The "Downstream" Side of Performance Management   358

Supporting Global Coordination   367

   Enabling Lateral Steering   368

   Appraising and Rewarding Teamwork   370

Performance Management Of International Employees   372

   Appraising Performance of International Staff   373

   Compensation of International Staff   375

Implementing Global Performance Management   381

   Who "Owns" Performance Management?   382

   Global Approach Versus Local Adaptation   383

   Creating Differentiation   384

10   Managing Knowledge and Innovation Across Borders   391

Overview   393

Sharing Knowledge In The Multinational   394

   Factors Influencing Knowledge Sharing   395

   How to Stimulate Knowledge Sharing   399

Knowledge Sharing In Professional Service Firms   405

   Three Configurations of Professional Service Firms   406

   Tensions in the International Professional Service Firm   410

Knowledge Acquisition   411

   Gaining Access to External Knowledge   411

   Knowledge Retention   415

From Ideas To Innovations   416

   Paradoxes in How to Encourage Promising Ideas   416

   The Organization and Staffing of R&D Centers   420

   Stages in the Innovation Journey   422

Dualities Of Exploration And Exploitation   426

11   Facilitating Change in Multinational Organizations   433

Overview   435

The Arduous Route To Transnational Organization   436

   Spiral Evolution of the Multidomestic Organization   437

Encouraging Subsidiary Initiative in the Meganational   444

Organize One Way, Manage the Other Way   449

Implementing And Executing Business Plans Through People   450

Challenges of Managing Change   451

Gaining Acceptance through Fair Process   452

The *Five E* Framework   454

The Tensions behind Fair Process and the Five Es   462

The Role of HR in Leading Change   463

Building Organizational Agility   467

Developing Strategic Sensitivity   467

Building Leadership Unity and Collective Commitment   468

Resource Flexibility   469

Agility Means Riding the Ups and Downs   470

12 Managing Alliances and Joint Ventures   476

Overview   477

The Whys And Whats Of Alliances   478

Alliance Business Drivers   478

Understanding Alliances   480

Planning And Negotiating Alliances   485

HRM Issues in Developing an Alliance Strategy   486

Preparing for Negotiations   491

Negotiation Challenges in Joint Venture Formation   492

Implementing Alliances   496

Managing the Interfaces with the Parent   496

Human Resource Management Issues in Managing the
Alliance   498

Supporting Alliance Learning   507

Obstacles to Alliance Learning   508

HRM Foundations for Effective Alliance Learning   512

The Evolving Role Of Alliances   517

Managing Network Boundaries   517

Alliances as Journey toward Transnationalism   519

13   Forging Cross-Border Mergers and Acquisitions   525

Overview   527

The M&A Phenomenon   527

  The Drivers of Mergers and Acquisitions   529

  Observing the M&A Experience   531

  A Framework for Thinking about M&As   534

  Key Human Resource Management Issues   537

From Planning To Closing   539

  Planning Acquisitions: The HRM Perspective   540

  The Due Diligence Process   541

  The Human Capital Audit   543

  Cultural Due Diligence   544

  Closing the Deal   546

The Post-Merger Integration Process   547

  The M&A Integration Agenda   547

  Managing Post-Merger Integration   550

  People Challenges of Post-Merger Integration   555

M&A As Organizational Capability   561

  Learning from Acquisitions   561

  From Learning to Action   563

14   Transforming the Global Human Resource Role   570

Overview   571

What Is Unique About The Global HR Function?   572

Organizing Global Human Resources   574

  HRM Process and Content Development   574

  HR Service Delivery   577

  Business Support   582

Where Are The Boundaries Of HR?   585

  The Responsibilities of Local, Regional, and Global Units   585

  Where Is the External Boundary of HR's Responsibilities?   587

  The Responsibility for HRM—Line Managers or HR?   589

Developing The Capabilities Of The HR Function   590

    HR Competencies   590

    Developing HR Managers for the Transnational Firm   593

Global Challenges Worth Standing Up For   596

    Building a Competitive Culture   596

    Organizational Sustainability   598

    Fighting for the Long-term Perspective   599

    The Social Implications of Globalization   601

HRM As Tension Management   604

BIBLIOGRAPHY   612

NAME INDEX   659

SUBJECT INDEX   675

Preface

Globalization has reshaped our world, and it will continue to do so—witness the growing presence of China, India, and other emerging countries on the world economic scene in the years since the first edition of this book in 2002. Financial markets are increasingly interdependent, with dramatic consequences for the volatility of the world economy, while advances in information technology have facilitated the globalization of knowledge. With money and other tangible assets becoming increasingly global and accessible, it is natural that companies are looking to people as a source of market differentiation.

Faced with the ever-increasing requirements to do things better, cheaper, and faster, the ability to coordinate effectively and to mobilize human resources across boundaries becomes critical. Attracting and developing future global leaders is high on nearly every CEO's agenda. The battle to grow and prosper in emerging markets is to a great extent over talent—and here foreign multinationals face the need to accelerate localization of management just as the fast-growing locals firms need to enhance their global leadership competencies. Therefore, most business executives and management scholars agree that the ability to manage human resources is crucial if multinational firms are to meet successfully the challenges they are facing in the dynamic and competitive global environment.

As a consequence of globalization, in multinational corporations strategy, organizational capabilities, and people management are increasingly intertwined. Therefore, we set the stage for this book by framing international human resource management from a *general management perspective*.

Each chapter in this book is a stand-alone guide to a particular aspect of international human resource management—from the history of international human resource management in the first chapter to the functional implications for human resource professionals in the last; from managing the human side of cross-border acquisitions to building multinational coordination.

The issues presented in the first edition of this book have been updated throughout with new information from research and practice. We build on the traditional agenda of international human resource management—*expatriation,* how to respond to *cultural and institutional differences,* and *global leadership development*—as well as exploring how companies continue to grow through *mergers and acquisitions,* where value depends greatly on the people challenges of integration, and how *cross-border alliances* are part of the fabric of organizational life.

However, readers familiar with the previous edition will notice that in order to address the emerging challenges of people coordination, talent and knowledge management, and the underlying dynamics of change, we have substantially revised the structure of our book, adding several new chapters:

- Reflecting competitive demands, the organization of multinational companies is increasingly multidimensional. If stultifying bureaucracy is to be avoided, firms must rely on *lateral leadership* roles to create alignment. *Cross boundaries teams* in different shapes and forms become the basic unit of the multinational firm, so we devote one chapter to discussing HRM issues related to such mechanisms of horizontal coordination.
- In an increasingly networked world where talented people have many career options, social capital and organizational culture—shared values, beliefs, and norms—are the binding glue. Global mindset also helps resolve the inevitable tensions embedded in international business. Thus, we discuss how HRM contributes to the *social architecture* of the multinational firm.
- We summarize the latest evidence from research and corporate practice regarding how the *core global human resource management processes*—from talent attraction and selection, to leadership development and performance management—need to be redesigned to support the needs of global organization.
- Knowledge management in multinational firms is largely a people game. Social networking opens up tremendous possibilities for *global knowledge sharing* and *the management of innovation.* Multinational firms are learning how to capitalize on this—with new opportunities for HR to make a contribution.
- We build on the experience of leading firms to present a framework for HR to support the process of change. *Implementing rapid change* globally is often an enormous challenge in a complex multinational. Line managers have to pay close attention to the how's of change, as well as the what's– and the line looks to their HR managers for guidance.
- We address the issue of how multinational firms are globalizing their HR function and practices. How can they build worldwide consistency while respecting the realities of local environments? At the same time, the HR function is undergoing a profound transformation, built around e-HR, self-help, and shared services, while deepening its business support role.
- Most fundamentally, we address the question of how firms can cope with the *"both/and" dualities* that underlie international management? That is, how can firms be both local and global in their orientation to human resource

management, capable of exploiting capabilities today while developing talent for tomorrow, integrating worldwide operations while at the same time encouraging local entrepreneurship?

Addressing these issues means that instructors, students, and practitioners have to go beyond a narrow functional perspective on international human resource management. While keeping a clear focus on HRM, we wanted to combine the leading edge of practice with the state-of-the art in theory, building on research in strategy, international management, organizational theory, and cross-cultural management, among other domains. Indeed, we argue that what is exciting about the international human resource management field is that it must be interdisciplinary in its orientation.

Our teaching, research, and consulting has taken place more or less equally over the years in North America, Europe, and Asia, and to a lesser extent South America and Australia. Therefore, our intention has been to write a book on such issues that is genuinely international in its orientation. The cases we use to introduce each chapter cover the globe, as do our examples from corporate practice–Nokia and Nestlé from Europe, GE and eBay from North America, Haier and Cemex from emerging countries.

The material presented in *The Global Challenge* is designed for use on advanced undergraduate, MBA and masters-level courses, as well as executive programs at business schools and in companies. We strive to provide practical advice, built on the experience of leaders and organizations as well as research, but we aspire to more than that. Our objective is to help people to understand the mindset, the deeper set of attitudes, needed to thrive in a world that is increasingly characterized by paradox and duality.

We hope that human resource professionals will find this book to be helpful in providing new insights and actions as they face up to the paradoxes of their field. We also hope that our academic colleagues will be stimulated by the way we have attempted to frame this area.

ACKNOWLEDGEMENTS

A book such as this builds on the insights, experiences, and research of many people.

First, we would like to thank the executives from the numerous companies that we have worked with over the last thirty years, who have shared their experiences and views during teaching seminars, research studies, consulting projects, forums and conferences. If we were to single out a few, they would include ABB, Canon, General Electric, Haier, Nokia, Shell, Schlumberger, and Toyota. We extend particular thanks to Rick Brown, John Herbert, John Hofmeister, Hugh Mitchell, Gary Steel, Hajime Tsuruoka, Yukio Yamashita, and Zhang Ruimin.

We have intellectual debts to pay to many academic colleagues and friends. Some of the foundation concepts underlying this book were laid down by Chris

Bartlett and the late Sumantra Ghoshal, as well as Yves Doz, C.K. Prahalad and the late Gunnar Hedlund, and also James March and Charles Hampden-Turner. In the human resource management field, we owe particular thanks to Dick Beatty, John Boudreau, Chris Brewster, Wayne Brockbank, Julian Birkinshaw, Pawan Budhwar, Mats Ehrnrooth, Carl Fey, Lynda Gratton, Gareth Jones, Steve Kerr, Henrik Holt Larsen, Ed Lawler, Jon Lervik, Kristiina Mäkelä, Mark Mendenhall, George Milkovich, Dana Minbaeva, H.J. Park, Adam Smale, Scott Snell, Paul Sparrow, Günter Stahl, Jennie Sumelius, Vesa Suutari, Betania Tanure, Dave Ulrich, Denice Welch, and Pat Wright. Thanks also go to Ulf Andersson, Wilhelm Barner-Rasmussen, Henri-Claude de Bettignies, Michael Brimm, Dan Denison, Mats Forsgren, Charles Galunic, Martin Gargiulo, Ludo van der Heyden, Peter Killing, André Laurent, Stefanie Lenway, Don Marchand, Jean-Francois Manzoni, Martha Maznevski, Tom Murtha, Torben Pedersen, Rebecca Piekkari, Joe Santos, Ed Schein, Susan Schneider, Janne Tienari, Eero Vaara, Zhixing Xiao, Katherine Xin, Tatiana Zalan, and Udo Zander. Special thanks also goes out the following reviewers who offered excellent feedback on this title: Thomas H. Stone, Oklahoma State University; Robert A. Figler, University of Akron; and Donna E. Ledgerwood, University of North Texas.

Thanks also for the encouragement and patience of our able editor Laura Spell, as well as Lori Bradshaw and the rest of the McGraw-Hill crew. A number of people provided great support in editing the final manuscript: Sylvia Ischer, Beverley Lennox, Lindsay McTeague, Michelle Perrinjaquet, and Sally Simmons. Their commitment and care was invaluable. We take this opportunity to express our appreciation to Alexandra Cappadoro at INSEAD and Anne-Marie Tassi at IMD who have shared all the trials, tribulations, and joys of this project. We would also like to thank Linus Hielm-Dahlberg for his editorial help, and Vanavan Jayaraman for his adept coordination of the production process. Ingmar Björkman would further like to thank the Finnish Funding Agency for Technology and Innovation (No. 53/31/08), the Academy of Finland (No. 122402), and H.C. Marcus Wallenbergs Stiftelse för företagsekonomisk forsking for financing his work on this book.

And finally there is the deepest of thanks for the constant and loyal support of our families. For Paul, Bente has made many adjustments and some sacrifices over these last years, supporting him with infinite patience, for which he is grateful beyond measure. For Vlado, Hoan has yet again lived with this project, now come to fruition, for longer than they would care to remember. For Ingmar, Anna has patiently looked forward to the dinner invitation that finally marked the end of the project and the possibility of spending more time together with Troy and Egil.

About the Authors

Paul Evans is the Shell Chaired Professor of Human Resources and Organizational Development and Professor of Organizational Behavior at INSEAD in Fontainebleau, France, and Singapore. British by nationality but raised in Africa, he has a PhD in Management and Organizational Psychology from MIT, an MBA from INSEAD, a Danish business diploma, and he is a graduate in law from Cambridge University. He has led INSEAD's activities in the field of international human resource management for many years, directing many of their executive programs in this domain. He was titular professor at the European Institute for Advanced Studies in Management in Brussels, and he has taught at Boston University, MIT, l'Université de Montréal, Skolkovo Moscow, Stockholm School of Economics, the University of Zurich, and Cornell University, among other schools, as well as spending periods as visiting scholar at the University of Southern California, UC Berkeley, and as visiting professor at London Business School. His research interests focus on international human resource management, leadership and the management of change, while his long-standing intellectual interest is in the dualities that underlie human and organizational behavior. Among his books are a pioneering study of the relationship between the professional and private life of executives, *Must Success Cost so Much?* (translated into seven languages), and the first book on international HRM, *Human Resource Management in International Firms: Change, Globalization, Innovation*. Former board member of the Human Resource Planning Society, he is the founding board member of the European Human Resource Forum (EHRF), a project-oriented network with 120 corporate members. He received an "outstanding teacher of the year" award from INSEAD's MBA students for his course on IHRM, and he has worked as an advisor or directed/taught programs for more than 120 multinational corporations.

Vladimir Pucik is Professor of International Human Resources and Strategy at IMD in Lausanne, Switzerland. Born in Prague, Czech Republic, where, after trained as a software engineer, he studied international economics, law, and political science. He continued his studies in the US, where he received MIA in international affairs (specializing in East Asia) and Ph.D. in business administration from Columbia University in New York. Before joining IMD, Professor Pucik held faculty appointments at the Graduate School of Business, University of Michigan and at the Industrial and Labor Relations School, Cornell University. He has also held a number of visiting appointments in universities around the world, including INSEAD, with three years as a visiting professor at Keio and Hitotsubashi universities in Tokyo. Professor Pucik's research interests include global people strategies, international dimensions of human resources and organizations with a particular emphasis on China and Japan, and implementing M&A and strategic alliances. He has published extensively in academic and professional journals, such as *Academy of Management Review, Harvard Business Review, Human Resource Management, Human Resource Planning, Journal of Applied Psychology, Strategic Management Journal*, as well as contributed to a number of books and monographs in the area of international business and human resource management. He currently advises several new high-tech ventures and has consulted and conducted workshops for global corporations worldwide, including Allianz, Amgen, Baosteel, Baxter, Canon, Hitachi, Intel, KPMG, Nokia, Samsung, Shell, Total, Toyota, and Vodafone. Professor Pucik also teaches in executive development programs for business schools in Asia, Europe, and the US.

Ingmar Björkman is Professor of Management and Organization at the Hanken School of Economics in Helsinki, Finland. Raised in Norway, he receiving his Ph.D from the Hanken School of Economics after having done parts of his doctoral studies at Stanford University. He has held visiting positions at Hong Kong University, ESSEC (Paris), INSEAD (Fontainebleau), and SCANCOR (Stanford University) and has also taught at a number of other business schools in Europe and Asia. His research interests focus on international human resource management, knowledge creation and transfer in multinational corporations, and integration of international mergers & acquisitions. Much of his work has been on Western companies' operations in the People's Republic of China but he has also published several articles on management issues in Russia and done extensive research on leading European multinationals. His latest book is *Handbook of Research in International Resource Management* (2006), co-edited with Günter Stahl (INSEAD and Vienna University of Economics and Business). A regular contributor to international academic journals, he works regularly with multinational corporations on issues related to how they manage their human resources. He has three times been elected "best teacher of the year" by the students at Hanken School of Economics.

CHAPTER 1

The Challenges of International Human Resource Management

Global Challenges at ABB

In 1988, a merger between ASEA of Sweden and Swiss firm Brown Boveri created one of the world's largest engineering firms, ABB. Both companies already had extensive international operations, Brown Boveri having begun to establish subsidiaries around the world immediately after World War II, and ASEA having started foreign operations during the 1960s. The newly merged company had sales of over US$15 billion and 160,000 employees.

Under the leadership of its Swedish CEO, Percy Barnevik, ABB went through a rapid transformation. In Western Europe, plants were closed and the number of employees was reduced, while the firm grew its operations in Asia, Eastern Europe, and North America. Over the next 10 years, ABB bought a large number of companies as it expanded geographically and diversified into new business areas, including engineering contracting and financial services. The company set up numerous joint ventures with local companies in China and other emerging markets, and established a 50–50 joint venture in power generation with the French firm Alstom.

Barnevik's vision was to create an international company that was able to deal effectively with three internal contradictions: being global and local, big and small, and radically decentralized with centralized reporting and control.[1] The key principle was local entrepreneurship, so most of the decision making was to be done at the lowest possible level, in the 5,000 independent profit centers, the business units (BUs) that became the foundation of the ABB organization.

Beyond the BUs, the firm was structured as a matrix of business segments and regions. Operations within a country were controlled by influential country managers.

1

ABB also established business steering committees and functional councils to coordinate the different units, exploit synergies, and help transfer knowledge and best practices across the network of local units. The firm developed a management information system called ABACUS that contained data on the performance of the profit centers. Barnevik and his team of top managers traveled extensively to ensure communication and knowledge sharing across units, while international assignments helped instill all units with the corporate ethos that Barnevik was pursuing: initiative, action, and risk taking.

However, after becoming one of the most admired companies in the world during its first 10 years, ABB encountered significant problems in its second decade. The company was affected by the economic downturn in Europe, while in the United States it became the target for many expensive asbestos-related damage claims linked to a firm it had acquired in 1989. Most importantly, limitations in the firm's management started to emerge.

Many of the smaller acquisitions—often initiated by aggressive and virtually independent local managers—were not well integrated with the rest of the firm, leading to different standards and systems as well as product overlap. The firm was flexible and responsive to the contexts in which it was operating, but had failed to achieve sufficient global synergies and efficiency. The structure did not work as intended, and conflicts between business areas and national units meant that many managers felt decision making was unclear. The local profit centers continued to operate their own human resources management systems, which were at best aligned at national levels but not at regional or global levels.

Barnevik's successor Göran Lindahl (1997–2001) attempted to impose more clarity and discipline by eliminating the regions and giving more power to global businesses. This only aggravated the confusion, since the divisions had neither the tools nor the experience to control the local units. Next came Jörgen Centerman, who made even more radical changes. ABB was reorganized into seven business divisions structured along user markets, with account managers for key customers, and the previously powerful country manager positions were eliminated. Centerman's next key decision was to create centrally designed and operated group processes to try to improve global control, coordination, and efficiency. However, this top-down initiative further increased the complexity of the firm, and without country managers in place to coordinate local operations, the company reached the verge of organizational paralysis.

With the company only days away from bankruptcy, Centerman was replaced in 2002 by a veteran CEO (Hoechst and Aventis), Jürgen Dormann, who immediately discontinued the group processes initiative, sold noncore businesses, and settled the asbestos claims in the US. He reinstated the position of country manager and simplified the company structure around two core global divisions: power and automation. He also became intimately involved in developing a new global ABB People Strategy, aimed at linking HRM with the business. A key priority was to make sure that a new corporate code of conduct would be widely shared and followed.

By the time Fred Kindle was recruited from outside the firm to become CEO in early 2005, ABB was profitable once again but had shrunk from 213,000 employees (in 1997) to 102,000.[2] Kindle found a firm with a high degree of local entrepreneurship, creativity, and innovation, but with limited coordination and still unsatisfactory global efficiency. He decided to focus on reducing complexity through common management processes and guidelines that would help address the drawbacks in the way the company was operating. The focus was now on improving global operational efficiency and how to better engage and energize ABB staff around the world. Barnevik's contradictions were back on the table.

OVERVIEW

From its inception, ABB wanted to be a fast-growing firm with a wide international presence. But over its 20-year history, the company faced overwhelming complexity as it struggled with contradictory management challenges, trying to live up to its corporate mantra of "acting local but thinking global."

In this chapter, we explore the major challenges faced by ABB from the perspective of the historical development of internationalization and the concomitant evolution of personnel management and then human resource management (HRM).

A look at the history of international business shows that the dilemmas faced by ABB have always existed. What has changed is the nature and speed of communication between a company's headquarters and its subsidiaries around the world. But the essential problems of being flexible and responsive to local market needs while avoiding duplication, promoting global efficiency, and coordinating and controlling diverse units and people remain.

In this context, theories about managing people have swung back and forth, alternating from "touchy-feely" to dispassionately scientific, and we will explore the different people management theories that have evolved over time. We will see that leading a complex worldwide organization raises new dilemmas about how to manage without full control over people and other resources.

Historically, firms have responded to challenges of control and coordination in two different ways. Some adopted matrix structures, others focused on building coordination capabilities at the center. We will discuss the advantages and limitations of these two approaches and the need to align the organization with the business strategy.

We will then discuss traditional approaches to the challenges of internationalization. Some firms adopt a *multidomestic* strategy, with autonomous local operations that can respond readily to local needs, while others pursue a centralized, *meganational* strategy to prevent duplication and make global operations more efficient. However, for companies that need to be simultaneously global and local, neither of these strategies is sufficient.

All this leads us to the idea that contemporary global corporations like ABB face many contradictions. They have to be simultaneously local and global in scope, centralized and decentralized, capable of delivering short-term results while developing future assets, managing multiple alliances without full control, and responding to market pressures to do things better *and* cheaper *and* faster. In the light of this, we examine the concept of the *transnational organization*, as developed by Bartlett and Ghoshal, at the heart of which is the notion of living with contradictions, or what they call the need to maintain "a dynamic balance."[3]

DEFYING BORDERS: WHAT'S NEW?

International business is not a recent phenomenon; nor is international HRM a product of the 20th or 21st century. The Assyrians, Phoenicians, Greeks, and Romans all engaged in extensive cross-border trade. There is evidence that Assyrian commercial organizations operating shortly after 2000 BC already had many of the traits of modern multinational companies, complete with head offices and branches, clear hierarchy, foreign employees, value-adding activities in multiple regions, and a drive to find new resources and markets.[4] Roman organizations spanning Asia, Africa, and Europe are often heralded as the first global companies in that they covered the whole of the known world.

Empire building was the primary goal of Roman-style international expansion, with commerce a by-product of the need to clothe and feed the dispersed garrisons.[5] For centuries the dividing line between conquest and exchange, for instance the Viking raids of the early Middle Ages, remained fuzzy. Even in the first half of the 20th century, internationalization was still closely associated with empires and colonization, and gunboats were often not far behind the merchants' ships. So when can we situate the birth of international companies?

Business historians often refer to the European and American companies of the 19th century as early versions of today's multinationals.[6] However, some go back further, arguing that the real pioneers of international business were the 16th- and 17th-century trading companies—the English and Dutch East India companies, the Muscovy Company, the Hudson's Bay Company, and the Royal African Company.[7]

International Operations in the Preindustrial Era

The early trading companies exchanged merchandise and services across continents and had a geographical spread to rival today's multinational firms. They signed on crews and chartered ships, and engaged the services of experts with skills in trade negotiations and foreign languages, capable of assessing the quality of goods and determining how they should be handled and loaded. These companies were obliged to delegate considerable responsibility to local representatives running their operations in faraway countries, which created a new challenge: How could local managers be encouraged to use their discretionary powers to the best advantage of the company? The trading companies had to develop control structures and systems to monitor the behavior of their scattered agents.

Distance makes control more difficult. This was particularly true in an era when the means of transport and communication were inseparable and slow.

The risks of opportunistic behavior loomed large.[8] Initially, companies demanded not only accounts but also written records of decisions and notification of compliance with directives from home. However, the high volume of transactions then led to the creation of administrative units to process receipts and accounts and to handle correspondence at the home office. By the mid-18th century, the Dutch and English East India companies each employed over 350 salaried staff involved in office administration.

Establishing formal rules and procedures was one way of exercising control, but this did not eliminate the temptations of opportunistic behavior for those far from the center. Other control measures were therefore developed, such as employment contracts. These stipulated that managers would work hard and in the interests of the company. Failure to do so could lead to reprimand or dismissal. Setting performance measures was the next step. These included the ratio of capital to tonnage, the amount of outstanding credit on advance contracts, whether ships sailed on time, and the care taken in loading mixed cargoes.

Systems were also installed to provide additional information about employees' behavior and activities. Ships were staffed with pursers, ships' captains were rewarded for detecting illegal goods, and private correspondence was read to minimize the risk of violations. In addition, bonds were often required from managers as insurance against private trade. However, there were also generous financial incentives, such as remuneration packages comprising a fixed cash component and a sizable bonus. Such a mix of control approaches was not far from contemporary methods used to evaluate and reward managerial performance in large multinationals.

The Impact of Industrialization

The Industrial Revolution originated in Britain in the late 18th century. The emergence of the factory system had a dramatic impact both on international business and on the management of people.

The spread of industrialization in Europe and the United States provided growing markets for minerals and foodstuffs and prompted a global search for sources of supply. Technological advances (for example, in mining equipment) also permitted the profitable exploitation of new territories. The rising need for raw materials fueled the growth of multinational service companies (trading and shipping companies, banks, and utilities) to support the expansion of world trade. British banks were already establishing branches and financing foreign trade in Australian, Canadian, and West Indian colonies in the 1830s.[9] These international companies were distinct from the trading companies in that they invested in assets that they controlled in foreign countries, a strategy known as foreign direct investment (FDI).

Cross-border manufacturing began to emerge by the mid-19th century. The Great Exhibition of 1851, staged in London, was an early forum for international benchmarking, and exposed visitors to a number of US products whose parts were built to such exacting standards that they were interchangeable.[10] Among these products were the Singer sewing machine and the Colt repeating pistol. Not surprisingly these firms established two of the earliest recorded US manufacturing investments in Britain: Colt set up a plant in 1853 and Singer in 1867.

Still, it was difficult to exercise real control over distant operations. The rare manufacturing firms that ventured abroad often used family members to manage their international operations. For example, when Siemens set up its St. Petersburg factory in 1855, a brother of the founder was put in charge. In 1863 another brother established a factory to produce sea cables in Britain. Keeping it in the family was the best guarantee that those in distant subsidiaries could be trusted not to act opportunistically.

The international spread of rail networks and the advent of steamships in the 1850s and 1860s brought new speed and reliability to international travel. More significantly, the invention of the telegraph uncoupled long-distance communication from transportation. London was joined by cable to Paris in 1852, and over the next 20 years to Bombay and cities in the US and Australia. Improved communication and transportation opened up new markets and facilitated access to resources in distant locations. It became possible for firms to manufacture in large batches and to seek volume distribution in mass markets. The rapid growth in firm size provided a domestic platform from which to expand abroad, paving the way for a surge in international business activity in the last decades of the 19th century.[11]

In parallel with developments in transport and communication, industrialization was also having a significant impact on the organization of firms. They were being reshaped by new manufacturing techniques, by the increased specialization and division of labor, and by a change in the composition of the workforce from skilled tradesmen to unskilled workers, previously agrarian, who were unaccustomed to industry requirements like punctuality, regular attendance, supervision, and the mechanical pacing of work effort.

Consequently, early factories experienced discipline and motivation problems. To reduce these difficulties, some managers began to pay more attention to working conditions and the welfare of employees. An early pioneer was Robert Owen, a British entrepreneur who reproached his fellow manufacturers for spending heavily on machinery yet failing to invest in their human assets. Owen proposed a number of labor policies and even put them profitably into practice in a Scottish cotton-spinning factory in the 1810s. He provided workers with housing and places to eat, increased the minimum working wage for children, reduced working hours, introduced schooling and systematic training for employees, and opened evening recreation centers. For these reasons, Robert Owen has been referred to as the father of modern personnel management.[12]

Owen's message took hold in the US in the 1870s, when a generation of prominent industrialists sought to apply a philosophy known as *industrial betterment* in their businesses, partly inspired by religious motives, and partly triggered by growing labor management difficulties.

Prelude to the Modern Era

The late 19th and early 20th centuries saw a number of developments in international business and in people management practices that warrant the label "modern." They led to a degree of internationalization that the world would not see again until it had fully recovered from the damage to the global economy created by two world wars.

The Golden Age Pre–World War I

By 1914, the list of companies with foreign subsidiaries was starting to have a contemporary look about it (see Table 1–1). Singer's second Scottish sewing machine factory, opened in 1885, was actually bigger than any of its domestic factories in the US. The company went on to open plants in Canada, Austria, Germany, and Russia. The first cross-border merger, between Britain's Shell and Royal Dutch, took place in 1907.

TABLE 1–1. Large Multinational Manufacturers in 1914

Company	Nationality	Product	Number of Foreign Factories in 1914	Location of Foreign Factories
Singer	US	Sewing machines	5	UK, Canada, Germany, Russia
J & P Coats	UK	Cotton thread	20	US, Canada, Russia, Austria-Hungary, Spain, Belgium, Italy, Switzerland, Portugal, Brazil, Japan
Nestlé	Swiss	Condensed milk/baby food	14	US, UK, Germany, Netherlands, Norway, Spain, Australia
Lever Brothers	UK	Soap	33	US, Canada, Germany, Switzerland, Belgium, France, Japan, Australia, South Africa
St Gobain	French	Glass	8	Germany, Belgium, Netherlands, Italy, Spain, Austria-Hungary
Bayer	German	Chemicals	7	US, UK, France, Russia, Belgium
American Radiator	US	Radiators	6	Canada, UK, France, Germany, Italy, Austria-Hungary
Siemens	German	Electrical equipment	10	UK, France, Spain, Austria-Hungary, Russia
L.M. Ericsson	Swedish	Telephone equipment	8	US, UK, France, Austria-Hungary, Russia
Accumulatoren-Fabrik	German	Batteries	8	UK, Austria-Hungary, Spain, Russia, Poland, Romania, Sweden

Source: G. Jones, *The Evolution of International Business* (London: Routledge, 1996), p. 106.

The growth in international manufacturing sustained a flourishing service sector, which provided the global infrastructure—finance, insurance, transport—to permit the international flow of goods. Multinational activity had become an important element in the world economy. It was a golden age for multinationals, with foreign direct investment accounting for around 9 percent of world output.[13]

In terms of management practice, one concrete legacy of the industrial betterment movement had been the emergence of welfare secretaries in both the US and Europe.[14] Initially concerned with health and safety, education, and social issues, these welfare specialists quickly appropriated line responsibilities such as handling grievances. Another new development was the establishment, first in Europe and soon after in the US, of stand-alone employment offices responsible for the creation and standardization of certain employment functions, such as hiring, payroll, and record keeping.[15]

The beginning of the 20th century also saw the emergence of *scientific management*, seen by some as a reaction to the paternalistic excesses of industrial betterment (see the box "The Pendulum of Management Thought"). Scientific management encouraged firms to conduct time-and-motion studies, prepare job specifications, and create wage incentive programs.[16] Hence the emergence of personnel management can be regarded as having a dual heritage, in the movements for industrial betterment and scientific management.

The Pendulum of Management Thought

The history of management thought shows pendulum swings in the amount and style of attention paid to people. Successive movements have alternated in focus between the "hard" and "soft" aspects of people management.[17]

Industrial Betterment

This philosophical movement, setting the foundation for modern personnel management, grew from the ideas of Robert Owen (1771–1858). Concerned with the impact of industrialization on individuals and communities, it rejected the laissez-faire indifference to working conditions and remuneration levels, showing concern for employees' social, educational, and even moral needs outside the work environment.

Scientific Management

Developed by Frederick Taylor (1856–1915) and embraced widely by industry, this movement emerged in the 1910s in part as a reaction to the underlying sentimentalism of the welfare orientation. Taylor was highly critical of welfare programs, and his recommendations fit the needs of employers who wanted to make more efficient use of a poorly educated labor pool containing many immigrants. Taylor described how employees could be trained for repetitive tasks, becoming easy to replace. *The Principles of Scientific Management*[18] became the first management best seller, and with it the social gospel gave way to the gospel of efficiency.

Human Relations

Criticism of scientific management for treating the worker as a "living tool" triggered the emergence of the human relations movement.[19] Elton Mayo's classic experiments at Western Electric's Hawthorne plant in the 1930s concluded that human interaction and paying attention to workers' needs could stimulate productivity. This contravened Taylor's dour philosophy of self-interest, because it suggested that social factors and the relationship between workers and management were keys to performance. Initiatives to enhance loyalty, motivation, and satisfaction flourished during and after World War II. These included shop floor compensation systems, schemes for participatory decision making and job enrichment, and the introduction of attitude surveys. These developments bolstered the legitimacy of the personnel department.

Systems Thinking

The backlash to human relations started in the mid-1960s. Systems rationalism—characterized by operational research methods, such as critical path analysis and the Program Evaluation and Review Technique (PERT)—was a reaction to the "touchy-feely" approaches introduced under the human relations umbrella (including T-groups and psychodrama). Formal personnel systems made a comeback, with management-by-objectives (MBO), pay-for-performance, and manpower planning leading the way.

Recent Developments

The *organizational culture* movement in the 1980s can be seen as a response to the mechanistic excesses of systems management, with its strong belief in planning. The emphasis turned to the management of meaning for employees, focusing on how to influence the values and norms shared by people in the organization. And in turn the emergence of *business process reengineering* in the 1990s can be seen as a reaction against the "culture" fashion.

Since the 1980s, however, there has been an explosion in management research and writing, with an increasing number of theories and movements existing in parallel. *Human resource management,* (HRM), began to emerge as a field of study in the mid-1980s, illustrating how mutually consistent and integrated HR practices could support and enhance corporate performance. The resource-based view of strategy became a dominant perspective in the 1990s, with much emphasis placed on how the *human* resources of the firm can provide a basis for competitive advantage. There were strong calls for HR professionals to become strategic partners, closely involved in the formulation and particularly the implementation of corporate strategies.[20]

During the last 10 years, *human and social capital* have emerged as major new theoretical concepts, and most recently, emphasis is being placed on *talent management*—seen as critical for the competitiveness of the firm.

War and Economic Depression

The outbreak of World War I, followed by a period of economic depression and then World War II, transformed management practices and multinational activity in very different ways.

These external shocks had a stimulating effect on the development of people management practices, hastening the spread of new thinking. The sudden influx of inexperienced workers (many of them women) into factories in 1915 to service war needs increased the pressure on managers to find ways to improve productivity rapidly. Tasks had to be simplified and redesigned for novices. To contain labor unrest, more attention had to be paid to working conditions and employee demands, which also meant training first-line supervisors. These initiatives centralized many of the aspects of employment relations previously discharged by individual line managers.

During World War I, the number of companies with managers specifically responsible for personnel issues increased dramatically. By 1920, the National Personnel Association had been formed in the US, and the National Civic Federation had started to refer to "personnel directors" instead of "welfare secretaries."[21] This institutionalized a tension that had previously been resolved by line managers—the competing demands of short-term efficiency (the production department) and employee morale (the personnel department). In some progressive firms, employees began to be viewed as resources and the importance of unity of interest between the firm and workers was stressed. The 1920s also saw the development of teaching and research, journals, and consulting firms in personnel management.[22]

In the interwar years, economic depression increased the attractions of union membership. At the same time, the pendulum began to swing back as the human relations movement gained ground to counterbalance the harsh face of scientific management.

The Great Depression was the start of a bifurcation in employment practices in the US and Japan, the latter having gone through a period of rapid industrialization and economic growth. Leading firms in both the US and Japan were experimenting with corporate welfarism in the 1920s.[23] However, the depth of the Depression in the US in the 1930s meant that firms had no option except to make layoffs and repudiate the welfare arrangements that had been established in many nonunionized firms. They turned instead to a path of explicit and instrumental contracts between employee and employer, with wages and employment conditions often determined through collective bargaining.[24] Because of the militarization of the Japanese economy, the impact of the Depression was much less severe on that side of the Pacific. Under legislation fostering "social peace" in the name of national unity, large firms maintained these welfare experiments, leading step-by-step to an HRM orientation built around implicit contracts (lifetime employment, corporate responsibility for the development of staff, and low emphasis on formalized performance evaluation). Endorsed by the strong labor unions that emerged in postwar Japan, these practices became institutionalized, reinforcing and reinforced by Japanese societal values.

In the West, World War II intensified interest in the systematic recruitment, testing, and assigning of new employees in order to leverage their full potential. Psychological testing used by the military spilled over into private industry.[25] In addition, the desire to avoid wartime strikes led the US government to support collective bargaining, strengthening the role of the personnel function as a result.

If these external shocks had some salutary consequences for the development of personnel practices, they had quite the opposite effect on multinational activities. With the loss of direct investments in Russia in the wake of the 1917 Communist Revolution, firms began to think twice about foreign investment. In an environment of political uncertainty and exchange controls, this caution was reinforced by the Great Depression at the end of the 1920s, followed by the collapse of the international financial system. Trade barriers were erected as countries rushed to support local firms, effectively reducing international trade. The adverse conditions during the interwar years encouraged firms to enter cross-border cartels rather than risk foreign investments. By the late 1920s, a considerable proportion of world manufacturing was controlled by these cartels—the most notorious being the "seven sisters" controlling the oil industry.[26] Similarly in pharmaceuticals, electric lightbulbs, steel, and engineering industries, elaborate arrangements were established among national champions allowing them to focus on their home markets and to suppress international competition.[27]

World War II dealt a crushing blow to these cartels, and after the war, the US brought in aggressive antitrust legislation to dismantle those that remained. By then there was little incentive for American firms to enter into cartels. While US firms emerged from the war in excellent shape, European competition was devastated, and Japanese corporations (known as *zaibatsu*) had been dismembered. The war had stimulated technological innovation, and American corporations had no desire to confine their activities to the home market. A new era of international business had begun.

THE MODERN MULTINATIONAL

Although Europe had a long tradition in international commerce, it was the global drive of US firms after World War II that gave birth to the multinationals as we know them today. American firms that had hardly ventured beyond their home markets before the war now began to flex their muscles abroad, and by the early 1960s, US companies had built an unprecedented lead in the world economy. "American companies have spent the past decade running a helter-skelter race to get located overseas . . . What US business was seeing, in the words of Chairman Frederic G. Donner of General Motors, 'is the emergence of the modern industrial corporation as an institution that is transcending national boundaries.'"[28] Throughout the 1960s, US industrial productivity was the highest in the world, accounting for 40 percent of world manufacturing output.[29] The US accounted for almost 70 percent of the R&D undertaken in the OECD.[30]

American firms also found faster ways of entering new markets. Many moved abroad through acquisitions, followed by investment in the acquired subsidiary in order to benefit more fully from economies of scale and scope.[31] This was the approach taken by Procter & Gamble (P&G), which established a presence in continental Europe by acquiring an ailing French detergent plant in 1954.[32] An alternative strategy was to join forces with a local partner, as in the case of Xerox, which entered global markets through two joint ventures, with the English motion picture firm the Rank Organisation in 1956, and with Fuji Photo Film in Japan in 1962.

American service firms followed their clients abroad, but internationalization strategies varied. The advertising agency J. Walter Thompson had an agreement with General Motors that it would open an office in every country where the car firm had an assembly operation or distributor.[33] In professional services, McKinsey and Arthur Andersen scrambled to open their own offices in foreign countries through the 1950s and 1960s. Others, such as Price Waterhouse and Coopers & Lybrand, built their international presence through mergers with established national practices in other countries. For most others, the route was via informal federations or networks of otherwise independent firms.

Advances in transport and communications—the introduction of commercial jet travel, the first transatlantic telephone link in 1956, then the development of the telex—facilitated this rapid internationalization. More significant still was the emergence of computers as business tools in the late 1950s. By the mid-1970s, computers had become key elements in the control and information systems of industrial concerns, paving the way for later complex integration strategies. Taken together, the jet plane, the new telecommunications technology, and the computer contributed to a "spectacular shrinkage of space."[34]

Alongside these technological drivers of internationalization, powerful economic forces were at work. The Marshall Plan, established to support the rebuilding of war-battered Europe, set the tone. Barriers to trade and investment were progressively dismantled with successive General Agreement on Tariffs and Trades (GATT) treaties. Exchange rates were stabilized following the Bretton Woods Agreement (July 1944), and banks started to play an international role as facilitators of international business. The 1957 Treaty of Rome established the European Community. US firms, many of which already perceived Europe as a single entity, were the first to exploit the regional integration, laying the foundations for a European market of a size comparable to that in the US. European companies were spurred by "the American challenge" (the title of a best-selling, call-to-arms book by the French journalist and politician Jean-Jacques Servan-Schreiber in 1967), encouraging them to expand beyond their own borders.

Staffing for International Growth

In the decades following World War II, virtually all medium- and large-sized firms had personnel departments, typically with responsibility for industrial (union) relations and for the functional and operational aspects of employment, including staffing subsidiaries abroad.[35] The newly created international personnel units focused on expatriation, sending home country managers to foreign locations.

The largest 180 US multinationals opened an average of six foreign subsidiaries each year during the 1960s.[36] This rapid international expansion opened up new job possibilities, including foreign postings. While US firms in the immediate postwar period had been "flush with veterans who had recently returned from the four corners of the globe [and who] provided a pool of eager expatriates,"[37] more managers were now urgently needed. People had to be persuaded to move abroad, both those with much needed technical skills and managers to exercise control over these expanding foreign subsidiaries. In most companies at the time, this meant paying people generously as an incentive to move abroad.

In the late 1970s, horror stories of expatriate failure gained wide circulation—the technically capable executive sent out to run a foreign subsidiary being brought back prematurely as a borderline alcoholic, with a ruined marriage, and having run the affiliate into the ground. Academic studies seemed to confirm this problem,[38] which for some companies became a major handicap to international growth. It was no longer just a question of persuading people to move abroad; it was a question of "how can we help them to be successful?" While the reluctance to move abroad was increasing, often for family reasons but also because of the mismanagement of reentry to the home country, concern over the rising costs of expatriation was growing.

At the same time, back home (particularly in the US and Scandinavia), initiatives in people management continued to multiply—participative management, training initiatives ranging from "sensitivity training" to the "managerial grid," the organizational development (OD) movement with its focus on planned organizational change, work redesign, and the sociotechnical and industrial democracy movements in northern Europe, to name but a few. While some academics argued that people were resources rather than just costs, in the US the term "human resource management" grew as much as anything out of the need to find a home for these burgeoning initiatives within the firm.[39] This was the intention of AT&T, which in 1971 created a new role of senior vice president in human resource development. Others followed suit, although initially this often amounted to no more than relabeling the personnel department with a more fashionable term.

International business also became a subject of academic study during this period. In the early 1980s, the challenges of expatriation started to attract the attention of researchers, reinforced by the newfound legitimacy of HR and the concern of senior managers anxious about growth prospects abroad. While it was too early to talk of an international HRM field, international growth was leading to new challenges beyond expatriation that were to shape this emerging domain.

Organizing for International Growth

Rapid international growth brought with it the problems of controlling and coordinating increasingly complex global organizations. Here we should point out that, while many authors use these terms interchangeably, we make an explicit distinction between control and coordination. We use the term **control** to refer to visible and hierarchical processes and structures, and **coordination** to refer to tools that facilitate alignment through lateral interactions and adjustments across different parts of the multinational (such as cross-boundary project teams and informal social networks). As we will show later in the book, this distinction has important implications for people management.

The awareness that international HRM is crucial not just for international staffing but also for building corporate cohesion and interunit collaboration grew and matured between the 1960s and 1990s. In April 1963, a special report in *BusinessWeek* stated, "Shaped in the crucible of complex foreign competition, the largest of US corporations have found themselves changing into a new form: the multinational corporation. . . . The term serves as a demarcation line between domestically oriented enterprises with international operations and truly world-oriented corporations."[40] It was becoming increasingly apparent that the traditional structures were not sufficient to cope with the growing complexities of managing international business.

This transition was captured by research on the Harvard Multinational Enterprise Project, initiated in 1965, which raised the question of how to organize effectively for international growth.[41] At an early stage, when foreign sales were of limited volume and scope, an export department tacked onto sales was sufficient. As foreign sales grew, the export department would become an international division within the divisional structure (which was replacing the functional organization to become the predominant organizational form).[42] However, when this international division reached a certain size, it triggered a transformation of the company into a "multinational structure."[43]

Many firms selling a wide range of products abroad opted for a structure of worldwide product divisions, whereas those with few products but operating in many countries would typically organize themselves around geographic area divisions, as did IBM. The tricky question was how to organize when the firm had many different products sold in many different geographic markets. It was not at all clear how companies should deal with this zone of maximum complexity.

In practice, two responses emerged. Some firms implemented matrix organizations involving both product and geographic reporting lines; others increased the number of headquarters staff in coordinating roles. Both of these routes were ultimately to show their limitations, but the two paths gave rise to a growing understanding of the potential role of HRM in dealing with the fundamental problems of cross-border coordination and control.

The Matrix Structure Route

By the early 1970s, several US and British companies (Citibank, Corning, Dow, Exxon, and Shell, among others) had adopted the idea of the matrix as a guiding principle for their worldwide organization. Right from the start, some management scholars urged caution. One study of nine British matrix organizations demonstrated that implementation was hindered by traditional management behavioral styles,[44] and it was also pointed out that a matrix was much more complex than reporting lines and structural coordination. A matrix had to be built into leadership development, control and performance appraisal systems, teamwork, conflict resolution mechanisms, relationships, and attitudes, anticipating the later insight that a matrix has more to do with HRM than it has to do with structure.[45] Few of the companies that opted for the matrix solution had such supporting elements in place.

Our example, ABB, had a formal matrix organizational structure, complemented by cross-boundary teams and steering groups. The firm needed to control and coordinate its hugely complex operations, with numerous and often distant foreign subsidiaries, without being paralyzed by slow, centralized, bureaucratic decisionmaking. Each time top management made changes in the structure to address these challenges, the reorganization led to unintended side effects and new challenges. A focus on *reporting lines*, the first dimension of coordination, was not sufficient. Attention also had to be paid to the second dimension of coordination, *social architecture*—the conscious design of a social environment that encourages a pattern of thinking and behavior supporting organizational goals. This includes interpersonal relationships and interunit networks, the values, beliefs, and norms shared by members of the organization, and the mindsets that people hold. Barnevik in particular was conscious of the importance of the social elements of the international firm, and thus the need for extensive communication, travel, and relocation of people across units.

A third means of coordination, *common management processes*, includes processes for managing talent (including recruitment, selection, development, and retention of key personnel), performance and compensation management, and knowledge management and innovation. As ABB's problems compounded, it became increasingly obvious to executives that they had to develop and implement global management processes, although it was less clear how to do this. Many of their efforts were not successful.

Many companies found matrix structures difficult. Managers were uneasy about the separation of authority and accountability. The new arrangements generated power struggles, ambiguity over resource allocation, buck-passing, and abdication of responsibility. Worse still, the traditional dimensions of product and geography in many multinationals were overlaid with additional matrix layers, such as functions, market segments, customer accounts, and global suppliers. In theory, a manager reported to two bosses, and conflicts between them would be reconciled at the apex one level higher up. However, it was not unusual to find companies where managers were reporting to four or five bosses, so that reconciliation or arbitration could only happen at a very senior level. The matrix initiative, originally introduced to help cope with complexity, seemed to be contributing to it.

The difficulties with implementing an effective matrix solution together with the growing importance of speed in global competition sounded the death knell for the matrix structure in a number of firms. Although a matrix might ensure the consultation necessary for sound decision making, it was painfully slow. By the time the firm had decided, say, to build a new chemical plant in Asia, nimbler competitors were already up and running.

By the early 1980s, the call was for clearer accountability, a notion increasingly present in management jargon. Many firms reverted to structures where clear accountability lay with the product divisions, although some (such as ABB) retained a structure with many matrix features.[46]

But if matrix structures were gradually going out of fashion, the matrix problem of organization was more alive than ever. Both practitioners and researchers turned their attention to how lateral interaction, adjustment, and teamwork could provide the flexibility of matrix without its disadvantages. Research reviews had shown that there were two dimensions of matrix management:[47]

- The dual or multiple authority relationships (formal reporting lines) reflected in the structure.
- The horizontal communication linkages and teamwork (for example, between product and country managers) that a matrix organization fosters.

Most of the disadvantages appeared to stem from the former, while most of the advantages originated in the latter. This observation found support in new ideas in organizational theory about the growing demands of information processing and decision making in complex firms.[48] The argument here was that the traditional hierarchical tools of control (rules, standard operating procedures, hierarchical referral, and planning) could not manage the growing complexity of information processing. Organizations required strong capabilities in two areas: first in information processing and second in coordination and teamwork. There was an explosion of interest in how to improve coordination while keeping the reporting relationships as clear and simple as possible.[49]

Gradually it became clear that the matrix challenges of coordination in complex multinational firms were essentially issues of people and information technology (IT) management rather than a question of strategy and structure. Matrix, as two leading strategy scholars were later to say, is not a structure; it is a "frame of mind" nurtured more than anything else by careful human resource management.[50]

The Headquarters Coordination Route

Not surprisingly given all the implementation difficulties, only a small number of leading-edge companies adopted a matrix for any length of time, although many tried. Most organizations took the well-trodden path of keeping control of international activities with central staff. This was particularly true for German and Japanese companies, but it was also the dominant organizing pattern in Anglo-Saxon firms. As with the matrix, this approach was initially successful but eventually led to inefficiencies and paralysis, as the staff functions at corporate and divisional levels overexpanded in an attempt to cope with growing coordination needs. Again, speed was shown to be the Achilles heel.

It took a long time to work through decisions in German *Zentralebereiche* (central staff departments), and particularly in Japanese *nemawashi*[51] (negotiation) processes of middle-up consultative decision making. However, multinationals from both of these countries were largely export oriented with sales subsidiaries abroad, and the disadvantages were initially outweighed by the quality of decision making and commitment to implementation that accompanied the consensus-oriented decision making. Moreover, the complex consultative processes worked reasonably well as long as everyone involved was German or Japanese.[52]

The strains of staff bureaucracy began to show in the US in the early 1980s as companies started to localize, acquiring or building integrated subsidiaries abroad. With localization of the management of foreign units, the coordination of decisions by central staff became more difficult, slowing down the process at a time when speed was becoming more important. Local managers in lead countries argued for more autonomy and clearer accountability, while the costly overhead of the heavy staff structures associated with central coordination contributed to the erosion of competitiveness.

Faced with the second oil shock and recession in the late 1970s, American firms were the first to begin the process of downsizing and de layering staff bureaucracies, followed by Europeans in Nordic and Anglo-Saxon countries. The Japanese and Germans followed more slowly. After decades of postwar international growth, attention in HRM shifted to the painful new challenges of dealing with organizational streamlining and job redesign, layoffs, and managing change under crisis. At a deeper level, this was an apprenticeship in how to master a new contradiction—maintaining loyalty and commitment while engaging in successive rounds of corporate reorganization.[53]

The pain of restructuring often started at headquarters, although the consequences quickly spilled over to subsidiaries. In many firms, the pendulum swung from central bureaucracy to decentralized local accountability, deemed cheaper and faster. Foreign subsidiaries transformed themselves into independent "kingdoms"—but the not-invented-here syndrome took hold, and a few years later the pendulum swung back to centralization. Why? Because the underlying problem of how to coordinate foreign subsidiaries remained unresolved.

Firms that had pursued the headquarters coordination route came to the same conclusion as firms that had invested in a matrix structure: They had to develop nonbureaucratic coordination and control mechanisms by building lateral relationships facilitated by human resource management.[54] The control and coordination problem became another important strand in the development of international HRM.

HRM Goes International

In the 1980s, the idea that HRM might be of strategic importance gained ground (see the box "HRM Hitches Up with Strategy"). The insight that strategy is implemented through structure had taken hold—and it was then logical to argue that strategy is also implemented through changes in selection criteria, reward systems, and other HR policies and practices. In turn, this challenged the notion that there might be a "best" approach to HRM—the approach would depend on the strategy.

HRM Hitches Up with Strategy

In the early 1980s, two significant conceptual developments in the US gave HRM an identity as a field, rather than just an umbrella for multiple initiatives to do with people and the HR department. They suggested in different ways that HRM could contribute to the performance of the firm. Underlying both was the idea from the emerging contingency theory that there is no right way of organizing or managing people—it all depends on fit with strategy, specific tasks, and the environment. These are known respectively as the concepts of "internal" and "external" fit or consistency.

The first concept originated from the Harvard model of managing human assets, which emphasized the importance of configuring different HRM policies to ensure internal consistency.[55] Research evidence and theoretical arguments presented between the mid-1980s and mid-1990s suggested that strong internal fit is associated with organizational performance, even convincing those European scholars who were initially skeptical about American evangelical rhetoric.[56]

The second concept was the birth of *strategic human resource management*, based on the concept of external fit between the strategy of a firm and its HRM policies and practices. The origins lay in the idea of *implementing* strategy through changes in reward and other HR systems. Building on this, Fombrun, Tichy, and colleagues developed the notion that strategy should guide the selection, appraisal, reward, and development activities of the firm, thereby influencing performance in a future-oriented direction.[57]

Strategic HRM was eagerly embraced in the US, at least within the professional HRM community. In the battleground for status, it provided a rationale for elevating the influence of the HR function. The discipline of human resource planning, involving detailed methodologies to link HRM to strategy formulation, came into being.[58] During the next 10 years, all self-respecting American firms spent considerable efforts on developing their human resource strategies.

The idea of strategic HRM was reinforced and popularized by the 7-S model from early management best seller, *In Search of Excellence*.[59] The authors set out to distill the characteristics of leading American firms. They concluded that competitive success stemmed from a tight configuration between the people side of the organization (style, skills, shared values, and staff) and the hard side (strategy, structure, and systems). In making this fit argument, they were implicitly placing the HRM dimension on a par with the dimensions of strategy and structure that had dominated organization theory since the earlier writing of Chandler.[60]

Although intuitively appealing, the notion of external fit proposed by strategic HRM proved difficult to put into practice. Indeed, in an age of increasing discontinuities, the whole notion of strategic planning was questioned, especially when the focus of practical attention in HRM shifted to the painful nitty-gritty of downsizing and restructuring.[61] Strategic HRM had perhaps more to do with change than with detailed long-term planning. However, the fundamental tenet of the strategic HRM movement is still valid, namely that firms can benefit from putting in place practices that lead to the recruitment, development, and retention of the type of people needed to carry out a strategy in ways superior to those of their competitors.

Perhaps appropriate HRM practice also depends on cultural context? This question was prompted by the difficulties that expatriates had experienced in transplanting management practices abroad, and was supported by growing research on cultural differences, pioneered by Geert Hofstede's study based on the global IBM opinion survey. This showed significant differences in the understanding of management and organization, even among employees within the same company.[62]

The emergence of "the Japanese challenge" in the 1980s as both threat and icon further highlighted the issue of cultural differences, as well as the strategic importance of soft issues such as HRM. Numerous studies attempted to explain how the Japanese, whose country was destroyed and occupied after World War II, had managed to rebound with such vigor, successfully taking away America's market share in industries such as automobiles and consumer electronics. How had they managed to pull this off with no natural resources apart from people? A large part of the answer seemed to lie in distinctive HRM practices that helped to provide high levels of skill, motivation, and collective entrepreneurship, as well as collaboration between organizational units.[63] This was a shock for Western managers, who suddenly realized that different approaches to management could be equally successful. It could no longer be assumed that a company expanding abroad necessarily had superior management practices.

New international human resource challenges were emerging. Many governments began to apply pressure on foreign firms to hire and develop local employees. The combination of government pressures and the cost of expatriation persuaded some multinational firms to start aggressively recruiting local executives to run their foreign subsidiaries. This often required extensive training and development, but as one observer pointed out, "The cost must be weighed against the cost of sending an American family to the area."[64] At Unilever, for example, the proportion of expatriates in foreign management positions dropped from 50 percent to 10 percent between 1950 and 1970.[65]

However, there was a Catch-22 in localizing key positions in foreign units: The greater the talent of local people, the more likely they were to be poached by other firms seeking local skills. Consequently localization was a priority for only a minority of multinational firms until well into the 1990s, except for operations in highly developed regions such as North America, Europe, and Japan.[66]

There were exceptions to this trend, and these tended to be firms that used expatriate assignments for developmental reasons rather than just to solve an immediate job need. In these corporations, high potential executives would be transferred abroad in order to expose them to international responsibilities. The assumption was that with growing internationalization, *all* senior executives needed international experience, even those in domestic positions. For example, the vice president of P&G had already pointed out in 1963, "We never appoint a man simply because of his nationality. A Canadian runs our French company, a Dutchman runs the Belgian company, and a Briton runs our Italian company. In West Germany, an American is in charge; in Mexico, a Canadian."[67] This meant that P&G was able to attract the very best local talent, quickly developing an outstanding reputation around the globe for the quality of its management. For local firms in France, Singapore, Australia, and Brazil, P&G was the management benchmark, and not only in the fast-moving consumer goods sector. Other firms started to adopt the P&G approach, although this created new challenges for international HRM. How does one manage the identification, development, transfer, and repatriation of talent spread out across the globe?

The link between international management development and the problems of coordination and control was established by the landmark research of Edström and Galbraith. They studied the expatriation policies of four multinationals of comparable size and geographic coverage in the mid-1970s, including Shell.[68] The research showed that these companies had quite different levels and patterns of international personnel transfer.[69] There were three motives for transferring managers abroad. The first and most common was to meet an immediate need for particular skills in a foreign subsidiary. The second was to develop managers through challenging international experience. However, the study of Shell revealed a third motive for international transfers—as a mechanism for control and coordination. The managers sent abroad were steeped in the policies and style of the organization, so they could be relied on to act appropriately in diverse situations. Moreover, frequent assignments abroad developed a network of personal relationships that facilitated coordination.

It appeared that Shell was able to maintain a high degree of control and coordination while having a more decentralized organization than other firms. Indeed, one of the basic principles of the Royal/Dutch Shell Group of Companies (the official title of the corporation until 2006) was to allow subsidiaries a high degree of local autonomy. This suggested that appropriate HRM practices could allow a firm to be globally coordinated and relatively decentralized at the same time. Global control and coordination, it appeared, could be provided through socialization, minimizing the necessity for centralized headquarters control or bureaucratic procedures.

These findings drew attention to expatriation, mobility, and management development as a vital part of the answer to the matrix/bureaucracy problem of coordination. In truth, the concept was not entirely new—the Romans had adopted a similar approach to the decentralization dilemma two millennia before.

By the mid-1990s, with globalization deepening, surveys consistently showed that global leadership development was one of the top three HRM priorities in major US corporations.[70] In some companies in Europe and the US, international management development was seen to be so critical that this department was separated from the corporate HR function and reported directly to the CEO.

These developments also lent substance to an earlier research by Perlmutter, suggesting that multinationals varied in the "states of mind" characterizing their operations.[71] The first was the *ethnocentric orientation*, where each subsidiary was required to conform precisely to parent company ways regardless of local conditions. The second was the decentralized *polycentric corporation*, where each subsidiary was given the freedom to develop with minimal interference, providing it remained profitable. The third was the *geocentric orientation*, where "subsidiaries are neither satellites nor independent city states, but parts of a whole whose focus is on worldwide objectives as well as local objectives, each making its unique contribution with its unique competence."[72] Perlmutter hypothesized that people management practices built this geocentric orientation. As in P&G, this meant that an individual's skills counted more than his or her passport, and there would be a high degree of mobility not only from headquarters to subsidiaries, but also from subsidiaries to headquarters and between the subsidiaries themselves, as with Shell. Perlmutter saw the route from initial ethnocentrism to geocentrism as tortuous but inevitable.

The research of Perlmutter and Edström and Galbraith suggested that international HRM was not just a question of sending expatriates abroad and putting the right person in the right place in foreign environments, important though these tasks may be. Their ideas provided a framework for understanding the role of HRM in the strategic and organizational development of the multinational corporation. However, until the early 1990s, the focus of management attention, at least in the US, was on the home market problems of restructuring and reengineering. And most of the research (and indeed business school teaching) in international HRM remained heavily functional in its orientation, focused on managing expatriate and international assignments.

Accelerating global competition in the 1990s was to change that, as the seeds of another important idea were sown—that the competitive advantage of a global corporation lies in its ability to simultaneously balance the forces of local responsiveness and global integration while at the same time learning across its geographic and other boundaries.[73]

ENTER GLOBALIZATION

By the end of the 1980s, the traditional distinction between domestic and multinational companies had started to become blurred. International competition was no longer the preserve of industrial giants; it was affecting everybody's business. Statistics from the 1960s show that only 6 percent of the US economy was exposed to international competition. By the late 1980s, the corresponding figure was over 70 percent and climbing fast.[74]

In 1985, Hedlund had noted, "A radical view concerning globality is that we are witnessing the disappearance of the international dimension of business. For commercial and practical purposes, nations do not exist and the relevant business arena becomes something like a big unified 'home market.'"[75] By the early 1990s, this was no longer a "radical" view.

Globalization surfaced as the new buzzword at the beginning of the 1990s—see the box "The Meaning of Globalization." Many of the ingredients of globalization had actually been around for several decades. The steady dismantling of trade barriers in Western Europe and in North and South America, the increasing availability of global capital, advances in computing and communications technology, the progressive convergence of consumer tastes, and, in particular, the universal demand for industrial products had all been under way for some time. What made a difference was that these trends now reached a threshold where they became mutually reinforcing.

The Meaning of Globalization

Globalization has different meanings to different people, often with strong positive or negative emotional overtones. For many people it implies that we are becoming all alike—globalization stands for convergence or homogenization. This was the first popular use of the term, spurred by the views of media giant Marshall McCluhan 40 years ago. If globalization did indeed mean homogenization, most of us would resist since it would imply loss of heritage and identity.

Indeed, globalization has a variety of negative meanings for various social groups, including many activist organizations, linked together under the "antiglobalization" umbrella. Some protest again the negative consequences for the environment, others are opposed to what they see as Americanization or the supremacy of the free market system, while many are against the political power of the multinational corporations, placing the rights of investors over citizens and individuals.

But there is an alternative view of globalization—as a source of new opportunities and increasing choice: more sources of information, widening markets for talent from anywhere, better quality and selection of products for consumers (often at lower prices), rich influence of other cultures.

Take access to international food as an example. In most large cities around the world we have access to an ever greater choice of food—French, Japanese, Thai, Mexican, Indian, Italian, Chinese. . . . We choose what we eat, and we enjoy having the diversity of choice. But we do not live in a single global village, so while sushi is everywhere in California, California sushi is quite different from sushi in Japan.

In this context, what many economists and political scientists mean by globalization is an increasing interdependence and interconnectedness. That is the sense in which we employ the term globalization in this book. We live in villages of different sizes and design that are, despite their differences, increasingly connected.

"Globalization, global integration is a widening, deepening and speeding up of interconnectedness in all aspects of contemporary life from the cultural to the criminal, the financial to the spiritual."[76] Events in the housing market of the US have powerful consequences for an industrial firm in Frankfurt or a retailer in Ho Chi Minh City. To meet global competition, Toyota no longer makes a whole car in a single location—it might make the front traction in China and the engine in Japan, and carry out final assembly close to the customer. Operations in the integrated multinational are separate but interdependent.

So when people use the word "globalization," check out first what they mean by it.

First of all, economic barriers such as national borders became less relevant (but not irrelevant!) as governments dismantled the barriers to trade and investment that once segmented the world economy. At the same time, widespread deregulation and privatization opened new opportunities for international business in both developing and developed countries. The multinational domain, long associated with the industrial company, was shifting to the service sector, which by the mid-1990s represented over half of total world FDI.[77] Problems of distance and time zones were further smoothed away as communication by fax gave way to e-mail and fixed phone networks to wireless mobile technology.

Globalization was further stimulated by the inevitable but still unexpected fall of communism in Russia and Eastern Europe. Together with China's adoption of market-oriented policies, huge new opportunities were opened to international business as most of the world was drawn into the integrated global economy. Back in the 1970s, world trade was already growing nearly 20 percent faster per annum than world output. This intensified in the 1980s, with world trade growing 60 percent faster than world output, and global FDI increasing even faster than trade. That period also saw the US share of world FDI decline from 50 to 26 percent, bringing it much more in line with the weight of the US in the world economy. Meanwhile Japan, with a strong international rather than domestic focus, increased its share of world FDI from 1 to 20 percent during the period 1967–1990.

International business was not just growing in volume; it was also changing in form. Much of the early theorizing depicted a step-by-step progression to international status, as mentioned earlier.[78] By the late 1980s, many companies were learning how to grow through various types of alliances, including international licensing agreements, cross-border R&D partnerships, international consortia such as Airbus, and the joint ventures that were increasingly used to expand quickly into emerging markets. The creation of the Single European Market in 1992, which then became the European Union, triggered an unprecedented wave of cross-border mergers and acquisitions that continue to accelerate in frequency and size.

Multinationals increasingly located different elements of their value-adding activities in different parts of the world. Formerly hierarchical companies with clean-cut boundaries were giving way to complex arrangements and configurations, often fluctuating over time. The new buzzword from GE was "the boundaryless organization."[79] With increasing cross-border project work and mobility, the image of an organization as a network was rapidly becoming as accurate as that of hierarchy. For example, a European pharmaceutical corporation could have international R&D partnerships with competitors in the US and manufacturing joint ventures with local partners in China, where it also outsourced sales of generic products to a firm strong in distribution. The new arrangements meant that companies might cooperate along some segments of the value chain and compete along others.

Another characteristic of the emerging competitive environment was the breakdown of historic sources of strategic advantage, leading to the search for new ways to compete. Traditionally, the only distant resources that multinationals sought were raw materials or cheap labor. Everything else was at home: sources of leading-edge technology and finance, world-class suppliers, pressure-cooker competition, the most sophisticated customers, and the best intelligence on future trends.[80] The home base advantage was so strong that multinationals could maintain their competitiveness while they gradually learned to adapt their offerings to fit better with local needs (thus supporting an incremental approach to international expansion).

Global competition was now dispersing some of these capabilities around the world. India, for example, developed its software industry using a low-cost strategy as a means of entry, but then quickly climbed the value chain, just as Japan had done previously in the automobile industry. The implication of such developments was that multinational firms, especially US firms, could no longer assume that all the capabilities deemed strategic were available close to home.

With the erosion of traditional sources of competitive advantage, multinationals needed to change their perspective. To compete successfully, they had to do more than exploit scale economies or arbitrage imperfections in the world's markets for goods, labor, and capital. Toward the end of the 1980s, a new way of thinking about the multinational corporation came out of studies of how organizations were responding to these challenges. The concept of the transnational organization was born.

The Roadmap for Managing Globalization

If there is a single perspective that has shaped the context for our understanding of the multinational corporation and its HRM implications, it is Bartlett and Ghoshal's research on the transnational organization.[81] To this we can add Hedlund's related concept of heterarchy and Doz and Prahalad's studies on the multi-focal organization, all of which have origins in Perlmutter's geocentric organization.[82] We will be referring frequently to their findings and concepts in this book, for all of these strategy and management researchers grew to believe that people management is perhaps the single most critical domain for the multinational firm. None of them had any interest in HRM by virtue of their training, but all were drawn to the HRM field by findings from their research.

Doz and Prahalad began to link the fields of multinational strategy and HRM when researching the patterns of strategic control in multinational companies.[83] As they saw it, multinational firms faced one central problem: responding to a variety of national demands while maintaining a clear and consistent global business strategy. This tension between strong opposing forces, dubbed local responsiveness and global integration, served as a platform for much subsequent research and came to be seen as the central challenge for the multinational company. It was captured by Sony's "think global, act local" aphorism, also adopted by ABB as its guiding motto.

These concepts were developed further by Bartlett and Ghoshal in their study of nine firms in a sample of three industries (consumer electronics, branded packaged goods, and telephone switching) and three regions (North America, Europe, and Japan).[84] They discovered that these companies seemed to have followed one of three internationalization paths, which they called "administrative heritage":

- One path emphasized responsiveness to local conditions, leading to what they called a "multinational enterprise" and what we prefer to call **multidomestic** (we use the term multinational in its generic sense, as a firm with operations in multiple countries). This led to a decentralized federation of local firms led by entrepreneurs who enjoyed a high degree of strategic freedom and organizational autonomy. Close to their customers and with strong links to the local infrastructure, the subsidiaries were seen almost as indigenous companies. The strength of the multidomestic approach was local responsiveness, and some European firms, such as Unilever and Philips, and ITT in the United States, embodied this approach.

- A second path to internationalization was that of the "global" firm, typified by US corporations such as Ford and Japanese enterprises such as Matsushita and NEC. Since the term global as used by Bartlett and Ghoshal is now, just like the term multinational, commonly applied to any large firm competing globally, in this book we prefer to call such a firm the **meganational** firm. Here, worldwide facilities are typically centralized in the parent country, products are standardized, and overseas operations are considered as delivery pipelines to access international markets. The global hub maintains tight control over strategic decisions, resources, and information. The competitive strength of the meganational firm comes from efficiencies of scale and cost.

- Some companies appeared to have taken a third route, a variant on the meganational path. Like the meganational, their facilities were located at the center. But the competitive strength of these "**international**" firms[85] was their ability to transfer expertise to less advanced overseas environments, allowing local units more discretion in adapting products and services. They were also capable of capturing learning from such local initiatives and then transferring it back to the central R&D and marketing departments, from where it was reexported to other foreign units. The "international" enterprise was thus a tightly coordinated federation of local units, controlled by sophisticated management systems and corporate staffs. Some American and European firms, such as Ericsson, fit this pattern, heralding the growing concern with global knowledge management.

It was apparent to Bartlett and Ghoshal that specific firms were doing well because their internationalization paths matched the requirements of their industry closely. Consumer products required local responsiveness, so Unilever had been thriving with its multidomestic approach, while Kao in Japan—centralized and meganational in heritage—had hardly been able to move outside its Japanese borders. The situation was different in consumer electronics, where the centralized meganational heritage of Matsushita (Panasonic and other brands) seemed to fit better than the more localized approaches of Philips and GE's consumer electronics business. And in telecommunications switching, the international learning and transfer ability of Ericsson led its "international" strategy to dominate the multidomestic and meganational strategies of its competitors.[86]

Perhaps the most significant of Bartlett and Ghoshal's observations was that accelerating global competition was changing the stakes. In all of these three industries, it was clear that the leading firms had to become more **transnational** in their orientation—more locally responsive *and* more globally integrated *and* better at sharing learning between headquarters and subsidiaries. What has been driving this change? Increasing competition was shifting the competitive positioning of these firms from *either/or* to *and*. The challenge for Unilever (like ABB in the opening case) was to maintain its local responsiveness, but at the same time to increase its global efficiency by eliminating duplication and integrating manufacturing. Conversely, the challenge for Matsushita was to keep the economies of centralized product development and manufacturing, but to become more local and responsive to differentiated niches in markets around the world.

The Transnational Solution

The defining characteristic of the transnational enterprise is its capacity to steer between the contradictions that it confronts. As Ghoshal and Bartlett put it,

. . . managers in most worldwide companies recognize the need for simultaneously achieving global efficiency, national responsiveness, and the ability to develop and exploit knowledge on a worldwide basis. Some, however, regard the goal as inherently unattainable. Perceiving irreconcilable contradictions among the three objectives, they opt to focus on one of them, at least temporarily. The transnational company is one that overcomes these contradictions.[87]

However, it is not clear that all international firms are destined to move in a transnational direction. While all companies are forced to contend with the dimensions of responsiveness, efficiency, and learning, and intensified competition heightens the contradictory pressures, these features are not equally salient in all industries. Moreover, the pressures do not apply equally to all parts of a firm. One subsidiary may be more local in orientation, whereas another may be tightly integrated. Even within a particular function, such as marketing, pricing may be a local matter whereas distribution may be controlled from the center. In HR, performance management systems may be more globally standardized, whereas reward systems for workers may be left to local discretion. Indeed, this differentiation is another aspect of the complexity of the transnational—one size does not fit all.

Transnational pressures have been strongest in certain industries, such as pharmaceuticals and automobiles, where firms must be close to local authorities and consumers, while at the same time harnessing global efficiencies in product development, marketing, and manufacturing. In other industries, such as steel, paper, and printing, the pressures to be locally responsive or globally integrated were less strong, at least in the past. In certain environments, developing a differentiated transnational approach would not be appropriate. Indeed, researchers argued that "unnecessary organizational complexity in a relatively simple business environment can be just as unproductive as unresponsive simplicity in a complex business environment."[88]

While industry characteristics influence the strategic approach of the firm[89]—multidomestic, meganational, or transnational—companies also have some degree of choice. Take the case of the brewing industry, where two neighboring firms have taken contrasting paths. Everyone has heard of the Dutch company Heineken through its global Heineken and Amstel brands. But how many had heard of InBev before it acquired the iconic American Anheuser-Busch beer? Based just across the border in Flemish-speaking Leuven in Belgium, and in partnership with Brazilians, InBev owns over 200 brands across the world, including Stella Artois, Bass, Labatt, Leffe, and Brahma. InBev is pushing some global brands, but continues to invest in its large portfolio of local brands. Thus, notwithstanding industry imperatives, different models may be equally viable provided that there is good execution, consistency in implementation, and alignment between HRM and competitive strategy.

In many ways, the transnational concept drew its inspiration from the concept of the matrix. But transnational is neither a particular organizational form nor a specific strategic posture. Rather it is an "organizational model," a "management mentality," and a "philosophy."[90] The transnational challenge is therefore to create balanced perspectives[91] or a "matrix in the mind of managers."[92]

Ghoshal and Bartlett argue that the role of top management in the transnational is now less about managing strategy, structure, and systems than it was in the past. Structure cannot cope with the complexity, while strategic initiatives come increasingly from the entrepreneurial activities of local businesses around the globe rather than from the center. The challenge for senior management is instead to build a common sense of purpose that will guide local strategic initiatives, to coordinate through a portfolio of processes rather than via hierarchical structure, and to shape people's attitudes across the globe.[93]

The early research on the transnational enterprise focused on one major contradiction, local versus global. Researchers then began to examine this tension as it appeared in different functions within multinationals, including HRM.[94] Clearly, a relevant question was the extent to which HR policies and practices should be adapted to fit not only the local cultural context but also local institutional rules, regulations, and norms. If the multinational decentralized the responsibility for HRM and adapted practices to the local environment, it could suffer from a lack of global or regional scale advantages within the HR function, forgo the possibilities of interunit learning within the corporation, and fail to use HRM effectively to enhance coordination. A failure to address issues related to corporate social responsibility in a globally consistent manner could also cost the company dearly. Siemens experienced this when a corruption scandal erupted in 2007, as did Nike, severely criticized for not having tightly supervised labor practices across its global network of suppliers.

From Taiwanese Fishermen to a Global Market Opportunity

A story often told at Nokia, the Finnish mobile phone manufacturer, communicates clearly the transnational spirit and what it means to be both local and global.

When product penetration by mobile phones was still fairly low, a Nokia sales manager, on holiday in Taiwan, noticed that the local fishermen all carried mobile phones. It dawned on him that this might be the tip of a neglected market. Perhaps the greatest potential for the firm's products was not sophisticated urbanites, as the central marketing people thought, but rather people in remote areas where the cost of laying a network of telephone cables was prohibitive (or impossible, in the case of fishermen).

The Taiwanese fishermen themselves did not represent much of a marketing opportunity. The strategy makes sense only on a larger scale, if the company focuses on clusters of users with similar needs scattered internationally. It is therefore a good example of the transnational challenge. The company has to be sensitive to local needs in order to spot such opportunities in the first place; but then it needs to be global in order to exploit the opportunity across all sorts of potential markets.

In another stream of research that followed Bartlett and Ghoshal's initial work on transnational organizations, emphasis was put on the ability of multinationals to identify and transfer ideas from a foreign unit to other parts of the corporation and to leverage capabilities on a global scale. The box "From Taiwanese Fishermen to a Global Market Opportunity" illustrates the advantages of learning locally.

Capabilities and Knowledge as Sources of Competitiveness

Today, management, strategy, and international business scholars are increasingly focused on capabilities and knowledge as drivers of competitive advantage. A core organizational capability (or core competence) is a firm-specific bundling of technical systems, people skills, and cultural values.[95] To the extent that they are firm-specific, such organizational capabilities are difficult to imitate because of the complex configuration of the various elements. The capabilities can therefore be a major source of competitive advantage (although their very success can also create dangerous rigidities).

The distinguishing feature of a capability is the integration of skills, technologies, systems, managerial behaviors, and work values. For example, FedEx has a core competence in package routing and delivery. This rests on the integration of barcode technology, mobile communications, systems using linear programming, network management, and other skills.[96] The capability of INSEAD or IMD in executive education depends on faculty know-how integrated with program design skills, marketing, relationships with clients, the competence and attitude of support staff, reward systems, and a host of other interwoven factors that have evolved over the years. We will return to this concept extensively in the following chapter.

Another crucial source of competitive advantage comes from the firm's ability to create, transfer, and integrate knowledge. At the heart of the surge of academic and corporate interest in management of knowledge lies the distinction between explicit and tacit knowledge. The former is knowledge that you know that you have, and in organizations explicit knowledge is often codified in texts and manuals. The latter is personal, built on intuition acquired through years of experience and hard to formalize and communicate to others. One of the main approaches to knowledge management is to build collections of explicit knowledge (on customer contacts, presentation overheads, etc.) using software systems, and to make that knowledge available via an intranet. Another approach is to focus on building connections or contacts between people in the organization that can be used to transfer tacit knowledge.[97] Many professional firms have gone down this route, for instance by creating yellow page directories or internal "Facebook" platforms that allow consultants to find individuals who have relevant experience and encouraging the development of informal relationships among people interested in a certain topic area.[98] In a world where the retention of people is more difficult, it is particularly important to retain and transfer their knowledge.

Kogut and Zander have argued cogently that *the* source of advantage for multinational firms is this ability to transfer and recombine knowledge across borders.[99] Corporations that do not have the capacity to do this well will inevitably run into problems and will be defeated by those who can.

It should be added that these ideas about the source of competitive advantage are related to the *resource-based perspective* of the firm, which views it as a bundle of tangible and intangible resources. If such resources are valuable to the customer, rare, difficult to purchase or imitate, and effectively exploited, then they can provide a basis for superior economic performance that may be sustained over time. This view quickly attracted the attention of HRM scholars because its broad definition of resources could be applied to HRM-related capabilities, such as training and development, teamwork, and culture. Resource-based theory helped to reinforce the interrelationship between HRM and strategy. It provided a direct conceptual link between an organization's more behavioral and social attributes and its ability to gain a competitive advantage. This influential view, based largely on research on multinational corporations, has continued to play an important role in current strategy and HRM thinking.

Toward a Flat World?

The process of globalization has continued in the new century. In his influential book *The World is Flat*, Thomas Friedman suggests that the world has become "flat."[100] He argues that 10 "flatteners" (see Table 1–2) have produced a more level competitive playing field for individuals, groups, and companies from all parts of a shrinking world. While the process of globalization was previously driven mostly by countries and then by corporations striving to expand their

TABLE 1–2. **Friedman's 10 Forces That Flattened the World**

Flattener 1: 11/9/89	The collapse of the Berlin Wall on November 9, 1989, marked the end of the Cold War, allowing countries from the other side of the Wall to join the world economy.
Flattener 2: 8/9/95	The Internet (symbolized by Netscape going public on August 9, 1995) has become accessible to everyone, enabling people to communicate digital information around the world.
Flattener 3: Work-flow software	Machines interact and individuals from anywhere collaborate on the same digital content.
Flattener 4 : Open-sourcing	The ability of individuals (and communities) to collaborate on projects online—examples include open-source software, blogs, and Wikipedia.
Flattener 5: Outsourcing	Parts of companies' value chains are handled by other firms (often in lower-cost countries) that can handle them more efficiently.
Flattener 6: Offshoring	Firms relocate parts of their activities to lower-cost locations to reduce costs.
Flattener 7: Supply-chaining	Global streamlining and optimization of companies' total supply chains.
Flattener 8: Insourcing	Company employees perform services, such as product repairs, for other firms.
Flattener 9: In-forming	Rapid and wide search for information through Google and similar search engines.
Flattener 10: The steroids	Personal digital devices, like mobile phones, personal assistants, and voice-over-Internet protocol (VoIP).

Source: T.L. Friedman, *The World Is Flat: A Brief History of the Twenty-First Century* (New York: Farrar, Straus and Giroux, 2005).

influence and integrate their activities, what Friedman calls "Globalization 3.0" is driven more by the ability of individuals, groups, and firms to collaborate and compete internationally using the tools of the increasingly virtual world—personal computers, broadband communications, and work-flow software. Developments in communications and transportation led to step changes in internationalization in the past. As the digital revolution becomes accessible to all across the globe, this is happening all over again today.

The forces described by Friedman have contributed to many of the changes in the world economy that we have seen during the last 10 years. China has consistently attracted large amounts of FDI as it has become the factory for the world,[101] while India has become an incubator of new multinationals in global businesses that did not even exist 10 or 15 years ago, such as IT support and process outsourcing contracts.

Even with the world deeply in recession as the first decade of the 21st century draws to a close, multinationals from high-growth developing and emerging markets have become major global investors. Large international acquisitions by firms like Tata Steel from India, which bought the Anglo-Dutch group Corus, among others, and CEMEX from Mexico, the world's largest building material company, have transformed industries that were traditionally dominated by firms from developed countries. The shift away from countries such as the US and Japan dominating lists of the world's largest companies is clear. Out of the world's 500 largest corporations, the US lost 26 of its 177 spots between 1999 and 2008 and Japan no fewer than 55 of its 81. The winners were emerging countries like China (from 10 to 29), South Korea (12 → 14), India (1 → 7), Taiwan (1 → 6), Mexico (2 → 5), Brazil (3 → 5), and Russia (2 → 5).[102]

Have these developments reduced the challenges of addressing people management in multinationals? Our answer is an emphatic no. Multinational firms still face complex questions of how to enhance global coordination; how to pursue both global efficiency and local responsiveness in their operations; and how to achieve successful global exploitation of existing competencies while also exploring new knowledge and innovations. As we will argue throughout this book, people management is an integrated part of how multinationals can deal with these issues. In today's economy, international HRM is increasingly a global challenge for multinationals from *all* parts of the world.

THE EVOLUTION OF INTERNATIONAL HRM

Looking back over time, we can detect waves of alternating theories and ideologies in the management of people (see the box "The Pendulum of Management Thought" earlier in this chapter). These swings reflect an underlying tension whereby the organization is sometimes viewed as a "community," where people are team members and assets, and sometimes as a "market," in which people are resources.[103] On one side, we have the soft rhetoric of industrial betterment, human relations, and organizational culture, which emphasize normative control, arguing that organizations are collectives held together by shared values and moral involvement and that control can be exercised by shaping the identities and attitudes of workers. On the other side, we find ideas that focus on the hard rhetoric of rationalism and productivity improvement, applying methods and systems to individuals who are assumed to have an instrumental rather than affective orientation to work—scientific management, systems rationalism, and reengineering. Today powerful computer-based applications for connecting people in global networks go hand in hand with a renewed emphasis on shared corporate values.[104]

As we have seen, the challenges of foreign assignments, adapting people management practices to foreign situations, and coordinating and controlling distant operations have existed since antiquity. It is only during the last 50 years that specialized personnel managers have begun to assume a responsibility for these tasks. With the acceleration of globalization, these and other international HRM issues have developed into a central competitive challenge (see Table 1–3,

TABLE 1–3. From Personnel Welfare to International HRM

Dates	Developments in International Business	People Focus	
		Practice	Theory
1870s	Early manufacturing FDI	Welfare programs—first experiments with improving working conditions, training schemes, and common wage policies.	Industrial betterment
1900s		Appointment of welfare (or social) secretaries to handle grievances, manage workers' transfers, run the sick room, provide recreation/education.	
1910s	The golden age of international business	Time-and-motion studies, fatigue studies, job analysis, and wage administration emerge as new tasks for the employment manager.	Scientific management
1920s	International cartels	Employment policy setting is increasingly centralized in a staff function responsible for hiring and firing, keeping performance records, and handling disciplinary problems.	
1930s	Multidivisional organizations	Replicating the protective structures proposed by labor unions through due process, disciplinary procedures, and complaint systems. Counseling and interviews are established as a staple ingredient of personnel practice.	Human relations
1950s	US companies expand abroad	Manpower planning is introduced. The recruitment, testing, and assignment of employees become more systematic with a wide battery of practices spilling over from wartime experience.	
1960s 1970s	Focus in US on expatriation; matrix structures and staff bureaucracies	An increased focus on leadership development. Managers expect careers, not just jobs. Succession planning and expatriation policies are developed. HRM becomes the umbrella for flourishing people management initiatives.	Systems thinking about organization
1980s	US faces stronger competition from Japan and Europe; rationalization and consolidation	HR planning grows and dies. Involvement with corporate restructuring, managing layoffs, and outplacement. Greater attention to talent development.	Strategic HRM; organization culture

Dates	Developments in International Business	People Focus	
		Practice	Theory
1990s	Globalization	Greater localization. Growing awareness of the role of HRM in providing corporate cohesion. Global leadership development becomes vital. Attention to alliances and cross-boundary merger integration. Focus on developing human capital leads to interest in social capital, supporting innovation and knowledge management.	Resource-based view of the firm; the concept of the transnational
2000s	The growth of multinationals from emerging markets	Competitive advantage through speed and adaptation, differentiation rather than imitation. Increasing emphasis on global knowledge management. IT/Internet-based solutions and outsourcing drive reengineering of HR practices and processes. Increased global reach of the HR function. Social architecture becomes the frontier challenge for HRM.	Social capital; tension, paradox, and duality

which traces the developments in practice and theory over the last 140 years). As Floris Maljers, former cochairman of Unilever, put it, "Limited human resources—not unreliable or inadequate sources of capital—have become the biggest constraint in most globalization efforts."[105] Many scholars studying the multinational firm today, whatever their discipline or background, would agree.

The centrality of these HRM issues has increased over time. For example, as the bottom-line consequences became more visible, concern over expatriation broadened to include the understanding that it was not just about sending managers abroad but also about helping expatriates to be successful in their roles and future careers. The scope of expatriation has changed—today expatriates come not only from the multinational's home country but also from other, third countries. Localization of staff in foreign units became a new imperative, leading to the complex task of tracking and developing a global talent pool. As globalization started to have an impact on local operations, for example in China, it also became clear that even local executives need to have international experience. Challenges of knowledge and innovation management and implementation problems in the number of international ventures, alliances and cross-border mergers, and acquisitions further highlighted how HRM influences the success of internationalization strategies.

As the ABB case illustrated, the failure of structural solutions to address the problems of coordination and control led to an increased focus on how HR practices might assist in providing cohesion to the multinational firm. HRM and strategy came together in the transnational concept that helped to dissolve many of the traditional boundaries in organizational thinking. Today, the strategic importance of international HRM is widely recognized.[106]

The increasing centrality of international HRM issues has blurred the boundaries between this domain of academic study and others. Once no more than an appendix to the field of personnel/HR management, international HRM has become a lens for the study of the multinational enterprise, the form of organization that dominates the world economy. Understanding the complex challenges facing today's global organizations calls for interdisciplinary work with scholars of strategy, institutional economics, organization, cross-cultural management, leadership, change management, organizational culture, and others.

While this book draws on many different theoretical perspectives from multiple disciplines on issues related to international HRM, as we have seen in this chapter, and as we shall see throughout the book, the last perspective is probably the most critical for understanding the multinational corporation in general and the international HRM area in particular. The manager experiences this duality perspective as a paradox or contradiction, and as the need for balance in response to the tension created by opposites. This view is at the heart of Bartlett and Ghoshal's notion of the transnational, and is discussed by other writers on strategic HRM in multinational enterprises.[107] The tension between pursuing local adaptation, seeking global efficiency through scale advantages, and exploiting disparities between national (labor) markets is also dominant in Ghemawat's recent influential work on global strategy.[108] We will be developing this idea further in the next chapter, where we look at the different faces of human resource management in the international firm.

OUTLINE OF THIS BOOK

Having set the stage here, in Chapter 2 we develop the conceptual framework that underlines the book. We examine the relationship between strategy, organizational capabilities, and HRM, and we present the HR Wheel used to map the domain of human resource management. Chapter 2 also outlines different stages of HRM in multinational firms: the builder, the change partner, and the navigator who steers through the dualities of international management.

The next two chapters review the globalization strategies of local responsiveness and global integration in depth. Chapter 3 addresses the HRM implications for firms that emphasize local responsiveness, discussing how multinational firms are under pressure to respond to the local cultural, institutional, and social environment. Chapter 4 focuses on the strategy of global integration. The chapter discusses the organizational control tools needed to achieve advantages of global scale and scope and examines in detail the challenges of managing expatriation. The control and coordination mechanisms used in multinational enterprises are discussed in this and several subsequent chapters. Table 1–4 presents these mechanisms and shows where they are discussed in the book.

We then look at the different methods of coordination. Structural coordination mechanisms examined in Chapter 5 include multidimensional structures,

TABLE 1–4. Control and Coordination Mechanisms

Control Mechanism	Explanation	Where Discussed (Chapters)
Personal	Centralized decision making and monitoring by headquarters management and expatriates	4, 5
Formal	Standardization and formalization of rules and processes	4, 5
Output	Performance measurement	4, 9
Normative	Specification and diffusion of shared values, beliefs, and norms	4, 6

Coordination Mechanism	Explanation	Where Discussed (Chapters)
Structural	Multidimensional structures, lateral governance mechanisms, global teams	5
Social	Shared values, beliefs, and norms; global mind-sets; social capital	6
Process		
• Talent management	Processes for attracting, assessing, selecting, developing, and retaining talent	7, 8
• Performance management	Processes for establishing performance criteria and goals, for following them up, and for providing rewards based on performance	9
• Knowledge and innovation management	Processes for enhancing knowledge acquisition and sharing, innovations	10

cross-boundary teams, cross-boundary roles and steering groups, and virtual teams. Social coordination mechanisms of social capital, shared values, and global mindset are discussed in Chapter 6. Four chapters (Chapters 7–10) deal with key processes in international HRM: talent acquisition and retention, talent development, performance management (including compensation), and knowledge and innovation management.

Subsequently we examine three complex people management challenges in global firms: facilitating change through HRM, managing alliances and joint ventures, and cross-border merger and acquisition integration. Chapter 11 addresses one of the most salient emerging domains in international HRM: how to plan and implement large, complex processes of change. Chapters 12 and 13 deal with the critical HRM issues in alliances and acquisitions that complement organic strategies for international growth.

The final chapter addresses the implications of recent and future developments for HR professionals in multinational firms.

The focus of this book is explicitly on international HRM in large complex multinational firms rather than small or medium-sized enterprises, although a number of issues that we will cover are of direct relevance for a broad spectrum of firms. We will present examples from firms drawn from all regions of the world, including eBay, GE, IBM, and Procter & Gamble from the US, Toyota from Japan, Haier from China, leading European multinationals like ABB, Nokia, and Shell, and companies without nationalities such as Schlumberger or Arcelor-Mittal. Each chapter starts with a short case, highlighting the issues that we will discuss.

As the HR contributions to internationalization increase in importance, the boundaries between the HR function and line management become blurred, as do the boundaries with other management functions, such as strategic planning, information technology, marketing, corporate communication, and operations. Throughout this book, we will be taking a broad managerial perspective, addressing "the manager," regardless of whether that manager works as a line or general manager or as a professional in the HR function. However, from time to time, we will also address challenges (and their implications) that are specific to HR in most firms. The convention that we use is to refer to "HR" whenever we mean the functional domain, and "HR practices" when referring to corporate practices for managing people for which the HR function is at least partly responsible. When we talk about human resource management, or HRM, we are adopting a generalist perspective.

TAKEAWAYS

1. To know why international business evolved in the way it did, we need to understand how our predecessors resolved dilemmas such as exercising control from afar before modern transport and communication were developed.
2. Industrialization drove both internationalization and the evolution of personnel management. World War I had a negative impact on internationalization but a stimulating effect on personnel practices.
3. With the emergence of the modern multinational in the expansion years after World War II, the first international personnel units were set up to manage international assignments. Until the 1990s, expatriation was the dominant focus.
4. Increasing geographical spread allied to growing product ranges led some multinationals to adopt the matrix, a big conceptual advance but a structural solution that is very difficult to manage.

5. In most firms, the headquarter bureaucracies grew to cope with the increasingly complex problems of international coordination and control. With increased global competition, these bureaucracies became too costly to maintain.
6. The emergence of the Japanese challenge represented a shock for Western managers, leading to the realization that there were actually "two best ways"—and if there were two best ways, then there might be more.
7. International firms have always muddled through dilemmas and contradictions, often in a pendulum fashion. These contradictions became apparent as firms were pushed to be responsive to local needs and globally integrated at the same time. Such contradictions are the hallmark of the transnational organization.
8. All multinationals face transnational pressures, but not with equal force. Firms started to realize that HRM could help them combine local autonomy with a high degree of global coordination.
9. As more emphasis was placed on capabilities and management of knowledge as sources of competitiveness and the resource-based perspective on strategy took hold, HRM came to be seen more and more as one of the keys to building sustainable competitive advantage.
10. The complexity of issues in the international HRM domain requires us to take an interdisciplinary perspective.

NOTES

1. Barham and Heimer, 1998.
2. Kindle left ABB in February 2008 after disagreements with the company's new chairman.
3. Bartlett and Ghoshal, 1989, p. 174.
4. Moore and Lewis, 1999.
5. Moore and Lewis, 1999, p. 230.
6. Wilkins, 1988.
7. Carlos and Nicholas, 1988. On the other side of the world, southern Chinese clans spread their hold across Southeast Asia in the 14th and 15th centuries.
8. In academic terms, this is known as "agency problems" and concerns the extent to which self-interested agents will represent their principal's interest in situations where the principal lacks information about what the agent is doing. According to agency theory, principals can invest in collecting information about what the agent is doing or seek to design an incentive system such that the agent is rewarded when pursuing the principal's interests.
9. G. Jones, 1996.
10. Wren, 1994.
11. Wilkins, 1970.
12. George, 1968.
13. Even by the early 1990s, foreign direct investment had rallied to only around 8.5 percent of world output (G. Jones, 1996). The latest data show the stock of FDI to be

22.4 percent of global GDP in 2007 (World Investment Report 2008, UNCTAD—available at http://www.unctad.org/Templates/WebFlyer.asp?intItemID=4700&lang=1).

14. In Britain, the first industrial welfare worker was appointed by Rowntree in 1896 (Crichton, 1968). In the US, the National Cash Register Company established an office for welfare work in 1897. For some, these appointments mark the official start of the history of HRM (Springer and Springer, 1990).

15. Kaufman, 2007.

16. Tead and Metcalf, 1920.

17. Barley and Kunda, 1992; Ouchi, 1989.

18. Taylor, 1911.

19. Child, 1969; Donaldson, 1995; O'Connor, 1999.

20. Ulrich, 1997.

21. Baritz, 1960.

22. Kaufman, 2007.

23. Moriguchi, 2000.

24. Kaufman, 2007.

25. Jacoby, 1985.

26. Sampson, 1975.

27. Vernon, Wells, and Rangan 1997. Of course, not all sectors were equally amenable to such collusion. Cartels were rare in industries with a wide variety of products or a large number of producers, such as most finished consumer goods—or in dynamic industries like automobiles (G. Jones, 1996).

28. "Multinational Companies: Special Report," *BusinessWeek*, April 20, 1963, p. 16.

29. G. Jones, 1996.

30. Dunning, 1988.

31. Chandler, 1990.

32. Schisgall, 1981.

33. G. Jones, 1996, p. 173.

34. Vernon, 1977.

35. Kaufman, 2007.

36. Vaupel and Curhan, 1973.

37. Hays, 1974.

38. Tung, 1982.

39. Use of the term "human resources" began to creep into the vocabulary in the 1960s—perhaps the earliest systematic use of the term was in Japan, where the word *jinzai* (the combination of characters for "human" and "material") gained currency in the 1950s. The Japanese did not have the capital or physical resources of the Americans—all they had was *jinzai*. Economists had for some time spoken of the productive "resources" or "factors" of the firm, although attention focused more on capital and physical resources. Edith Penrose was particularly influential, arguing that both intangible assets such as people and tangible assets such as capital or machinery are the basis for productive output (Penrose, 1959). The research on human capital by the Nobel prize–winning economist Becker reinforced the focus.

40. "Multinational Companies: Special Report," *BusinessWeek*, April 20, 1963, p. 63.

41. Stopford and Wells, 1972.

42. The transition from the functional to the M-form divisional structure was assessed by Alfred Chandler (Chandler, 1962, 1977). Between 1949 and 1969, the number of *Fortune* 500 US firms organized along functional lines dropped from 63 percent to

11 percent (Rumelt, 1974). As Chandler put it, "Although not all integrated industrial enterprises became multinationals, nearly all industrial multinationals evolved from such enterprises." (Chandler, 1986, p. 409).

43. The threshold as a percentage of sales that would trigger this transformation from a divisional to a multinational structure was hotly debated.

44. Argyris, 1967.

45. Davis and Lawrence, 1977.

46. It would be misleading to say that the matrix structure is dead. Some organizations introduced matrix organizations in the late 1980s and 1990s. The matrix structure that ABB employed until 1998 is perhaps the most well-known example. But, as we will see in Chapter 5, this was a different form of matrix than those introduced in the 1970s—a matrix built around a structure of clear accountability. Research suggests that a matrix structure can be appropriate as a transition organization, facilitating the development of a "matrix culture," although typically it will ultimately lead to a more unitary structure now made flexible by coordination mechanisms that the matrix introduced (Ford and Randolph, 1992).

47. Ford and Randolph, 1992.

48. Galbraith, 1977.

49. Martinez and Jarillo, 1989.

50. Bartlett and Ghoshal, 1990.

51. The *nemawashi* process in Japanese firms is an informal process of consultation, typically undertaken by a high potential individual, involving talking with people and gathering support for an important decision or project.

52. Many German international firms had an unusual structure abroad, where the sales subsidiary was run jointly by a local general manager with a German commercial manager on a *primus inter pares* basis, facilitating this consensual approach.

53. This fueled a new question for HRM around the world: Since the old psychological contract of "a fair day's pay for a fair day's work . . . with a generous pension at the end" was now under threat, what was the nature of the new psychological contract for the future (Greller and Rousseau, 1994; Rousseau and Robinson, 1994)?

54. Although we know of no research directly on the point, our observation is that firms that took the matrix route generally learned more quickly the importance of lateral relations and "normative integration" than those that took the headquarters coordination route. Indeed, researchers have described matrix structures as an apprenticeship in building lateral teamwork (Ford and Randolph, 1992). For example, when Dow Chemicals abandoned its matrix structure, it was partly because it no longer needed it since the necessary "matrix culture" mechanisms were solidly in place to ensure coordination. Companies taking the headquarters route appear more typically to oscillate between centralization and decentralization, sometimes getting stuck in protracted pendulum swings.

55. Beer et al., 1984.

56. Legge, 1995.

57. Galbraith and Nathanson, 1979; Fombrun, Tichy, and Devanna, 1984.

58. Walker, 1980.

59. Peters and Waterman, 1982.

60. Chandler, 1962.

61. Mintzberg, 1994. In the US, the Human Resource Planning Society emerged as the first strategic human resource professional association and was later to regret its choice of name. While the idea of linking strategy and HRM initially generated a lot

of enthusiasm among HRM scholars, one article in 1985 accurately described the outcome as "somewhere between a dream and a nightmare" (Golden and Ramanujam, 1985).

62. Hofstede, 1980a. See our discussion in Chapter 3.

63. Pucik and Hatvany, 1981, and Pucik, 1984. The success of Japan threw the spotlight on HR ingredients such as long-term employment, intensive socialization, team-based appraisal and rewards, slow promotion, and job rotation. Distinctive features of Japanese management that received attention in the West included continuous improvement, commitment to learning, quality management practices, customer-focused production systems, and consultative decision making. Some observers saw these HRM practices as amounting to a third way of organizing, based neither on command-and-control (Theory X) nor on participative management (Theory Y), and which were dubbed "Theory Z" (Ouchi, 1981).

64. Oxley, 1961.

65. Kuin, 1972.

66. Even today, localization, discussed in Chapter 3 (how to develop the talent of local staff), remains one of the most neglected areas of international human resource management.

67. "Multinational Companies: Special Report," *BusinessWeek*, April 20, 1963, p. 76.

68. Edström and Galbraith, 1977.

69. "Three times the number of managers were transferred in Europe at [one company rather than the other], despite their being of the same size, in the same industry, and having nearly identical organization charts" (Edströ and Galbraith, 1977, p. 255).

70. See the SOTA (State of the Art) surveys run annually since 1995 by the Human Resource Planning Society, reported each year in the journal *Human Resource Planning*; see also a survey undertaken in *Fortune* 500 firms by Gregersen, Morrison, and Black (1998).

71. Perlmutter, 1969.

72. Perlmutter, 1969, p. 13.

73. Kogut and Zander, 1993.

74. Prescott, Rothwell, and Taylor, 1999.

75. Hedlund, 1986, p. 18.

76. Held et al., 1999.

77. FDI refers to investments in units abroad over which the corporation has control, thus excluding purely financial (portfolio) investments.

78. Vernon, 1966; Stopford and Wells, 1972; Johanson and Vahlne, 1977.

79. Ashkenas et al., 1995.

80. Such clusters of critical factors helped particular nations to develop a competitive advantage in certain fields—such as German firms in chemicals or luxury cars, Swiss firms in pharmaceuticals, and US firms in personal computers, software, and movies.

81. Bartlett and Ghoshal, 1989.

82. See Hedlund, 1986; Prahalad and Doz, 1987; and Perlmutter, 1969.

83. Doz, Bartlett, and Prahalad, 1981; Doz and Prahalad, 1984, 1986.

84. Bartlett and Ghoshal, 1989.

85. Since the term is generic, we use "international" when referring to Bartlett and Ghoshal's (1989) use of the term.

86. Although NEC clearly had the grand vision, with its notion of combining computers and communication (long before the emergence of Cisco), it was unable to

implement that vision. A big part of the problem is that it was never able to global-ize and go where the talent was.

87. Ghoshal and Bartlett, 1998, p. 65.
88. Nohria and Ghoshal, 1997, p. 189. In terms of theory, it is the principle of "requisite complexity" that underlies the appropriate fit between organizational environment and form—the internal complexity of the firm should reflect the complexity of the external environment. Requisite complexity is a concept borrowed by management theorists from the field of cybernetics (Ashby, 1956).
89. See Nohria and Ghoshal (1997) for a classification of the business environments of multinational firms.
90. Bartlett and Ghoshal, 1989.
91. Doz and Prahalad, 1986.
92. Bartlett and Ghoshal, 1989.
93. Ghoshal and Bartlett, 1997.
94. Rosenzweig and Nohria, 1994; Björkman and Lu, 2001.
95. Hamel and Prahalad, 1994; Leonard, 1995.
96. This example is taken from Hamel and Prahalad (1994, Chapter 9) who provide a more complete definition, emphasizing that core competencies should be gateways to the future.
97. Polanyi, 1966; Nonaka and Takeuchi, 1995.
98. So-called communities of practice are discussed in Chapters 6 and 10.
99. Kogut and Zander, 1992.
100. Friedman, 2005.
101. At the same time, Chinese outward FDI also increased dramatically. In 2008, Chinese outward FDI amounted to US$52 billion, almost double that of the US (K. Davies, 2009. "While Global FDI Falls, China's Outward FDI Doubles," *Columbia FDI Perspectives*, No. 5: http://www.vcc.columbia.edu/pubs/documents/DaviesPerspective-Final.pdf.).
102. See http://money.cnn.com/magazines/fortune/global500/2008/full_list/.
103. Legge, 1999.
104. The need for global shared values is discussed in Chapter 6 and also in Chapter 8.
105. Cited by Bartlett and Ghoshal (1992).
106. Even in the mid-1980s there was speculation about whether international HRM was "fact or fiction" (Morgan, 1986).
107. See, for example, De Cieri and Dowling (1999, p. 321).
108. Ghemawat, 2007.

CHAPTER 2

Human Resource Management in the International Firm: The Framework

Lincoln Electric Ventures Abroad

The 110-year-old Ohio-based Lincoln Electric Company has long been a favorite case used by business schools to show how human resource management can contribute to sustainable business performance. The largest manufacturer of welding equipment in the world, Lincoln motivates its American employees through a distinctive compensation system and a culture of cooperation between management and labor, based on one of the founders' fervent beliefs in self-reliance, the necessity of competition for human progress, and egalitarian treatment of managers and employees. Introduced by family management in the 1930s, the incentive system is based on piece rates and an annual bonus linked to profits that can amount to over half of employees' income. To determine the bonus, production employees are appraised on four criteria: output, quality, dependability, and ideas/cooperation.

Abroad, Lincoln Electric invested successfully in Canada (1925), Australia (1938), and France (1955), but until the late 1980s the firm still focused mostly on its domestic market. The company had enjoyed unrivaled and much-acclaimed growth and prosperity, driving its domestic competitors (including GE) out of the business. Led by a management team that had never worked outside the United States, the firm then decided on a bold strategy for internationalization, spending the equivalent of over half its sales on building greenfield plants in Japan and Latin America, and on 19 acquisitions in various European countries and Mexico.[1] Tremendous opportunities were envisaged to leverage Lincoln's manufacturing expertise and HRM system internationally, implementing its motivational and incentive system, which already worked well in France and other foreign operations. Combining the most productive and low-cost manufacturing operation with high quality, Lincoln seemed destined to dominate the global market.

The rapid international expansion turned out to be a disaster. Lacking managers with international experience, the firm was forced to rely on acquired managers who were not familiar with Lincoln's culture and who wanted to maintain their own autonomy. The only new country where its incentive system and culture took gradual hold was Mexico. In most of Europe and Japan, where piece-rate payments are viewed with deep suspicion, Lincoln's approach was rejected. In Germany, with its 35-hour workweek, employees would not agree to working nearly 50 hours when necessary, as they did in the US. The tight link between sales and manufacturing—another pillar of Lincoln's success—disintegrated, and inventory ballooned while sales stagnated in the recession of the early 1990s. To fix the problem, senior managers with strong international track records were recruited from outside the company. A new team then sold off or restructured most of its international acquisitions.

Lincoln's failure was the consequence of poor transfer of HRM practices abroad, in spite of the phenomenal success of its approach at home. When Lincoln again expanded its international operations in the late 1990s, it kept the expensive lessons from its previous internationalization attempt in mind. The company relied more on joint ventures and alliances and, if necessary, adapted its management approach to fit local conditions. It also gradually built a cadre of managers with international experience who were transferred to the foreign units. In 2008, the company again enjoyed record sales and profits, with 40 percent of sales stemming from its expanding foreign operations. However, in spite of the significant progress made, Lincoln still experienced challenges in managing people in its overseas units. For instance, in China it continued to struggle to find, develop, and retain talented local professionals and managers.[2]

OVERVIEW

In this chapter, we lay out the conceptual framework that underlies this book. We start with a central question: How does human resource management add value in international firms?

HRM can contribute most significantly to firm performance when HR practices support the organizational capabilities that allow the company to compete successfully. Lincoln's major capabilities in the US were the extremely high productivity of its workforce and the consistent high quality of its products. Equally important was the firm's high level of operational flexibility as US employees' pay was tied to firm performance and the workers agreed to adjust their working hours to meet market demands. These organizational capabilities helped create superior value for customers, and were difficult for Lincoln's competitors to copy. In short, the HR practices in Lincoln's US operations helped build and support the firm's capabilities.

Business strategy and the creation of distinct organizational capabilities are the core of our conceptualization of HRM and its role in the multinational corporation. Building on this core, we will review the HRM domain consisting of a number of key elements that we represent as different parts of an HR Wheel. These include guiding principles for HRM decision making, the development and implementation of HR practices in different parts of the corporation, the roles of the HR function of the firm, and HR outcomes that contribute to value creation in the enterprise.

In our discussion of HRM we distinguish between three different stages and the related roles. In the first stage the metaphor is that of a builder who puts basic HRM foundations in place. This is not only a question of developing individual HR practices such as compensation and development—consistency between HR practices and the work organization is also crucial. Consistency is Lincoln's strength in the United States. The finely tuned interrelationship of the firm's organizational practices contributed more to its performance than its incentive system—coherence that was lost when Lincoln moved abroad.

Over time, builders may become administrative custodians, and this can become a challenge in the second stage of HRM, which we describe with the change partner metaphor. Markets, technologies, and competitive conditions all change with time, as does firm strategy. At this stage, HRM's contribution to performance is to facilitate organizational realignment in order to respond to changes in the external environment and strategy. Moreover, as firms develop their international activities, there are particular challenges in finding a balance between pressure to adapt HRM practices locally while maintaining consistency across locations and units. This is a complex and less understood process, at least from the HR perspective.

As the need for change speeds up, it is necessary for HRM to anticipate the future. There is a dualistic pattern in changes facing the global organization reflecting the tension between opposing forces—for example, between local adaptation and global integration, centralization and decentralization, and between evolutionary progress, focused on exploiting resources, and revolutionary change, focused on developing new resources. The third stage of HRM, and the final topic of this chapter, puts the emphasis on steering through these dualities—the navigator role. This aspect of HRM is particularly important for the transnational organization, defined by the contradictions that it confronts.

BUSINESS STRATEGY AND ORGANIZATIONAL CAPABILITIES

Strategy has to do with making forward-looking choices under conditions of uncertainty—choices about which parts of the value chain the firm will focus on, what it will develop and do in-house rather than buy in from outside, the geographical markets it will serve, and myriad other choices that are important for the long-term direction of the firm. Strategic management is a broader term, encompassing the process of deciding on strategy as well as its implementation.

Since the inception of the field of strategic management in the 1960s its main preoccupation has been with the question of why some firms are more successful than others. Initially, little attention was paid to the role played by human resources. During the 1980s, strategy meant competitive positioning based on the analysis of industry characteristics.[3] But it soon became clear that having the right strategy is not enough; what also matters is the capacity to execute that strategy. Execution is to a greater or lesser extent always a question of people—having the right leaders to implement the strategy; training and coaching people in the new skills and behaviors that are required; realigning performance management and rewards to the new strategy; and all the challenges of managing major change. The initial focus of strategic human resource management was on strategy implementation.

Strategy implementation is closely associated with the management of change and realignment (which we review briefly later in this chapter). The resource-based view of the firm that came into prominence in the early 1990s provided a different and complementary view, shifting the focus to sustainable performance and turning the spotlight even more on the firm's internal resources. To achieve superior, long-term economic performance, Barney proposed that the organization's resources should be valuable to the customer, rare, and difficult to purchase or imitate.[4]

Today, this view is widely accepted in the field of strategic management, where human resources and other intangible resources, like organizational culture and reputation, have moved squarely to the center of the debate about why some firms are more successful than others. Not surprisingly, HR scholars have also widely endorsed the resource-based view of the firm as a theoretical foundation for their work, arguing that the firm's pool of human resources as well as its processes for managing them can constitute bases for sustainable competitive advantage.[5] They must also be intimately linked to the firm's business model and strategy.

However, in practice, linking HR (and other organizational) processes with business strategy has proven difficult. Many different HR strategies can support a particular business strategy. How can the firm make the right choices about the policies and practices needed to implement the strategy? This question can be resolved by focusing on the features of the organization that support the business strategy—the kind of activities and processes at which the firm should excel, bringing us to the concept of organizational capabilities.

Organizational Capabilities

A formal definition of organizational capability is "the ability to perform repeatedly a productive task which relates to a firm's capacity for creating value through effecting the transformation of input to output."[6] In short, organizational capabilities refer to the firm's ability to combine and leverage its resources to bring about a desired end.[7] 3M's long-term track record in innovation, Toyota's continuous improvement process in manufacturing, and the ability of Southwest Airlines to deliver excellent customer experiences at a low price are examples of such capabilities.[8] Not all companies compete through organizational capabilities, but those who do generally earn higher returns because their competitive advantage is more sustainable. From this perspective, the HRM elements of an organizational capability are closely linked to strategy.

Organizational capabilities are often difficult to unravel and thus hard to imitate. Let's consider the case of Lincoln. A casual observer may consider the company's piece-rate incentive system as driving the business model—aggressive pay-for-performance stimulates high productivity. However, high productivity alone does not provide sustainable differentiation. Other companies can achieve high productivity, through automation or by outsourcing production to a low-cost location, for example. In addition to workforce productivity, at the core of Lincoln's successful business model is the elasticity of its cost structure—the ability to transform fixed costs into variable costs, essential in an environment with high volatility of demand. Anything that HRM at Lincoln can do to convert fixed costs to variable costs is given priority—so production workers are expected to reduce their working hours in economic downturns and increase them when demand is high.

In most cases, a firm must put in place a range of capabilities to create value, although usually there are only a few that drive the company's competitive advantage. These differentiating capabilities must satisfy three criteria:[9]

- They must create value for the customer—doing something that does not add value to the customer, however well it is done, cannot be a source of competitive advantage.
- The capability has to be rare and unique—if competitors have a similar capability, it cannot be a source of competitive advantage.
- The capability has to be difficult to duplicate—otherwise it will quickly be replicated by competitors.

It should be noted that even if a specific capability may be essential to a particular business model, it will not contribute to competitive advantage unless it satisfies these criteria. The difference between enabling and differentiating organizational capabilities is important. For example, in the pharmaceutical industry, conducting R&D in strict compliance with regulatory rules is an enabling capability, while doing it faster and more cheaply than competitors may deliver differentiation.

Implementing Capabilities

Implementing a competitive and robust HR strategy that supports the business requires the HR leadership to think ahead about some important questions:

- What are the essential characteristics of the business model?
- What differentiating and enabling organizational capabilities should support the business model?

- What behaviors and actions will be required to drive these capabilities?
- What people strategies (HR practices) would lead to these desired behaviors?

Long-term success is driven far more by consistency and coherence in answering these questions than by the quest for "best practices." A number of firms have tried to copy Lincoln's compensation system, but failed. What they have missed is that at Lincoln, the piece-rate system is only one of the tools that drive cost flexibility and productivity. It is the unique bundling of people management and organizational practices that produces the desired effect.

There is another even more intangible element in Lincoln's way of implementing capabilities. Piece-rate systems of pay are often associated with adversarial relationships between employers and employees. However, at Lincoln, the relationship between management and employees is characterized by a high degree of mutual trust. Again, there are many elements to this trust. Careful attention is paid to fixing the piece rates, which do not change unless there are unusual circumstances and full consultation. The firm has a distinctive employer brand that leads to the self-selection of people attracted by its entrepreneurial culture and the possibility of earning generous bonuses. Without the trust that has evolved over decades in the US plant, Lincoln's capabilities would fall apart. Its executives are conscious of this. When the disastrous foreign expansion led to large corporate losses in the 1990s, Lincoln borrowed money to be able to continue to pay bonuses to its US workers since these generous bonuses were a part of the psychological contract that existed between the workforce and the company.[10] If the company had broken its side of the deal, this would have seriously jeopardized the employees' trust in management and destroyed the workers' belief in what is fair—high financial rewards in return for high productivity and flexible work practices.

Consider another highly successful US firm, Southwest Airlines. From its launch in 1971, Southwest adopted a strategy of short point-to-point flights, frequent departures, and low fares. The firm has been profitable every year since its inception, in a volatile industry marked by poor profitability. Southwest's success is partly the outcome of a successful low-cost business model. Southwest uses a single aircraft type, often operates from underused secondary airports that are free from congestion and cheaper than large international airports, and it provides no food on board. While these characteristics may be easy for other airlines to imitate—and many have tried—its pool of hardworking, customer-oriented, and productive employees who turn Southwest planes around in considerably less time than its competitors need has not been easy to replicate.

Indeed Southwest's management strongly believes that its real competitive advantage lies in its employees and the customer service they provide.[11] Since its creation, Southwest has developed a unique culture, dubbed the "Southwest Spirit," and personified by founder and long-standing CEO Herb Kelleher. The Southwest culture, with its emphasis on having fun at work, puts a premium on the behavior of its employees. Through multiple rounds of interviews, the company rigorously screens job candidates for positive, team-oriented, and customer-centric attitudes. The organizing principle of Southwest is teamwork rather than specialized job descriptions, and employees are expected to "do the right thing" (one element of the Southwest Spirit). The fact that employees own more than 10 percent of the company's stock keeps them aware of the importance of retaining Southwest's outstanding record of on-time arrivals and customer service. In short, the capability of Southwest to get planes full of repeat customers in the air fast is supported by a set of well-aligned HR practices that are implemented consistently across the whole organization.

The Lincoln and Southwest cases illustrate how organizational capabilities help to sustain firm performance. Human resource practices are consistent and have played important roles in building the differentiating capabilities of these firms. However, these examples also raise two other points.

First, HR practices that have a positive impact on firm performance for a particular firm with a particular business model in a particular industry may not do so in other situations. There is no single recipe for success. For instance, Lincoln pays its employees large bonuses based on their individual performance while Southwest Airlines does not pay any individual bonuses, driving motivation through a strong team and customer-oriented culture.

Second, although there is a tendency for firms in the same industry to adopt HR practices that are relatively similar, since they are all influenced by the dominant technology of the sector, companies in the same industry may also differ in their intended organizational capabilities and how these are implemented through HR and other practices. For instance, the workforce strategy of Ryanair—perhaps the most successful budget airline in Europe—with its emphasis on a contingent workforce and confrontational employee relations, could not be more different than that of Southwest.[12]

Organizational Capabilities in Multinational Firms

In this book, we introduce examples from around the world of successful companies that are able to outperform their competitors in part because of their people management practices: for example, Haier in China, CEMEX in Mexico, Lincoln Electric and Southwest Airlines in the United States, Infosys in India, Michelin in France, Toyota in Japan. While they deploy very different HR practices, all these companies are clear about which organizational capabilities are needed to support their business model, and they make sure that their HR practices drive the necessary actions and behaviors.

However, as these companies internationalize, the challenge they face is how management practices that successfully support organizational capabilities in one country can be adapted to another. Southwest Airlines has not yet encountered this issue as it only operates in the US, but the troubled journey of Lincoln overseas shows how difficult it can be to transfer organizational capabilities abroad—the underlying HR practices do not necessarily travel well to a different environment. Lincoln Electric executives regarded their HR practices as a major source of competitive advantage. Yet these practices generally failed when transferred to the newly acquired units abroad. As an organization expands internationally, culture and institutional context make the issue of how HRM contributes to company performance even more complex.

The concept of organizational capability is relevant to multinational firms not only from the perspective of good management of the process of internationalization. As we discussed in Chapter 1, starting with the ABB case, the capacity of the multinational firm to master the global control and coordination challenge, and to manage the multiple tensions and conflicting demands embedded in international business, is in itself a key organizational capability.

THE HR WHEEL

In the previous section we introduced the concept of organizational capabilities, which alongside strategy implementation, provide the centerpoint for HR activities in any business organization. These capabilities (a) are based on underlying principles that guide HRM in the firm; (b) are reflected in distinct HR practices that are supported by (c) different roles of the HR function, leading in turn to (d) a set of desired organizational outcomes. These four fully integrated parts of the total HR system determine how HRM operates in multinational corporations.

We use the metaphor of the "HR Wheel," presented in Figure 2–1, to capture the dynamic and interdependent relationship between these four elements. We will discuss each part of the HR Wheel in turn, but we will focus in particular

---

FIGURE 2–1. The HR Wheel

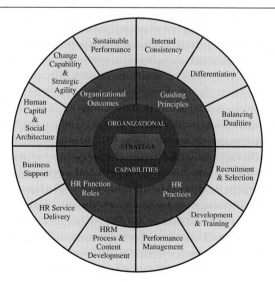

on the guiding principles, as these determine to a large degree what kind of HR policies and practices will be implemented inside the firm.

Setting the Guiding Principles

We start the discussion of the HR Wheel with a proposition that three guiding principles are at the foundation of human resource management in multinational corporations:

- Internal consistency.
- Differentiation.
- Balancing dualities.

The three principles are complementary, although in practice most multinational companies approach their implementation in a gradual manner—starting with consistency, then developing a more differentiated approach, and finally mastering how to respond to the dualities embedded in cross-border people management.

Internal Consistency

The principle of internal consistency refers to the way in which the firm's HR practices fit with each other and with other elements of the work organization, such as the degree of specialization of work tasks and the extent to which work is organized around teams rather than individuals. For example, if a firm invests a great deal of money in skill development, it should emphasize employee retention through constructive feedback, competitive compensation, and career management. It also should empower employees to contribute to the organization and reward them for initiative.[13] Some form of explicit management philosophy will help ensure this consistency across all practices. Such combinations of HR practices lead to a whole that is more than the sum of its parts. Conversely, having a reward system that pays for individual performance when the work is organized around teams would constitute what some describe as a "deadly combination" of work practices.[14]

Consistency is important for organizational performance. Let's return to Lincoln Electric to illustrate this point. Lincoln has a highly consistent approach to HRM, and its widely publicized piece-rate and bonus systems are only one part of a finely tuned set of practices that evolved over 50 years.[15] The factory workers view themselves as individual entrepreneurs who are rewarded generously if they perform well. The US plant is basically run by the workers, with only one supervisor per 58 workers.[16] The incentive system goes hand in hand with a radical belief in the equality of management and employees—no-holds-barred consultative mechanisms, open-door practices, and total transparency about company results. Similar compensation principles apply equally to executives, managers, and factory workers. The appraisal system has evolved step-by-step over the decades and supports the strategy of the firm: high quality at the lowest possible cost, and flexibility to meet changing demand.

In practice, there are three different aspects of consistency to consider. The first is single-employee consistency—whether employees experience appraisal, promotion, compensation, and other HRM elements as complementary or conflicting. Studies of the impact of HRM on employee attitudes and behavior show that performance suffers because of loss of motivation, commitment, and initiative when members of staff experience these practices as inconsistent, owing to poor design or conflicting management priorities.[17] The second aspect is consistency across employees—whether employees in similar roles and making the same contribution but of different genders, ethnic origins, or backgrounds (e.g., expatriates vs. locals) are treated equally.[18] The third aspect is temporal consistency, or continuity over time. If practices and policies are constantly changing, there will be confusion and dysfunctional frustration among employees.[19] All three aspects of consistency can be found in Lincoln Electric's US operations.

So far, we have discussed consistency in terms of the content of HR practices—the way in which the firm recruits, selects, develops, and manages the performance of its employees. However, these practices should also display consistent themes or messages, often embodied in some management philosophy or value system that supplies the necessary coherence.[20] If the messages picked up by employees through work practices are clear and consistent, a stronger positive effect on employee attitudes and behavior can be expected.[21] But sometimes HRM rhetoric conflicts with the reality that employees perceive, and this can undermine HR's credibility. We have seen an example during our work in Brazil, where some well-intentioned HR executives championed an HRM philosophy they had learned in the US and Europe, while local staff typically saw the message as so remote from reality that the HR function was discredited.[22]

All this highlights the importance of consistency between the espoused HRM strategy, the HRM policies, and the actual practices in different parts of the organization. For instance, company executives may state that they have a merit-based pay system. But if the firm does not have valid processes for making sure that employees are in fact paid on merit, the staff may feel unfairly treated, leading to a drop in organizational commitment and effectiveness.[23]

The challenges of achieving a good fit between HRM strategies, policies, and practices are particularly difficult in multinational corporations with operations in different cultures and institutional contexts. While the firm may espouse a worldwide HRM philosophy supported by globally standardized HRM policies, actual practices often reflect the local cultural and institutional context, and therefore differ across countries. Local managers often ignore the global philosophy and policies—"Great idea, but unfortunately it does not apply here"—and the result is inconsistency in the deployment of HRM across the organization.

Differentiation

While there are good reasons for emphasizing internal HRM consistency, there is a risk of taking consistency too far. Companies that focus too much on building and optimizing a well-integrated set of consistent HR practices run the risk of creating a rigid system that may be costly and difficult to adapt to changing demands. Therefore, the principle of consistency must go hand in hand with the principle of differentation.

While differentiation in HRM practices due to geographic location receives most attention in the HRM literature—especially when it relates to multinationals—there are actually at least three complementary notions of differentiation that need to be considered:

- Differentiation across employee groups.
- Differentiation across subunits (geographies and/or business lines).
- Differentiation from other firms, both multinational and local.[24]

First, not all employee groups are equally important for the success of the organization. Firms that apply the same HR practices across all employee groups run the risk of underinvesting in the talent that is crucial for long-term success while overinvesting in people who are easily replaceable. Practices that are appropriate for one part of the workforce may not be optimal for another. Lepak and Snell's work on different HR architectures has been influential in this area (see the box "Differentiation among Employee Groups").[25]

Differentiation among Employee Groups

Lepak and Snell suggest that one can juxtapose two dimensions—strategic value and uniqueness—to arrive at a matrix of four groups of employees, each with different employment relationships and appropriate configurations of HR practices, as presented in the following figure.

Core employees have high strategic value and are unique to the firm, fulfilling two of the criteria that constitute a viable basis for

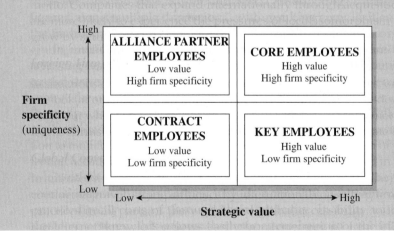

competitive advantage. Firms have a strong incentive to invest in and retain this talent pool. Some configuration of high performance/commitment-based HR practices is a natural approach to managing this employee group. In multinational corporations, this core group typically includes senior managers, high potentials, specialists with unique and critical skills, and some technical professionals.[26]

The employees in the quadrant of high strategic value but low uniqueness are also likely to be employed on a long-term basis. However, since their human capital is not unique to the firm they can be replaced more easily, so it makes less sense to invest heavily in their development. The drivers at UPS and DHL fall into this category.[27] However, the distinction between this and the former group is not always clear-cut. Sales professionals may be easy to replace, but those with close relationships with customers are not.

It may make more sense to engage people with firm-specific know-how but of low strategic value through long-term partnerships with service providers than to employ them full-time. For instance, firms often choose to outsource certain HR processes such as recruitment or international compensation and benefits, in long-term collaboration with specialized service providers. An example is Nokia, which uses PricewaterhouseCoopers for issues related to the international transfer of personnel, and IBM for many of its IT processes.

Finally, there are certain necessary tasks that neither are of high value nor require unique knowledge or skills. These tasks tend to be either carried out by temporary employees or outsourced on a relatively short-term competitive basis. Examples include clerical work and maintenance tasks of various kinds that are only loosely coupled with the way in which the company produces value for its customers.

Lepak and Snell's arguments in favor of differentiating HR practices among employee groups are compelling and in line with what we see in many corporations. One study of Spanish firms concluded that 70 percent used all four modes of employment;[28] another showed that companies did indeed use different combinations of HR practices to manage employee groups that varied in terms of strategic value and uniqueness.[29]

While the benefits of differentiating HR practices between employee groups apply to most organizations, differentiation across subunits is of particular importance to multinational firms. They are often under considerable pressure to differentiate or adapt their HR practices to the institutional and cultural environments in which they operate.

Failure to make sensible adaptations to different environments may be costly, as the Lincoln case shows. The US executives spearheading the company's internationalization in the late 1980s and early 1990s believed strongly in the effectiveness of their work practices, and so these were introduced without much adjustment in the newly established or acquired subsidiaries abroad. However, local managers often disagreed with the appropriateness of (for example) worker consultation or autonomy over working hours, while local employees and unions rejected other practices. In many countries, the proposed practices were simply illegal, at odds with national labor laws and regulations.

Lincoln's approach may seem naïve, but many firms have walked the same path with great enthusiasm. Successful companies, particularly those that have operated unchallenged for long periods of time in home markets, sometimes adopt a universalist approach to HRM when they expand internationally. They find out the hard way that some degree of local differentiation is necessary—which can in turn compromise the consistency of HR practices and necessitate a careful rethinking of the company's management approach.

Does this mean that companies must always adapt their practices to fit with the cultural and institutional environment? Is "When in Rome, do as the Romans do" always a good guideline? Such a conclusion would be as naïve as the "one best way."

In our view, the Lincoln story should not be interpreted as implying that reward and appraisal systems that link compensation closely to individual and/or company performance will never work in, say, Germany. After careful analysis, an appropriate conclusion might be that such an approach to HRM might work in Germany: *if* the firm is able to recruit staff who find such a reward system attractive; *if* the work system can be designed to measure individual performance; *if* the compensation system complies with local labor law; *if* appropriate practices can build employee trust in management; and so on.

Some of these *if*s might rule out the use of such a system or render it excessively expensive, but highly variable reward systems may pop up in the most unlikely places if properly implemented.[30] Lincoln's mistake was not that it tried to take its unique approach to people management abroad. When firms globalize it makes sense to build on what makes the company unique and successful in its home country. However, the Lincoln management seemed to be unaware of how far its management approach could vary from local norms and how difficult it might be to change the behavior of managers and employees in acquired companies who had no experience of the Lincoln Way.[31]

Some HR professionals consider that it is arrogant, if not fundamentally wrong and improper, to be different in a foreign culture. However, having HR practices that are distinctively different from those in local firms can help to recruit and retain local talent who are attracted by the unique features of the multinational. The hallmark of cross-cultural understanding is being able to go beyond rudimentary stereotypes, knowing where one has to conform with the environment and where one can be different. Understanding where to push and where to give in to cultural and instititutional considerations—in short, how to balance the two—is part of the global know-how at the core of people management in the transnational corporation.

This brings us to the third and probably most potent aspect of differentiation, focusing on the distinctiveness of the firm's approach to HRM. Sustainable competitive advantage rarely comes from either copying others or being like them—it invariably comes from being different from other firms. As we noted earlier, a capability has to be rare and unique, as well as difficult to duplicate, in order to confer sustainable competitive advantage. Differentiation stems from how the firm's unique combination of HR practices makes it stand out from other organizations, often in subtle and invisible ways that are embedded in the culture of the enterprise.

While the necessity for differentiation is widely accepted within the fields of strategic management and marketing, where being different is key to firm performance, the importance of competitive differentiation has received much less attention in HRM. Although it may be intuitively obvious that commodity-type HR cannot produce distinct organizational capabilities, when we attend HR conferences around the world we are struck by the amount of effort that goes into collecting information about what other firms are doing, rather than into thinking about how to differentiate. In particular, recruitment, development, and performance management are three HR processes with great potential for creating differentiation.

For example, attracting and retaining the right people involves marketing the firm as an employer. Unless the firm stands out from its competitors in the labor market, it is unlikely to appeal to potential employees with the required skills and attitudes. In the Cleveland, Ohio, area where Lincoln Electric's main factory is located, the company's unique work practices are well known. This enables the company to recruit self-reliant individuals who are attracted by its highly competitive work system. Lincoln's strong employer brand is an important reason why it has been so successful in the United States—but it is also one element of its competitive advantage that is not easy to transfer abroad.

Other firms that follow a distinct path to developing competitive capabilities are also known for paying careful attention to recruitment and selection. Toyota's meticulous assessment of all job candidates from hourly workers to senior executives is legendary.[32] And P&G with its traditional (some might say archaic) emphasis on long-term careers and promotion from within attracts 600,000 applicants worldwide and rigorously selects the 2,700 it deems the very best (including testing for attitudinal fit).[33] No apologies there for not being trendy. But in both the P&G and Toyota cases, differentiation also goes hand in hand with consistency, which takes us to the third guiding principle of multinational HRM—balancing dualities.

Balancing Dualities

The importance of balance—in other words, deciding how far to focus on one particular goal, issue, or principle at the expense of another—is one of the central messages of this book. We will elaborate more on this issue when discussing the navigator stage of HRM, managing the numerous tensions that exist between opposing forces, later in this chapter. Here we limit our scope to the consistency–differentiation duality.

In case of a multinational firm, there are no simple answers to the questions of how, and how far, to adapt HR practices abroad. While differentiation across locations can help the multinational achieve a better fit with the various environments in which it operates, too close alignment of HR practices to each external location (country or region) is likely to lead to a loss of integration—global inefficiencies, lack of learning across units, and problems of control and coordination.

The tension between differentiation on the one hand and consistency and integration on the other has traditionally been resolved through structural choices—indeed, differentiation and integration form the fundamental DNA of organizational design.[34] Corporations build their basic structure—traditionally differentiating either by geography (regional structures) or by business (product line structures)—to maintain consistency and coordination within units, but allowing differentiation between them. However, the situation of the transnational organization is more complex. It faces multiple pressures for differentiation—on geographic/regional, business, customer or global account, and global project lines—as well as increasing needs for coordination. We discuss the structural choices that organizations can use to respond to these pressures for multidimensional organization in Chapter 5.

However, multinational firms also use social mechanisms to address this duality of high needs for both differentiation and integration.[35] Relationships between employees from different parts of the corporation help people to understand and constructively deal with the often conflicting goals of local responsiveness, global efficiency, and interunit coordination. In addition to facilitating social networks, corporations may invest in developing shared values and a global mindset among their employees—that is, a way of thinking that incorporates the dualities and contradictions they face in their daily work.

Designing Core HR Practices

With the three guiding principles in mind, the next step is to put them in action. Every firm has to cope with a number of basic and vitally important HRM tasks, such as getting the right people into the right place at the right time—attracting, motivating, and retaining people. These are the core tasks of HRM, the facet that is most familiar, and that is dealt with in myriad books on the topic. Organizational performance will suffer if these tasks are not executed well. To guide our discussion, Table 2–1 provides a simple framework to structure the key HR practices.

We will discuss many of the specific HR practices listed in Table 2–1 in considerable detail in Chapters 7–9. In this chapter, we provide a brief introduction to these practices and point to some of the key challenges that multinationals have to confront. We should point out that with our focus on managers and knowledge workers in multinational firms, we address the important area of labor and industrial relations only briefly in the context of institutional differences among countries.

Recruitment and Selection

Companies worldwide face the challenge of meeting their demand for human capital and attracting new employees with the desired skills and competencies. Without an appealing and differentiated employee value proposition, including a set of HR practices potential job applicants will find attractive, it is difficult for the firm to fight the "war for talent" that characterizes emerging and growing

TABLE 2–1. Key Human Resource Practices

Recruitment and selection
- Workforce planning
- Employer branding
- Recruitment
- Induction and socialization
- Selection
- International transfers
- Termination and outplacement

Development and training
- Training (on-the-job and off-the-job)
- Talent assessment and reviews
- Succession planning
- Career management
- Coaching and mentoring
- Leadership development

Performance management and rewards
- Job evaluation
- Goal/standard setting
- Performance measurement
- Appraisal and feedback
- Compensation and benefits
- Rewards and recognition

Communication[A]

Labor and industrial relations[A]

[A] In this book, these practices will be considered only in passing.

markets in both good and bad times.[36] How can global firms build a strong employer brand in different parts of the world? The importance of brands has long been recognized in global marketing, and contemporary HR thinking about employer branding has clearly been influenced by insights from the field of marketing.[37]

The most suitable people have to be selected on the basis of their fit with the organization, a specific vacancy, and their future growth potential. A variety of selection and assessment methods are used to choose between external and internal candidates for jobs, but with big differences in their applicability across cultures and legal contexts. The importance of diversity is increasingly acknowledged in multinational firms across the world—yet most multinationals still staff their top positions with men from the home country. One of the biggest challenges facing tomorrow's transnational corporations is how to do more than pay mere lip service to diversity.

Another question multinationals have to resolve is whether to develop their own talent or increase their reliance on recruiting from outside. But regardless of the balance between build and buy, investment in recruitment, selection, and the subsequent development of talent will not be a viable business proposition unless the company can retain people and profit from its investment. An attractive compensation package and good development opportunities, a sound relationship with the boss, and the possibility of maintaining a healthy (or at least a reasonable) work–life balance are just some ways to reduce the attrition of core talent.

Development and Training

Developing future global leaders is a particularly high priority for the multinational firm, and is usually one of the major strategic preoccupations of top management. But what is a good leader, and how can a multinational with many distant operations identify people with leadership potential outside the home country? There are two main difficulties: First, there are significant perceptual differences about what constitutes good leadership among different cultures; and second, the skills needed at senior leadership levels are different from those at lower levels.

People develop most by taking on and learning from challenges. For international leaders, this implies demanding assignments, working outside their domain of functional and geographic expertise. Most new or promoted employees do not immediately have the skills needed for their jobs, so these must be developed through on-the-job learning, coaching, mentoring, or formal training. However, the bigger the challenges that people take on, the higher the likelihood that they will make significant mistakes that can be costly for the firm. Training, coaching, and mentoring should therefore be part of a people risk management strategy.

Leadership development has traditionally been managed top-down, with the corporation focusing on the development of a select group of high-potential individuals. This is increasingly complemented by bottom-up job markets and resourcing. Investment in globalized HR processes and self-help e-technology can facilitate the deployment of talent across borders, potentially adding great competitive advantage, although there are wide implications for career management (which becomes the responsibility of the individual) and for control. An increasingly important task for most multinationals is integrating top-down and bottom-up approaches to talent development.

Performance Management

Performance management is a process that links the business objectives and strategies of the firm to unit, team, and individual goals and actions through periodic performance appraisals and rewards. It has three successive phases: setting goals and objectives; evaluating and reviewing performance as well as providing feedback; and linking rewards and development outcomes to appraisal results. Implementing this process creates a number of challenges for any multinational firm.

Effective goal setting depends on frank and honest two-way communication between superior and subordinate.[38] This is not easy to achieve where there are differences between both parties, not only in the terms of hierarchy and gender—which in itself may elicit different responses across cultures—but also in corporate status (expatriate vs. local). Similarly, cultural issues may impact the applicability of various performance appraisal tools, such as 360° feedback.

Praise is generally well accepted around the world, although positive feedback is not free from cultural implications (e.g., distinguishing one individual in a collectivist culture). But dealing with low performance is a different matter. Whether the issue is "maintaining face," a major issue in some Eastern cultures, or legal constraints affecting employers' discretion around performance issues, multinational firms generally find it difficult to manage low performance consistently across borders.

More than any other element of the HR Wheel, performance management puts into stark relief the perennial tensions of global integration versus local adaptation. This is of particular relevance to multinationals, like Lincoln, where the performance management system is one of the core tools to drive its differentiating capabilities.

Defining the HR Function Roles

This book is about how multinational corporations can deal with the challenges of global operations and improve their performance through the way they manage their employees. We argue that this task is a joint responsibility of top executives, line managers, and HR—but in this section we will focus mainly on the tasks and roles of the specialized HR function.

The academic HRM literature contains several conceptualizations of the tasks and roles of the HR function.[39] We distinguish between the three following roles:

- HRM process and content development.
- HR service delivery.
- Business support.

These three roles correspond to the way in which many multinationals organize their HR function. For instance, Unilever structures its HR functional activities into shared service centers, expertise teams, and business partners. P&G initially organized all basic HR tasks into three regional service centers, and later outsourced them to IBM, retaining responsibility for development and business support. For several years, Nokia has made a distinction between functional and business HR. While business HR professionals work closely with the corporate executive group and the management of the business unit with which they are affiliated, functional professionals are organized centrally and have responsibility for the development of HRM tools, processes, and policies, as well as for the delivery of operational HR services.

We provide a brief overview of these different roles here. In Chapter 14 we will elaborate on each of these roles in more depth, and discuss how multinationals can develop the required competencies among their HR professionals.

HRM Process and Content Development

The key outcomes of the HRM process and content development role are HR policies and practices that help the firm maintain and enhance the organizational capabilities needed to execute its business strategy.

Professional knowledge of state-of-the-art HRM is a necessary point of departure for this role. Learning from others is essential—but blind pursuit of the latest best practice is not. HRM decisions should be based not on trends but on a thorough analysis of what is needed to support the unique organizational capabilities essential to the business. Central to the process and content development role are the three guiding principles of HRM presented earlier in this chapter: consistency between HR practices and with other parts of the work organization; differentiation in HRM across employee groups and subunits, as well as from other firms; and balancing critical dualities, such as global integration and local responsiveness.

Given the constant pressure to do more with less, organizing HRM process and content development is a challenging task for any multinational firm. The organization of global expertise depends on the structure of the company, but the traditional solution is to have functional experts at headquarters with a global responsibility for tasks such as talent and performance management. It is essential that these experts have deep international experience and can look beyond the home country. Another solution is to decentralize responsibility for developing policies, processes, and tools to a center of global expertise located in a subsidiary that has particular capabilities in the functional area in question. ABB has followed this route, delegating the responsibility for developing its shared service concept to India. And if the lead role is in the hands of businesses or regions, then global committees and task forces could be used to enhance broader coordination.

HR Service Delivery

The key task in the HR service delivery role is for core HR processes to be carried out at low cost and with a desired service level. The interface with HRM process and content development must be managed carefully.

Over the last 15 years, considerable pressure has been put on HR departments to cut costs and reduce the number of personnel involved in administrative tasks. In response, e-HR solutions have been developed that shift much of the transactional HR work to employees and managers themselves using self-help tools; HR service centers have been established; and elements of HR have been outsourced.

It has been estimated that today employees can obtain online answers to 60 percent of the HR questions they have about holidays, pensions, regulations, and routine transactions.[40] While investments in standardized HR processes and IT systems can be considerable, they can also enable the introduction of new capabilities, for example facilitating global internal labor markets and cross-border deployment of professional talent.[41]

Shared service centers began to emerge in the 1990s as larger firms realized that many administrative tasks could be carried out in a more standardized manner, undertaken at a central location in the country or on a regional basis. A clear trend has been to locate service centers in low-cost settings in Central America, Central and Eastern Europe, and India.

Certain HR processes have been outsourced for many decades—companies rely on headhunters and recruitment firms for recruitment and selection, and on business schools for management training programs. The trend toward outsourcing larger parts of HR has intensified in recent years, although firms should obviously keep in-house practices that are strategically important to its competitiveness.

Although effective HR service delivery is unlikely to translate into any sustainable competitive advantage for the firm, failure to execute these basic services can put the firm at a competitive disadvantage and will certainly hurt the credibility of the HR function. The importance of efficient, high-quality HR services must not be underestimated in the search for what may seem like more prestigious and high-profile roles for the HR profession.

Business Support

The business support model describes the activities of HR professionals who work directly with line and top managers on business, organizational, and HRM challenges. These "HR business partners," as they are often called, typically report to the person in charge of the business unit, with an indirect (dotted line) relationship to the corporate HR department. In contrast to the specialist knowledge of the process and content development role, the business support role requires broader generalist competence.

A key part of the business support role is to contribute to strategy discussions by highlighting the people aspects of strategy implementation and capability development. HR professionals should have a seat at the table when these discussions take place—which is not always the case.[42] Senior HR managers also work with senior management on strategically important issues related to organizational design and cohesion, talent management, performance management, knowledge and change management, acquisitions, and alliances—strategic challenges we discuss later in this book.

Business partners often become natural links between business units and the functional centers of expertise in the corporation, as well as the service centers. Yet not all this work is strategic. An indispensable part of HR business support is dealing with more mundane operational tasks and helping line managers to resolve employee issues and concerns.

Focusing on Organizational Outcomes

HR practices, guided by a set of principles and with the HR function playing important roles, ultimately lead to desired organizational outcomes of human resource management—the final element in the HR Wheel framework outlined in Figure 2–1. We have identified three interwoven critical outcomes that together contribute to the process of value creation:

- Human capital and social architecture.
- Change capability and strategic agility.
- Sustainable performance.

The first outcome focuses on the quality of people and social connections in the corporation; the second highlights the dynamic capabilities of the organization; and the third is focused on long-term business success.

Human Capital and Social Architecture

The human capital of employees is the first outcome of HRM. Do employees have the knowledge and skills needed for the firm to implement its strategy? The world is full of strategies and business plans that are discounted by analysts and investors who know that the enterprise does not have the human capacity to execute them better and faster than its competitors. To what extent are current and planned HR practices building the organizational capabilities needed for future success?

HR practices, such as performance feedback, coaching and development, and attention to fair process in decision making,[43] also shape employee attitudes, which may be just as important for firm performance as knowledge and skills. While the literature on organizational behavior deals with many different employee attitudes, which companies often measure using so-called "engagement surveys," employee commitment to the organization is particularly relevant.[44] Several studies have confirmed that a high level of affective commitment is associated with better firm performance,[45] and individuals who are highly committed are less likely to leave the organization.

However, the people management practices of the corporation have additional implications that are seldom discussed in the traditional HRM literature. The HRM activities of the firm play important roles in shaping what we call the social architecture of the global organization: its social capital (the structure and strength of social relationships between individuals and units); shared values, norms, and beliefs (organizational culture and the extent to which it provides social glue or cohesion); and the global mindset that leaders and other members of multinational organizations must display.

Change Capability and Strategic Agility

The second critical HRM outcome is the change capability of the multinational firm. A crucial question here is how well the firm can manage the long-term transition toward a transnational organization characterized by global integration, local responsiveness, and worldwide management of knowledge and innovation.[46] We discuss this in Chapter 11.

The multinational must excel at worldwide implementation or execution of operational strategies and business plans. Execution depends on both good planning and acceptance of decisions. Since most decisions will arouse some degree of resistance, particularly from successful or autonomous units, it is important that the way in which those decisions are reached is seen as fair in order to maintain commitment and loyalty. Indeed, the execution of strategy and business plans is at the heart of strategic human resource management, and facilitating the management of change is a vital part of the business support role of HR professionals.

A growing number of industries are characterized by continuous strategic change in technology, markets, and competitor moves. Strategic agility is needed if firms are to survive, and HRM is a crucial element in explaining why some multinational companies are more agile than others.[47]

Sustainable Performance

Sustainable performance—the ability of the firm to retain its competitiveness over a prolonged period of time—is the third organizational outcome of the HR Wheel.

The impact of HRM on firm performance is at the center of a hot debate that has been raging for some years. Much of this debate has focused on the choice of HR practices. Although there may not be a single best way of managing people, the evidence suggests that having a coherent set of HR practices that promote employee skill development, motivation, and involvement pays off in most circumstances. These practices are often labeled as high-performance

Research on HR Practices and Firm Performance

Much research confirms that HRM can have a significant positive effect on firm performance. For example, an analysis of the results from 92 studies of 19,319 organizations, carried out in a variety of industries and countries, revealed a correlation of 0.2 between the use of high-performance/commitment work practices and various measures of firm performance.[49] The most influential of these studies was undertaken by Huselid and Becker, who explored the payoff from careful selection of staff, investment in training and development, and performance management.[50] They collected data on HR practices and on economic and accounting performance from 968 large and medium-sized firms in 35 US industries. To measure accurately the independent effect of HR practices, the researchers controlled for variables that affect firm performance, such as industry, firm size, union coverage, sales growth, and R&D intensity. One standard deviation in the use of such practices enhanced profitability by more than US$4,000 per employee and increased market value by more than $18,000 per employee.[51] These are impressive findings, indicating that investment in a collection of high-performance/commitment HR practices really pays off, and that the financial returns can be very significant.

work systems, high-commitment HRM systems, or high-involvement HRM.[48] The box "Research on HR Practices and Firm Performance" summarizes the relevant research.

However, one limit of prescriptive viewpoints concerning HR practices is that they are static, whereas our world is highly dynamic. All industries—and some more than others—periodically go through cycles of growth and decline, created by fluctuations in supply and demand for their products or services. In 2008–2009, we witnessed one of the most dramatic changes in the global economic climate since the Great Depression in the 1930s. In some industries, companies went from booking record profits to suffering record losses in the course of three to four months. In a turbulent environment, sustainable performance depends on being able to cope with these cycles, anticipating the downturn in boom times and building for the future in lean periods.

Paradoxically, the most difficult time to invest in human capital and social architecture is during times of growth, when managers are typically scrambling to take advantage of opportunities and are too impatient to invest in long-term global processes. The best time to make these changes and investments is during lean periods—as long as the firm has made sure it has sufficient funds in anticipation of a downturn. Indeed, we suggest later that the best metaphor for understanding change in multinational organizations is steering—navigating smoothly between good and harsh times, between global integration and local responsiveness, between short term and long term.[52]

Egil Myklebust, who headed Norway's largest firm, Norsk Hydro, for 10 years between 1991 and 2001, understood this well. Norsk Hydro was an international company focused on cyclical industries like fertilizers, metals, and oil. Myklebust had known many ups and downs, and he told us that his role as CEO was to cut off the tops and bottom of the cycles in his own mind. "In the boom times, when everyone is scrambling to launch projects and to hire people, my role is to push for caution and make sure there is ultra-sound justification. Otherwise hasty actions will worsen the downturn that surely lies ahead. And when people are taking the axe in the pits of the downturn, I have to push people to be bold and optimistic; otherwise we won't be in a position to take advantage of the good times ahead."[53]

THREE STAGES OF HRM IN MULTINATIONAL FIRMS

So far we have discussed the management of human resources without paying much attention to shifts in the HRM challenges facing firms as they grow and internationalize their activities. Our research and experience over more than three decades lead us to believe that it is useful to conceptualize three different stages in the contribution that HRM can make to value creation in multinational firms, as shown in Table 2–2. We refer to these as stages

TABLE 2–2. The Three Stages of Human Resource Management

	Activity	Focus of attention	Theoretical perspective	Metaphor
Building HRM	Foundations—getting the basics in place	Internal consistency	Fit (across HRM and work practices)	**The builder**
Realigning HRM	Adjusting to environmental and strategy change	Change	Fit (with environment and strategy)	**The change partner**
Steering via HRM	Long-term capability development	Constructive tension between opposites	Duality	**The navigator**

because development in most organizations goes from the simple to the complex.

We call the first stage "building HRM"—getting the basics of HRM into place and ensuring their coherence across practices and with the work organization. The strategy and organizational capabilities of the firm are relatively stable givens, supplying a point of departure for the development of appropriate core HR practices. While this task is often the responsibility of the HR department— the metaphor here is that of a *builder*—the involvement and support of line management in the development of the HRM basics are essential.

The second stage is "realigning HRM" to meet the needs of the changing external and internal environment. Shifts in the marketplace and the structure of competition, the emergence of new technologies, and/or a change in business strategy all call for realignment within the firm. The focus is on reconfiguring and changing the approach to HRM to implement new strategies effectively. This typically involves a partnership between line management and the professionals within HR, and we use the metaphor of the *change partner* to describe the tasks undertaken by HR.

The third stage may be described as steering via HRM. While most will recognize our description of the first two stages, from both the HRM literature and practice, the third stage may be less familiar. At this point, business strategy and human resource factors cannot be separated; both are completely interlinked. The focus is on developing the capabilities of the organization and its people to thrive in a world of global competition and continuous change, which means managing constructively the tensions between dualities, such as short-term operating results and long-term growth, global efficiency and local responsiveness, the need for change and the continuity required by execution. We use the role metaphor of the *navigator* who steers the organization forward between opposing forces.

Each of these stages reflects a different theoretical perspective, and each has different implications for international HRM.

Building HRM: Focus on Foundations

Some years ago one of the authors of this book was invited to participate in a panel advising an international organization on its HR policies. The other panelists consisted of academics and senior HR executives from companies like 3M and GE. The participants were grappling with some of the intricacies of strategic aspects of human resource management and its role in managing change, when GE's Frank Doyle brought us down to earth. "This is all well and good," he said. "But do you know what Jack Welch [CEO of GE at the time] would fire me for? It would not be for some failure in 'strategic human resource management,' but it might happen if we ever had serious problems with the pension fund."

The first stage of HRM may not be the most glamorous, but we cannot emphasize enough that there is nothing wrong with being intensely focused on getting the foundations right. If the "HR factory" does not work effectively, the function will have no credibility with line management when it comes to tackling other challenges. Talk of becoming a "business partner" will be dismissed as hot air. Early on, when it was expanding rapidly, Nokia sought our advice about how to focus the HR function. The company was becoming a fast-moving "shoot-before-you-aim" organization, and the HR professionals were unsure about the role they should play. We advised them to focus first on building solid HR foundations rather than trying to be "strategic partner" or "change agent." They came back to us later and told us how sensible that advice had been.

A company that has failed to build up solid, basic HRM foundations in recruitment and selection, development and training, and performance management will be severely handicapped when it ventures abroad. It will not have the codified experience either to avoid making mistakes or to learn from its experiences. It will find it difficult to manage the movement of expatriates to foreign affiliates and their return home because it will not have the basic systems and processes in place. Companies without good HRM processes and tools may be disadvantaged in joint venture negotiations: Foreign partners will be wary of entering an alliance with a firm that does not have the proven sophistication in people management to make the joint venture work.[54] Acquisition integration will be a nightmare. Differences in management approach between two firms that are to be merged, including HRM, can be worked through if they are clear and transparent—but it is difficult to merge two firms that lack clearly articulated approaches.[55]

The core HRM foundations must be built in close alignment with the strategy and context of the firm. The theoretical perspective behind the first face of HRM is that of fit—with strategy, as well as fit between elements of HRM and other parts of the work system. This is an inward-oriented perspective on the firm, focusing on capturing the benefits of internal consistency, which we discussed earlier in this chapter. The expectation is that HRM (and the other elements of work practices) will support the organizational capabilities that the firm is trying to build.

Building solid and consistent foundations can take years, even decades. Pushed by the desire for internal consistency, HR policies and practices tend to crystallize into a particular HRM configuration. And once policies and practices in selection, performance management, and so on become established, they become rigid. Like the foundations of a building, the resulting configuration of HR practices is difficult to modify without impacting the entire system. Often changing one element might entail reconsidering everything else, which is not a simple task in large complex organizations—we have seen again and again how employees and managers react negatively when the rules of the game are changed.

Not surprisingly, some HR professionals may over time become overcautious and conservative rather than proactive. For example, HR managers may resist moving to a reward system linked to competence rather than the job to attract people with valuable skills. Not only would this change undermine a finely tuned salary system; it might also threaten the job evaluation/ranking system linked to titles that give people status in the wider community. It would threaten employees' concept of the career ladder, the authority structure of the firm, relationship norms between bosses and subordinates, and so on—many of the elements of the hidden structure of working life in an organization.

In many firms, HR professionals have a tendency to become stuck at the HR foundation stage, becoming administrators of their systems, attempting to refine or patch over the holes, rather than trying to adapt to or anticipate changes in markets, technology, and strategy.[56] The builder becomes a custodian—sometimes in the pejorative sense of an administrative janitor. Maintaining internal consistency becomes an end in itself, and, in the long run, at the expense of firm performance. HRM may be critical to the success of the business, yet HR practices sometime constitute the biggest obstacle to much-needed change.

This HR handicap is a widely discussed and well-known global phenomenon, as true of Japan and South Korea as it is of the US and Germany. The response has been changes in the HR service delivery element in our HR Wheel—service centers, self-help e-HR, and outsourcing. And as we will discuss in Chapter 14, changes in HR foundations are accelerating through the use of new information and communication technology and further standardization of core HR processes.

In the current dynamic and competitive business environment the need for proactive human resource management moves us on to the second stage of HRM, managing change.

Realigning HRM: Focus on Strategic Change

Compared to the building stage of HRM, the realignment stage has a more outward focus. The theoretical perspective framing this stage is that of external fit between an organization and its competitive environment (see Table 2–2). Major shifts in markets, technologies, competitors' strategies, and socio-political contexts compel equally major changes in strategy. New capabilities must be explored and developed as the competitive advantage of traditional capabilities is eroded.

The implementation of new strategies and the development of new capabilities will invariably require a reconfiguration of HRM practices. We use the term realignment because it captures this necessity to reconfigure the different elements of the whole system.[57] In stage two, the focus is on the dynamics of change, realigning for the future while managing the immediate needs of the present. If practices remain rooted in the past, pouring more resources into reinforcing the old HRM foundations is likely to damage performance.

Fit is still the framework of the second stage of HRM. But achieving fit is more complicated now, since the need for internal consistency must be complemented by a focus on adapting to new demands in the external environment and/or firm strategy. There is a potential contradiction between the first two stages. Surely the achievement of external fit will mean destroying the internal coherence—the optimal alignment of different organizational elements—that constitutes an important reason for the firm's current good performance? This is indeed correct. There is a tension between these two perspectives—any process of change involves tension.

Change as Realignment

Over the last 20 years, we have discussed the following proposition with thousands of line and HR managers across the globe: "The ultimate (though perhaps unattainable) objective of every human resource professional is to do him or herself out a job." The responses vary, more between firms than between countries. Overall, roughly half agree and half disagree, with little difference between line and professional HR managers. We can summarize the usual debate about our proposition as follows: If the world were static, the ideal might indeed be to cut back radically on the HR function, once good foundations have been built. Routine matters can be automated, those requiring expertise can be outsourced, and line managers can decide on many strategic matters concerning HRM. But the world is *not* static. We face continual and never-ending change and the need for constant realignment, and so this requires a dedicated HR function.

Conceptually, if a firm adopts a consistent strategy toward internationalization, the problems of realignment and strategic change will be minimized. Firms adopting a strategy of global efficiency take a consistent stance—policies and practices are determined by the center, although some adjustments are usually made locally by trusted expatriates. Some locals are socialized into the global mold, so they can be given more responsibility. Any realignment, from changes in recruitment strategy to technological change, will also be managed by the center. Those adopting a strategy of local responsiveness take the opposite, but equally consistent, stance of allowing each local unit to develop its own distinctive approach to people management. Local management will have to figure out how to work through strategic changes. In reality, both extremes are rare, since most firms experience some degree of transnational pressure.[58]

Practical and conceptual issues about realignment and strategic change are dealt with throughout this book.[59] Here we will mention only briefly some of the issues that are particularly important for the change partner tasks undertaken by HR professionals.

HR as Change Partner

A profound understanding of the firm's business strategy and its people implications is the necessary starting point for a process of HRM realignment. Unfortunately, this may not always be the case.

Companies organizing an international HR workshop sometimes contact us. They want input on how they can develop "more strategic HRM" as a part of their companies' change efforts. They tell us about all the ambitious change projects that they have under way, in terms of competence management, succession planning, 360° feedback, appraisal system development, and the new seminars they have launched on managing change. "That's fine," we say, "but tell us about the strategy for your business and what organizational capabilities you need to build." All too often there is a long pause . . . and then, "Well, we'll have to get back to you about that."

HR professionals—at the very least those in senior positions within the function—must know the business well enough to be able to articulate clearly the implications of the new strategy for the organization. Close interaction is needed between the people in more functionally oriented HRM process and content development roles, and those in business support, to tackle the challenges of realignment. Further, it is very difficult for HR professionals to do a good job unless strategic and people planning processes are closely linked.

How can this work in practice? Today, much attention is turned to performance management and capability (or competence) analysis as a way of linking strategic goals to objectives. On the basis of studies with a consortium of eight international firms operating in the UK, including BT and Hewlett-Packard, most of whom were undergoing strategic reorientation, Gratton and her colleagues see the realignment task as focusing on two cycles, short-term and long-term.[60]

The short-term cycle links annual business objectives to individual performance through performance management—objective setting, performance measurement, rewards, and short-term training. At the heart of the cycle is the analysis of the gap between current capabilities and the strategic vision for the future, leading to appropriate corrective changes.[61] The long-term cycle focuses on linking long-term strategy to its people implications, with an emphasis on leadership development, wider workforce development (e.g., skills that will be needed to manage future technologies), and organizational development (e.g., greater needs for flexibility and responsiveness). We discuss the need for a global process of performance management in transnational firms later in the book.[62]

With their expertise in people and organizational dynamics, HR professionals can play critical roles as sparring partners to line management in discussions about how to manage the process of change—how to engage key stakeholders, assess inevitable resistance, adapt to cultural differences, empower new champions, and communicate the new strategy so that people lower down in the organization and across the world understand the implications for them—just a few of the issues we will return to in Chapter 11.

One of the least recognized challenges in managing change in multinational firms is accepting that change and reconfiguration often take some time to achieve. Gratton articulates this well when emphasizing the temporal dimension of HRM.[63] It took the pharmaceutical giant GSK 10 years to meet its goal of developing a capability in rapid product development. This required creating new work processes in the shape of cross-functional teams; changes in performance management, as well as selection and development; realigning technology and workflows; redesigning career paths; and implanting new shared norms and values. Similarly, it took P&G and Nokia more than a decade to build a premier local management cadre for their operations in China.

Some of the dualities central to the next phase of HRM become apparent in the process of realignment. One notable dilemma is the need to manage today's operational requirements while realigning toward future needs. One of the basic laws of change is that it comes at a cost—upheaval, disruption, and internal preoccupation, as well as large investments of time and energy. One is always better off in the short term by not changing, simply doing better what one did yesterday. HR managers may have a legitimate concern that line and top managers overreact to external changes and become too focused on change, resulting in the loss of internal consistencies and efficiency. Communicating these concerns to top management without being labeled a change blocker requires an HR function that has both credibility and confidence.

The Dangers of Fixation on Change

If there is a danger of becoming stuck in a custodial orientation at the building stage, as we discussed earlier, there is also a corresponding danger of becoming fixated on change.

Fixation is often the result of poor change management that is excessively focused on delivering solutions without understanding the broader context. Each new management team scrambles around to find new solutions to ongoing challenges. Since employees do not understand the problems, and since final goals are unclear, these solutions fail to yield the expected results. Another management team is brought in, under greater pressure to come up with new solutions, and the cycle repeats itself. Gradually a cynicism about change programs and initiatives builds up among employees. They learn to ignore the rhetoric of change, quietly carrying on with their work and their own lives—until real change is brought about through crisis. The lesson is that real change requires continuity (one of the steering dualities in the next stage of HRM). This continuity can be provided only if top management has a clear focus on long-term vision and goals, leaving the detailed solutions to those who will implement them.

Excessive mobility under the guise of international management development can exacerbate change fixation. Each new expatriate leader will start off a new change initiative—for instance, driving the local unit toward cost reduction. Just as the change is beginning to take hold, the expatriate is transferred and a new successor is appointed. Since there are few brownie points for implementing what someone else has started, the new expatriate will take the unit off in a different direction, say toward improved customer service. The focus of that person's successor is morale boosting and teamwork, and after that the goal returns to cost reduction. There is accountability for change, but not for execution.

The ABB case introduced in Chapter 1 is an example of these disruptive swings. Every time top management reset the direction for the organization, in an attempt to reclaim control and capture synergies, the result was actually the opposite—more fragmentation and anarchy. Redrawing the chart at the corporate center is easy; the hard part is aligning all the processes needed to make it happen. Without solid HRM foundations, managing the change process in a complex global firm like ABB is impossible.

In some firms, top management focuses exclusively on change, improvement, stretch, and constant realignment, exploiting robust but short-term performance management systems. The danger is that foundations may be neglected, leading to instability. Each year, the targets are stretched further. The previous year's achievements justified a good bonus, and now represent the baseline for further achievements in the current year. This creates a treadmill atmosphere where more and more is squeezed out of the organization. Longer-term strategic and organizational development is ignored. No one takes the time to listen to others. There is no time to worry about morale, loyalty, and climate. No one tracks the turnover and retention rates that herald the dangers.

However, continuous change has become a reality in many sectors, and with accelerating global competition there are no signs that the pressures for change will go away. In many industries, particularly the new high-tech, software, professional service, and e-based sectors, the process of change is accelerating. Technological and product life cycles grow shorter, and competitive changes succeed one another in waves. As this process speeds up, it is necessary to anticipate future changes and to build the future into the present—the third stage of multinational HRM.

Steering with HRM: Focus on Dualities

In the third stage of HRM (see Table 2–2), the task of the navigator is to steer between dualities. An organization cannot go through constant realignment. Some measure of temporal consistency is important for employees, and every process of realignment exacts a cost. However, there is a dualistic pattern in change, seen, for example, in swings of the pendulum between centralization and decentralization, evolutionary progress focused on exploiting resources and revolutionary progress focused on developing new resources. Why not exploit the advantages of decentralization while anticipating tomorrow's needs for greater coordination? Why not try to find a way of balancing the focus on today while investing in tomorrow? This is the challenge facing the navigator, steering through dualities and paradoxes. It is a task that is particularly important for the transnational corporation.

Understanding Dualities

Some of the early work on organizational dualities originated with research on that ultimate, though elusive, dependent variable in organizational studies—organizational effectiveness. A number of studies since the early 1980s have suggested that the concept of organizational effectiveness is difficult to pin down, first because organizational effectiveness is a multidimensional concept, and second because those dimensions involve opposites. For example, Quinn's data led him to suggest that multiple opposing dimensions underlie thinking about effectiveness—control and flexibility, internal and external focus, focus on both means and ends.[64] To be effective, an organization must possess attributes that are simultaneously contradictory, even mutually exclusive.

We refer to such opposites as dualities,[65] although other terms are used, such as competing values,[66] dilemmas,[67] and dialectics.[68] They express themselves as paradoxes. These opposites are not either/or choices, the appropriateness of which depends on a particular context (as in contingency theory), but dualities that must be reconciled or dynamically balanced. Some of the many dualities facing organizations and groups are shown in Table 2–3.

The proponents of the duality school of thought emphasize the limits of fit theory, arguing that excessive concern with fit or consistency leads to seesaw pathologies, cycles of complacency (when there seems to be a good fit) alternating with crisis/transformation (when lack of fit is addressed). Fit or contingency

TABLE 2–3. Some of the Dualities Facing International Firms

Managing today's assets–building tomorrow's assets
- Satisfying customer needs–being ahead of the customer
- Short term–long term
- Exploitation–exploration

Loose–tight
- Opportunistic–planned
- Entrepreneurship–control/accountability
- Flexibility–efficiency

Competition–partnership

Low cost–high value added

Differentiation–integration
- Decentralization–centralization
- Unit performance–corporate integration
- Individual accountability–team responsibility

Change–continuity
- Speed of responsiveness–care in implementation

Professional–generalist
- Technical logic–business logic

Taking risks–avoiding failures

Task orientation–people orientation

theories are too static for the fast-moving modern age, and they leave little room for understanding organizational dynamics.

Although there is not yet any single, seminal, theoretical exposition of duality theory, the concept, along with associated ideas of paradox and the dynamics of virtuous and vicious circles, is broadly accepted, and applied to many areas of management apart from challenges of the multinational firm—strategic management, knowledge management, new product development, change management, leadership style, and cross-cultural behavior, to mention just a few.[69] Research is emerging to support this perspective.[70]

One important claim of duality theory is that any positive qualities taken too far become negative or pathological.[71] Instead of trying to maximize something, an organization should try to ensure that it maintains at least a minimal level of attention toward a desirable attribute. For example, an organization requires a minimal degree of consensus, but not so much that it will stifle the dissension that is the lifeblood of innovation; and it needs a minimal degree of contentment, sufficient to ensure that key people remain with the firm, but not so much that arrogance or complacency emerges.

The pace of change has recently highlighted many of the paradoxical features of contemporary business organizations. In the past, dualities expressed themselves in a leisurely way. There were the ebb and flow of centralization and decentralization; there were long periods of evolution within an existing product life cycle, alternating with short periods of revolutionary crisis when the technology changed.[72] Fueled by the pressures of globalization, pendulum swings have become more frequent as competition compresses time frames. As product life cycles speed up, as swings between undercapacity and overcapacity shorten, strategic agility becomes vital.[73]

In this world of rapid change, an important duality is that firms have to leverage their existing resources to make profits today, and at the same time develop new resources that will be the source of their profits tomorrow. Leverage (called *exploitation* by academics) involves concern for efficiency, execution, production, and short-term success, but excessive focus leads to "the failure of success." Resource development (or *exploration*) involves innovation, learning, risk taking, experimentation, and focus on long-term success.[74] However, an excessive focus on development is risky, compromising the survival of the firm. Indeed, the duality behind resource leverage and development is at the heart of the resource-based view of the firm.[75] While the transnational firm faces the local–global dilemma, it also faces this exploitation–exploration dilemma.

Steering between Dualities

While the notion of fit may allow us to capture the match with a specific context at a particular point in time, duality theory recognizes that this context is likely to change in the future. Opposing forces—such as differentiation and integration, external and internal orientation, hierarchy and network, short term and long term, planning and opportunity, rational analysis and emotional involvement, change and continuity—can never be reconciled once and for all. They create tensions that must be anticipated and managed.[76]

The navigator or helmsman is a useful metaphor for understanding how to deal with these tensions.[77] The job of the navigator at the helm of a vessel is to manage a constant but varying tension between the need to maintain a particular course and changing winds and currents. Steered by a skilled navigator, the path of a boat toward its destination is a series of controlled zigzags in response to wind and current. The unskilled helmsman fights to maintain headway, overcorrecting when the boat is blown off course, failing to anticipate the storms and calms that lie ahead. The resulting path is a series of wild zigzags as the boat veers from crisis to crisis.

Charles Hampden-Turner, one of the pioneers of duality theory (or dilemma theory as he calls it), shows how tensions caused by dualities can lead to virtuous or vicious circles of organizational development.[78] Most firms have to steer between opposing forces like functional excellence and interfunctional coordination, low cost and high flexibility, mass and niche marketing. Some firms focus on a fixed strategy—for example, aligning the firm to the development of functional excellence. This might lead to initial success. But when that success is threatened by opposing pressures (for example, slow decision making caused by lack of coordination among functions), leaders often respond by reinforcing what led them to be successful in the first place, increasing the pressure for functional excellence. At an extreme, this "failure of success" paradox leads to a vicious circle of threat, reinforced efforts, and further threat, culminating in crisis.

In contrast, the leaders of other firms appear to anticipate the need for a change in course, gently steering specialized functions toward greater teamwork before the problems of slow decision making show up. Alternating between one course and the other, they steer toward their aims of higher profits and better return on investments in a virtuous spiral of increasing capabilities in both functional excellence and integrated teamwork. We have called this process of capability development "sequenced layering."[79] Mastering this process is of critical importance to transnational firms.

As we mentioned earlier, duality theory is also the theoretical basis for many recent developments in the field of strategic management. The term ambidexterity has been used to describe the extent to which firms are able both to explore new areas and build new capabilities while exploiting their existing strengths.[80] This concept has also been embraced by some senior executives. For example, Jeff Immelt, current CEO of GE, uses the term ambidexterity to stress the fact that his company must excel at both exploration and exploitation in its global operations[81]—with the additional challenge of mobilizing the entire global organization around a concept that most non-English speakers find hard to spell!

Dualities and Transnational Management

As we discussed in Chapter 1, understanding dualities is a cornerstone for effective transnational management, since the defining characteristic of the transnational enterprise is its capacity to steer between the contradictions it confronts. Thus the duality perspective that lies behind this third stage of HRM goes hand in hand with the management of the transnational enterprise— or rather the steering of the transnational firm. There are two particular dualities confronting the transnational enterprise that we will highlight in this book—the duality of local responsiveness and decentralization versus global efficiency and centralization, and resource exploitation versus resource exploration.

In Chapter 1 we discussed how many firms traditionally internationalized by decentralizing responsibilities to their subsidiaries and local business units. Decentralization has many advantages, including proximity to customers, a heightened sense of accountability, more local innovation and entrepreneurship, and better employee morale. The trouble is that decentralization has a shadow side. After initial success, it often leads to reinventing the wheel, the not-invented-here syndrome, duplication of back office functions, slow response to technological change, difficulties in dealing with matrix pressures, and lack of shared resources to respond to emerging needs. These "handmaidens of decentralization," as Bartlett and Ghoshal have called them, often prompt firms to swing back to centralization, until bureaucracy, loss of responsiveness, and the inability to retain good people turn the pendulum to decentralization once again.

After several swings, organizations begin to realize that decentralization (local autonomy) and centralization (global integration) are a duality. Even though there may be an immediate advantage to decentralization and local responsiveness, a future movement in the direction of the organization must be anticipated. One executive expressed this with apt advice to senior management: "Organize one way, manage the other way." If the structure is currently being decentralized, senior management attention should be focused on building coordination links across units. If the structure is centralized, the focus of attention should be on preventing the loss of local entrepreneurship.[82]

Organizing one way but managing the other way requires a change of thinking among local leaders, part of what we call global mindset. While acting as local entrepreneurs, they also need to have a clear understanding of global strategy. Strategic management becomes a process that involves all key leaders around the world, and local managers need to have a global perspective. The role of people in central staff positions, including corporate HRM, is not to tell local people what to do or to solve their problems for them—that would be incompatible with the need for local autonomy. Instead, central staff must act as network leaders, getting people together to face up to common problems.

The challenges of managing dualities are of crucial relevance to HRM. All organizations maintain corporate control and coordination through hierarchy, budgets, rules, and centrally managed processes and procedures. But as the needs for coordination grow, more rules, more control, and more bosses at the center simply will not work—this will only kill local entrepreneurship and drive away good people. These classic tools need to be complemented with more subtle mechanisms of horizontal coordination, such as lateral governance, social architecture, leadership development, performance and knowledge management. These coordination tools are to a large degree the application of human resource management, as we discuss at greater length and in greater detail throughout this book.

TAKEAWAYS

1. To add long-term value, HRM has to support the development of organizational capabilities that differentiate the firm from its competitors, and help the firm implement its business model successfully.
2. Differentiated capabilities must satisfy three criteria: They must create value for the customer, be rare and unique, and be difficult to duplicate by competitors.
3. Keep the guiding principles of HRM in mind—internal consistency of human resource and work practices; differentiation among employee groups, between locations, and from other competitors; and balancing dualities.
4. Every firm has to cope with a number of basic and vitally important HRM tasks: attracting and recruiting employees, developing and retaining people, and managing and rewarding performance. The core HR task—getting the right people into the right place at the right time—must not be neglected.
5. The HR function covers three roles: HRM process and content development, HR service delivery, and business support. Each of these distinct but interrelated roles is important, and they all need to be staffed by competent HR professionals.
6. Human capital and social architecture, change capability and strategic agility, and sustainable organizational performance are the key organizational outcomes of HRM.
7. It is useful to conceptualize the three stages of how HRM creates value in multinational firms. The theoretical perspective behind the *builder* is internal consistency; behind the *change partner*, it is the fit with the changing environment and strategy; and behind the *navigator*, it is the duality theory.
8. Beware of the dangers of becoming stuck at specific HR stages. Builders may become administrative custodians, losing the business credibility necessary to act as change partners. Change partners may neglect the importance of internal consistency and solid foundations.
9. One of the ways in which HRM contributes to organizational performance is in helping the firm adjust to environmental change. However, since change involves significant realignment, this often takes much more time (continuity) than people expect.

10. Organizational effectiveness is inherently paradoxical, requiring opposing strategies and capabilities. Two dualities of concern are centralization versus decentralization (reflecting the global–local dilemma) and resource leverage versus resource development (also known as exploitation versus exploration).

NOTES

1. Berg and Fast, 1983; Hastings, 1999; Bartlett and O'Connell, 1998.
2. Björkman and Galunic, 1999; Siegel, 2007; see www.lincolnelectric.com.
3. Porter, 1980.
4. Barney, 1991.
5. Boxall, 1996.
6. Grant, 1996, p. 377.
7. The term "dynamic capabilities" is used to describe the firm's ability to create new organizational capabilities in response to changes in the environment (Teece, Pisano, and Shuen, 1997; see Zollo and Winter, 2002, for a slightly different definition).
8. Grant, 1996; see also Ulrich and Lake (1990) for an early HRM-based discussion of organizational capabilities.
9. Barney, 1991.
10. A psychological contract is the (often informal) perceptions of the individual and organization of the employment relationship, including the reciprocal promises and obligations implicit in it (Rousseau, 1995; Guest and Conway, 2002).
11. Ross and Beath, 2007.
12. *Human Resource Management International Digest*, 2007.
13. See Boxall and Purcell (2003) for a presentation and discussion of the "ability, motivation, and opportunity" (AMO) model.
14. Becker et al., 1997.
15. For details on the evolution of Lincoln Electric's approach to HRM, see Berg and Fast (1983) and Björkman and Galunic (1999).
16. Siegel, 2007.
17. Bacon, 1999. Another example is a collection of studies by British researchers on employee experiences with HRM (Mabey, Skinner, and Clark, 1998).
18. It is particularly important that comparable employees in the same location are treated similarly (Baron and Kreps, 1999).
19. Baron and Kreps, 1999.
20. See Baron and Kreps (1999) for a detailed discussion of the importance of consistency between HR practices, notably in Chapter 3.
21. Bowen and Ostroff (2004) conceptualize HRM as a signaling system. When HR practices send distinct and consistent messages, employees are motivated to understand and adopt attitudes and behaviors consistent with the strategy and goals of the firm.
22. Tanure, Evans, and Pucik (2007). Legge (1995) critically elaborates on a long-standing clash between the rhetoric and the reality of HRM in Europe.
23. Kepes and Delery, 2007.
24. There may also be some differentiation across business lines. This fourth aspect of differentiation is particularly relevant when business units differ in the organizational capabilities they use to compete.

25. Lepak and Snell, 1999, 2002, and 2007.
26. Global talent management, which focuses clearly on this group, is discussed in Chapters 7 and 8.
27. Lepak and Snell, 1999.
28. Gonzáles and Tacorante, 2004. However, it must be noted that the classification of employment types is a considerable challenge in empirical research of this kind.
29. Lepak and Snell, 2002.
30. See Chapter 9 for a discussion of this point.
31. Lincoln's management might have done a better job in managing the change process of implementing a new approach to people management in newly acquired units. We discuss management of change in Chapters 11 and 13, with particular reference to M&As in the latter.
32. Liker and Hoseus, 2008.
33. "P&G Leadership Machine," *Fortune,* April 13, 2009, p. 16.
34. This refers to the classic principles of differentiation and integration in organizational design. See Lawrence and Lorsch (1967), Mintzberg (1979), Galbraith (1977), and many other works in this domain.
35. These social mechanisms are discussed in Chapter 6.
36. The consulting firm McKinsey coined the "talent war" expression to capture the reality in many industries (Chambers et al., 1998).
37. Sparrow, Brewster, and Harris, 2004.
38. Lawler (2003) summarizes the research on this.
39. Readers may be familiar with David Ulrich's well-known so-called Four Box Framework (Ulrich, 1997), with two operational and two strategic roles. Ulrich suggests that there are two operational HR roles, that of the "administrative expert" and that of the "employee champion." Our HRM service delivery role incorporates Ulrich's administrative expert role, while our HRM development role contains elements of the administrative expert but also elements of Ulrich's strategic/long-term roles of the "strategic partner" and "change agent." Finally, our business support role is closest to Ulrich's strategic partner and change agent but also contains aspects of the employee champion. More recently, Ulrich and Brockbank (2005) identified five roles for the HR function: employee advocate, human capital developer, functional expert, strategic partner, and HR leader.
40. Ulrich and Brockbank, 2005.
41. This is discussed in Chapter 8. As we note there, these global open job markets are helping IBM achieve its vision of becoming a globally integrated enterprise.
42. We will return to this question in Chapter 14.
43. Fair process in decision making is referred to throughout this book, but particularly in connection with managing change in Chapter 11.
44. Psychological empowerment is another important attitude. The individual's perception of being able to decide on and/or influence relevant issues related to his or her own work is one integrated part of psychological empowerment; the feeling of having the necessary knowledge and skills is another. Both academic research (e.g., Spreitzer, 1996) and company anecdotes confirm that psychological empowerment has a positive effect on company performance. For research on affective organizational commitment, see Allen and Meyer (1990).
45. For a review of such studies, see Kuvaas (2008).
46. We discussed the characteristics of a transnational enterprise in Chapter 1.
47. Doz and Kosonen, 2008. See the discussion in Chapter 11.

48. Huselid (1995), Lepak and Snell (2002), and Guthrie (2001), respectively.
49. Combs et al., 2006. See also the literature reviews conducted by Boselie, Dietz, and Boon (2005) and Paauwe (2009).
50. Huselid, 1995; Huselid, Jackson, and Schuler, 1997; Becker et al., 1997.
51. Huselid (1995) also found that sales per employee increased by more than $27,000 for each standard deviation in the use of high-performance work practices.
52. See Chapter 11 for a discussion on steering through change.
53. Discussion with one of the authors and presentations at Norsk Hydro, 2000. By 2009, the name of the company had been changed to Hydro and only the metals industry had been retained.
54. HRM in international alliances is the topic of Chapter 12.
55. We discuss how to deal with HRM issues in international mergers and in depth in Chapter 13.
56. Readers might like to guess how many people were employed in the corporate HR function of AT&T in New Jersey in 1994. The answer is over 4,500 out of a total work-force of 320,000, including 2,500 people in corporate training—at a time when re-sponsibility for training had been decentralized to the business units. A "small" corporate HR department consisted of 50 people. In contrast, AT&T's European com-petitor Alcatel, slightly smaller in overall size, had between 8 and 12 people in the corporate HR office in Paris. But the HR foundation AT&T built was solid—many of the HR training and development tools used today (such as assessment centers) were developed in AT&T.

    This heavy HR structure made sense when AT&T was a telephone monopoly whose profits could be eroded by discontented employees, hostile unions, or nega-tive public image. Training is a good investment—it keeps people happy, it is socially legitimate, budgets can be adapted to cash flow, and it develops people profession-ally. But the logic behind AT&T's approach to HRM evaporated in the different en-vironment in the 1990s. First deregulation and then explosion of wireless networks changed the industry dynamics completely—but the company could not adapt. To-day, what remains from the old AT&T is only the brand name acquired by one of its offspring.
57. We talk about "realignment" rather than alignment. Alignment captures only one part of the picture (where the organization wants to go); it does not capture the other half, namely the fact that the organization is coming from a different place.
58. Evans and Lorange, 1989.
59. Chapter 11 is dedicated to discussing change management in multinational firms.
60. Gratton et al., 1999a; Gratton et al., 1999b.
61. The closeness of the links between strategy and individual performance is measured in five levels (Gratton et al., 1999a). At the weakest level (1), business strategy is not clearly articulated to the individual. Discussions between individuals and their man-agers about performance and expectations are ad hoc, often vague, and not linked to clear objectives for the business. Needless to say, the absence of links makes the man-agement of realignment extremely difficult, if not impossible. In contrast, at the strongest level (5), the business objectives of the strategic plan are clearly articulated to individuals and teams, and translated into clear objectives that are discussed and agreed upon. Processes exist to ensure that individual objectives are realigned to take account of ongoing changes in business strategy, with clear monitoring.
62. See Chapter 9.
63. Gratton, 2000.

64. Quinn and Rohrbaugh, 1983.

65. Evans and Doz, 1989; Evans and Doz, 1992; Evans and Génadry, 1998.

66. Quinn, 1988.

67. Hampden-Turner, 1990a.

68. Mitroff and Linstone, 1993.

69. For example, duality-oriented studies on strategic flexibility (Volberda, 1998), knowledge management (Coff, Coff, and Eastvold, 2006), change management (Fiol, 2002; Price Waterhouse Change Integration Team, 1996), capabilities in new product development (Leonard-Barton, 1992), and cross-cultural behavior (Hampden-Turner and Trompenaars, 2000), to take but a few examples.

70. After studying the performance of more than 1,000 companies over a 20-year period, Dodd and Favaro (2007) argue that management's performance in meeting three dualistic tensions had a closer relationship to total shareholder returns (TSR) than any other common measure (earnings, EPS, EBITDA, economic profits, PE multiples, or return on capital employed). These tensions were profitability and growth, today and tomorrow, and whole and the parts (the latter referring to corporate integration and local responsiveness).

71. Historians have been well aware of these swings. Indeed Arnold Toynbee's monumental *A Study of History* is built on the insight that the decline of civilizations occurs when a society pursues its success formula to excess (Toynbee, 1946). One of the earliest articles on duality theory, on the theme of organizational seesaws, emphasized this point (Hedberg, Nystrom, and Starbuck, 1976).

72. Greiner, 1972; Tushman and O'Reilly, 1996.

73. We discuss strategic agility in Chapter 11.

74. March, 1991.

75. Penrose, 1959; Dierickx and Cool, 1989.

76. Evans and Génadry (1998) argue that it is tension between opposites that should be the dependent variable in organizational research.

77. Hampden-Turner, 1990a.

78. Hampden-Turner, 1990b.

79. Evans and Doz, 1989. Similar examples of steering are provided by Brown and Eisenhardt (1997, 1998). They show how successful firms in fast-moving industries steer between the need for semistructures (clarity of roles, deadlines, priorities) and improvisation (opportunism, open communication).

80. Birkinshaw and Gibson, 2004; O'Reilly and Tushman, 2004; Rausch and Birkinshaw, 2008. Duncan (1976) may have been the first author to use the term "ambidextrous organization."

81. "Lafley and Immelt: In Search of Billions," *Fortune*, December 11, 2006.

82. We discuss and provide examples of these dynamics in Chapter 11 when exploring the change paths to transnational organization.

CHAPTER 3

Becoming Locally Responsive

E-Bay in China

In March 1998, Meg Whitman was recruited to become the CEO of eBay—three years after the e-business firm had been founded by the French entrepreneur Pierre Omidyar. At the time, eBay had only 50 employees and US $4.7 million in revenues, and operated only in the United States. When she stepped down as CEO of the California-based firm 10 years later, eBay was present in close to 40 countries and had more than 15,000 employees, approximately 100 million active users, and about $8 billion in annual revenue.[1] By any standards, eBay is a highly successful multinational corporation. However, in spite of its market dominance in many countries around the world, it has been struggling to grow in some key markets in Asia.[2]

eBay's entry point to Asia was Japan in 2000. Its business model for Japan, as for all the other international markets it had previously entered successfully, was essentially the same as for the US (for example, the user fee structure and no media advertising). Its local Web site was also similar to the company's US version, with no special features to attract and serve local users. However, eBay was not the first mover in the Japanese market. Its US competitor Yahoo! had already formed a joint venture with the Japanese Internet company Softbank and invested heavily in an aggressive advertising campaign to promote its services.[3] By the time eBay went online, following the lengthy process of building its 100 percent owned company from scratch, Yahoo! had already built a loyal customer base that eBay was not able to seduce away. Two years after its entry to Japan, eBay pulled out.

As the company looked at other opportunities in Asia, eBay's management was determined to learn from its failure in Japan. Rather then starting from zero, eBay entered Taiwan, Korea, and India through partnerships and partial acquisitions of local firms. This was the strategy chosen in potentially the biggest market opportunity of all: China. In March 2002, eBay bought a 33 percent stake in EachNet, China's first and largest online consumer-to-consumer (C2C) trading site. The CEO of EachNet, Shao Yibo, was a native of Shanghai who had graduated from Harvard, worked at Boston Consulting Group, and developed EachNet with eBay as his model. One year later, eBay bought the rest of EachNet. Within a short time, eBay/EachNet had become the clear market leader for C2C business in China, with a dominant 85 percent market share.

However, local competition began to push back very quickly.[4] The biggest challenge came from a start-up formed by Chinese Internet entrepreneur Jack Ma. Ma already had a highly successful business-to-business auction site called Alibaba (in which Softbank from Japan and later Yahoo! were major investors). Ma was concerned that eBay/EachNet would establish a beachhead from which to attack his very profitable B2B activities. So in 2003 Ma set up his own e-commerce company Taobao ("hunt for treasure") as a direct competitor to eBay.

In China as elsewhere, eBay added fees based on the value of a deal to the listing fees that EachNet charged. Taobao did not charge any such fees, and Ma promised that his company would not do so for at least three years.[5] While eBay's Chinese site had a layout and features similar to those in the rest of the world, Taobao presented a site full of popular local and cultural features (such as horoscopes). Critically, Taobao developed a new payment system linked to physical delivery of the goods, as Chinese customers did not fully trust the credit card–based systems like PayPal that eBay was using. Taobao—unlike eBay—also allowed the seller and buyer to interact directly. This was a clever way of dealing with issues of trust in a society where there is very limited trust between people who do not know each other personally. Finally, to build customer confidence, Taobao decided to provide customer service support by telephone—again, not something supplied by eBay.[6]

The challenges of integrating EachNet and eBay further aggravated the latter's problems of establishing the company in China. Many members of the original EachNet team felt that they had been sidelined after the acquisition, when eBay managers from places like Germany and Taiwan were brought in to help with the integration. EachNet senior executives, including Shao Yibo, rapidly left the company. In order to achieve economies of scale, eBay moved EachNet's Internet platform to its US–based global server, as it had done systematically when integrating other foreign units. In the process, several locally developed design features were removed. Once the site was on the global platform, requests to localize the content of the Chinese site had to be approved from the US. Local employees felt that headquarters "did not listen to them."[7]

Despite following Taobao's example with free product listing, by the end of 2006 eBay's market share was down to 20 percent. Although Meg Whitman had promised, after the failure in Japan, that eBay would do a better job in adapting its activities to the local market in China, the company was unable to do so. In December 2006, eBay announced a fresh start, forming a joint venture with Tom Online, a wireless Internet company controlled by Hong Kong tycoon Li Ka Shing.[8] All eBay/EachNet business would be merged into a joint venture managed by Tom Online; only eBay China's global trading remained independent.

OVERVIEW

The story of eBay in Asia provides a vivid example of the potential problems facing multinational corporations that fail to adapt to local demands and competitive conditions. In this chapter we examine how firms respond to the diverse environments they face in international markets. We start with a presentation of the business advantages of a multidomestic strategy focused on local responsiveness, and then turn to its people management aspects.

It may not be enough to have HR practices that are adapted appropriately to local conditions. This aspect of responsiveness typically goes hand in hand with the localization of management, including not only how top positions are staffed in overseas units but also the influence of local managers on key decisions. In the second part of this chapter we discuss management localization as the foundation of a local responsiveness strategy, along with its pitfalls and lessons for a successful implementation.

Of all aspects of localization, the management of people has to be most cognizant of the cultural and institutional contexts facing the multinational firm abroad. Therefore, the core part of the chapter focuses on global diversity. We discuss three different theoretical perspectives that provide insights on sources of diversity and their implications for people management.

The first perspective on diversity builds on the idea that people and companies are products of the societal cultures of which they are a part. The second emphasizes national business systems, which require understanding the institutional arrangements in the host context. The third centers on the networks to which the company belongs, focusing on how managers tend to copy the practices of their peer groups. We use examples of differences in HR practices across countries as illustrations, and review the question of whether or not there is evidence of increasing global convergence in approaches to the management of people.

We conclude the chapter by considering the limitations of a multidomestic strategy.

ROOTS OF RESPONSIVENESS

At the core of the multidomestic strategy is the argument that local responsiveness helps to overcome the "liability of foreignness" that firms may suffer from when entering new markets.[9] When firms expand beyond their national borders they are often under pressure to adapt their operations; the greater the difference between the home country and the potential market, the more they may have to adapt their existing way of operating to respond to the local context. As we have seen in the case of eBay, not knowing how to manage in the unfamiliar environment, and/or not having products and services that fit local requirements, puts foreign companies at a disadvantage compared with their local competitors.

Local responsiveness was the route followed early in the internationalization process by companies such as Nestlé and Unilever at the beginning of the 20th century. In an era when communication and transport were restricted, customer preferences around the world were fragmented. Perhaps more importantly, logistical barriers meant that the cost of shipping goods internationally and the delays involved offset the economies of global mass production for all but a limited range of products. In markets where local competitors were likely to emerge, it was often preferable to set up a fully integrated local operation.

Rising trade barriers in the 1920s and 1930s forced even the most ardent pursuers of global economies to set up manufacturing facilities behind high tariff walls, further encouraging local responsiveness. The onset of World War II isolated some overseas operations from their parent organizations, especially those located in Europe. For example, the fear of takeover by Nazi Germany led Philips to spin off its companies in Britain and the United States and to restructure them as legally independent companies owned by trusts.

The US companies that internationalized in the 1960s and 1970s faced less initial pressure to be responsive to national differences and encountered fewer barriers to capitalizing on global economies of scale. But since then, the market leaders in most business sectors have become more evenly matched on access to capital, know-how, and technology. In a world of increased global connectivity,[10] local responsiveness—the capacity to sense and answer the varied needs of customers and other stakeholders—has acquired additional value as a source of competitive advantage. Even Coca-Cola, which for most of its existence constituted the archetype of a firm pursuing a meganational strategy, felt the need to "rediscover" its own multi-local heritage in the late 1990s, triggered by the slow responsiveness of the global headquarters in Atlanta to changing local markets and to food safety incidents around the world.[11]

In the process of "rediscovering" local responsiveness, our understanding of it has also changed. For a long time, the term "local" was generally understood to imply "national." For cultural and institutional reasons, nations remain important drivers of differentiated needs, but they are by no means the only ones. One of the challenges for multinational companies is precisely to differentiate responsiveness needs more finely, market by market. In fact, "local" refers to any market that is distinct from others. Clearly, "local" needs can be aggregated at various levels, with pressures for responsiveness differing significantly, not just between countries but also within countries.

For example, Japanese manufacturing firms entering the US and Europe for the first time during the 1980s tended to place their new plants in rural locations rather than in traditional manufacturing centers. Typically they set up in regions where the value system (tightly knit communities) and institutional environment (for example, unionization and supplier networks) were both closest to Japan and most flexible—the Midwest in the US, Wales in the UK.

From the multinational firm's point of view, some regions and markets may be more distant than others.[12] For example, research on foreign companies in

Brazil revealed that those coming from countries with strong ties to Brazil (in terms of language and institutional similarity, geographical proximity, colonial history, and immigration) were usually more successful than firms from countries with weaker ties to the country.[13] Also, there is some evidence that firms moving step-by-step to culturally distant countries, after establishing a presence in more proximate countries, are more successful than those that expanded by directly entering distant markets.[14] Given such findings one might urge managers to pay careful attention not just to market opportunities but also to ease of entry in terms of social, cultural, and institutional factors, especially with respect to their impact on human resources.

Business Advantages of Local Responsiveness

A locally responsive company is likely to be more receptive to local trends, emerging needs, and product usage patterns—and therefore less likely to miss subtle market opportunities. eBay has (so far) failed to respond properly to contextual demands in Japan and China, but it is not the only US Internet giant to struggle internationally. Google is the most popular Internet search engine in many countries, but it has failed to overtake the leading local Internet search engine Yandex in Russia.[15] According to industry observers, Google has wrestled with the complexities of the Russian language, been slow to develop local payment methods, and generally failed to understand the local market in Russia.[16]

However, a multidomestic strategy based on local responsiveness has many advantages that go beyond facilitating entry into foreign markets and adapting products and services to local customer tastes and preferences. By presenting a local face and acting like a domestic firm, the foreign firm may reach a wider customer base and compete more effectively in local labor markets. Responsiveness also includes a firm's business practices, such as the way it handles relationships with suppliers, distributors, and local government, and the approach it takes to people management.

The drivers of local responsiveness come from a mix of market, organizational, and political considerations (see the box "Business Drivers of Local Responsiveness").

Conforming to local business practices and developing ties to local authorities are especially important. If a firm becomes a local insider, it is more likely to have a say in the shaping of new policies and regulations, and to be invited to play a significant role in industry or trade associations. In this way it can gain valuable information and have a better chance of participating in local deals. As global oil companies like Shell and Exxon recognize, it is important to be close to local authorities in the regulated world of petroleum exploration and marketing. However, there are also potential dangers involved. Being too close to the authorities can create its own risks—for example, if the local government comes under attack for questionable practices. This happened to Shell, which had links with the regime of the former Nigerian leader General Sani Abacha.

Business Drivers of Local Responsiveness

Industry Characteristics

In certain business sectors, there is little competitive advantage to be gained from standardizing or coordinating across different subsidiaries. For example, nonbranded foods and small household appliances face weak forces for global integration because of an absence of scale economies. Cement companies, such as Lafarge and CEMEX, engage heavily in local production in every country they have entered. This is largely because the shipping and tariff costs neutralize any cost advantages of centralized sourcing.

Customer Needs

Historically, branded packaged goods companies, such as Danone (foods) or Unilever (nondurable goods), have tended to respond to different customer expectations, preferences, or requirements. But even businesses with global recipes, such as McDonald's or Disney, may be forced to modify their offerings to cater to local traditions or expectations. For example, European dining habits forced both Disney's theme park in Paris and McDonald's European franchises to abandon cherished no-alcohol policies applied in the home market.

Local Substitutes

Competition from local products or services with different price/performance characteristics may lead a company to local adaptation. Nestlé varies its infant cereal recipes according to local raw materials—in Europe they are made with wheat, in Latin America with maize and sorghum, and in Asia with soy. Whirlpool, contrary to its worldwide policies, introduced a locally manufactured brand of appliances in Eastern Europe to compete against low-priced competition.

Markets and Distribution

National differences in market structure and distribution channels can have repercussions on pricing, product positioning or design, promotion, and advertising. For example, the distribution infrastructure, particularly in emerging markets, may require adjustments to product design or packaging in order to cope with the challenges of dust, heat, or bumpy roads.

Host Government Regulations

Host government concerns—for national development or national security—may force a business to be locally responsive. Petrochemical firms have to build close relationships with national authorities controlling a resource that is critical for economic development. Local content requirements can force a firm into development partnerships with suppliers. Retail practices that are standard in the US, such as opening 24/7, or refunding the price difference on any item sold for less elsewhere, are illegal in Germany, forcing Wal-Mart to adapt its approach when it entered the German market.[17]

Consumers around the world perceived Shell as colluding with a corrupt government, compromising its corporate image.

Another more recent example is from the Internet search industry. For several years Google had a Chinese-language version of its search engine (google.com) that operated outside of China. However, the Chinese government closely monitored the search engine, once closing it down for two weeks, continuously using a firewall to block access to sites blacklisted by the government, and slowing down the search in general. In January 2006, Google decided to open up a new Chinese-speaking version in China (google.cn), and the company agreed to adhere to Chinese self-censorship laws and regulations.[18] This guaranteed faster and more reliable access for users in China, who could still access the old google.com site to compare search results. However, the decision by Google to follow Yahoo! and Microsoft in accepting self-censorship in China was heavily criticized in the United States, where company executives were called into Congressional hearings to defend their actions.[19]

People Challenges of Local Responsiveness

Alongside the business arguments for local responsiveness, there are equally compelling arguments for taking a local orientation in people management. Of all the management domains, people management is generally seen as the most sensitive to local context.[20] Cultural differences are one reason, but by no means the only one. National regulatory pressures are equally if not more important—on forms of workplace representation, employee participation, fiscal incentives for training, acceptable practices when hiring and firing, working hours, and so on.

Some countries regulate employment practices closely, whereas others leave more discretion to the employer. For example, firms in the US can set their own overtime policies and seldom pay professionals for overtime. These practices are nominally illegal, yet not uncommon in Japan, but in Germany they would certainly land the company in court. Moreover, HR practices are typically subject to scrutiny by labor unions, whose strength and attitudes toward management vary by nation and industry (more about this later in the chapter).

These characteristics make people management more context-specific than accounting, marketing, or manufacturing, which tend to adhere more closely to parent company norms. Because people management tools are context-specific, one response is simply to delegate HR practices entirely to the local subsidiaries—an approach that might be characterized as "When in Rome, do as the Romans." Yet this is too simplistic.

The adjustment of HR practices to the local context is often framed as a Hamlet choice: To adjust or not to adjust, that is the question. In fact, people management is not a monolithic domain. For example, research on foreign companies in China shows significant differences in the degree of localization in recruitment, training, compensation, performance appraisal, and promotion criteria,[21] and we explore reasons for these differences in this chapter. Also, HR practices for rank-and-file employees may correspond more to local norms than practices affecting executives.[22]

Some HR practices are more contextually bound than others. Some can be regarded as high-context, others as low-context, to borrow from Hall's terminology.[23] Low-context practices are more explicit, based on clear frameworks, and applied in a similar fashion across cultures—such as job design criteria and objectives, and measures of employee performance. High-context practices have a stronger dependence on local norms and values, such as conflict resolution, and how objectives are set and performance appraisals conducted.

While the focus of our discussion so far is on people management practices, it is important to keep in mind that people management (HRM) impacts the organization at different levels—from guiding principles, policies, processes, and tools, to actual operating practices.[24] The practices are shaped by company principles, policies, and processes, but they are typically more locally adapted, compared to guiding company principles that may be designed to apply universally around the world. Even in a multinational corporation, with globally standardized HR policies, processes, and tools, we are likely to find variance in how these are implemented across and within foreign subsidiaries.[25]

IMPLEMENTING LOCALIZATION

To be locally responsive, it is not sufficient for multinationals to have HR practices that are appropriately adapted to local conditions—responsiveness typically goes hand in hand with localizing management, including not only how top positions are staffed in overseas units but also the influence of local managers on key decisions. Although local responsiveness does not always imply localization—experienced international managers can often be effective representatives of the local voice to the corporate center—expatriate staffing strategies are difficult to sustain in the long term. The difficulties facing eBay in China were partly associated with the fact that the company was not able to retain talented Chinese managers.

Localization takes a variety of forms. Our focus in this chapter is on the people aspect—systematic investment in the recruitment, development, and retention of local employees who can take over the running of local operations. Unilever provides one of the earliest documented examples of this policy in action. Sensitive to the national aspirations of newly independent countries, the company started to replace expatriates with indigenous managers. Known internally as the "ization" policy, it started in the 1930s and 1940s with "Indianization" and "Africanization" of local subsidiaries.[26]

Since then, localization has become part of the corporate mantra for multinational enterprises around the world. Building strong local management teams is considered a sign of enlightened management and especially of good corporate citizenship. It is a lever for attracting local talent worldwide and for improving the firm's international perspective, and represents an integral strand in the globalization strategy of many companies. We explore this further in Chapters 7 and 8, where we discuss talent management.

However, localization goes beyond staffing and retention. Our concept of localization equates it with the degree of local responsibility for decision making. A subsidiary may have only one expatriate, but if that individual makes all decisions of importance, the subsidiary's degree of localization will be low. This will also be the case if a local general manager has to check out every decision with corporate headquarters. On the other hand, a high degree of localization is not synonymous with complete subsidiary autonomy. A high degree of localization simply implies that the local subsidiary managers are responsible for their decisions and live with the consequences of their actions.

The case for localization of management is strong and straightforward:

- Better local understanding of markets, customers, and opportunities.
- Goodwill among local authorities and the local media.
- Improved local network connections.
- Enhanced employee commitment and motivation.
- Lower costs.

Local employees nearly always have a better understanding of the vernacular—the cultural, institutional, and business environment in which the company operates—and they are usually better at managing a local workforce. Localization helps foreign multinationals penetrate the network of personal and business contacts needed to build and consolidate a presence in the country.

While some expatriates are capable of surmounting some linguistic and cultural barriers, generally their expatriate status works against them. Expatriates are often dismissed as "temporary fixtures"—why would key industry players or government officials bother to cultivate relations with someone whose assignment is going to end in the near future?

Authorities often evaluate foreign firms by their degree of localization, while the media, politicians, and trade union officials also tend to stress the importance of local talent development. Some governments—for example, most of the Gulf states—impose quotas, restrict work permits, or impose fiscal controls on expatriate salaries. Therefore most companies with a long-term commitment to a particular local market will see localization as a necessary step to gain social acceptance and avoid a colonial or ethnocentric image.

Employee commitment and motivation are also influenced by the degree of localization. Unless senior managers can convince local employees that they understand and honestly represent local interests to headquarters so that local employees' concerns are given due consideration, they may have difficulty eliciting commitment. Employee commitment is also likely to suffer if decision making is centralized at corporate headquarters. This was demonstrated in the negative reactions of local managers toward the way eBay integrated the newly acquired EachNet and transferred decision-making authority for many areas to its California headquarters.

Opportunities for growth and advancement are important concerns for local employees—and dissatisfaction with those opportunities is one of the most frequently cited reasons for turnover. Heavy reliance on expatriates is often perceived as blocking promotional avenues for local managers and as a sign of the company's lack of trust in them. In contrast, the presence of influential local executives in a subsidiary supplies role models for younger employees and improves recruitment and retention. Moreover, local executives may find it less difficult than expatriates to implement difficult decisions, such as layoffs or reorganization. Expatriates' allegiance is more suspect, and their decisions are more closely scrutinized.

Big compensation packages for expatriates are often a source of ill feeling within the organization, as local employees often have detailed knowledge of expatriates' salaries and allowances. The localization of management can reduce the high costs of maintaining a large contingent of expatriate managers. However, focusing on localization only from a cost perspective could lead to decisions driven only by short-term bottom-line effects, to the detriment of other considerations, such as corporate governance, development of common culture, and knowledge transfer. Further, in an increasing number of locations, the cost of employing a high-quality local executive is approaching that of an expatriate.

Overcoming Barriers to Management Localization

Many international companies actively promote localization to increase local responsiveness, but progress is often slower than they would like. The process of localization is complex. Localization has to be acknowledged as an important goal,[27] and achieving this requires sensitivity to its people dimensions as well as accountability—all backed up by a sustained strategy for the development of local managers. It is revealing that while there is voluminous research on expatriation, there is far less on the challenges of localization.[28]

Attracting and Developing Local Talent

The attraction and development of capable local managers is the foundation of successful localization.[29] Recent improvements in the educational system in China and other emerging markets have improved the qualifications of the local labor force. However, two interrelated problems continue systematically to plague corporate efforts to localize. First, because of high demand and limited supply, competent local managers are often hard to find. Second, once found, they may be hard to retain. These two problems sometimes create a dilemma: If good local managers are going to leave us in any case, why bother to invest time and money in developing them?

While there are no silver bullets to solve these problems, there are initiatives that many companies can implement, starting with a focus on the attraction and development of local talent.

1. **Establish a visible presence.** In many emerging markets, there may be a genuine scarcity of talent with specific functional or managerial competences, while competition in the labor market is keen. The challenge even for well-known international firms is that they do not enjoy the reputational advantage over their peers that they may have at home. In every market they enter, they start from scratch. The first step is therefore to build a visible

presence in the local labor market—forging links with educational institutions, offering scholarships, sponsoring sporting events or charitable activities. For instance, each member of top management at GE China has been allocated one leading university for which he or she is personally responsible.[30]

2. **Adjust selection criteria.** Developing a generic set of recruiting criteria is often difficult. For example, when recruiting experienced managers in Russia, Cadbury's quickly realized that it had to scrap its "global" requirements concerning work experience and educational background—they were simply not relevant in local conditions. Selecting on competencies may also not work. Instead, recruiters may look for candidates with the right attitude—to critical company values, teamwork, learning—even if they are not immediately ready with respect to functional skills, which can be developed through on-the-job and off-the-job training.

3. **Sell careers, not just jobs.** When talking to prospective recruits, the company should communicate its localization objectives and connect those plans to the career prospects of local managers. When Schlumberger recruits engineers in Russia, the company knows that they have the same career prospects as those recruited in France or the US, and that the performance criteria are the same. A reputation for thorough training and skill development can enhance the outcome of the recruitment efforts.

Because of the difficulties of attracting and retaining experienced managers, some companies choose to "grow their own timber." They take on young recruits, placing more emphasis on their future potential than on their current professional or technical skills. This entails large investments in their development, through formal training programs, international assignments, and individual coaching and mentoring. It may even involve building local training institutions, as many multinational firms have done in China, where Motorola has established a Motorola University, Schlumberger has helped local engineering establishments reach world-class standards, and the Ericsson Academy has for many years offered an MBA program to its local employees and customers.

Recruiting locals who have graduated abroad is another popular strategy to address the talent gap. However, in some emerging markets such as China, where access to education abroad was for a long time restricted to the privileged elite, tensions between locals and "pseudo-locals"—returnees with freshly minted foreign MBAs commanding salaries well above market rates—produce the kind of resentment that used to be provoked by the lavish packages granted to expatriates.

In mature markets, attracting talent is more likely to be a problem of accessing the appropriate labor pool. For example, the number of top-class Japanese managers who can be lured from local corporations to foreign firms is still relatively small (though growing). Many headhunters who service multinationals in Japan find it difficult to spot or access high performers in local firms and therefore limit themselves to searching among executives already in the *gaishikei* (foreign-affiliate) world.

Managing Retention

A disproportionate number of local managers trained to take over expatriate positions never actually fill those posts or do so only briefly. One study identified biased selection and inappropriate training as part of the explanation but found that a more significant factor was that terms and conditions after training did not measure up to what the external market offered to ambitious and well-trained individuals.[31] The company expects a return on its training investment, but competitors may poach the most talented products before this can happen.

Given the length of time that is often needed to develop qualified local managers, which may include investing in basic education that the local system has not provided, retention can be a real challenge. Some multinational firms are obliged to hire at least two local trainees for each former expatriate position.[32] Inevitably, this drives up costs, and can create a temporary surplus of skilled managers, allowing rival firms to benefit from the company's development efforts. US automobile companies and German carmakers with US manufacturing sites systematically raid Japanese transplants to capture local talent, weakening the latter's ability to localize. On the other hand, that may be a price worth paying if the company is still able to attract and retain the very best; companies such as GE and Procter & Gamble believe it is worth it.

Consider the environment facing multinationals in Russia. Before the fall of the Berlin Wall, the country contained only a handful of foreign firms. Today, thousands are based there, resulting in significant competition for well-qualified employees. In addition, more Russian firms—several of which already feature in the ranks of *Fortune* Global 500—are able to make attractive employment offers, further increasing the competition.[33] The local educational and training infrastructure still needs time to close the gap between demand and supply. Not surprisingly, staff turnover is high.

Inevitably, compensation figures prominently among the mechanisms to retain local talent. Paying above-market rates is typical, but market rates are less than transparent in emerging countries. This partly explains the curious fact that the vast majority of companies claim to pay in the top market quartile. However, cash is only one part of the compensation package. Today, retention bonuses, stock options, and restricted shares are just as common in Shanghai as in New York, if not more so. Some companies have introduced even more comprehensive packages, including private health programs, interest-free loans, or housing assistance.

As a result, salary costs for capable local staff are increasing around the world. The lament of a general manager of a Japanese bank in London, as he struggled to retain qualified specialists wooed by European and US institutions in the City—"for us localization is no longer a cheap alternative"[34]—heard a decade ago, can be heard today in nearly any location where multinationals are present to any significant degree.

Ultimately, an attractive compensation package is necessary but not enough—there are always other companies that can offer more.[35] The decisive factors may have more to do with career development and involvement in decision making. The multinational firm has to be prepared to develop and promote talented people more rapidly than it traditionally did at home, and support them with the necessary training, coaching, and feedback. Mapping the career paths of high-potential local candidates is an important signal of the company's commitment to them.[36] Social climate may also be important. Company atmosphere, friendship ties, and social activities, combined with the promise of a stable future in a firm with high local growth prospects, have been observed to be decisive factors in local employee retention.[37]

Localization Starts at the Head Office

For all its advantages, localization is unlikely to be successful if it is only a faddish whim of transient expatriate general managers or regional directors. Breaking out of that vicious circle requires long-term corporate commitment right from the top. Systematic recruitment and development of local managers require a long-term organizationwide effort that transcends the good intentions of individual managers. While the positive or negative outcomes of localization efforts are most visible within the subsidiary operations involved, the core of the problem may actually be far away, in the corporate center.

The fundamental bottleneck of localization is often the capacity of corporate headquarters to interact effectively with locally hired executives. For example, in last 20 years we have observed several Japanese multinationals who aggressively recruited capable local staff, recognizing correctly that the weakness of local management is an obstacle to faster global growth. However, within a relatively short period the newly appointed local managers left in frustration because they could not get the job done. What was going on?

Historically, the international growth of Japanese multinationals was coordinated through an informal network of Japanese executives, carefully orchestrated from the center that controlled the critical resources. Although nominally in positions of substantial authority, the newly hired non-Japanese executives were simply not able to secure the resources necessary to drive the local business forward. They did not have the personal connections or even the language ability to communicate with the head office, which was generally staffed by managers without much, if any, international experience. Only when these headquarters managers were replaced by more global-savvy executives, as happened at Matsushita during the early 2000s, did localization efforts begin to show results.

Expatriates Are Responsible for Localization

Building a capable local management team does not happen overnight. It needs preparation.[38] Although the corporate or regional HR function is usually in charge of developing plans for the localization of management, most of the day-to-day responsibility for successful localization rests with expatriates in senior management positions *within the subsidiary.*[39] This means paying as much attention to the role of the expatriates as to the locals, as it is expatriates who ultimately carry out the localization strategy. When assigning this responsibility to expatriates, three areas require close attention: (1) the link to expatriate selection, (2) mandate and timing, and (3) measurements and rewards.

1. **Expatriate selection.** The key issue in expatriate selection is determining the experience profile necessary to drive localization. In addition to the professional skills expected of any expatriate, they need to be able to share knowledge, and coach and mentor their local successors. As the China-based HR manager of a large US manufacturing company put it, "Expatriates should be able to transfer information even to people who don't know what questions to ask."[40] These skills are in short supply in most organizations, and cultural and language differences only compound the challenge.

   The young high potentials that Shell traditionally sent out to emerging markets were not successful in managing the localization process. They had neither the motivation nor the depth of experience to pass on their skills. A local manager in East Asia observed, "Most expatriates learn on the job, and the locals end up teaching them."[41] Gradually, and sometimes only under pressure from host governments, Shell changed tack, making sure that a sufficient number of expatriates had knowledge and experience to share.

2. **Mandate and timing.** Prior to the assignment, the localization objectives and time table should be clearly identified as key objectives. Unless these expectations are articulated, expediency and the need to meet business results and other quantitative performance indicators will dominate, with only token attention given to identifying training needs and developing local managers.[42] However, doing this well takes time, as the tasks associated with developing a local successor—including transfer of technical know-how, business knowledge, and corporate norms, as well as introductions to networks of people back at headquarters—may take longer than the typical two- or three-year expatriate posting. An unrealistic schedule will be ignored or poorly implemented.

   Expanding its brewery operations into China and Vietnam, San Miguel used a "two-plus-two-year" assignment rule for its Philippine expatriates: two years to settle in and identify a local successor, and two years to develop him or her. ABB's objective in China was to try to localize senior management positions in new units within five years.[43]

3. **Measurements and rewards.** Expatriates take the localization challenge seriously to the extent that they are measured not just on their business performance but also on their ability to develop local managers. The localization objective will seem all the more authentic if the company attaches incentives to its implementation. One study recommended replacing the traditional hardship allowance with a "successful completion bonus" for expatriates who train competent local replacements.[44] However, it must be clear that successful completion means more than just installing a local

successor. We know of several multinational corporations in China that pay bonuses to expatriates who have groomed successors only if the latter are assessed as performing well after 12 months in the new job.

On the other hand, appointing a local face who does not have qualifications and credibility can sometimes be more detrimental to the morale of the local workforce than no localization. It reinforces doubts about whether the foreign owners know how to run a local business . . . so it may be time to head for the door. One way of evaluating performance against localization objectives is to include feedback from multiple sources, both expatriate and local.

However, probably the most compelling incentive for expatriates to drive effective localization may be the prospect of an attractive follow-up assignment. If there is high uncertainty about repatriation and future career, where is the incentive to train local successors who are destined to make the expatriate obsolete? Repatriation planning therefore plays an important role in supporting successful localization.

Avoiding the Localization Traps

It is important for international companies to take localization initiatives seriously right from the start. Companies that fail to do so can find themselves caught up in a dangerous process of serial localization. If, for whatever reason, the newly appointed local managers cannot do the job after the expatriates pull out, the subsidiary's performance will inevitably decline. Then expensive troubleshooters from the outside are sent in to fix the problems, followed by a second wave of managers with a new mandate to localize. The efforts have to start again from scratch, but by this time in an atmosphere of increased cynicism locally about the company's commitment (or ability) to get it done.

Similarly, when turnover of local managers is high, companies often become reluctant to invest enough in developing local employees, preferring instead expatriates with a proven commitment to the company—this merely confirms suspicions of a glass ceiling for locals. Expatriate-heavy structures restrict career opportunities for local managers, making it even harder to attract or retain local talent. If this continues through several rounds, the morale and motivation of local employees are bound to suffer.

Localization is not a one-time effort. The challenge does not end with the appointment of a competent local management team. Once implemented, localization efforts need to be sustained and carefully managed. Often, the cost of developing and promoting local managerial talent is such that efforts are scaled back as soon as the first generation of local managers takes over. However, if local managers do not have an interest in investing in the next generation of leaders, whom they may even see as threats to their leadership positions, then localization will be doomed to fail.

At one UK affiliate in Nigeria, the first group of local managers received extensive training and support, but the next generation was not given the same opportunities. Naturally, with their career path blocked by their local seniors, the best were tempted away by other opportunities, and when the seniors retired or moved on, there were no capable candidates left in the succession pipeline. The expatriates and consultants (disguised expatriates) who were parachuted back in to refill the vacuum were viewed by many local employees as evidence of a hidden agenda at headquarters to discredit the localization process.[45]

Strong leadership in the HR function that will protect the localization initiative from parochial interests is an essential condition for its success. Indeed, one somewhat paradoxical trap is localizing the leadership of the HR function too early in the process. While a local HR manager may be best at operational matters—knowing the culture, employment legislation and labor market, and coping with local employee relations—she or he may not have the experience needed to develop a coherent long-term localization strategy or the influence at headquarters to ensure its implementation.

Localization is important, but anything taken to an extreme can create a pathology. Excessive localization can lead to empire building, unwarranted respect for the local status quo, and ultimately loss of control by the head office. Put simply, if everyone is local, who is global? When the corporation is so local around the world that opportunities for horizontal cross-border mobility are limited, it becomes difficult to develop managers with broad global experience. Indeed, localization should be viewed as a step on the journey toward transnational management development and not as an end in itself.

UNDERSTANDING DIVERSITY

So far, we have pointed to the advantages of responsiveness and to the benefits of localization of management. The underlying assumption is that in order to compete effectively in international markets, companies must respond to diversity across countries. In this section, we focus on the sources of diversity across countries, and how international firms respond to this diversity in the way they manage people.

We present and comment upon three theoretical perspectives for understanding diversity. They relate to the cultural differences between the context in which the parent company and its local subsidiary are embedded (know yourself and others), to the institutional configuration of the environment (know where you are), and to the company's way of networking (know whom you talk to).

Know Yourself and Others: The Cultural Perspective

The cultural perspective maintains that the values (i.e., notions of what is desirable) shared by members of a social group shape, and are at least to some extent shaped by, collective beliefs, behavior, and artifacts.[46] Members of a society internalize certain values, beliefs, and behavioral norms that become more or less taken for granted. Culture is believed to influence and thus differentiate management practices across societies as well as other collective groups, such as industries and organizations.

From this perspective, attention typically focuses on how the local culture influences the activities of foreign firms in the country. But the starting point for sensible local responsiveness is recognizing that the parent organization is embedded in the societal culture of its home country. This cultural embeddedness may have an effect on its international strategy, how the multinational controls and coordinates its foreign units, and the prevailing views held by parent company executives about effective management practices. Simply put, before you try to understand other people and the practices and strategies that may be effective abroad, you had better understand yourself. In this chapter we will focus on societal culture, postponing our discussion of organizational culture to Chapter 6.

Research about Work-Related Values

The most influential body of literature concerning values in international business relates to cultural differences between countries. Its foundation is Hofstede's landmark book *Culture's Consequences,* which describes research conducted in the late 1960s, and is grounded in one of the largest databases about workplace values ever analyzed—attitude surveys of 116,000 IBM employees in 53 countries.[47] Hofstede's study showed that despite IBM's strong integrative culture, national culture played an important role in differentiating work values.

In his analysis, Hofstede identified four "universal" dimensions along which cultures could be compared: *individualism/collectivism, power distance, uncertainty avoidance, and masculinity/femininity.* Hofstede argued that these four dimensions influence the way in which organizations are structured and managed. Some years later he added a fifth dimension: long- versus short-term orientation. Though at times heavily criticized,[48] Hofstede's work continues to influence the field and is well known among managers worldwide. His quantitative measures of culture gave birth to the notion of "cultural distance" between home and host country and allowed the cultural perspective to infiltrate other fields of international business research.

The work of Hofstede was complemented by Laurent's research, which showed bigger differences in managerial beliefs among people working for the same company in different nations than among people working for different companies within one nation.[49] Following a similar line of inquiry, Trompenaars and Hampden-Turner have compiled a large database documenting systematic cross-cultural variances in the relative importance of opposing values, such as achievement versus ascription and universalism versus particularism.[50] They identify seven cultural "tensions" (see Table 3–1) that they believe companies (and managers) should be aware of since these could influence the transferability of management practices across borders.

Recently, a multinational team of researchers (GLOBE) conducted another large-scale study of cultural differences in that they collected and analyzed data on cultural values and practices and leadership attributes from over 17,000 managers in 62 societies.[51] Partly overlapping with Hofstede's conceptualization of cultural dimensions, the GLOBE project identified nine cultural dimensions along which various societies can be ranked.[52] Table 3–2 shows the scores for a number of countries.

TABLE 3–1. Seven Cultural Tensions

1. **Universalism versus particularism:** When no code, rule, or law seems to cover an exceptional case, should the most relevant rule be imposed, or should the case be considered on its merits?

2. **Analyzing versus integrating:** Are managers more effective when they break up a problem or situation into parts, or integrate the parts into a whole?

3. **Individualism versus communitarianism:** When people reach decisions or make choices, should they consider their own best interests, or should they base their choices on the considerations of the wider team, organization, collectivity, or community to which they belong?

4. **Inner-directed versus outer-directed:** Should managers be guided by internal standards, or should they be flexible and adjust to external signals, demands, and trends?

5. **Sequential versus synchronic view of time:** Should managers get things done as quickly as possible, regardless of the negative impact that their actions may have on others, or should they synchronize efforts so that completion is coordinated and the negative impact minimized?

6. **Achieved versus ascribed status:** Should individuals be judged primarily or solely by their achievements, or by their status, as reflected in age, length of service, or other ascriptions?

7. **Equality versus hierarchy:** Should subordinates be treated as equals and allowed to exercise discretion in decision making, or should relationships be delimited by hierarchy?

Source: Adapted from C. Hampden Turner and A. Trompenaars, *Building Cross-Cultural Competence* (New York: Wiley, 2000).

GLOBE dimensions like differences around assertiveness allow us to understand the problems of interpersonal relations and teamwork when working across cultures. When there is a conflict or a problem that arouses strong feelings, people from some cultures (Israel and the Netherlands, for example) will tend to be direct and assertive in confronting what they see as the issue; others will find this distressingly aggressive, to the point of loss of face (Japan and China). In low-context cultures such as the United States, words like "Yes" have a clear meaning, indicating assent. But in high-context cultures like Japan, the meaning of a word depends on the context in which it was expressed. When used as a response to a question from an angry superior, "Yes" may mean "the circumstances give me no choice except to respond in this way." Indeed, as both GLOBE and Hofstede suggest, there are differences from one culture to another in the extent to which subordinates feel free to challenge their bosses (power distance). Without such understanding, at least on the part of the leaders, conflict can split the team and undermine performance.

Managers can use the GLOBE data for a rough but up-to-date indication of important differences between countries that may have implications for HRM,

TABLE 3–2. The GLOBE Study on Cultural Practices with Results from Selected Nations (Scale 1–7)

Dimension	US	Germany[A]	France	Sweden	Russia	China	Japan	Brazil	Egypt
Power distance: Extent to which members of a collective expect power to be distributed equally.	4.9	5.3	5.2	4.9	5.5	5.0	5.1	5.3	4.9
Uncertainty avoidance: Degree to which a society, organization, or group relies on social norms, rules, and procedures to alleviate the unpredictability of future events.	4.2	5.2	4.4	5.3	2.9	4.9	4.1	3.6	4.1
Societal collectivism: Degree to which organizational and societal institutional practices encourage and reward collective distribution of resources and collective action.	4.2	3.8	3.9	5.2	4.5	4.8	5.2	3.8	4.5
In-group collectivism: Degree to which individuals express pride, loyalty, and cohesiveness in their organizations or families.	4.3	4.0	4.4	3.7	5.6	5.8	4.6	5.2	5.6
Performance orientation: Degree to which a collective encourages and rewards group members for performance improvement and excellence.	4.5	4.3	4.1	3.7	3.4	4.5	4.2	4.0	4.3
Assertiveness: Extent to which individuals are assertive, confrontational, and aggressive in their relationships with others.	4.6	4.6	4.1	3.4	3.7	3.8	3.6	4.2	3.9
Future orientation: Extent to which individuals engage in future-oriented behaviors, such as delaying gratification, planning, and investing in the future.	4.2	4.3	3.5	4.4	2.9	3.8	4.3	3.8	3.9
Humane orientation: Degree to which a collective encourages and rewards individuals for being fair, altruistic, generous, caring, and kind to others.	4.2	3.2	3.4	4.1	3.9	4.4	4.3	3.7	4.7
Gender egalitarianism: Degree to which a collective minimizes gender inequality.	3.3	3.1	3.6	3.8	4.1	3.0	3.2	3.3	2.8

[A] Refers to West Germany (former Federal Republic of Germany)

Source: R. House, P.J. Hanges, M. Javidan, P.W. Dorfman, and V. Gupta (eds.), *Culture, Leadership and Organizations: The GLOBE Study of 62 Societies* (Thousand Oaks, CA: Sage; 2004).

although we need to be cautious when using societal-level data to predict the people-related challenges facing firms abroad.

Cultural Features and the Need for Local HRM Responsiveness

The proponents of the cultural perspective on organizations argue that cultural values are deeply anchored and enduring, that they vary systematically between societies, and that they condition organizational practices. Consider the case of people management. Hofstede has argued that the motivation theories dominating management thinking reflect American cultural values, especially individualism.[53] They stress achievement and self-actualization as the ultimate human needs. These assumptions may not hold true in other cultures.

Schneider has teased out some of the cultural assumptions underpinning standard HR practices, from selection to socialization.[54] For example, in the realm of performance management she highlights a number of underlying assumptions that have particular resonance in the US: the ideas that goals can be set and reached (assuming control over the environment) and that objectives may be given a 6- to 18-month time frame (assuming that time can be managed). Managers and subordinates are expected to engage in a two-way dialogue to agree what has to be done, by when, and how. Again, this assumes that power differences allow this to happen, that employees have the right to input in determining their goals and are eager to take responsibility.

Does performance mean the same thing to everyone? Is there an objective best approach to performance management?

In the US-influenced rhetoric, performance management is focused on results delivered by the individual. In accordance with this, Ulrich and his colleagues advise, "Begin with an absolute focus on results."[55] Individual appraisal is crucial for linking results to pay, but appraisal can also be team- or organization-based. For the US consultancy firm Hay Group, the bottom line is "if performance can't be accurately measured, if employees don't understand how it is evaluated, or if they can't see the link between their efforts and the desired results, the program won't work or will be less than fully effective."[56]

The Japanese concept of performance is often contrasted with that of the West, particularly the US. For instance, Toyota focuses on *kaizen,* or continuous improvement, steered by collective action. *Kaizen* is an umbrella for a variety of processes oriented toward continuous improvement—including statistical tools, total quality management (TQM), suggestion schemes, and small group consultation. Japanese management efforts are directed at supporting and stimulating the efforts of subordinates to improve the processes that generate results, and the time horizon for improvement is longer than in the West. Appraisal focuses on employee skills and efforts (discipline, collaboration, involvement) that lead to continuous improvement, rather than on short-term results.

In summary, culturalists suggest that the development of HRM theory is based on a set of assumptions that are deeply embedded in one culture—that of the US, where many of the most influential HR scholars and consulting firms are based. This limits the applicability of this template to other cultures. The ultimate expression of this cultural perspective is the memorable description of HRM as "a contemporary manifestation of the American Dream."[57]

Home Country Culture and People Management Abroad

As we have argued, national culture is often presented as a key factor influencing how firms manage people. The cultural features of the corporation's home country may also imprint how it manages people abroad. Let us take Trompenaars' universalism–particularism dimension as an example. Though we should be wary of cultural stereotypes, people in universalist cultures tend to believe in guiding rules, procedures, and principles, whereas in particularist cultures everything depends on the nature of the relationship and the specific context.

The United States is seen as one of the more universalistic cultures, with a strong belief in contracts, standard operating procedures, and systems. Trompenaars and his colleagues argue that people from such a culture will tend to look for a single way of dealing with cultural differences, a "solution" to the "problem." For example, codes of conduct are supposed to solve differences in ethics. Koreans may be different from Americans, but if a US firm has a clear set of values, it may select its local staff from among the "5 percent of Koreans" who fit with the company's value system.

Midrange cultures, like those in many European countries, are more cautious about such universalistic principles and global value systems. They tend to be critical of "one-best-way" thinking and are more open to situational adaptation. International HRM is likely to be considered as the local implementation of strategy and business objectives, as opposed to selecting people who will conform to particular practices.

The Chinese, the Koreans, and the Japanese are highly particularistic. The keynote is subtlety, depending on contexts and relationships. On-the-job training is favored over formal training, which is considered too black-and-white to capture the nuances of reality. Whereas a universalist may believe that an experienced person can teach someone to manage cultural differences, the particularist believes that someone will begin to cope with cultural differences only after years of intensive experience in a culture. Japanese firms like to hire non-Japanese managers who will agree to spend a number of years learning the delicate context in which the firm operates before being entrusted with significant responsibility.

The Limits of a Cultural Perspective on HRM

So far we have focused on the influence of the firm's home cultural context on HRM. However, to what extent should the cultural environment of a subsidiary abroad influence local HR practices? To what degree *should* multinationals adapt their practices to each location in order to achieve cultural fit? Conventional wisdom suggests that national cultural factors matter a great deal. Although we subscribe to the view that cultural issues are of significance for international HRM, we also believe that it is important to examine critically the assertion that multinationals must adapt to the local national culture when deciding on HR practices in their foreign units.

The cultural hypothesis builds on the following assumptions, among others:

- Between-country differences in values are substantially larger than within-country differences in values held by individuals.
- A misfit between national culture and management practice will reduce effectiveness.
- Companies attract, select, and retain employees in a random fashion.[58]

The first of these assumptions has been refuted in several academic studies, including Hofstede's study, referred to above. Yes, the nationality of a person does explain some of the variance in work-related values, but according to several investigations this amounts to only 1.8 to 4.4 percent of the total variance.[59] These studies remind us that individuals differ significantly in their cultural values and that only a relatively small part of the global variance between individuals is explained by their passports. They also point to the possibility of a considerable overlap in values by individual members of society that can be found even between countries that are culturally distant (see Figure 3–1 for a graphic illustration of this).

The second assumption suggests, for example, that using an explicit public performance management system would not work in a Chinese culture where not losing face is extremely important. Indeed, there are numerous stories that testify to the risk of implementing alien HR practices in overseas units. On the other hand, there are also examples of foreign and *local* firms that have successfully introduced HR practices at odds with local values and practices. In Chapter 9

FIGURE 3–1. Illustration of the distribution of individual values in two countries.

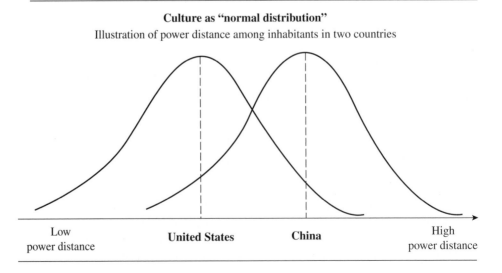

Culture as "normal distribution"

Illustration of power distance among inhabitants in two countries

Low power distance   United States   China   High power distance

we look more closely at the case of consumer appliance manufacturer Haier, whose fully transparent performance management system has become famous in China, successfully attracting many young Chinese to join the company.

A recent survey of HR managers from a large number of countries also raises some doubts about the validity of this assumption. While the cultural fit argument would lead us to expect that HR managers of different nationalities would have different views about the effectiveness of HR practices, they largely agreed on which practices contribute to enhanced firm performance.[60] For instance, HR managers in Japan, China, the United States, and Central, Eastern, Southern, and Northern Europe rated the effectiveness of pay-for-performance systems almost identically.

Even if individuals from different countries differ on average substantially in their values, with consequences for the effectiveness of HR practices, companies can try to select people who hold matching values. For example, in France, Lincoln Electric can recruit and select individuals whose values fit well with Lincoln's famous performance-based compensation system. In fact, Lincoln has successfully operated in France since 1955 with an HR system that is more like the one it has in its Cleveland plant in the US than those found in local French organizations. This example points to the importance of selection—clearly communicating to the labor market the values and practices of the firm, recruiting and then promoting internally those individuals who fit well with the organization (we discuss this further in Chapter 7).

Thus, although the cultural fit argument has surface validity, research shows that multinational firms have considerable leeway when deciding which HR practices to implement overseas. It is perhaps more effective to present the HR practices in a way that is compatible with what people perceive to be important in their local culture, as opposed to aligning practices with that culture's average values.

Commentary

Cultural explanations hold considerable intuitive appeal for international managers. They supply multiple plausible interpretations for the many difficulties of working with people from different countries. That is both the strength and the weakness of the cultural perspective.

The work of cultural researchers has heightened sensitivity to the influence of cultural values in shaping organizational practices and in explaining employee reactions toward management policies and practices. A compelling case can be made for the importance of the cultural perspective in understanding different attitudes toward authority, teamwork, and conflict resolution. However, the cultural perspective tends to overemphasize value differences and neglect the fact that the cultural traits found in a particular country represent only a central tendency. Individuals and indeed companies inevitably differ in the extent to which they adhere to those values. For example, Intel and Hewlett-Packard have strikingly different organizational cultures in spite of their shared national and industrial roots. Research indicates that differences in values across organizations are perhaps even greater than those across nationalities.[61]

Successful people management requires knowledge of differences within a culture as well as across cultures. While the distance between national cultural modes or means can be a barrier to effective cross-cultural interaction, another substantial barrier is outsiders' lack of comprehension about diversity *within* a given culture. A potential danger of relying on cultural studies (like those of Hofstede, Trompenaars, and the GLOBE team) is that they create a notion of what all people from a certain country are like. We may have stopped stereotyping gender and race—we need to tackle culture with the same determination.

Another reason for caution is that cultural stereotypes are mostly rooted in historical beliefs about people from other countries, and while national cultures seem to change slowly, cultural values and practices do co-evolve as societies are transformed. Mainland Chinese society is a case in point. While China has traditionally been a high power distance country,[62] characterized by high in-group collectivism, young urban Chinese exhibit a considerably higher degree of individualism and a more modest level of power distance. They are also more assertive than the previous generation. Human resource practices that were aligned with traditional Chinese values 10 years ago may not be suitable in China today.

Among local managers, culture is often used as an alibi for failing to introduce change, protecting local fiefdoms against interference from the head office. Because culture is impenetrable, it is difficult to argue against these explanations. When the local manager in Thailand tells the head office that "confronting poor performers is not possible here for face-saving reasons," there is some truth in the excuse—but it is also an exaggeration. Often, the approach, rather than the objective, has to be altered.

For companies trying to adapt their HRM strategies to local needs, it is not enough to focus on cultural values. Culture can too easily become a catchall for complexity, both in academic and managerial circles—and may even foreclose the search for alternative drivers of a particular phenomenon. The cultural lens needs to be supplemented by consideration of institutional factors.

Know Where You Are: The Institutional Perspective

As noted earlier, working practices that are acceptable in one country (like working a 50-hour week in the US) may be questionable in another country and illegal in a third (as a 50-hour week would be in Germany, for instance). This reflects social, legal, and political differences that are captured by the institutional perspective on diversity. The ease of doing business index, developed by the World Bank, expresses this well. From an institutional perspective, Singapore is currently seen as the easiest country in which to do business; it is easy and straightforward to start a new business there, to register property, get credit, pay taxes, have a contract enforced, and hire and fire employees. All of these are immensely difficult in the Democratic Republic of Congo and in Venezuela, two of the most difficult countries in the world on the 2009 index.

Table 3–3 shows the 2009 index, notably the scale for ease of employing workers, for 17 selected countries. Let us look at the contrasting institutional environment

TABLE 3–3. Ranking of 17 Countries (out of 181) on Ease of Employing Workers and Overall Ease of Doing Business

Country	Ease of Employing Workers[A]	Rigidity of Employment Index[B]	Firing Costs (Weeks of Salary)	Ease of Doing Business Rank[C]
Singapore	1	0	4	1
United States	1	0	0	3
Denmark	10	10	0	5
Japan	17	17	4	12
United Kingdom	28	14	22	6
United Arab Emirates	47	13	84	46
Italy	75	38	11	65
India	89	30	56	122
Netherlands	98	42	17	26
Brazil	121	46	37	125
Germany	142	44	69	25
France	148	56	32	31
Korea	152	45	91	23
Indonesia	157	40	108	129
China	159	27	91	61
Spain	160	56	56	49
Venezuela	180	79	Not possible	174

[A] Overall index for employment, averaging the rigidity and firing cost indexes.
[B] This averages three subindexes: difficulty of hiring, rigidity of hours, and difficulty of firing.
[C] This overall index averages indicators on 10 topics, of which ease of employing workers is one.
Source: Doing Business 2009 Report, World Bank Group (www.doingbusiness.org).

for human resources in two European countries, namely Denmark (ranked 10th for ease of employing workers) and France (ranked 148 out of 181 countries on the same scale). In Denmark, there are few restrictions on hiring a new worker, considerable flexibility about working hours, and few constraints on firing someone (for example, there is no obligatory legal settlement). This is combined with a union environment, which, for more than 100 years, has favored working through agreements with top management rather than strikes. Denmark has a favorable institutional environment where the responsibility for HRM lies with line managers, with the HR function in a weaker advisory role. By contrast, in France, newly hired employees have by law to be given a permanent contract after an initial trial period; this makes it expensive and difficult to fire people. The working week was reduced to 35 hours in 2000, and after that date, employees could not be made to work longer if they did not wish to do so.[63] The French union environment has a long adversary heritage, and the HR function has by law and by tradition a much more powerful role in determining employment conditions and who is hired.

According to the institutional perspective, there are alternative ways of organizing economic activity, and the key to understanding business behavior in different countries lies in the interrelationships between economic, educational, financial, legal, and political systems. Societal factors strongly influence issues at the core of people management, such as compensation, training, job design, industrial relations, and by extension company performance.

When working in Germany, it is vital to understand the apprenticeship system developed by Bismarck 130 years ago. The concept of *"Kompetenz"* is different from "competence," and is linked step-by-step to the development of *Meister* or "master" status. Indeed, comparative studies reveal distinct national patterns of work organization in terms of hierarchy, promotion avenues, wage differentials, and the worker/management ratio. After years of training, a German *Meister* or master technician is not a trained specialist in one single machine but in machines in general, which means flexibility in the face of technological change.

At the heart of institutional theory is the concept of "configuration." Institutional configurations have been dubbed "national business systems,"[64] "industrial orders,"[65] and "varieties of capitalism."[66] Whitley and other scholars argue that these configurations shape and constrain the structure and processes through which companies conduct business. The systemic character of configurations explains their persistence. As Child puts it, "They are likely to be 'sticky' in the face of economic and technological change."[67] Therefore, although the differences across companies within the same system must not be underestimated, significant institutional differences remain between firms from different parts of the world.

Redding and Whitley suggest that there are at least six successful configurations of capitalism.[68] Each is distinguished not only by distinctive differences in ownership patterns and business objectives, but also by different employment practices.

1. The main purpose of the *Anglo-Saxon individualist form,* dominant in North America and the United Kingdom, is to provide returns to shareholders (shareholder value). The focus on short- to medium-term returns tends to drive HR practices; employment security is relatively limited and firms rely on fluid labor markets to recruit managers and professionals externally as needed.
2. The stakeholder perspective characterizes the more *communitarian European form* in large organizations. Here social contracts and obligations are more important; German firms have, for instance, been characterized as having patient capital, with HR practices based on codetermination of employees and management, long-term employment security, and a fairly high reliance on internal promotions.[69]
3. The *European industrial district form* of networked enterprise, based on family ownership (but also involving skilled employees committed to the firm), is found in Italy (for example, Benetton) and Scandinavia. Its aim is to optimize the interests and values of the family owners and senior professional managers associated with the firm.

4. The prime purpose of the *Japanese form* of capitalism, with its institutional cross-shareholding and lack of strong owners, is the stability of the organization. Lifetime employment of core employees and slow promotions are its most visible HR manifestations.

5. The *Korean chaebol* is simultaneously oriented toward retaining the influence of the original entrepreneurs and their families and growth strategies supporting national economic development. While labor relations are often contentious, the emphasis until recently has been on lifetime employment of managers recruited from top Korean universities.[70]

6. The *Chinese capitalist form* is represented by family businesses throughout the Southeast Asian diaspora and increasingly in mainland China. It exists primarily to serve the needs and wealth ambitions of owners, with trusted long-term employees playing important roles in the firm, but with relatively few efforts to build a formal HR system.

Of course, this is not a complete list of the different configurations of capitalism. However, it is a reminder that although there have been some tendencies of convergence toward the Anglo-Saxon model of capitalism in recent years, we can still identify differences across firms from different institutional environments.

Institutional theorists also argue that organizations are under pressure to adapt and align with their institutional environment—the central assumption being that organizations searching for legitimacy within the same configuration tend to become isomorphic (alike) by adopting similar organizational practices. This isomorphism results from three different processes: *regulatory* (the government imposes certain rules and regulations on firms); *cognitive* (organizations in situations of uncertainty mimic others in their environment that are viewed as successful); and *normative* (professional organizations, such as universities, consultancy firms, and professional interest groups, disseminate "appropriate" organizational practices).[71]

Since the early 1990s there has been a flood of research on HRM from an institutional (or contextual) perspective, spearheaded by the so-called Cranet project on HRM in different European countries.[72] Three broad distinctions between the institutional frameworks of the US and continental Europe have been identified, reflecting the European "communitarian" business system that transcends internal differences within Europe[73]—see the box "Differences between the US and Continental European Institutional Frameworks."

From this perspective, many European researchers tend to view the (universalist) American model of HRM, shaped by the US institutional context but usually presented without any explicit recognition of this fact, with a certain suspicion, debating the extent to which it applies to Europe (and elsewhere in the world), with its different institutional contexts.[74] However, others hotly disagree that there is a European model, pointing to the great variations across countries within Europe. They emphasize that in several HR domains such as equal opportunity, US firms are arguably more regulated than their transatlantic counterparts.[75]

Differences between the US and Continental European Institutional Frameworks

- There is a higher level of *state regulation* in Europe that constrains organizations in their HR practices, particularly with regard to layoffs and dismissals.
- *Labor unions* are larger and have more influence in many European countries (union recognition can be a legal requirement for the purposes of collective bargaining).
- There is stronger European tradition of *employee representation*, in particular in countries such as Germany and the Netherlands, where employee representatives are members of supervisory boards and can exert a heavy influence over personnel matters.[A]

[A]This is also true of some other countries, such as France, where Works Councils are legally required once the firm reaches a certain size in terms of employees, or where employees request it.

Comparative studies conducted outside Europe have further confirmed the impact of the institutional context on HRM.[76]

Responding to Local Context: Labor Relations

The role of labor unions is a notable example of how a local institutional context can influence a company's international operations. Wal-Mart is well known for its strong antiunion stance at home, but its employees in China are working under a union contract, as required by law and enforced by various administrative practices.[77] Recent restructuring of Pfizer Japan ran into severe problems, forcing a CEO resignation under pressure from the company union—headed by company managers.[78]

Countries differ radically not only in trade union membership, but also in collective bargaining coverage, the structure of the unions, and their involvement in collective consultation and communication at the corporate level. Table 3–4 outlines *union membership* coverage as a percentage of the total workforce in selected countries. Union membership is highest in Northern Europe, lower in other parts of Europe and in the US. Over all, the trade unions have lost membership during the last 20 years.

However, union membership does not tell the whole story of the unions' influence; more important is whether the employers are required to adhere to the results of collective negotiations for all employees (see Table 3–4). For instance, although union membership is very low in France, *collective bargaining* covers more than 90 percent of all employees, as employers are required by law to negotiate employment terms and reach collective agreements. Therefore, unions typically have an influence that goes beyond their formal membership.

The structure of the unions also differs significantly. In many countries in Europe, as well as in the US, unions are formed mainly around industry sectors and/or professions. However, in Japan it has been common to have separate

TABLE 3–4. **Trade Union Coverage and Collective Bargaining Coverage in Selected Countries**[79]

Country	Trade Union Coverage (%)	Collective Bargaining Coverage (%)
Australia	25	80+
Austria	37	95+
Belgium	56	90+
Czech Republic	27[A]	
Denmark	74	80+
Finland	76	90+
France	10	90+
Germany	25	68
Japan	22	15+
Korea	11	[B]
Netherlands	23	80+
Portugal	24	70+
Spain	15	80+
UK	31	30+
US	13	14

[A] Union density figure from 2001, collective bargaining data missing.
[B] Collective bargaining data missing.

unions for each corporation. In recent years, the relationship between enterprise unions and management has typically been nonadversarial, with strikes and other forms of labor struggles virtually unheard of (as in Denmark and Switzerland)—except for foreign-owned firms. In some countries, like China, the government recognizes only one union, the All China Federation of Trade Unions (ACFTU). All companies are expected to have trade unions, and even foreign firms that usually resist unionization—such as Wal-Mart—today have unions in their Chinese units. The role of the ACFTU has traditionally concentrated on welfare issues, but recently the trade union has become much more involved in negotiations about collective contracts for employees and issues related to layoffs and dispute settlement.

In a number of countries, the trade unions form an integrated part of employee consultation and collective communication. In Europe, works councils are typically required in all but the smallest firms, and all companies established in the EU member states are covered by the European Works Council Directive. Corporate decisions that influence employees in significant ways must be discussed with the works councils. Although these have limited decision-making power, they often serve as important communication channels and as a sounding body for employees. However, from a management perspective, the obligation to discuss decisions in works councils may lead to delays in the decision-making process.

There are many idiosyncratic differences across countries in the roles played by trade unions, and corporate headquarters often have only limited understanding of local conditions. Multinationals therefore usually decentralize the responsibility for dealing with unions to their foreign subsidiaries.

Projecting One's Own Institutional Context Abroad

In the same way as companies often project the cultural values of the home country when they go abroad, so the institutional environment of the home country may influence its policies and practices in the international arena. Consider the example of diversity management in US corporations. Most US firms have developed diversity management programs, partly in response to legal requirements but also to reflect the new consensus in the American society on the need to provide equal opportunity regardless of gender, race, or age. In the late 1990s, many US companies began to transfer these programs to their foreign subsidiaries. However, many foreign subsidiary managers see these diversity policies as well-intentioned but parochial; they do not necessarily fit with the host country's context, where there may be a raging war for talent and where the most salient dimensions of diversity may be not gender but ethnicity, religious belief, or nationality (opportunities for locals rather than expatriates). Consequently, one often finds local adaptations in the way diversity programs are implemented abroad. Nonetheless, US subsidiaries typically adhere, at least on the surface, to the traditions of the home country and to the policies introduced by their parent companies.[80]

The institutional tradition of management development in the home country also influences the way in which companies create pools of international managers. In the US, and to a lesser extent the UK, career paths are less specialized and more generalist. This is institutionalized in broad business school education and expectations of rapid movement from job to job. It is also in stark contrast to the on-the-job long-term acquisition of specialist expertise that typifies the system in Germany, where until recently business schools were rather alien. There, as in Japan, managers expect to spend a longer period in each job, leading to very different skill profiles. The highly political nature of the promotion process in France may inhibit international mobility because of the need to remain visible to top management. Overall, the home heritage in management development, anchored in national business systems, will color the way in which the company goes about international management development.

Commentary

The institutional perspective emphasizes that firms are constrained by their local environments. For the multinational firm, there is a risk of being blind to the extent to which the home country context puts its mark on people management issues, just as home country cultural values do. As a company internationalizes, it should reflect on the way in which the institutional context in its home country has shaped its HR strategy and how this influences its approach to people management abroad.

Foreign subsidiaries in fact face dual institutional pressures—from the parent organization and from the local environment—which they need to balance.[81] Line executives in these subsidiaries, and particularly international HR managers, need strong negotiation skills, especially if headquarters executives are unaware of these local institutional constraints. Headquarters may decide to cut headcount or to introduce new work practices globally, and such actions are strongly constrained by the local environment. Local managers cannot simply refuse to comply; they have to be objective about what is feasible in their environment and argue cogently for it.[82]

One of the dangers of the institutional perspective may be to exaggerate the persistence and the strength of local institutional pressures. While labor laws and regulations may indeed restrict the range of possible HR actions, local managers often have taken-for-granted views about what works and what does not with respect to management of people. There may be strong local professional norms concerning what constitutes appropriate corporate practices.

For example, many foreign firms regarded the German market as off limits to takeovers until the British mobile phone operator Vodafone shattered the perception of impenetrability by acquiring Mannesmann. German firms such as Daimler and E.ON have eagerly embraced "shareholder value," reorienting their accounting systems to Anglo-Saxon standards as they entered the US stock exchange to access cheaper sources of capital. We can also observe an increasing number of Japanese corporations divesting unprofitable units and even laying off employees as they restructure their operations.

Some regard the influence of national business systems as declining, pointing to the individualization of HRM practices in Japan, to the changes in the Korean *chaebol*, and to what has been called the Anglo-Saxonization of management. They foresee a gradual global shift toward the more market-oriented institutional mechanisms prevailing in the US business system. American commentators, in particular, often feel strongly about the virtues of the free-market open economy, resenting the degree of state intervention and regulation that prevails in many parts of Europe and Asia, though the 2008–2009 global financial crisis, ascribed by many to underregulation, will undoubtedly lead to further debate around this.[83] Politicians and business leaders in the emerging BRIC economies (Brazil, Russian, India, and China) are actively looking for new models of management, leadership, and organization.

Most importantly, irrespective of institutional constraints, in an increasingly professional and knowledge-based world, employees and managers are more and more aware of management practices in firms from other countries. Executives everywhere are bombarded daily by press reports on the latest global business and management trends in the US and elsewhere. The Internet has further accelerated this trend. The idea of cultural or institutional cocoons where firms are prisoners of their own national heritage is less and less true. It all depends on whom you talk to and whom you view as role models—and this leads us to the network perspective on diversity.

Know Whom You Talk To: The Network Perspective

Beyond similarities in cultural values or institutional context, organizations define themselves by the company they keep. In other words, multinational organizations also face pressures to conform to so-called best practices, to innovations and changes adopted by other firms in similar circumstances. A growing number of studies document the importance of interorganizational networks in diffusing such information, and this network perspective is particularly relevant to the HR/personnel domain since professional associations have long played an important role in prescribing what is "best" in people management.

The networks to which a company belongs can make a big difference to what it views as important, as demonstrated in a study on HRM in foreign and local firms in Ecuador. The study, conducted in the 1990s, showed little transfer of HR techniques between multinationals and local firms. Managers in local Ecuadoran firms compared themselves to other local firms, and the multinationals compared themselves to other multinationals operating in the country. They constituted two separate networks with virtually no overlap—and no transfer of know-how.[84]

It is understandable that multinationals do not learn from local firms in countries where local firms are smaller and perceived as less sophisticated than their own subsidiaries. Why would multinationals cultivate contacts with lower-status players? What could they learn from them? Yet a similar phenomenon is also visible in Japan, where one would expect exchange between Japanese multinationals and locally based foreign subsidiaries. In fact, they are two separate worlds. Foreign companies in Japan pay higher wages than local firms, since their salary surveys compare them only with other foreign firms. Most are not even aware that they are paying this *gaijin* tax (foreigner tax) because they would never think of networking with an indigenous Japanese corporation. Japanese managers working for foreign subsidiaries even have their own union, the Foreign Affiliated Managers Association (FAMA). These managers seldom cross over to Japanese multinationals, or vice versa.

Even in the "boundaryless" European Union, we found in one of our studies that Danish companies tend to take a management idea seriously only if it has been adopted by another Danish organization. Even in the 21st century there is a definite tribal characteristic that the Danes acknowledge.[85] To a lesser extent, the same is true of France, where networks of graduates from the *grandes écoles* or "great schools" tend to dominate the major French companies, leaving graduates from "lesser" institutions to opt either for the foreign company circuit or the nonestablishment business sector. In France, as in other countries, this creates separate networks and labor pools with little exchange between them.[86]

Learning from Friends When Abroad

HR managers working abroad have a particular incentive to build networks with those from other multinationals since they are not sure how specific HR practices will fit into the local context. Expatriates who are responsible for introducing practices that may be risky, expensive, and hard to reverse are naturally keen to discuss the benefits, or frustrations, that others may have experienced when implementing similar changes. As Burt puts it, "Adopting innovation entails a risk, an uncertain balance of costs and benefits, and people manage that uncertainty by drawing on others to define a socially acceptable interpretation of the risk."[87] And there is research evidence that firms tend to imitate changes previously adopted by network peers.[88]

All this suggests that local adaptation of HR policies and practices may be influenced as much by what other foreign subsidiaries are doing, or what regionally based consultants recommend, as by the experience of local firms or best practices back home. A study of foreign firms operating in Russia highlights this three-way tension. It showed that the HR practices of foreign firms "were more similar to their parent firm's practices *and those of other foreign firms operating in Russia* than to HR practices in local Russian firms" (our italics).[89] Similarly, in China, while some HR managers we interviewed in multinational firms complained about constantly being contacted by local firms interested in learning more about their approach to HRM, foreign firms seemed to be much less interested in learning about HRM in local Chinese companies.[90]

Sharing the same clubs, sending their children to the same schools, living in the same areas, expatriates from different multinationals quickly develop strong ties, especially in developing countries. Such relationships provide natural channels for sharing useful information about what works and what does not. A firm's choice of HR practices therefore also reflects the information received from networks to which its employees belong.

The networks may be predominantly professional or social in nature and run with a various degrees of formality. For instance, in many of the major cities in China, there are formal HR networks where managers from multinational firms meet regularly to discuss issues of interest to network members. Some of these are open groups, organized by Chambers of Commerce or consulting companies, while others may limit membership to a selected group of peers. However, all the networks contribute to the development of beliefs about what constitutes efficient HR practices, with participants spreading the ideas to their own organizations.

Global Trends—and Fashions

Of course, firms can also look outside their immediate networks for ideas about what they should do and what may work. Increasingly, organizations have access to a kind of surrogate network in the form of cases gleaned from business professors, consultants, management gurus, and journalists. These fashion setters carry best practices and benchmark information across borders, geographical or industrial.[91] Each proposes new exemplar companies and organizational innovations. Companies are exposed to the routines and practices of key international competitors. What self-respecting international manager has not heard of GE's Workout or Toyota's Production System? In a broad sense these companies and practices become part of an organization's extended network—legitimate sources of comparison.

Indeed, in the 1980s and early 1990s Japanese management was the rage, only to be replaced by global worship of General Electric and its CEO Jack Welch. Through the business media, new leading-edge practices reach a broad audience and converge on a company's executives from several points at once. This can create intense pressure to follow suit in order to maintain the appearance of a "legitimate," "modern," or "progressive" organization, as defined by the reference network. This is plain bandwagon imitation.[92]

Moreover, access to what is "in" has been spurred by the rapid rise of the Internet. Executives in Europe, Asia, or Africa may be just as familiar with the latest in best practices as their American counterparts. This has undoubtedly accelerated the convergence of multinationals from different countries on an Anglo-Saxon model for people and organizational management.[93] Although as we pointed out some premises of this model are being reconsidered, the trend toward at least some cross-border convergence is likely to continue. This seems almost inevitable among the network of multinationals that invest in the same emerging markets, recruit from the same business school, and send their executives to the same conferences and training courses. These companies are subject to the same competitive pressures and they wrestle with similar issues—managing change, transferring knowledge across boundaries, coping with e-opportunities, and fighting the talent war, to name only some current concerns.

On the other hand, the resulting convergence is more nuanced than it often appears. One investigation into the Anglo-Saxon influence on European multinationals reveals important variations.[94] Though French and German multinationals are adopting Anglo-Saxon practices in the fields of executive compensation, job restructuring, and corporate governance, they do so in a local manner. For example, German preoccupations with long-term orientation and social responsibility have been merged with new concerns for shareholder value and responsiveness, leading to distinctly German ways of responding to the latter. Layoffs through restructuring are more moderate than in Anglo-Saxon countries, accompanied by an emphasis on partnerships and cooperation with the workforce.[95]

International networks may rapidly spread new concepts such as value innovation or 360-degree feedback, but successful adoption means that they have to be worked coherently into the fabric of the firm. Indeed a detailed study of the transfer of Japanese total quality management (TQM) practices to five firms in the US showed that while simplified rhetoric may be necessary to kickstart the process of transfer, successful implementation requires detailed technical attention and adaptation to the specific circumstances of the enterprise.[96] Despite initial skepticism, 360-degree feedback can work well in Asian environments, but only if meticulous attention is paid to issues like respondent anonymity. There may be generic ideas, but there are no generic solutions.

Moreover, those with a longer-term perspective should be wary of endorsing the Anglo-Saxon or any other model as objectively virtuous. Only 20 years ago, Japan was the worldwide model, and who knows what fashions the future will bring. New models for internationalization are constantly emerging, as leading

Brazilian, Indian, and Mexican firms leapfrog others in mastering how to go global.[97]

Commentary

Traditional models of organizational adaptation tend to portray companies as deciding how to respond to new circumstances in social isolation. The emerging theory and evidence on networks suggest otherwise. Besides home and host contexts, there is the influence of the international networks to which organizations belong. These interfirm ties may be of particular relevance to foreign subsidiaries, given the high uncertainty they face. When there is high uncertainty, people naturally seek the views of experienced peers, experts who are central in networks, and others facing the same challenges. Network ties multiply the repertoire of potential responses in adapting to an uncertain environment, "making linked organizations more astute collectively than they are individually."[98]

Moreover, if the subsidiary eschews home practices as inappropriate, adopting the practices of an internationally recognized peer may appear more legitimate (vis-à-vis the head office) than those of a successful local company. Local managers who must create the impression that they are conforming to the "norms of rationality" may yield to those pressures.

However, this need for social legitimacy can trigger bandwagon effects that highlight the drawbacks of networks. Traditional HR networks are excessively local or focused on emulating a few companies that may be in vogue at a given point of time. The choice of the networks and intensity of how these networks are used are of critical importance. In fact, the roles played by company networks are recurrent themes in this book.[99]

In order to remain alert to choices, to preserve healthy cynicism, and to avoid me-too decisions, we need to be aware of the ways in which networks shape reality. Homogenization of perspectives leads to impoverished choices. Research on executives who have good track records on managerial innovation show that they carefully maintain broad networks and take every opportunity to seek out the views of others.[100]

What Shapes Local Responsiveness?

Cultural diversity, institutional factors, and network relationships, as well as global fads and fashions, shape the ways in which multinational corporations manage people. Practice depends on the context, and all these factors constitute different sources of contextual influence.

There are at least five different contextual and isomorphic influences on international HR practices: the *mother country*; the *mother company* and its distinctive culture and institutionalized practices; the *local cultural and institutional context*; *other foreign firms in the country*; and *other international companies*.[101] While internal consistency pushes the multinational toward a particular configuration of policies, work systems, and practices, it is subject to the pushes and pulls of all these different forces.

Country-of-Origin effect

Companies develop HR and other management practices that reflect their national cultural and institutional conditions, and then transfer these practices to their foreign units. The time perspective of the parent company is a case in point. US firms, where the tenure of top managers depends on annual if not quarterly results reported to shareholders, are likely to have a shorter-term perspective than traditional German firms, where bankers and employee representatives may have a controlling influence on the external board of directors.[102] Whether senior management looks only for short-term results or takes a long-term view will have a profound effect on the orientation of HRM within the firm, at home and abroad. A range of studies has reported strong differences in practices according to the country of origin, with notable differences between US and non-US firms.[103]

Company-of-Origin effect

Companies develop distinctive HR practices and then transfer these to foreign environments. Lincoln Electric's story in the late 1980s illustrates a less successful case, although there are many examples of the successful transfer of company culture. Nokia has a distinctive culture that is embodied in the evolving "Nokia Way," emphasizing rapid decision making in a flat organization. When Nokia recruits a native Russian engineer for its local unit in that country, it is looking for an engineer who deviates from the hierarchical Russian norms, someone who is likely to thrive in its flat networked culture.

Host Country Effect

Here companies adopt HR and management practices that reflect institutional and cultural conditions in the place of local operations. To some degree, all organizations must conform to local practices. Some firms adopt local isomorphism as a strategy—"Strategy may be global, but everything else is local implementation." Ahold, the global Dutch retailer that is a competitor to Wal-Mart, has been one of many examples of firms that operate in line with this motto. Companies that expand internationally through acquisition and alliance are more likely to experience the pressures of local isomorphism than those that grow by setting up greenfield sites.

Foreign Firm Network Effect

In situations of uncertainty about what constitutes best practices, organizations often look at others and then mimic what they do or collectively develop a consensus about what to do. As discussed earlier, we often see that the networks to which foreign firms belong produce common notions about appropriate HR practices.

Global Convergence Effect

In an era of worldwide diffusion of technology, footloose capital, widespread intercontinental travel, strong influence by international consulting firms on corporate practices in all parts of the world, and global accessibility to information via the Internet, knowledge flows easily from one region of the globe to another.

International companies compare themselves with others with international experience and model their practices on these, as well as on their own experience with their various subsidiaries. Diffusion of technology and management practices means that national effects become less important than the globalization effect.

The debate about whether management practices around the world, including HR practices, are converging or diverging is not new. Different forces or effects exist simultaneously and will continue to do so in the years ahead.

THE LIMITS OF RESPONSIVENESS

We started this chapter by describing eBay's problems in Asia, attributing them largely to a failure to respond to local circumstances. However, a local responsiveness strategy also has its limits. Indeed, when localization of staff is combined with a decentralized federal structure, it can lead to local fiefdoms and inhibit collaboration. This often results in lost opportunities for the multinational to share best practices and learn across units. It can generate other inefficiencies as well, such as duplication of effort (reinventing the wheel), needless differentiation, and resistance to external recommendations or ideas—the "handmaidens of decentralization," as Bartlett and Ghoshal dubbed them.[104]

Just as firms following a meganational strategy (discussed in the next chapter) may fail by blindly applying home strategies and practices to the new environment, so may the multidomestic firm fail by focusing too closely on its local playing field. In trying to be more local than the locals, the ultraresponsive firm may fail to leverage its home base or globally derived knowledge. Regionalization, a bridge between globalization and localization, can be a way of responding. One study examined the role and structure of 15 regional headquarters of Western firms in Asia and 15 regional headquarters of Japanese firms in Europe. These regional headquarters often played an important functional coordination role and provided a strong link between the local subsidiary and the global head office.[105]

The impatriation of local managers to the regional or global headquarters is a big step toward transnational organization. To ensure international mobility, Unilever has long had a policy of reserving at least one slot on all management teams in both emerging and developed countries for an expatriate—a European in Asia and an Asian or Latin American in Europe. Traditionally, the risk of local empire building is attenuated at 3M by an informal rule that executives cannot become managing directors in their own country. Promising local managers are appointed as heads of subsidiaries in other countries. This reduces the danger of indigenous managers becoming fixtures for several decades and clogging the career pipeline, and it ensures that local stars gain international exposure.

Local Responsiveness Does Not Necessarily Mean Playing by Local Rules

One somewhat paradoxical outcome of successful localization is the recognition that local responsiveness does not always mean playing by local rules. Indeed one of the benefits of localization is that indigenous managers have a better sense of which local rules they can break. Local managers have a better sense of *intracultural* variation—tolerance for differences within a nation. They tend to have a better awareness of the strengths of cultural values and norms and the likely effects of breaking them. They also know how flexible national and local institutional structures are.

The transnational ideal is local managers who have been exposed to global methods and practices through their networks and time spent in lead countries, perhaps working with expatriates who are in the local subsidiary to gain international experience. Rather than embracing the local way, they can redefine the boundaries of what is considered "local"—showing smart disrespect. Finding ways to operate that neither mimic local firms nor copy the way multinational corporations do things in other parts of the world may be the seed of innovations that can subsequently be transferred to and benefit the corporation as a whole.

TAKEAWAYS

1. Local responsiveness helps the firm overcome the disadvantages of being an outsider. However, local responsiveness, once synonymous with country boundaries, now applies to any market with distinctive needs.
2. With increased globalization, local responsiveness may have acquired additional value as a source of competitive differentiation.
3. HR practices are more sensitive to local context than finance, marketing, or manufacturing practices, because HRM deals with people, and people differ across the world. Within HRM, some practices are more sensitive to context than others.
4. Localization means local authority over local decision making, with local managers playing key roles while drawing on and adapting the experience of headquarters, expatriates, and other subsidiaries.
5. Localization of management requires a long-term strategy with commitment at all levels, especially among expatriates, to developing local successors. Shortcuts lead to protracted difficulties.
6. Cultural values influence HRM practices, but this does not necessarily mean that companies have to adapt to the local culture. There are wide variances in values within any nation, and firms can choose whom to recruit. Some local employees find practices that deviate from national stereotypes to be attractive.
7. National business systems (institutional environments) shape the HRM practices of the home company, and many of these practices may need adjustment in other institutional environments. This is particularly evident in the area of employee and labor relations.
8. Adjusting to local conditions is not just a trade-off between headquarter practices and host country practices; it is also influenced by the practices of international peers.

9. Mindful learning from other firms may enhance competitiveness, but copying "best practices" without considering their context is rarely effective.

10. Local responsiveness does not necessarily imply playing by local rules, but it does require knowing which rules can be broken, and how. Excessive local responsiveness tends to inhibit collaboration across boundaries, and this may be as harmful to performance as excessive centralization.

NOTES

1. www.ebay.com: eBay Marketplace Facts, June 30, 2008; Corporate Factsheet.
2. The caselet builds partly on the IMD teaching case series "Alibaba vs. eBay," IMD-3-1842 to IMD-3-1844, 2007.
3. "How Yahoo! Japan Beat eBay at Its Own Game," *BusinessWeek,* June 4, 2001.
4. "An Upstart Takes on Mighty eBay," *Fortune,* November 15, 2004.
5. "The Taobao Offensive," *Red Herring,* June 27, 2005.
6. "eBay's Tom Online Deal: Timely Lessons for Global Online Company Managers," *China Knowledge Wharton,* February 14, 2007.
7. "eBay's Tom Online Deal: Timely Lessons for Global Online Company Managers," *China Knowledge Wharton,* February 14, 2007.
8. "eBay's Tom Online Deal: Timely Lessons for Global Online Company Managers," *China Knowledge Wharton,* February 14, 2007.
9. Zaheer, 1995.
10. Friedmann, 2007.
11. As Coca-Cola's new CEO noted in 2000, "In every community, we must remember we do not do business in markets, we do business in societies. . . [This means making] sure that we stay out of the way of our local people and let them do their jobs." (D. Daft, "Back to Classic Coke," *Financial Times,* March 27, 2000, p. 16). But as described in Chapter 11, the company swung the pendulum too far from the global to the local, and has been struggling in recent years to get the balance right.
12. One framework of note conceptualizes the "local" in terms of distance from the home country of the multinational. In Ghemawat's CAGE framework, there are four dimensions to distance—cultural, administrative (what we call institutional), geographic, and economic. See Ghemawat (2007).
13. Rangan and Drummond, 2004.
14. Barkema, Bell, and Pennings, 1996.
15. In February 2008, Google was the second most popular search engine in Russia with a 31.2 percent market share compared to Yandex's 47.4 percent market share (http://www.comscore.com/press/release).
16. Pfanner, E., "New to Russia, Google Struggles to Find Its Footing," *The New York Times,* December 18, 2006.
17. See Prahalad and Doz (1987) for a more extended analysis; see also Prahalad and Lieberthal (1998).
18. Google has for many years removed links to pro-Nazi Web sites in Germany.
19. Thompson, C., "Google's China Problems (and China's Google Problems)," *New York Times,* April 23, 2006.
20. O'Hara-Devereaux and Johansen, 1994; Rosenzweig and Nohria, 1994; Gooderham, Nordhaug, and Ringdal, 1999.

21. Lu and Björkman, 1997. A study on multinationals in Greece reported similar findings (Myloni, Harzing, and Mirza, 2004).
22. Rosenzweig and Nohria, 1994; Goodall and Warner, 1997.
23. Hall and Hall, 1990.
24. Becker and Gerhart, 1996.
25. Sippola and Smale, 2007.
26. Kuin, 1972.
27. Law, Wong, and Wang, 2004.
28. See Hailey and Harry (2008) for an overview of research on localization.
29. Talent acquisition and development are discussed in depth in Chapters 7 and 8.
30. Fernandez and Underwood, 2006.
31. Cohen, 1992.
32. Wong and Law, 1999.
33. Fey, Engström, and Björkman, 1999.
34. Terazono, E., "Japanese Banks' Local Feel," *Financial Times*, January 29, 1997.
35. Compensation is discussed in Chapter 9.
36. Wong and Law, 1999.
37. Fey, Engström, and Björkman, 1999.
38. Two separate studies of localization of management in foreign multinationals in China found that the effort spent planning the localization process was positively associated with its outcome (Fryxell, Butler, and Choi, 2004; Law, Wong, and Wang, 2004).
39. Expatriate management is discussed extensively in Chapter 4.
40. Melvin and Sylvester, 1997.
41. Hailey, 1996.
42. Hailey and Harry, 2008.
43. Lasserre and Ching, 1997.
44. This study was sponsored by the US–based National Foreign Trade Council of multinational companies operating in China, reported in *The Wall Street Journal*, December 12, 1999.
45. Hailey, 1993.
46. In his influential model of culture, Schein (1985) proposes that there are three levels of culture: (1) basic assumptions, (2) values, and (3) surface manifestations, such as artifacts and behavior. Most research on national culture has focused on the values held by individuals in the country in question. However, there are a large number of definitions and conceptualizations of culture, a review of which is beyond the scope of this book.
47. Hofstede, 1991 and 2001.
48. See, for example, the debate in *Journal of International Business Studies*, 2006, issue no. 6.
49. Laurent, 1983.
50. See Trompenaars (1993); Hampden-Turner and Trompenaars (2000). The work of Trompenaars was strongly influenced by the dilemma (duality) concept of Hampden-Turner.
51. For critical reviews of the GLOBE study, see several articles in *Journal of International Business Studies*, 2006, issue no. 6.
52. House et al., 2004.
53. Hofstede, 1980 and 2001.
54. Schneider, 1988; Schneider and Barsoux, 2003.
55. Ulrich, Zenger, and Smallwood, 1999, p. 171.

56. Flannery et al., 1996, p. 249.
57. Guest, 1990.
58. Gerhart and Fang, 2005.
59. Gerhart and Fang, 2005.
60. Stahl et al., 2007.
61. Gerhart and Fang, 2005.
62. Hofstede, 1991.
63. Institutional environments are subject to change, and the business community in France has long been lobbying for less restrictive employment practices, arguing that they cannot maintain global competitiveness with such a handicap. Such reforms were launched, not without resistance, in 2008.
64. Whitley, 1992.
65. Lane, 1989.
66. Orrù, 1997.
67. Child, 2000, p. 20.
68. Redding, 2001; Whitley, 1999. See also Hampden-Turner and Trompenaars (1993).
69. Koen, 2004.
70. Cho and Pucik, 2005.
71. Scott, 2001. See also DiMaggio and Powell (1983) for an influential and slightly different conceptualization of institutional processes.
72. The Price Waterhouse/Cranfield (later renamed Cranet) project on international human resource management, led by Brewster, involved successive surveys undertaken in 14 European countries (Brewster and Hegewisch, 1994). The survey has subsequently been expanded to cover countries outside of Europe as well (Brewster, Mayrhofer, and Morley, 2004).
73. Pieper, 1990; see also Brewster (1995 and 2006).
74. See Legge (1995) for a potent critique of American HRM and Brewster (2007) for a recent European perspective.
75. Clark and Mallory, 1996.
76. Gooderham, Nordhaug, and Ringdal, 1999; Brewster, Mayrhofer, and Morley, 2004.
77. Lague, D., "Unions Triumphant at Wal-Mart in China," *International Herald Tribune*, October 13, 2006.
78. "Pfizer to Slash Japan Costs Without Job Cuts," Boston.com News, May 29, 2006.
79. OECD Employment Outlook, 2004; Rigby, Smith, and Brewster, 2004; Visser, 2006.
80. Egan and Bendick, 2003; Ferner, Almond, and Colling, 2005.
81. Rosenzweig and Nohria, 1994; Kostova and Roth, 2002.
82. The consequent importance of negotiation and influence skills for international human resource managers is discussed in Chapter 14.
83. See "When Fortune Frowned: A Special Report on the World Economy," *The Economist*, October 11, 2008.
84. Maria Arias, personal communication.
85. Evans and Engsbye, 2003.
86. The network can be a more interesting unit of analysis than the nation. France and other countries have networks of establishment and extra-establishment firms. In Germany there is a network of big industrial groups, such as Bayer and Daimler, and the very different *Mittelstand* of smaller, often family, firms (Simon, 1996). These constitute the Europe Industrial District form of capitalism described earlier in this chapter. In Japan, the "three pillars" of lifetime employment, seniority-based pay, and enterprise unions apply to the big corporations that recruit from the elite

universities, but not to the vast majority of Japanese working in small and medium-sized enterprises (Pucik, 1984).

87. Burt, 1987.
88. Hauschild, 1993; Westphal et al., 1997.
89. Fey et al., 1999. See also Child and Yan (1998) and Björkman and Lu (1999), who observed the same in joint ventures in China.
90. Björkman et al., 2008; Sumelius, Björkman, and Smale, 2008. See also Braun and Warner (2002).
91. Micklethwait and Woolridge, 1996; Abrahamson and Fairchild, 1999.
92. Abrahamson and Fairchild, 1999.
93. Pudelko and Harzing (2007) show that the HR practices in the foreign subsidiaries of German and Japanese multinationals have converged toward dominant US practices.
94. Ferner and Quintanilla, 1998.
95. Ferner and Quintanilla, 1998.
96. Zbaracki, 1998.
97. Bartlett and Ghoshal, 2000; "The New Champions: Emerging Markets are Producing Examples of Capitalism at Its Best," Economist Report on Globalization, *The Economist*, September 20, 2008.
98. Kraatz, 1998.
99. In Chapter 6 we elaborate on social relationships in our treatment of social capital, and in Chapter 10 we discuss how interpersonal and interunit networks are integrated parts of knowledge management.
100. Dyer, Gregersen, and Christensen, 2008.
101. Ferner and Quintanilla (1998) discuss four of these; we have added the influence of other international firms in the local context.
102. Loveridge, 1990.
103. See Bae, Chen, and Lawler (1998) for a study of American, European, Korean, Japanese, and Taiwanese firms operating in Hong Kong that strongly supports the country-of-origin hypothesis.
104. Bartlett and Ghoshal, 1989.
105. See Schütte (1998). This study found that regional headquarters were instrumental in integrating the region by supporting and guiding functional activities such as HR, although they were rarely able to create synergies between businesses or divisions. The 30 multinationals operating in Asia and Europe were by and large successful in the region concerned, attributing that success in part to their regional headquarters. Indeed, the regional dimension of coordination, particularly concerning HRM, merits further attention by researchers.

CHAPTER 4

Achieving Global Integration

Leveraging Global Capabilities at Nokia

Who would have anticipated in the early 1990s that Nokia, a traditional, 100-year-old Finnish company with origins in the rubber, pulp, and paper businesses, would become the world's biggest producer of mobile phones? Today, Nokia handsets are sold in more than 150 countries, and its brand name is a symbol of status and quality among consumers worldwide. Nokia's joint venture with Siemens also makes it one of the leading suppliers of the wireless telecommunication infrastructure for mobile operators around the world.[1]

Nokia first entered the telecom business in 1981 when the company acquired 51 percent of a state-owned phone equipment firm. Although attempts to become a leading TV and PC manufacturer nearly bankrupted the group, the transformation gathered speed when the visionary head of its mobile phone business, Jorma Ollila, became CEO in 1992. Under Ollila's leadership, Nokia became step-by-step a global company with an almost exclusive focus on wireless telecommunications.[2]

Nokia's strategy was to leverage its early R&D investment in mobile phones by growing international sales rapidly. Top management took a giant bet, correctly forecasting that GSM technology would become the new global standard outside the United States, and put all available resources behind it. Research and development as well as core manufacturing were concentrated in Finland to maximize efficiency and speed of product development and to exploit manufacturing economies of scale. Ollila spelled this out even before becoming CEO: "To succeed in mobile phones means becoming a consumer-driven, marketing-driven business and designing the product in such a way that we can mass-produce and lower the price of the product. How cheap and how efficient our production ability is will have a major impact." Nokia's ability to manage the whole process more efficiently than its competitors—from product development to delivery of handsets to sales outlets—soon became a key competitive advantage.

As Nokia expanded rapidly around the world, the product groups located in Finland retained control over major commercial decisions, supervised by a tightly knit group of Finnish senior managers. Foreign subsidiaries, managed in most cases by Finnish expatriates, were responsible for meeting sales and budget targets. Quick entrepreneurial decision making was emphasized. As Ollila notes, "A prime part of our organization is our policy to give the employees who have shown capability of taking the company forward three times more responsibility than they themselves see as reasonable."[3] Informal networks were considered more important than formal authority or bureaucratic processes, with a culture (the Nokia Way) that helped integrate the different parts of the corporation. This culture spread abroad through the expatriate network, facilitating Nokia's global expansion.[4]

By the turn of the millennium, Nokia had become the undisputed market leader in mobile handsets. When Olli-Pekka Kallasvuo, another Finn, took over as CEO from Ollila in 2006, Finland was still an important location for R&D and the manufacturing of some of the most technologically advanced products. However, R&D and other functional activities were now considerably more dispersed, requiring extensive integration across borders and functions.[5]

Nokia continued to rely heavily on expatriates to achieve global integration, but they now came from a wide variety of countries. The number of foreign nationals on the top management team had increased from zero in 2000 to 4 (out of 12) in 2009, and a large number of non-Finns worked in the parent organization in Finland.

OVERVIEW

Nokia became a leader in mobile telephony by pursuing a strategy of global integration, leveraging its R&D investments at home into global dominance through superior efficiency. In this chapter, we build on this story to elaborate on the benefits of global integration strategies and outline the key mechanisms of global integration and their implications for the organization and HR practices. We review different control mechanisms relevant to firms operating across national boundaries, describing personal, procedural, output, and normative control. Subsequently we discuss the benefits and cost of global standardization, and its implications for HR practices.

Expatriates play crucial roles when new operations are established abroad and corporate practices are transferred across dispersed units. In fact, most tools of global integration are associated with a heavy reliance on expatriate managers. The second and main part of this chapter focuses on the challenges in managing expatriation processes effectively. While different aspects of expatriation are explored throughout the book, the core concepts are introduced here.

After a review of the literature on expatriate success and failure, we present the key theories, concepts, and practices concerning the different stages in the expatriate cycle (selection, training, adjustment, performance appraisal and compensation, and repatriation). We compare research findings with current practice and discuss particular challenges, such as family adjustment. We also discuss the inevitable tensions in the expatriate cycle (home/host, global/local, short-/long-term, leading/learning) and explore the implications of trends such as dual careers, the growing number of female and younger expatriates, and the increased use of alternatives to expatriation.

We end the chapter by summarizing the benefits that can be derived from well-implemented strategies of global integration, but point also to the rigidities that must be overcome when a company begins to experience transnational pressures.

THE LOGIC OF GLOBAL INTEGRATION

Multinational corporations face two sets of conflicting demands in their international operations: local responsiveness and global efficiency. In Chapter 3, we discussed the need for international firms to respond to local requirements. We argued that *local responsiveness* is achieved primarily by delegating decision-making responsibility to local units and by appointing local managers to the top management teams of subsidiaries.

In this chapter we discuss how firms can achieve global efficiency through a high level of integration of their international activities. *Global integration* means that the different parts of the corporation constitute a whole, and that decisions made are based on a global perspective.

In companies pursuing global integration, the development of new knowledge takes place mainly at the global hub, usually the corporate headquarters or the worldwide product division. Foreign subsidiaries depend on the center for resources, direction, and information. They act as product delivery pipelines to foreign markets, implementing the strategies of the parent company. We call companies that use this "one-country" approach to creating competitive advantage *meganational* firms.[6]

Many companies choose to expand internationally while maintaining close control over the value chain—that is, the string of primary activities (R&D, manufacturing, logistics, marketing, etc.) and support activities (such as HR and procurement) that are the source of added value. Decisions are made from a global perspective—in the extreme, the firm operates as if the world were a single market. While Nokia's globalization strategy stands out for its remarkable success, the logic that the company followed is quite common. Nokia's strength came from its focused R&D investments and from its control over the links between technology, product development, supply chain management, and marketing, integrating these activities on a global basis.

Key strategic decisions at Nokia involve a fast-moving process of data gathering and analysis, consultation, and conflict resolution, involving many different perspectives. In the 1990s, this was enabled by key executives being in the same place—Finland.[7] They shared a common language and cultural background, and they were used to working with each other. In other words, they functioned as a tightly integrated team.

Global integration does not necessarily imply selling identical products in the same way all over the world. What it does mean is that decisions about how to address local customer needs or market differentiation are made by managers who have an integrated global point of view. The strategies of export-driven Japanese, Korean, and Chinese manufacturing companies—relative latecomers to internationalization—typify this. Their tightly integrated product development and manufacturing functions at home allowed them to develop economies of scale in cost, quality, and product innovation, flooding the world with automobiles, cameras, copiers, consumer electronics, and other products via their sales subsidiaries abroad.

The meganational approach is not limited to companies that compete globally by exporting standardized consumer products. Meganational companies can be found across the spectrum of industries, from high-tech to fast foods, in particular where products are naturally relatively standardized across the world, where there are only limited benefits of local responsiveness, or where maintaining key activities in the value chain at the central hub can create a competitive advantage in terms of speed of product development, cost reduction, or quality improvement.[8]

Some companies, such as Nokia, have used a meganational strategy as a first step to internationalization, moving to a different strategic posture as they progress. Indeed, elements of meganational strategy can be detected in most cases of early internationalization when resource constraints require careful central control. Other firms maintain their meganational orientation for an extended period of time because it fits with their products and/or markets.

The Business Advantages of Global Integration

There are a number of reasons why companies may choose to follow a route of tight international integration (see the box "Business Advantages of Global Integration").

Global integration does not, however, mean centralization of all aspects of a company's operations. It may be limited to a particular product, function, or value chain segment. For example, P&G strives to standardize products worldwide because P&G's key success factor compared to its competitors is technological innovation and its rapid application to all markets. Packaging and advertising, on the other hand, are more adapted to local needs.

With increased global competition, an argument can be made that global integration is becoming a competitive necessity in a number of markets in which decentralized strategies were dominant in the past. Among the factors favoring integration are the emergence of global consumers, owing to greater homogeneity of tastes; the diminishing importance of country borders with regional integration in Europe, Latin America, and Southeast Asia; and the increasing importance of fast decision making in our rapidly changing competitive environment.

Business Advantages of Global Integration

- *Economies of scale.* A company can lower its unit costs by centralizing critical value chain activities, such as manufacturing or logistics. This may involve having a small number of large facilities to make products for export, or creating a network of specialized and focused operations spread around the world that are tightly controlled by the central hub. This allowed Nokia to manage carefully its investments in R&D and to maximize economies of scale in manufacturing, sourcing, and logistics.

- *Links in the value chain.* Sometimes competitive advantage comes from tight links between value chain activities—between R&D, manufacturing, and marketing in the home country, which is a technological leader (such as Silicon Valley in the Internet equipment business); or between manufacturing and logistics. Tight integration allows the firm to stay ahead of technological and competitive changes.

- *Serving global customers.* To the extent that customers are integrated and operate on a global basis, their suppliers may be forced to adopt a similar structure. Subsidiaries do not have their own stand-alone customers; prices, quality standards, and delivery terms are determined globally. For instance, international law firms are expected to deliver the same service to their global clients regardless of where they are served.[9]

- *Global branding.* A consumer products company like Coca-Cola promotes a unified brand image around the world. Coke standardizes both its formula and advertising themes (its two critical success factors) to a high degree, gaining efficiencies in the use of marketing tools like advertising and merchandising.

- *Leveraging capabilities.* Some companies expand globally by transferring capabilities developed in the home market. The international expansion of both IKEA and Wal-Mart depends on supply chain management skills that allow these companies to pursue their traditional low-price strategies around the world.

- *World-class quality assurance.* Key processes are standardized and centrally controlled to maintain competitive advantage. The pharmaceutical giant Merck manufactures locally to meet government requirements. Its manufacturing processes are complex, however, and these are standardized in order to maintain high quality.

- *Competitive platforms.* Tight control of local subsidiaries by central headquarters may allow rapid response to competitive conditions and redeployment of resources to facilitate expansion worldwide. For example, in the past, tightly centralized Japanese multinationals penetrated new markets through price subsidization funded by profitable operations elsewhere.

Meganational firms can be found even in industries in which the forces for local responsiveness are supposedly high—McDonald's and Pizza Hut in fast foods, and IKEA and Wal-Mart in retailing. Within the same industry, companies may pursue different internationalization strategies, often following the path that led them to success in their home markets.

A meganational firm is sometimes perceived as ethnocentric by foreign subsidiary employees. Global decisions often seem to be made at the expense of the subsidiary, with the corporation's home country apparently having an undue influence. The composition of the top management team, typically dominated by home country nationals, further strengthens this perception. In addition, expatriates from the home country often have key roles on local management teams to maintain the necessary close link with the head office. Not surprisingly, Japanese multinationals, with their historical preference for a meganational approach, consistently have more expatriates per subsidiary and a greater presence of Japanese in local management than multinationals from other countries.[10] How to overcome this "natural" tendency to become ethnocentric is one of the challenges facing the meganational firm.

The Tools for Global Integration

Historically, the levers of global integration have been primarily those that enable centralized control over dispersed operations.[11] There is an extensive literature on control in organizations, much of it focused on the microeconomic debate about the respective virtues of markets and hierarchies as governance mechanisms.[12] More pertinent to our focus are the frameworks found in organizational theory. The idea underlying these organizational control frameworks is that, as the degree of complexity and uncertainty of tasks increases, a progressively wider range of control mechanisms will be employed. Simple mechanisms such as rules and procedures can manage simple tasks; but as the complexity of the task increases, direct supervision, planning, and more complex levers of control will come into play.[13]

The integration mechanisms are sometimes referred to as tools of control, sometimes as tools of coordination, both in popular usage and in textbooks. Control and coordination are two closely related concepts that are difficult to separate.[14] As we proposed in Chapter 1, we will use the term "control" when power and authority are overt and the mechanism is hierarchical in nature.[15] We will use the term "coordination" when the focus of the mechanisms is on enhancing two-way lateral (horizontal) interactions and adjustments among different organizational units and individuals.

Control mechanisms can be classified broadly into four types:[16]

- Personal control.
- Procedural control.
- Output control.
- Normative control.

Personal Control

This control mechanism is reflected in the managerial hierarchy of roles and responsibilities, in which decision-making authority is concentrated at the center of the organization. Since all organizations are organized in a hierarchy, some degree of personal control is universal. This is the most direct and personalized form of control. The center takes key decisions, supported by direct supervision—for example, by visits to foreign operations by senior executives.

Personal control through expatriates can be used to replace and complement headquarters centralization. Trusted expatriates make decisions on behalf of headquarters and monitor the implementation of central decisions.

Procedural Control

In its simplest form, this involves standardization of procedures, typically in written form and increasingly supported by IT-based tools. These procedures can come to constitute an internal governance system—for example, mandating the processes for recruitment, for signing external contracts, or concerning safety measures.

Standardization can also take more sophisticated forms, including the development of complex global work processes and systems. Standardization can apply to skills (training people in how to approach customers or handle a performance appraisal) as well as knowledge (codifying new knowledge on customer solutions so that it can be diffused across operations).[17]

Output Control

In contrast to the other types of control, the focus here is on results rather than on behavior or a course of action. Control is exercised through negotiation and agreement about objectives or targets. This is analogous to market ways of governance, as opposed to hierarchical means. Targets that have been agreed constitute quasi-contractual obligations, typically backed up by explicitly stated rewards and sanctions. Bonuses are linked to achievement of results, and the ultimate sanction may be replacement or dismissal for nonperformance.

The broad trend in many global companies toward greater rigor in performance management (objective setting, evaluation, and rewards—to be discussed in Chapter 9) reflects an emphasis on output control. At the same time, the market nature of output control is guided by some form of planning system that focuses on working through the trade-offs between long-term strategic objectives and short-term outputs (financial targets and budgets as well as operational goals).[18] Otherwise output control can lead to an excessively short-term orientation.

Normative Control

In comparison with supervision, normative control—often called socialization—is more implicit and subtle. It means inculcating certain values, beliefs, and behaviors that employees are expected to learn and follow; the norms are internalized. (In contrast, we discuss horizontally shared values, beliefs, and norms at more length in Chapter 6.)

People can be recruited on the basis of their potential fit with these values and norms, which can also be taught, both through formal socialization programs and through informal interaction with other organizational members. Those who demonstrate adherence to corporate values and behavioral norms are chosen for positions of responsibility. To the extent that employees share common norms and values, they can be trusted to exercise discretion without the necessity for rules, procedures, and supervision.

Global Integration and the Use of Expatriates

Common to all these different integration mechanisms is the role played by expatriation. Global integration is not about dictatorship by headquarters; it is about alignment. The trick is to make sure that managers worldwide are on the same wavelength. One way to ensure alignment is expatriate staffing, shifting the locus of decision making to the affiliates while assuring that a global view prevails.

Expatriation is a form of direct, hierarchical, personal control[19]—headquarters' executives often trust their expatriates more than they trust their local employees. Trusted expatriates are also likely to have been through intense socialization, and may be levers for standardization of practices across borders.

Centralization is a case in point. When one thinks of meganational firms, the first characteristic that usually comes to mind is centralized decision making at the all-powerful headquarters, or at the central office of the worldwide product group in a more diversified firm. This is misleading. Senior managers at the headquarters would become overloaded with operational details, taking their attention away from important strategic issues. As the scope of international operations expands, decision making would break down—everything would stop until headquarters made a decision. It would also be difficult to attract and retain local staff, who would feel alienated at slow decision making by distant bosses with no understanding of their local circumstances.

However, decentralizing decisions to affiliates does not necessarily mean increasing their autonomy. There is a lot of confusion about this, since autonomy in multinational companies is often perceived as synonymous with the locus of decision making.[20] If decisions are made at headquarters, subsidiaries are said to have little autonomy; if decisions are made locally, then they have high autonomy. In fact, making decisions locally does not necessarily imply autonomy if the decisions are made by expatriates rather than local managers. Who makes the decision may be as important as where the decision is made.

The typical pattern in meganational firms is that home country expatriates, well socialized in the parent company norms and with strong social ties to headquarters managers, occupy key positions in the subsidiaries. For many firms this may be a key post, like general manager or financial controller. For others, it may be a critical technical position, such as the brewmaster at Heineken.[21] Indeed, sending expatriates to subsidiaries can have the same results as centralizing decisions at headquarters.[22] Reinforced by the network of relationships with colleagues at headquarters, local decisions may be similar to those made at the center.

For example, research has shown that a large Japanese presence in subsidiaries is associated with more "local" decision making.[23] This indicates that the Japanese are pursuing global integration through informal networks of

Japanese expatriates. Local executives may not like centralization (critical decisions are made in Tokyo), but they also find it hard to live with this more subtle pseudo-decentralization (decisions are made locally by Japanese executives). No matter how hard some Japanese companies try to open and enlarge their management pool, skeptical observers doubt the impact of such efforts.[24]

The four different control mechanisms are largely complementary. Almost all organizations have some hierarchy, some formalized procedures, some degree of output negotiation and planning, and some attention is paid to socialization. Firms tend to employ certain levers of control more than others, however, leading to different organizational configurations. Research tentatively suggests that globally integrated companies tend to rely on hierarchical mechanisms, notably via expatriates, while locally responsive firms rely more on output control.[25] Studies have also revealed differences in the use of integration mechanisms across functions (HR, production, etc.).[26]

Research shows differences between countries of origin, with respect to the type of control exercised by the headquarters.[27] US firms tend to depend on standardization and output control, Japanese multinationals use a larger number of expatriates to integrate their foreign operations, and many continental European corporations rely more on normative integration than firms from the other regions.[28]

Global Standardization

An important facet of global integration is the standardization of key operational procedures. Shared global standards will facilitate control, ensuring more consistent performance in terms of cost and quality as well as compliance with environmental and safety standards. An important element of procedural standardization is worldwide consistency of HR practices, and this also facilitates the transfer of the work organization as a complete system to a foreign location.

Maintaining Global Standards in Operations

Ask anyone anywhere for a list of companies that deliver the same product around the world, and it is likely that McDonald's, the largest global fast-food company operating in some 120 countries, would be on the list. Whether you are in Tokyo, Moscow, Paris, or Cincinnati, the experience of ordering, buying, and eating a meal at McDonald's is virtually the same, although menus may vary with local tastes. What attracts customers to McDonald's is the consistently high service level, from product quality to speed of order execution, from the ambiance of the stores to their hygiene. McDonald's operating system has for many years been a model for scores of other businesses in which personal contact is an essential part of delivering value to customers.[29]

Every aspect of McDonald's operations is designed to satisfy customer expectations based on standards that are universal around the world. Nothing is left to chance or individual discretion. A big part of McDonald's success is its ability to transfer expertise developed first at home to other markets worldwide.

Global standardization of practices through operation manuals is an important tool. All McDonald's restaurants are required to conduct 72 safety protocols every day.[30] Even more critical is a relentless focus on education and training, led by Hamburger University and its regional "colleges" throughout the world.[31]

Another example of process standardization is the Swedish furniture retail chain IKEA. Its well-designed, simple, but durable products are sold in more than 30 countries,[32] including the US and China. IKEA's competitive advantage comes from its ability to optimize work processes worldwide—integrating product design, low-cost manufacturing, logistics, and efficient service. As several marketing textbooks have explained, this is built around a tightly controlled standard marketing concept in an area normally associated with strong cultural preferences. What is less known is how IKEA's approach to HRM supports its global strategy.

Guided by an unwavering commitment to its core values, IKEA strives to standardize its approach to people management in much the same way as it standardizes its approach to markets. Wherever it operates, the company carefully recruits people who will blend well with the IKEA culture of humility, simplicity, and cost-consciousness. It prefers to hire people without much previous experience, and focuses heavily on the initial socialization process and on developing them quickly by delegating responsibility and rotating them frequently. Specially trained "IKEA ambassadors" have been assigned to key positions in all units, charged not only with the transfer of know-how but also with inculcating "IKEA's way" among its staff around the world.

Global Standardization of HRM

It is only relatively recently that multinationals have increased the level of global integration of HRM through standardization of HR practices, although usually not to the degree seen at IKEA. Arguments in favor of global standardization of HRM, together with arguments for local adaptation, are summarized in Table 4–1.

A number of factors drive and support global standardization of HRM:

- The implementation of *IT-based HR tools* in multinationals has led to a significant increase in the level of standardization across foreign subsidiaries.[33]
- Global standardization is associated with *scale advantages* as investments in the development of HR tools and procedures are divided among multiple units. Foreign subsidiaries can implement HR processes and tools that they would not have been in a position to develop or deploy by themselves. Standardization of HR practices can also enable further *specialization within the global HR function*, and there may be less replication of functional expertise across units. With similar HR tools and processes implemented throughout the corporation, questions related to functional subareas can be referred to the corporate functional specialist, regardless of where this person is located.[34]
- Asking overseas units to use similar guiding principles, criteria, tools, and procedures for managing employees increases headquarters' *control* over foreign subsidiaries. For instance, a standardized performance management

TABLE 4–1. Advantages Associated with Global Standardization and Local Adaptation of HR Practices

Global Standardization	Local Adaptation
• Allows specialization and scale (cost) advantages in the HR function.	• Fits with local culture, institutional, and labor market considerations.
• Facilitates the use of IT-based HR tools and processes.	• Helps fulfill local legal requirements.
• Can transfer best HR practices and work systems.	• Appropriate HR practices may enhance local goodwill and image.
• Global (foreign) HR practices are sometimes preferred by host country nationals.	• Motivates host country managers to have locally developed practices.
• Serves as control mechanism.	• May be needed to support the strategy of the local unit.
• Facilitates coordination across units.	

system allows headquarters to influence goal setting and to follow up on how well employees have achieved their objectives. Using similar procedures, tools, and performance criteria worldwide provides headquarters with a way of evaluating and comparing employees' performance.[35]

- Organizational practices can be valuable resources that firms seek to replicate and exploit throughout the multinational.[36] When management of people is an integral part of the work system—contributing to organizational capabilities that allow the firm to implement its strategy in a superior way—it is likely that a company will attempt to implement *"best"* HR *practices* perceived to be important for the success of the multinational.[37]

- "Foreign" HR practices—that is, practices not found in domestic corporations in the host country—may sometimes be highly appreciated by local employees and managers. The fact that they have worked for a foreign firm adds considerably to their human capital. For example, in emerging economies such as China and Russia, the extensive investment in employee training and development made by many multinationals is seen as valuable, and so is experience with a sophisticated performance assessment system.

- Finally, having similar HR practices enhances interunit *coordination* in many different ways (to be discussed in the chapters that follow). First, it is easier for employees from different units to collaborate if they have similar competences. Second, with standardized HRM, employees share a vocabulary and beliefs about the business, facilitating communication and collaboration.[38] Third, when all units share the same HR practices, they are more likely to identify with the corporation as a whole, instead of having an us-and-them attitude. Fourth, standardization of practices can contribute to perceived equity within the corporation, further stimulating interunit cooperation.[39] The more the value chain activities are integrated across different units of the corporation, the more important the coordination argument for international transfer of HR practices will be.

While global HR standardization can have significant positive effects, such efforts often encounter difficulties, partly because they go against legitimate pressures for local adaptation of HR (see Table 4–1).[40] Also, the ease of standardization varies with the level of HRM. As discussed in Chapter 3, it may be quite easy to standardize HR philosophies (or guiding principles) and general policies, but actual practices are likely to differ across foreign units.

There are also differences between HR practices in the benefit to be gained through global standardization, which may impact the degree of standardization. Table 4–2 presents the findings of research on the HR practices for host country professionals and managers in Western multinationals in China. Practices related to performance management showed the highest degree of global standardization. The *criteria* behind HR practices tended to be more global than other aspects, such as the *level* of employee compensation and the *methods* of recruitment, which were more influenced by local conditions.

TABLE 4–2. Degree of Global Standardization and Local Adaptation of HR Practices in Western-Owned Units in China

	Global Standardization[A]	Local Adaptation[A]
Methods used when recruiting new local managers and professionals	4.4	3.9
Criteria used when recruiting new local managers and professionals	5.0	4.1
Amount of management and professional training	4.4	3.4
Content of management and professional training	4.7	3.6
Relative importance of financial bonuses as a percentage of total compensation	4.1	4.2
Criteria employed to determine financial bonuses	5.1	3.8
Methods used to appraise (assess) the performance of professionals and managers	5.4	3.7
Criteria used to appraise (assess) the performance of professionals and managers	5.4	3.7

[A] Global standardization was measured by asking managers how similar (on a scale from (7) very similar to (1) very different) subsidiary HR practices were to those in the multinational's home country operations. Local adaptation was measured with a similar question about the similarity between subsidiary HR practices and practices found in local firms.

Source: I. Björkman, P. Budhwar, A. Smale, and J. Sumelius, "Human Resource Management in Foreign-Owned Subsidiaries: China versus India," *International Journal of Human Resource Management* 19(5) (May 2008).

The choice of standardization versus adaptation should not be reduced to an either–or dilemma. In our view, the real question is *what to respect, what to ignore, and what to reinvent* when adapting work practices to another environment. For example, multinationals may transfer some aspects of how people are recruited and selected from the parent company; they may copy some aspects of how this is done in local organizations; and they may develop some entirely new ways to deal with certain issues. Some HR functions may also be managed at a regional level (Asia Pacific or Europe, for example), leading to some regional standardization of HRM. The outcome is to a greater or lesser extent *hybrid* HR practices found in most foreign subsidiaries.[41]

So far we have discussed the extent to which the HR practices of foreign subsidiaries resemble those in other parts of the corporation. A more comprehensive and, in our view, more fruitful approach is to see that there are two central elements to the adoption of parent organization HR practices by foreign subsidiaries: the *implementation* of corporate practices abroad, and their *internalization* by subsidiary managers and employees.[42] While the degree of implementation matters, it is also crucial that users have internalized the underlying principles. Indeed, the most challenging element is often the thoroughness of internalization, the "state in which the employees at the recipient unit view the practice as valuable for the unit and become committed to the practice."[43]

Although policies and practices can to some extent be imposed by the headquarters through various control systems, there are no simple means available to influence positively the attitudes of subsidiary employees toward an imported system. We argue that firms need to pay attention to both the implementation *and* the internalization of practices at subsidiary level. Lack of attention to the underlying principles of a certain practice may lead to it being adopted only on the surface,[44] or even resisted through open conflict and resistance.[45] The enforced adoption of a practice without a belief in its value will, at best, lead to superficial compliance and a low level of engagement.

Globally standardized practices most commonly originate at corporate headquarters, which also play a key role in their transfer abroad. We will return to the question of how to transfer organizational practices and knowledge across the multinational firm later in Chapter 10, and to issues related to change management in Chapter 11. At this point it is enough to note that the use of expatriates has been found to be a crucial conduit for the transfer of knowledge and practices.

Transplanting the Work System

Standardization of HR practices facilitates the replication of the whole operating system in foreign units, since HR practices are an integrated part of any effective operation system. For example, HR practices played an important role in the success of manufacturing practices in Japan, which have been well studied.[46] HR factors included team-based production, worker participation in problem solving, job rotation, few job classifications, single status, and high levels of training. Japanese automotive firms transferred these practices to most of their overseas plants, but often with considerable adaptation.[47] The use of comprehensive

Transferring the Toyota Production System to Nummi

In 1963, General Motors opened an automobile assembly plant in Fremont, California. By the late 1970s, the plant employed over 7,000 workers but ranked lowest in productivity, and one of the worst in terms of quality, in the entire GM system. Relations between management and the union were marked by distrust and even fear. Daily absenteeism was almost 20 percent, drug abuse and alcoholism were rampant, and first-line supervisors were known to carry weapons for personal protection. The plant was closed in the 1982 recession.

Under an agreement between Toyota, GM, and the United Autoworkers' Union, the plant reopened in 1984 as NUMMI, a joint venture between the two automakers. Toyota accepted the same 25-person union bargaining committee that existed under the old GM system. Eighty-five percent of the initial workforce of 2,200 was hired from the original pool of laid-off GM employees (employment reached 4,000 by the early 1990s). By 1986 the plant was 60 percent more efficient than a comparable plant fully owned by GM. How did this happen? Part of the change came from integrated HR and manufacturing processes, using intensive involvement of the workforce in a way that simultaneously empowers and controls them.[49]

Just as important was the deliberate and extensive socialization of NUMMI employees into the new system. First, when deciding whom to rehire there was a heavy emphasis on the selection of employees who had the ability to function within the NUMMI philosophy.

Second, Toyota sent no fewer than 400 trainers from Japan to explain the Toyota methods to the US workforce. At the same time, 600 of NUMMI's blue-collar employees were sent to Japan for between three weeks' and several months' training at Toyota factories. This included classroom training and working alongside Toyota workers. As part of the training, NUMMI employees were asked to suggest improvement to the famous Toyota manufacturing system. The approach was not "Now you have to learn to work this way" but "Can you help us all to improve?"—cross-cultural action learning at its best.

The whole transplant effort was headed by a bicultural leadership group combining expatriates from Toyota in key plant positions, a small number of GM managers (mainly finance and procurement), and other Americans recruited from outside (including HR).[50] The plant itself was organized around teams, with a three-level hierarchy (in contrast to five or six levels in traditional GM plants). Most of the original team leaders went through the training in Japan, and many of them were subsequently promoted to managerial positions at the Fremont plant.

By 1996, after a decade of improvements in the United States automobile industry, NUMMI was still 20 percent more efficient and 25 percent higher on key quality indicators than other GM plants, comparable with Toyota's operations in Japan. NUMMI continued to be ranked among the most productive plants in the United States 25 years after its formation.[51]

methods for employee selection and socialization certainly reduced the impact of operating in a different cultural and institutional environment. However, while job rotation practices were similar to those in Japan, problem-solving team methods were substantially adjusted, and compensation was comparable to local rather than Japanese norms. In the case of plants located in the United States, the progressive transfer and adaptation led to levels of performance similar to those in Japan.

Probably no other foreign investment site has received more coverage in the media and in academic literature than NUMMI—a joint venture created by General Motors and Toyota in 1982 to manufacture a small car on the site of a closed GM plant in Fremont, California.[48] The box "Transferring the Toyota Production System to NUMMI" focuses on the transfer of Toyota's manufacturing system to Fremont. Many in the US automobile industry expected that the transfer would fail, assuming that Japanese manufacturing methods were too deeply dependent on Japanese culture. However, the venture was an instant success, and NUMMI became the US leader in quality and productivity within three years.

While NUMMI's case may be exceptional, many companies attempt to replicate their domestic work environment in foreign locations. Replication of HR practices from the home country organization is an important element of such efforts.

MASTERING EXPATRIATION

The use of expatriates is as old as international business; because of this, the international HR profession has historically been the domain of relocation specialists, consultants in compensation and benefits, and experts on international taxation. In the academic literature, until recently, international HRM was also synonymous with studies of expatriation. Today the emphasis of international HRM has changed dramatically. Nevertheless, the effective management of expatriation—or more broadly of international transfers—remains one of the foundations for the implementation of global strategy.

The Evolution of Expatriate Management

Expatriation has been a tool of organizational control since the early stages of civilization. In ancient Rome (see the box "Holding the Roman Empire Together"), as with the Dutch and English trading houses that pioneered international trade in the 16th and 17th centuries, the art of developing trusted representatives to manage distant subsidiaries often spelled the difference between success and failure in overseas colonization. In the early modern era of expatriation after World War II, foreign business was usually run by an international division that supervised exports, licensing, and subsidiaries abroad. The main role of corporate HR was to facilitate the selection of staff for foreign postings, finding employees familiar with the company's products, technology, organization, and culture, who were at the same time amenable to the constraints of working abroad.

Typical parent country employees stationed abroad operated like viceroys—directing daily operations, supervising the transfer of know-how, communicating

Holding the Roman Empire Together

The geographical reach and longevity of the Roman Empire can be regarded as a prodigious feat of international management. Rome expected those in charge of even the most distant part of the Empire to be more than just representatives—they had to make the right decisions on behalf of Rome. One of the binding forces of the Empire was the careful attention paid to the selection, training, and socialization of Rome's expatriates, the generals and governors entrusted with the governance of far-flung provinces.[52]

Such positions required a long apprenticeship in a highly trained and organized army. Governors were selected exclusively from consuls who had held high state office. By the time they were dispatched abroad, the ways of Rome were so ingrained in their minds that they would not need policy guidance—nor had they means of getting such advice. They were "centralized within."

This policy of administrative decentralization coupled with tight socialization of the local decision makers created strong, self-contained provinces or "subsidiaries." A tribute to their robustness was that the Roman Empire survived even the fall of Rome (a sort of involuntary divestiture) when the center of the Empire moved east to Byzantium.

corporate policies, and keeping the home office informed about relevant developments in their assigned territories. Assignments were decided on an ad hoc basis, occasionally supported by crash courses in language and foreign culture. Since foreign assignments often meant being at a distance from the politics of career progression in the parent company, all sorts of financial incentives were used to make foreign postings attractive.

During this period, the notion of "expatriate" brought to mind a middle-aged, male executive dispatched from a first world headquarters to a third world subsidiary. In fact, this stereotype was not true then, and it is even less so today. Most international transfers were to economically advanced countries. Today, the countries with the highest population of resident expatriates are the United States, China, and the United Kingdom. Table 4–3 provides an overview of some characteristics of today's expatriates, based on a comprehensive survey of 180 mostly North American and European multinationals in 2009. And as we will discuss later, the expatriate population is increasingly diverse in its ethnic origins, gender, and age, as well as in the roles expatriates are expected to perform.

Understanding the Expatriate Phenomenon

Before looking in detail at specific HR practices associated with international transfers, we briefly review the motives that drive expatriation, and examine the controversy over whether expatriate failure really is as serious a problem as it is sometimes argued.

TABLE 4–3. A Portrait of Expatriates

A 2009 survey profiled expatriates in 180 multinationals from the Americas (50%), Europe, the Middle East, and Africa (49%), and Asia Pacific (1%).

- 18% of the assignments were expected to be less than one year, 55% one to three years, 20% more than three years, and 7% permanent.
- 20% of the expatriates were women.
- 86% were accompanied by a spouse.
- 30% of the spouses were employed before but not during the assignment, 13% were employed during but not before the assignment, and 10% were employed both before and during the assignment.
- 49% had children with them on the assignment.

Other findings:

- 57% of the expatriate assignments were to/from the home country of the multinational.
- 33% of the companies expected an increase in total expatriate population, 25% a decrease.
- The most frequent expatriate locations were China, the US, and the UK.
- The most common assignment objective was filling a managerial or technical skills gap, followed by building management expertise.
- The most critical challenges were assignment costs, finding candidates, controlling policy exceptions, and career management.

Source: Brookfield Global Relocation Services (2009), "Global Relocation Trends 2009 Survey Report" (www. brookfieldgrs.com).

The Motives for Expatriation

Much of the literature on expatriation focuses on international assignments of parent (or home country) employees. In a classic article, Edström and Galbraith explored the principal motives behind such assignments.[53] They proposed that expatriates are dispatched abroad for three sometimes overlapping reasons. The first is simply to *fill positions* that cannot be staffed locally because of a lack of technical or managerial skills. The second is to support *management development,* enabling high potential individuals to acquire international experience. The third reason is *organizational development*—that is, the control and coordination of international operations through normative control and/or informal social networks.[54]

Pucik differentiates between *demand-driven* and *learning-driven* international assignments, and there is empirical verification for this distinction.[55] Traditional expatriate jobs fit mainly into the former category: employees who are dispatched abroad to fix a problem or for reasons of control. On the other hand, more and more companies recognize that cross-border mobility is a potential learning tool, increasing the number of assignments in which the primary driver is individual or organizational learning. Many assignments combine both elements, but in most cases it is clear which of the two dominates.

In addition, expatriates differ in the time they spend in an assignment abroad. Many assignments are long-term, often lasting two to four years.[56] Others are

FIGURE 4–1 **The Purpose of Expatriation: Demand-Driven vs. Learning-Driven**

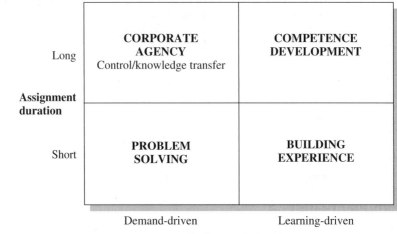

short-term, less than one year, linked to a specific task or need. Figure 4–1 puts assignment length and purpose together into a framework for understanding the nature of expatriate roles.

In most cases, expatriates are assigned abroad for a relatively long period of time as agents of the parent firm in order to accomplish a variety of tasks related to operations and/or oversight of the subsidiaries. Here the demand for their services is driven primarily by headquarters control or the transfer of knowledge or practices. The expatriates serve a *corporate agency* role.

In other cases, the demand for expatriates is driven by short-term start-up or problem-solving needs, and the length of the assignment is determined by the time it takes to address the task. We call this a *problem-solving* role. Historically, most expatriate assignments were either corporate agency or problem solving; in both cases, the expatriate had knowledge and competencies that were not available locally.

Now, with the development of local managerial and professional capabilities, there is less demand for expatriate assignments to fill a local skill gap. At the same time, companies face an increasing need to develop global coordination capabilities, boosted in part by mobility across borders. The focus of these *competence development* assignments is on organizational and individual learning rather than deploying skills or transferring practices from other parts of the multinational. International assignments are powerful development opportunities for the individual expatriate (we discuss this further in Chapter 8), and extensive use of expatriates helps create interpersonal networks that facilitate collaboration and knowledge sharing across units (there is more about this in Chapter 10).

Finally, a rapidly growing type of expatriation is short-term learning assignments of young high potential professionals who move across borders primarily for the purpose of building experience and developing their careers.[57] These jobs generally last less than a year and may involve rotation across several countries or even regions. In a number of firms, such assignments are becoming an integral part of career development planning for young professionals and managers.[58] A particular category is short-term transfers of managers and professionals from foreign subsidiaries to headquarters for training and development purposes.

While employees take up expatriate positions for different reasons and lengths of time, many companies still deal with expatriates as if they were a homogeneous group placed abroad for agency reasons. If distinctions are made, they are based on family situation or hierarchical level. As we review the extensive research on expatriation, it is important to bear in mind that the concepts, empirical observations, and practical recommendations of most studies are generic and therefore fail to acknowledge the differences that exist between qualitatively different expatriate roles.

Studying Expatriation: What Is Failure?

Much research on expatriation has focused on analyzing the causes of failure in overseas assignments, recommending HR practices that would help organizations to select, develop, and retain competent expatriates.[59] In contrast, practitioner work has emphasized compensation issues, an area in which there is little academic research.

Until recently, a typical study on any topic linked to expatriation was framed by an introduction about the high cost of expatriates and the high frequency of assignment failure, especially in American multinationals.[60] However, while the direct costs of relocating an expatriate are real, there seem to be no studies that have empirically linked failure rates directly with company or subsidiary performance.

In this context, there has been no shortage of references to high expatriate failure rates, with claims that more than a third of expatriations are aborted.[61] But does the empirical evidence support these claims? The answer is a surprising but unambiguous no. It seems that a persistent myth of high failure rates (that is, early returns of the expatriate to the home country) has been created by "massive (mis)quotations" of a handful of articles about US multinationals, some dating back to the 1960s.[62] The real rates appear to be considerably lower. For instance, the 2009 Brookfield survey[63] reported that 7 percent of expatriates returned early without having completed their assignments, and other studies have reported similar figures.[64]

It is conceivable that the exaggeration of expatriate "failure" may have slowed down the adoption of some useful recommendations. When companies compare their failure rates with the alarming "average" presented in some textbooks, their situation does not look too bad. Why spend resources on what does not seem to be broken?

However, is "premature return" an adequate reflection of expatriate failure? One can argue that expatriate failure should continue to be examined, but using other measures. It may be far more damaging for a company if an expatriate who fails to perform adequately stays until completion of the overseas assignment. If underperformance in the new job is included in the figures—either as the result of poor selection or adaptation—failure rates may be considerably higher.[65]

Recently, researchers' attention has shifted from explaining failure to a focus on *intercultural adjustment*—how well do expatriates adjust to working and living in a foreign environment? Indeed, one can view failure, in the sense of recall, as an extreme manifestation of poor adjustment, and adjustment has been found to be positively related to expatriates' job satisfaction and work performance.[66] However, from a corporate perspective it may be even more important to assess expatriate "success" directly, with measures such as time to proficiency, the time that it takes to master a new role, or indeed assessments of overall job performance.[67] For instance, one American survey showed that nearly a third of expatriates who stayed in their positions did not perform to the expectations of their superiors.[68]

Managing International Transfers

Making an expatriate assignment a success for the individual, the family, and the firm requires paying attention to many factors, from the time of initial selection until repatriation. A starting point is the recognition that expatriation is a process, not an event. This process can be broken down into a set of phases:

- Selecting expatriates.
- Preparation and orientation.
- Adjusting to the expatriate role.
- Managing the performance of expatriates.
- Compensation and rewards.
- Repatriation.

We will discuss each of these activities in the "expatriate cycle" separately, although naturally they are closely linked (expatriate performance management and compensation are covered in more depth in Chapter 9). The problems of later phases have to be anticipated earlier—for example, repatriation has to be taken into account at the selection phase, while the purpose of preparation is to facilitate role adjustment.

Selecting Expatriates

Surveys show that it is essential for firms to pay attention to technical expertise and domestic track record, with some indication that European multinationals give additional weight to language skills and international adaptability.[69] The selection process is often informal and ad hoc, characterized by what Harris and Brewster label the "coffee machine" system.[70] Candidates are likely to be known personally to the senior managers in the parent company, and the real selection decisions tend to be made in informal discussions "by the coffee machine."

There are few proper discussions of the selection criteria; the position is seldom announced openly (or when it is, it is already clear who is the preferred person); and there is little formal assessment of the person chosen.[71] This is clearly inadequate, and there is broad academic agreement that organizations should make stronger efforts to develop their selection routines. What does research say about the characteristics of successful expatriates?

CHARACTERISTICS OF SUCCESSFUL EXPATRIATES. Researchers have found a large number of factors to be important for successful expatriation. One cross-cultural textbook identified 68 dimensions, 21 of which were deemed highly desirable,[72] while another review identified 73 skills necessary for cross-cultural learning.[73] If one adds up all these characteristics, the ideal expatriate is close to superhuman! Most of the key factors, however, can be grouped into the following categories:

- Professional and technical competence.
- Relationship and communication abilities.
- Cultural sensitivity and flexibility.
- Self-efficacy and tolerance for ambiguity.
- Family factors.[74]

Appropriate *professional and technical competence* is a prerequisite for most international assignments. Even in cases when the expatriate is not expected to be able to carry out certain tasks immediately, the person must have the relevant training and experience to learn on the job.

A meta-analysis of 66 studies on expatriate adjustment and performance concluded that relational skills were the strongest predictor of international adjustment.[75] *Relationship and communication abilities* help the expatriate build close interpersonal contacts that improve collaboration and give the person access to local knowledge and the personal feedback necessary for successful work performance.[76]

Cultural sensitivity and flexibility refer to the expatriate's ability to understand and respond to differences between countries and situations. Expatriates who are nonevaluative when interpreting the behavior of foreigners are more likely to learn, adjust, and perform well. Research on cultural sensitivity and flexibility has found both to be positively associated with expatriate performance.[77]

There is evidence from several studies that *self-efficacy*[78] and *tolerance for ambiguity*[79] can help expatriates adjust and perform well on their assignments. The former refers to an expatriate's belief in his or her own ability to act and perform. Individuals with a healthy measure of self-confidence are more likely to act and learn from the outcomes of their actions. International assignments often put expatriates in situations where they need to have a high tolerance for ambiguity and an ability to cope with stress.

The adjustment and support of the *family* emerge as one of the strongest predictors of expatriate adjustment.[80] These also feature consistently as the main factor influencing expatriates' decisions to return prematurely from their assignments.

The relevance of particular traits and skills depends on the role the expatriate is expected to assume. Clear managerial qualifications and proven leadership skills, together with relevant professional skills, are the essential foundation for agency-type assignments. Expatriates in agency roles should also be able to improvise and find new solutions in response to unexpected changes, impart confidence in their own ability to solve problems in difficult situations, and motivate all members of the organization to cooperate. For learning-oriented assignments, in contrast, relationship abilities and cultural awareness may be more important, as these are the keys to accessing new knowledge.

How do international companies respond to these recommendations? The emphasis is clearly on enlarging the pool of potential candidates for international assignments beyond persons from the home country of the multinational and on making sure that the international track attracts those with the best potential to succeed in the firm. Assessments for international assignment are becoming closely linked to the overall evaluation of an employee's potential and are also increasingly rigorous.

ASSESSMENT TOOLS. So far, only a minority of multinationals rely on any kind of standardized tests and evaluations, including psychological profiling, cultural proficiency tests, or family readiness evaluations;[81] but there is no shortage of expatriate selection tools for companies interested in formal assessment methods, though not all are well validated. Some desirable expatriate traits, such as intercultural adaptability and willingness to communicate, can be assessed using standard psychometric tests. Some companies use formal assessments to evaluate candidates only after they have been identified for an international assignment; others screen all college graduates for future success as "global managers."

When formal assessment is used, it is argued that it should not be applied to screening out unsuitable candidates.[82] Instead, the results should provide the employee with objective feedback. This allows the potential expatriate (and family) to consider carefully all the factors that may influence the success of the assignment, to consult experts on how to deal with problematic areas, or to decline the assignment.

However, by far the most common selection method is simply to interview the potential candidate. Appropriately structured interview techniques can increase effectiveness.[83] For instance, Nokia involves cross-cultural psychologists in interviews during the selection process. Ideally, people from the intended host unit should also be involved.

Many experienced international firms send potential expatriates on a preassignment orientation visit. This helps the local hosts to evaluate the candidate's fit with the environment, and the candidate can review the job and location before agreeing. These visits can preempt costly surprises later, and may be valuable even after both sides agree to the assignment. Free time with the family will be needed on arrival, before starting the new job. This minimizes the stress of dividing attention between family and work during the demanding period of settling into a new job and getting to know colleagues and the customer network.

WHAT ABOUT THE FAMILY? Family considerations have a critical impact on an individual's willingness to relocate and the outcome of the assignment. The decisions of American managers to relocate were found to be influenced by their spouses' feelings about international relocation, by their own attitudes toward moving in general, by the number of children at home, and by the employer's transfer policies. One of the major reasons why people are reluctant to relocate is their children's schooling.[84]

Virtually all research studies highlight the importance of family well-being, including spouse and children. The lack of consideration of this, in Western cultures at least, emerges as one of the most significant explanations of expatriate failure.[85] The stress of a new job in a new culture, combined with stress on the family front, puts people under intense pressure, and the likelihood of effective adjustment is greatly reduced.

The implication? Whenever possible, select a family, not a person. Not surprisingly, a number of international firms involve the candidate's spouse, if not the whole family, in the process of assessment and counseling, particularly in predeparture training.[86]

Research shows that when firms actively seek spouses' opinions of the assignment, they are more likely to adjust to living in the new culture.[87] "Buying off" the family to gain acceptance can be short-sighted, as a temporary increase in standard of living can make a successful repatriation more difficult.

IS IT OK TO SAY NO? We have pointed out that a properly executed assessment can provide a candidate with feedback before making the final decision on whether to accept the assignment.[88] But what happens if the potential expatriate declines the offer?

The answer varies across firms. In some, where management considers international mobility an integral part of the employment relationship, a refusal could mean the end of a promising career. For junior staff in some international British firms, or in Japan in the not-so-distant past, expatriate assignments were an inherent component of executive development—the issue was not if, but when.[89] Tales of hardships endured when the boss called on the second day of the honeymoon were part of the lore. However, it is important to note that these expectations were clearly communicated to staff before they joined the company.

There is a strong case to be made for the principle that an individual should not be penalized for declining a job, especially if acceptance would involve perceived hardship for the family. Lack of commitment or desire to work internationally only increases the likelihood of failure. However, since companies try to ensure that senior executives have international experience, some degree of international mobility is fast becoming a necessary prerequisite for career success.

Preparing for an Assignment

There is strong agreement about the need to invest in thorough training and predeparture orientation in both the academic and practitioner literature.[90] Early planning and training are important for the growing number of companies where international experience is a key component in management development.[91] Offering predeparture and arrival support is also a good way to show that the company cares about expatriates and their families.

Insufficient commitment to expatriate training and development is one of the most common criticisms leveled at HR practice in multinational companies. Surveys indicate that most companies offer some kind of cross-cultural training to at least some expatriates and their spouses. According to the 2008 GMAC survey, 39 percent of the companies offered cross-cultural training for all assignments, 45 percent for some, and 59 percent for certain countries only. Training programs are more often organized for expatriates from the parent company than for people from other countries.[92] Furthermore, the programs are seldom mandatory; in reality, many expatriates receive no predeparture training.

Let us focus on certain important questions about expatriate training and development. What kind of expatriate training is desirable? When should training take place? Is language competence essential? And again, what about the expatriate's family?

WHAT KIND OF TRAINING? Expatriate training has long focused on cross-cultural issues—the greater the cultural distance from the host country and the more social interaction the job involves, the more important this is.[93] Today there are abundant training tools in this domain, including cultural briefings, books, videos, case studies, cross-cultural simulations, and Web sites. But not all preparation takes place in a classroom—there are preassignment visits, "shadowing" visits while the soon-to-be expatriate is still in his or her previous job, coaching by an experienced manager, and open dialogue on key issues that emerge during the selection process.[94]

The right kind of cross-cultural training is important; a poor program can have a negative impact on expatriate adjustment and performance if it strengthens cultural stereotypes. No one training methodology will be universally appropriate—the preparation for a European plant manager who is to be dispatched to China is bound to be different from that of a Japanese bank trainee on the way to New York. The training should be customized to match the needs of the expatriates and their families.

WHEN SHOULD TRAINING TAKE PLACE? Some companies start this process a long time before departure, to ensure thorough preparation.[95] Others argue persuasively that training about the host culture is best linked to the expatriate's experience and conducted after the assignment begins: the predeparture orientation is kept brief and practical, and more complex cultural issues are left for later. Early training may build stereotypes, whereas real assimilation involves understanding the subtle differences within a culture, something that comes only with experience. However, from a practical viewpoint many expatriates, especially those in executive positions, are too busy to attend a formal training program after the start of their assignments. Individual real-time coaching may be the best solution, albeit an expensive one.[96] Without company commitment and a specific training plan built into the workload, it will be difficult to find time for any formal learning during the assignment.

Some multinationals involve the receiving subsidiary in supporting newly arrived expatriates. Intel has a "buddy system," where local peers are appointed as ad hoc trainers and cross-cultural interpreters for their foreign colleagues. The company also offers training to managers who are about to receive an expatriate.[97] Expatriates who have access to host country mentors have demonstrated greater adjustment to their work and greater interaction with host country nationals.[98]

IS LANGUAGE COMPETENCE ESSENTIAL? Everyone would agree that knowledge of the local language is beneficial—but is it a "must," desirable, or not essential? The answer depends on the nature of the job. English is rapidly becoming the company language for many expatriate jobs that are focused on internal cross-border control and coordination. Local language proficiency may not be as critical for those assignments. However, when the assignment requires extensive interaction with local customers or local employees who may not speak English or any other global "office language," the ability to speak the local language may be essential.

Accumulated research evidence suggests that language fluency helps expatriates develop interpersonal relationships and adjust to living overseas. However, no clear relationship has been found between language ability and work adjustment with the notable exception of nonnative English-speaking expatriates on assignments in English-speaking countries.[99]

Our own experience suggests an additional dimension to the language issue. Often the effort and commitment shown by expatriates in trying to learn and use the local language counts for far more than their proficiency in it. An effort to learn shows respect for the local culture, and that is appreciated anywhere in the world.

PREPARING THE FAMILY. The expatriate's family, or at least the spouse, deserves the same attention and preparation as the expatriate. The spouse is typically more exposed to the local culture than the expatriate, and learning the local language may be even more important for him or her. Again, learning opportunities after the start of the assignment may be more valuable than predeparture training, especially as the spouse is unlikely to have the same immediate job constraints.

Adjusting to the Expatriate Role

When people move to an unfamiliar environment they have to learn to adjust to new behaviors, norms, values, and assumptions. Most people are familiar with the notion of *culture shock.* Although individual experiences vary, this is fairly often a U-shaped process of adjustment in which an initial honeymoon stage of excitement, stress, and adventure leads to a depressive downswing, a phase of shock, frustration, and uncertainty about how to behave. Ideally, this heralds an upswing of learning and adaptation. Digging further into culture shock, Black and others have spelled out three dimensions of cross-cultural adjustment (defined as the degree of psychological comfort associated with living and working in the host country)—adjustment to work, general adjustment, and interaction adjustment.[100]

The first dimension is *adjustment to work* in the new environment. If the job is unclear, if there is inherent conflict in the role, and if there is little discretion in the work, adjustment is likely to be difficult. Some companies schedule an overlap with the outgoing jobholder to ease some of these strains. In the globally integrated firm, adjustment to work may be the easiest aspect of adjustment, because of similarities in procedures, policies, and tasks across the firm.

The second dimension is *adjustment to the general environment*—reactions to housing, safety, food, education, transportation, and health conditions. These difficulties increase with cultural distance. Companies try to minimize the problems through housing and educational allowances. Previous international experience, effective preparation for both expatriate and family, and spending time with other expatriates before the assignment may facilitate this aspect of adjustment.

The challenge of *adjustment to interaction with local nationals* is generally the most difficult for the expatriate and the family. Behavioral norms, patterns of communication, ways of dealing with conflict, and other aspects of relationships may be different in the new culture, creating frustration or even anger, which may in turn be counterproductive. Each individual's adjustment is linked to the quality of the support network inside the host country, as well as to time spent with other expatriates before the assignment and to links with the home office.

Family adjustment matters. To facilitate this, Honda has "family centers" in Ohio and Tokyo to help with the cultural adaptation process. In addition, families of American employees transferred to Japan are "adopted" by Japanese families with similar characteristics (for example, children of the same age). Mentors, who will keep the expatriate informed of changes in the home organization, are assigned to each expatriate before departure.

These adaptation challenges are greatly helped by investment in predeparture feedback and training. Nevertheless, there are limits to what an organization can do. Much depends on the expatriate's personality, motivation to be transferred abroad, and willingness to learn from the new environment. The ultimate indication of cross-cultural adjustment is the ability to feel at home in a foreign culture without rejecting one's own roots.[101]

BALANCING MULTIPLE ALLEGIANCES. One element of the adjustment process is finding the right balance between potentially conflicting allegiances to the parent firm and to the foreign operation. Black and his colleagues have outlined four generic patterns of expatriate commitment: free agents, those who leave their hearts at home, those who go native, and those with dual allegiances (see Figure 4–2).[102]

Free agents are marked by low allegiance to both the parent and the local firm. They are committed to their careers. They do not expect to return home, either because they understand that their careers in the parent firm have already reached a plateau, or because they see their international experience as increasing their value on the external market. Some free agents may do fine in an isolated affiliate, and companies undergoing rapid internationalization may need

FIGURE 4–2 **The Dual Allegiance of Expatriates**

	Low	High
Low	Expatriates who see themselves as **FREE AGENTS**	Expatriates who leave their **HEARTS AT HOME**
High	Expatriates who **"GO NATIVE"**	Expatriates who see themselves as **DUAL CITIZENS**

Allegiance to local firm (vertical axis: Low, High)

Allegiance to parent firm (horizontal axis: Low, High)

Source: Adapted from S. Black, H. Gregersen, and M. Mendenhall, *Global Assignments: Successfully Expatriating and Repatriating International Managers* (San Francisco: Jossey-Bass, 1992).

such hired guns. As a rule, however, their lack of commitment quickly becomes transparent to local staff, diminishing their credibility.

Another group of expatriates—usually those with long tenure in the parent firm and little previous international experience—*leave their hearts at home*, remaining emotionally attached to the parent firm with little allegiance to local operations. This attitude is reinforced by discomfort with the local culture and strong networks with senior executives back home. Their behavior is often ethnocentric, which may antagonize employees or customers, although their ability to work easily with headquarters may make them valuable in situations when close global coordination is required. This group can benefit most from cross-cultural training and other tools facilitating adjustment.

Some expatriates exhibit the opposite pattern and *go native*, building a strong identification with the local firm and culture. They are difficult to repatriate, often preferring to leave the firm and remain in their new home. The parent office finds it difficult to get their cooperation for the implementation of corporate policies and programs. They do not fit well into a meganational firm, though they may thrive in a multidomestic organization, capitalizing on their ability to build trust and support with local employees and stakeholders.

Obviously, the ideal outcome would be to develop expatriates who have *dual allegiance*, although research shows that this is the exception rather than the rule.[103] Expatriates who see themselves as "dual citizens" feel a responsibility to serve the interest of both parties. They deal effectively with the local environment, but they are also responsive to the needs of the parent firm, facilitating the coordination of global initiatives. The work environment—role clarity, job discretion, and a manageable degree of role conflict—is critical to the development of dual citizens. Role clarity and job discretion can be addressed through appropriate job design; manageable role conflict is closely linked to implementation of an effective expatriate performance management system.

Expatriate Performance Management and Rewards

Performance management of expatriates is a critical HRM process that can facilitate (or hinder) global integration by linking local business goals and appraisal to global objectives and standards. Performance management can also be a tool for lateral coordination across units. Decisions on how expatriates should be appraised and rewarded can make a big impact on effectiveness of global integration—not to mention the cost.

At a corporate HR conference in the United States in the early 1990s, one of the presenters commented that most international HR professionals devoted about 90 percent of their time to expatriate issues—and 70 percent of that to compensation. Today the emphasis of international HR has changed dramatically, and many administrative issues concerning expatriate compensation are now handled by specialized external providers. However, there are still complex issues concerning reward strategies for international staff that require careful attention from the HR policy makers at the top of the HR organization. We will discuss these when reviewing performance management in multinationals in Chapter 9.

Repatriation and Reentry

Most expatriates from the home office eventually return home. However, coming home is not necessarily easy. It can be a complex process of renegotiating one's identity, rebuilding professional networks, and reanchoring one's career in the organization.[104] Many expatriates find it particularly difficult to give up the autonomy and freedom they have enjoyed on their international assignments. Even more frustrating are "make-work" assignments, doled out to returnees who are stuck in a holding pattern while waiting for a real job opportunity to open up.

Empirical research with German and Japanese expatriates suggests that the most troublesome expatriation problems originate in poor career management systems and impaired relations with headquarters, rather than adjustment to the foreign culture.[105] Further, a growing number of corporations fail to guarantee a job in the home organization at the end of a foreign assignment.[106]

When all this is combined with the loss of social status and financial benefits associated with expatriation,[107] it is no surprise that many observers argue that the shock of coming home may be even greater than the challenges associated with the initial expatriation.[108] Available data point to a high turnover of employees after their return from international assignments. One survey put the turnover among repatriates at 35 percent in the first year after reentry, compared to 15 percent turnover during the whole assignment and 10 percent among corporate employees in general.[109] Turnover of these proportions not only means loss of the investment the corporation made in developing the expatriate; it can also create a vicious circle, increasing resistance to expatriation and to the firm's ability to implement a strategy of global integration.

As with data on expatriate "failure," however, there are reasons to be conservative about the scope of the problem. Any job transition is stressful, even within the home country.[110] Further, research indicates that a growing number of international assignees view their international work experience as an investment in their own competence and value in the external labor market,[111] so retaining them at the end of their assignment may be a tall order. Nevertheless, multinationals can do more, at relatively low cost, to improve the probability of success.

The best repatriation practices emphasize advance planning to provide real opportunities on return, emotional and logistical support during the transition, and continuous dialogue with expatriates through formal or informal networking or mentoring programs.[112] In these firms, career managers or advisers monitor the expatriates' development throughout their assignments, keep them informed, and serve as advocates for the expatriates during the home country succession planning process.

Some companies fix an end date to foreign assignments to facilitate succession and repatriation planning. Another policy that is frequently applied is to require the dispatching unit to take formal responsibility for finding a position for the expatriate comparable to the one s/he left. However, returning after an absence of three to four years, the repatriate may actually face demotion, the fate of a surprisingly large number of returnees.[113]

Our experiences with a number of multinational firms suggest two observations on how to increase the odds of successful repatriation. First, seeing is believing. If most senior executives have international experience, this demonstrates the value of expatriation and eases worry about repatriation. Second, the best predictor of successful repatriation is the performance of expatriates before their international assignments. Employees with an outstanding track record before their assignment will usually be easier to place in a good job on their return.[114]

Finally, regardless of the quality of the corporation's expatriate management system, we advise expatriates to be proactive in maintaining good contacts with managers at headquarters and other parts of the organization. Changes take place swiftly and unpredictably in today's corporations, and it is impossible for the HR function to plan for all contingencies. Personal connections may often be crucial for identifying satisfactory job opportunities at the end of an international assignment.

A Summary of Practices Supporting Effective Expatriation

Table 4–4 summarizes a number of key themes[115] relating to practices that support effective expatriation. Although the suggestions are presented separately for each part of the expatriation cycle, it is also important to bear in mind the links between the different parts.

TABLE 4–4. Human Resource Practices That Support Effective Expatriation

Staffing and Selection

- Communicate the value of international assignments for the company's global mission.
- Ensure that those with the highest potential move internationally.
- Provide short-term assignments to increase the pool of employees with international experience.
- Recruit employees who have lived or who were educated abroad.

Training and Career Development

- Make international assignment planning a part of the career development process.
- Encourage early international experience.
- Create learning opportunities during the assignment.
- Use international assignments as a leadership development tool.

Performance Appraisal and Compensation

- Differentiate performance management based on expatriate roles.
- Align incentives with expatriation objectives.
- Tailor benefits to the expatriate's needs.
- Focus on equality of opportunities, not cash.
- Emphasize rewarding careers rather than short-term outcomes.

Expatriation and Repatriation Activities

- Involve the family in the orientation program at the beginning and the end of the assignment.
- Establish mentor relationships between expatriates and executives from the home location.
- Provide support for dual careers.
- Secure opportunities for the returning manager to use knowledge and skills learned while on the international assignment.

BEYOND THE TRADITIONAL EXPATRIATE MODEL

Few firms launch their international expansion without at least a small core of expatriates. However, as companies pursue internationalization, the inevitable tensions of expatriation become apparent. These tensions, together with the changing demographics of the expatriate population, are changing the ways in which companies approach international assignments.

The Tensions in the Expatriate Cycle

Five types of tension are common to most expatriate situations.

Home/Host Tensions

For a number of reasons, the presence of expatriates may generate tensions with the local environment. Expatriates who are well socialized in the ways of the parent company are often insensitive to local cultural norms. They often enjoy a standard of living that is not available to local employees, which may create resentment; and they may be costly compared with the value they are seen as bringing to the local business.[116] Host government officials and regulators may also prefer to interface with locals, whom they view as more loyal to host country interests.

Global/Local Tensions

When top positions in a subsidiary are continuously occupied by rotating expatriates, capable local managers may become discouraged due to lack of opportunities to advance their careers. Either they leave or their willingness to make an effort on behalf of the firm slackens. Over time, these disadvantages may offset the benefits of an expatriate presence—the simple control structure, ease of communication with headquarters, and improved coordination with other corporate units. In addition, as foreign operations increase in size, intimate knowledge of local operations may become as important as communication and coordination with the headquarters.

Short-Term/Long-Term Tensions

Expatriates are often criticized for making short-term decisions since their perspective may be limited by the duration of their assignment. They may shrink from difficult but necessary actions to secure long-term benefits. In one such case, a poorly negotiated initial labor contract in the subsidiary of a foreign airline in Japan has inflated its labor cost relative to competitors for years. Renegotiating the contract, to align it with the existing practice in the industry and generate future savings, would be costly in the short term and would risk triggering a strike by the company union. So far, no one in a long line of expatriate executives has been willing to take the risk "on their watch."

Conversely, newly appointed expatriates often experience a heady sense of freedom to make decisions that will attract the attention of the head office and promote their careers—in effect change for the sake of change. On a European Web site frequented by employees of a US subsidiary, one fast-track expatriate was defined as someone who "can outrun his mistakes."

Tension between Cost and Investment

The considerable expense associated with expatriation is often viewed as the cost of market entry, to be reduced, if not eliminated, in the long run. Indeed, the need to reduce the costs of expatriation is often one of the drivers of localization. Yet while companies can benefit from smarter management of expatriate costs, the expense of expatriation can be seen as an essential investment in building the links necessary for managing a transnational firm and learning across organizational boundaries.[117] A cost-driven expatriation strategy can lead to "boom–bust" swings. The number of expatriates increases in good times, only to be cut when growth slows and recession looms, creating havoc and imbalance in the local organization.

Demand/Supply Tensions

The accelerating pace of internationalization has increased the demand for experienced and capable expatriate managers. However, constraints on international mobility are also increasing, many of them stemming from family considerations and changing career expectations.[118] Employees are increasingly reluctant to move abroad if moving will handicap their children's educational opportunities or mean that spouses have to put their careers on hold. The care of elderly parents is also a growing concern. In a competitive environment, good people everywhere have alternative employment options.

Changing Demographics of the Expatriate Population

Traditionally, policies and practices governing international assignments were built on a number of assumptions about expatriate characteristics:

- Expatriates were selected from the employees in the parent country.
- The expatriate population was homogeneous in ethnicity, gender, and experience—home country, male, experienced, possibly married but with an adaptable spouse.
- Expatriate assignments were temporary (three to four years' duration), often occurring only once during a career.
- The objective of the assignment was to maintain control over the affiliate and to transfer know-how from the sophisticated parent to the subsidiary.
- After completion of the assignment, an expatriate was expected to return home, to be replaced by another expatriate.

Today, these assumptions are less and less valid. The expatriate population is increasingly heterogeneous, and a contingent approach to expatriation is needed.[119] In a number of multinationals, the prototypical experienced male executive from the parent country is already in a minority. Because of the growing use of expatriation as a tool for learning and development, many expatriates are relatively young. And as companies throughout the world are removing obstacles to gender diversity in management, an increasing proportion of expatriates are women.

Female Expatriates

Although international experience is seen as one of the critical foundations for developing future leaders, until the late 1980s only 5 percent of all American expatriates were women. According to some recent surveys, this proportion has increased to about 20 percent in European and North American multinationals.[120]

A number of explanations for the small number of female expatriates have been proposed: cultural prejudices, including low acceptance of working women in certain countries; lack of support and access to male-dominated expatriate networks; inflexibility and resentment by male peers; particular difficulties linked to family and dual-career issues; and the unwillingness of women to accept foreign assignments.[121] Adler identified "three common myths" about female expatriates:[122]

- Women do not want to become international managers.
- Companies refuse to send women overseas.
- Even when women are interested in international assignments, the prejudices of foreigners against women may render them ineffective.

Exploration of these "myths" stimulated a number of studies of female expatriates, particularly in the US and Europe.[123] One stream of research focuses on *the desire of women to become expatriates.* Examining responses from more than 1,000 students from multiple universities, Adler concluded that male and female students displayed no differences in their interest in pursuing international careers.[124] Similar results were observed in a more recent study.[125] However, there is also some evidence of differences in the willingness of males and females to accept foreign assignments to culturally distant and less developed locations.[126]

With respect to *willingness to select female expatriates*, Adler concluded that 70 percent of HR professionals in 60 multinational companies were hesitant to choose women.[127] Among the reasons presented were difficulties in accommodating dual careers and gender prejudice in the countries to which women would be sent. It has also been argued that qualified female employees may be overlooked because men make most of the decisions about whom to send, and many hold traditional stereotypes about women in international jobs.[128] However, a more recent study of US and Canadian firms did not support Adler's findings, and more research on this myth is needed.

Several studies have focused on the *adjustment and performance of female expatriates.* Female American expatriates were found to be just as successful as their counterparts overseas—even in so-called male-dominated cultures such as Japan and Korea.[129] Other results suggest that male and female expatriates can perform equally well in international assignments regardless of the host country's predisposition to women in management, but that female expatriates self-rate their adjustment lower in countries with few women in the workforce.[130] Female expatriates were perceived as effective regardless of the cultural toughness of the host country.[131]

However, there is some evidence that it is more difficult for women to reconcile international assignments with the careers of their spouses. Companies with a high number of female expatriates are more likely to report problems resulting from the inability of spouses to continue their careers.[132] Not surprisingly, therefore, a much higher percentage of women on international assignments are single—approximately 45 percent in the 2009 Brookfield survey, compared to about 25 percent of the men.[133]

Some studies have pointed out that women may actually have an advantage over men as expatriates. For example, until more women take over expatriate roles, their relative visibility and novelty may enhance their access to local business networks.[134] Tung has argued that women tend to possess attributes that make them more suitable for overseas work than men, such as indirectness in communication, good listening skills, and emphasis on cooperation over competition.[135] Also, because female executives have long experience of being "outsiders," they may be better equipped to manage the stress that often accompanies isolation in foreign settings.

Dual-Career Considerations

Research shows that female expatriates are more likely to be single than their male colleagues. This may be because female managers are more likely than male managers to have working partners, and so may be more constrained by dual careers. Often there are no available jobs for spouses at the new location, a situation aggravated by the obstacles like visa regulations, professional licensing rules, and language barriers. And even if a job is available locally, it may not contribute to a meaningful career, reducing the likelihood that the couple will be willing to move.

How can companies respond to this challenge? Multinational firms can use a number of steps to mediate the pressure of dual careers:

- Plan the assignment in terms of location, timing, and duration based on professional preferences and personal circumstances of the couple.
- Approach the partner's employer and jointly prepare expatriation plans.
- Provide career counseling and assistance in locating employment opportunities for spouses abroad.
- Subsidize educational programs for spouses while abroad.
- Support entrepreneurial initiatives by spouses.
- Cooperate with other multinational organizations in finding jobs for spouses.
- Provide reemployment advice to partners after repatriation.

None of these are silver bullets that will solve every problem but in most cases, even modest progress in reducing barriers to mobility will have a positive impact on the pool of future global managers.

Younger Expatriates

The issue of dual careers is often easier to manage among younger expatriates. Their partners (if any) may be more flexible about job opportunities in the local market, as they risk less by taking an international career detour. Placing younger employees who are single or who have small families in international jobs can substantially reduce the total compensation cost; the expenses involved in family expatriation (housing, education, and home leave) can easily surpass the salary cost at lower professional levels.

This point is important because the aim behind international assignments is shifting from demand-driven to learning-driven objectives, as discussed earlier. Instead of a focus on control, knowledge transfer, or problem solving, assignments are increasingly aimed at the development of organizational and individual competence and furthering the career development of the expatriate.[136] These learning assignments are naturally suited to younger employees.[137]

Third-Country Nationals

Expatriates from countries other than the parent country of the multinational are commonly referred to as third-country nationals (TCNs). Historically, two factors drive TCN employment: the scarcity in the home country of suitable candidates for international assignments, and attempts to hold down the cost of expatriation. For example, a US multinational may seek to employ expatriates from the United Kingdom, Canada, and Australia, countries with a common language and comparable compensation and living standards, but no double taxation on expatriate income.

With accelerating globalization, companies today are simply looking for the most suitable candidate, irrespective of country of origin, and so the proportion of TCNs in the expatriate population is increasing. For example, at HSBC the cohort of senior international managers—people expected to move globally—included 380 managers from 33 countries. Half of the latest intake were women.[138]

Repatriation of TCNs often creates acute dilemmas. Even with the best career planning, there may simply be no comparable position back at their foreign country home. Finishing an assignment sometimes forces an agonizing choice—to return home and leave the company, or to accept a posting in yet another country, which in turn makes the prospect of a later return even more problematic. TCNs shoulder such dilemmas, creating difficult trade-offs between career prospects and the well-being of the family.

The Changing Nature of International Assignments

With these changes in the composition of the expatriate population, conventional expatriate assignments may become the exception rather than the rule. The impact of changing demographics is accentuated by two other trends—the shorter duration of assignments and the diminishing security of expatriation.

Short-Term Assignments

Earlier, we identified short-term learning assignments as a growing type of expatriation. Many problem-solving and project assignments also have short spans, so it is not surprising that short-term transfers (less than one year in duration) are the fastest-growing type of international assignment.[139]

Short-term assignments are popular because they offer flexibility and are simpler to plan and execute. Even more important, they cost less—expensive housing and cost-of-living allowances are not necessary. Short-term assignments also facilitate repatriation to the home organization. From the employees' point of view, they need not uproot the working spouse and family. The partner may stay at home or take a short sabbatical. Many companies limit such assignments to less than six months, while longer transfers are treated as a regular international assignment.[140]

The Insecurity of Expatriation

Not only are international transfers becoming more short-term, they are also becoming less secure.[141] Expatriate postings in the past provided at least a temporary haven from the turmoil of home office reorganizations, since the terms for international assignments in most Western companies (and virtually all Japanese or Korean companies) included the guarantee of a return position.

Now, however, the pattern—in some countries at least—is changing, with fewer companies offering expatriates a guarantee of a job upon their return home. International experience may not be a career booster for all expatriates: management development assignments may indeed lead to upward mobility, but problem-solving transfers may not. In part, this reflects general changes in the employment relationship—"If we cannot guarantee jobs for people at home, how can we promise them to people abroad?" But it is also a sign that expatriate positions are not exceptional today, so companies do not see the need for special treatment.

There are mixed signals here. One message from international corporations is that international experience is an asset. But, however unintentional, another is that it may be risky for the career. There is a gap between the rhetoric and the reality. While the logic of "equal" treatment may have some merits, there is no question that employees temporarily located abroad may have substantially more difficulties in lining up alternative job opportunities at home, or at least that they may perceive this to be the case. And an increased *perception* of insecurity naturally leads to increased resistance to international mobility.

Alternatives to Expatriation

How can companies respond proactively to such tensions? With changes in the nature of expatriate jobs and the conditions of the assignment, is there a future for expatriates? There are certainly some emerging alternatives.

Global Integration without Traditional Expatriates

We already argued that short-term assignments are increasingly used as an alternative to dispatching expatriates on long-term assignments. Table 4–5 presents a number of alternatives to the traditional expatriate model.

A group of employees that has received little attention but is growing in numbers are foreigners who work overseas without having been sent out by an organization. These employees are not expatriates in the traditional sense of the term but are on *self-initiated foreign assignments*. They typically have local

TABLE 4–5. Alternatives to Traditional Long-Term Expatriate Assignments

- Short-term assignments.
- Self-initiated assignments.
- Returnee assignments.
- International commuter assignments.
- Rotational assignments.
- Virtual assignments.

employment contracts and no guarantee of remaining employed by the corporation on their return to their home country, even if that happens to be the corporation's home country.[142]

Returnees are people who have studied and maybe worked for a significant period of time abroad before returning to their home countries. For example, a large number of Chinese nationals study and work overseas before being sent by their employers on assignments to China. Are these people expatriates? Many demand and are given the benefits associated with expatriate status; some are not.

The ongoing revolution in communications is dramatically expanding the possibilities of *virtual expatriation*—assignments where employees have responsibilities abroad but manage them from the home country. Some managers with heavy international coordination responsibilities spend so much time on the road that it does not matter where these frequent flyers live. Unilever used to allow its regional managers to decide whether they would live in the parent country or the region—either way, they would be traveling a lot in the other direction.

A variation on post-expatriate management is the *international commuter*. Just as many US executives routinely commute across the continent to their jobs after every weekend, so a new generation of European managers prefers a weekly commute to relocation—for example, taking the high-speed train between Brussels and Paris. Their priority is securing a stable environment for the family, while companies benefit because of considerable cost savings and because they can expand substantially the pool of candidates for international jobs when relocation is not required. A particular category is *rotational* assignments, where the expatriate commutes to another country for a short, set period of time followed by a break in the home country.[143]

Virtuality has its limits. No amount of electronic communication can replace human contact. The cost of fewer international postings may be more short-term trips. During business downturns, companies are usually quick to issue edicts against unnecessary travel. How many times can an individual jet between continents before fatigue sets in? The wear and tear of international travel is a hidden health threat, the cost of which has yet to be calculated.[144]

Beyond the solutions afforded by new technologies, globally integrated companies are seeking new strategies for organizing their international activities. The Spanish fashion retailer Zara is a tightly integrated empire, with over 1,000 stores in more than 30 countries on three continents. In contrast with established industry logic, Zara makes two-thirds of all its clothes in the company.[145] It has its own factories in Spain and restocks stores around the world twice a week. The team of core designers in the head office continuously redesigns its products.

Zara uses expatriates only for temporary assignments in connection with start-up operations. Indeed, the company has learned that using Spanish expatriates to run local operations does not necessarily provide good results because of the diverse cultural idiosyncrasies of the host countries.[146] Zara relies instead on hiring local managers and socializing them into the corporate culture (many have some ties to Spain), and will not operate in countries in which local talent is not available.

Zara's key capabilities are in design and production processes, and the tools needed to support these capabilities in the subsidiaries can easily be transferred through formalized procedures in logistics, inventory control, marketing information systems, and centralized product design and pricing. In addition, the company resolves cross-border issues through extensive use of international management meetings and deployment of auditors from the headquarters to monitor local activities. The corporate auditors, based in Spain, perform coordination roles that are often assumed by expatriates in other firms.

Impatriation: The Next Step in Fostering Global Integration

Zara, Nokia, and many other international companies discussed in this chapter invest substantial resources in the socialization of their local managers. An important tool of this process is often a temporary assignment to the head office or parent country operations. Such foreign nationals on nonpermanent assignments in the parent country of the multinational are frequently called "impatriates."[147]

The number of impatriates is increasing worldwide. For instance, multinationals with operations in Central and Eastern Europe have a considerable number of impatriates at corporate headquarters.[148] A large number work in the United States and Europe, where there are more than 40 nationalities represented at the headquarters of some major multinationals such as Nestlé and Shell. Only in Japan and Korea is the number of impatriates small.

Most impatriates are young employees or middle managers who come to the parent organization for developmental assignments, to absorb the corporate culture, or to participate in project teams. Some come with the explicit aim of preparing themselves to replace expatriates; others stay and join the home organization on a semipermanent or permanent basis.

What kinds of HR policies are best suited to support impatriation? Are typical expatriate policies suitable for impatriates? Are there differences between impatriates and expatriates that would argue for different HR approaches? The situations facing expatriates and impatriates may be similar, but they are not the same. Most impatriates are assigned for learning reasons; very few are corporate agents. In terms of national origin, they are more heterogeneous than expatriates, so defining one-size-fits-all policies is fraught with difficulties.

Communication is often a major constraint for impatriates. Employees in foreign locations are generally used to interacting with expatriates. They choose to work for a foreign-based firm, and they expect to see foreigners around. The office language is usually the language of the expatriate, and the locals have to adapt. Not so in the home office, where communication problems with impatriates are often unexpected, and sensitivity to communication difficulties on both sides is required. Indeed, HR may have to support impatriation through cross-cultural training—for the locals.

A British manager relocated to the head office in the American Midwest experienced an initial warm welcome, but then social interactions with coworkers cooled off. He felt frozen out. Sharing his concerns with the HR manager, he learned that the locals were upset with his perceived "selfish" values—putting his career ahead of his family, as demonstrated by his leaving two young children behind at boarding school in England. Of course, this was before Harry Potter!

Some companies simply treat their impatriates as local staff, integrating them into the home office compensation and benefits programs. They do not provide foreign service premiums, housing support, or related benefits to their impatriates, assuming that the corporate headquarters is the center of the universe. If the impatriates are expected to remain permanently in the parent country, this may be the most sensible approach. But for temporary transfers, it may be better to treat impatriates in the same way as home country expatriates on learning assignments are treated, with a degree of support appropriate to the expected length of stay.[149]

As the number of expatriates continues to increase, there is an emerging trend to treat people transferred across borders in the same way, at least in principle. Some companies have developed global transfer policies that cover everyone regardless of country of origin. The terms are determined by the purpose of the assignment, its duration, and the career circumstances.

THE LIMITS OF GLOBAL INTEGRATION

Nokia had been considered a good employer worldwide, with a nurturing and empowering culture that created excellent opportunities to learn and grow. But more and more local employees perceived the company as providing only limited career opportunities since the majority of "good" jobs were filled by expatriates—most of them from Finland. Retaining the best local talent began to be a problem, requiring the firm to rethink its approach to global HR management. From the mid-1990s, the number of TCNs and impatriates increased rapidly, and as we mentioned in the opening case, the company has also appointed several non-Finns to the top management team.

But realigning the staffing policies was perhaps the easy part. One weakness of global integration strategies is the potentially negative impact on the firm's ability to be responsive to the local needs and demands of customers, host governments, or local employees. For example, as Nokia continued to grow globally, new organizational challenges emerged, especially in its infrastructure business. While the company had mainly offered universal GSM technology based on global standards, customers now began to demand specific solutions fitting local needs, which required extensive customization.

As the market expanded beyond the traditional operations, Nokia was expected not only to provide equipment but also to manage the whole project of installment and start-up on a turnkey basis. With increased complexity, the coordination demands on the Nokia organization increased dramatically. This required a new set of skills that had to be shared across the whole organization. And where Nokia had acted alone before, the rapid evolution of technology now required engagement in multiple partnerships, involving extensive coordination. The old approach of global integration that had proven so successful during the first decade of global expansion began to outlive its usefulness.

Nokia's recent experience points to the importance of balancing global integration and local responsiveness. However, the challenge for the multinational is not only how to deal with the ubiquitous challenge of being locally responsive *and* globally integrated; it must also be proficient in *coordinating* its lateral international operations. The next part of the book will discuss how to address the latter challenge from a people management perspective.

TAKEAWAYS

1. Global integration means that decisions are made from a global perspective—in the extreme, the meganational firm operates as if the world were a single market.
2. The *control* mechanisms supporting global integration can be classified into four types: personal control through decision making; procedural control through formalization and standardization; output control through achieving agreed results; and normative control through corporate values, beliefs, and norms.
3. Global standardization of HR practices is associated with a number of advantages, including subsidiary control, international transfer of best practices, and scale advantages in the global HR function.
4. There are two types of international assignments—demand-driven and learning-driven. The former are driven primarily by corporate agency requirements (control and knowledge transfer) or by problem-solving needs; the latter focus on individual and organizational competence and career development.
5. Making an expatriate assignment successful for the individual, the family, and the firm demands attention to many factors, from initial selection until repatriation. A starting point is recognizing that expatriation is a process, not an event.
6. The personal traits and skills needed by expatriates depend on the roles they are expected to assume. Professional and leadership skills are the foundation for agency-type assignments. In contrast, relationship abilities and cultural awareness may be more important for learning-oriented assignments.
7. It is important to understand the factors influencing intercultural adjustment and expatriate work performance—adjustment to work, to the general environment abroad, and (most difficult of all) to interaction with the local environment.

8. Family well-being is a critical element in expatriate effectiveness. The inability of the family to adjust to the new country is often the reason for assignment failure. Dual-career couples are also more likely to experience stress in international assignments because of the expected negative effects of a career interruption.

9. Tensions embedded in the expatriation process, together with the changing demographics of the expatriate population—the growing number of women, third-country nationals, younger expatriates, impatriates, dual-career families—are changing the way in which companies approach international assignments.

10. With the growing complexity of business, global integration strategies may have a negative impact on the firm's ability to be responsive to the local needs and demands of customers, host governments, or employees.

NOTES

1. www.nokia.com.
2. Doornik and Roberts, 2001.
3. "The King of Nokia: Jorma Ollila." Reported in *The City* (tourist newspaper), Helsinki, August 2000.
4. Doornik and Roberts, 2001.
5. Doz and Kosonen, 2008.
6. We prefer the term "meganational firm" to Bartlett and Ghoshal's "global firm" (1989). "Global" may be confusing because of the generic nature of the word; as suggested in Chapter 1, it is a word that has many meanings.
7. J. Fox, "Nokia's Secret Code," *Fortune*, May 1, 2000.
8. Nohria and Ghoshal (1997) do find empirical support for the match between industry and structural fit. Scientific measurement instruments, cement products, industrial chemicals, aircraft engines, and mining machinery are among the industries that are traditionally globally integrated.
9. Segal-Horn and Dean, 2008. The automotive industry is another example of a business in which suppliers must be able to serve their customers globally.
10. Pucik, Hanada, and Fifield, 1989; Kopp, 1994; Yoshihara, 1999.
11. Prahalad and Doz, 1987, p. 160.
12. Economists view the market as the prime mechanism of control over transactions, since the market price contains all the information that an individual needs to decide whether or not to enter into a transaction. Coase (1937) asked why transactions are not all performed by markets—why do organizations exist? Williamson (1975) developed his influential transaction cost theory to address this question, essentially arguing that since the rationality of human behavior is bounded or limited, organizations have advantages over markets as control mechanisms under conditions of high uncertainty and complexity (and also under conditions of high asset specificity and high transaction frequency).
13. See Galbraith (1977), Lawrence and Lorsch (1967), Mintzberg (1989), Martinez and Jarillo (1989), and Harzing (1999).
14. Organizational theorists typically see control and coordination as the same in principle, and there is often some confusion around terminology. Both are means to

achieve organizational goals. Harzing summarizes the literature by saying that "control is a means to achieve an end called coordination, which in turn leads toward the achievement of common organization goals" (Harzing, 1999, p. 9).

15. The terms "control" and "coordination" were explained in Chapter 1.

16. The classification we use is largely drawn from Harzing (1999), who reviews the literature on control mechanisms.

17. Standardization is a prerequisite for formal control, as it is nearly impossible to formalize work processes that are not standardized.

18. One study of diversified corporations identified three different approaches to output control (Goold and Campbell, 1987). In "financial control" companies, objectives are set in terms of financial performance. In "strategic control" firms, objectives cover longer-term strategic objectives and annual financial targets. In "strategic planning" firms, there is far more emphasis on the planning process, driven by the intention to develop bold strategies. Objectives blend both short-term financial targets and long-term strategic aims.

19. As Brewster (1991, p. 33) comments, "For the key managerial postings, at least, it is clear that management in these organizations trust their 'own' people to operate as they are required to do, more than they trust the locals they employ."

20. Hennart, 1991.

21. Japanese subsidiaries abroad often have locals heading functions such as marketing and sales, but Japanese nationals in roles demanding close liaison with Tokyo (usually product planning and finance).

22. Egelhoff, 1988; Hennart, 1991.

23. Pucik, 1994.

24. Rudlin (2000), a former manager of a large Japanese trading company, argues that advances in information technology allow Japanese managers to increase the exclusivity of informal communication. In the past, phone conversations in Japanese were at least audible to local staff. While they may not understand, they get an idea that something is going on and follow up with questions. With one-on-one e-mail, the locals are totally excluded.

25. Harzing, 1999.

26. Kim, Park, and Prescott, 2003.

27. Studying 287 headquarters of MNCs in nine countries, Harzing (1999) found that personal control (centralization) was used more by British and German corporations than their Swiss and Swedish counterparts. The latter made much more use of normative control through socialization and building networks for mutual adjustment (controls used infrequently by French and Japanese firms with respect to their subsidiaries). Formalized control through standardization and output control was most strongly employed by UK and German firms, and least by Japanese corporations. Other studies have also found that US firms use extensive output control and Japanese firms use control through expatriates (e.g., Chang and Taylor, 1999).

28. Chung, Gibbons, and Schoch, 2006.

29. Schlesinger and Heskett, 1991.

30. www.mcdonalds.com/corp/about/factsheets.

31. The company's legendary founder, Ray Kroc, recognized the power of training. "Hamburger University" (HU) was started in 1961 in Oak Brook, Illinois, only six years after Kroc acquired the business from the McDonald brothers. By 1999, the school had trained more than 65,000 "bachelors of hamburgerology," adding new graduates at the rate of 7,000 per year. Equipped with state-of-the-art technology, it

is part business school, part technical workshop, but mostly a teacher training college. Its students are mainly operating managers with at least 2,000 hours of prior local training, and their mission is to go forth and teach others at home. Thirty resident professors at HU teach courses on store management, team-building skills, staffing and retaining crew, sales growth strategies, business planning, and most importantly McDonald's global operation standards ("Face Value: The Burger King," *The Economist*, October 23, 1999). McDonald's annual training budget exceeds US$1 billion.

32. On June 2, 2009, IKEA had 297 stores in 36 countries/territories.

33. Comparative studies of multinationals from different parts of the world have found US corporations to have the highest degree of global standardization of their HR practices (Harzing, 1999; Björkman and Lu, 2001; Ferner et al., 2004).

34. Farndale and Paauwe, 2007.

35. Almond, Edwards, and Clark, 2003.

36. Zaheer, 1995.

37. Taylor, Beechler, and Napier, 1996.

38. Kogut and Zander, 1993.

39. Almond, Edwards, and Clark, 2003.

40. See, for example, Kostova and Roth (2002), Paauwe (2004), Rosenzweig (2006), and Farndale and Paauwe (2007) for discussions of the pressures on multinationals to pursue both global standardization and local responsiveness of HR practices.

41. Ferner, Almond, and Colling, 2005.

42. Kostova, 1999; Kostova and Roth, 2002. A third element, beyond the implementation and internalization of practices, is their integration with other relevant and related subsidiary practices (see Björkman and Lervik, 2007). The integration of practices refers to the links and connections that develop between the practice in question and the other established processes and practices in the subsidiary (Lervik, 2005), and is therefore another important sign of successful transfer.

43. Kostova and Roth, 2002, p. 217.

44. Meyer and Rowan, 1977; Kostova and Roth, 2002.

45. Blazejewski, 2006.

46. See Womack, Jones, and Roos, 1990; MacDuffie, 1995.

47. See Kenney and Florida, 1993; Pil and MacDuffie, 1999; Shimada and MacDuffie, 1999. For the role of Japanese expatriates in this transfer, see Peterson, Peng, and Smith (1999).

48. For the early history of this alliance, see O'Reilly and Pfeffer, 2000.

49. Adler, 1999; Pil and MacDuffie, 1999; O'Reilly and Pfeffer, 2000.

50. The small number of GM managers assigned to the joint venture seriously impeded transfer of learning back to GM. We will discuss the learning aspects of this alliance in Chapter 12.

51. O. Wyman, "The Harbour Report North America 2008"—available at http://www .reliableplant.com/article.asp?articleid.asp?articleid=12134. However, in 2009, when GM was forced to restructure under a prepackaged bankruptcy process, the company decided to withdraw from the joint venture, putting its future in doubt.

52. Jay, 1967.

53. Edström and Galbraith, 1977.

54. Other scholars, such as Hays (1974) and Tung (1981), also examined expatriation with respect to the responsibilities and positions assumed by expatriates. Integrating these various viewpoints, Derr and Oddou (1991) identified two types of expatriate: those who are assigned abroad to fix a problem, including persons in specialized functional positions; and those who go abroad as "high potentials" to broaden their

development before moving up to senior management. Harzing (2001) uses the metaphors of bears (formal direct control), bumblebees (socialization), and spiders (informal communication) in her discussion of the different roles expatriates may play.

55. Pucik, 1992. Empirical support has been found for differentiating demand-driven and learning-driven assignments—a study of 1,779 assignees found that turnover intentions varied with the nature of the assignment (Stahl et al., 2009).

56. When followed up with yet another international transfer, expatriation can become a career, a pattern not uncommon in many international firms.

57. A survey of US multinationals showed that the proportion of assignees on short-term transfers of less than 12 months increased from 5 to 16 percent between 1992 and 1998 (Solomon, 1998). The yearly Brookfield survey reported an increase in assignments planned to last less than one year from 10 percent in 2000 to 32 percent in 2008, but a drop to 18 percent in 2009—the drop probably reflecting a reluctance to support learning assignments during an economic downturn.

58. GE has estimated that 25 percent of its managers will need global assignments to gain the knowledge and experience necessary to understand the global markets, customers, suppliers, and competitors the company will face in the future (Black et al., 1999).

59. Tung, 1981; Mendenhall and Oddou, 1985; Oddou, 1991; Arthur and Bennett, 1995.

60. Baker and Ivancevich, 1971; Tung, 1981; Black, Gregersen, and Mendenhall, 1992.

61. Some researchers suggest that expatriate failure rates in European multinationals may be lower than in the United States because of more effective European expatriate policies (Brewster and Scullion, 1997), better selection (Scullion, 1995), and more emphasis on the value of international experience (Björkman and Gertsen, 1993). An alternative explanation may be that European multinationals accept lower standards of performance to avoid the loss of face involved in a premature return (Scullion, 1995).

62. Harzing, 1995. For comprehensive reviews of research on expatriate failure rates, see Harzing (1995) and Forster (1997).

63. Brookfield Global Relocation Services (2009), "Global Relocation Trends 2009 Survey Report" (www.brookfieldgrs.com).

64. Björkman and Gertsen, 1993; Forster, 1997.

65. Forster, 1997.

66. Bhaskar-Shrinivas et al., 2005.

67. For research on time to proficiency, see Waxin, Roger, and Chandon (1997).

68. Black and Gregersen, 1999.

69. Suutari and Brewster, 1999.

70. Harris and Brewster, 1999.

71. Recently a number of large multinationals have introduced open job postings on the corporate intranet. For instance, 12 of 14 US, European, and Asian firms studied by Farndale and Paauwe (2007) had such systems. Open job posting systems may create more openness in the expatriate staffing process.

72. Sparrow, 1999.

73. Yamazaki and Kayes, 2004.

74. See Pucik and Saba, 1998; Stroh et al., 2005.

75. Bhaskar-Shrinivas et al., 2005.

76. Liu and Shaffer, 2005. Wang and Nayir (2006) discuss differences in the effects of social interaction on expatriate adjustment in China and Turkey. For an informative discussion of how to improve the interaction and collaboration between expatriates and host country employees, see Toh and DeNisi (2005).

77. A meta-analysis conducted by Mol et al. (2005) found cultural sensitivity to have a sampled weighted mean correlation of 0.24 with employee performance. The corresponding figure for cultural flexibility was 0.21.
78. Bhaskar-Shrinivas et al., 2005.
79. Mol et al., 2005.
80. Bhaskar-Shrinivas et al., 2005.
81. Sixteen percent of multinationals surveyed by Aon International in 1997 used family readiness evaluations, 11 percent used psychological profile instruments, and 11 percent applied cultural proficiency tests ("No Common Thread in Expat Selection," Global Workforce, 1998, p. 9).
82. Black et al., 1999.
83. Black et al., 1999.
84. Brett and Stroh, 1995. Family concerns and spouses' careers were the most cited reasons for assignment refusals in the 2009 Brookfield survey [Brookfield Global Relocation Services (2009), "Global Relocation Trends 2009 Survey Report" (www .brookfieldgrs.com)].
85. Torbiörn, 1982; Black and Stephens, 1989; Brewster, 1991, ch. 6. However, our own work with international companies suggests that self-reported expatriate failure rates attributed to family issues may be somewhat exaggerated. We have observed several cases where the cause of the failure was poor performance or adjustment, but the explanation given was "family"—perhaps to allow the returnee to save face, or perhaps to shift the blame for an expensive selection error outside the HR department.
86. Brookfield Global Relocation Services (2009), "Global Relocation Trends 2009 Survey Report" (www.brookfieldgrs.com).
87. Black and Gregersen, 1991b.
88. See Dickmann et al. (2008) for an analysis of factors influencing the decision to accept an international assignment.
89. For example, Marks & Spencer has long had an explicit policy that all managers and high potentials have to be prepared to move home and family once a year, if needed—"If you don't like that policy, don't join us!"
90. A meta-analysis of available studies on cross-cultural training showed a positive relationship with expatriate performance (r = 0.26) and indications of a positive association with expatriate adjustment (r = 0.13) (Morris and Robie, 2001)
91. For example, Toyota provides one to three years of ongoing training for employees who may be targeted for overseas assignments, in a program called "training for overseas duties." Two types of training are offered: preparation for a US assignment and preparation for a non-English speaking country assignment.
92. Harvey, 1997.
93. Tung, 1981; Mendenhall and Oddou, 1986.
94. Harris and Brewster, 1999. See Littrell and Salas (2005) for a comprehensive review of cross-cultural training practices.
95. Preparatory training is at best only a foundation for future learning—unless it is properly designed, it can have unintended consequences. One of the early studies on expatriation to Japan (Black, 1988) showed that predeparture knowledge was negatively correlated with expatriate work adjustment—probably because the cultural stereotype of Japanese organizations presented in the standard training package did not correspond to the multifaceted reality.

96. Mendenhall and Stahl, 2000.

97. Toh and DeNisi, 2005.

98. Feldman and Bolino, 1999.

99. Bhaskar-Shrinivas et al., 2005.

100. For conceptual background, see Black, Mendenhall, and Oddou (1991). Several studies have shown that these three dimensions are independent of one another (Shaffer, Harrison, and Gilley, 1999; Cerdin and Peretti, 2000; but see Thomas and Lazarova (2006) for a critical review of the theoretical and empirical support for the conceptualization). Bhaskar-Shrinivas et al. (2005) provide a comprehensive review of past research on expatriate adjustment.

101. Black et al., 1999. See also the recent empirical research of Stahl (2000) on the coping problems of German and Japanese expatriates.

102. A concise summary of research on expatriate dual allegiances can be found in Gregersen and Black (1992), Black et al., (1999), and Stroh et al. (2005).

103. Gregersen and Black, 1992, p. 143.

104. Brewster, 1991; Black, Gregersen, and Mendenhall, 1992; Stroh, 1995.

105. Stahl, 2000.

106. "Traveling More Lightly," *The Economist*, June 24, 2006, pp. 99–101.

107. Studies referenced in Black et al. (1999, p. 219) have shown that about three-quarters of expatriates, regardless of nationality, have experienced significant decreases in their standard of living after returning home.

108. Adler, 1981; Black and Gregersen, 1991a.

109. Brookfield Global Relocation Services (2009), "Global Relocation Trends 2009 Survey Report" (www.brookfieldgrs.com). According to Black and Gregersen (1999), "one-fourth of those who completed an assignment, left their company . . . within one year after repatriation."

110. Some turnover can always be expected—see Nicholson (1984) for research on work transitions. When expatriates gain new competencies during their assignments, their market value on the external market may be higher than inside the old organization, so naturally they leave. The return of the spouse to work may result in family relocation that is not compatible with the job offered to the returnee. While many firms undergoing restructuring are loath to terminate employees during an international assignment (partly for legal reasons in some countries), the employees are laid off as soon as they return.

111. Stahl, Miller, and Tung, 2002; Dickmann and Harris, 2005.

112. Allen and Alvarez, 1998; Black, Gregersen, and Mendenhall, 1992.

113. Research studies quoted in Black et al. (1999, p. 219).

114. Allen and Alvarez, 1998.

115. Pucik and Saba, 1998.

116. For example, Western or Japanese expatriates in China may cost the employer some $500,000 annually, several times the salary of most local Chinese managers (despite their rapid increase during recent years).

117. This issue is discussed in detail in Chapter 6.

118. Collings, Scullion, and Morley, 2007.

119. The need for a contingency approach to expatriation was first raised by Mendenhall and Oddou (1985). See also the empirical research of Stahl (2000).

120. Brookfield Global Relocation Services (2009), "Global Relocation Trends 2009 Survey Report" (www.brookfieldgrs.com).

121. Moran, Stahl, and Boyer, 1988.

122. Adler, 1984.
123. For a recent review of research on women and international assignments, see Altman and Shortland (2008).
124. Adler, 1986.
125. Tung, 1997.
126. Lowe, Downes, and Kroeck, 1999.
127. Adler, 1984.
128. Chusmir and Frontczak, 1990.
129. Adler, 1987; Taylor and Napier, 1996; Tung, 2004.
130. Caligiuri and Tung, 1999.
131. Stroh, Varma, and Valy-Durbin, 2000.
132. Harzing, 1999.
133. Brookfield Global Relocation Services (2009), "Global Relocation Trends 2009 Survey Report" (www.brookfieldgrs.com).
134. Many of the women in a study of Western expatriates in the Pacific Rim reported advantages to being highly visible, benefiting from the curiosity of local businesspeople eager to meet them (Adler, 1993).
135. Tung, 1995; 2004.
136. Merck and Exxon send engineers on short-term assignments for technology transfer and personal development. Some European multinationals have long done this.
137. As a side note, a complementary trend is that there are opportunities for international transfers later in employees' careers, when they may be looking for lateral challenges, free of child-rearing constraints, and open to new challenges. Young local professionals may benefit from such senior executives sharing their experiences.
138. "Traveling More Lightly," *The Economist*, June 24, 2006, pp. 99–101.
139. See the statistics in note 57 above.
140. See Tahvanainen, Welch, and Worm (2005) for a discussion of the HR implications of the use of short-term international assignments.
141. Dickmann et al., 2008.
142. Suutari and Brewster, 2003.
143. Welch, Worm, and Fenwick, 2003.
144. See Welch and Worm (2006) for an extensive discussion about international travelers.
145. L. Crawford, "Style With Rapid Response," *Financial Times*, September 26, 2000.
146. Bonache and Cervino, 1997.
147. Harvey, Speier, and Novicevic (1999) proposed that impatriate employees who are well integrated into the home organization may provide the international firm with a number of significant advantages such as (1) unique cultural/social knowledge and insights that are difficult to imitate; (2) acting as a critical communication point for host country managers to ensure the clarity of the strategy; (3) a diversity of perspectives when developing international business strategies, policies, and plans; (4) a pool of talent that can replace high-cost/high-failure expatriates in the host countries.
148. Peterson, 2003.
149. A major challenge arises if salaries or lifestyle expectations abroad are higher than at the corporate center. And this is not just about money. How much holiday should be granted to a French or German employee assigned to the United States?

CHAPTER 5

Structuring Global Coordination

Lateral Coordination at Nestlé

In April 2000, Nestlé—the world's largest food and beverage company with 250,000 employees and close to 500 factories in over 80 countries—launched a US$3 billion IT initiative. The Global Business Excellence program (GLOBE) was to transform the Nestlé organization from a loose "federation of independent markets" into a company showing a common face to customers and suppliers around the world.[1]

While the program could nominally be seen as a massive SAP rollout (in itself a complex undertaking), the purpose went far beyond building a new IT platform. Peter Brabeck, CEO of Nestlé, was explicit about the final goal:

I want this to be very clear. With GLOBE we will create common business processes, standardized data, and a common IT infrastructure—but do not think this is an IT initiative. We are going to fundamentally change the way we run this company.

In Brabeck's view, Nestlé's decentralized structure, which had brought the company so much success in the past, no longer fit the new realities of ever-increasing global competition.

Traditionally Nestlé had been structured as a cascading pyramid of major zones and markets—usually countries. Each business was essentially local, neatly aggregated to larger geographical units, all finally coming together in the corporate center. Running alongside this organization in a coordinating role were half a dozen strategic business units, such as beverages, dairy products, and infant nutrition.[2] The role of the business unit managers was to increase integration across geographies with a particular focus on new product development, but without profit and loss responsibility.[3]

The company's strong focus on product customization to local tastes was the foundation of Nestlé's success; but this also created duplication and inefficiencies that the company could no longer afford, with sales overhead costs well above its competitors.[4] A fragmented supply chain did not provide the desired economies of scale. Bargaining power with cross-border suppliers and retailers was weak—some large customers had better pricing information about Nestlé products in different markets around the world than the Nestlé central office.

Internal coordination was also difficult, as each country's organization and systems had been operating independently. Identical products had different product codes in different countries, and in HR there was no common grading and compensation system. With different titles for similar positions across countries, it was almost impossible to agree on who was at the same hierarchical level or performed the same job. Even for senior managers, salaries and bonuses were difficult to compare.[5]

The aim of the GLOBE program was to build a common platform for Nestlé's global operations, but the formal structure of the company would remain for the most part configured as a matrix of geographies and businesses. And as Nestlé was determined to maintain its focus on local markets, the company did not want to move too far away from its culture of decentralization. However, in order to cope better with the competitive challenges facing the company, it had to become more globally connected and aligned.

In essence, Nestlé needed to find an alternative route that would balance the benefits of local initiative with global leverage but remain in line with Nestlé's long-standing business principle of "putting people ahead of the systems." Senior management believed that maintaining local decision-making autonomy while standardizing core processes would achieve this. By simplifying and standardizing basic processes, Nestlé hoped to reduce internal complexity so local management could focus externally on customers and competition. And by flattening the organization and assigning more coordinating responsibility to cross-border and cross-functional teams, the company hoped to move away from the traditional vertical hierarchy to a more flexible network structure, which it believed is more suitable to the new generation of company employees.[6]

One of Nestlé's key leverage points for enhancing lateral coordination has been global implementation of common HR processes—from a single worldwide performance management system to comprehensive talent reviews, as well as succession planning based on a common grading system and structured leadership development (for a global talent pool of about 2,200 people). However, this does not mean that Nestlé's corporate HR function rules over local companies by issuing detailed global policy directives. Instead it uses a lot of virtual teamwork to reach a consensus on HR process objectives and tools, thereby working toward consistency and coherence across the world.[7]

OVERVIEW

The Nestlé case illustrates how changes in the global competitive environment have exposed the limitations of traditional multinational organizational structures. The purpose of this chapter is to understand how firms can develop new horizontal or lateral mechanisms of structural coordination and the vital role of human resource management in facilitating this.

In the first part of this chapter, we discuss the logic of the transition from hierarchical control to lateral coordination from three different angles: the nature of competition facing a transnational firm; the people management implications of a knowledge-based society; and what organizational theory tells us about managing in a complex global environment. We also introduce a framework guiding the next few chapters of the book—from mechanisms of structural coordination and social architecture to core HR processes supporting global coordination.

The second part of the chapter focuses on multidimensional structures. We examine how many traditional, multidomestic firms evolved into differentiated networks,[8] and how other firms pursuing gains from global efficiency and delivery capabilities are evolving step-by-step into globally integrated enterprises.[9] We also look at a third multidimensional organization model—the front–back organization, where the front-end customer-facing units are organized differently than back-end product-driven units.[10]

The emergence of multidimensional structures also has an impact on wider aspects of organization. In the past, simple structures were aligned with single-focus decision making—at the corporate center for centralized meganational firms and at the country or business unit level for decentralized multidomestic firms. However, making effective decisions in networked structures requires coordination mechanisms that can supplement, if not replace, traditional top-down hierarchical decision-making models. In the third part of this chapter, we examine different types of cross-boundary lateral management tools that are being deployed in multinational firms. These typically include individuals in cross-boundary integrating roles or leadership groups that coordinate the activities to be aligned across units.

The last part of the chapter focuses on global teams—as perhaps the best way to address the complex business challenge facing global organizations is through cross-boundary collaboration. Today, numerous kinds of virtual teams working across borders are one of the key elements supporting horizontal coordination. They also provide a foundation for tapping into a diversity of perspectives and experience. Indeed, one might argue that virtual teamwork is a core characteristic of most organizations in the global economy.

FROM VERTICAL CONTROL TO HORIZONTAL COORDINATION

The traditional model of corporate governance in international business was built on organizational hierarchy employing control mechanisms like centralized planning and decision making backed up by staff experts at headquarters; an extensive use of corporate rules, standard operating procedures, and policy guidelines; and reliance on expatriates as agents of headquarters control. As we discussed in Chapter 1, firms responded to the challenge of managing the growing complexity of international operations in two different ways—either using a matrix structure or expanding the number of headquarters staff. However, both of these routes largely failed, leading companies to search for more effective ways to manage the global organization.

Emergence of Coordination

In simple terms, the way in which a firm goes about setting authority differentiates the transnational firm from the traditional multinational corporation. In the past, there was a clear decision maker (the global or business manager, or the local or country manager); the responsibility and accountability of all managers were closely aligned; and the areas where they could act were clearly defined and supported by dedicated resources. In transnational firms, the identity of the "boss" may vary based on circumstances and priorities, business, function, and customer. Task forces or steering groups create forums outside the formal structures that allow employees to influence the direction and execution of business strategies in a way that may not possible within the hierarchical organization.

Dilemmas of hierarchical control—centralization versus decentralization of decision making—are much less central to transnational coordination. What is important is knowing which subunits in the firm need to be connected, and identifying the best mechanisms to ensure coordination among all who need to be involved with a decision and its implementation. Also, in contrast to hierarchical control, which is often nothing more than a set of rules and regulations imposed from the corporate center, transnational coordination involves mostly horizontal interactions, with the active participation of those who have a stake in the decision.

How can we best understand the logic of this transformation? We can take three different perspectives to illustrate what drives it and what the implications are. First, we look at the new competitive realities facing transnational firms; then we consider the workforce or people perspective; and finally we discuss how all of these changes fit with one of the emerging paradigms of organizational theory—the firm as a network.

The Competitive Perspective

Today's transnational organizations face a different situation from the past. The American, European, and Japanese companies that led the process of internationalization in the post–World War II era either exploited home based scale economies or transferred home grown knowledge to their subsidiaries abroad. In both cases, their know-how and critical resources were located at the center. However, there are not many companies left in this position today, and there will be even fewer in the future.

Consider some of the new realities:

- Subsidiaries abroad may be of paramount importance to the multinational, sometimes representing market opportunities larger than at home. This has long been the case for multinationals from smaller countries such as Switzerland and Sweden. Whole business lines may be run from these other countries, and there will be multiple locations that must be linked together. Also, the technical and managerial sophistication of some lead subsidiaries may outstrip that of the parent country; information therefore has to flow both ways between the subsidiary and the headquarters.

- The transnational organization is differentiated, in the sense that subsidiaries vary in their strategic importance, competencies, and resources.[11] Rigid structures, undifferentiated policies, and traditional notions of planning cannot cope with this. For subsidiaries that are "strategic leaders," planning may involve intensive interaction with the headquarters, whereas distant "contributors" may be left alone as long as they meet their targets. In the former, staff development and compensation policies may be negotiated to balance corporate and local interests, whereas contributors usually adjust to local practices.

- Companies can no longer afford to be deliberate but slow. The pace of competition, and the need to make decisions quickly without compromising on cost and quality, have increased. Instead of competing with local companies that in the past were weak on technical and management expertise, companies such as Nestlé now compete with other sophisticated multinationals, such as Kraft or Unilever, as well as local players with multinational ambitions in many different battlefields around the world. And their customers are also increasingly global. With the ongoing waves of global consolidation, the pressure to be aligned globally is likely to increase.

- In many industries, future competitive advantage cannot be secured through further economies of scale, downsizing, and delayering. Even best-of-breed companies, like Toyota or Nokia, which pushed the limits of operational improvement, now realize that future competitive advantage can come only through leveraging know-how across their global affiliates. Furthermore, the flow of innovation is changing from center-to-local to local-to-center or even local-to-local.

Collectively, all these trends mean that the traditional focus on headquarters–subsidiary relationships, and on ways of structuring the multinational corporation, is giving way to the questions of how to coordinate relationships, how to build and maintain ties, and how to manage a complex web of connections. The focus on center-to-subsidiary relations remains, but to this one adds subsidiary-to-center(s) and subsidiary-to-subsidiary ties.

The People Perspective

Since the 1960s, the top-down, hierarchical organization, and its corresponding compliance to authority, has come under increasing attack, starting with Douglas McGregor's elegant formulation of two assumptions about the nature of management.[12] He outlined the pathologies of the traditional control-oriented Theory X that underlie the hierarchical model, and instead advocated Theory Y, which assumes that people can be trusted to perform well if they are given appropriately challenging work and feedback. A wave of best sellers in the 1980s brought this perspective into the management mainstream,[13] and myriad articles and volumes have since been written on this topic.[14]

At the same time, the top-heavy control model of the multinational organization could not cope with the realities of global markets. The cost of multiple layers of supervision and control started to weigh heavily on the profitability of companies—corporate monitors and controllers were adding little, if any, value. To meet the growing coordination needs, it became necessary to develop self-control rather than boss-control, and for this American practitioners coined a new term—"empowerment."[15] This in turn required new skills such as leading without authority. The outcome was more attention to selection, skill development, objective setting, feedback, and other tools of people management.

The transition to a postindustrial society based on knowledge skills rather than manual ability had also led to changes in ways of managing people. First, there is a much higher level of education and training of the global workforce today than there was only a decade ago. As innovation became more important, traditional hierarchical firms found that that they could neither attract nor retain the new generation of skilled knowledge professionals that they needed. Highly educated employees require motivation and a raison d'être for working in a specific company that go beyond financial rewards. Second, employees no longer need to be in the office to work—with e-mail, the Internet, and wireless phones, people are increasingly working from home or from other subsidiaries. Direct supervision is gradually disappearing. Third, cooperation is increasingly important; today's organizational world is no longer about individual roles but about teams and groups.[16]

The Organizational Theory Perspective

Organizational theory has shown that as the environment becomes more complex, and as information processing demands increase, the organization has to complement its reliance on hierarchical modes of information processing and decision making with attention to lateral coordination.

The best way of coordinating in simple and stable environments is to use rules and standard operating procedures, hierarchical referral (ask the boss), and planning systems that lead to goal setting (explicit performance contracts).[17] But as complexity and turbulence increase, these vertical mechanisms can no longer cope. On the one hand, the organization can try to reduce the need for information processing by outsourcing nonessential activiti es, or by creating self-contained units, like independent business units.[18] On the other hand, like Nestlé in our opening case, organizations can increase their coordination capacity by creating lateral or horizontal relationships, complemented by investments in vertical information systems. Research shows this gradual shift from structure to horizontal coordination over the last 40 years.[19]

Consequently, it has become increasingly common to think of organizations as networks of internal (and external) relationships. Network theory ascribes a low degree of connectivity to bureaucratic or mechanistic structures. Relationships are asymmetric (top-down with little upward feedback) and centralized (focused on a few key actors in hierarchical positions). In contrast, organic or adaptive organizations are characterized by dense, strongly interconnected networks, with many lateral and reciprocal relationships. The overall degree of coordination is much higher.[20] They satisfy the principle of requisite complexity—that the internal complexity of the firm must mirror the complexity of its external environment.

However, this is not to suggest that complex is better. The appropriate degree of lateral coordination will depend on the strategy. A company should not create more coordination mechanisms than required by the strategy since these mechanisms (coordinating roles, steering groups, and other forms of cross-boundary teamwork) imply additional expense in terms of resources, management time, and energy.[21]

In summary, the three perspectives on the transnational firm introduced here all lead in the same direction and emphasize the importance of horizontal coordination.

Horizontal Coordination Mechanisms

Expanding on our brief introduction to coordination in Chapter 1 (see page 14), our framework of the horizontal coordination mechanisms is shown in Figure 5–1. Because coordination is applied for a purpose, we use the term "organizational glue" to describe the underlying processes and practices (some companies refer to this as "cohesion management"). Glue is something that can be used to stick two parts of an organization together for a specific purpose. Indeed, this term, which we started using in the early 1990s, seemed to strike a responsive chord and has caught on. Glue technology is to a great extent the application of human resource management.

FIGURE 5–1. Horizontal Coordination Mechanisms

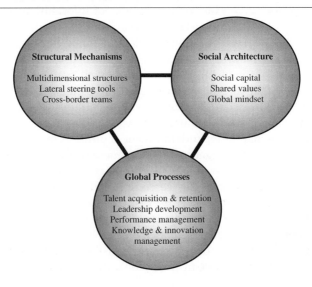

There are three elements to coordination or glue technology—structural mechanisms (which we discuss in this chapter); social architecture (discussed in Chapter 6); and key global processes of talent management and leadership development (Chapters 7 and 8), performance management (Chapter 9), and knowledge and innovation management (Chapter 10). Before expanding on the structural mechanisms, we will give a brief overview of these three elements here.

Structural Mechanisms

Organizational structure spells out who does what and who reports to whom. Structures can be based on different dimensions, and in a simple world one dimension dominates. Small firms have functional structures; larger firms have either business or geographic structures, and sometimes a combination of both. However, making a choice on a single dimension of alignment—product, geography, function, and (increasingly) the customer—is difficult, since transnational firms need the ability to act simultaneously on all these dimensions. Therefore, many multinationals have chosen to implement multidimensional structures.

Making decisions and implementing them in multidimensional structures requires alternative ways of horizontal collaboration, complementing traditional top-down hierarchical decision making. These lateral steering tools typically center on an individual or a team that coordinates decisions across the various business units, broadening the perspectives that can be brought to bear on strategic decisions. Individuals charged with these roles may have high responsibility and accountability, but not necessarily much formal power or independent resources. Temporary or permanent steering teams are responsible for coordinating various activities and decisions across organizational boundaries.

Cross-boundary teams and projects are basic building blocks of coordination in today's corporations. Different types of teams are set up to respond to many different challenges. Teamwork allows the organization to mobilize the collaborative energy of those employees whose talents and knowledge are most relevant to the immediate issue. Team membership is flexible; teams can be formed and disbanded as circumstances require. In the transnational firm, team members usually work virtually in multiple locations.

Social Architecture

The social architecture of the firm, which we discuss in Chapter 6, complements these structural mechanisms. The foundation of social architecture is relationships between people, increasingly facilitated by electronic technology—relationships which constitute the social capital of the firm. In firms with rich social capital, information flows quickly and freely across intraorganizational boundaries. Social capital, where people trust and understand each other, is essential for effective global coordination, making it easier to mobilize scarce resources when help is required in a distant subsidiary, or to secure access to those with desired knowledge. Relationships also help resolve the inevitable conflicts created by the conflicting demands facing the multinational corporation.

Another important part of the social architecture of the firm is shared values. Values, beliefs, and norms that are held in common across all or part of the corporation form the core of the organizational culture. Shared values facilitate the trust that is essential for effective lateral coordination, conflict resolution, and knowledge transfer. Relationships between people are unlikely to add much value unless there is some degree of cohesion in the way in which people think and behave.

Global managers need to be able to cope with conflict and contradiction. This leads to the third element of social architecture—what we call global mindset. Global mindset is a set of attitudes that predisposes individuals to cope constructively with competing priorities (for example, global versus local priorities) rather than advocating one perspective at the expense of others. It includes awareness of diversity across businesses, countries, cultures, and markets; the ability to interpret business issues independently from assumptions of a single country, culture, or context; and, most importantly, the willingness to accept the legitimacy of multiple points of view.

Global Processes

The Nestlé case illustrates how multidimensional structures and the social architecture of the firm are enabled by core human resource and organizational processes. Formalization and standardization support coordination, and organizations have traditionally tried to align behavior through rules, policies, and standard operating procedures. While rules are ill-suited to the differentiated complexity of the multinational enterprise, standardized global processes can supply efficiency, alignment, and focus. Three global processes are particularly important for supporting coordination: talent management, performance management, and knowledge and innovation management.

Coordination can happen only through people, and so the first element of global process coordination is talent management—from recruitment and selection to leadership development (discussed in Chapters 7 and 8). Organizational capabilities supporting sustainable competitive advantage have to be embedded in people; otherwise it is too easy for competitors to replicate. Of course, everyone talks about hiring the best; but if the best methods for attracting, selecting, and retaining people are applied only in the home country, other parts of the firm will never succeed on the talent front. Yet much of people management is highly contextual—what parts of the process should be global and what local? In the transnational firm, managers across the world need skills in exercising leadership without authority, and a strong global mindset needs to be nurtured in local managers.

Probably no other global process generates as much tension and debate as performance management, which we discuss in Chapter 9. Many managers advocate that performance management must be adjusted to the cultural specifics of each particular country. Others emphasize the importance of aligning performance management with the company's overall strategy, structure, and organizational culture, and advocate a more universal approach. Both arguments have their merits, but because performance management is a crucial process for establishing organizational alignment, a shared perspective on what should be common and what discretionary is vital for any global organization.

The final element of glue technology is knowledge and innovation management, discussed in Chapter 10. It is not possible to develop any truly global process without sharing knowledge about what works and what does not. Knowledge, and the innovations that result from pooling that knowledge, can come from anywhere. In the past, knowledge was transferred out from the center to the local affiliates. Today, new knowledge and innovation may come from units and markets anywhere in the world, and it is therefore vital to be able to transfer know-how rapidly from one local affiliate to another, and to lower the barriers to the assimilation of knowledge received from the outside.

Properly designed, these global processes in talent, performance, and knowledge management represent the lateral application of traditionally hierarchical tools of control, capturing the advantages of global integration through standardization and simplification while respecting local differences. A worldwide recruitment process, for example, does not specify whom should be hired for business X in country Y. But guided by explicit assumptions, it does spell out the steps, considerations, consultations, and tools that will lead to an appropriate decision.

It should be emphasized that horizontal coordination does not replace vertical control—it transforms it. The leader becomes a strategic coach rather than a controller. General management becomes a responsibility of all middle and senior managers rather than a role occupied by one person. The focus of planning shifts from content to process, with an emphasis on working through conflicts and building commitment to strategies.[22] As for corporate staff, their roles change from functional experts to network facilitators, with new skills in capturing, assimilating, and ensuring the transfer of expertise around the world. Global or regional processes for connecting different activities together replace rigid policies. Measurement becomes an instrument for enhanced self-management and learning rather than one of control.

MULTIDIMENSIONAL STRUCTURES

As we pointed out in Chapter 1, many multinational companies that implemented a matrix structure found it difficult to live with its consequences. In principle, matrix structures may be useful in companies that require both local responsiveness and global integration. With some employees reporting to two or even more bosses—often a country and a business unit or functional manager[23]—such structures allow for a balance of influence between the product (business unit) and market/geography (country) perspectives of the company. However, a global matrix is a difficult structure to maintain because of the inevitable conflict of priorities between the different units of the organization. How these conflicts are resolved is the most critical task facing any matrix organization.

Companies using a matrix structure usually attempt to regulate the balance with carefully written rules of engagement, specifying the responsibilities of each role. However, no matter how well defined the responsibilities are, overlaps and tensions are inevitable as business evolves, and consequently a matrix is often regarded as a transitional organizational form. The ABB case, presented in Chapter 1, is perhaps the best-known example of a multinational applying a complex matrix organization—balancing the influence of product lines with countries and regions—and running into major difficulties.

What went wrong? With Barnevik's emphasis on radical decentralization to 5,000 business units, there were few unifying processes in place, aside from the financial reporting system. Even at a country level there was no common IT, HR, or purchasing. With time, the complex matrix structure became unwieldy, and costs spiraled out of control. Barnevik's successor, Göran Lindahl, attempted to re-establish discipline by shifting power fully to the businesses, but the reorganization resulted in fragmentation and chaos at the operating level—the businesses had no tools to exercise meaningful influence. When the next CEO, Jörgen Centerman, in the middle of yet another reorganization, finally proceeded to build from the top the core groupwide processes the company needed, their disconnect from operational reality only further deepened organizational paralysis.[24]

Three CEOs and a major crisis later, ABB is back to a multidimensional structure. According to Fred Kindle, CEO from 2005 until 2008, "ABB, like every global company, must recognize the need to manage the interface between business and geography—matching the benefits of 'one simple ABB' with the power of local entrepreneurship."[25] Intentionally, the new multidimensional organization is not balanced (in fact use of the word "matrix" is banned); business divisions are taking the lead, while the role of countries and regions is to create appropriate synergies.

Emerging Forms of Global Multidimensional Structures

With the pressure to optimize multiple strategic dimensions, especially those of local responsiveness and global efficiency, it is not surprising that many global firms such as ABB, IBM, Nestlé, and Nokia are adopting structures that are configured along multiple dimensions, with resulting complexities far surpassing the traditional matrix organization.

In multidimensional organizations, managers not only are responsible for achieving results for their own units but also have shared accountability for successful strategy implementation across units. Viewed with the lens of hierarchical control, the overlapping accountability could be seen as a problem, although from the perspective of horizontal coordination, it is quite natural. While accountability can be shared, it cannot be delegated (or avoided), and it often includes an obligation to monitor and challenge others. Nestlé's conceptualization of the responsibility and accountability interface for senior managers is presented in Figure 5–2.

In other words, managers' accountability at Nestlé goes beyond their own area of responsibility and may include areas that they should influence but cannot directly impact through their authority. In firms with multidimensional structures, this means that managers have to take into account the

FIGURE 5–2. Responsibility and Accountability at Nestlé

Responsibility

- Embraces the **main tasks** of the individual.
- Expects/allows an individual to act with own resources.
- Assumes decision-making authority and the competence/ability to **directly enforce** the execution of the task.
- Is assigned to an individual and can **be neither delegated nor shared.**
- Implies full accountability for the related tasks.

Accountability

- Goes beyond responsibility as it also includes tasks the individual should **influence** but **cannot directly enforce.**
- Encompasses the areas of responsibility of the direct reports and/or the areas of responsibility of the individuals that are functionally led (dotted line).
- Can be **shared** but **cannot be delegated.**
- Includes an **obligation to challenge** and follow up on the plan/actions of the responsible individual.

- Responsibility can be described as follows:
  Decide . . . set . . . define . . . manage . . . perform . . . act upon . . . assume the results . . .

- Accountability can be described as follows:
  Propose . . . ensure . . . support . . . facilitate . . . monitor . . . follow up . . .

perspectives of other relevant actors before making decisions in their areas of responsibility. All of this requires alignment with people strategies from talent development to performance management.

We will look at some of the most distinctive examples of multidimensional structures in worldwide organizations today. While they all reflect the multidimensionality of transnational firms, they apply different organizational priorities.

Three sets of factors are influential in shaping these new structures: (1) the evolution of capabilities and knowledge within the firm; (2) the drivers of competitive advantage; and (3) the importance of working closely with customers. The choice of how to structure the firm is also heavily influenced by its administrative heritage—that is, its historical development.[26] Table 5–1 lists three common archetypes of multidimensional organizations that can be observed today.

The focus of a company organized as a **differentiated network** is on leveraging competencies and capabilities initially developed in its local subsidiaries

TABLE 5–1. Configuring the Multidimensional Organization

Strategic Perspective	Organizational Perspective
• Subsidiary competence.	• Differentiated network.
• Global optimization.	• Globally integrated enterprise.
• Customer and efficiency.	• Front–back organization.

for worldwide advantage.[27] Put simply, it can be described as a bottom-up process of business unit globalization. Multidomestic firms with strong local subsidiaries, such as ABB or Nestlé, are typically in the forefront of the move toward a differentiated network.

The objective of a company organized as a **globally integrated enterprise** is to achieve competitive advantage by locating specific activities in the best place worldwide, and finding ways to link or integrate these activities across the world.[28] In this case, the process of globalization is top-down. Firms such as IBM or Toyota, originally "international" or meganational, are examples of companies that follow such an organizational approach.

The **frontback organization**[29] is another emerging form of a multinational organization. Using the front–back office idea pioneered by financial service firms, the customer-oriented parts of the company are aligned locally to respond to customers (the front end) while those parts of the company that may benefit from global efficiencies and scale are organized along global lines (the back end). This avoids the disadvantages of a full-blown matrix, limiting matrix connections to front- and back-end coordination. "International" firms (for example, HP and P&G) and meganational firms (for example, Nokia) have been realigning their global organization in this direction.[30]

Recognizing the Importance of Subsidiaries: The Differentiated Network

Companies such as Nestlé and other multidomestic firms grew mainly by investing in the development of local capabilities. The idea behind the differentiated network organization is that valuable capabilities should no longer be managed solely from a local perspective; subsidiary capabilities should be leveraged regionally and globally, using horizontal coordination.[31] The greater the capability, the broader the potential scope for leverage.

In a differentiated network, the role of a subsidiary depends on its capabilities and competence, as well as the strategic importance of the local environment. Rather than simply executing a headquarters-designed strategy in a local context, which is what happens in multidomestic firms, the subsidiaries are expected to become active contributors to global strategy—even strategic leaders—benefiting from location-specific advantages that can be leveraged across the whole organization. The differentiated network is particularly powerful when a company has subsidiaries in regions of the world that can provide a real competitive advantage—for example, when a subsidiary has developed a specific area of excellence through the local country's endowment.[32] Not surprisingly, cultural and regional differences at Nestlé that result from the company's global footprint are viewed as sources of sustainable competitive advantage.

The concept of the "center of excellence" is integral to the differentiated network organization (although found in other forms of global enterprise as well). A center of excellence is an organizational unit that has been explicitly recognized as a source of value creation. For example, the lead role for Nestlé's core confectionery business is entrusted to the British subsidiary.[33] Some centers of excellence have developed from long-term experience in dealing with a demanding customer; others derive their unique position from external sources. Among financial firms, for example, private banking is often run from Switzerland, options and derivatives products from New York, and foreign exchange products from London.[34] In principle, a firm operating as a differentiated network draws on multiple centers of excellence with supporting capabilities widely dispersed around the world.

One of the key advantages of the differentiated network organization is providing space for local entrepreneurship. However, managing the resulting complexity of capabilities distributed around the globe can be a major challenge, since the responsibility for collaboration and coordination is also widely diffused. To tackle this challenge, Nestlé launched a number of organizational initiatives under the heading "Nestlé on the Move," spreading the message that the company must move from being a hierarchy to becoming a network, from command to alignment, and from separated national and functional units to cross-border and cross-functional teams. The company also adjusted its performance management system to encourage interunit collaboration.

Trust and collaboration are important and must be nurtured. One of the guiding principles in the early days of ABB was that disagreements between parallel units within the network (such as on internal transfer pricing or product specifications) should be resolved by the managers themselves and not delegated upward for solution by top management. As the company folklore had it, one could ask twice for help . . . but the third time top management would put someone else in the job who could handle conflict resolution without involving superiors. When senior management intervenes on details and plays the role of arbiter (a problem not unique to ABB), organizational politics kick in with a vengeance and trust disappears. There is no end to the upward escalation of conflict, and in the end this can paralyze the organization.

Leveraging Distributed Capabilities: The Globally Integrated Enterprise

According to Sam Palmisano, the CEO of IBM, the essence of the globally integrated enterprise is a shift in the focus of strategic decision making "from what products to make to how to make them, from what services to offer to how to deliver them."[35] On the assumption that national boundaries are less and less relevant to corporate practice, local capabilities and cost advantages are nurtured purposely. While the objective of global optimization is paramount, in contrast to a traditional meganational firm, these capabilities can be anywhere, not only in the mother country. IBM is perhaps the most visible example of a multinational company pursuing this approach.

For example, IBM spends roughly $40 billion annually on goods and services to run its business. Over the past few years, IBM has transformed its procurement function, consolidating transaction processing into three operations centers for America, Asia, and Europe. There is no longer a need for local procurement departments in the 100 and more countries where IBM operates.[36]

Procurement is not the only example. In pursuit of global optimization, all IBM support functions are integrated on a global scale and specialized tasks are outsourced to internal and external experts, who can be located anywhere in the world. As an illustration, the IBM sales organization in Australia and New Zealand is supported by a payroll function in Manila (the Philippines), procurement in Shenzhen (China), accounts payable in Shanghai (China), accounting in Kuala Lumpur (Malaysia), leasing administration in Okinawa (Japan), and an asset management team in Bratislava (Slovakia).[37]

What enables the development of such a globally integrated enterprise? One factor is the lowering of trade barriers, which enables a better flow of goods and services across national or regional borders. The second factor is the IT revolution, which allows standardization of business processes across subsidiaries, driving costs down. But it is not only economics. In a world where production and distribution are commoditized, it is important to offer a differentiated value proposition that can come only from organizational capabilities and people. Therefore, the third factor is the emergence of a global talent pool—expertise and knowledge have no boundaries.

As a result of the interplay of these three factors, companies can move from targeting their investments at specific local markets to a focus on supplying the entire global market. When everything is connected, work flows to places where it will be done best—that is, most efficiently and with the highest value added. And the workforce may move as well; the IBM global delivery center in Brno (Czech Republic) numbers 70 different nationalities among the 2,100 employees.[38]

Because new technologies are allowing companies to treat different functions and operations as component pieces, firms applying this reasoning can pull those pieces apart and put them back together again in combinations. The decision on how to do this is based on strategic judgments about those operations where the company wants to excel and those it thinks are better left to its partners. Operating systems based on global standards link the entire company, and resources are deployed to the locations where they are most needed. The accountability for making this work resides with the specialists in globally integrated functions.

Implementing the globally integrated enterprise poses a number of people management challenges, notably the need for a globalized approach to talent and workforce management. Not surprisingly, IBM is at the forefront of applying new workforce planning methodologies as well as approaches that allow the rapid deployment of talent across boundaries. Such firms also have to be effective in mobilizing and sharing knowledge across the whole global organization, using social networks as well as information technology.

For operating managers, skills in working laterally without authority are essential as most of the resources they need to deliver results lie outside their core responsibility. A collaborative leadership style and strong partnering skills are vital. Employees have global opportunities, but they are also exposed to worldwide competition for their work. They must have tools at their disposal for rapid upgrading and development of skills, as well the ability to work anywhere, regardless of location. For this reason, training and development are fundamental pillars of the company's HR strategy.

Becoming Customer-Centric: The Front–Back Organization

You cannot build competitive advantage by doing only what is easy—anyone can do that. In order to resolve a long-standing contradiction—how to combine customer focus (the front end) with global economies of scale (the back end)—some firms are trying to gain competitive advantage by experimenting with a new organizational design: the front–back organization. Two types of firm are adopting this type of organizational structure: companies, such as Nokia, with a meganational heritage of centralized product development but with emerging focus on strong local customers; and corporations like HP, which are expanding a global product-centered business model to include value-adding services and solutions.

The core of the front–back organization is a dual structure in which both halves are multifunctional units.[39] The front half of the organization—marketing, sales, and customer service—is focused on customer needs and market opportunities (usually organized around specific customer segments or markets). The back half—R&D, manufacturing, and supply chain functions—is focused on global efficiency and product excellence (usually organized on business or product lines).

Front–back organization is not aiming to achieve a balance. It is fundamentally a customer-centric, not product-centric, design. Even for the back end, the primary objective is maximizing end-user benefits. Nor is it a matrix structure—there is a clear separation between global product divisions and market-facing units, each with their own P&L, and limited dual reporting. The two halves of the organization are usually linked only at the very top level of the senior executive team.

Nokia Networks (now Nokia Siemens Networks) is one company that has moved from being product-centric to customer-centric. When telecommunications around the world became deregulated, start-up operators such as Orange or Vodafone looked for support in designing, building, and maintaining their networks. Nokia Networks responded by creating a Customer Operation division in which teams—reporting to account managers—were charged with providing total solutions (products and services) for specific customers—while the rest of the firm was organized along product or functional lines. Each unit functioned like a small consulting firm that could react quickly to customer demand. The key measurement was customer satisfaction and the share of customer business obtained by Nokia. This encouraged employees to do what the customer wanted, including installing equipment from competitors if the customer's specification demanded it.[40]

A key challenge facing front–back organizations is that they demand a high degree of coordination as well as skill in contention management. Tensions and everyday conflicts are normal because many issues have the potential to be contentious. Companies that are trying to implement such structures need solid foundations in lateral coordination. When HP, with its long history of decentralization, launched its attempt to implement a front–back organization in the early 2000s, many observers were doubtful about its chances of success. *BusinessWeek* commented that the company was "betting on an approach so radical that experts say it has never been done before at a company of HP's size and complexity."[41]

It took HP five years and a new CEO to get the new organization firmly in place. Similar challenges were encountered by other firms moving toward this kind of model, and even widely admired multinational companies such as P&G aborted their original front–back design for a more modest organizational overhaul.

From the human resource management perspective, implementing a front–back organization brings a range of challenges, from the development of senior executives capable of working comfortably with the tensions embedded in this design, to the design of a performance management system that focuses either on the customer or on the product (depending on the unit in the firm), while at the same time supporting collaborative behavior. Ideally, this kind of organization is ambidextrous—local *and* global, excelling at short-term execution while pursuing the long-term vision of creating new markets—not an easy task without a full line of other coordinating mechanisms.

Implications of Multidimensionality

Two points need to be made with respect to this discussion.

The first concerns the increasing differentiation of structures within the multinational firm. The three emerging forms are organizational archetypes. A single corporation may contain different archetypes since the choice of an appropriate structure is often made at the business rather than the corporate level. In some businesses, the emphasis may be on countries and geographies in order to respond to local opportunities (or political pressures); in others, the aim is to optimize global efficiency and to support new product development. Even IBM, which pioneered the concept of a globally integrated enterprise, has some "global" activities in multiple locations, as localization of capabilities is an increasing concern of host governments. The focus may vary from one business to another, and also over time.

The second point concerns the transformation of leadership in these new types of multinational. All of these new organizational forms are flatter than the traditional hierarchical organization, not only because there are fewer levels but also because—for reasons of speed—decision making is less centralized than in more vertically oriented firms.

Because of this emphasis on bringing decision making closer to where decisions need to be made in the organization, there is a popular belief that networks and hierarchy are opposites, and that the former are replacing the latter. This is not at all the case. Networks need some form of hierarchical leadership authority. Without strong leadership to establish clear goals to which people are committed, networks can become debating clubs, with the risk that the extreme of chaos could replace the other extreme of excessive order.[42]

However, networks, along with leadership style and the underlying skills needed, do transform the nature of leadership. As we pointed out earlier, enabling or coaching management replaces the traditional command-and-control approach, and skills in influence and collaboration become vital. Similarly, while strong headquarters leadership is needed, this is no longer based on the authority to tell people what to do, since headquarters has less and less of a monopoly on expertise and experience.

Headquarters managers have to provide what we call network leadership (sometimes referred to as parenting[43])—for example, bringing value to the network by building cross-border links between affiliates in order to reap the benefits of coordination and knowledge sharing. Network leadership at the center also involves leveraging functional capability, providing specialist expertise that is well adapted to the different parts of the enterprise.[44]

LATERAL STEERING TOOLS

WWL, a logistics company based in Oslo, is the world's leading car carrier. Its ocean transportation business is divided into six major trades, each controlling shipments from one continent to another, with each trade manager having full P&L responsibility for the specific trade. Trade managers report to respective heads of regions. At the same time, all trades are linked to each other. A ship bringing cars from Japan to the United States should continue taking US cargo to Europe and finally European cars to Asia. The key to WWL's business success is optimization of capacity utilization across the whole fleet, taking into account differences in profit margins on different trades and customers.

In theory, the optimal solution could be calculated and imposed from the center, and until recently this was the way the business was run. However, as the business grew and became more complex, this centralized approach was destroying local accountability and initiative toward customers, who are primarily local. Today, it is the collective role of the global ocean team (composed of all trade managers) to coordinate among the different trades, so that both global and regional priorities can be optimized. The team meets face-to-face several times a year, but it is continuously in touch by e-mail and teleconferencing.

The Benefits of Lateral Steering

Temporary or permanent steering teams, such as the WWL ocean trade management group, are responsible for coordinating activities and decisions across organizational boundaries. Given the complexity of decision making in the transnational firm, it would often be inappropriate if go or no-go, resourcing, and other key decisions were made without consulting different perspectives. Steering groups can facilitate cross-boundary collaboration to coordinate regionally, to manage the introduction of a new technology, or to tackle other complex problems—all without introducing the complexities of a matrix structure. And most importantly, lateral steering can increase commitment to action, to the extent that key actors can be involved as members of the group.

Other benefits are flexibility and avoidance of formal bureaucracy. While it is difficult—and slow—to change the structure of an organization, such steering groups can be set up and disbanded from one day to the next as priorities emerge and change. The composition of the steering groups can also shift, along with the priorities. For example, a Scandinavian firm that is organized on worldwide product lines decided that its operations in Asia were of strategic importance, and needed greater coordination across businesses, as well as careful resourcing. Within a few weeks it set up an Asian board, consisting of the COO, the heads of two divisions active in Asia, and three key individuals from its Asian operations. Projects that were floundering now came under the supervision of this board, and new projects were set up. When the projects moved to the implementation stage, the internal board membership changed to pass the responsibility on to operational executives.

Lateral steering can take many different shapes and forms—as internal boards, formal or informal steering groups, functional councils, product development committees, strategic development councils, regional boards, and the like. Alternatively, the steering group may be a single person, such as someone who has vertical functional responsibility for a business unit but also horizontal responsibility across businesses in a region. The purposes of both forms of lateral steering are complementary, and most multinational firms use a combination of the two. We will start our discussion with individual coordinating roles, moving on to team-based steering in the second part of this section.

Lateral Leadership Roles

Cross-border brokering and integrating roles are often assumed by individuals. These managers will hold titles like project manager, program manager, global account manager, or process owner. But regardless of title, they all have two common features. First, they are responsible for decisions in a specific domain, which they implement through coordination across different units. Second, they execute their role with little formal authority, since authority remains with the line organization.[45]

In most firms there are at least four critical operational domains that may require lateral leadership:

- The first is efficient resource utilization in line with overall strategy. The role of *business or area coordinators* is to fill the alignment gaps that the formal structure does not cover and to coordinate among units that report to different leaders.
- The responsibility of *global competence manager* is to coordinate the development of competencies required by current and future business strategy, and to ensure that functional knowledge accumulated in the firm is harnessed effectively.
- The third domain focuses on the external customer. *Global account managers* are charged with managing the interfaces between important customers and the different units of the global organization.
- Finally, as multinational firms are increasingly engaged in collaborative business partnerships, *alliance managers* are often appointed on a corporate level, responsible for planning, negotiating, and implementing alliances. We will discuss this role separately in Chapter 12.

Business/Area Coordinators

The ability of a company to coordinate and optimize its regional or global activities, going from sourcing to marketing and from product development to supply chain management, is the key to its competitive advantage.[46] This is the role of business or area coordinators. Some are focused externally, aligning the organization toward vendors or customers; others are focused on creating synergies inside the firm.

The nature of the role depends on the configuration of company activities. In Nestlé, business unit managers (Nestlé's term for business coordinators) do not manage a business in a specific geography but concentrate on the global business as a whole. Most Nestlé profit centers still focus on individual countries, and the coordinators exert influence through participation in the planning process, as well as through control over product development and new product launches. But it is their personal influence that counts most, as they are traditionally recruited from among the most accomplished country leaders.

The scope of the business coordinator may depend on the competitive conditions. Nestlé's main competitor, Unilever, tailored the structure of business coordination to the needs of different markets.[47] Markets in Europe were highly competitive and interdependent, requiring a tightly coordinated approach, so product coordinators had direct line responsibility over the local operating companies in their line of business. But in Latin America, country managers kept their line responsibility, with product coordinators serving as advisors.

At Toyota, the role of coordinators is to link overseas operations to the parent firm, bridging the language and cultural barriers for local unit managers. Coordinators are responsible for facilitating access to global resources, ensuring the horizontal flow of information with other parts of the company, and alignment of local operations with the company culture (we will return to this issue in the next chapter).

As with any coordinating role, the power and legitimacy associated with the position matter a great deal. But power does not need to be overt. With proper staffing, coordinators can exert influence even when they have no formal authority because they are effective at influencing the behavior of others. Good coordinators know the business, using their networking skills to obtain the information they need and their personal credibility to get things done.

Sometimes, the business coordinator role is played by one of the senior executives. In one European food company, the importance of cross-boundary coordination was reinforced at the highest level by the global steering role of the number two executive in the firm. Meeting regularly with regional councils that were set up in parallel, his role was to identify challenges that cut across country lines and to set up projects to deal with them. Such projects ranged from the consolidation of manufacturing facilities to tactics on how to defend themselves against focused attacks by a competitor.

Global Competence Managers

Functional managers have long been recognized as important for the coordination of global activities especially with respect to facilitating communication among dispersed functional specialists, assuring timely diffusion of best practices, and promoting innovation within a particular discipline.[48] However, there is one important dimension of functional responsibility, closely connected to human resources management, that often requires a dedicated role, namely developing new capabilities. Consider the following example.

A Japanese manufacturing company expanded rapidly over the last decade, building satellite plants in emerging regions of the world such as China and Eastern Europe. However, new plants were invariably completed at a cost higher than the budget, and they were slow in reaching the expected level of performance. Analyzing the cause, the company discovered that each project was handled as a one-off, essentially a learning assignment for some of their high-potential managers. Today, as the company continues to expand, it considers new plant construction and start-ups as a fundamental capability, with a dedicated manager (seated in the global manufacturing function) responsible for ensuring that each project is staffed with an appropriate mix of experience.

A global competence manager has at least two areas of responsibilities. The first is to align company business strategy with competence development within the function. It is one thing to declare that the company is going to expand in Asia; however, it is far from simple to ensure that company has the talent and capability on the ground to make this happen. Competence managers look ahead at the nature of the business challenge, and together with the HR function they design appropriate steps to fill any possible gaps. This might include attracting employees with new skills to the organization, as well as making sure that existing competencies are retained as the company evolves.

A complementary area of responsibility is to look after the health of the function from the bottom up. This happens at Shell, for example, a company with global competence managers embedded in most professional functions, including HR. These managers are members of senior leadership teams and assume responsibility for a number of operational tasks in global talent management—making sure that the business unit attracts and develops a sufficient number of young high-potential graduates, facilitating opportunities for cross-border experience, and in general, ensuring that the professional workforce has the competencies to deliver on business expectations. Career managers at Michelin perform a similar role, although they also take care of specific talent pools.[49]

Global Account Managers

The scope of operations of customers in many industries, such as automobiles, IT service, and telecommunications, is increasingly global. Customers demand common and consistent quality and delivery standards across all these operations worldwide, global (lowest possible) pricing, and support in all locations. To respond to these demands, many companies have implemented global account management, with the objective of presenting one face to the customer.

These managers coordinate across businesses and geographies and provide a voice for the customer inside the organization.[50] Some companies establish global account structures to differentiate themselves from the competition by developing long-term relationships with their key customers.

There are three generic approaches to the design of global account management, depending on how the firm manages the balance between global and local responsibility for the customer interface.[51] In the first, ownership of the customer and P&L stay with the country; the global account manager plays the role of cross-country coordinator, information provider, and influencer. The second and probably most common approach is a matrix, where an account manager reports both to the local sales organization and to a corporate global account management function. For both these approaches, managers in global account roles have responsibility and accountability for the client but no formal power or independent resources. Only in the third approach—still rare but increasing in frequency—does the balance of power lie with the global account manager. This structure may be appropriate if global customers are seen as more important than local sales.

Implementing global account management can be long and painful because it adds a whole layer of complexity to the organization. Even more importantly, it usually involves shifting the balance of power within the global organization, and meeting resistance (see the Box "Implementing Global Account Management").

Implementing Global Account Management

- Implementing a global account structure is a complex process. As far as time and deliverables are concerned, targets should be realistic; putting a global account management structure in place without the ability to deliver on customer demands would be counterproductive, creating customer expectations that cannot be satisfied.

- Historically, the best customers are often close to their local suppliers and value this relationship. Gaining the necessary cooperation from local subsidiaries is an important early step in the implementation process. It may be advisable to allow local managers to participate in setting up the new global account.

- The shift in power between countries and global accounts will have an impact on firm culture. Companies must put in place appropriate policies and systems to support this transition, not least in human resources. Senior executives must be seen to back the change.

- Remember that the global account manager is not a salesperson. The role is essentially internal—communicating, facilitating, and coordinating—not external. Selecting individuals with the skills and competencies that fit this role is the foundation for effective global account management.

Source: J. Birkinshaw and J. DiStefano, "Global Account Management: New Structures, New Tasks," in *The Blackwell Handbook Of Global Management: A Guide To Managing Complexity*, eds. H.W. Lane et al. (Oxford: Blackwell Publishing, 2004); G.S. Yip and A.J.M. Bink, "Managing Global Accounts," *Harvard Business Review* (September 2007).

From the HR perspective, the key issues relating to global account management are selection and performance management. Deep knowledge of the business, interpersonal skills, cross-cultural communication skills, and comfort in leading without authority are some of the key criteria for selecting managers for this role. In terms of performance management, while maximizing the revenue flow is as important as it is in any other sales and marketing role, other soft factors such as the quality of the relationship with the customer should also be taken into consideration.

Lateral Steering Groups

The second important instrument of lateral coordination—cross-border steering groups—includes cross-regional business teams, strategic development councils, product development committees, and regional management boards, as well as various other formal and informal steering groups. While the structure of the firm may be quite simple, cross-boundary steering groups help to align the organization by providing platforms to bring a variety of perspectives to bear on issues in the steering group's area of responsibility.

Using cross-boundary groups to steer strategic or operational projects or problems provides flexibility in the governance of the transnational firm. Cross-border steering groups can help the firm to coordinate globally or regionally to launch a business initiative, manage the introduction of a new technology, align and standardize processes across various boundaries, and to tackle other complex problems—all without introducing the complexities of a matrix structure. Such groups can also manage emerging areas of business or nurture new strategic activities until they are large enough to become a part of the mainstream organization.

Although one advantage of steering groups is flexibility, roles and responsibilities need to be clearly defined and well communicated to ensure that decisions can be made quickly. Accountability, with clear deliverables, is essential; otherwise there is a risk that steering groups will become bureaucratic representational committees with no credibility and little influence.

Cisco is one global company that has embraced the steering group concept. Under the banner of "speed, skill, flexibility" the company coordinates its global operations with at least 10 boards, more than 30 councils, and so many working groups that no one bothers to keep count. The steering group idea took off when CEO John Chambers realized that Cisco's hierarchical structure precluded the company from moving quickly into new markets. Putting managers in cross-functional and cross-regional teams helped to break down traditional silos and led to faster decision making. However, not all managers made the transition to the new style of work—as many as 20 percent of Cisco executives could not handle the new requirements or did not accept the revamped compensation system tied to teamwork.[52]

Some cross-border steering groups, such as business coordination teams and functional councils, are set up to complement the formal organization. They represent a semipermanent mechanism for introducing relevant perspectives into strategic and operational decision making, without crushing innovation and local accountability by imposing decisions from the center. Global teams can address specific operational problems by mobilizing the collaborative energy of employee whose talents and knowledge are most relevant to the issue at hand. These ad hoc teams respond to the firm's major challenges, such as a large-scale cross-border acquisition or a worldwide change effort. When the task is accomplished and decisions implemented, the groups will disband. The examples include global project management teams such as the Nestlé GLOBE team, various transformational task forces, and postmerger integration teams.[53]

Business Coordination Teams

Business coordination teams are typically set up to create and manage global products and services—for example, to integrate product strategies across regions by linking marketing and supply chain units, to launch a new product in multiple countries, or to service global accounts when an account manager's role is not sufficient. A coordination team may have access to its own resources, as well as accountability for specific objectives. The team members are appointed by senior management, which gives them authority and legitimacy.

Cross-company teams (CCTs) and cross-functional teams (CFTs) were introduced by Carlos Ghosn after his appointment as Nissan's CEO to maximize the benefits of the Renault and Nissan alliance. The role of the 11 CCTs (with the chair of each team coming from Renault and vice chair from Nissan, or vice versa) was to coordinate operations and to search for synergies between the two firms. The mission of the 10 CFTs was to streamline processes in specific functional areas, such as purchasing, and sales and marketing. The CFTs were limited to 10 members to facilitate fast action, but they were supported by subteams set up to explore specific issues and to work out action plans. In total about 1,500 managers and professionals were involved.[54]

Regional management is one area where business coordination teams are used with increased frequency, replacing the traditional bureaucracy. GE grew to become one of the largest companies in Europe with over $40 billion in local revenues, although it has only recently established a European head office. All necessary coordination was implemented through horizontal councils and task forces with limited budgets and no formal resources. Not surprisingly, nomination to any of these coordinating bodies was a badge of honor for any up-and-coming GE executive.

Functional Councils

In many multinational corporations, functional councils perform a number of essential coordinating and governance roles. The role of functional councils is first and foremost to align functional and business strategy, a critical task when business units are operating globally while functions are organized locally. The councils set global priorities for the function and monitor implementation. They can also drive standardization of practices and processes, which increases efficiency by reducing unnecessary duplication. If established at an operating level, these councils can be a good vehicle for communication and sharing best practices to develop and leverage functional competence worldwide.

For example, Heineken has three functional councils in Europe: for manufacturing, distribution, and marketing. To take the manufacturing council as an example, it is headed by one of the managing directors and consists of the manufacturing directors from all countries who constantly share ideas about brewing technology and best practice. They also discuss when and where to add new breweries or close old ones, and how to combine purchases to reduce costs for materials and equipment.[55]

Functional councils are increasingly used to steer the global HR function in large complex companies like ABB, P&G, and Shell. Keeping them small to maintain focus, a top-level HR council, coordinated by the head of corporate HR, might consist of managers heading key expertise areas in the head office, HR leaders from regions or lead countries, and HR managers from the business divisions. Similar councils may be cascaded down to regions or even countries. One of the important roles of such councils at intermediate levels is to monitor the performance of high-potential employees and provide them with opportunities for career development.

Project Management Teams

Many companies manage complex cross-border projects through project management teams. These may take a permanent form, like the project management group at ABB that oversees the collaboration between scores of business units on large-scale strategic or engineering projects. Or, more typically, they are ad hoc, like the project teams preferred by Toyota when building new overseas factories. The box "Cross-Cultural Differences In Project Management" contrasts the strengths and weaknesses of Western and Japanese firms.

Large cross-border projects typically go through different stages. Research has shown that one major problem is the failure to anticipate and manage the transitions between these stages. People who become involved in later stages without being consulted previously want earlier work redone. Shell became aware of these problems in large 10-year projects, like designing and building a refinery, which involved many different functions. Such projects may go through a dozen different stages from the initial feasibility study to the handover to the refinery operating team. Shell calculated that the costs and delays in transitions were such that it was theoretically more effective to load all staff, including the operating team, onto the project at the beginning and to take people out, rather than bring them in, as time went on.

The staffing challenge applies particularly to large international projects, where the problems of links between phases may lead to loss of direction or momentum.[56] The theory of project sequencing is that the next phase should be clearly anticipated, with the future leader functioning as an early team member. However, in many firms the striking reality is that when leadership in the project is passed from function to function, there is virtually no leadership

Cross-Cultural Differences in Project Management

There appears to be an interesting asymmetry between Western and Japanese strengths in global project team management. Western firms tend to master the international aspects of project management quite well. They invest considerable effort in choosing project members from lead countries, probing to test reactions in different geographic regions, and ensuring that cultural differences do not block projects. The problem for Western firms is lack of cooperation between functions. Conversely, Japanese firms are more adept at interfunctional coordination, while they have difficulty handling the international aspects of a project. A project may run smoothly at home with a high degree of crossfunctional teamwork, but when foreign staff have to become involved, it may hit a roadblock.

These differences reflect different patterns of career socialization. Western professionals tend to move up within their functions, and are exposed to their international functional colleagues through training, conferences, and projects. In contrast, the Japanese work on interfunctional projects early in their careers and are frequently moved to a different function as part of their initial training. Yet they rarely have contact with their peers outside Japan, partly, at least, because of the language barrier. Consequently these differences in project staffing and management development show up in different sequencing challenges.

overlap. When the passage from one phase to another works well, it is often because the sequencing problems are anticipated and dealt with through staffing and coordination meetings.

For some industries, such as upstream oil exploration, the management of large complex projects, like opening up a new gas field in Siberia or accessing deep offshore oil, is of capital importance. Projects like these may span a decade or more, carrying the complexities of a partnership with the local government on one hand and hundreds of subcontracting agreements on the other through many different phases. Not long ago, the CEO of Shell identified project management capability as one of the topmost strategic capabilities for the future, and an academy (a steering group unit) was set up to reinforce the development of these capabilities. Shell today is reorganizing the whole of its upstream oil and gas exploration and production around such project units.

Avoiding the Traps in Managing Steering Groups

Observing a large number of effective (and ineffective) steering groups, we propose the following guidelines:

- First, size does matter. While one purpose of a steering group is to engage multiple perspectives in decision making, groups need to stay small to be effective. Steering groups are not representational committees—those who have tried to run complex companies by committee have usually failed. It helps if individual members have broad perspectives, by virtue of their prior experience and social networks.

- As we have noted, the roles and responsibilities of steering boards and councils have to be clearly defined and well communicated throughout the company. Sony's first attempt to create a pan-European organization in the mid-1990s failed, despite top management support and clear business logic, because operational roles and responsibilities were not properly spelled out.
- It is vital that the members of steering groups have an integrative leadership orientation.[57] The ability to resolve issues horizontally with one's peers is leadership behavior that should be expected and rewarded.
- Senior management must actively encourage, recognize, and reward horizontal collaboration, through words as well as compensation and promotion.

People Strategies Supporting Lateral Steering

Implementing lateral steering tools is closely linked with people strategies and must be anchored in corporate human resource practices. The behavioral competencies of leaders are far more important in organizations with strong horizontal coordination than in vertically oriented structures, and the selection and development of leaders should reflect these requirements. Carefully designed mobility and training can foster the development of the informal networks that are a foundation for horizontal coordination. With respect to team-based lateral coordinating structures, performance management becomes an essential tool, since objectives need to be aligned and decisions executed across borders.

Lateral Leadership Skills

Probably the most important distinction between staffing vertical and horizontal structures is that in vertical structures, the authority vested in a position defines what can be done by the occupant of the role, while in a lateral structure it is *who* is in the job that will determine what gets done. Essentially, authority comes from the person in the job. What do we know about leadership competencies essential for effective lateral coordination? Table 5–2 provides a summary of some of the key skills.

As we have pointed out, lateral leaders, such as alliance managers or global account managers, have neither large budgets, nor staff, nor direct authority over resource allocation. Instead, the manager has to rely on persuading and

TABLE 5–2. **Lateral Leadership Competencies**

- Assuming responsibility without authority.
- Effectiveness in mobilizing resources across the organization.
- Skills in managing conflicts and steering through tensions.
- Working proactively under ambiguity.
- High degree of cultural flexibility and adaptability.
- Experience and ability to work virtually.
- Ability to build trust through professional credibility and personal integrity.

influencing networks of people inside and outside the firm. The ability to assume responsibility without full authority and effectiveness in mobilizing resources across organizational boundaries are two especially important competencies for lateral leaders.

We have said repeatedly that differences in priorities and perspectives are inevitable in multinational firms. Therefore, managing the resulting conflicts and steering through tensions is another important competence for lateral leaders. The job may also require a high degree of flexibility, and the ability to adapt to management styles and practices in different national and subunit cultures. Managers who are not comfortable working under ambiguity will find it difficult to cope, as will those who do not have strong virtual teamwork and networking skills.

Only people with credibility and strong skills in conflict resolution can successfully manage the inevitable tensions between conflicting but legitimate priorities that naturally emerge in any global business. Trust is at the base of the relationships through which lateral leaders get things done. These managers usually have a mix of functional and interpersonal competencies, ranging from technical expertise and analytical skills to communication and cross-cultural skills.

Developing the Necessary Social Understanding and Networks

To be effective, lateral leaders require an in-depth understanding of the organization. Who has influence, and who has expertise? Who should be involved in what kind of issue? This know-how is gained through broad experience and links with others in the enterprise. Because of the tacit nature of knowledge required to be an effective lateral leader, most companies try to grow their own.[58]

One of the best ways of developing the coordination skills of lateral leaders is through various forms of international assignment, especially if they are properly structured around the learning dimensions of the expatriate role.[59] The value of mobility can be further enhanced through global and regional meetings, participation in international projects, social gatherings, and training events that deepen personal ties. And since experience gained in international assignments develops horizontal coordination, an organization should have incentive and reward systems to make these assignments attractive.

The success of lateral design depends a great deal on the depth and quality of the company's social capital—in essence, the network of links between people in the organization. In Chapter 6, we will elaborate on the contribution of social networks and social capital to horizontal coordination.

BUILDING CROSS-BORDER TEAMS

As we have seen, cross-border teams are a fundamental coordination mechanism in transnational enterprises as they provide a way of tapping into the diversity of perspectives and experiences residing in different parts of a multinational.

Like any other team, a cross-border team can be defined as a small number of people with complementary skills who are committed to a common purpose, with a set of performance goals for which they hold themselves accountable.[60] Cross-national teams can be used for a number of reasons, and we begin this section by mapping the different forms of such teams. We then discuss how to create the foundations for successful international teams and highlight key factors that enhance their performance.

Mapping Cross-Border Teams

Santos has developed a typology of different kinds of cross-border teams, as shown in Figure 5–3.[61] The teams vary on two dimensions: the extent to which the members share the same context, and whether or not the members are located in the same place.

Some teams have high confluence or shared context—members speak the same language and have shared systems of meaning and common stocks of basic knowledge. Other teams are more diverse in terms of language, culture, and experience, and there is a greater probability of misunderstanding when members work together. Some teams are co-located in the same area or building, where face-to-face meetings can easily be organized and where there is a high probability of spontaneous interaction and instant feedback. Other teams are separated physically, and the opportunity for face-to-face exchanges is much lower.

This leads to the four types of team that are shown in Figure 5–3. In the *classic team*, people with relatively similar backgrounds are all co-located—for example, at the headquarters of a company. Although Microsoft is in the business of helping people to work virtually, Microsoft knows the virtues of co-location. Key

FIGURE 5–3. Four Types of Cross-Border Teams

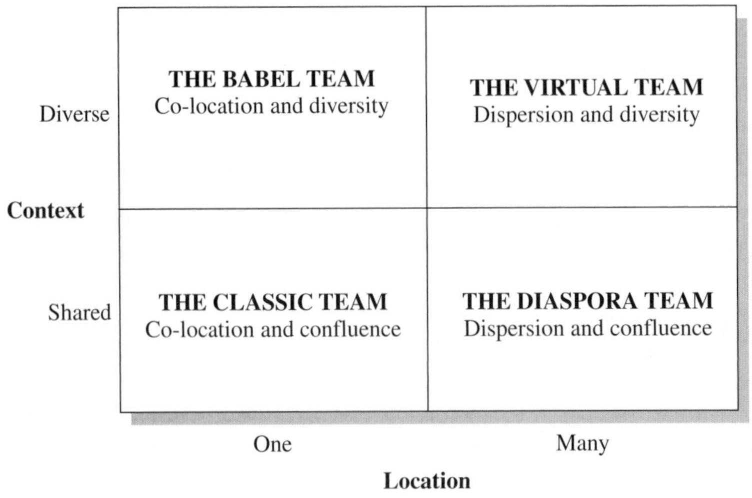

	One	Many
Diverse	**THE BABEL TEAM** Co-location and diversity	**THE VIRTUAL TEAM** Dispersion and diversity
Shared	**THE CLASSIC TEAM** Co-location and confluence	**THE DIASPORA TEAM** Dispersion and confluence

Context

Location

functions are all housed at its Redmond campus outside Seattle, where people dress similarly, speak the same in-house lingo, and share a common socialization regardless of their national or functional background. Microsoft believes that the probability of innovative solutions and effective coordination is highest under such circumstances, although this may not always be possible or desirable.

In contrast, the *diaspora team* can consist of strongly socialized expatriates from the parent company who are sent abroad and yet function as a tightly knit global innovation network. Although they work in multiple locations, they share a common context by virtue of their socialization by the parent. These expatriates often staff global development projects, having dual roles as local representatives and as guardians of the global enterprise.

In the *Babel team*, representatives of different cultures gather in a single location, usually the regional or parent headquarters. Being physically together reduces the negative impact of the lack of shared socialization. Finally, there are the truly *virtual teams* that share neither context nor location. The members of these teams work together through information and communications technology, interspersed with occasional face-to-face meetings.

Virtual teams have become increasingly common in multinational firms. They can bring together the best people in an organization to work on a specific task without having to consider where those members are located. They can also draw on wider networks of information and expertise.[62] Instead of an army of headquarters staffers who study opportunities and solve problems, a few network leaders are needed to form a cross-border team for a specific purpose, with appropriate members drawn from units with relevant expertise. Such teams can drive change fast by cutting across layers and boundaries. Speed is a critical advantage of these teams—they can be put together quickly, and their composition can be changed equally rapidly if needed, providing firms with invaluable flexibility.

However, because the team members share neither a common socialization nor a common location, creating effective virtual teams has turned out to be more difficult than expected.[63] Geographic and cultural distances interact to create obstacles to team performance,[64] and much of our discussion here will focus on the particular challenges in teams that work virtually to a greater or lesser extent.

Foundations for Global Teamwork

Teamwork within a unit is difficult enough, and the obstacles multiply with international and virtual teams. Although many of the general principles of project management apply to cross-border teams, the failure to apply these lessons rigorously amplifies the risk of team failure, due to the greater complexity and diversity of transnational projects.

A great deal has been researched and written about teamwork during the last 20 years.[65] From this, we can single out several enabling factors and obstacles to the establishment of effective cross-boundary teamwork that are particularly relevant for international human resource management: clarity on goals and deliverables; careful choice of team members; and the building of relationships and trust from the outset.

Clarity on Goals and Deliverables

One of the most ubiquitous findings about cross-border teamwork is that success depends on the clarity of the task and goals.[66] Clear goals and deliverables distinguish a team or a project group from a committee. If the mandate remains fuzzy, as is often the case initially, the project group risks developing into a time-wasting talk shop, no matter how important its mission. Since most team members will typically have their own operational roles to undertake, lack of clarity undermines commitment to the project and creates a self-fulfilling prophecy. Shell, a company with substantial experience with global teams, encourages clarifying goals by insisting that all such groups should prepare their brief and obtain buy-in for it from appropriate sponsors.

Overambition is a related trap, setting up too many cross-border groups that overstretch the organization. The difficulties facing the specialty chemicals division of a European firm illustrate this problem. The division grew organically, complemented by a number of acquisitions. In the words of its human resource director,

There was a clear need for consolidation, which initially took the shape of a series of conferences, internal seminars and workshops. These started to break down some of the barriers, and then we set up a series of project groups to work through challenges that had been identified by senior management. With hindsight, we were too ambitious—there were about 20 project groups and this overloaded the organization. Five or six were successful, but many developed into time-consuming discussions that led nowhere. A certain cynicism started to prevail because the many failures drowned out the successes. We live with this problem today because no one really believes in collaboration.

In this context, it is critical that cross-boundary teams be visibly linked with organizational priorities, and that firms provide the resources and high-level cross-border sponsorship that are needed for such teams to work effectively. In fact, there is some evidence that larger, critical projects (in relation to the size of the business) are more likely to succeed than smaller projects because they receive more attention and sponsorship from senior management.[67] The latter are forgotten in the allocation of necessary resources. It is also important to ensure that the first cross-border projects to be set up are visibly successful.

Importance of Staffing

Cross-boundary teams are often put together to provide diversity of perspectives, so selecting people to work in the team involves balancing multiple criteria, such as technical or functional skills, representation of different parts of the firm, and the dual interests of global integration and local responsiveness. There are also arguments for taking personal characteristics into account, like cross-cultural sensitivity, emotional self-control, and the ability to work autonomously.[68] However, it is difficult to incorporate all this diversity because team size is limited. The internal difficulties of team management, as well as cost and scheduling problems, appear to grow exponentially with the size of the team. Psychologists suggest that the optimal number of people in a team is typically five to nine, and never more than 10 to 15. Where technical constraints argue for larger teams, the task has to be structured so that it can be broken down into work for subgroups.

Understaffing to the point where the team does not have members with necessary perspective and experience is dangerous, but overstaffing also has serious drawbacks. One of the paradoxes of staffing project teams is that some of the most energized and committed groups are those where the members complain about being overworked and understaffed. This has been called "optimal undermanning" or "n-minus one staffing," keeping the team lean and mean rather than representational and consequently bureaucratic.[69] Another paradox is that the available people are rarely the right people—indeed, this is probably precisely why they are available. In this sense, the formation of a project team is a political process, as the box outlining "Staffing Nestlé's GLOBE" illustrates.

Staffing Nestlé's Globe

Nestlé's GLOBE team was formed in April 2000. The whole team was expected to grow to about 300 professionals at its peak, supported by scores of outside consultants. At the core, however, the project would be led by a small leadership group of fewer than a dozen managers.

Thirty-nine-year-old Chris Johnson, previously responsible for Nestlé's business in Taiwan and without any direct IT experience, was nominated to head up the GLOBE team. He would also become the youngest member of Nestlé's group management, the team of nine top executives heading the company, for the duration of his appointment as the head of GLOBE. He reported to the CFO of the company.

Chris's boss provided him with a short list of people he recommended for the GLOBE core leadership group. Some of them reported to the CFO; some worked in the IT department at headquarters and had been involved in previous integration projects that had

failed. Some were very experienced but close to retirement, and others, according to Chris's peers, were not well respected in the markets.

As Chris was considering whom to select, he learned that several of these candidates had already been promised a position on the GLOBE team. Chris now had to decide what to do next. Accept the CFO's recommendations in spite of his doubts? Find a compromise? Reject all candidates in whom he had no confidence?

Chris Johnson decided to confront his boss: "Either I pick the people or I quit!" It was the only time during the GLOBE project that he laid it on the line—as he saw it, it was a way of telling everyone that he would take full responsibility for the success or failure of the GLOBE project.

Source: J.P. Killing, "Nestlé's Globe Program (A): The Early Months," Case study no. IMD-3-1336, video. IMD, Lausanne, 2003.

When individuals see a successful line forming, they are eager to join it—and conversely they are quick to jump ship if it looks as though it will founder. The director of the specialty chemicals division we quoted earlier noted that the most successful project had been in coordinating management information systems. "There we were lucky," he said. "The director of information systems should have headed up the project, but he was too busy. This allowed us to give the responsibility to a general manager who had been arguing for some time about the benefits of coordinating IS. He roped in some of his colleagues, and you could see from the line-up that it was going to lead to something. The information systems director saw the way things were heading and quickly maneuvered himself on board—as a team member and not as the leader, which was the right role for him. It worked out very well indeed."

The members of cross-border teams are responsible for testing and probing with their own parts of the organization to ensure effective buy-in.[70] This means that their personal credibility with their own units in the firm must be high. Team members have to be able to command the time and attention of people outside of the team over whom they may have no direct authority, but whose support is essential.

Global Teamwork Builds on Relationships

Teams are chosen to confront complex problems and conflicting pressures, and there is widespread agreement from both research and experience that personal relationships facilitate the working of international teams. This is illustrated by the problems that an alliance in the European financial services sector ran into (see the box "The Failed Alliance").

The Failed Alliance

An alliance involving three main corporations, French, German, and Danish, was formed to meet a clearly identified new market that cut across national borders. A high-level working party was set up, meeting for a day every three weeks to work out the strategy and implement the intent behind the partnership. The meetings were task-oriented, and virtually no time was committed to build relationships. The busy executives spent the lunch breaks on the phone dealing with issues back home, and flew off quickly at the end of each session.

It took the group a year to recognize that the Germans and Danes had a different concept of a working team than the French. For the Germans and Danes, its objective was to negotiate decisions that would then be implemented. Consequently, they prepared meetings seriously, checking out their positions with their CEOs. They arrived with an agenda for negotiation, and they made sure that decisions were carefully worded in the minutes. However, for the more traditional French, the team was a consultative mechanism, in the spirit of what the French call *concertation,* to help the president reach a final decision—only the CEO could make such decisions, after having been appropriately briefed on the results of the discussions. Consequently, the French prepared for the meetings on the plane journey to the meeting site, alternating between surprise and amusement at the earnestness of the Germans and Danes, and considered the minutes only as a document to prepare the later briefing session with the president.

While frustrations surfaced early, they were never openly discussed. Relationships between the working party members were superficial and did not allow confrontation on such sensitive issues. The frustration created a self-fulfilling prophecy. Within a few months, all the busy executives sensed that the work was getting nowhere, and even the Germans and Danes invested less energy in preparation. The alliance was eventually disbanded because it had yielded no results.

We are convinced that this alliance would have stood a better chance of surviving if the team had spent some evenings together at an early stage in the project, building relationships. The conflicts would have surfaced in informal discussions and could have been worked through. This brings us to an important point for virtual teams. There will always be cultural differences of one type or another, even between people of the same nationality. Without relationships, these will invariably handicap the task. Therefore, in the start-up phase it is important to commit time to building personal relationships face-to-face.

High-quality relationships characterized by trust and respect, cooperation, and commitment are important in all teams but even more so in virtual teams. And cross-border teams must pay additional attention to relationship building, since identity, cooperation and trust are not easy to build and maintain virtually. Deep relationships are more likely to develop when attention is paid not only to the tasks at hand but also—and explicitly—to the social or team-building process.

In a comprehensive study on trust in virtual teams who never met face-to-face, Jarvenpaa and her associates found that trust, which was critical to the team's ability to manage decision processes, could be built relatively quickly, though it is fragile.[71] Team members tended to begin their work together with a basic willingness to trust each other to get the work done with an appropriate level of quality and commitment. Particular factors such as early social communications, early expression of enthusiasm, coping well with uncertainties and technical problems, and individual initiative all contributed to the early creation of trust.

This "swift trust"[72] was maintained and nurtured if communication patterns were predictable—with team members providing early warning of communication breaks, establishing regular patterns of interaction, and explicitly addressing expectations up front—and if feedback and substantive information were extensive and timely. Trust was also maintained if leaders maintained a positive tone, if difficulties were discussed only within the team, and if the initial focus on social interaction and team processes evolved into a strong task focus. However, they found that this type of swift trust was fragile, breaking completely after seemingly minor infractions.

Working in Cross-Border Teams

Many lessons on working in face-to-face teams also apply to virtual teams. However, the absence of face-to-face, co-located contact, and the fact that team members come from different contexts, puts additional emphasis on appropriate communication, managing conflict, team leadership, appraising and rewarding team performance, and quality of team learning processes.

Communication

Some studies suggest that electronic mail increases the quantity of communication, but lowers its quality. There is substantial evidence that electronic communication is less effective with ambiguous or complex tasks, where there is no neat technical answer, and when negotiating interpersonal or complex technical conflicts.[73] The more complex the team project, the more important it becomes to pay attention to building trust and face-to-face relationships, as just discussed. In a study of global R&D management in 14 multinational enterprises, the senior product development manager of the company with the most sophisticated electronic communication system said,

> Videoconferencing, integrated CAD/CAM databases, electronic mail, and intensive jet travel all contribute to lowering the communication barriers. All things considered, however, the most effective communication, especially in the beginning of a project, is a handshake across a table to build mutual trust and confidence. Then and only then can electronics be really effective.[74]

The author of this study estimated that the "half-life" of a personal meeting in R&D networks—the time it takes before trust falls below a dangerous threshold—is less than three months.

The communication challenges faced by virtual team members come from two main sources.[75] First, because any technology is lower in richness and social presence than face-to-face interaction, team members lose much of the contextual information that they usually rely on to help them understand each other well. Second, most electronic communications are asynchronous—there is a lag time between the exchange of messages, reducing the immediacy and efficacy of feedback. This is exacerbated further by communications across time zones.

In some ways, intercultural communication can be more effective when it is written rather than oral. E-mail can help those who prefer the written word; it gives them time to digest and think through a reply. In many cultures, people prefer working through the written word, and even within the same culture, some people prefer writing to speaking.[76]

The complementarity of electronic and face-to-face communications is well summarized in this quote from a book on network organization:

> What the electronic network can do is to accelerate as well as amplify the communication flow, but its viability and effectiveness will depend critically on the robustness of the underlying social structure. This implies that one has to be careful in substituting face-to-face ties with electronic ones. It is vital to maintain a critical ratio of face-to-face

to electronic interactions. It may be even more critical to maintain face-to-face relationships with those individuals who can serve as bridging ties, gatekeepers, champions, and so on. These are the relationships that provide the foundation on which the rest of the network depends.[77]

The failure of global teams is often attributed to communication difficulties and conflict arising from cultural differences. But this is a difference in degree, not kind. Even a local project team faces complexity and conflict because of the diversity of its members, with a consequent risk of misunderstanding and personality clashes. In transnational teams, that diversity is greater, with correspondingly greater risks of failure.

Managing Conflict

As we argued earlier, given the diversity of cross-boundary teams, contention and conflict are inherent in such teams. However, conflict is not necessarily a problem. Task or cognitive conflict, due to different information or assumptions, can be productive, hence the importance of diversity in teams; but relationship or emotional conflict (about behaviors, the way things are said, or conflicts of personal interest) can be highly disruptive for teams, especially if there is low trust between team members.[78] Relationship conflicts easily become personal. They typically erupt when teams run into obstacles, notably when they experience their first performance problems and receive negative feedback from outside.[79]

Often it is not conflict itself but avoidance of conflict that disrupts the team. The most important skills needed by leaders of global teams are those that enable them to bring cognitive and emotional conflicts to the surface and work through them. Because virtual teams cannot pick up visual cues, they may find it difficult to detect a conflict before it mushrooms. Failure to respond to an e-mail expressing a position can easily lead to misattribution and undermine trust. Does the nonresponse signify disagreement, anger, lack of interest—or simply that the other parties are busy?

Cultural norms and language problems can be serious obstacles. In some cultures, silence or lack of explicit endorsement indicates disagreement; in others, silence could mean a tacit approval. In one action-learning global leadership development program, the team met face-to-face the day before the final presentation to the CEO after working virtually for six months. A British member of the team had prepared the presentation material, based on the key recommendations she believed the team had agreed on during numerous teleconferences. Her Japanese colleagues appeared stunned by what they saw on the screen. Finally one of them pointed out, "But—we have never agreed to this." Apparently, during the teleconferences, as American and European team members vigorously debated the recommendations, the Japanese were silent, and no one bothered to check their understanding and agreement. Needless to say, the next 24 hours were very intense . . .

One lesson these team members learned was the importance of safeguarding an open dialogue: setting up ground rules so that everyone can be heard, making sure that potential conflicts and disagreements surface early in the process. Beyond this, there is little conclusive research on conflict management strategies in virtual teams; published recommendations are based more on personal experience and intuition than empirical data.[80] We know, however, that conflict resolution is highly dependent on team culture and trust among team members. We will come back to this issue in the next chapter, when we discuss the importance of social capital and relationships in maintaining cohesion in the global organization.

Importance of Leadership

Leadership is clearly a critical contributor to the effectiveness of global teams. The leader has to be highly skilled in coaching behind the scenes, conflict resolution, and team building (see the box "Leadership Roles In Global Teams"). The leadership skills required may vary at different stages of the team project. In the early stages, advocacy skills are needed to build legitimacy, to obtain resources, and break through bureaucratic barriers. At the intermediate stage, catalytic skills in building commitment and negotiating with external stakeholders are required. And integrative skills in coordinating and measuring progress are necessary as the project nears fruition.[81]

Leadership Roles in Global Teams[82]

Developing and communicating a compelling vision of the team's collective goals and potential outcome is one of the most important aspects of leadership.[83] When team members understand and are committed to a vision, they trust the leader and are more motivated to work toward its realization. A strong vision also allows more autonomy and empowerment among team members. If everyone understands the team's goals and direction, team members trust each other to act on their own on behalf of the team.

Every team needs a clear task strategy and defined roles, an organized workspace (which, in a virtual team, means access to appropriate information and communications technology), and explicit interaction norms that include coming to meetings well prepared with a clear understanding of the objectives. Virtual teams that do not manage these processes carefully often simply fail to get off the ground. It is the leader's role to ensure that these basic processes are well structured, and that related resources are available and supported.

Another role of the leader in a global team is facilitating relationships and building trust. It is important for team members to build social capital by engaging in healthy dialogue and conversations, both social and work-related. With the absence of visual cues, the leader of the virtual team has to check regularly for understanding and potential conflict; the leader should have cross-cultural experience and be sensitive to contextual differences in behavior.

The leader must also ensure that the team does not become too inwardly focused. An external focus on scouting (identifying expectations and tapping into outside knowledge), ambassadorship (building buy-in and sponsorship as well as keeping track of allies and adversaries), and coordinating with other groups in the firm is also vital for high-performing teams.[84]

Finally, the leaders should be particularly attentive when the team runs into its first major obstacles, such as negative feedback from key sponsors. This is the time when conflicts erupt, and the leader needs to make sure that the group learns how to deal with obstacles constructively. This may require time-out meetings, especially for a virtual team, as well as revisiting norms. High-performing teams are characterized by how they deal with the rough times rather than by the honeymoon period.[85]

An experimental study of virtual teams in which the members came from different countries showed that effective leaders demonstrated the capacity to deal with paradox by performing contrasting leadership roles simultaneously. For example, they were able to act as empathetic mentors while asserting authority in influencing the responsibilities of members.[86] The dualistic demands of cross-boundary project work are one of the reasons why such assignments are an important element in the process of developing leadership competences and global mindsets.

Appraising and Rewarding Teamwork

Unless the project assignment is full-time, a major problem in cross-boundary teamwork is the tension between accountability for the regular job and the demands of lateral teamwork, leading to appraisal and reward difficulties. Individuals are asked to work on cross-border teams and then reprimanded because of poor performance in their own jobs. Cross-border teamwork can overstretch the organization unless people have settled into and mastered their operational jobs before they are assigned to cross-boundary teams.

The appraisal and reward system can sometimes discourage teamwork. Appraisal and reward systems that take cross-boundary performance into account are not simple, but they are becoming commonplace in project-oriented organizations like professional service firms. At Accenture, senior partners spend up to a quarter of their time on appraisal of partners and managers, collecting the views of clients, research and back-office departments, managers and subordinates—"You are not going to be receiving a top bonus this year because although the client is happy, the research department did not get the collaboration it needed."[87] Other firms make use of 360-degree appraisals and similar multirater input to capture the opinions of team clients and members.

Promoting Feedback and Learning

Most firms would be well advised to follow the route of IBM and leading professional service firms that are in the forefront of developing processes for cross-border teamwork—ensuring that every project ends with a learning review that contributes to individual and organizational know-how. We often find that managers do not spontaneously seek out learning as an outcome, although they quickly realize its importance when it is signaled to them.

The HR function has an important obligation and opportunity here. We recall urging the human resource executives in a major information technology firm to become involved in four key global projects that the firm was setting up. Project expertise and management of cross-boundary teams was clearly a critical future capability in this industry, and there was no internal know-how about the implementation of such complex global projects (such as how to staff and motivate the teams, or how to speed up the process of successive adoption by countries). To our regret, the HR function turned down the opportunity: "Sorry, but that is not part of our job." No one undertook the role, mistakes were made—but more importantly, there was no learning from those mistakes.

Implementing Global Teamwork

Global teams cannot operate in isolation; as we pointed out, they can be effective only if other mechanisms of global coordination are properly designed—notably the shared norms and values that facilitate trust as well as appropriate talent and performance management processes.[88] Indeed, enabling global teamwork is a big challenge for international human resource management. As technological developments allow us to move further into the world of virtual organization, some of the learning from research is summarized in the box "Supporting High Performance In Virtual Teams."

Supporting High Performance in Virtual Teams

Communicate Thoughtfully

- Match technology with the message—use richer technology (videoconferencing rather than e-mail) and face-to-face communication for more complex messages.
- Match frequency with task—communicate more frequently to match the degree of interdependence the task requires.

Manage Differences

- Invest time in relationships; understand cultural and professional backgrounds; build trust and commitment.

- Structure the task—vision, task strategy, clear goals with timelines, procedures.

Build a Rhythm

- Plan well in advance a rhythm of periodic face-to-face meetings (building trust and commitment) supported by continuing virtual interaction.
- Even teams that never meet need to find ways to create rhythms, using rich technology periodically (the monthly conference call); but occasional face-to-face meetings

may be indispensable for teams engaged in complex tasks.

Lead the Team with Dynamism

- The degree of task interdependence varies from one stage to another, and the team must adjust accordingly.
- Expect the team's task and composition to change continuously, requiring the team to change how it works together.

Manage the Context

- Invest effort in getting the team launch right.
- Create positive visibility for virtual project work.

Source: M. Maznevski, S.C. Davison, and K. Jonsen, "Global Virtual Team Dynamics and Effectiveness." In *Handbook of Research in International Resource Management*, eds. G.K. Stahl and I. Björkman (Cheltenham, UK: Edward Elgar, 2006).

There is some evidence that the effectiveness of the transnational team is likely to be bipolar—either disastrous or superb—whereas national teams are more likely to be simply satisfactory.[89] On the one hand, there is a higher probability of affective or emotional conflict in the multinational team, associated with hostility, distrust, cynicism, and apathy. If the differences are left unmanaged, the team may blow up, compromise, or fizzle out. On the other hand, multicultural teams can be very effective because of the higher levels of cognitive conflict—complementary differences in knowledge, perspectives, and assumptions.[90] There is experimental evidence that cross-national teams take significantly longer to reach decisions but that they consider a wider range of options than homogeneous teams.[91]

Yet the challenges facing global teams are often complex. Their success depends not only on their ability to work through conflicting priorities but also on building commitment to implement their decisions, so accountability for implementation must be included in team members' roles beyond their operational responsibilities—requiring them to work in matrixed or "split egg" ways that are becoming typical for leaders and professionals in transnational firms (see the box "Learning How To Work In 'Split Egg' Ways"). In this sense, for many managers in multinational firms, the "matrix" competencies required for working in global teams and performing their daily roles are becoming increasingly similar.

In the past, the traditional line–staff organization responded to conflicting priorities by segmenting them structurally. Line managers and employees in the business units and subsidiaries had an operational focus. Their attention was centered on local targets and budgetary constraints with a short-term time horizon. The responsibility for long-term global strategic development lay with senior leaders and the staff at headquarters. The staff was responsible for strategic projects, such as strategic planning and business development (external in orientation); cost reduction and the introduction of new IT systems (internal); and best practice transfer or new product development (projects with a lateral orientation). However, these neat line–staff and headquarters–subsidiary distinctions created

Learning How to Work in "Split Egg" Ways

Instead of resolving the conflicting priorities that face transnational organizations—local versus global, short-term performance versus long-term strategic innovation—through formal reporting lines, these dilemmas are nowadays built into the roles of individual managers.

As a consequence of the shift to lateral coordination, all leaders, and an increasing number of managers and professionals, have to learn how to work in matrix roles or what we call split egg ways (see the diagram here, which looks like an egg divided into two).

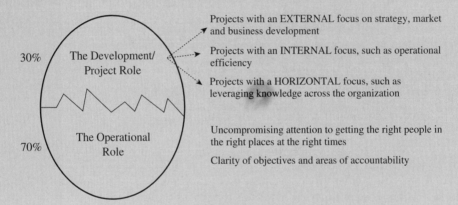

Projects with an EXTERNAL focus on strategy, market and business development

Projects with an INTERNAL focus, such as operational efficiency

Projects with a HORIZONTAL focus, such as leveraging knowledge across the organization

Uncompromising attention to getting the right people in the right places at the right times

Clarity of objectives and areas of accountability

30% The Development/ Project Role

70% The Operational Role

a bureaucracy where much fell into the cracks between the two. Line managers had no commitment to the plans developed by headquarters, which often failed to reflect the realities in the field. At a time when speed was becoming a vital competitive edge, this way of organizing was simply too slow.

One response to this challenge is to deal with these conflicting needs through the redefinition of business unit or subsidiary managerial roles rather than through the structure. The responsibility for strategic initiatives and lateral coordination is added to the operational responsibilities of the manager, in what we call the manager's project role. The manager in the business unit now has two roles, *operational* and *project*, as shown in the split egg diagram. During the first year in a new job, the operational role will take 100 percent of the available time. But after settling in a new role, the manager (especially those with high potential) is now expected to spend, say, 30 percent of his or her time or work on change or improvement projects with a longer-term and cross-boundary perspective, typically involving formal or informal teamwork.

The person always remains accountable for performance in the operational role. But the need to free up time to work on cross-border initiatives, project teams, and coordination work obliges the managers to delegate much of the operational tasks, "empowering" direct subordinates. Now they need to take the nuts and bolts of human resource management seriously—paying attention to getting the right people into the right places and to getting clarity on objectives. This is the managerial role of the person—in the sense of "doing things right." But people are not promoted just for their performance in doing things right; they are promoted to higher levels because of the leadership initiative that they show in the project role—"doing the right things."

In the old days, managers were people in the middle whereas leaders were people at the top. In today's transnational firms, capable individuals at different levels have to exercise skills in both *management*—getting agreed results through people in their areas of responsibility—and *leadership*—taking cross-boundary initiatives and adding value through coordinated strategic projects.

The split egg role is not a radically new role concept (McKinsey used the metaphor of the T-shaped manager back in the 1970s).[92] In most firms, it has always applied to high-potential managers who are expected to deliver on their operational targets and to earn visibility by working on broader development projects. In Chapter 8, we discuss further the role of the split egg in global leadership development as well as some of the pitfalls of this way of working when it is extended to all managerial and professional staff.

One critical implication of the shift to split egg roles is the increased importance of human resource management for the global organization. Managers learn to pay careful attention to talent selection, getting the right people into the right places. Performance management is essential. In short, when they experience split egg pressures, managers learn that one of their most important tasks is human resource management.

MATRIX EVERYTHING . . . EXCEPT THE STRUCTURE

One way of summarizing the challenges of organizing the transnational firm is to stand conventional thinking on its head.

Go back to the law of requisite complexity. Transnational firms face the highest degree of environmental complexity, and the law of requisite complexity says that the internal complexity of a firm must mirror external flexibility. This is still best captured by the matrix concept. The environment is highly matrixed—product markets, geographic markets, customer segments, basic technologies, management technologies. Consequently, as Jorma Ollila, Nokia's architect and former CEO, correctly says, organizations cannot avoid matrix. But matrix does not have to mean only structure, as it did in the past. In order for a multidimensional organization to function, the organizational culture must also think and breathe matrix: Matrix has to be built into leadership development, control and evaluation systems, teamwork, conflict resolution mechanisms, relationships, and attitudes.

So—matrix everything . . . except the formal structure! This could be a good guideline for a global organization. Like every guideline, do not take it to the extreme. There is a role for matrix structures of dual reporting relationships in most organizations. However, to manage complexity, matrix through project groups, steering committees, internal boards, management processes, business planning, and measurement. A project group can be set up quickly; an internal board can be formed, reconstituted, or disbanded in a few days; roles and responsibilities can be rapidly revised—it takes time and energy to align or change structure. Matrix roles and responsibilities, so that people have vertical and horizontal accountabilities. And matrix minds and mindsets—we will be discussing how to do that in the next chapter.

TAKEAWAYS

1. Vertical and hierarchical means of coordination cannot cope with the complexity of demands facing the transnational firm. They must be complemented by worldwide horizontal coordination mechanisms—glue technology. Horizontal coordination does not replace vertical control—it transforms it.
2. The basic structural mechanisms of horizontal coordination are multidimensional structures, lateral steering tools, and cross-border teams.
3. In multidimensional organizations, managers are not only responsible for achieving results for their own units but also have shared accountability for successful strategy implementation across units. They must learn to work in "split egg" ways.
4. The focus of a firm organized as a differentiated network is on leveraging competencies and capabilities initially developed in its local subsidiaries for worldwide advantage.
5. The objective of a firm organized as a globally integrated enterprise is to achieve competitive advantage by locating specific activities in the best place worldwide, and finding ways to link or integrate these activities around the world.
6. The front–back organization is another emerging form of a multinational corporation. The customer-oriented parts of the company are aligned locally to respond to customers, while those parts of the company that may benefit from global efficiencies and scale are organized along global lines.
7. Lateral steering can take many different shapes and forms. It provides a flexible and potent means of global coordination while promoting empowerment and accountability at the lowest level possible.
8. Effectiveness in lateral steering roles requires the ability to exercise leadership with little formal authority, since authority remains with the line organization. Business or area coordinators, global competence and global account managers, as well as alliance managers, are examples of such roles.
9. Cross-boundary teams are basic building blocks of horizontal coordination. They vary on two dimensions: co-location and shared context. Global teams with members who are not colocated and who do

not share the same context need to invest in building and maintaining trust through face-to-face interactions.

10. The generic lessons of team management apply to cross-boundary teams—on issues such as goal clarity, the importance of staffing, managing conflict, team leadership, and feedback/learning—though the risks of failure, if they are not applied rigorously, are greater.

NOTES

1. The information about Nestlé was obtained from Killing (2003b), company documents, and personal interviews with company executives.
2. Killing, 2003b.
3. Galbraith, 2000.
4. Killing, 2003b.
5. Interview with Paul Broeckx, former senior vice president, Corporate Human Resources Division, Nestlé, December 2005.
6. Nestlé internal company document, Nestlé on the Move, Human Resource Department, Nestec Ltd., Vevey, Switzerland.
7. Interview with Paul Broeckx, former senior vice president, Corporate Human Resources Division, Nestlé, December 2005.
8. Nohria and Ghoshal, 1997.
9. Palmisano, 2006.
10. Galbraith, 2000.
11. Bartlett and Ghoshal, 1998, p.122. They distinguish between different types of national subsidiary according to their strategic importance and their level of resources and capabilities—strategic leaders, contributors, implementers, and black holes.
12. McGregor, 1960.
13. Peters and Waterman, 1982; Ouchi, 1981; Kanter, 1985; O'Toole, 1985.
14. The European work on sociotechnical systems, participative management, and organic (as opposed to mechanistic) work systems also fostered the change, then adopted in the United States under the umbrella of the Organizational Development movement. Its history and arguments are well summarized from an HRM perspective in the publications of Ed Lawler. He contrasts hierarchical or bureaucratic management with what he calls "high-involvement management" (Lawler, 1992).
15. The concept of "empowerment," with its emotive connotations, has created a great deal of misunderstanding. The best formulation of what this implies is to be found in Mills (1994), who provides the following formula: Empowerment = Goals × Delegated "Respons-ability" × Measurement and Feedback. The term "respons-ability" (our word) means having the necessary skills to respond. This formula emphasizes both the hard and soft elements of empowerment. If any element is zero, then anything multiplied by zero nets out to nothing. In other words, attempts to delegate will not lead to significant results unless there are clear goals, measurement criteria, feedback that allows learning, and appropriate skill development. We will return to these issues in Chapter 9.
16. Broeckx and Hooijberg, 2007.
17. Galbraith, 1977.
18. This can extend to corporate spinoffs such as the separation of Kone's elevator and cranes businesses (the spinoff of Konecranes from Kone in Finland) and the split

between Hewlett-Packard (computers) and Agilent (the original HP instruments business).

19. To cite but three examples of this shift in research focus, in his value chain analysis Porter argued for the importance of "horizontal strategies," viewing these as the most important contribution HRM makes to the way in which a firm adds value (Porter, 1986). Martinez and Jarillo (1989) reviewed the stream of research on coordination in multinational firms, clearly noting this shift in focus from hierarchical and structural mechanisms to informal and lateral means of coordination. St. John et al. (1999) studied how 48 international firms managed links between marketing and manufacturing. They found that firms with relatively simple multidomestic strategies used traditional planning and scheduling methods, while firms with more complex global strategies used a wider variety of coordination tools, including lateral teams and relationships. Firms with the most complex transnational strategies used the widest range of coordination mechanisms.

20. Baker, 1994; Ibarra, 1992.

21. This is based on the theory of requisite complexity described in Chapter 1.

22. Planning becomes learning, to use the image of a former Shell corporate planner (De Geus, 1988). See also Mintzberg (1994).

23. This was a radical departure from the "one-boss" model enshrined in the classic principle of unity of command (one-person-one-boss). For this reason, the matrix has been regarded by some as the only totally new 20th-century form of organization.

24. Zalan and Pucik, 2007.

25. Personal interview, February 2007.

26. Bartlett and Ghoshal, 1989.

27. Birkinshaw and Hood, 1998; Nohria and Ghoshal, 1997.

28. Palmisano, 2006.

29. Galbraith, 2000.

30. This is also the case for many pharmaceutical companies (for example, GSK) which need a front end oriented to national regulatory authorities as well as customers, while R&D and manufacturing are global.

31. Ghoshal and Nohria, 1987; Nohria and Ghoshal, 1997.

32. Galbraith, 2000.

33. Frost, Birkinshaw, and Ensign, 2002.

34. Galbraith, 2000, p. 42.

35. Palmisano, 2006.

36. Sanchez, 2007.

37. Maerki, 2008.

38. Sanchez, 2007.

39. Galbraith, 2002.

40. Galbraith, 2002.

41. "The Radical: Carly Fiorina's Bold Management Experiment At HP," *BusinessWeek*, February 19, 2001.

42. Gittell (2000) illustrates the importance of hierarchy for coordination. This study contrasts the flat organization of American Airlines, which has broad spans of control and rigorous performance management, with the smaller spans of control at the phenomenally successful Southwest Airlines. The price that American Airlines pays is poor coordination. In contrast, supervisors at Southwest play cross-functional coordination roles—diffusing blame and providing coaching and feedback.

43. Goold and Campbell, 1998.

44. We discuss network leadership and the implications of exercising leadership without authority in Chapter 8.
45. Galbraith, 2000.
46. Porter, 1986; Galbraith, 2000.
47. Bartlett, Ghoshal, and Birkinshaw, 2003, pp. 462–3.
48. Bartlett and Ghoshal, 1992.
49. Francis et al., 2004.
50. Galbraith, 2000.
51. Birkinshaw and DiStefano, 2004; Yip and Bink, 2007.
52. "Cisco Systems Layers It On," *Fortune*, December 8, 2008.
53. Postmerger integration teams are discussed in Chapter 13.
54. Donnelly, Morris, and Donnelly, 2005.
55. Galbraith, 2000, p. 128.
56. Hedlund and Ridderstraale, 1995.
57. We discuss integrative leadership orientation and how it can be developed in Chapter 8.
58. Galbraith, 2000. See the discussion on building or buying talent in Chapter 7.
59. Pucik, 2006.
60. As defined by Katzenbach and Smith (1993).
61. Santos, 2001. It may be noted that Santos focused on cross-border innovation teams.
62. Maznevski, Davison, and Jonsen, 2006.
63. Maznevski, Davison, and Jonsen, 2006.
64. MacDuffie, 2007. See also Kiesler and Cummings (2002) for research on the effects of proximity and distance on groups.
65. Davidson Frame, 1987; Katzenbach and Smith, 1993; Johansen et al., 1991; Bettenhausen, 1991; Mannix and Sondak, 2002; Gluesing and Gibson, 2004; Maznevski, Davison, and Jonsen, 2006; Ancona and Bresman, 2007.
66. Davidson Frame, 1987.
67. Hedlund and Ridderstraale, 1995.
68. Blackburn, Furst, and Rosen, 2003.
69. Snow, Miles, and Coleman, 1992.
70. Although it was not international in focus, Ancona and Caldwell's (1992) study of new-product team managers showed that effective teams follow cycles of external activity (aimed at molding the views of senior management, getting feedback, and general scanning) and internal processes that were associated with long-term success. See the work on X-teams undertaken by Ancona and Bresman (2008).
71. Jarvenpaa, Knoll, and Leidner, 1998; Jarvenpaa and Leidner, 1999. For more on the importance of trust in cross-border virtual teams, as well as the practical implications, see Duarte and Snyder (2006).
72. Meyerson, Weick, and Cramer, 1996.
73. Duarte and Synder, 2006.
74. De Meyer, 1991, p. 56.
75. Maznevski, Davison, and Jonsen, 2006.
76. Jin, Mason, and Yim, 1998; Canney Davison, and Ward, 1999.
77. Nohria, 1992, pp. 304–5.
78. Simons, Peterson, and Task, 2000. See Hinds and Bailey (2003) for a comprehensive model of conflict in virtual teams.
79. Peterson, Behfar, and Jackson, 2003.

80. Maznevski, Davison, and Jonsen, 2006. See Duarte and Snyder (2006) for an outline of strategies, tools, and techniques for work in virtual teams. And see Behfar et al. (2008) for a framework and empirical research on conflict resolution strategy in non-virtual teams.

81. See Snow et al. (1996). Behavioral complexity theories of leadership seem appropriate to understand these demands. These theories argue that leadership effectiveness depends on the ability of managers to display multiple, dualistic leadership styles, supported by a high degree of cognitive complexity (Denison, 1996; Hart and Quinn 1993). Situational leadership ideas, widely used on training programs, embody the same notion.

82. Our basic source is Maznevski, Davison, and Jonsen (2006).

83. Bass and Stogdill, 1990; House et al., 1999.

84. Ancona and Bresman, 2007.

85. Peterson and Behfar, 2003.

86. For the research on leadership in virtual teams, see Leidner et al., (1999).

87. Ghoshal, 1991; Lorsch and Tierney, 2002.

88. We will return to these issues in Chapters 6 to 9.

89. Adler, 1991.

90. Amason and colleagues argue that handling these two faces of conflict is critical for team performance (Amason et al., 1995). Affective conflict is associated with team failure, while cognitive conflict is associated with team success. Their empirical research (Amason, 1996) supports this argument, leading them to suggest that knowing how to steer a group toward constructive conflict is the key to successful team management.

91. Punnett and Clemens, 1999.

92. See Hansen and von Oetinger (2001) for an update on the T-shaped concept, applied to knowledge managers.

CHAPTER 6

Building Social Architecture

Building a Shared Culture Worldwide at Toyota

What later became Toyota Motor Corporation began as an automotive department established within the textile machinery maker Toyoda Automatic Loom Works in 1933. Production of the first car began some years later, exports to the United States started in 1957, and in 1962 the company began its first manufacturing operation abroad, in Brazil. Toyota added overseas plants in Thailand in 1964 and a first US factory (a joint venture with General Motors) in 1984, and the first European car plant began production in Britain in 1992. By the end of 2007, Toyota had reached the number one position in the global automotive market, with 12 domestic and 52 vehicle assembly plants in 26 countries outside Japan, employing altogether 300,000 people. Most of the foreign plants had been set up during the previous 15 years, with teams of technicians and managers from Japan playing a crucial role in the process. The close relationships between team members, and between them and the parent plants in Japan, were important for the transfer of knowledge necessary to start new operations.

The business principles guiding Toyota's operations today were originally developed by the founder of Toyota, Sakichi Toyoda, in the 1930s; but unlike many other Japanese firms, these principles were never codified in a way that would make them easy to communicate. As the international expansion of the company made it increasingly difficult to centralize decision making at headquarters in Japan, clarification and strengthening of the Toyota global operating philosophy were seen as an essential precondition for diffusion of authority to locations abroad.

After discussing and refining how to express company values over a period of several years, the first internal draft of the Toyota Way was presented in 2001. There are five elements at the core of the Toyota Way: challenge (focus on analyzing and solving problems to improve performance); *kaizen* (continuous improvement); *genchi genbutsu* ("go see for yourself" or "go to the source," a principle for analyzing and solving problems); respect for people (with different opinions and perspectives); and teamwork.

217

Along with the Toyota Way, the company formulated the Toyota Business Practices, an articulation and explication of the Toyota Way with a focus on how to analyze and solve operational problems. All Toyota employees throughout the world are expected to master and use these practices in their daily work. The Toyota Business Practices provide a common language for all Toyota employees and units. Both the Toyota Business Practices and the Toyota Way are covered extensively in the formal training programs for domestic and foreign employees in which Toyota has invested heavily during recent years.

The Toyota Way is viewed as one of the key tools for integrating and coordinating the company's widely diffused global operations, especially in the manufacturing area, and participants in company internal meetings and development programs spend a considerable amount time discussing how to use it. A range of strategies helps new employees learn how to act and behave appropriately in the corporation. Toyota puts considerable emphasis on selection and socialization processes. Job candidates at all levels are rigorously screened to make sure that they fit into the Toyota culture, and new members of the organization go through a comprehensive orientation program before they are turned over to their work departments, where the socialization process continues.[1]

The start-up phase is crucial to the establishment of new overseas manufacturing units. When Toyota began to expand internationally, it made a rule that a specific plant in Japan would be responsible for training people in each overseas operation. However, with the increasing number of new production facilities abroad, this system had reached its limits. Instead, Japanese coordinators are sent to the foreign units to instill Toyota's philosophy, concepts, and manufacturing methods. Each coordinator spends between three and five years abroad, with the first generation serving as teachers, the second as coaches, and the third generation as advisers. The first non-Japanese trainers/coordinators from plants in Kentucky and Canada were dispatched abroad in 2007.[2]

In spite of its immense commercial success, Toyota is facing several challenges in managing its international operations. Even with heavy investment in education, the company still does not have a sufficient number of international trainers and coordinators. Employee turnover in some overseas operations makes it more difficult to develop a workforce that has internalized the values, behavioral norms, and management processes that have emerged and been refined in the Japanese operations. Toyota does a good job in socializing new recruits into the corporation, but nonetheless attrition is a significant problem. And learning a culture does not happen overnight. Toyota former President Katsuaki Watanabe goes so far as to say, "I don't think I have a complete understanding even today, and I have worked for the company for 43 years."[3]

OVERVIEW

Both Toyota's top management and external observers agree that the Toyota Way is a key ingredient in Toyota's global success. However, while Toyota may be special in the degree of attention it pays to disseminating its culture worldwide, every organization is a social entity in which values and norms make a difference—especially in the context of international business. In this chapter we focus on how to build what we call the *social architecture* of the multinational firm.[4] We will explore three aspects of social architecture, focusing on the HRM activities necessary to construct the architecture and the ensuing outcomes: (1) relationships among the employees (social capital); (2) shared values, beliefs, and norms (organizational culture); and (3) global mindsets.

We begin this chapter with a discussion about social capital—the ways in which personal relationships and networks can serve productive purposes. The social capital perspective has gained prominence during the last decade, and we apply it here to the functioning of multinational firms. The existence of strong social capital among employees, in particular relationships among individuals from different subunits and countries, greatly contributes to enhanced interunit coordination.

Shared values facilitate corporate coordination, and we continue by exploring multinational firms through the lens of organizational culture. We discuss positive and negative aspects of shared values and strong organizational cultures, identifying ways in which corporations can try to manage or at least influence their culture. The socialization of new employees into the organization is one notable way for the firm to fortify its culture.

The mindset of executives, managers, and employees is important for the functioning of multinational firms. In the third section of the chapter, we concentrate on two perspectives to understand what global mindset means. The first is cultural, and it refers to individuals' openness and interest in other nations and cultures; the second is strategic in the sense that it denotes an individual's ability to balance competing strategic priorities (such as local responsiveness and global efficiency). The focus of the section is on what firms can do to develop stronger global mindsets among their employees.

LEVERAGING SOCIAL CAPITAL

As we saw in the Toyota case, social networks are essential during the early phases of internationalization. Historically, with limited means to communicate and share information, companies had to put their trust in key managers expatriated to distant subsidiaries. Today's multinational firm relies heavily on advances in information technology; without wireless phones, e-mail, and the Internet, the coordination of geographically dispersed activities would be a lot more difficult. But whenever there is a need to collaborate across borders, to transfer and assimilate know-how, or to resolve conflicts or differences in perspectives, employees act in the same way as their less e-enabled predecessors—they rely on those they know, trust, and understand. One of the paradoxes of globalization is that the power of technology to connect people can be harnessed effectively only if there are close relationships between those involved in the exchange of information. It is captured by the cliché that we live in a world of high tech and high touch.

In any organization, deep social relationships improve communication between people and facilitate the development of trust and collaboration, allowing the firm to pursue common objectives with minimal friction. Relationships between employees (or ties, as they are termed in the academic literature) are especially important for companies that operate across borders. Many of the elements of coordination discussed in this book would not be effective without person-to-person relationships. For some coordination activities, such as working in cross-border teams or knowledge sharing, they are indispensable.

Sociologists have analyzed social relationships and networks for many decades, but in the past, informal networks in business organizations were often viewed with suspicion—bringing harmful personal politics into the workplace through the influence of old-boy networks and office mafia. The view that social networks of organizational members are critical for effective coordination in transnational firms has only recently gained acceptance in the international management and HRM literature. In this section we examine the multinational from a social capital perspective, focusing on interpersonal relationships between people within and across units and organizations.

What Is Social Capital and Why Do We Care about It?

The term *social capital* refers to the benefits that derive from the connections and interpersonal relationships of people within an organization and with people outside.[5] This constitutes an intangible resource—a form of capital in the same way that human skills constitute human capital. Let us start with the justification for describing these benefits as social *capital*.

First, personal relationships can be used to access other resources, such as information, or support for the implementation of decisions that have been made. The relationships that were formed between local employees and expatriates sent out from Japan to the newly established Toyota factories abroad continued to facilitate exchange of information and problem solving long after the expatriates had returned to Japan.

Second, investments in relationships are like a stock that may yield future returns. For example, doing someone a favor, treating them well, or spending time together builds social capital that can be used to call in a favor later. But third, like human capital, social capital needs to be maintained; otherwise it will depreciate over time as the personal relationship fades.

For all these reasons, it makes sense to use the term *capital* when referring to the content and structure of social relationships—even though social capital is difficult to quantify and is riddled with uncertainty, dependent as it is on the parties with whom the person or group has a relationship.[6]

Nahapiet and Ghoshal view social capital in a multinational firm as having three distinct but interlinked dimensions.[7] The *structural* dimension is mainly concerned with physical links between people or units, such as the network of ties between actors, the pattern of ties in terms of their density, hierarchy, or connectivity.[8] The *relational* dimension focuses on personal relationships and relations of mutual respect that individuals have developed through a history of interaction. It includes elements such as trust and trustworthiness, norms and sanctions, obligations and expectations, and identity and identification. While the structural dimension is concerned with the existence (or otherwise) of links between individuals and units, the relational dimension deals with the strength of those relationships. Finally, the *cognitive* dimension encompasses organizational phenomena such as shared representations, interpretations, language, codes, narratives, and systems of meaning among parties. Here we discuss the structural and relational dimensions of social capital, and will explore its cognitive dimension, in the form of shared beliefs as well as global mindsets, later in the chapter.

A distinction can be made between a bridging and a bonding perspective on social capital. One interesting aspect of the structural dimension is the position of an individual as a *bridge* between different networks. Building on the US sociologist Mark Granovetter's classic insight into the strength of weak ties for landing a new job,[9] the structural perspective stresses the advantages in terms of access to information and new ideas of being able to bridge otherwise unconnected networks.[10] Subsidiary managers in a multinational corporation who have personal relationships with key people at corporate headquarters and maybe with other subsidiaries act as bridges—or "boundary spanners"[11]—between the local environment and the corporate parent organization.

Over time, this individual social capital can be built on to create a more complex structure of personal relationships between the subsidiaries and headquarters. What is more, when boundary spanners share their thoughts and feelings about headquarters with local employees, they mold staff attitudes toward the parent organization.[12] Impatriates who return to the subsidiary after assignments at corporate headquarters or elsewhere in the multinational play similar boundary-spanning roles.

The focus of the relational perspective on social capital is often on the group or network as a whole. The emphasis here is on internal *bonding*. There is commonly a sense of mutual obligation, trust, commitment, and influence among individuals who share a common history and/or background, especially if there are multiple and overlapping links between them.[13] One of the widely acknowledged factors behind Nokia's emergence as the dominant player in mobile telecommunications was the working style of its top management group, who spoke the same language and had worked together for many years. This built trust and allowed the team to make faster and better decisions than their competitors. Working through the network of Finnish expatriates, the company moved equally fast to have those decisions implemented.

This example confirms what we know from research on trust in organizations: The degree of trust that exists within the organization can impact the firm's ability to adapt to complexity and change. Trust improves communication and problem solving and enhances commitment.[14] As trust grows, so does social capital.

Without personal relationships, there is limited trust. People who have close relationships with each other are more likely to share information and offer assistance, facilitating collaboration in the social network. Over time, close relationships among individuals can become a feature of an entire group or organizational unit. For instance, in a global R&D team of people who have a long history of working together, all members of the unit or organization can tap into the common social network.

Advantages of Social Capital

Individuals who bridge different social networks have been found to gain superior *access to information* about opportunities, new research findings, business ideas, and so forth, that are likely to be useful to the unit where they are working. For instance, the personal contacts of a manager often determine how the firm will enter a new market,[15] while social relationships within and outside multinationals allow employees to search effectively for solutions to problems that they encounter in their work. Attempts to create corporate "Facebooks" build on this. Close relationships are particularly useful when information is sensitive and when sharing it requires a high level of trust between provider and receiver. Strong bonds are also beneficial for *sharing complex and tacit knowledge*.[16] In a tightly integrated social network, new information flows extensively between the members, producing teams where people share a common knowledge base.[17]

Both internal and external social capital can contribute to improved *innovativeness* for the firm.[18] Individuals with extensive external networks can bring in experts to work on projects, and use these contacts to access, acquire, and combine information and knowledge with resources in their own organization. The ability to draw on a wide array of personal contacts, sometimes even among competitors, allows managers to develop new business ideas and introduce improved organizational practices.

Further benefits of social capital are *solidarity* and *collaboration*. Shared values, beliefs, and behavioral norms often develop in tightly integrated social networks. Members may also develop a common language for discussing work-related issues. There is also greater willingness to subordinate individual goals to collective goals and actions.[19] Moreover, individuals with strong bonds may be more willing to take initiatives that serve the goals of the unit, venturing outside the scope of their formal job descriptions. In the multinational corporation, the more units depend on each other, the more they can benefit from social capital to help coordinate their activities.[20]

Through the private social relationships of employees with friends and acquaintances, a firm can tap into a pool of potential job applicants. Studies have shown that people hired through referrals tend to stay longer and perform better than those employed through other recruitment methods.[21] Furthermore, employees are less likely to leave a firm if they have good relationships with others working there.[22] Thus social capital facilitates *employee acquisition* and *retention*.

Finally, social capital can also be viewed from a *power and influence* perspective. When a person has built up a set of obligations from others, they can be used to get the others to act in accordance with his or her own interests. Several studies have shown how individuals spanning social networks—especially if they are the only bridges—can exploit this situation to negotiate favorable terms for themselves and their business units and to influence decision making.[23]

The benefits of social capital to a firm (or an individual) are summarized in the box "Advantages of Social Capital."

Resolving Conflict and Tensions

Conflict is an inevitable part of work and life in any social organization, particularly in the multinational given the contradictions and tensions that it faces. An important aspect of the relational dimension of social capital is conflict resolution, and at the heart of contention management is the fact that most conflicts are best worked out through social relationships.

In the process of coordination there will always be decisions that may go against someone's interests. In the past, prevailing practice in international companies was to minimize conflict by passing tensions up for top management to resolve, so that middle managers and lower-level employees would not be distracted by trade-offs, dilemmas, and confrontation. Indeed, the history of organizational structures in multinational firms, as they developed ever more complex matrices, can be interpreted as a struggle to find a structural resolution to conflict—leading ultimately to the conclusion that the ability to cope with conflict has to be consciously built into the culture of the firm.

Managers sometimes ask us how conflicts in transnational management can be minimized. It is the wrong question. Many people might think that conflict within a company, and particularly within the management team, is to be avoided at all costs. But while too much conflict is destructive, a total lack of conflict may lead to equally destructive apathy and complacency. In fact, research shows that successful companies in fast-changing contexts constantly review their business environments, encouraging fact-finding and divergent arguments so that they are fully prepared when the moment for decision making comes.[24] Different perspectives, and fresh assumptions that may challenge received ideas, can be both positive and productive. High-quality relationships increase the likelihood that people will present different viewpoints and the probability that conflicts can be turned into constructive and novel solutions.[25]

Clearly, organizations and societies differ in how conflicts are framed and solved. At GE, Jack Welch was a master at constructive debate. He spent considerable time at GE's management training center, where he presented his views on the challenges and goals to GE managers and then expected them to argue back. He would also join his subordinates in fierce, no-holds-barred debates about which decision to make. "If an idea can't survive a spirited argument, the marketplace surely will kill it."[26] However, not many Asian executives are comfortable with this kind of confrontational problem-solving approach, so despite its commitment to boundaryless behavior and business expansion in Asia, GE's leadership under Welch was viewed by some as US-centric.

The GE challenge is far from unique. L'Oréal, the world's most successful cosmetics firm, is over 100 years old. Its cultural values were built around contention management, embodied in a dualistic value system (to be a "creative poet" and a "financially conservative peasant" at the same time), and in practices such as using confrontation rooms for making key decisions. This worked well and contributed

TABLE 6–1. Resolving Conflict

- **Ensure that there is agreement on goals.** Absence of agreement about goals (or vision or strategic criteria) will lead to political infighting and unconstructive debate.

- **Actively listen before you disagree.** Showing other people that you have understood their views increases the probability that they will listen constructively to yours.

- **Data, data, data . . . measurement, measurement . . .** A focus on facts keeps dialog constructive. Companies with cultures of constructive debate tend to believe in measuring everything.

- **Ensure balanced power structures.** If certain functions or units are left out of the debate, which is simplified by focusing the power on an inner circle, it is highly likely that there will be no debate before a decision is made.

- **Explore multiple alternatives to enrich the debate.** Focusing on your preferred option to simplify the process of debate will slow down the process of exploration and increase the probability of conflict.

- **Inject humor into the decision-making process.** Trust the psychologists—research shows that humor can keep tension constructive.

- **Focus on the issues, not personalities or individuals.** Much conflict can be avoided by making sure that it is the idea that is challenged, not the individual who voiced it.

to L'Oréal's phenomenal success—as long as all key managers were French and deeply socialized into such practices. But as the firm expanded internationally in the early 1990s, L'Oréal's distinctive approach to managing contention gradually weakened, as the firm localized its management without thorough acculturation of the new leaders. Therefore, one of the challenges of firms such as GE and L'Oréal is to develop norms for contention management as well as close social relationships that allow people of very different backgrounds to collaborate effectively.

To guide constructive debate, some of the general guidelines that stem from research and practice are shown in Table 6–1.

How to Build and Manage Social Capital

Informal social networks emerge in all social settings. In the past, organizations were driven by relationships that were often formed early in life—the cohort of colleagues who joined the firm at the same time, the clan formed at university, the team of people who built up and internationalized the company. These clans and networks drove new projects and initiatives. However, rather than allowing yesterday's networks to steer business development, relationships in the proactive transnational firms need to be built with today's and tomorrow's needs for coordination in mind. This means bringing people together—for example in global teams—where there are current or anticipated links, or where coordination is needed.

Building and maintaining social capital poses particular challenges for firms spanning vast geographical distances, time zones, and cultures.[27] Social networks within the organization do not necessarily follow its formal structure. Therefore, rather than relying on serendipity, multinational firms shape informal social relationships and networks through complementary structural solutions. For example, the existence of councils, committees, and formal project teams influences the pattern of interactions and relationships that evolve within the firm and with other organizations. Even if the interaction is initially mostly task oriented, gradually more social aspects and bonds are likely to develop.

One large petrochemical firm designed more than 20 formal networks to work within special parameters, with the aim of defining and sharing best practices across the multinational. Each network had an appointed leader who had a budget and a coordinating role but took no formal part in decision making. Members of the network were picked from different parts of the corporation to make sure that relevant employees and competencies were included, and efforts were made to collect and disseminate best practices.[28] Because the network leaders had limited hierarchical power, their success was to a large extent dependent on how well they managed to integrate members socially and into the network, and how members perceived the added value of their participation.

One of the challenges facing firms is how much to "manage" the informal networks that emerge spontaneously within and across organizations, now frequently described as *communities of practice*. These communities are characterized by largely informal interaction and collaboration around a common set of interest, such as functional expertise in an area of technology. Firms that have tried to actively manage such communities find that they rarely get off the ground. It is more important to facilitate and encourage participation, and notably leadership, by recognizing contributions as a legitimate part of a person's work, accounting for this in performance evaluations and promotion decisions. The firm may also provide budgets for travel and workshops as well as technological support, removing counterproductive policies that stifle the informal activities of such communities. However, too much micromanagement can kill the intrinsic motivation of those participating in these communities of common professional interest.[29] We will return to discussing the use of communities of practices for knowledge sharing in chapter 10.

While creation of social capital has traditionally been viewed merely as a by-product of HR practices, there is growing awareness that the formation of social relationships should be viewed as a key outcome of proactive people management.[30] Take recruitment and selection practices. Companies may try to increase the likelihood of social capital formation in a particular unit by selecting people on the basis of their organizational cultural and social fit, using feedback from extensive interviews with employees. Building personal ties among peers becomes an integral part of socialization or the onboarding process. And in many global professional service firms, onboarding activities are also used to build relationships between new recruits and senior leaders.[31]

Indeed, multinational firms have long viewed interpersonal communication skills as a basic competence for people in professional as well as leadership roles. For example, companies recruiting from international business schools such as IMD and INSEAD say that an essential attribute they look for in potential recruits is interpersonal skills in dealing with people who are different from themselves.

The recruitment of MBAs from business schools brings the additional benefit of the extensive global social networks that they have built up during their studies.

Other HR practices also impact the creation of social capital. The way some firms encourage and support mentoring relationships between junior and senior employees can contribute to the formation of social ties. The motivation of boundary spanners to share their social capital with others depends in part on whether such behavior is acknowledged within the employee performance appraisal system and forms the basis for individual rewards.[32] However, alongside company and functional workshops or get-togethers, management training and development also enhance social capital in the firm.

An important component of many leadership training programs is the opportunity to mix employees from different parts of the global organization who usually do not meet otherwise, and executive development specialists today pay much attention to the role of management training programs in building social capital. Learning teams are constructed to ensure a good mix of people from different backgrounds; team-building exercises are an integral part of executive training programs; and action learning assignments provide excellent opportunities for participants to get to know each other better while working on important projects. As stated by Nokia's head of executive development; "The personal relationships that the participants build are an extremely important part of the outcome of our executive development programs."[33]

Well-planned getaways and meetings may also play important roles in building social capital (see the box "Ten Days in the Desert"). In this example, the

---

Ten Days in the Desert

Some years ago there was a merger between a large French company and its British competitor to form the largest packaging group in Europe. On paper, the merger made a great deal of sense, but business analysts discounted the potential advantages because they felt that two such arch-competitors would continue to fight with each other. The president of the newly formed group decided to invest seriously in building relationships.

The top 25 executives, half French and half British, were told to clear their desks for 10 days. They were flown to Saudi Arabia, then on by helicopter into the middle of the desert. Landing on a sand dune, they got out and found two caterpillar trucks with camping equipment, food, and water—and, as the helicopter took off, a letter from the president saying that he looked forward to seeing them in four days' time for their first management meeting at a hotel in Riyadh. This unexpected outward-bound experience was a dramatic but successful way of breaking the ice and building new relationships. Making it to the hotel without undue incident, it was a real "team" that spent the next four days hammering out ways to develop the strategy for the new group. The team building paid off in open and constructive debate, leading to several creative conflict resolutions. The strategy was highly successful, and the firm's share price soared.

relationship building had a clear objective, namely developing a strategy for the merged corporation. This brings us back to the point we made earlier. Unless there is a well-thought-out purpose to relationship building, backed by careful preparation, the cost may exceed the benefits. Consider the case of a Belgian corporation formed by the merger of a dozen companies in different but complementary branches 10 years earlier. Each year, the senior executives met for an annual three-day conference. But after seven years, people began to complain about the time-wasting "annual Mass" (as they called it) when all they did was discuss business results and exchange views about what had happened in the past. Although the exercise had been useful for the first few years, there had never been any follow-up in terms of specific collaboration between the companies.

There is considerable art to building necessary relationships at such meetings—managing process is at least as important as managing content. Expensive failures happen when people feel that they have only heard inputs they could have read on the intranet, and socialized with regular colleagues. Successes result when participants build useful relationships with new people, learn new perspectives, and modify stereotypes. Appropriately designed, these occasions develop the interpersonal networking skills that help managers to navigate the complexities of the transnational enterprise.

Management training and development programs can also be used to build social relationships with managers from key business partners. The Swedish telecommunication equipment corporation Ericsson has for many years offered its main Chinese customer organizations the opportunity to send participants to its internal MBA program. The training program has been organized in collaboration with a leading Chinese university and a foreign partner school, which award MBA degrees to graduates. In addition to the impact on Ericsson's human capital and the internal company social networks of its employees, the program has strengthened the external relationships of Ericsson employees, who now have ties with managers in telecom service providers from all parts of China.

Finally, conferences and forums, sabbaticals, leaves of absence, and short-term exchange assignments, either within or between firms, encourage the development of social networks. Employee transfers and visits across borders are particularly relevant within multinational firms. As the Toyota case illustrates, expatriates (and impatriates) play especially important roles, as they bring their social capital with them and create new social relationships in their host organizations.

Where links are important, as in R&D, careful internal recruitment strategies can pay off. The executive in charge of a leading Nordic multinational's new R&D unit in China stressed the benefits of relationships gained from the first expatriates he recruited to the new unit:

A part of my strategy is to get people from different units. By having these people in my organization we are able to easily reach into the other units. This is particularly important in the beginning as we are dependent on doing parts of larger projects in collaboration with other centers. If we have good people who have credibility from each of the other product development centers we will be recognized and seen as trustworthy.

As employees with long service to the firm are more likely to build the requisite relationships and trust, some authors argue that a long-term employment relationship is essential in order to build social capital.[34] The employment practices of firms like Toyota that strongly believe in the value of social capital provide evidence supporting this point of view.

The Impact of Social Capital across Cultures

While social capital is important in all cultural and institutional contexts, there are differences in how one goes about building it and how social relationships influence management and business.

One study explored the functioning of social capital in brokering new relationships through a comparison of French and US enterprises. The more successful French managers, like their American counterparts, had extensive personal networks, though social capital was found to develop in a different way. French managers tended to have long employment relationships with their firms, and the managers' networks—which were mostly within the organization—reflected this. Their limited social capital outside the firm was built on contacts formed during executive education programs, demonstrating the role that management training plays in building social networks. In contrast, the networks of more mobile American managers reflected work relationships with people from a wider variety of firms, brokering a wider range of potential innovations, though perhaps at the expense of the capacity to leverage networks within their organization.[35]

China exemplifies a society where social capital (*guanxi*) plays a crucial role. Traditionally, there has never been a well-functioning legal system in China, and there is very limited trust toward strangers. Therefore, strong personal relationships have been even more important in China than in many other countries. These relationships are typically formed through family ties, shared provenance (coming from the same villages), and studying together. There is also a well-established tradition of using trustworthy individuals to broker introductions to unknown others, the "third person" acting as a guarantee for the trustworthiness of all parties. Experienced managers, consultants, and academics stress the importance of creating *guanxi* with employees, business partners, suppliers, customers, and government officials. Foreign firms can adopt one of two basic strategies. They can either buy external *guanxi* by recruiting individuals who already have relationships with important stakeholders, or develop their own *guanxi* over time.

However, China's high regard for social capital is by no means unique. Countries in Central and Eastern Europe—and even Switzerland, where mandatory military service for males traditionally builds networks across social groups—are other examples of countries or regions where what matters is "whom you know."

Managing the Darker Side of Social Capital

Most recent discussions about social capital in organizations focus on its positive contributions to firm performance. However, an emphasis on social capital also has a potential dark side that needs to be acknowledged and properly addressed.

A high level of bonding within a social group may mean that the group is closed to outsiders, or at least that it is more difficult for outsiders to become accepted. An example of this is language-based social networks in multinational firms. Although most large multinationals use English as their official corporate language, in reality individuals and units tend to form social network clusters based on their languages. Japanese corporations have been criticized for having strong networks of Japanese-speaking executives that are difficult for non-speakers to break into. Employees of a large Finnish multinational who did not speak Finnish complained about the "Finnish mafia."[36]

The former CEO of IKEA Anders Moberg created a public stir when he addressed an MBA class and advised all foreign employees who really wanted to advance in the company to learn Swedish.[37] Although his comments were intended to urge future employees to understand the culture of the parent organization, they nonetheless point to the disadvantage shared by the large majority of staff who did not master the language. It has also been shown that fluency in the company language is positively associated with the level of trust and shared understanding within global organizations.[38]

Other social categorizations produce in-groups and out-groups. Gender researchers have criticized the persistence of male-dominated networks of executives, arguing that old-boy networks lead to discrimination against women. Although some corporations have put considerable efforts into diversity management, the top layers of most global firms are still dominated by men, often from the corporation's home country.[39] Strong local bonding may also make it difficult for expatriates and short-term visitors to become integrated in a unit.

Close social relationships and a high level of solidarity may make an organization too inward-looking. Little new information will reach the members of the group, who may be too loyal toward each other to engage in an external search for new ideas and opportunities. For instance, a set of strong personal relationships with the people working for a local supplier may prevent the firm from noticing and seeking out better alternatives. The not-invented-here syndrome may be particularly prevalent in units with strong internal bonding.[40]

Companies with a high degree of reliance on social capital may be characterized by inertia and conformity. Japanese trading companies, *sogo shosha*, were typical examples of firms that operated globally with an extensive reliance on social networks, within the firm and with most of their customers. Success in the firm was dependent not only on business skills but also on the ability to cultivate relationships—starting from entry-level training to various social activities with superiors, peers, and subordinates. Since the first oil shock in the early 1970s, all major trading firms proclaimed their desire to wean themselves from the traditional Japan-centric import–export business model, as they correctly foresaw its limitations. However, in spite of their often-expressed desire to globalize the scope of their business, these trading firms have not been very successful so far, mainly because they were not able to align their social relationships with the requirements of new strategies.

One crucial question for the corporation is who will appropriate the potential advantages that accrue to individual employees who bridge different social networks. As a private good,[41] social capital is an asset that individuals can use to improve their own situation—indeed, social relationships are the basis for many nefarious forms of corruption. But leaving corruption aside, take the example of a corporate scientist who gains access to important information that would benefit other members of the product development team. There is no guarantee that the individual will share the information because sharing would weaken his or her own position.[42]

Finally, it is important to recognize that there are costs (money and time) associated with developing and maintaining social networks, for both the company and the individual. Relationships are the means through which coordination takes place rather than the ends.

SHARING VALUES GLOBALLY

The Toyota Way reflects a system of values and accompanying behavioral norms that evolved informally over the years. New members of the organization learned the Toyota Way gradually, partly through an oral tradition of stories and anecdotes, and partly by observing and learning from events and behavior around them. The writing and publishing of the Toyota Way, and continual reference to it by executives, strengthen the company's culture and sharpen the Toyota identity.

Toyota is not alone. A number of other successful multinational firms are known for their strong and enduring culture—IBM (US), Shell (Europe), and Infosys (India), as well as Matsushita and other Japanese companies. Not surprisingly, the organizational cultures of these companies are often studied and discussed by academics and practitioners.[43]

Scholars and managers have shared an interest in organizational culture for several decades. The managerially oriented literature on organizational culture exploded with Peters and Waterman's *In Search of Excellence* (1982), in which they argued that corporate culture was responsible for the success of the most profitable and successful US firms. Today, the term is widely used in the business community not only to describe and explain corporate practice but also to explain performance. Managers are advised to investigate the cultural fit between the partners in international alliances,[44] while problems encountered in mergers and acquisitions are often explained by clashes in culture.[45]

The academic literature on organizational culture has expanded since the 1980s, and the topic continues to attract scholarly interest. Studies are published on the relationship between organizational cultural strength and firm performance;[46] research is conducted on the impact of the cultural distance between the partners in alliances and mergers and acquisitions; and scholars theorize about how culture should be viewed and treated as a tool for corporate control and coordination.[47] At the same time, researchers have become interested in related ways of examining multinational firms from a social perspective, including organizational climate,[48] corporate identity,[49] and employee identification with their organizations.

Shared Values, Beliefs, and Norms

We focus here on one common way to view culture—as a system of shared *values*, defining what is important; shared *beliefs* about the corporation and the context in which it is operating; and as associated *norms* that define appropriate behavior and action in the organization.[50] Largely tacit mental assumptions (values, beliefs), shared by members of the organization, are at the core of the concept of organizational culture, manifesting themselves in organizational symbols, rituals, the language used by employees, and the stories told by people in the organization.[51] Members of an organization may be unconscious of the beliefs and values they share.

Organizational culture often serves as a tool for social control, a primary purpose of shared values being to ensure compliance with corporate strategy. When top managers say, "We have to change our culture," they are usually expressing their view that values, norms, and behavior need to be better aligned with corporate strategy. But in the context of social coordination, shared values have much broader purpose—they facilitate bottom-up and horizontal collaboration and initiatives, not only vertical compliance.[52]

As companies move to the transnational stage, shared values become even more important. While consistency in strategy execution is still critical, shared values facilitate trust, which is essential for effective lateral governance, horizontal problem solving, and knowledge creation. IBM, for example, believes today that in a knowledge-based world where talented individuals always have other options, the only way of integrating people into the firm is through values and norms that are broadly shared and internalized by all, steering necessarily autonomous action at every level of the organization. In other words, values are what should guide you when the boss is not looking over your shoulder.

The diffusion of shared values across the units of a worldwide corporation obviously cannot happen through a top-down process of imposition. It is cemented through continuous and consistent reinforcement, based on interactions between like-minded individuals from different parts of the multinational. What really counts is what people do—particularly their leaders—not what is said on the corporate Web site. Therefore every aspect of people strategies, from communication to performance management, has to be aligned with the desired values and behaviors. The diffusion of shared values requires what is called values-based leadership.

The Benefits of a Strong Culture

Most observers would unhesitatingly describe Toyota's organizational culture as "strong." An organizational culture can be considered *strong* if its values, beliefs, and norms are widely shared and intensely held by members of the organization.[53] A strong culture increases consistency of behavior among employees. In a multinational firm, the advantage of a strong culture is that it engenders coordination and facilitates interaction among employees and units who know what to expect from others. Common behavioral norms provide guidelines for ways to behave in different situations; and widespread agreement about values provides a basis for deciding how to act without formal rules. Those who do not adhere to organizational norms may be forced to exit the company.

Strong corporate cultures enhance goal alignment. When there is clarity about corporate goals as well as appropriate behavior and practices, employees face less uncertainty and can react quickly when confronted with unexpected situations. In Toyota, the focus on challenge and *genchi genbutsu* has been internalized by employees as a natural way to approach problem solving. Goal alignment also facilitates coordination, as there is less room for debate about the firm's best interests.[54]

There is some empirical evidence for the hypothesis that strong organizational cultures are associated with better and more reliable performance.[55] However, other studies have failed to find any significant relationship between cultural strength and company success. One reason for these inconclusive research findings is the potential costs associated with a strong culture. Firms with a strong culture may have difficulty adapting to changes in the business environment that require radical shifts in strategy and new operational modes, a phenomenon known as the failure of success.[56] For instance, commentators have suggested that the problems confronting the UK-based retailer Marks & Spencer a decade ago stemmed from ingrained "M&S ways of thinking and behaving" that guided the strategy and actions of the firm.[57]

The lack of internal diversity in perspectives found in many strong cultures makes it more difficult for a firm to adapt.[58] The values and norms that were beneficial at one point in time may be inappropriate when markets and technologies change. The potential risks of a strong culture include "inertial, myopic thinking and orientation to the past . . . [T]he ties that bind may also blind."[59]

Corporate versus Local Unit Identification

But are multinational corporations that span dozens of countries and have a number of different businesses characterized by only *one* organizational culture? In reality, there may be significant differences in values, beliefs, and norms across units belonging to the same firm. Not only do we often find that foreign subsidiaries constitute *subcultures* within the multinational—we also find that employees are torn between their allegiances to the local unit and the global parent organization. This tension between the local and the global allegiance has been analyzed in research on organizational identification.

Organizational identification refers to the strength of an employee's identification with the organization in which the person works.[60] Identification tends to be stronger if there is a good match between the employee's and the organization's values, a relationship that often becomes deeper the longer the person has been employed.[61]

Organizational identification has many positive effects for a corporation. If employees throughout a multinational firm identify with the parent corporation and feel positively toward its leadership, their self-esteem and self-motivation will be enhanced. Organizational identification also facilitates cooperation across units since employees share values and loyalties. But this does not imply that allegiance to the local unit in which they are working will be detrimental to the performance of the company.

Indeed, in multinational enterprises and other large organizations, employees often identify with several organizational entities. For instance, as mentioned in Chapter 4 an expatriate manager may have a strong identification with the corporation as a whole and at the same time be psychologically attached to the foreign subsidiary where she is working. Such *dual organizational identification* is beneficial since it fosters sensitivity to both corporate and local interests and concerns, and it may help the manager to be a "bicultural interpreter" between the local unit and the rest of the corporation.[62] In fact, employees who have dual loyalties—to the corporation as a whole and to their own local unit—may be more effective than those who identify only with the global organization.[63] For instance, a subsidiary manager in a consumer goods company may play an important role in achieving a balance between the pressure from headquarters to adopt a globally standardized brand strategy and the necessity to adapt that strategy to local conditions.[64]

There is some evidence that subsidiary managers identify more with their own unit than with the parent corporation, especially host country managers[65]—but even expatriates experience dual identification.[66] Research on organizational identification suggests that rather than trying to weaken subsidiary identity, corporations should try to strengthen corporate identity.[67] There are several ways of doing this. First, make sure that employees in subsidiaries spend time at corporate headquarters; second, communicate positive characteristics of the corporate identity actively and persuasively; and third, signal international career opportunities for employees from all geographical units.

Building Shared Values

The firm's HR practices play a central role in shaping and strengthening the values that underlie organizational culture. Selection is one of the most important instruments. When they recruit and select employees either for entry positions or promotions, many successful firms strive for a fit with existing (or desired) values. Trying to reengineer the fit for existing employees (for example after an acquisition) is much more difficult. Training and development, promotion, and reward decisions are important filters for selecting people with the right fit for senior positions. Many firms also try to assess how well individuals "live" corporate values in their talent reviews.

In any multinational firm, the extent to which culture is shared is influenced by a range of factors. The most critical of these are

- The broader culture and institutional environment in which the corporation was founded.
- The beliefs and actions of founders and other important past and current leaders, as well as explicit efforts at defining and communicating the corporate values.
- Processes of employee socialization.
- International employee transfers.
- Monitoring how well employees adhere to corporate values and norms.

Each of these factors will influence the choice of HR tools and practices used to develop and reinforce the organizational culture of a global firm.

The Interface of National and Organizational Cultures

As we discussed in Chapter 3, organizations reflect to some extent the societal environment in which they have been established. A sizable body of research has shown that there is a home country effect on companies that operate across different countries. For example, the collaborative values often found in Japanese firms reflect traditional Japanese societal values.[68] Companies can use such features to enhance their image among customers and prospective employees. The values of LVMH, a company selling luxury goods, champagne, and spirits, reflect the refinement and elegance associated with its French origins. The cultures of BMW and Audi are rooted in the importance of engineering in German society.[69]

However, although there is a relationship between societal and organizational values, many successful firms are cultural outliers, with unique cultures that do not fit a national pattern. A close analysis of the culture of companies from the same country and in the same industry can reveal striking differences. Table 6–2 lists the corporate values of Toyota and Honda.

Although the values and philosophies of these two Japanese competitors appear similar at first glance, Honda's culture stresses the importance of individual ambitions and performance, and being aggressive in the marketplace. Honda's founder, Soichiro Honda, once told a reporter, "Each individual should work for himself. People will not sacrifice themselves for the company. They come to work at the company to enjoy themselves."[70] Honda also focuses more on R&D and innovation than Toyota. We need to look beyond national heritage to understand differences in organizational cultures.

Organizational cultures are anchored on a distinct set of shared values. Within their home culture, few managers would question the benefit of such cultural differentiation. Leading-edge companies are seldom scolded by the business press for having a different management style than their competitors. Indeed, culture is viewed as an important source of competitive advantage. Idiosyncratic cultures and values are celebrated and often emulated. However, for many multinational firms, it can be a challenge to maintain social cohesion around unique values while expanding globally and responding to local cultures.

TABLE 6–2. The Corporate Values/Philosophies of Honda and Toyota

Honda	Toyota
• Proceed always with ambition and youthfulness.	• **Challenge:** At Toyota, we maintain a long-term vision and strive to meet all challenges with the courage and creativity needed to realize that vision.
• Respect sound theory, develop fresh ideas, and make the most effective use of time.	• **Kaizen:** Kaizen means striving for "continuous improvement. As no process can ever be declared perfect, there is always room for improvement."
• Enjoy work and encourage open communication.	• **Genchi Genbutsu:** Genchi Genbutsu involves "going to the source to find the facts to make correct decisions, build consensus, and achieve goals."
• Strive constantly for a harmonious flow of work.	• **Respect:** Toyota respects others, makes every effort to understand others, accepts responsibility, and does its best to build mutual trust.
• Be ever mindful of the value of research and endeavor.	• **Teamwork:** Toyota stimulates personal and professional growth, shares opportunities for development, and maximizes individual and team performance.

Source: Corporate Web pages.

While it is fine to be unique or different at home, being different in a foreign culture is frequently considered rude and arrogant, if not fundamentally wrong and improper. When Michelin's management in China decided to promote the company global values among its Chinese staff, many outside observers (as well as some insiders) were critical of their decision, arguing that the company should follow the "Chinese Way" rather than the "Michelin Way."[71] Nevertheless, many successful international firms have chosen to implement the same business values globally. Johnson & Johnson has a "no bribes" policy that makes no allowance for local "accepted" business practices. The company imposed this policy long before other firms subscribed to the same principle.

Organizational Values: Historical Legacy or Engineered Outcome?

There is wide agreement that founders and significant leaders often exert considerable influence on organizational culture. Konosuke Matsushita, Soichiro Honda, Ingvar Kamprad, Sam Walton (Walmart), and Jack Welch are examples of founders and long-term CEOs whose values and beliefs shaped their corporations. Some of their values and beliefs helped their organizations deal with critical situations in their history. Learning from such events can become important elements of the culture of the company, even as it expands around the world.[72]

Some of these corporate leaders have written up their values, beliefs, and personal stories in books that are read extensively by employees and others in the business community.[73] Many firms consciously use *stories*, or sagas, from the history of the organization to describe significant accomplishments of their founders or other key leaders to highlight important aspects of their corporate culture. The stories anchor the present in the past and provide legitimacy for how things are done in the organization today. It has become customary to present these war stories on the corporate Web site for the benefit of internal and external visitors.

Shared language is one precondition for strong cultures, helping employees to communicate effectively, even across considerable geographic and cultural distance. Firms with strong cultures often develop their own vocabularies that new organizational members have to learn. And this learning lasts—former employees of GE or Toyota are often easy to spot even years after they left their original employers, based on the language they use.

Material symbols can also be used to reinforce the values of the organization. The layout of corporate headquarters, the types of car that executives are given and how they travel, and the dress code and behavior of managers are all symbolic expressions of organizational values. The frugality (and relentless focus on cost reduction) of the founder of IKEA, Ingmar Kamprad, is well known throughout the IKEA organization from stories that are told about him: how he drives an old Volvo, that he travels in economy class and stays in budget hotels.

During recent years a growing number of global firms have tried actively to create a set of corporate values. The so-called *values jamborees* at IBM have received widespread attention. In July 2003, IBM chairman Sam Palmisano invited all employees at IBM worldwide to participate in a 72-hour Web-based discussion of what "we represent to ourselves and to the rest of the world." More than 22,000 members of the organization participated in the experiment, which was followed by a large number of interviews, analyses, and discussions before the company arrived at the formulation of IBM's three values: (1) dedication to every client's success; (2) innovation that matters—for our company and for the world; and (3) trust and personal responsibility in all relationships. This was then followed up by redesigning HR programs and policies in line with these values. Other large multinational corporations such as Nokia have engaged in similar jamborees when redefining their corporate values. However, it goes without saying that members of the organization may not necessary agree with the new values, or internalize them, even if they have had a chance to state their own opinions about what those values should be.

Managing Employee Socialization

Employee socialization is probably the most important tool for building global corporate culture. Employee socialization refers to the process by which a person acquires the attitudes, behavior, and knowledge needed to participate and perform well as a member of an organization.[74] Every organization is unique, so new members need to learn what its unique features are and how they can function effectively within it. For newcomers to become committed to the organization and be able to contribute effectively, they need to feel socially accepted—that they have become insiders.[75] Although socialization occurs whenever an individual changes roles and moves across boundaries within the firm, the process is most intense when first entering the organization.[76]

New employees go through the first part of the socialization process before officially beginning work for the corporation. The signals sent by firms to the labor market influence the kind of applicants that they receive.[77] The more distinct and consistent the messages that the corporation sends to the labor market via its Web site and advertisements, the more likely applicants are to fit the cultural values, leading to better commitment to the firm. Multinationals like Toyota, Cisco, IBM, and Nokia have developed elaborate presentations of their company on their Web pages in which they describe what it is like to work in the company. These messages are part of the anticipatory socialization that happens before any face-to-face contact between the recruit and the firm.

Many firms have developed formal induction programs for new employees, and there is ample evidence that such programs improve the outcomes of the socialization process.[78] At Toyota, new members of the US organization go through a comprehensive five-week orientation program. Every hour of the induction program is specified. Subsequently, the new hires are transferred to their own units, where the focus shifts to on-the-job training.[79] For newly recruited managers induction training is weighted more toward individualized mentoring.

The Toyota case shows that proper induction of new recruits should involve far more than a one-day seminar where the history and norms of the company are rolled out by someone from the HR department. Indeed, some companies do not even do that. We saw one international high-tech firm that decided to recruit ahead of the projected growth curve. But the firm did nothing about induction, in terms of formal training or integrating individuals into the organization. As a consequence, cohorts formed between people who shared the common culture of the company they came from. There were the IBM mafia, the HP clique, and the Motorola group. Deep beneath-the-surface conflicts broke out between these cliques, contributing to disappointing results.

Socialization is not an issue for entry-level employees only. It is equally, if not even more, important for externally recruited managers and senior executives if they are to perform well in their new company. One US executive, recruited to a high-level position in Toyota, went through a period of 12 weeks in a US engine plant, followed by 10 days visiting plants (including suppliers) in Japan. A senior Toyota manager served as his mentor throughout this period, giving him assignments and feedback, and discussing his experiences on a continuous basis.[80] The socialization process was aimed at helping the US manager to understand Toyota's values as well as its management and production principles through an intensive first-hand experience. He also began to develop personal relationships with people in different parts of the corporation.

In contrast, a French multinational, one of the world's biggest players in its industry, is an example of a firm that failed to socialize its new senior managers successfully. Ten years ago, the firm brought eight outsiders into executive positions with the explicit aim of injecting change and new attitudes and perspectives into the culture of the firm. However, within 18 months, all but one had quit. Without support, instead of changing the culture of the firm, they had been rejected by the organization as being too different.

One of the challenges in managing the socialization of new managers is therefore the delicate balance that has to be achieved between socialization and desired change.[81] Socialization should be seen as a two-way process, where the organization is striving to influence new members who, conversely, are trying to define a role for themselves in the corporation. If the corporation is inert and hostile toward changes associated with recent hires, the potential value of the new ideas brought into the firm is lost and the incomers are likely to leave.

Rolls-Royce, the aircraft engine firm competing with GE, has been successfully expanding into new geographies. It has been recruiting senior executives from across the world, with the aim of globalizing its traditional British culture. Rolls-Royce's top management recognized that this recruitment drive would not only involve socializing new executives into the firm, but also entail resocializing managers who had spent their entire careers in Rolls-Royce into new ways of thinking. Recognizing that close social network building was vital at this level, the vehicle for the reciprocal socialization was a five-day management program offered periodically to a mix of roughly half new recruits and half old-timers. The program was sponsored by the CEO, who was actively involved in the first day, briefing participants on strategically important projects on which team members then worked intensively together, reporting their recommendations back to him and top management.

Impact of International Mobility

Toyota is a good example of a multinational firm that consciously uses expatriates to transfer the parent company culture to new foreign units. Toyota is not alone in using expatriates as a way to diffuse values, beliefs, and behavioral norms to different parts of the corporation—the pioneering work of Edström and Galbraith recognized the role of international transfers as a mechanism of organizational socialization.[82] Harzing called expatriates "bumblebees" because they fly across units and pollinate local employees with their values, beliefs, and behavioral patterns.[83]

Multinationals increasingly transfer employees from foreign subsidiaries to headquarters or other corporate units, not only to learn the business or inform headquarters about the local perspective, but also with the explicit or implicit objective of helping the impatriate absorb parent company values and beliefs. In a number of multinational firms, it is well understood that one of the prerequisites for locally hired high-potential employees to reach senior positions is a successful pilgrimage to head office.

International training programs, with sessions taught in different parts of the world, and perhaps combined with cross-national teams working on action learning projects, may also be used to influence the participants' values, beliefs, and behaviors. AGC Group, one of the leading global glass manufacturers, has its headquarters in Japan and significant operations in Europe and Asia. It has made the dissemination of the "Asahi Way," a global coordination tool, the centerpoint of its senior leadership program.

Monitoring Adherence to Values and Norms

Virtually all multinationals administer some kind of employee surveys at regular intervals. Their names differ: Toyota carries out an Employee Morale and Opinion Survey in its US units every 18–25 months, while Nokia has an annual global Listening to You survey. Many corporations use these surveys not only to obtain feedback from their employees on a range of issues, but also to measure how well corporate values and corresponding behaviors are followed in the focal unit. The results are then typically fed back to the unit and discussed. If necessary, a set of corrective measures is agreed and implemented.

As with so many other aspects of organizational life, organizational culture will not take hold if senior management does not walk the talk. One of the most difficult decisions is how to deal with high-performing managers who compromise company values. Companies with strong cultures practice zero tolerance: compliance first, performance second. In one US pharmaceutical firm, a highly successful general manager of a Chinese subsidiary was asked to resign because he tolerated sales practices that were not in congruence with corporate values. Although the official announcement was very discreet, within days, everyone in the company worldwide understood that values are nonnegotiable.

Challenges in Managing Organizational Culture

Firms with strong cultures typically have explicit values, indeed often a clearly understood management philosophy like the Hewlett-Packard Way, the Lincoln Electric Value System, or the Toyota Way. Explicit values are the backdrop against which practices can be calibrated. This is desirable, perhaps vital, because it is not specific work practices that create a competitive culture but the coherence and consistency between those practices.

The potential upside of having a strong organizational culture is significant, but heavy-handed management efforts to manipulate the culture are sure to backfire. Indeed culture management may be viewed as social engineering, which in the extreme can lead to an Orwellian "1984," when socialization and training are manipulation in disguise, and empowerment means making someone else take risks and responsibility.[84] In multinationals, attempts by headquarters to influence employee values and norm may be perceived as colonialism, as expatriates and parent company managers imposing their values and norms on the local workforce. In a similar way, top management's claims about corporate identity may be challenged by employees in subsidiaries, who strive to preserve the elements of the subsidiaries' identity and organizational culture that they value.[85]

Although consultants and academics have suggested a range of tools that companies may use to manage their cultures, reality shows that even with best of intentions, culture management and change are extremely difficult. Much attention has been paid to the challenges of managing culture in alliances and in mergers and acquisitions, but influencing culture in day-to-day operations is equally riddled with challenges. Unfortunately, there is not yet much research on the long-term efforts of trying to manage and change culture in large multinational firms.[86] Nonetheless, the existing literature, examples of multinationals that have been successful in managing their cultures, and our own experience suggest that culture management requires the following:

- A profound understanding of factors influencing human behavior across cultures.
- Consciousness of the key elements of the existing culture that the firm wants to retain and those that it would like to change (and why).
- The involvement of employees from different parts of the corporation in the process.
- Attention to how decisions and actions are interpreted by organizational members across units and borders.
- Attention to the realignment of the whole range of HR practices in all parts of the firm.
- Parent company executives as well as local managers who "walk the talk."
- A long-term perspective, recognizing that change in culture requires continuity in change.

The careful management of organizational values at the Indian IT giant Infosys provides a good example of many of the points we have mentioned here—see the box "Walking the Talk at Infosys."

Strong cultures are effective in the long term only if emphasis is placed on values and norms that support innovation, change, and the successful management of tensions. When circumstances change, there must be intense debate over how to define values that should guide new behavior. The decade-long reconsideration of the tenets of Hewlett Packard's HP Way in the 1990s reflected a process of internalizing modified values that led to a new configuration of work practices.[89] Values jamborees, such as those carried out in IBM and Nokia, could also be a part of a longer process of realigning a firm's values. However, even with its culture firmly in place, as pointed out earlier, it took Toyota a number of years to explicitly articulate the various elements of its culture in a formal description.

LEVERAGING GLOBAL MINDSET

Several years ago, the mobile telecommunication infrastructure division within the Nokia corporation (now a part of Nokia Siemens Networks), participated in a benchmark study of how managers perceive a company's global strategy.

Walking the Talk at Infosys

The top managers of India's Infosys deeply believe that shared values and principles give the corporation its character and provide the sustained integration they feel its 90,000 employees need. The values were those of Narayan Murthy and his seven colleagues, who built the IT services corporation that was Asia's most admired corporation for six consecutive years from 2000. The values are formalized with the acronym CLIFE, standing for Customer delight, Leadership by example, Integrity and transparency, Fairness, and the pursuit of Excellence.

These may sound like trite phrases, but they are imbued with meaning for Infosys staff precisely because of the example of their leaders. Indeed, being a role model is embedded in the second of the five values. Narayan Murthy, the billionaire CEO, sets the example by living in the same two-bed room apartment he and his wife moved into in 1984. He says, "I truly believe in leadership by example. I have realized that it is the most powerful way of creating trust in your ideas. Before doing something, you must do it yourself." For example, he used to travel frequently on company buses. When complaints were made about bus travel, Murthy's comments were taken seriously. His management team believes in rapid communication and responds to all internal e-mails and inquiries within 24 hours.[87]

Recruits in this fast-moving company are hired and promoted not for their IT skills but for their ability to learn quickly and for their fit with company values. But as with Toyota, the concern today is how to maintain these values as the company expands its operations around the globe.

Researchers have found that enterprises are unlikely to have strong shared values unless they were deeply held by the founder.[88] Indeed, the cultures of Infosys, Toyota, Virgin, Maersk, Hilti, IBM, and other companies that are exemplars of values-based leadership, all stem from their founders. It takes so much consistency over time and across leaders to give values meaning—a warning for those who think that values can be developed at a seminar and disseminated through fancy presentations.

The survey showed that some parts of the organization, such as product lines, had a highly global orientation. Other parts were strongly local—for example, local sales companies in emerging markets. The initial reaction of most executives was positive: "This is exactly what we need—strongly integrated product lines worrying about global economies of scale and locally oriented sales units worrying about local opportunities."

Their view changed as they realized that, as a result of this differentiation, conflicts were being pushed up to senior management for arbitration, overloading their agendas, causing delays in decision making, and leaving little time to focus on institutional leadership. While the product managers did indeed need to be global, they also needed to work conflicts through with local sales units—and vice versa. Consequently, top management launched a number of initiatives, ranging from management education to changes in profit and loss accountability, in order to develop a more balanced perspective and the necessary global mindset.

In the global competitive arena, sustainable competitive advantage depends on the ability of employees across all regions of the world to implement increasingly complex competitive strategies. One source of complexity is the simple fact that competitive demands may vary from one subsidiary to another and from function to function—the challenge is how to respond to strategic diversity across units.

It is not only the blueprint of a strategy that matters; the organization's capacity to execute it is equally important. Headquarters rules and policies help, but they cannot fully cope with a differentiated reality. Leadership is essential for addressing the contradictions of transnational enterprise, but it is also insufficient. The key lies in the minds of people inside the enterprise—requiring a particular intellectual orientation to business problems and an open and positive attitude toward other cultures and people. We call the attitudes and the required cognitive structure that underlie such thinking a *global mindset*.[90]

What Is Global Mindset

The organizational challenges of globalization require new skills for managing diversity as well as changes in how managers frame business problems. This is not a new argument. It was originally proposed in the late 1960s by Howard Perlmutter,[91] who developed the first formal outline of the orientations or mindsets of managers in multinational firms. Perlmutter's now-classic typology of ethnocentric, polycentric, and geocentric orientations formed a framework for subsequent theoretical and empirical work. Perlmutter identified a need for more "geocentric" managers, "the best men, regardless of nationality, to solve the company's problems anywhere in the world."[92] Since then, many authors have argued that the orientation of managers has become a critical issue facing multinationals.

Expatriates are defined as managers working in a different country from their own. In contrast, global[93]/geocentric[94]/transnational[95] managers—the terms have been used in rather similar ways by different authors—are defined by their *state of mind.* They are people who can work effectively across organizational, functional, and cross-cultural boundaries. Some global managers may be expatriates; most have been expatriates at some point in their careers; but not all expatriates are global managers. The international management literature is full of examples of expatriates with an ethnocentric orientation.[96] At the same time, managers in key subsidiaries may not be expatriates, but they invariably need to have a global mindset.

There are two different and complementary perspectives on global mindset, one rooted in a psychological focus on the development of managers in multinational firms, and the other coming from scholars and practitioners with a strategic viewpoint on the transnational enterprise. Let us briefly review these two perspectives.

The Cultural Perspective

The first views global mindset as *the ability to accept and work with cultural diversity,* reflected in research that tries to map the skill or competence sets associated with management of diversity. Cultural self-awareness and openness to and understanding of other cultures are the core elements of the psychological or, as some scholars prefer to label it, the *cultural* perspective on global mindsets.[97] In contrast to an ethnocentric mindset, a person (and by extension a firm) with a global mindset "accepts diversity and heterogeneity as a source of opportunity."[98]

In line with this perspective, the term "transnational manager" has been coined to describe cultural "citizens of the world," individuals defined by their knowledge and appreciation of many cultures, able to tread smoothly and expertly between cultures and countries throughout their careers.[99] Rhinesmith suggests that people with a global mindset tend to have broader perspectives than people with a traditional domestic mindset; they try to understand the context for decision making and are suspicious of "one-best-way" solutions. They accept life as a balance of contradictory forces, facilitating their ability to handle tensions and conflict. They value diversity, channeling it through teamwork. They view change as an opportunity rather than a threat, are open to new initiatives, and focus on process rather than structure to deal with the ambiguities and needs for adaptation in multinational firms.[100]

Few individuals possess all these qualities (or the personal attributes, skills, and knowledge supposedly held by individuals with a high level of "cultural competence"[101])—but those who do are likely to be better equipped to deal with the challenges of working in transnational firms.

We discussed related issues when listing preferred personal characteristics of expatriates, but these qualities are also relevant for home-country-based executives in global organizations.

The Strategic Perspective

The second complementary perspective on global mindset, and the one that we will address in more detail, focuses on a way of thinking (or cognition) that reflects conflicting strategic orientations; it can therefore be labeled a *strategic* perspective. Since most multinational firms face strategic contradictions (the determining feature of the transnational enterprise), scholars have emphasized the need for "balanced perspectives," arguing that a critical determinant of success in multinationals lies in the cognitive orientations of senior managers—their ability to cope with complexity embedded in the business.[102]

Diverse roles and dispersed operations must be held together by a management mindset that understands the need for multiple strategic capabilities, and views problems and opportunities from both local and global perspectives. The task is not to build a sophisticated structure but to create a matrix in managers' minds.[103] As suggested in Chapter 1, the "matrix in the mind" concept captures the notion of global mindset and the idea that contradictions need to be built into the way of thinking of managers and leaders in the transnational firm.

As we discussed earlier in this book, the main strategic drivers in the transnational enterprise are global efficiency, local responsiveness, and worldwide coordination. So the strategic perspective on global mindset expects individuals to *balance competing priorities* that emerge in international management processes, rather than to advocate one dimension at the expense of the others. The global mindset recognizes that organizational resources are deployed across all subunits and places high value on sharing information, knowledge, and experience across boundaries.[104]

Obviously, not all companies need to develop transnational mindset in order to do business across borders, although we believe that an increasing number of firms will should develop in this direction. A multidomestic or meganational mindset may sometimes be just as appropriate, and a polarized mindset may serve a positive purpose at a particular stage of a firm's internationalization. The desired state is that employees in a global organization share a mindset aligned with the strategic posture of the corporation.

Measuring Global Mindset

Global mindsets have been measured in different ways, some focusing on the psychological/cultural dimension, some on the strategic.[105] It is possible to measure the strategic view of global mindset and identify the orientation of different parts of the multinational. Measurement is a powerful tool for development. Using repeat surveys to evaluate global mindset provides top management with an objective indicator of the effectiveness of development activities. Before-and-after scores assist in evaluating the effectiveness of international management training or communications programs intended to promote global values and priorities within an organization. Individual and group scores can help to assess the effect of HR policies and tools, such as international assignments and rotation, global compensation practices, performance management, and specific training programs.

Scales for measuring individual and organizational progress toward a global mindset have been developed and validated (see Table 6–3).[106] The aim is

TABLE 6–3. Measuring Global Mindset

- **Global efficiency/integration:** the centralized management of dispersed assets and activities to achieve scale economies.
- **Local responsiveness:** resource commitment decisions made autonomously by a subsidiary in response to primarily local competitive or customer demands.
- **Worldwide coordination:** the level of lateral interaction within and between the network of affiliates with respect to business, function, and value chain activities.

Source: T.P. Murtha, S.A. Lenway, and R.P. Bagozzi, "Global Mind-Sets and Cognitive Shift in a Complex Multinational Corporation," *Strategic Management Journal* 19, no. 2 (February 1998).

to assess a key ingredient for the successful implementation of a global competitive strategy—namely, the capacity of individuals to consider complex interactions and differences in global strategy.

In our study of Nokia, mentioned at the beginning of this section, the data showed that global efficiency/integration was valued more than local responsiveness. This illustrated a polarity between the global orientation of the business units that were part of worldwide product lines and the local orientation of downstream units responsible for regional sales and customer services. Corporate staff held balanced views, but with a relatively low orientation toward both global efficiency/integration and responsiveness, reflecting difficulties in reaching consensus. Previously, this rapidly growing company handled the tensions of conflicting polarities through informal dialogue among the close-knit network of leaders who shared common experiences and values. However, as the business expanded, the ability of a small network of leaders to address all the issues was increasingly strained. This global mindset needed to be shared by a much larger managerial population.

What did the company do? It actively communicated the need to increase local responsiveness, and it rotated the leadership team to give more responsibility to executives with local experience. Profit and loss accountability was decentralized. Two hundred and fifty managers were involved in action learning programs to find ways of increasing lateral coordination, replacing vertical integration. The next round of the survey 18 months later showed a significant shift to the desired balanced direction.

How to Develop Global Mindset

While it may seem obvious that multinational firms will need more managers with global mindset both at headquarters and in overseas units, translating this attractive vision into an operational reality is not simple. How does one go about developing global mindset? How can HRM tools help? It all starts with recognizing diversity.

Equal Opportunity for All—Regardless of Passport

Perhaps the biggest barrier to the development of global mindset is the impression of local staff around the world that one's passport counts more than one's talent. If developmental opportunities are restricted (even unintentionally) to people from the parent country, or those from a few lead countries, local employees will inevitably tend to retain local perspectives—that is the only direction relevant for their own futures. Therefore, the key challenge in developing global mindset is to secure equitable access for talented employees worldwide to take advantage of available opportunities.

From a long-term perspective, a truly global enterprise must satisfy a simple but demanding test: Does it matter, for their future success, where employees enter the organization? Today there are probably only a few companies that can meet this benchmark, especially if global actually means outside of the

Northern Hemisphere. How many established multinational firms have succeeded in developing a cadre of senior executives representing all the continents on which they operate? It takes decades of effort to ensure that selection criteria are not biased toward one cultural group and that early identification of talent works just as well in Karachi as it does in New York.

Why do these barriers persist? Historically, most operational HR activities in multinational firms were decentralized to individual country organizations. In principle, this approach is logical—after all, the vast majority of employees are and always will be "local," embedded in the local culture and impacted by the local legal and regulatory environment. However, when HR localization is taken too literally, and everyone is treated as local, who is "global?" A natural outcome of this well-intentioned, but ultimately destructive, localization bias is that nationals of the country where the corporate center is located are considered implicitly "global," but all others are "local" and have only a limited chance of advancing on the corporate ladder. That is why the top leadership group, even in firms with extensive international experience, is usually unrepresentative of the employee population.

This deepening emphasis on global mindset requires a major shift in HRM orientation. Inherited ethnocentric and parochial HR systems and policies, which focus on a single country or a select group of employees, are often the biggest barriers to the implementation of effective global HR processes. The conventional focus of international HR is on selecting and supporting expatriates, rather than serving the global employee population. In many corporations worldwide, the operational needs of the expatriate management system, much of it centered on compensation and benefit issues, still dominate the "international" agenda of the corporate HR group. We will return to this important issue in Chapters 7 and 8.

Building on International Mobility and Project Work

Academic research[107] has shown that international assignments develop many different aspects of global mindset, as outlined in Table 6–4.

But despite its advantages, there are several limitations to the use of international mobility as a tool for developing global mindsets, not least that it is costly and employees may not be willing to relocate internationally. Therefore, while learning-driven international transfers are likely to remain a critical building block for developing global mindset, they are reserved for the critical few with clear functional or leadership potential. An equally important building block, and one that is increasing rapidly in use, is cross-border project work.

Cross-border projects are an alternative tool to work through local–global problems and opportunities, and are an excellent way of developing global mindset—perhaps the most important instrument for the future. The purpose of the project group (or cross-border steering group or internal board) is to bring different perspectives to bear. The skills learned through project work include the ability to work with peers who may have different perspectives on how to

TABLE 6–4. How Mobility Enhances Global Mindset

- Transfers develop the portfolio of skills associated with global mindset, such as championing global strategy, facing up to cross-border conflicts, and handling complexity.

- Transfers develop skills in handling cultural diversity. An individual learns that there are multiple ways to solve a problem and that every way has some merit. This also counteracts the cognitive tendency to think in terms of cultural stereotypes.

- As managers move from a local subsidiary role to a regional or global coordination role and back, they know that they may inherit any problems of excessive localism (or globalism) in their next job—which may moderate the natural tendency to swing the pendulum too far.

- The need to balance different pressures is built into many jobs. The career prospects of the international assignee depend on being able to satisfy the performance requirements of the subsidiary, *and* the demands of headquarters staff, *and* perhaps those of the assignee's mother country.

- Someone with experience of working abroad is more likely to be put on international project groups and councils, to be appointed to cross-border steering groups, and to be a link in best practice transfer, all of which reinforce the development of global mindset.

approach the problem, setting goals on important but ambiguous tasks, and working through conflicts.

Enhancing Global Mindset through Management Training

Another important tool to develop global mindset is training. This underlines the appeal of recruiting from business schools with internationally heterogeneous student populations. The educational process, with its emphasis on classroom discussion, team approaches to case studies, and international consulting projects, is designed to maximize the give-and-take of multiple opinions and orientations, giving the students a better understanding of the richness of various perspectives and the value of tapping into other people's knowledge.

Many companies, including Johnson & Johnson, Unilever, and GE, use in-house training to speed up the development of global mindsets. Staff in GE's management development center designed short, intensive, and experiential action learning programs to foster GE's internationalization. As part of these programs, multicultural action learning teams of GE managers were sent to China, Russia, and India to work on specific company problems in these regions, as well as to collect information on GE's best and worst practices around the world. The teams immersed themselves in the issues relevant to each region and reported on their findings, outlining business opportunities to top management. Even today, many years after they have taken part, many of the former participants reflect on their "global leadership" training as one of the most influential events of their careers.

Most of the company-specific programs that we undertake with multinational firms have the development of global mindset as an objective. A typical scenario is a two-week seminar for 36 select executives, commissioned by the chairman of a group of companies headquartered in Southeast Asia. The concept behind this and other such programs is simple: Lock up a group of executives off-site; get them to understand each others' problems and their interdependencies through project work and discussion of appropriate cases, guided by the conceptual understanding and encouragement of outside faculty; and facilitate the face-to-face relationships that will allow them to work through the conflicts. In short—build global mindset and appropriate behavior.

Reinforcing Global Mindset

The development of global mindset through assignments, projects, and training is unlikely to be effective unless it is reinforced within the organization by internal consistency and coherence of practices and norms. We had a clear illustration of this when working with Nokia, which relies heavily on international transfers to implement mobile telecom projects around the world.

Our research showed that Nokia expatriates had far more "balanced" perspectives than their domestic counterparts, showing high understanding of the interplay between global and local forces and the need for coordination. However, to the company's surprise, there were no significant differences in mindset between expatriates returning to Finland after six months' absence and those who had never left home. At headquarters, roles, responsibilities, and corresponding performance criteria were heavily skewed to the global at the expense of the local. Repolarization of the mindset appears to quickly follow.

One of the key steps top management took was to adjust performance management metrics to push for more balanced perspectives. Shared performance indicators, tied to a common global strategy, facilitate the resolution of conflicts across boundaries.

The Role of Senior Executives

Global mindset starts at the top. The first step is its articulation and reinforcement by top management, in clear and consistent language, across all levels and units. During his tenure as CEO of ABB, Percy Barnevik spent more 200 days each year visiting ABB's operating companies around the world, personally presenting his vision of a global enterprise to thousands of managers and employees. For many years, "Barnevik's slides" served as a common source of reference down through the organization. Barnevik did not believe that communicating ABB's business vision and strategy could be delegated. Many other top executives agree: Corporate leaders like Carlos Ghosn of Renault-Nissan and former Shell CEO Jeroen Van der Veer are famed for the amount of time they have spent roaming the world to spread the word.

Global mindset is not just part of a vision statement; it is manifested in the way a company makes strategic decisions and goes about their implementation. While top management provides the context for the way to think about global strategy, it is up to the senior managers in business units, functions, and country and regional organizations to make global mindset a reality inside an organization. Their respective roles may be different, but they ultimately share the responsibility for the synergy between responsiveness and integration.

Rethinking the Global Mindset Paradigm

At this point, it may be useful to remind ourselves that global mindset—and its strategic dimension in particular—is about balancing perspectives that at first glance may appear contradictory. In their passion to promote global mindset, academics and others writing from a normative perspective sometimes have a tendency to see global or cosmopolitan as superior to local, calling for a "universal way that transcends the particulars of places."[108] "Local" is taken to mean parochial and narrow-minded.

However, in our view, global mindset requires the opposite approach to such one-dimensional universalism—it calls for a dualistic perspective, immersion in local "particulars" while retaining a wider cross-border orientation. As companies pursue various strategies to instill global mindset, it is important to consider that a genuine emphasis on global mindset implies recognizing diversity. And diversity includes tolerance of people who are not "global," either through lack of opportunity, personal choice, or circumstances. Anything taken to extremes risks becoming pathological—and global mindset is no exception. This is true for companies as well as for individuals.

During the last decade, a catchy paradigm—"Think globally, act locally"—has often been used to capture the concept of a progressive corporation that considers the whole world its market, but at the same time carefully nurtures and adapts to local priorities and requirements. However, implementing this vision has turned out to be a longer and more difficult process than most companies envisioned.

What is the problem here? In a multinational firm that used this popular slogan on the first page of its annual report, one local subsidiary manager commented, "Our firm is organized on a simple premise. When operating under stress—and that is most of the time—*they* do the thinking, and *we* do the acting." In other words, the thinking and acting are two separate roles, performed by two separate groups. The headquarters takes the strategic initiatives, which the locals are left to implement. Although such a paradoxical outcome may not be what was intended, it may be unavoidable: The tensions embedded in managing a business on a global basis are dealt with by separating decision-making responsibilities, making no provision for supporting the development of shared ways of thinking.

In contrast, the key argument we present in this section is that global mindset is about the ability to balance contradictory perspectives. It is also as much about learning as about doing. To be truly global implies openness to learning from the experience of others, and to understanding and appreciating how others (local customers, employees, or competitors) think. Of course, the specific needs of local customers have to be assessed carefully—hence the requirement to be able to learn and understand the local context through *local* immersion. However, the ability to satisfy those needs with a superior value proposition is dependent on the *global* mobilization of corporate resources, whether these are leading-edge technology, economies of scale, or global standards of performance and quality. There is no competitive advantage in being an "average" local firm.

Perhaps the way out of the global/local dilemma is to return to the logic of the globalization process. Today, it is not enough to act locally in a fragmented country-by-country fashion. Leveraging R&D investments, manufacturing assets, logistics, IT infrastructure, service platforms, and operational know-how for competitive advantage requires a world-scale approach. At the same time, customer needs are increasingly individualized, and customers throughout the world exhibit a strong preference to be treated as individuals—the secret of the business model implemented by Dell (customers design their own computers) and Ritz-Carlton (providing extraordinary personal service to its hotel clients), or the mass customization perfected by Toyota. Similar tendencies are increasing among corporate customers: They want it their way, unique to their particular situation, but at the best possible global price and quality—and speedily. This can be achieved only if the whole organization can act as one.

What, then, is the competitive advantage of a multinational corporation? In simple terms, it is the ability to tap into and mobilize the company's *capabilities* and skills, wherever they may be in the world, to satisfy local *customer needs*. It may be useful, therefore, to rephrase the original paradigm. Building a company with a global mindset is really about developing an organization that can *learn locally and act globally*—in a way that competitors cannot match.[109] Perhaps this is a contradiction, but such is the nature of globalization.

In summary, the idea behind global mindset is that managers in multinational firms must have the capacity to accept the legitimacy of multiple business perspectives. Inevitably, multiple perspectives lead to tensions between different subunits of the firm; yet most tensions can be worked out through relationships supported by norms of collaborative teamwork. This brings us back to the concepts of social capital and shared values discussed earlier in this chapter; these three aspects of social architecture are closely intertwined.

TAKEAWAYS

1. Every organization is a social entity. One of the key responsibilities of HRM in multinational firms is to design and build the company's social architecture.
2. Three elements of social architecture are of particular relevance to global organizations: relationships among the employees (social capital); shared values, beliefs, and norms (organizational culture); and global mindsets.
3. There are three aspects of social capital: structural (emphasizing position within a network); relational (focusing on trust and mutual obligations); and cognitive (encompassing shared meanings).

4. In firms rich in social capital, information flows quickly and freely across intraorganizational boundaries. Social relationships also help resolve the inevitable tensions and disagreements created by the conflicting demands facing the multinational firm.

5. Organizational culture can be understood in terms of values, beliefs, and norms that are held in common across all or part of the global organization. Shared values facilitate the trust that is essential for effective lateral coordination, conflict resolution, and knowledge transfer.

6. The extent to which values, beliefs, and norms are shared throughout the multinational is influenced by a range of factors related to HRM. The selection of future employees, their socialization, and international mobility are commonly used for the firm to maintain and strengthen its culture.

7. In multinationals, employees often identify with both their local unit and the corporation as a whole. The dual organizational identification can be beneficial if well balanced, since it fosters sensitivity to both corporate and local interests, issues, and concerns.

8. There are two different and complementary perspectives on global mindset. The first is a *cultural* perspective and refers to the openness toward other nations and cultures; the second is a *strategic* perspective that denotes a person's ability to balance a firm's competing strategic priorities.

9. The foundation for developing a global mindset is equal opportunity for all, regardless of where they enter the firm. The major HRM tools to build such a mindset are international mobility, cross-border projects, and training.

10. Building a company with a global mindset means developing an organization that can *learn locally and act globally*.

NOTES

1. Liker and Hoseus, 2008; see also Osono, Shimizu, and Takeuchi (2008).
2. Stewart and Raman, 2007.
3. Stewart and Raman, 2007, p. 80.
4. See page 15 for a definition of social architecture.
5. Kostova and Roth, 2003. There is no shortage of definitions attempting to express the value of social ties and relationships in the organization. Lengnick-Hall and Lengnick-Hall (2006, p. 477) define social capital as "the intangible resource of structural connections, interpersonal interactions, and cognitive understanding that enables a firm to (a) capitalize on diversity and (b) reconcile differences."
6. Adler and Kwon, 2002.
7. Nahapiet and Ghoshal, 1998.
8. The structural ties between actors have been the key focus of social network research. See, for example, Kilduff and Tsai (2003).
9. In his influential work, Granovetter (1973) found that people who were trying to change jobs were more likely to find interesting opportunities through their "weak

ties" (acquaintances and friends of friends) than through their "strong ties" (close friends). Close friends would typically provide few leads that they had not thought of, whereas acquaintances often had leads into totally new networks and opportunities.

10. The bridging/structural perspective on social capital was pioneered by Ronald Burt (1992). Much of his work emphasizes the returns for an individual who brokers "structural holes—the bridging of two networks that are spanned by one person only.

11. Kostova and Roth, 2003.

12. Kostova and Roth, 2003, p. 309.

13. Kostova and Roth, 2003.

14. Neves and Caetano, 2006.

15. Ellis, 2000.

16. We discuss how social capital can contribute to knowledge sharing in Chapter 10.

17. Adler and Kwon, 2002.

18. For instance, Tsai and Ghoshal (1998) found a positive relationship between inter-unit social capital and innovativeness.

19. Leana and Van Buren, 1999.

20. Kostova and Roth, 2003.

21. Lengnick-Hall and Lengnick-Hall, 2003.

22. Dess and Shaw, 2001.

23. Adler and Kwon, 2002.

24. Brown and Eisenhardt, 1998.

25. Maznevski, Davison, and Jonsen, 2006.

26. Tichy and Sherman, 1993, p. 60.

27. Taylor, 2007.

28. Bryan, Matson, and Weiss, 2007.

29. Lengnick-Hall and Lengnick-Hall, 2003.

30. Lengnick-Hall and Lengnick-Hall, 2003.

31. Erickson and Gratton, 2007.

32. Kostova and Roth, 2003.

33. Sonja Weckström-Nousianen, Nokia Corporation, personal communication, 2008.

34. Pfeffer, 1994.

35. Burt, Hogarth, and Michaud, 2000.

36. Marschan-Piekkari, Welch, and Welch, 1999.

37. Björk, 1998.

38. Barner-Rasmussen and Björkman, 2006.

39. As pointed out by Hearn, Metcalfe, and Piekkari (2006), international HRM is (too) seldom examined from a gender perspective.

40. Adler and Kwon, 2002; Hansen, Mors, and Løvås, 2005.

41. Leana and Van Buren, 1999.

42. Adler and Kwon, 2002.

43. For instance, Liker and Hoseus (2008) examine the Toyota culture, while Gerstner (2002) provides a readable description of his efforts to change IBM's culture.

44. See, for example, Child, Faulkner, and Tallman (2005).

45. See, for example, the collection of papers in Stahl and Mendenhall (2005).

46. Sorensen, 2002.

47. O'Reilly and Chatman, 1996.

48. Denison, 1996; Fey and Beamish, 2001.

49. Organizational identity is a concept fairly closely related to organizational culture. However, one distinguishing facet between the two is that the essence of organizational identity is what makes the organization unique; it answers the question "What is this organization?" Organizational identity requires self-reflection as organizational members—in particular top management, as a part of their leadership role—try to define "who we are." In practice, the terms "organizational culture" and "organizational identity" are often used in overlapping ways. In this book we focus on organizational culture and only occasionally refer to organizational identity. See Albert and Whetten (1985) for a seminal treatment of organizational identity, Bouchikhi and Kimberly (2008) for a recent discussion, and Alvesson and Willmott (2002) and Rodrigues and Child (2008) for critical perspectives.

50. O'Reilly and Chatman, 1996; Ravasi and Schultz, 2006.

51. See, for example, Hatch (1993).

52. Nohria and Ghoshal, 1997.

53. O'Reilly and Chatman, 1996.

54. Sorensen, 2002.

55. Sorensen, 2002.

56. Miller, 1990.

57. Johnson, Scholes, and Whittington, 2005; Miller (1990) gives many examples of such firms, from Digital Equipment to IBM in the decade before its 1991 crisis.

58. Sorensen, 2002; Welch and Welch, 2006.

59. Staber, 2003, p. 416.

60. Mael and Ashforth (1992, p. 104) offer the following formal definition of organizational identification: "The perception of oneness with or belongingness to an organization, where the individual defines him or herself in terms of the organization(s) in which he or she is a member." See Ashforth, Harrison, and Corley (2008) for a comprehensive review of the literature on identification in organizations.

61. Reade, 2001.

62. Gregersen and Black, 1992; Vora, Kostova, and Roth, 2007.

63. Doz and Prahalad, 1986. See the discussion on expatriate allegiance in Chapter 4.

64. Stroh et al., 2005. For a review of research on multilevel identification in organizations, see Ashforth, Harrison, and Corley (2008).

65. Vora, Kostova, and Roth, 2007.

66. Stroh et al., 2005. See also Chapter 4.

67. Ashforth, Harrison, and Corley, 2008.

68. Dore, 1973.

69. Schneider and Barsoux, 2003.

70. "Soichiro Honda: Uniquely Driven," *Business Week*, August 17, 2004.

71. Francis et al., 2004.

72. Schein, 1985.

73. See Kamprad and Torekull (1999).

74. Van Maanen and Schein, 1979.

75. See Bauer et al. (2007) for a comprehensive analysis of newcomer adjustment during organizational socialization.

76. Bauer, Morrison, and Callister, 1998.

77. Hence the importance of managing the employer brand, as discussed in Chapter 7.

78. Bauer, Morrison, and Callister, 1998.

79. Liker and Hoseus, 2008.

80. Spear, 2004.

81. Van Maanen and Schein, 1979. See Klein (2004) for an interesting assessment of how to assist outsiders to achieve this balance.
82. Edström and Galbraith, 1977.
83. Harzing, 2001.
84. Sisson, 1994.
85. Ravasi and Schultz, 2006.
86. Welch and Welch, 2006. One of the few studies published on a cultural change program reported few lasting effects on employee values in the Singaporean subsidiary of a Western corporation (Selmer and de Leon, 2002).
87. Agrawal and Kets de Vries, 2006.
88. Baron, Burton, and Hannan, 1996.
89. The original HP Way was well adapted to its instruments business but ill suited to the computer world that Hewlett-Packard was forced into when instruments became computerized. The struggle to adapt the HP Way is described in Beer and Rogers (1995).
90. Levy et al. (2007) discuss different definitions of global mindset.
91. Perlmutter, 1969.
92. Perlmutter, 1969, p. 13.
93. Pucik and Saba, 1998.
94. Perlmutter, 1969.
95. Adler and Bartholomew, 1992.
96. See for instance Black et al. (1999) and the discussion about expatriates in Chapter 4.
97. Levy et al., 2007. "Cosmopolitanism" has been proposed as an underlying dimension of the psychological/cultural perspective.
98. V. Govindarajan and A. Gupta, "Success Is All in the Mindset," *Financial Times*, February 27, 1998, pp. 2–3. Similarly, Kanter (1995) sees this as a difference between new "cosmopolitans" and "locals," to employ terms that had been developed earlier by the sociologist Gouldner to describe the difference between people who identified with the wider profession as opposed to those who identified with the "local" interests of the firm.
99. Adler and Bartholomew, 1992.
100. Rhinesmith, 1993.
101. Johnson, Lenartowicz, and Apud, 2006.
102. Levy et al., 2007.
103. Bartlett and Ghoshal, 1989.
104. See Murtha, Lenway, and Bagozzi (1998) and Levy et al. (2007) for further elaboration, also for the distinction between the strategic perspective and alternative frameworks.
105. Levy et al., 2007.
106. Murtha, Lenway, and Bagozzi, 1998. These measures can be used to evaluate the way in which individuals working in different areas, functions, and business units understand corporate global objectives. For example, do managers in global product divisions conceptualize the importance of global efficiency/integration and responsiveness in the same way as managers in country units? What about managers with international experience, as opposed to those who pursued local careers?
107. Arora et al., 2004; Nummela, Saarenketo, and Puumalainen, 2004.
108. Kanter, 1995, p. 60.
109. Pucik, 2003.

CHAPTER 7

Managing Global Talent: Recruitment, Selection, and Retention

Developing a Global Talent Pool at Schlumberger

Founded by two brothers, Conrad and Marcel Schlumberger, in France in 1927, Schlumberger is now a US$23 billion giant in the oil services industry, with headquarters in Houston, Paris, and New York and a British CEO, Andrew Gould. The Schlumberger brothers invented a way of detecting oil located deep in the ground by lowering electrical wires down a drilling hole. Today Schlumberger offers most of the services that an oil company needs to explore and produce oil, from seismic mapping to integrated project management, on a fixed-fee basis. With the most sophisticated oil technology in the industry—vital when oil is difficult to find and get out of the ground—Schlumberger's fortunes have boomed during the last five years, with revenues growing by around 30 percent each year and profits tripling since 2003 to reach an estimated $7 billion in 2007.

Western oil majors like ExxonMobil and Shell depend on Schlumberger's services, as do the national oil-producing companies that control the bulk of oil reserves around the world, such as Saudi Arabia's Aramco, Brazil's Petrobras, and Kazakhstan's KazMunaiGaz. Countries with oil reserves want to control the revenues from their oil, but they do not have the necessary technical skills. Rather than sharing the revenues with a Western oil major to access those skills, as they did in the past, they have turned to Schlumberger. In Russia, for example, Gazprom contracts technical services from Schlumberger, which first entered the Russian industry in 1929, and 14,000 of the company's 80,000 employees work in Russia. Andrew Gould comments that "Russia could one day be as big for us as the US," where Schlumberger gets nearly 30 percent of its revenues.[1]

A good part of the unrivaled competitive advantage that Schlumberger enjoys over competitors such as Halliburton and Baker Hughes dates back to an initiative the firm took in the early 1990s, when it decided that people and technology would be the two strategic drivers of business growth. Schlumberger had long recruited in its regions of operations, and now it decided to invest actively in developing local talent in petroleum geology and geophysics in emerging markets like Russia, Kazakhstan, and China, building close relationships with the top local engineering schools.

Young employees are attracted to the firm because they know they will receive the best learning opportunities in the industry through classroom training and project work. One of the pulls for bright engineers in China, Nigeria, and Mexico is that Schlumberger is renowned for treating everyone in the same way, regardless of passport, when it comes to training, careers, and compensation. In a culture where "talent" equates with "engineers," performance is appraised by technical experts rather than managers.

These proved to be farsighted moves. During the last 15 years there has been a global geographic shift in the supply of technical talent to the oil extraction industry. The number of petroleum engineers graduating from schools in the United States and Western Europe dropped steadily from the mid-1980s, practically drying up after 1999 when oil prices bottomed at $10 a barrel. But the number graduating from universities in emerging countries has steadily increased. Western majors envy Schlumberger's ability to attract, develop, and retain the best and brightest, and to deploy them where needed, from the freezing tundra of Siberia to the charred deserts of Algeria.

Schlumberger does have retention problems. Top drilling experts are lured away by 300 percent salary raises in an industry where talent is a key to success. Each such departure warrants a full investigation, just like a technical mistake causing downtime on an oil rig.

Through lean and fat years, Schlumberger has consistently focused on cultivating great people. They are expected to be highly mobile—a senior Nigerian manager now working back home, for example, may have worked on every continent. Unlike many other firms, high performers from other disciplines often do a stint in human resources, and 40 percent of the HR staff are so-called visitors. "The capacity to develop talent from anywhere in the world is one of our key strengths," says Gould, and even its closest competitors would agree, envying the company's profitable growth.[2]

OVERVIEW

An international oil service company like Schlumberger has few fixed assets and no legacy positions; it lives off its know-how, embedded in the talent of its workforce. In that sense, Schlumberger is a typical multinational in today's knowledge economy. What is notable about Schlumberger is that it made some bold strategic decisions concerning global talent attraction and development. It moved early on from exporting home based talent to transnational talent management.

Talent management is the process through which organizations anticipate and meet their needs for human capital. Basically, it involves getting the right people into the right places at the right time. The focus has historically been on managerial and leadership positions, but increasingly it also targets top-level technical specialists who are strategically important to the success of the firm—like the engineers for emerging markets that Schlumberger needs.

After defining talent management, we discuss other reasons why it is so important for the international firm—some might argue that together with the closely related domain of performance management, it is the most important item on the HRM agenda. The reasons have to do with the progressive move into the knowledge economy, with demographic changes and globalization (notably competition for talent from local start-ups and multinationals in emerging markets), and with increasing individual mobility.

In international firms talent management has historically been a local responsibility; corporate headquarters restricted its focus to expatriation and the development of senior leaders. Today transnational organizations are under pressure to have more consistent talent practices across the world. This tension between global consistency and local adaptation is one of the balancing acts that we discuss in this chapter; the other is the balance between building or buying talent—developing talent internally or recruiting it from the market.

We then move on to discuss three areas of particular interest to firms operating across borders. The first is *managing recruitment*, where we consider how an organization can forecast the supply and demand for talent, how it can reach out to recruit people globally, and how it can build an appropriate employer brand as well as a differentiated employee value proposition.

The second area of talent management is *selection and assessment*, where we review the role of culture and business context in selection, and what this means for the management of diversity (with a focus on gender as well as national culture and ethnic background). Many international firms use competence frameworks to steer assessment and link it to capability development. We discuss alternative ways of developing such a framework and applying it in a transnational firm. We also discuss the important challenges of internal talent selection, how "potential" can be assessed among people in operations located around the globe.

The third area is *retention management*. Investing in the development of talent is not a viable business proposition unless the company can retain the individuals and profit from that investment. Before moving on to the next chapter, where we focus on talent development, we explore another balancing act in talent management—balancing short-term pressures with a long-term time horizon.

WHAT IS TALENT MANAGEMENT AND WHY IS IT SO IMPORTANT?

There is no shortage of talented people in the world; but there is a shortage of the right people in the right places. Talent management has been described by academics and practitioners alike as the key strategic human management agenda for the future.[3] As some say, "We bet on people, not on strategies"—for what is the value of a strategy unless it can be executed through people? Recent surveys of many thousands of executives throughout the world show that finding talented people is likely to remain the single most important preoccupation of executives in the medium term. No other global trend was considered nearly as significant.[4]

What Do We Mean by Talent?

When we ask managers from either the line or HR function to define talent in their organization, many of them say "everyone." In its broadest sense, talent is synonymous with human capital or resources. A 2006 British survey of HR managers showed that two-thirds of them felt that talent should not focus on a small privileged group or exclude anyone.[5] However, when it came to their enterprises, the majority of firms—three-quarters of those surveyed—had a more restrictive definition of talent, focusing on employees with high strategic value, those who are most important for the success of the firm.

Huselid, Beatty, and Becker argue that the focus of talent management should be on building capabilities to implement the strategy of the firm. It should center on resourcing A positions, those roles that (1) have a direct impact on company strategy and (2) exhibit wide variation in the quality of the work carried out by people who occupy them.[6] To this we can add (3) uniqueness or firm specificity, the extent to which positions require tacit knowledge and deep experience that cannot be found easily in the external labor market.[7] It would not make economic sense to invest equally in a clerical employee who can be easily replaced and in a functional expert who may additionally have high leadership potential.

This portfolio approach distinguishes between strategically important A positions, supporting B positions, and C positions that may be required but that do not differentiate the firm,[8] as shown in Table 7–1. While A positions are defined primarily by their impact on strategy and its execution, as well as the range in performance levels and the firm specificity of the position, other characteristics flow from this that distinguish A, B, and C positions—such as differences in the scope of authority and in the consequences if someone in that role makes mistakes.

These three types of position do not necessarily correspond to hierarchy, pay scales, or the difficulty of recruiting for the position. Take the airline industry as an example. The people who negotiate landing rights, with higher variability in their performance, are more critical to the success of the firm than the pilots who come immediately to mind but who are more replaceable. So it would make sense for an airline to select carefully and groom such negotiators, the A position players who constitute talent with a capital "T." Regulations ensure that all pilots have to be well trained and qualified, and so their roles might be considered as supporting B positions, or talent with a small "t." Ground staff might be considered C players, managed according to the market.

So we would define talent management as deliberate actions to attract, recruit, develop, and retain those individuals who, individually or collectively,

TABLE 7–1. **Which Jobs Make the Most Difference?**

	A Positions: Strategic	B Positions: Support	C Positions: Surplus
Defining characteristics	Has a direct strategic impact AND exhibits high performance variability among those in the position, representing upside potential, AND requires firm-specific know-how	Has an indirect strategic impact by supporting strategic positions and minimize downside risk by providing a foundation for strategic efforts OR has a potential strategic impact but exhibits little performance variability among those in the position	May be required for the firm to function but has little strategic impact
Scope of authority	Autonomous decision making	Specific processes or procedures typically must be followed	Little discretion in work
Primary determinant of compensation	Performance	Job level	Market price
Effect on value creation	Creates value by substantially enhancing revenue or reducing costs	Supports value-creating positions	Has little positive economic impact
Consequences of mistakes	May be very costly, but missed revenue opportunities are a greater loss to the firm	May be very costly and can destroy value	Not necessarily costly
Consequences of hiring wrong person	Significant expense in terms of lost training investment and revenue opportunities	Fairly easily remedied through hiring of replacement	Easily remedied through hiring of replacement

Source: Adapted from M.A. Huselid, R.W. Beatty, and B.E. Becker, "A Players or A Positions?" *Harvard Business Review*, December 2005, pp. 110–17.

have the capability to make a significant impact on the results of the firm, and whose skills are firm-specific.[9]

Why Is Talent Management So Important?

Although the concern for talent ebbs and flows with economic cycles, the growing importance of talent management reflects changes in the nature of the supply and demand for skilled employees. What drives these changes is first the shift to the knowledge economy and second the impact of demographic changes—an aging of the workforce in much of the West, but rapid growth in the rest of the world. Third, there is the progressive globalization of talent: Western multinationals search for highly skilled scientists and engineers in emerging countries while local companies seek managers to help them to become multinationals. And fourth, we are witnessing increasing job mobility, with at least some shift in the balance of power from the organization to the individual.

The Shift to the Knowledge Economy

As we move step-by-step into the knowledge economy, company performance becomes increasingly dependent on the skills of its employees. Workers in traditional blue-collar industries were once easily replaced. Today's equivalent of the blue-collar worker needs specialized skills in robotics or computerized production, and these workers be replaced so easily. Silicon Valley enterprises such as Google use billboards not to advertise their services but to attract smart and experienced job applicants to their employment Web sites. In organizations that live entirely off their knowledge capabilities—consulting and legal firms, investment banks, and academic institutions—the CEOs of top firms spend 25–40 percent or more of their time on talent management.

Talent is so important in the knowledge economy that companies are obliged to go where the talent is. Let us take R&D as an example. In the past, if there was one function that would be located close to the headquarters in San Jose, Munich, or Tokyo, it was R&D. Multinational firms used to focus only on R&D talent in the mother country, and even in multidomestic firms more effort was devoted to talent management at home than elsewhere. Today there is growing awareness that R&D talent is available in many parts of the world. Silicon Valley used to be the home ground for high-tech IT skills. Nowadays, these may be located in Bangalore and Pune, Tallinn, or Kuala Lumpur.

Demographic Changes

Due to inescapable demographic trends in most developed countries, there has been a decline in the size of the talent pool that will continue for the next 20–30 years (partially compensated for by immigration, particularly in the United States). There is a bulge in the number of older people approaching retirement and fewer young people, especially those at the productive career stage of their thirties.

Figure 7–1 shows the demographic profile of Germany for 2015, shaped like a diamond. With affluence, dual careers, and increasing divorce rates, countries such as Germany have for many years been experiencing negative population growth. There is a bulge in the number of people aged 45–54, the baby boom generation that is heading into retirement, resting on a narrow population base of younger people. The German figures are not atypical—Japan and Italy have an even more serious demographic problem, while the situation is similar but less severe in Scandinavia, Singapore, and the United States.

FIGURE 7–1 German Demographic Profile in 2015

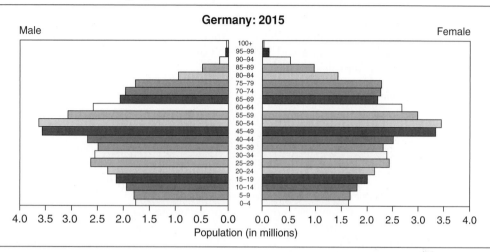

Source: www.census.gov/ipc/www/idb.

While the population of the more developed world has increased by a mere 14 percent during the 30-year period 1978–2008, the population of less developed countries has been doubling, growing by 112 percent during the same period.[10] Western companies have capitalized on this supply of low-cost labor first by offshoring manufacturing and then by outsourcing IT services. In turn, the economies of countries such as China and India have been growing rapidly.

That rapid growth in emerging countries now means that concern with talent management is not limited to corporations in the developed Western world. China, with 1.4 billion people, is the world's most populous country. Yet what was the biggest business concern of the CEOs of multinational companies with businesses across China in 2007? Underdeveloped financial systems? Lack of good data on the market? No—their top concern was the shortage of qualified staff, followed in third place by staff turnover and in fifth place by wage inflation, a consequence of the other two.[11]

Why is there such a shortage, driving executive salaries in Shanghai toward New York levels? A Chinese executive working for a multinational firm needs to speak good English, to be able to work in a multinational team, and to have strong "Western-style" supervisory skills—in addition to understanding the business and the local market. Such individuals are rare in China, at least relative to demand.

The demand–supply imbalance is particularly pronounced in the market for young professionals. While there has been a boom in university enrollments in India, China, and Brazil, the quality of graduates is often uneven. Language skills are not always emphasized, and local educational systems often do not foster skills valued by multinationals, like taking initiative and teamwork. One survey estimated that only 10 percent of Chinese and Russian engineering graduates were deemed suitable to be hired by a multinational firm, in comparison with 35 percent of such Malaysian graduates and 50 percent from Central European countries.[12] Companies like Schlumberger, Cisco, and Emerson, which invested earlier in partnerships with elite local technical institutions in places like China and India, are now reaping the benefits as they are able to recruit top professionals.

Globalization

While saving on labor costs still remains the principal reason for decisions to move operations abroad, access to qualified personnel influences 70 percent of offshoring decisions.[13] Indeed, we are seeing the progressive globalization of talent management, and this is beginning to affect corporate strategy. Shifts in the supply of talent are leading firms to look to emerging countries, not only for lower-cost outsourcing in noncore areas, but also to staff strategically important functions. Cisco has moved its corporate headquarters for global innovation from San Jose to Bangalore.[14] São Paolo is now one of the global hubs for Internet banking expertise and financial information forecasting.

The competition for talent in emerging countries used to be with other multinational corporations. That is changing. While Western and Japanese corporations still regard China as a country for low-cost manufacturing, a 2007 survey showed that nearly a third of major Chinese firms are intent on significant expansion in foreign revenues in the next three years.[15] They view the biggest barrier to their international expansion as the lack of managerial talent, more significant than lack of capital or customer understanding. Many managers still lack foreign experience and have only limited education. So we can expect increased competition for skilled people.

Talented local people are often interested in obtaining skills and experience by working with a multinational and then leaving to join a local firm or start their own business. The story of the rise of Alibaba and Taobao at the expense of eBay in China, told in Chapter 3, is an example. The multinationals that are attractive to locals are increasingly home-grown companies that often count among the top players worldwide in industries such as cement (Cemex in Mexico), IT services (Infosys in India), steel and beer (Gerdau and InBev in Brazil), and home appliances and container transport (Haier and CIMC in China), to name just some examples. Firms like Lenovo in China, HCL Technologies, Infosys and Tata Consulting Services in India, and InBev (now Anheuser-Busch InBev) from Brazil are seen as new pioneers in talent management.[16]

Increasing Individual Mobility

After World War II, there was so little ready talent available in North America, Europe, and Japan that companies had no alternative except to develop it themselves.[17] Long-term careers became the norm, and the firm could undertake intensive assessment at the time of entry and during the early career years. Western firms, organized as internal labor markets, could systematically and with increased sophistication assess and develop their talent, while some Japanese firms would evaluate performance and potential several times each year for a seven-year period before deciding on a person's potential.[18] On the other hand, the individual had limited access to external job market information—mainly via newspapers and private networks.

The Internet changed all that, facilitating a major shift in the information symmetries around employment. Today, exploring what the external job market offers is as easy as the click of a mouse. Internet job sites such as Yahoo! Hot Jobs and Monster.com provide targeted information on available jobs in all major countries of the world, while other sites provide inside information on prospective employers. This facilitates mobility, which has steadily increased as firms also use Internet recruitment to poach skilled individuals from competitors. Another social change that gives individuals more control over their careers and facilitates mobility is the change in pension systems across the world. The annuity-based "defined benefits" pension systems of the last century locked people into their organizations but proved to be excessively expensive as people lived longer. It has been estimated that by 2014, portable "defined contribution" systems will overtake these defined benefit systems in terms of the amount of money invested worldwide.[19]

Of course, there are still differences in mobility between countries. But even in Japan, where lifetime employment remains one of the pillars of many corporations, on average, employees will work for three different companies during their careers (in contrast to seven in the US), and a growing segment of the younger workforce no longer believes in permanent jobs.

The influence of mobility and the changing power balance is profound. Retention has become a vital element of talent management, inseparable from attraction and development. Unless firms can manage retention, any investment in talent development may be wasted. Organizations may become more reserved about employee training and development since there is risk that the employee may exploit the benefits by moving elsewhere—it is safer to try to poach experienced talent from others.

KEY CHALLENGES IN TALENT MANAGEMENT

As we have discussed, the focus of talent management is on individuals who have firm-specific skills and the ability to make a significant impact on firm results. The scope of "talent" varies from firm to firm. Almost all will include leaders and potential leaders, and many will broaden this to include key technical or functional professionals. To take a few examples, at Microsoft talent management focuses on the top 10 percent of performers at all levels and functions, while at Schlumberger it focuses on engineers. GE has a broader definition—high performers, who also have high potential and display key GE values. At Shell, talent management covers senior leaders and those with senior leadership potential, along with select functional staff.

An increasing number of multinationals structure the workforce around *talent pools*, each of which constitutes a family of jobs and a career track.[20] Talent pools that are considered strategically important are managed rigorously, including invariably the high-potential leadership pool. All IBM employees worldwide are assigned to a career track, grouped into three clusters of executive resources, technical resources (systems specialists and IT architects), and top talent (high potentials or the top 10 percent of middle management). Each track has a sponsoring executive, supported by dedicated HR managers. IBM draws the attention of its staff explicitly to the fact that "tracks vary in the level of investment the business makes to developing guidance, based on criticality to the business." However, the majority of firms have no clear concept of who constitutes talent aside from senior leadership and those with potential to occupy such positions in the future.

The Talent Management Mindset

Rigorous talent management fundamentally boils down to attention and resources. The most difficult aspect is that it requires a high degree of attention from three internal stakeholders: top management, notably the CEO; the global HR function; and line managers in general. The HR function cannot do this alone, as talent management cannot be separated from business strategy—the development of organizational capabilities comes largely through ensuring that talent is closely aligned with other elements of operational and business management. This implies the active involvement of senior leaders. Nevertheless, a global survey of CEOs, business unit leaders, and HR professionals indicated that the most significant perceived obstacles preventing talent management from delivering value are, first, that senior managers do not spend enough quality time on it and, second, that line managers are not adequately committed to people development.[21]

Global talent management should embrace the following activities:

- Ensuring that global talent considerations are taken into account early in the strategy formulation process, and translating business strategy into talent strategy.
- Forecasting supply and demand for talent worldwide using workforce planning and simulations.
- Diagnosing gaps in organizational capabilities and taking measures to fill them.
- Developing and updating global processes in attraction, recruitment, induction, career development and training, performance management, and retention; ensuring that they are employed by local units.
- Ensuring internal consistency between talent management processes worldwide.
- Building a talent mindset by making sure that development discussions, succession planning, performance differentiation, and mentoring are part of the priorities of line management throughout the global organization.

Creating a talent mindset is the most challenging of these activities. All too often, line managers give only token acceptance to talent management, treating it reactively, for example by recruiting salespeople only when new products take off. They are often unwilling to differentiate between high-average-and under-performing people; they hoard their own high performers and are unwilling to share talent across businesses or geographies. Out in the field, far away from the headquarters, talent management can sometimes seem like a vague long-term concern that has little bearing on the behaviors that are rewarded.

The Balancing Acts in Talent Management

Talent management involves balancing many opposing tensions—a recurring theme in this book. We have already touched on one such tension—the need to focus on the critical few who are important for strategy, at the risk of elitism, as opposed to the pressure to focus on the wider majority, at the risk of diluting resources. We explore two additional tensions here, and we will discuss the balancing of short and long term at the end of the chapter.

Local Adaptation or Global Consistency?

Talent management, in the widest sense of the management of staff, has traditionally been a local matter. As we discussed in Chapter 3, national cultures differ, and laws and labor markets vary greatly. But even in multidomestic firms, there is usually a corporate-led global focus on leadership succession for senior management, including attention to managing the localization of executives.[22]

Some transnational firms have been broadening the globalization of talent management to all positions that are important to firm strategy and its execution. Our Schlumberger case is an example, where global talent management covers engineers in emerging countries. Schlumberger did not succeed in recruiting the best engineers in China and Russia by doing this the local way. It succeeded by applying in China the methods that it had honed at home in Texas and France, helping local educational establishments to become world-class and then training a Chinese recruit in the same way as it would train someone in the United States.

Indeed there has been a gradual shift during the last 10–15 years toward multinationals using the same processes for recruitment, selection, induction, and development, transferring practices across the world. This applies to talent pools for strategically valuable core and possibly key employees, but not to contract staff, where the company will want to take advantage of all opportunities for local differentiation.[23]

When considering people who will occupy strategic positions, companies see numerous advantages to global consistency, driven by the central HR function with the support of top management, and assisted by IT platforms:[24]

- They can build competitive advantage throughout the world by finding and developing the best people in local markets, as in the case of Schlumberger.
- Global consistency facilitates the ability to deploy talent across geographic locations to where it is needed. It is difficult to identify and move talented

people unless the standards for talent are the same, so it is important to have the same competence- and performance-based standards for the evaluation of individuals.

- Using a global database of qualified talent, candidates can be quickly identified. Combined with computer-based platforms in open job markets, skilled professionals can be more quickly deployed to new opportunities and projects, particularly on a regional basis.
- The use of common processes and measures makes global workforce forecasting and planning possible, using new analytic techniques and simulations.
- Many firms suffer from the herd effect—for example, all moving IT services to Bangalore, with resulting wage inflation. Companies skilled in global talent management can take advantage of second-tier locations, where there is greater variability in the quality of talent.[25]

Local managers are often ambivalent about such global processes, arguing that *they* are different. How does one know whether this reflects resistance to change or a substantive competitive reality? Because of local conditions, a global practice might indeed have to be adapted, or it may be too expensive to implement.

The advice from companies that have introduced global staffing processes is to push back, asking people to prove that they really are different. However, local buy-in is increased if the local leaders can shape execution in ways that reflect sensitive local issues. P&G allows differentiation where there is a legitimate business need or where the longer-term benefits outweigh the short-term concessions, shooting for a 85:15 or 90:10 ratio of standardization to customization.[26] The test of a good global staffing process is that it allows the firm to fill local positions with better candidates than it could using a local platform, and possibly cheaper and faster as well.[27]

This balance is an issue that we will pick up in our discussions of attraction, selection, training, and development. While a multinational firm may achieve consistency in concepts, principles, and the use of some techniques, there are inevitably local differences when one gets down to practices and behaviors rooted in a specific context.

Should We Build or Should We Buy?

Another important balancing act is the decision of whether to staff future expansion through internal resourcing or through external recruitment—whether to build or buy talent. In the past, this sort of "supply chain" question would rarely be asked. Companies tended to have undifferentiated talent strategies. Some firms grew primarily through external recruitment at all levels; to get promoted you had to change company. Other firms grew through developing their own talent in internal labor markets. What are the pros and cons of development through internal labor markets (ILMs)?[28]

ILMs are characterized by long-term mutual attachment between the organization and its workforce. Promotion is from within, and there is an emphasis on experience, which is equated with seniority. ILMs are well studied,[29] and their advantages and disadvantages are summarized in Table 7–2. One of the major strengths of the ILM is its capacity to nurture firm-specific strategic skills and complex capabilities, in the shape of experienced experts or leaders who also have broad functional and market know-how, and who are loyal and committed to the firm. But well-functioning ILMs require effective talent management practices. Without these, the disadvantages of the ILM can undermine its advantages. A poorly managed ILM can become an expensive training ground benefiting competitors who will poach the most talented individuals.

When combined with solid talent management practices and focused on strategic human capital, the ILM is an integral element of a high-performance HRM system. Schlumberger's engineers are recruited into a well-managed internal labor market, which includes weeding out people who do not make the grade; historically fewer than 40 percent of recruits spend a substantial part of their careers with the firm.

The institutional environment is important in determining the balance between build and buy. Japan, Germany, France, Italy, and Switzerland are among the countries where internal resourcing dominates, either by custom or forced on firms by labor legislation. For example, in Italy and France, employees in all but the smallest firms receive a permanent contract after an initial probationary

TABLE 7–2. Internal Labor Markets—Advantages and Disadvantages

Advantages	Disadvantages
• Developing the firm-specific strategic skills underlying competitive advantage.	• Higher overhead, including costs of talent management.
• Building loyalty and commitment (better retention).	• Risks of investments in training or experience are borne by the company, not the individual.
• Better screening of job candidates; more rapid and cheaper decision making on staffing.	• Lack of flexibility; rigidity and higher salary costs in times of decline and change; slower to adjust in times of major technological or market changes.
• Potentially lower supervisory costs because of greater capacity for self-monitoring.	
• More control over salary levels; lower salary costs in times of growth (lags the external market).	• May foster greater mediocrity and conformity; risk that poor performance goes unchallenged.
• Encourages sharing of information and teamwork; beneficial in terms of innovation in complex value chains.	• Insular; fewer insights into competitors; less innovation through bridging with external agents.
• Better maintenance of the culture, including social networks, if the culture is a source of competitive advantage.	• Risk of unchallenged "glass ceilings".
	• Risk of overstaffing or understaffing, especially with difficulties of forecasting talent demand.

period, which makes it difficult and expensive to terminate employment. Successive governments have tried to open the labor markets to bring more market flexibility, though resistance from unions and employee groups is strong. On the other hand, in Denmark, the Netherlands, Britain, and Hong Kong, strong ILMs are less frequent, even among large firms. The emphasis on internal development has steadily declined in the United States, and as we discuss later, the US is probably the region with the strongest preference for buying talent.[30] In Russia, much of Central and Eastern Europe, and China, the external labor market orientation dominates today, despite the history of state-owned enterprises with ILMs controlled by the Communist Party.

The nature of the knowledge and skill in a particular industry is another important factor determining the balance between build and buy. Build strategies prevail in capital-intensive industries that depend on complex knowledge and skill, such as the oil industry. Graduates are recruited for long-term careers, and sophisticated talent management processes steer internal resourcing. Large functionally oriented structures also facilitate talent management in pharmaceuticals.[31] But in the fast-moving worlds of software development and IT, the pattern has been to rely on buy strategies, especially in the United States.

Cappelli argues that there should be a mix of build and buy, guided by the answers to four key questions:[32]

1. For how long will the talent be needed? The longer the time horizon, the easier it will be to recoup investments on internal development.
2. Is there a career hierarchy of skills and jobs that facilitates internal development? This is most obviously the case if there are clear functional development paths.
3. Is the culture of the firm part of its competitive advantage? If so, this favors ILM development rather than recruits who have no understanding of the culture.
4. How accurately can one forecast demand? The less accurate the forecasts, the greater the risks with internal development.

Integrated oil companies with upstream exploration and downstream marketing are asking themselves whether they should consider having different talent strategies in different businesses. In a world of high oil prices, strategic development is led by the upstream exploration business, which needs complex people skills now that the world has run out of easy oil. A build strategy may be appropriate here, while a buy strategy may be favored in the downstream marketing operations. But people strategies affect organizational governance, and this raises new dilemmas. Is it possible to maintain two increasingly different businesses under one roof? One of the reasons why Hewlett-Packard spun off its original measurement and instrumentation company as Agilent in 1999 was the difficulty of applying a predominantly build strategy in one part of the firm while there was a buy strategy in another. Thirty percent of the staff at Google are contract employees, and the problems of having insiders and outsiders on the same team attracts criticism.

MANAGING RECRUITMENT

Recruitment is typically defined as the practices and activities carried out by the organization with the primary purpose of identifying and attracting potential employees.[33] This distinguishes recruitment from the tasks of selection and assessment (discussed in the next section), which focus on deciding whom to select for a position with the firm or for promotion. In practice, the tasks involved in attraction, recruitment, and assessment, as well as induction (bringing new recruits on board), are inseparable and must be closely aligned. For this reason some companies and researchers prefer to put these under one umbrella, either staffing or resourcing.

Without attention to global recruitment, multinationals risk being trapped in the ethnocentricity of the mother company. Take the case of a leading European firm that has a strong reputation as a leader in international HRM. Despite decades of attempting to internationalize the talent pipeline by promoting the development of local managers, the senior leaders remained by and large graduates of the top engineering schools in the mother country. The turning point was reached when they realized that the problem was under their noses—the home country received more attention and resources from HR and the senior line than other countries so that the home unit enjoyed particularly close relationships with the top universities. They were able to recruit the best people at home, who then received the best induction and career mentoring. The people who moved later into leadership positions tended to be those who had experienced the best start to their careers. If they were to internationalize the talent pool, they would have to do an equally professional job of attraction and recruitment in other countries—exactly what Schlumberger did in many of the countries in which it operates.

Forecasting the Need for Recruitment

If a company is to have a strategic and proactive approach to talent management, this begins with the ability to forecast the supply and the demand for talent. This is particularly true if a company engages in building its own internal supply of talent—recruiting people young, training and developing them to create a pipeline of talent. Workforce planning, as it is called, has a checkered history (see the box "Forecasting Talent Supply and Demand"). At leading companies like Nokia, recruitment and staffing plans are included in the resource plans resulting from competence gap analysis. Senior management assesses these gaps as part of the strategic planning process.

Reaching Out to Attract Talent

A key question in recruitment is how to reach out effectively to potential candidates. There are a variety of different vehicles for attracting and recruiting talent:

Forecasting Talent Supply and Demand

The idea of forecasting the supply and demand for talent is appealing, and manpower planning, as it used to be called, has a long history. Sophisticated talent forecasting methods were deployed by many major US corporations in the early 1970s, but the recession of 1974 put a quick end to these efforts since the forecasts were shown to be dangerously inaccurate. For example, Exxon's forecasts in the early 1970s predicted that it would need more chemical engineers than the entire supply of all the universities in the United States. After the slump of 1974, the company had an excess.

The prime aim of forecasting is to prevent a shortfall in internally generated talent. But as Cappelli argues, there are equally high risks and costs associated with an excessively full pipeline of talent.[A] First, there are the significant direct and indirect costs of unnecessary recruitment, induction, and training. Second, a blocked pipeline means that people do not have growth and promotional opportunities, and good people are likely to leave. Third, absence of opportunity leads to poor morale.

More recently, workforce planning has enjoyed a comeback, but based on new assumptions and analytic techniques:

- First, the quality of data has significantly improved, and data are available easily at low cost. Companies that have global enterprise resource planning systems in place have standardized their employee data by grade, title, business, and country, as well as having information on attrition, promotion and outside hires. Standardized HR data, such as performance appraisal information, supplement these. New analytic techniques allow rich and low-cost analysis of these data to draw firm-specific conclusions.
- Second, rather than using the statistical modeling methods of forecasting that were

employed in the past, simulations allow firms to undertake scenario planning that take uncertainties into account. Moreover, close collaboration between top management, line managers, and the HR function allows constructive dialogue on the strategic options. Specific business plans can be simulated to explore implications.

- Third, firms are now advised to cope with the uncertainties of the future by being conservative in their estimates of future talent needs, rather than making spot predictions, knowing full well that a shortfall in internally supplied talent is likely. That shortfall can be compensated for by recruitment, leading to a rational mix of build and buy in talent strategy.
- Fourth, if talent management practices are standardized globally, large multinational enterprises may benefit from a talent portfolio effect. While there may be a shortfall of potential functional leaders in one business or location, there is likely to be an excess of such leaders in another part of the corporation who can be moved where they are needed. This capability in standardized talent management and deployment is central to the global HR strategy of IBM, for example. In comparison, both small businesses and highly decentralized multidomestic organizations may tend to be underresourced and constrained because they cannot profit from such portfolio benefits.

With the help of new analytic tools, talent management becomes a business challenge rather than a functional HR matter—as long as the necessary commitment of the line is present.

[A]This box is largely based on the work of Cappelli (2008, pp. 131–56).

- **Relationships with local universities, technical schools, and business schools.** For large and leading corporations this is the most common route for entry-level recruitment of technical professionals and high potentials.[34] For example, Emerson has joint training programs with technical universities in China and the Philippines, while Volkswagen and Motorola have established strategic alliances with Chinese universities and technical institutes. The German automotive supplier Continental has Continental universities in Mexico and Romania.

- **Internships.** Firms can identify prospective recruits among students who are offered short-term internships—a recruitment strategy popular among many Western multinationals. Cross-border internships are growing, especially for MBA students. Infosys offers internships in India for talent it wants to recruit from foreign markets. At the same time, such internships allow students to evaluate potential employers, leading to a better fit.

- **Contests, competitions, and fellowships.** Organizing contests with prizes and offering employment to the winners, or using fellowships to attract outstanding candidates can be effective ways of attracting good candidates. Google organizes periodic worldwide programming competitions to test contestants' Internet programming skills. Even the meat industry in the United States selects its future managers on the basis of national carcass-judging championships.

- **Employee referrals.** As discussed in the previous chapter, some of the early sociological insights into social networks came from a study of their power in referrals and recruitment.[35] Used widely by smaller and high-technology companies in the US, employee referrals have been shown to lead to more realistic pre-hire knowledge of the firm, longer tenure, and better performance among those recruited. As long as the risks of nepotism are minimized, referrals work particularly well in networked cultures like China.[36]

- **Internet.** Internet recruitment is rapidly becoming common practice throughout the world. Global job search Web sites, such as Monster.com and its local equivalents, are growing rapidly, as are sites focusing on specific occupational specialties. Social networking sites are increasingly being exploited for recruitment purposes. Careful attention is given to the design of company Web sites; the global accounting firm Deloitte Touche Tohmatsu eliminated 35 local Web sites to create a single global site with links to local country information. The problem with Web recruitment is the high cost of screening and selecting from a large number of candidates, though the use of automatic selection tools and Web competence testing can help.

  The Internet can be used in creative ways for attraction and recruitment, as Cisco's successful strategy of targeting passive job seekers testifies. Cisco grew by targeting experienced professionals at other IT firms who were willing to be lured, even if they were not actively looking for alternative employment. These passive job seekers are estimated to make up around 40 percent of those employed. For example, every time someone from a targeted rival organization clicked on a Cisco site, they were automatically diverted to a page asking if they were interested in having lunch with someone from Cisco. These practices were copied widely by others in the IT industry.

- **Advertising.** Attention-grabbing advertising can be effective, especially when a firm is largely unknown. Back in 1991, when Infosys was still struggling in India, it ran an ad featuring this headline: "Only 64 brilliant young engineers are destined to conquer the world of software. Find out if you are one of them this Saturday." This advertisement inspired a stampede of more than a thousand applicants. Companies still advertise in newspapers and specialized magazines, but those media are being replaced by nontraditional and Web-based methods; for example, Google advertises for talent in cinemas and on billboards.
- **Professional recruiting firms and agencies.** Executive search firms started to internationalize their operations 20 years ago because those that could offer services in different world regions were at an advantage with multinational clients. Such internationalization has spread to recruitment agencies that specialize in particular types of talent, such as medical technicians or IT specialists. A number of firms have outsourced the whole recruitment process to a service provider, in some cases worldwide, following a trend that started in Silicon Valley two decades earlier.[37] This approach has its pros and cons, but it provides little advantage for a firm that has competent recruiting processes in place and is an employer of choice.[38]

The effectiveness of different recruitment channels varies with national culture, though not as widely as the selection methods we discuss in the next section. It is important to analyze the effectiveness of alternative recruitment sources and methods in any particular market. GE questioned the effectiveness of recruiting MBAs from top business schools, deciding instead to build relations with second-tier business and technical establishments, as well as sourcing managers from the military. Today it is reviewing whether or not to return to recruiting at top schools. Research shows that firms who analyze recruitment sources for their effectiveness in generating positive applicants perform better.[39]

Valero, the oil refining corporation that grew from 3,000 to 22,000 employees in the space of 10 years, uses dashboards to monitor different methods in the recruitment chain, such as ads on job boards, and staffing managers intervene to fix "red" problems. Valero is one of a growing number of firms applying supply chain thinking to speed up hiring and reduce the expenses associated with it. When a new refinery opens, skills are sought from around the world—project managers from the United States, outsourced engineers from Canada, and programmers from India.[40]

Global Employer Branding

Attracting talent basically means marketing the firm to recruits. We remember an evening on Hong Kong Island in the mid-1990s with Nokia's HR manager for China. Looking across at the big neon lights saying "MOTOROLA" and

"SAMSUNG" across the water on the Kowloon mainland, he sighed. "People in China know the name Motorola. How can Nokia recruit good people in China when no one has heard of us?" The successful efforts to build a brand image in China were not only to promote products but also to attract talent, involving close collaboration between the marketing, external relations, and HR functions.

Companies that enjoy a strong reputation and a powerful brand can profit from this, as Infosys does in India, allowing the company to grow from about 10,000 to 66,000 employees over the last five years without compromising the quality of its services. Despite growing competition for software engineers, Infosys received almost 1.5 million job applications in 2005. It tested about 160,000 candidates and hired the 15,000 that the company considered the best of the applicant pool.[41] But its challenge in recent years is to globalize its employment brand and recruit top graduates in its key markets in the Americas and Europe.

Having a reputation as an employer of choice may be a mixed blessing because of the expense of selecting appropriate candidates. Companies are interested in how to attract the right candidates in a targeted way, leading them to apply branding techniques that are derived from marketing and customer analysis. If firms can create a distinctive image in the recruitment market, then they will attract only the right people. This means thinking of recruits as customers, segmenting the talent market, and using analytic techniques to identify whether the brand image is effective in attracting the right talent and to identify rivals.[42]

If employer branding is to be effective, it cannot be merely cosmetic. It involves managing internal changes to ensure that external image and internal reality are consistent. As we mentioned earlier, part of Schlumberger's attractiveness for engineers lies in its performance management system, which is run by technical leaders rather than managers. BMW, a leader in branding methodology, ensures that the messages in its external advertising campaigns are consistent with what is practiced within the organization.

Building a Differentiated Employee Value Proposition

Attracting or keeping a desired employee is based on the same principles as attracting and keeping a desired customer. This is the idea behind the *employee value proposition* (EVP), a balance of "give up" and "get."

The "give up" side of an EVP is often ignored, though it varies widely from one firm to another. Employees give up something in order to work, and the price they pay varies from one firm to another. Some firms, such as global investment banks, ask to be prioritized 24/7 in the lives of their talented people, who must be willing to work evenings, to travel extensively, and to tolerate high stress loads. Talented people will be willing to work for this kind of firm only if there is an equal "get," or value they receive, in return. Other organizations may demand less of a commitment, with more flexibility to balance work and family life. As a result, they need to offer less to make an attractive employment proposition.

The "get" side, the value that the company offers, is more than just pay, benefits, and morale. Just as some customers will pay more for a product that provides reliability or prestige, people will often choose to work for lower pay in one company than elsewhere because that company offers something distinctive that they value. That distinctive offering might be challenging work, a high degree of autonomy, strong friendship and social bonds, learning opportunities, a reputation in the community, or an image of social responsibility. How can one figure out the best value proposition to attract and retain a target employee group in a particular job market?

In contrast to the employer brand, which should be consistent across the firm, the EVP should be differentiated, varying with the employee group and the geographic market. This requires being aware of the different elements that can form an EVP, and carefully assessing the relevant market in order to figure out which elements to highlight.

For example, for Federal Express in China, the drivers of the vans are a key employee group. FedEx suffered from excessively high turnover as their experienced drivers were lured away by more highly paid opportunities with local fly-by-night courier operations. Assessing potential levers aside from pay, they found that emphasizing the FedEx values of safety and security, building a sense of pride in accident-free driving in immaculate clean vans, succeeded in bringing turnover rates down decisively.[43]

The potential elements in an employee value proposition are shown in Figure 7–2.

FIGURE 7–2 The Employee Value Proposition

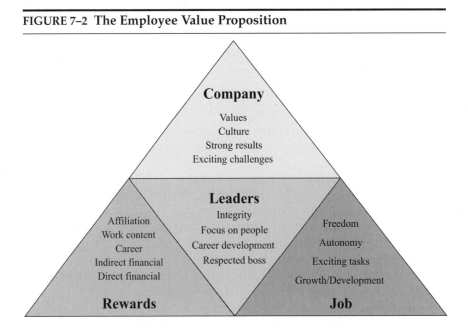

- The *rewards* are an obvious part of the package. Nokia's EVP in China emphasizes competitive pay and increments, as well as benefits such as personal insurance that it does not offer elsewhere. But rewards go beyond pay and benefits, including intangibles such as a sense of belonging, affiliation, and progressive career development. Traditional Japanese enterprises offer low entry salaries to their core talent, but provide relatively secure long-term careers.
- Attributes of the *job* may attract talent to the firm, notably the challenge of the work, its autonomy, or the learning opportunities associated with it.
- Features of the *company*, its culture, value system, and reputation may be assets, allowing the firm to highlight them in targeted campaigns. The reputation and values of the firm may enhance an individual's social reputation, even in his or her private life. For young employees worldwide, a firm's reputation for social responsibility plays an increasingly important role.
- The firm's *leadership* image may be part of the value proposition for attracting high-potential recruits. GE's reputation for leadership development and the thoroughness of its people management processes in feedback and development act as a pull for certain recruits who are likely to match the orientation of the firm. The person leaving GE parts with a plus on the CV because of its reputation for rigorous grooming of managers.

Through interviews and surveys, the EVP of a targeted group can be assessed, focusing messages on the most attractive elements. Focused recruitment efforts may be more cost-effective than broad reputational campaigns.

When the talent war is severe, companies are often forced to segment talent markets. "Life cycle differentiation" is an example. Life cycle differentiation means tailoring employee value propositions to highlight desirable elements for a target age group, whether this is housing, educational opportunities, autonomy, or flexible work practices. The concept of cafeteria benefits was based on this idea, now extended by modifying the EVP according to life cycle needs— offering learning and challenge to younger staff while emphasizing flexibility and meaningful work for the older generation. As we will discuss in greater detail later, Schlumberger has become the leading recruiter of women in the oil exploration industry throughout the world by offering flexible working practices to accommodate family needs and mobility constraints.[44]

MANAGING SELECTION AND ASSESSMENT

Selection involves identifying the most suitable person from a pool of candidates— internal and/or external.[45] It focuses on assessing the fit between the candidates and the job or career opportunity. The way in which this is done may bias recruitment or promotions, so selection is closely linked to the management of cultural, gender, and other forms of diversity.

In this section, we discuss four issues: selection methods, focusing on the external candidate pool; the management of diversity, with a particular focus on gender and ethnicity; the framework for selection (competencies); and the challenges of internal selection. The last factor is particularly important for multinational corporations since it deals with the identification of global talent among local employees.

Along with performance management, selection is one of the most important political processes in an organization, since selection decisions determine who is in and who is out. If decisions on who is recruited and who is promoted are concentrated in the hands of a small clique of line managers who follow their own personal criteria while ignoring HR processes, those HR activities will amount to little more than hot air. This can happen in multinational firms where local or expatriate managers give token acknowledgment to human resource development rhetoric but follow their own rules when it comes to promotions and internal appointments.

Selection Methods: The Importance of Context

There is broad agreement among both practitioners and scholars that there is no universal approach to selection. Selection is the area of human resource management where cultural and institutional differences play the biggest role.[46]

For example, in the United Kingdom there is a long-standing belief in empirical prediction. The role of selection is to gather relevant information through interviews, testing, and assessment vehicles, to make an accurate, reliable, and valid prediction of relevant outcomes like job performance. In France, selection systems are based more on clinical assessment, to size up fit for long-term employment, not to predict outcomes. The French educational system is seen as predicting performance outcomes, and so media articles on French business leaders will invariably refer to their educational background. The role of selection at entry recruitment is to minimize the risks that accompany long-term employment. This helps explain why graphology—handwriting interpretation—is widely practiced in France despite its poor predictive ability: It is a cheap source of information that might detect outlying risks in recruiting candidates.[47]

The use and interpretation of different selection methods vary from one culture to another. Let us take some examples:

- **Interviewing.** Interviews are widely used everywhere. However, structured interviewing, where each applicant is asked the same questions, is the norm in the United States and has been shown to have higher predictive validity than the unstructured interviews practiced in other cultures.[48] Companies such as IBM, Accenture, and Shell that want to globalize talent management practices use structured templates for interviewing.[49] However, the acceptability of phone interviews varies across cultures.
- **The role of HR versus the line manager.** There are significant national differences in who has the prime responsibility for selection decisions. In countries like France and Italy, where employees have legal rights to long-term employment after a probationary period, the HR staff have the role of vetting people.

Contrast this with Denmark, where there are few legal restrictions on hiring and firing; recruitment decisions are largely devolved to line managers.

- **Testing.** As we noted earlier, attitudes toward psychometric testing vary with culture, with the strongest belief in its predictive ability in the UK. Today there is widespread awareness of the cultural biases in testing instruments when used across different cultures, though psychologists claim that some tests, like general mental ability, have high predictive validity across different contexts.[50] Faced with cultural differences in selection, companies are tempted to respond by searching for cross-culturally validated testing instruments. Companies and consulting firms make more use of simulation instruments than psychological tests, particularly when guiding the selection of technical and managerial talent.

- **Assessment centers.** Well-designed (albeit expensive) assessment centers using interviews, role-plays, presentations, tests, and simulations are considered to be a rigorous and valid way of screening talent, either at recruitment or for the internal assessment of potential. Yet assessment centers do not translate well without adaptation to the new cultural context. Heavily structured exercises that work well in one context may be quite inappropriate in another; simulation cases may have to be rewritten for a different setting, and different norms will have to be worked out for tests.[51]

Selection should be seen as a *two-way process*, especially where highly talented individuals are concerned. Assessment content and the way in which selection is undertaken have an effect on the candidate's perception of the enterprise; they can be seen as a first step in the socialization process. A well-intentioned HR department can put off talented individuals by creating an impression of cumbersome and bureaucratic procedures. A test or simulation that has not been adapted well to the local culture, or that goes against practice in that region, can create the impression of an ethnocentric corporation where locals have few possibilities for progression. Moreover, in a growing number of countries, such as the UK and Germany, individuals have the right to see the written notes or references made during the assessment process, to counter discrimination in selection processes.

Cultural norms and legal contexts vary enormously. Corporations seeking the benefits of having one global approach to selection need to proceed carefully. For example, IBM developed a global selection toolkit with the participation of HR professionals from 18 countries. It included résumé screening, a phone interview, a behaviorally anchored structured interview together with two simulations, and a test to assess the candidate's fit with IBM culture. All this was accompanied by online training in how to use the toolkit. But IBM still found that units with a high degree of historic autonomy resisted adoption; the respective roles of HR and line varied considerably from one country to another, and unsurprisingly, entrenched resistance came from countries with a long history of using their own selection methods. To allow for cultural differences, each country could adjust the tools, though the objective is to encourage consistency across the globe.[52]

Selection and Diversity Management

Diversity and selection are closely interwoven. Selection bias—favoring people of a particular gender, color, or cultural origin in recruitment and promotion—is a significant factor in discrimination. There are many facets to diversity, which in the US focuses on minorities in organizations—women, older people, blacks, Asians, Hispanics, native Americans, gays and lesbians, and the disabled. However, the salient aspects of diversity management vary from one culture to another. In Canada, a key issue is Francophone versus Anglophone, both of whom are predominantly Caucasian. In many European countries it is the sizable immigrant population—Turks in Germany, Muslims of diverse nationalities in France. In much of Asia, it is ethnic background—for example Chinese, Indians, and Malays, in Singapore and Malaysia. For multinational companies, the obvious dimension of diversity is national background.

The characteristics of the selection system clearly influence bias. Selection systems like open job resourcing, where candidates can apply for positions and where the selection criteria are formally spelled out, favor unbiased decision making.[53] But systems that are closed, in the sense that candidates must be nominated by headquarters and where the selection criteria are more informal (simply the judgments of the assessors), are more likely to be biased, as a study on whether international careers are open to women has shown.[54]

In terms of gender discrimination in the developed world, Japan has fewest women in the workforce; only 49 percent of adult Japanese women are employed. The average wage for Japanese women is 65 percent of the equivalent male salary. Despite beefed-up legislation and some change, there are many subtle obstacles rooted in the Japanese employment system. These include an attachment to traditional performance assessment, where objectives are vague, often based on an assumption of willingness to sacrifice oneself for the company.[55] Scandinavia has also a low percentage of women in management positions in the private sector, many women finding better career opportunities in government and public service. In some Arab countries, such as Saudi Arabia, gender discrimination is anchored in religious beliefs.

In the traditionally male-dominated oil sector, Schlumberger's target for 2010 is for 20 percent of managers at all levels to be women, across a full range of nationalities. The actions launched during the last 10 years to achieve this cover a range of diversity initiatives:

- There is a special program to identify high potential women at an early career stage and to provide them with high-profile positions.
- There are recruitment targets: for example, 40 percent of R&D hires should be female.
- Nearly half of Schlumberger's recruiters are female, acting as role models; such recruitment jobs are two-year stepping-stone assignments before moving into management.

- Schlumberger has taken many actions to be an employer of choice for dual-career couples, including flexible work schedules, leaves of absence, and hiring spouses.
- Female employees are encouraged to join and develop networking groups that are managed locally but share experiences globally.

Employee surveys at Schlumberger and Shell assess how individual and workforce diversity is respected by measuring *inclusiveness*. The results of annual attitude surveys are analyzed to see if the scores given by women in a particular country, business group, or function are lower on relevant questions, like support from the boss or opportunities for development. Low inclusiveness scores lead to feedback and appropriate action.

The American view on diversity typically emphasizes the business case. IBM argued that its heavy investment in diversity, initially in the United States, would pay off in a billion dollars of revenues in the next 5 to 10 years through a better understanding of its female, gay, and ethnic minority customers.[56] Other business reasons for diversity include improved ability to attract and retain talent, as well as enhanced innovation and problem-solving ability. Schlumberger's expansion into emerging markets was based on a long-standing principle that recruitment should broadly parallel the geographic distribution of revenues. But while surveys show that virtually all *Fortune* 500 companies view global diversity as an important or very important issue, with respect to gender, research in other parts of the world, including Europe, suggests that the business case for gender diversity is less widely accepted there than in the US.[57]

One of the open questions for multinational corporations is whether a global strategy is best for diversity management. IBM's approach, which originated in the US, is global.[58] The company created global task forces, reporting to a high executive level and with strong representation from the targeted minorities. A global structure of regional or business councils at lower levels is responsible for specific initiatives, complemented by the creation of employee network groups. A similar approach was implemented in Shell. Other multinational corporations prefer to take a decentralized local approach, since equal opportunity laws and norms vary from one culture to another.

However, nationality and cultural background remain the most challenging issues for multinational firms, as they struggle to escape their home country roots. As an executive working for a large fast-moving consumer goods firm told us, "My handicap is not that I am a woman but that I am Chinese." From the earliest days of globalization, the forecast has been that multinational companies will gradually move from an *ethnocentric* to a *geocentric* orientation, where the key indicator will be national diversity at the top.[59] This is important for various reasons: There will be an appropriate diversity in perspectives underlying decision making; the composition of top management will reflect the customer mix of a global corporation; and it indicates a well-managed global meritocracy where contributions count more than passports.

There are some firms with strong diversity on the executive team. There are 10 nationalities among the top 26 executives at Schlumberger, and some foreigners are celebrated CEOs of *Fortune* 100 multinationals: Howard Stringer at Sony, Arun Sarin at Vodafone, and Indra Nooyi at PepsiCo. Although one might expect executive committees or boards to be most diverse in European countries, research shows that there is a long way to go. Considering the 363 largest firms in the 15 oldest members of the European Union in 2005, only 15 percent of the executive positions were occupied by leaders with a different nationality than the firm's country of origin.[60] The Netherlands appears to be most open to a geocentric mix. Schlumberger is a path-breaking exception—in most multinationals there are significant biases that favor the careers of home country nationals.

Competencies: Frameworks for Selection and Talent Management

One of the ways in which a multinational firm influences selection is by identifying the firm-specific competencies that should guide selection decisions. A competence is a cluster of related skills, abilities, and traits that enables a person to act effectively in a particular job or situation. One important distinction is between deeply rooted *qualities*, or traits/motives, that might guide selection decisions and behavioral *skills* that can be developed.

Competence frameworks are intended to ensure consistency across recruitment, selection, socialization, and development actions.[61] They also provide a common language for line managers and HR professionals across the matrix of operations, to steer talent selection, performance management, development, and decisions that will help build desired capabilities. As Reuben Mark, former CEO of Colgate-Palmolive, says, "Competencies, are the glue that joins all of our HR processes; they factor into our various employee training and development programs (about 110 worldwide) as well as our promotion and compensation decisions."[62]

While the idea of providing such a global platform for talent management is appealing, the journey is fraught with frustration and disillusionment. Competence frameworks are often too generic to be useful, means become ends, and company task forces spend large amounts of time and money generating sterile wish lists of desirable qualities. Why is this competence journey so difficult?

A study of 31 North American firms found that a major reason for this confusion in linking organizational needs to individual competencies is that there is not one guiding logic but at least three. Twelve of the firms took what we call a *performance-based approach,* nine adopted a *strategy-based approach,* four used a *values-based approach,* while others had adopted hybrid approaches.[63] Each logic has its merits and disadvantages, so that there are trade-offs rather than a single correct approach. Our experience is that the source of confusion stems from people using the concept of competence in different ways, without realizing that they are applying different logics and dealing with trade-offs. These three approaches are summarized in Table 7–3.

The Performance-Based Approach

The performance-based approach says that we should focus on the characteristics of high performers so we can reproduce more of them. For example, GE selects people who "see change as an opportunity, not a threat" and who "have a passion for excellence, hating bureaucracy and all the nonsense that comes with it."[64] In GE's experience, seeking out challenges and opportunities for change is what differentiates high performers from others.

High-performing individuals are studied to identify their distinguishing characteristics and behaviors, and they may be compared to more modest contributors. Because of this, the performance-based approach is also called the *research-based approach*.

One of the authors of this book assisted a major energy firm in developing a research-based framework. The aim of the project was to decentralize

TABLE 7–3. Profile of Three Competence Logics Guiding Talent Management

	Description	Advantages	Disadvantages
Research-based approach	Competencies based on behavioral research on high-performing individuals	• Grounded in actual behavior • Air of legitimacy • Involves people, which fosters acceptance	• Based on the past, not the future • May omit intangible and unmeasurable competencies • Requires extensive resources
Strategy-based approach	Competencies forecast to be important in the future for the successful implementation of company strategy	• Competencies based on the future, not the past • Focuses on learning new skills • Can support organizational transformation	• The scenario for the future may be incorrect or distant • Difficult to implement unless top management "walks the talk"
Values-based approach	Competencies based on a holistic view of norms and values	• Can have strong motivating power • Can provide strategic stability for long periods of time, especially in fast-growing environments • Provides "glue" or integration	• Depends on the ability of top leaders to communicate a holistic philosophy of management • Competence development process may lack rigor • Can be difficult to translate into actual behavior

Source: Adapted from J.P. Briscoe and D.T. Hall, "Grooming and Picking Leaders Using Competency Frameworks," *Organizational Dynamics,* Autumn 1999, pp. 37–51.

An Example of a Performance-Based Framework

Linking Competence to Career Progression

	Professional	Personal	People	Business	Change	Strategy	Vision
VI	ANTICIPATING FUTURE	PERSONAL IMPRINT ON ORGANIZATION	REPRESENTATIONAL LEADERSHIP	MEDIATING STAKEHOLDER DEMANDS	CREATING A CULTURE FOR CHANGE	POLICY TO STRATEGY	CORPORATE VISION AND DIRECTION
V	BALANCING SECTORIAL DEMANDS	TAKING NEW PERSPECTIVES, NEW MENTAL MAPS	TRANSFORMATIONAL CORPORATE LEADERSHIP	RENEWING THE BUSINESS	SUPPORTING ORGANIZATIONAL LEARNING AND ADAPTATION	STRATEGIC MANAGEMENT	CONTRIBUTING TO RESHAPING AND REDIRECTION
IV	ORCHESTRATING INTER-FUNCTIONAL RELATIONSHIPS	PROMOTING GROWTH IN SELF AND OTHERS	DEVELOPING BROADER RELATIONSHIPS	DEVELOPING BUSINESS CREATIVITY	MANAGING MAJOR CHANGE	RESPONSIVENESS TO THE ENVIRONMENT	SHARING AND CARRYING OUT VISION
III	SPECIALISM IN WIDER COMMERCIAL CONTEXT	HUMAN RESOURCE MANAGEMENT SKILLS	DEVELOPING PEOPLE AND ORGANIZATIONS	MANAGING A BUSINESS UNIT	SKILLS FOR CHANGE	STRATEGIC BUSINESS PLANNING	MATCHING OWN BUSINESS DIRECTION WITH STRATEGY
II	DEEPENING THE EXPERTISE OF SELF AND OTHERS	MOTIVATING, NEGOTIATING, AND INFLUENCING	MANAGING OTHERS	INTEGRATING BUSINESS SKILLS AND INTRAPRENEUR-SHIP	PARTICIPATING IN CHANGE	MONITORING PERFORMANCE	IMPACT OF MISSION ON JOB
I	DEVELOPING FUNCTIONAL AND TECHNICAL SKILLS	MANAGING SELF AND USE OF EXPERTISE	TEAMWORKING AND NETWORKING	COMMERCIAL AWARENESS	UNDERSTANDING ORGANIZATIONAL CHANGE	AWARENESS OF STRATEGY	AWARENESS OF MISSION

EXPLANATION

The horizontal axis indicates seven areas of skill or competence, while the vertical axis indicates hierarchical career progression, from individual contributor positions (I) through supervisory management posts to business unit management (II and III), up to positions as a member of the management team of an operating company and as managing director of such a subsidiary (IV and V), to group top management (VI).

The concept behind this matrix is that the added value in development lies in sticking close to the diagonal boxes. For example, development attention should focus above all on developing skills in "managing others" in level II supervisory positions. The groundwork will have been laid earlier through demonstrated ability in teamwork and networking. Good skills in managing others will allow people to develop broader competence in developing people and in network relations as they move up in their careers. The further one moves from the diagonal, the lower the added value.

responsibility for management training and development to local operating companies around the world, within the discipline of a common framework. The performance-based approach made sense; since it was rooted in actual data on high-performing individuals in seven sample countries, it was more likely to be accepted by local operating companies. This is shown and explained in the box "Linking Competence to Career Progression."

The performance-based approach has some clear advantages, and it is often used to steer talent management at functional and core skill levels. A firm that wants to recruit and train sales staff for an emerging market might employ the methodology to develop criteria for selection and training, and to guide regular assessments, perhaps adopting skills-based compensation linked to those competencies. Depending on how it is applied, the performance-based approach is potentially rigorous. The study of real managers gives legitimacy to the "soft" domain of talent management and facilitates its acceptability and implementation. Above all, the performance-based approach is pragmatic, and with appropriate cultural adjustment the results can easily be incorporated in performance appraisal guides, selection criteria, and training schemes around the world.

However, there are some disadvantages when the performance-based approach is applied to strategic talent. It is fundamentally a rear-window methodology, oriented toward the past and the status quo rather than to the future. While there may be merit in using such logic in a slow-moving industry, the approach is poorly suited to the discontinuities of a fast-moving competitive environment or to the complexities of a multidimensional professional service firm. Since it is based on historic data, the performance-based approach may perpetuate an outdated structure of career paths.

The Strategy-Based Approach

The strategy-based approach is forward-looking, built around where we want to go. The original theory behind "strategic human resource management" emphasized translating strategy for the future into current implications for talent selection and development, thereby implementing strategy faster.[65] This is the approach that some strategy scholars, such as Kaplan and Norton, advocate as an integral element of their balanced scorecard approach to strategic management and execution.[66] What competencies does our talent need in order to execute our strategy? How well are we providing those competencies? And how do we fill the gaps through training, development, performance management, and rewards?

While the strategy-based logic lacks the rigor and legitimacy of the performance-related approach, especially for people lower down in the firm, its big advantage is that it is oriented to the future. It is often appealing to the senior management of firms undergoing substantial transformational change and to those in fast-moving competitive environments. As GE's CEO Jeff Immelt notes, every strategic initiative he takes is translated into recruiting, training, and succession—in other words, into plans to build the necessary competencies.[67]

Consistency of behavior at senior levels—walking the talk—is important. As ABB's former CEO Percy Barnevik once commented, "If we talk about the need for fast decision making and then top management procrastinates on important decisions, then it just isn't credible."[68] Fast decision making needs to be matched by fast and thorough communication throughout the organization. While the need for new behaviors aligned around a change in strategy may be obvious to top management, it may be far from clear to middle-level managers in distant subsidiaries, where the decisions on recruitment and promotions are made. The competencies may be seen as the whim of the current CEO or as headquarters politics.

The quickest way to implement the strategic approach is to bring in new strategic skills from outside, as happens at the top in times of crisis. Extraordinary promotions are also effective in communicating strategic signals in complex multinationals—for example, a particular individual, widely regarded as a maverick, is promoted to a position of major responsibility.

The Values-Based Approach

While the values-based logic behind talent development may be linked to a competence framework, it is part of a broader philosophy of management linked to strong normative integration, as Toyota illustrates (see the discussion of Toyota in Chapter 6). Hewlett-Packard is another good example. In his autobiography, Dave Packard described how he and Bill Hewlett wrestled for decades to articulate their emerging management philosophy and to communicate it to their expanding staff.[69] If they could do this, they could let employees loose, guided by targets but otherwise autonomous. The result was "the HP Way," a list of values (or competencies) such as long-term perspective, listening to customers, and trust in people.

Similarly, Infosys recruits for what it calls "learnability" and applies this to all internal selections right up into senior management.[70] Indeed selection on the basis of specified qualities is arguably one of the most powerful ways of building and maintaining a strong culture. The values-based approach, closely associated with the values-based leadership that Infosys's CEO Murthy exemplifies, provides potentially powerful glue or integration, particularly in a knowledge-based organization that cannot rely excessively on hierarchical mechanisms of control.[71]

Adapting Competencies in the Transnational Firm

Global competencies need to be translated into behavioral indicators in order to steer selection decisions, whether these involve external recruitment or internal promotion and transfer. Cross-cultural validation studies undertaken by companies show that there will inevitably be differences in these behavioral indicators from one culture to another, as well as from one business to another. For example, a specific skill within the competence of "managing people" at supervisory levels might be providing feedback. In an individualistic culture, such as the United States, the appropriate behavioral indicator might be "confronts people constructively on their failings," whereas in a collective culture, such as Thailand, this might read as "ensures that subordinates know how they stand while maintaining team harmony." In defining "external relations" in a petrochemical company, the downstream exploration business might emphasize community relations, while customer relations would be highlighted in the upstream marketing business.[72] The "teamwork" competence may apply across cultures, but with very different indicators in different settings.

There is a real tension between the need for differentiation and the need for consistency. Unless the competence framework is developed in close partnership with top management and the line, there is a risk that line managers will pay no attention to what they see as an "HR exercise" that ignores the pragmatic needs for differentiation, trying to impose one size on all. The need for differentiation across countries will often be invoked by local subsidiaries arguing for their own local way in choosing the competencies that guide selection.[73]

The Challenges of Internal Selection (Assessment of Potential)

How does a multinational corporation spot and select talent from within its ranks? This question is important: As usually only those selected will be offered development opportunities and training with the intention of moving them into leadership roles. If selection into this pipeline, as it is called, is focused only on males from the home country, those are the people who will come out of the pipeline into executive roles. So how do global companies identify leadership potential?

Regional Differences in Internal Talent Management

There are many ways of assessing talent or leadership potential within the multinational firm. The traditional ways of doing this vary from company to company and from nation to nation.

THE ELITE COHORT APPROACH. Many Japanese corporations in the latter half of the 20th century adopted what we call the elite cohort approach, which also characterizes some established European firms.[74] Cohorts of graduates are recruited from target universities for long-term careers and then moved around the organization during a seven-to-eight-year trial period, when they are trained in company-specific skills and socialized into the organization's values. The trial period is characterized by a "safe learning environment" in the sense that there are no immediate consequences of poor performance. But performance and behavior are carefully monitored over time. Appraisals by superiors are collected by the central personnel department—at Toyota, for example, this happens at least three or four times a year. In effect, these seven years are an extended selection period, based on different assignments and bosses.

By the time the members of the cohort are in their early 30s, and moving into positions of leadership responsibility, these assessments will have enabled the company to separate the sheep from the goats. The rules change, and career progression becomes a tournament, with "winners" and "losers."[75] Those who are deemed outstanding are given challenging responsibilities, while those who score lower are assigned to less important roles with virtually no chance of getting back into the game. These managers may eventually be counseled out of the firm to join a subsidiary company—or a foreign multinational.

Although there has been considerable change in Japan over the last 15 years, many leading Japanese corporations still follow this elite cohort approach, as it has some strong merits. Selection has been rigorously undertaken, assuring the development of a highly socialized leadership elite whose loyalty is unquestioned, whose skills have been meticulously honed, and which has a strong grasp of the subtle problems of coordination.

However, this approach is incompatible with localization. Since potential is identified at the time of recruitment, all the people entering the cohort pipeline are Japanese. Consequently the output of the pipeline is Japanese. Even when Japanese firms attempt to include foreign employees in the cohort, the practice of appraising potential cautiously over a number of years discourages the best, who want quick signals that they have a future. As a consequence, while Japanese work practices at the factory level are widely admired, Japanese firms have a poor reputation for manager development, particularly in service industries such as banking and entertainment. However, since the elite cohort approach has been successful, it is not easily modified.[76]

THE ELITE POLITICAL APPROACH. What we call the elite political approach, which characterizes some US firms, is the typical pattern in establishment companies in Latin Europe. We can take France as an example. As in the cohort approach, potential is identified at entry. Recruits come from schools that specialize in grooming an elite for positions of future leadership responsibility. In effect, the French educational system is responsible for selection. That system, from the high school *Baccalauréat* (leaving diploma) to the *Grandes Ecoles* (graduate or elite schools), is a funnel that progressively selects people for their intellect, ambition, and ability to conform to establishment values.[77] The graduates of the best *Grandes Ecoles* are virtually guaranteed positions, as top leaders (the only doubt is the size and stature of the firm), and they will immediately enter positions of managerial responsibility without any trial period. While everyone else in the firm (graduates of lesser schools and universities) moves up in functional paths—what the French call *les métiers*—this elite will move on a path of cross-functional challenge that continues to develop their leadership skills.[78]

The equivalent of this in the United States would be firms that recruit graduates from Ivy League universities with top MBA degrees. One could argue that some elite consulting firms and investment banks, such as McKinsey and Goldman Sachs, play the same role in the US and elsewhere as selection grounds for senior-level appointments.

THE FUNCTIONAL APPROACH. Historically, German firms exemplified the functional approach, a third model for internal assessment and talent management, though variants can again be found throughout the world. It is less elitist in nature, and the distinctive feature is that leadership is associated with functional expertise rather than managerial leadership.

As in the elite cohort approach, there is an initial trial period of assessment after graduate recruitment, but of a very different nature. Following the apprenticeship tradition, which is deeply rooted in German heritage, recruits are rotated between departments for a two-year period (a practice also followed in some American and other European firms). The objective is twofold: first, to provide the recruits with a broad exposure to the business and organization; and second, to assess where their talents really lie. At the end of this trial period they are assigned to the function that appears to suit them best. They will then climb that functional ladder to higher and higher levels of expertise,[79] although German firms increasingly rotate their talent internationally and cross-functionally.

The advantage of the functional approach is the in-depth expertise that it develops, shown by the meticulous attention to detail that is associated with the renowned quality of German engineering. The disadvantage is the slowness of decision making in organizations with strong silos, especially when it comes to strategy in a fast-moving world of global competition.

Schlumberger follows a variant of this model. As we discussed, the company recruits top engineering graduates from elite schools in both emerging and developed countries. These recruits then follow a three-year training program involving classroom, on-the-job training, and projects, but their performance and fit are closely assessed. During this period, 40 percent of recruits will drop out or be counseled out. While there is a long-term approach to development, only one in four hires will make a full career with the firm.[80]

WHAT ABOUT THE UNITED STATES? Variants on these three approaches to the internal identification of talent could be found in leading US enterprises in the golden years of American economic dominance after World War II until the 1980s. But with the increase in global competition, the focus changed to restructuring and cost reduction. GE's CEO at the time, Jack Welch, was nicknamed "Neutron Jack," as he set the pace by eliminating more than a 100,000 jobs during his early years as chief executive, many of them in the management and professional ranks. IBM, formerly a bastion of stable if not lifetime employment, pushed a quarter million people out of the firm between 1985 and 1993, and brought in a hundred thousand new hires. Subsequent waves of acquisitions further disrupted talent plans, and the increasing speed of change made it difficult to forecast talent requirements. Meanwhile, the new IT industry was growing in California's Silicon Valley, largely through buying and poaching talent at all levels. Cisco employed 500 recruiters and regularly added 1,000 new employees each month in the five years until 2000. It was only after the crisis in 2001 that Cisco started to focus on internal talent management, including the launch of a talent assessment process to accelerate the development of top contributors.[81]

What this means today is that the United States is the country with perhaps the weakest belief in internal talent management, including assessment and development. The most common way to get promotion is to change companies. For many companies (some leading multinationals like GE, IBM, or P&G are exceptions), talent management means recruiting and buying talent from the outside. About 40 percent of US employees have been with their current employers for less than two years.[82] A global survey in 2005 showed that organizations in North America were the least likely to have a succession plan for staff, gave the lowest priorities to people development and retention, and were the most skeptical about the competitive advantage of people development.[83] Cappelli describes the rise and fall of talent management practices, arguing that talent management should learn from supply chain management, oriented to developing and supplying talent within a short-term time horizon.[84]

Toward a Transnational Approach

Each of these three models has distinctive strengths, but they share the danger of an excessive reliance on internal labor markets. They have come under pressure from progressive globalization. One of their limitations is that talent and potential, particularly in the elitist models, are identified so early. While there are clear advantages to this (talented people can be exposed to developmental challenges over a longer period of time), it inevitably leads to a parent country bias, as well as an excessive number people in the pipeline who may leave for other firms.

Consequently a different approach has emerged, one that is more in tune with the needs of the multinational enterprise, particularly those facing transnational challenges. The distinctive features of this model are that it is not elitist, in terms of identifying potential at entry; and that it decentralizes the responsibility for functional development to its local subsidiaries, while managing selection into the leadership and global talent ranks tightly at the corporate level.

The pattern that has developed in multinational corporations, from Exxon to Nestlé and from IBM to Novartis, is to decentralize the responsibility for recruitment to local units. The parent country itself becomes just another local unit, and the corporate recruitment or staffing unit is separated from the mother country.[85] The role of the reconfigured corporate function is not to recruit in the parent country—it is to beef up the rigor with which local companies undertake recruitment and staffing (typically aided by a guiding competence-based logic). Local subsidiaries recruit not just for jobs but also for potential.[86] Local recruits pursue their careers within the local company, typically moving upward within functions for the first five to eight years. One could call this a *locally managed functional trial.* The corporate task is then to distinguish those with wider potential from the ranks of local talent.

Since potential is not identified at the time of entry, a wide variety of techniques are used to identify internal people with potential:

- Local general managers may be asked annually to submit the names of their high potential individuals, who will then be scrutinized or even sent through an assessment center. The task of developing high potential local talent may be one of the key performance indicators (KPIs) for the local unit.
- Expatriates working in local firms are required to identify local high potentials, including their possible successors.
- If there is a regional structure, identifying potential is a particular responsibility of the regional HR manager working with local subsidiaries.
- In some firms, potential is identified in a more subtle way, through local nominations for a landmark corporate "young managers" educational program, in which the training staff observe the behavior of participants closely.
- Local personnel who are given exceptional salary raises may come under particular scrutiny, as will those individuals who are assigned by local subsidiaries to work on cross-boundary projects.
- Exxon used to use a peer ranking methodology,[87] and multiple appraisal remains a reliable method of making such judgments—getting a group of managers who are familiar with the local people around a table for a frank discussion of their qualities. While the choice of a competence-based logic in no way resolves the problem of identifying potential, it provides a common language and concept of potential to guide these methods.

One of the implications is that global performance management will become particularly important, since internal selection should be based on common standards for performance evaluation across borders and cultures. We will explore further some of the dilemmas around this issue in Chapter 9.

MANAGING RETENTION

One of the basic tenets of human capital theory is that individuals who have valuable generalized skills that are not firm-specific will be most likely to be lured away by market opportunities elsewhere. Therefore, retention must be an integral part of talent management. Firms that do a good job of recruitment and development but who manage retention poorly will have borne all the costs of talent development, while other firms capture the benefits. Unfortunately, it is typically the most talented people, whom firms can least afford to lose, who leave for higher pay and bigger opportunities elsewhere.

Attrition rates vary from one region of the world to another, depending on supply and demand and other factors outlined at the beginning of this chapter.[88]

Staff turnover is generally low in Europe and the Middle East, and lowest of all in Japan where lifetime employment is still the norm in large companies. Attrition rates are high in the growth economies of Asia, where opportunities outstrip supply, and they are particularly high among senior managers and executive leaders. Attrition is also high in North America, where there is a strong belief in buying talent rather than building it, as discussed earlier. Most Silicon Valley firms grew solely through building ever-greater sophistication in recruitment at all levels in the boom years of the 1990s. Attrition is also extremely high in Russia.

Many studies have tried to estimate the costs of turnover. The more skilled and talented the person, the higher the direct and indirect costs of disruption and replacement, so costs are typically estimated by taking a multiple of the salary. The larger the salary, the higher is the multiple. The cost of replacing an unskilled person is usually one or two times the monthly salary, while for a senior executive it may be 10 or 15 times that monthly salary.[89]

Why Do People Leave and What Can Be Done about It?

The scholarly research on turnover and retention suggests that there are multiple reasons for attrition,[90] and there is a large practitioner literature on the reasons why people leave a firm.[91] With this in mind, let us review some of the implications for managing retention:

1. **Compensation.** When asked in an exit interview about the reasons for leaving the organization, most people will say that they are getting a higher wage package in their new job. But this does not necessarily mean that higher compensation is the solution to retention. Experienced HR professionals will point out that typically it is not money that leads someone to look outside in the first place but some other cause for disgruntlement—lack of clear development opportunities, a difficult boss, or problems in work–life balance. And if talented individuals are prepared to change jobs and organizations, they will invariably gain (often significant) increases in compensation. Raising salaries across the board to solve retention would only price the company out of business. As we discussed earlier, it is important to consider all aspects of the employee value proposition, of which compensation is only one element.

   This does not mean that compensation is unimportant for retention. There is a widespread belief in the United States that an unsatisfied employee can be tempted elsewhere by a 5 percent increase in wages, while it will take 20 percent to lure a satisfied person.[92] Compensation is important, and if the firm is out of line with the market for a particular category of talent, then it can expect to see turnover rising. Consequently, research shows that firms that invest in human capital development in order to build a more productive workforce are willing to pay above-average market wages, as is indeed the case with Schlumberger.[93]

   To retain strategic talent it is vital to know how employees view the local job market and to know this market well (it may include small local companies). In countries where it is possible to use stock options and retention bonuses, these may be effective in boosting retention. People may leave after their options are exercised, but this is at least predictable.

Financial penalties can sometimes be used to discourage unilateral resignations. For example, employment contracts that include retention bonds (often with family guarantees) are widely used by the public sector in Singapore to retain employees who have benefited from education or training support from the government or the employer. The aim is to ensure that they remain with the sponsoring organization for a prescribed period of time to secure a return on the development investment. In the private sector such contracts, while not uncommon, are difficult to enforce.

2. **The quality of the relationship with the boss.** The line manager is responsible for many areas of potential dissatisfaction contributing to turnover: coaching, providing feedback, giving recognition, offering growth opportunities. The boss is also central to other dimensions of retention management, such as work–life balance, where the superior typically has considerable discretion, regardless of corporate policy and practice. HR professionals often argue that much of the problem of turnover lies in the hands of the direct supervisor. A popular way of expressing this is the aphorism that "people don't leave companies, they quit bosses."

   One of the bones of contention concerning retention management is that line managers tend to see it as the responsibility of the HR function, often linked to compensation and benefits, while HR professionals want line managers to take the prime responsibility for retention. However, creating a talent mindset where line managers accept that they must pay attention to subordinates can be difficult. This is true even in North America, where it is now common for at least senior managers to have retention objectives among their key performance indicators.

   If the firm has an internal job market that allows employees to apply freely for other internal positions, the role of the boss in retaining talent becomes more transparent—as described in the box "How IBM Got Line Managers to Feel Accountable for Retention." By 2005, half of companies in the US allowed employees to apply for another internal position without permission from the boss.[94] But creating this talent mindset can be more challenging in the environment of emerging countries, like Russia and China, where bosses often have an eye on the door themselves, and are not used to considering people management as part of their role—indeed they may take their best performers with them when they leave!

3. **Work–life balance.** The biggest source of work dissatisfaction in the opinion surveys of many leading multinationals is poor balance between professional and private life, particularly pronounced in high-growth markets of Asia and Latin America. And in affluent countries where dual careers have become the norm, there is no doubt that work–life imbalance contributes to attrition.

   This is particularly true among career women with children, and among the younger Generation Y in their 20s. One reserve to note here is highlighted

How IBM Got Line Managers to Feel Accountable for Retention

In the high-tech boom years of the late 1990s, IBM professionals were frequently poached by competing companies. In a firm that had always prided itself on its retention capacity, annual turnover rates among software engineers and IT specialists were in excess of 30 percent in some domains and countries. As in most firms, line managers saw this as a problem for the HR department to solve. Instead, HR devised a strategy to encourage the line to feel accountable for retention management.

IBM had an internal job market where professionals could apply for other positions. But it was not functioning well, since bosses could make life difficult for people who applied. HR gathered the line managers together and showed them the turnover statistics—32 percent of software engineers going to Dell, HP, and start-ups each year. "We can't prevent people from leaving," HR pointed out, "but we want them to look at other possibilities within the IBM before they decide to quit. So we are going to have to remove any rights that bosses have over their people. You can no longer prevent anyone from applying for a job and moving elsewhere within IBM." There were howls of protest from the line: "How can we do our work when you've taken away all our rights over our people?" With the backing of top management, HR insisted that these were the new rules of the game.

Within a year, turnover rates had come down significantly. To get their work done, managers were now obliged to coach their people, listen regularly to their needs, and allow flexibility within reasonable limits for family demands. By the time the 2001 recession hit and turnover was no longer a significant problem, the culture of IBM had changed and the new rules remained in place.

in the research of one of the authors, based on 14,000 managers across the globe, which showed that perceived work–life imbalance may hide other problems, notably different types of mismatch between the job or company and the individual.[95] In contrast, individuals who thrive on their jobs and work environments will often live with their work–life dissatisfaction for protracted periods of time.

In order to retain talent, companies respond with a range of work–life programs to juggle work and family commitments, as well as child-friendly working practices. Infosys successfully tackles retention with a group of workplace initiatives, including family involvement, that mimic the best aspects of university life and aim at avoiding impersonal bureaucracy amid rapid growth.[96] Flexible working hours are spreading, practiced by two-thirds of European companies and by large firms in other developed regions, from Singapore to San Francisco. While telecommuting appears to be particularly effective with respect to retention among dual-career couples with children, only 24 percent of a sample of 300 corporations across the globe offer this, and we rarely see it in Asia.[97] Thoughtless practices—such as Friday conference calls, New York time, that take away part of the weekend for those in Asia—should be eliminated.

4. **Internal development and promotion.** Providing a transparent structure for talent development that is clearly based on performance and potential is another important tool for combating attrition. In multinational firms, this means establishing positive role models for local staff. The lack of development and promotional opportunities contributes greatly to attrition, especially among talented individuals. We found this to be consistently true at multinationals in emerging markets like Hong Kong, in the past, and Shanghai, Singapore, and Bangalore today. If locals are unsure of their development opportunities in the firm, particularly when they see senior jobs going first and foremost to expatriates, they will naturally manage their careers by keeping a close eye on outside opportunities. But this also true of firms in the US, where senior positions are often filled by outsiders.

5. **Location.** It may be easier to recruit people in talent cluster locations like the San Francisco area for the IT industry, the north of Italy for the fashion industry, or in conurbations such as Shanghai and Sao Paolo. But it is also easier for other firms to poach talent in such places, and attrition will certainly be higher. The HR strategy of software firm SAS focuses on providing generous employee benefits and a highly congenial flexible work environment—but it is located in North Carolina, far from the industry hub on the Pacific coast. Its attrition rate is low in an otherwise volatile industry (see the box "Retention in High-Velocity Environments") and this stability gives SAS a competitive advantage over its competitors, where many members of software development teams are either learning the ropes or looking for opportunities elsewhere. Companies with sophisticated techniques for the attraction, selection, and development of talent may be able to choose secondary locations where it is easier to socialize and retain talented individuals (like Vietnam rather than China).

Retention in High-Velocity Environments

Conventional wisdom about human resources says that it is particularly important to pay attention to factors such as development in the second and third years of employment, a time when people often begin to look at alternative options. However, a recent study in the booming marketplace of India, where attrition rates among young professionals have been exceeding 30 percent, suggests that employers should start a professional development plan immediately after recruitment, as talented individuals are making decisions about whether to stay or leave within six months.[98] In these fast-moving environments, four factors were found to be important:

- Performance management to identify rapidly the right people to retain.
- Professional and career development.
- Attention by line managers to individuals.
- Company social responsibility.

A company's reputation and attitude toward social responsibility are increasingly important for attraction and retention among Generation Y.

BALANCING SHORT AND LONG TERM IN TALENT MANAGEMENT

One of the biggest tensions pervading most areas of talent management is between short and long term. GE paid close attention to this when creating its talent development culture. When managers complained that they were under so much immediate performance pressure that they did not have time to develop their people, former CEO Jack Welch pushed back. "Anybody can manage short. Anybody can manage long. Balancing those two things is what management is about."[99]

Companies can become trapped in a vicious cycle of HR boom-and-bust if leaders are excessively reactive and pay attention only to the short term. In a downturn, the first budget to be cut is recruitment, followed by training. When the business cycle is at its lowest point, there is a temptation to cut costs to the bone by laying off people, sometimes in ways that compromise the motivation and loyalty of survivors. When the upturn comes, there are not enough skills left in the company to take advantage of the growth opportunities. Managers scramble to fight short-term fires, hiring people with excessive bonuses and frustrating others. If before there were no budgets for training and development, now there is no time to do training and development well. Problems with underperforming people are pushed aside—until the next downturn, when they are laid off. And so the cycle repeats itself.

Even firms known for long-term thinking, such as those in the oil and gas industry, have fallen into this trap. Oil prices are by nature cyclical and unpredictable, and during the 1980s and 1990s the oil majors took a conservative stance on recruitment of petroleum engineers and geophysicists. Then, when the price of oil hit an all-time low of $10 a barrel in 1999, Shell, Exxon, and most other major players stopped all recruitment, faced with an obvious need to cut operating costs. For several years there were no new jobs in the oil industry, hundreds of engineers and geologists were laid off, and many departments of petroleum engineering at Western universities literally had to close their doors. Then 10 years later, when the oil price jumped to over $100 a barrel, the share price of these companies depended on the capability to find and exploit oil reserves. However, technical graduates were only to be found in emerging oil-producing countries such as China, Russia, and Indonesia. These graduates would typically prefer to join their national oil company—or Schlumberger, the now booming oil services provider that had demonstrated a longer-term strategic staffing perspective.

L'Oréal, the French cosmetics giant, had an exemplary way of dealing with this cycle. Top management openly acknowledged that one of the most important tensions to manage is the conflict between the short-term bottom line and long-term development; and that in decision making there is a natural tendency to privilege the short term, since it is so immediate and concrete. The role of the human resource function at L'Oréal was to act as the guardian of the strategic and long-term perspective, especially concerning decisions about recruitment, promotion, and the development of people. This did not give HR a right to veto; however, it did give them the right to stop the music and say, "Time out! Let's look at the long-term arguments before we decide." Sometimes the decision would favor the short term, sometimes the long term, and sometimes a creative solution favoring both would be found.

Companies should be investing in performance management to identify and retain high performers and to weed out low performers in good times, not just bad. For well-managed companies with solid global performance management, strong balance sheets, and the liquidity to make investments, there is no better time to build competitive advantage than during a downturn. As Peter Sands, CEO of Standard Chartered, notes, the times of crisis are a period of opportunity for bold moves that pave the way for the future, notably with respect to talent management.[100] That is the time when one can have the best of both worlds by retaining one's best people and attracting the best from one's competitors. As the good times return, the corporation is in a strong position.

TAKEAWAYS

1. The talent management process anticipates and meets a firm's needs for human capital. It is defined as deliberate actions, connected to the organizational strategy and capabilities, to attract, select, develop, and retain those who, individually or collectively, have the capability to make a significant impact on the firm's results.

2. Along with performance management, talent management is often seen as the most important element of HRM in the knowledge economy. Demographic changes and global competition add to the importance of talent. Individuals are increasingly mobile as the Internet opens access to more career opportunities.

3. Talent management requires a high degree of attention from three internal stakeholders: top management (notably the CEO), the HR function, and line managers in general.

4. Multinational firms can build competitive advantage through talent management by ensuring that the best individuals get opportunities, regardless of their passports, and by proactive recruiting in emerging markets.

5. Firms need a balance between building and buying talent. The former is favored if (1) the strategic time horizon of the firm is long; (2) there is a clear internal sequence of skills and jobs; (3) the culture of the firm is part of its competitive capability; and (4) it is possible to forecast the demands for talent.

6. To attract and retain talent in local markets, it is important to build a global employer brand and differentiated employee value propositions, balancing the needs for global consistency with local adaptation.

7. Selection involves identifying the most suitable person from a pool of candidates (internal or external). Selection and assessment are closely

linked to the management of gender, ethnicity and religion, and other forms of diversity.

8. Multinational corporations often guide talent management processes by specifying desired competencies. But there is a lot of confusion in defining competencies, which comes from mixing three different perspectives—performance, strategy, and values.

9. There are different approaches to internal selection: (1) the elite cohort approach; (2) the elite political approach; and (3) the functional approach. Many multinational firms use a mixed approach that can be described as a locally managed functional trial.

10. Unless a company can manage retention, there is no point in investing in talent development. Four possible causes of attrition must be carefully managed: compensation, relationships with the boss, work–life balance, and opportunities for internal development and promotion.

NOTES

1. "The Stealth Oil Giant: Why Schlumberger, Long a Hired Gun in Oil-Field Services, is Becoming a Major Force and Scaring Big Oil," *BusinessWeek*, January 14, 2008.
2. "Star Search: How to Retain, Train, and Hold on to Great People," *BusinessWeek*, October 10, 2005. See also Beyer (2006).
3. Boudreau and Ramstad, 2007.
4. Guthridge, Komm, and Lawson, 2008. More than 10,000 respondents completed the 2006 McKinsey survey mentioned here, with 1,300 for the 2007 survey.
5. Iles, 2007.
6. Huselid, Beatty, and Becker, 2005.
7. The dimensions of variance (used by Huselid, Beatty, and Becker, 2005) and uniqueness, used by Lepak and Snell (2007), and discussed in Chapter 2, are similar, though their perspectives are slightly different. The former focus on positions or roles, while the latter focus on the nature of the knowledge required.
8. These C positions were described as "contractual" in the framework used in Chapter 2 (see page 52); the employment orientation is likely to be market-oriented, and C positions may be outsourced.
9. Ingham, 2007; Stahl et al., 2007. See Lewis and Heckman (2006) for a critical review of the meaning of talent management.
10. US Census Bureau, International Database statistics, 2008. See www.census .gov/ipc/www/idb/ for worldwide demographic statistics by region and country.
11. "Capturing Talent: Asia's Skill Shortage," *The Economist*, August 18, 2007. According to this Economist Intelligence Unit corporate survey, the five biggest concerns of CEOs about China were shortage of qualified staff; bureaucracy, red tape, and inefficient government; staff turnover; legal uncertainty; and wage inflation. Note that three out of these five business concerns focus on HRM. Ready, Hill, and Conger (2008) show that there is a shortage of middle and senior managers in all the BRIC countries (Brazil, Russia, India, and China).
12. Guthridge, Komm, and Lawson, 2008.

13. Manning, Massini, and Lewin, 2008. Access to qualified personnel has been steadily increasing as an important reason for offshoring, from 42 percent of the cases in 2004 to 69 percent in 2007.

14. Manning, Massini, and Lewin, 2008.

15. "Competition from China: Two McKinsey Surveys," *McKinsey Quarterly Online Journal*, 2008 (www.mckinseyquarterly.com).

16. Ready, Hill, and Conger, 2008.

17. See Cappelli (2008) for a historical analysis.

18. Pucik, 1984; 1989.

19. "Briefing: The Trouble with Pensions," *The Economist*, June 14, 2008.

20. The origins of talent pools lie in the dual-career ladders adopted by technology firms, leading to job family analysis.

21. Guthridge, Komm, and Lawson, 2008.

22. Scullion and Starkey, 2000.

23. See the figure on page 52 for an explanation of these terms.

24. Wiechmann, Ryan, and Hemingway, 2003.

25. Farrell, Laboissière, and Rosenfeld, 2006; Manning, Massini, and Lewin, 2008.

26. Ryan, Wiechmann, and Hemingway, 2003.

27. The issue of "cheaper and faster" often creates another tension. While the global platform is likely to reduce HR cost in high-cost countries, it may increase HR expenses in low-cost locations. When subsidiaries are directed to absorb this increase under the "one-firm" banner without seeing much tangible benefit, a pushback is inevitable.

28. See the analysis of four different career models in Sonnenfeld and Peiperl (1988). Cappelli (2008) develops the idea of viewing talent development through a supply chain lens.

29. See Baron and Kreps (1999, Chapter 8) for a review.

30. The 2005 IBM global survey found that the region with the strongest attachment to buying was North America, widely adopting HRM practices to support a highly mobile "free agent" workforce (www.ibm.com/services/us/bcs/html/2005_human_cap_mgt_gen.html). Firms in this region were the least concerned with retention, the least likely to have a succession plan, and the most skeptical about the competitive advantage of people development.

31. Cappelli, 2008, p.121.

32. Cappelli, 2008.

33. Orlitzky, 2007.

34. Stahl et al. (2007) found this to be true in their survey of 37 MNCs from North America, Europe, and Asia. See also Manning, Massini, and Lewin (2008).

35. Granovetter, 1973.

36. Breaugh, 1992; Morehart, 2001; Cheung and Yong, 2006; Lengnick-Hall and Lengnick-Hall, 2003.

37. Among leading firms, Microsoft took this route at one point but has since retreated.

38. Sparrow, 2007; Lawler et al., 2004.

39. Terpstra and Rozell, 1993.

40. "The 10 Most Forward-Thinking Leaders in Workforce Management," *Workforce Management*, March 13, 2006.

41. Stahl et al., 2007.

42. Hieronimus, Schaefer, and Schroder, 2005.

43. Personal discussion with Professor Stewart Black, INSEAD Singapore.

44. Guthridge, Komm, and Lawson, 2008.

45. The literature on selection tends to focus on the former, neglecting the challenge of selecting high potentials from among the existing employees.

46. There is a vast research literature on selection methods and tests according to culture and context. See, for example, *The International Journal of Selection and Assessment*. See Brewster, Sparrow, and Vernon (2007) for a more detailed overview from the perspective of the international corporation.

47. Brewster, Sparrow, and Vernon, 2007.

48. Cook, 1999.

49. Ryan, Wiechmann, and Hemingway, 2003

50. Schmidt and Hunter, 1998.

51. Sparrow, 1999.

52. Wiechmann, Ryan, and Hemingway, 2003.

53. Open job resourcing is discussed at length in Chapter 8.

54. Harris,1999.

55. Benson, Yuasa, and Debroux, 2007.

56. Thomas, 2004.

57. Nishii and Özbilgin, 2007.

58. Thomas, 2004. See Ciceri (2007). Also, there is a danger that "global" can mean applying US criteria worldwide!

59. Perlmutter, 1969. See discussion in Chapter 1.

60. Van Veen and Marsman, 2008.

61. Winterton (2007) notes that a major reason for the adoption of competence frameworks in the 1990s was the need to replace formerly supply-driven training and development systems with demand-driven models, linked to desired capabilities. But the meaning of competence varies according to cultural context, with different meanings in the US, UK, France, and Germany. For a review of some of the debates around the concept, see "Management Competence: The Debate in Management Learning," *Personnel Review* 22:6 (special issue, 1993); Boam and Sparrow (1992). See Sparrow and Hiltrop (1994, Chapter 10) for a discussion of the concept in a comparative management context.

62. Morrison, 2007.

63. Briscoe and Hall, 1999. In Chapter 8, we discuss brand-specific competencies linked to the development of firm-specific leadership skills.

64. Chatman and Cha, 2003.

65. See Fombrun, Tichy, and Devanna (1984).

66. Kaplan and Norton, 2008.

67. Bartlett and McLean, 2003.

68. The quote is from Kets de Vries (1994).

69. Packard, 1995.

70. Kets de Vries, Agrawal, and Florent-Treacy, 2006.

71. See the discussion of Toyota and the section on culture as shared values in Chapter 6.

72. These observations are based on Shell's experience in the study, reported in the box "Linking Competence to Career Progression," and also on BP's experience when validating the OPEN competence framework that was one of the motors of culture change in its transformation in the 1990s. OPEN is an acronym for the four sets of competencies associated with success in enabling change (the performance criterion behind the BP framework)—open thinking, personal impact, empowering, and networking. See also Sparrow and Hiltrop (1994).

73. See the case study and commentaries in Morrison (2007).

74. The elite cohort approach is not confined to Japan. For example, the Danish group Maersk, a *Fortune* 100 multinational in containers and shipping, has long used such an approach to management development, though with some different features from the Japanese.

75. Pucik, 1984.

76. Given accelerating globalization, this has long been described as the Achilles' heel of Japanese management practices (Bartlett and Yoshihara, 1988).

77. At junior high and high school in France, students are progressively screened out into discipline streams. Since the educational reforms in the 1950s, those who are gifted in analytic subjects, such as mathematics, physics, Latin, Greek, and ideally also philosophy (an important subject in French high schools that demonstrates one's ability to structure complex ideas), become the elite. Students following scientific tracks are lower in ranking, while the lowest ranking goes to those studying the humanities. The top graduates then spend two years preparing for a competition to get into the so-called Grandes Ecoles (graduate schools); the choice of college depends strictly on one's national ranking in this competition. At the top colleges, education focuses on preparing people for future leadership responsibility.

78. The indicator of potential is speed of reassignment and promotion from one job to another, a sign that senior people are impressed and want the individual as a collaborator. If other people are moving faster, then the person is well advised to use connections to stay on a fast track in a smaller or less prestigious enterprise. The virtue of the French system is that leaders in the business corporations of the establishment have close relationships with senior government ministers and officials—often they were classmates at a Grande Ecole. Consequently, French enterprises have been successful in sectors where government–business cooperation is important—defense, atomic energy, utilities such as energy and water, and telecommunications.

79. The approach to decision making that evolved in such enterprises reflected their strongly functional cultures. At middle levels, managers would rarely venture out of their zones of expertise when coordination problems arose—these would be passed up the hierarchy. Responsibility for coordination was assumed by management committees at a senior level, guided by the strongly consensual norms that are characteristic of large German enterprises.

80. "Star Search," *BusinessWeek*, October 10, 2005.

81. Chatman, O'Reilly, and Chang, 2005.

82. Cappelli, 2008.

83. IBM, 2005, "The Capability within: The Global Human Capital Study" (www.ibm .com/services/us/bcs/html/2005_human_cap_mgt_gen.html).

84. Cappelli, 2008. We will consider some of the implications of this for training and development in Chapter 8.

85. This often happens in tandem with a corporate reorganization, where the global headquarters are separated from the mother country, since the problem of confounding global management and mother country management is not unique to HR. Thus BP kept its worldwide headquarters in London, transferring the European headquarters (to which the UK reports) to Brussels. TetraPak had earlier moved its headquarters (and whole legal structure) from Sweden, first to Switzerland and ultimately to London. The examples today are legion, and a majority of companies facing

transnational pressures are at least talking about relocating their global headquarters to achieve this separation in focus.

86. See our earlier discussion on localization in Chapter 3.

87. Exxon, an early pioneer in international management development, for many years used an annual procedure whereby each manager across the world was given a list of names of people in the immediate working environment. The manager had to rank these names in order of perceived potential. The rankings were summarized, and the final ranking was the basis for a more intensive qualitative review. However, the procedure was eventually abandoned because the judgments reflected performance rather than potential.

88. The source of the data here is primarily IBM's Global Human Capital Study, 2005 ("The Capability Within: The Global Human Capital Study," www.ibm.com/services/us/bcs/html/2005_human_cap_mgt_gen.html.), based on a survey of 300 corporations across the world.

89. Cascio, 2000. Also Lawler (2008). In Finland, Nokia estimates that the cost of turnover of a well-performing professional is 12–18 months' salary.

90. See, for example, a review by Shaw et al. (1998) of more than 1,500 studies on the topic; and the meta-analysis by Griffeth, Hom, and Gaertner (2000).

91. See, for example, Branham (2005).

92. Branham, 2005.

93. Huselid, 1995; Huselid, Jackson, and Schuler, 1997. See the summary of research on high-performance working systems outlined in Chapter 2.

94. Talent Research in 2005 reported by Cappelli (2008).

95. Evans and Bartolomé, 1979; Bartolomé and Evans, 1980. We found that the stress of work, for example in a mismatch between employee and function, spills over into private life, compromising psychological availability. The misfit would feel a sense of work–life imbalance, whereas another individual working the same hours would perceive no imbalance.

96. "The 10 Most Forward-Thinking Leaders in Workforce Management," *Workforce Management*, March 13, 2006.

97. IBM, 2005, "The Capability within: The Global Human Capital Study" (www.ibm.com/services/us/bcs/html/2005_human_cap_mgt_gen.html). This report is the source of other data in this paragraph.

98. Doh et al., 2008.

99. Stewart, T., "See Jack. See Jack Run," *Fortune*, September 27, 1999, pp. 66–75.

100. Speech given at the Singapore Human Capital Summit, October 2008. Standard Chartered is a financial services group that focuses on emerging markets. It was one firm that learned its lesson from the recession of the early 1990s when it cut budgets for talent—and then paid the price in the boom times that followed because it did not have a reputable employer brand or sufficient leadership talent on board. In times of rapid growth, it is difficult to put talent management processes in place or to create the necessary talent mindset. The time to do that is when the heat is off.

CHAPTER 8

Developing Global Leaders

General Electric's Leadership Meritocracy

One hundred years ago, Charles Coffin succeeded Thomas Edison as CEO of General Electric (GE) and, with his belief in meritocracy through measured performance, laid the foundations for what was to become renowned as GE's "leadership engine." Refined by successive CEOs and brought to fame during Jack Welch's tenure (1981–2001), Coffin's enduring achievement earned him *Fortune*'s award of "the greatest CEO of all time" in 2003.[1]

The idea behind the leadership engine is that a leader is a steward of human capital, whose primary job is to leave a legacy of talent that can carry the company forward. This is what GE's top executives believe—and the corporation has become a model for talent development that is emulated globally. This reinforces, indeed underlies, the strength of GE's brand—and executive search agencies around the world target GE as a talent-rich firm. When we meet former GE managers in Germany, China, or the United States, they invariably speak highly of their GE training. Former GE executives have moved on to head up a wide range of international firms, from ABB in Switzerland to Boeing in the US.

If Coffin laid the foundations with a premonitory emphasis on merit, Welch brought a focus on candor and honesty when he took Session C, GE's core process for talent review, development planning, and succession management, out into the businesses. Every spring, the CEO and senior vice president of HR visit each of GE's operating units and hold a day-long audit, assessing the performance of the management team and the potential of rising talent. A follow-up takes place six months later.

"We have made leadership development the most important element in our work," said Welch. "We focus on some aspect of it every day. It is in our blood. We put people in the right job and let them develop a strategy, in that order. You can't start with strategy and then appoint someone to execute it. So my most important job is to choose and develop business leaders who are bright enough to grasp the elements of their game, creative enough to develop a simple vision, and self-confident enough to liberate and inspire people."[2]

To drive this, Welch used metrics in the shape of a "vitality curve," where individuals were ranked into As (top 20 percent), Bs (middle 70), and Cs (bottom 10 percent) on performance, potential, and fit with company values. Linking this to rewards—and punishments, since the bottom 10 percent would not be there next time around—created shock waves around the world. "I own the managers," Welch said to GE's businesses. "You only rent them from me." His successor, Jeff Immelt, is equally committed to the vitality curve reviews. He responds to critics by saying that you have to be totally consistent: "Unless you are really dedicated to a whole system, it doesn't work."

Jeff Immelt, who was appointed CEO in 2001, the day before 9/11, is himself a product of the GE leadership development process. A Harvard MBA, he chose to ignore warnings that it would take 10 years before he met Welch and got any visibility (he met Welch within a month). Soon considered as one of the top 150 high potentials, he succeeded in a series of tough challenges, including saving a business.

Immelt's strategic focus today is on innovation, technology, and continuous internationalization (in 2008, 53 percent of GE revenues came from outside the United States). Talent management is a means to get this done. "Every initiative I'm thinking about gets translated into recruiting, Crotonville [training], and Session C [development reviews and succession planning]. When you step on the gas here, it really goes."[3] For example, to translate innovation into action, each business was asked to identify five high-level "pillar jobs" that involve the challenge of building customer-facing innovation. Top management reserves the right to fill these positions with the candidates of their choice. In this way, GE makes sure that its best people will be given the challenge of leading a breakthrough opportunity that, if successful, could be grown into a new business.

Nevertheless, globalization of leadership development remains a challenge. Welch often hinted that his successor could be from another country, or would at least have extensive international experience. Yet Immelt never held a position outside the US, and in 2009 only one of the top 18 corporate executives was not an American.[4] Still, GE tries hard to develop a global executive team. Immelt and his colleagues go out of their way to meet with high potentials when they are on trips abroad, and GE continues to win nominations as one of the best three companies in the world for developing leaders.[5] When Immelt nominates his successor, we will know the outcome of this effort.

OVERVIEW

More than almost any other firm in the world, GE has built a reputation for the quality of its leadership development, to the point where former GE executives occupied the CEO positions of 34 *Fortune* 200 companies in 2005.[6] In this chapter, we build on some of the lessons of GE's experience to discuss why leadership development is such a priority in multinational companies. While there are conceptual differences in leadership across cultures, there is general agreement that leadership involves setting the agenda for the future, rather than simply assuming operational responsibility for the current job. Leadership intransitivity—by which we mean that the skills required at one level different from those that led to success at former levels of responsibility—is a major challenge for multinational organizations.

This leads into our discussion of the principles that guide leadership development, and key supporting tools. First, people develop through challenges, which means demanding assignments including split egg roles; the challenge of working outside one's domain of functional and geographic expertise is particular important for leadership development. Second, the focus on leadership challenge requires what we call people risk management to mitigate the risk of failure, through interventions such as training, coaching, and mentoring. We also explore the importance of development factors such as learning agility.

We then move on to describe the traditional top-down management of leadership development, exploring the dilemmas associated with assessing leadership performance and potential, and those related to the development of leadership skills. This traditional pattern of development is increasingly complemented by bottom-up, open job resourcing. Investments in global people management processes and in self-help e-technology can help a firm deploy people more effectively across borders, with the implication that the responsibility for career management shifts from the organization to the individual.

We close the chapter by highlighting how leadership development facilitates coordination in the transnational firm, providing powerful glue to the multinational enterprise.

GLOBAL LEADERSHIP

The task of developing global leaders is a top priority of human resource management in multinational firms.[7] Already more than a decade ago, surveys of *Fortune* 500 enterprises showed that 85 percent were concerned about the insufficient supply of global leaders—people with the ability to manage uncertainty, and with the organizational and business savvy and cross-cultural skills needed to run such a business.[8] More recent surveys continue to highlight this issue. In one 2007 survey of corporations in 40 countries, over 75 percent of top HR executives cited the development of future leaders as a critical challenge.[9]

The impending retirement of experienced executives in mature economies is one factor behind the shortage, but it was above all the explosive growth in emerging markets that fueled the gap. In the BRIC countries of Brazil, Russia, India, and China, the shortage of management talent is most acute at senior levels.[10] And, as we noted in the previous chapter, the new demand comes not just from Western firms but also from local multinationals.

CIMC is a Chinese multinational that has grown to be a world leader in container manufacturing in the last 20 years, with 60,000 staff and more than 100 subsidiaries in China and abroad. When CEO Mai Boliang was asked about the biggest challenges facing the company, he singled out leadership and talent development. "CIMC operates in broader geographies, on a larger scale, and in more diversified fields than it did in the past, and that poses more severe challenges . . . We find that the starting point of Chinese staff members who are developed internally, often from the shop floor, is relatively low and that it takes them longer than the better-educated people to reach the point we think is sufficient for work at an international level."[11] Indeed, rapid growth, combined with a small pool of experienced leaders, means that the lack of leadership capability has been the primary workforce challenge for enterprises in Asia Pacific, as well as Latin America.[12]

A survey of nearly 1,500 HR professionals around the world reports high rates of failure among leaders, averaging 37 percent who leave their positions and/or do not achieve their objectives. The failure rate was highest in Asia, with 42 percent. The main reasons for failure were seen as lack of interpersonal skills (building relationships, giving feedback, communication), leadership (facilitating change, building a team), and strategic skills (ability to set a vision or direction and align people).[13]

How Does Leadership Relate to National Culture?

Leadership is subject to trends, and since it moved to center stage in the 1980s, many different types of leadership have been projected as the norm—for example, transformational, empowering, visionary, and charismatic. Today there is a trend toward thinking of leadership in pluralistic or distributive terms—as a set of different roles, played by different people, rather than the quality of one heroic individual.

Concepts of leadership and management are culturally and contextually bound. For example, in some Asian countries leadership is based on the traditional authority of command, while in the United States, there is a perceived need for leadership that fosters commitment. Concepts of leadership are tied to different concepts of authority, as outlined in the box "Cultural Differences in Authority and Leadership."

Cultural Differences in Authority and Leadership

Any concept of management or leadership implies getting results through other people rather than through one's own efforts as an individual contributor. People become managers when they move into roles where they assume responsibility for other people, and they often struggle with this transition, since they have to figure out how to exercise authority.[14] Our research suggests that there are three different types of authority corresponding to three different managerial orientations, as shown in the following figure.[15]

The traditional form of authority is hierarchical and comes with position—the right to give orders and to demand compliance. In some countries, such as Italy (with its *dirigente)*, Germany (with its *Prokurists*), or Japan (*daihyo torishimariyaku*), this is formalized in civil and commercial law and gives the title-holder the legal right to commit the firm. Hierarchical authority is typically reinforced by the holder's power to reward and punish.

The authority of expertise is built on hierarchical authority and develops as individuals move up functional ladders to higher positions. However, as they move into middle management and leadership, we find that expertise-oriented managers begin to

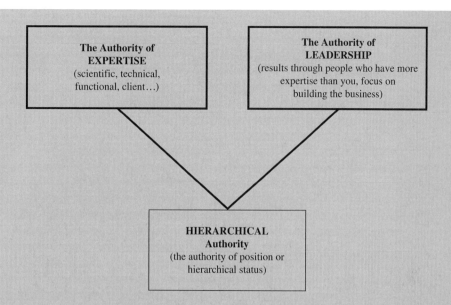

underdelegate, becoming excessively focused on details that capable subordinates could undertake, instead of concentrating on the leadership challenges of building the business. Since their authority is based on their expertise, they find it threatening to delegate important matters—subordinates might develop similar expertise and undermine their roles.

The third orientation builds on the authority of leadership. This is the skill of obtaining long-term results while assuming accountability for operational results. It means learning how to delegate much of the responsibility for operational activities to competent people; so managerial leaders understand the need to have the right people in the right places at the right time.

National cultures differ on these authority orientations, as research by André Laurent demonstrates. Laurent asked managers from different cultures whether or not they agreed with the proposition that "It is important to have at hand precise answers to most of the questions that subordinates may

raise about their work." He found big differences between cultures—as shown in the following figure, which gives information on 17 countries.[16]

In some cultures, such as Sweden, South Africa, and the United States (the first three columns), there is strong disagreement with the proposition. The response in these cultures seems to be "I'm not expected to be the expert so I won't have a precise answer to most questions. Go and talk with so-and-so. And even if I had the answer, I would not necessarily give it because then people will always bother me with questions—I'll end up doing their jobs, and I won't have time for my leadership role of building the business." The strong leadership orientation in these cultures contrasts with the expertise orientation in Germanic cultures, such as Germany and Austria, and also to some extent Belgium and France (where the functional sense of a *métier* remains powerful). Here the reaction is likely to be "I have been promoted because of my expertise and experience, so I should be able to give a precise answer." Countries

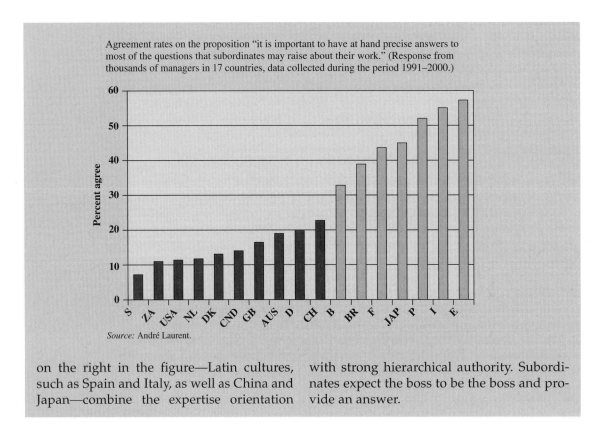

Agreement rates on the proposition "it is important to have at hand precise answers to most of the questions that subordinates may raise about their work." (Response from thousands of managers in 17 countries, data collected during the period 1991–2000.)

Source: André Laurent.

on the right in the figure—Latin cultures, such as Spain and Italy, as well as China and Japan—combine the expertise orientation with strong hierarchical authority. Subordinates expect the boss to be the boss and provide an answer.

GLOBE studies of the cross-cultural dimensions of leadership find that certain qualities are universally associated with leadership effectiveness, notably looking ahead and having vision, as well as fairness and integrity.[17] Other qualities—being an asocial loner, being noncooperative and irritable, and being autocratically dictatorial—are universally regarded as impediments or derailment factors.[18] But the value of some leadership attributes, such as individualism, varies significantly from one culture to another (see Table 8–1). The conclusion is that there is a great deal of communality across cultures in perceived qualities of leadership, but also some differences.

In our view, common elements of leadership are captured well by a Hay-McBer study of leadership competencies in various countries, from the United States to Japan, and from France to Korea, suggesting that leadership is about setting direction and aligning people. The art of leadership is how one goes about setting the agenda and how one brings people on board.[19] There are myriad ways of doing this—leadership personality and style depend on the context. The old belief in a generalized "professional leader," independent of context, is now outmoded; research has shown that leaders have to know their business environments well.[20]

TABLE 8–1. Cultural Views of Leadership Effectiveness According to the GLOBE Studies

The following is a partial list of leadership attributes with the corresponding primary leadership dimension in parentheses.

Universal Facilitators of Leadership Effectiveness
- Being trustworthy, just, and honest (integrity).
- Having foresight and planning ahead (visionary).
- Being positive, dynamic, encouraging, motivating, and building confidence (inspirational).
- Being communicative, informed, a coordinator, and a team integrator (team builder).

Universal Impediments to Leadership Effectiveness
- Being a loner and asocial.
- Being noncooperative and irritable.
- Being dictatorial.

Culturally Contingent Endorsement of Leader Attributes
- Being individualistic.
- Being status conscious.
- Being a risk taker.

Source: M. Javidan, P.W. Dorfman, M.S. de Luque, and R.J. House, "In the Eye of the Beholder: Cross-Cultural Lessons in Leadership from Project GLOBE," *Academy of Management Perspectives* 20, no. 1 (February 2006), pp. 67–90.

Global Leadership Competencies

The belief that global leadership requires different skills than "domestic" leadership is widely shared. When David Whitlam, then CEO of Whirlpool, was steering the company's transition from a domestic US player to a global firm, following the acquisition of Philips' appliance division in the mid-1990s, he commented, "I've often said that there's only one thing that wakes me up in the middle of the night. It's not our financial performance or economic issues in general. It's worrying about whether or not we have the right skills and capabilities to pull the strategy off. . . . It is a simple and inescapable fact that the skills and capabilities required to manage a global company are different from those required for a domestic company."[21]

While there seems to be agreement that leading a global organization requires a particular skill set, there is no accepted definition of the global leadership construct or established body of tested theory. Still, a substantial literature has developed over the last decade addressing the question of what competencies global leaders need to be effective and how these competencies can be developed.[22]

Many global leadership competencies have been singled out, and these can be viewed as a pyramid, as shown in Figure 8–1. At the base are the global knowledge and understanding that come above all through contact with people of different backgrounds while working and living abroad, as well as education and experience. Then certain threshold leadership traits are required—we will discuss openness to challenge and learning agility later in this chapter. The next three layers form the core global competencies, including attitudes and interpersonal and systemic skills.

FIGURE 8–1. The Pyramid Model of Global Leadership

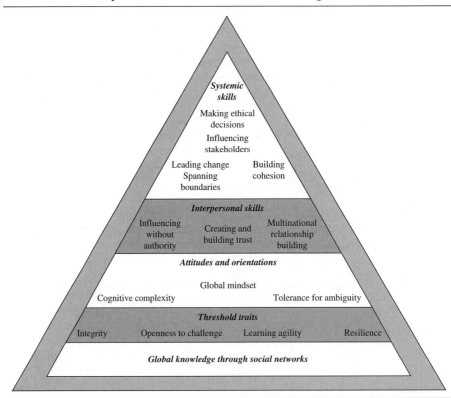

Source: Adapted from A. Bird and J. Osland, "Global Competencies: An Introduction," In *The Blackwell Handbook of Global Management*, eds. H. Lane, M. Maznevski, M. Mendenhall, and J. McNett (Oxford: Blackwell, 2004).

Many of these competencies have been discussed in other chapters, but we see four as particularly important for global leadership. Global leaders need a high tolerance for ambiguity, along with the ability to work with contradiction that is at the heart of global mindset. It is also clear that leaders need strong interpersonal skills in building multinational relationships, including emotional self-control and the ability to handle conflict. Finally, the ability to exercise influence without authority is essential for effective lateral coordination.

Some people would like to believe that such global skills can be learned at home by working with a diverse workforce. However, it has been estimated that the experience of living and working overseas is indispensable for the development of over half of all significant global competencies.[23] While many important business lessons could perhaps be learned at home, most deep attitudinal or cultural lessons about leadership were learned as expatriates. Expatriation, the experience of living and working abroad—not merely traveling—is necessary to develop emotional depth of understanding of global business, going beyond simple intellectual understanding.

Leadership Passages: Intransitivity

One of the limits of the idea of mapping out global leadership competencies is that the leadership skills needed at one level in the transnational organization are different from those needed at the next level. This is called *intransitivity.*

Leadership intransitivity means that the skills and attitudes of the next position up are qualitatively different from those in the previous job. The best player often does not make the best coach. The famous Peter Principle—people are promoted to one level above their competence—captures the idea that the best engineer does not necessarily make the best engineering manager. One major transition in managerial careers is the move from a position requiring the authority of expertise to one re-quiring the authority of leadership. GE developed a more detailed framework of six transitions in the leadership pipeline as people move from individual contributor roles built around their own expertise to enterprise leadership.[24]

For example, as one moves from a supervisory position where one man-ages other people to a position above where one manages managers, new skills must be mastered—assigning responsibilities, measuring progress, and coaching people. And when one moves from the role of managing a function to that of managing a business, with responsibility for the bottom line, the transition involves learning to feel comfortable managing domains where one has little familiarity as well as balancing short- and long-term perspectives.

Why does leadership intransitivity matter for multinational firms? As Bartlett and Ghoshal have argued, the shift toward transnational enterprise is increasing the degree of intransitivity. The old model of organization in the multinational firm, they argue, was a top-down structure that was largely tran-sitive. Management tasks at each level of the hierarchy were similar to but big-ger than the tasks a level below. Top managers were the strategic architects, senior managers were the administrative controllers of these strategic plans, while operating level managers were the frontline implementers of strategies that were conceived "up there" by top managers and their staffs. It was like a Russian doll—inside the big doll is a similar smaller doll, with yet another sim-ilar doll inside that one. Bartlett and Ghoshal argue that this transitive model is particularly dysfunctional for the transnational organization.[25]

Their model is much more intransitive, implying qualitatively different roles at different levels that require new attitudes and skill sets, as shown in Table 8–2. In a fast-moving competitive environment, strategic initiatives come from the operating-level managers, not from top management. These operating managers heading up business units and subsidiaries need to be aggressive entrepreneurs, creating and pursuing new business opportunities, as well as attracting and de-veloping resources, including people. They identify new opportunities, and strategies are born out of their initiatives rather than on the drawing boards of corporate planners far removed from the action of the marketplace.

The senior managers heading up businesses and countries/regions, to whom these entrepreneurs report, need to be integrative coaches with strong skills in lateral coordination, able to cope with the complexity of vertical and

TABLE 8–2. A Model of Management Competencies for Roles in the Transnational Organization

	Operating-Level Managers	Senior-Level Managers	Top-Level Managers
Changing Role	• From operational implementers to aggressive entrepreneurs.	• From administrative controllers to supportive coaches.	• From resource allocators to institutional leaders.
Primary Value Added	• Driving business performance by focusing on productivity, innovation, and growth within frontline units.	• Providing the support and coordination to bring large company advantage to the independent frontline units.	• Creating and embedding a sense of direction, commitment, and challenge to people throughout the organization.
Key Activities and Tasks	• Creating and pursuing new growth opportunities for the business. • Attracting and developing resources and competencies. • Managing continuous performance improvement within the unit.	• Developing individuals and supporting their activities. • Linking dispersed knowledge, skills, and best practices across units. • Managing the tension between short-term performance and long-term ambition.	• Challenging embedded assumptions while establishing a stretching opportunity horizon and performance standards. • Institutionalizing a set of norms and values to support cooperation and trust. • Creating an overarching corporate purpose and ambition.

Source: C.A. Bartlett and S. Ghoshal, "The Myth of the Generic Manager: New Personnel Competencies for New Management Roles," in *Transnational Management: Text, Cases, and Readings in Cross-Border Management*, eds. C.A. Bartlett, S. Ghoshal, and J. Birkinshaw (New York: McGraw-Hill/Irwin, 2004).

horizontal responsibilities simultaneously. They must stretch and at the same time support the local units, linking the dispersed know-how of these units, and building strategy out of entrepreneurial initiatives. Top managers need to be institutional leaders with a longer time horizon, nurturing strategic development opportunities, managing organizational cohesion through global processes and normative integration, and creating an overarching sense of purpose and ambition.

This intransitive structure has important implications for leadership development. Many people who perform well in entrepreneurial leadership roles at the operating level will not be able to adjust to more ambiguous roles as lateral coordinators and integrators in business area or regional roles. Appropriate developmental experiences need to be planned to build the new skills they will need.

Although this model of transnational talent development may not be an appropriate guide for all enterprises, the intransitivity of knowledge-based careers is likely to increase in the future, with accelerating technological, social, and competitive change. Therefore, while the ability to make a particular known transition is important, the ability to cope with transitions in general will become an important overarching competence for leaders—hence the importance of learning agility, to which we return later.[26]

THE PRINCIPLES OF GLOBAL LEADERSHIP DEVELOPMENT

We start our assessment of the principles and tools for steering global leadership development with an overview of the experiences that successful global executives identify as contributing most to their own development. McCall and Hollenbeck interviewed 101 senior executives from 36 countries, covering all major regions of the world, who worked for 15 different multinational corporations, including ABB, Shell, Unilever, and Johnson & Johnson.[27] Table 8–3 shows the key events that these executives saw as contributing most to their development, classified in four categories of experience.

Major line assignments, particular those involving managing change, figure prominently, as do special projects and consulting roles (what we call split egg experiences). Also high on the list are mobility and transition experiences that

TABLE 8–3. The Developmental Experiences of 101 Successful Global Executives

Percentage of People Describing the Event As a Key Developmental Experience	
Foundation assignments	
• Early work experiences	12%
• First managerial responsibility	7%
Major line assignments	
• Business turnarounds	30%
• Building or evolving a business	16%
• Joint ventures, alliances, mergers, or acquisitions	11%
• Business start-ups	10%
Shorter-term experiences	
• Significant other people	32%
• Special projects, consulting roles, staff advisory roles	24%
• Development and educational experiences	23%
• Negotiations	8%
• Stint at headquarters	7%
Perspective-changing experiences	
• Culture shock	27%
• Career shifts	21%
• Confrontations with reality	18%
• Changes in scope or scale	17%
• Mistakes and errors in judgment	10%
• Family and personal challenges	8%
• Crises	7%

Source: M. McCall and G. Hollenbeck, *Developing Global Executives* (Boston: Harvard Business School Press, 2002).

led to a deep change in perspective, such as culture shock and career shifts. Above all, people develop through challenging assignments and experiences.

The problem with challenging assignments, especially transitional assignments like a first managerial job abroad, is that there is a risk of making mistakes. Drawing on the experience of others helps mitigate this, and so another important source of development for these global executives is significant relationships—with bosses, mentors, coaches, and peers—complemented by timely education and training to help them master new skills. We conceptualize these sources of development as people risk management. Companies sometimes express this as the 70–20–10 principle: 70 percent of development happens on the job, 20 percent through feedback, coaching, and relationships with others, while 10 percent occurs through training.

Challenge Is the Starting Point

We often take managers back to basics by asking them, "How do you develop people?" They quickly give a number of valid responses: through assessment of their qualities; coaching; feedback; providing goals; responsibility; encouraging learning from mistakes; training; mentorship; and so forth. Some people emphasize that development happens on the job. But they often miss the most central point—at the heart of development is the simple principle that people learn most by doing things they have not done before.[28] People develop above all through challenge, by venturing outside their comfort zone.

Test this yourself. Just ask people to tell you about their own richest developmental experience. Surprisingly enough, training and education are hardly ever mentioned, at least by people in developed countries. Some may talk about a relationship with a significant mentor or role model. But the vast majority will describe some stretching challenge that they worked through, often succeeding but sometimes failing, often in professional life but sometimes in private life, sometimes planned but equally often by chance.

There are good reasons for regarding challenging jobs that are well aligned with the strategic priorities of the firm as being owned by the corporation rather than the business, as GE does with "pillar jobs"—opportunities to lead customer-facing innovation that are stepping-stone challenges to higher positions. The most important question in talent development is probably "Who gets the important experiences?" Firms should make sure that such potentially challenging jobs are not blocked by people with low potential to grow.

A common denominator we found in our research on leaders who make a difference, in technical or managerial positions, is that they respond more positively than other people to challenge, seeing opportunities where others perceive threats.[29] And top leaders of notable multinational firms have challenge firmly in mind. The consistent aim of Mads Ovilsen, architect and former CEO of the leading pharmaceutical and biotech multinational Novo Nordisk, was "to be the best and a challenging workplace." According to Ovilsen, these are two sides of the same coin.[30] Some large organizations, like Shell and GE, retain small entities or alliances in their portfolio of operations that provide only mediocre returns from a strictly business perspective. The rationale is that these fringe units provide excellent developmental opportunities for high-potential leaders. One of the problems for small companies is that they may not have enough challenging assignments at middle levels of responsibility to provide stretching development opportunities for younger people.

Cross-Boundary Mobility as the Key Tool for Leadership Development

If the concept of leadership varies with culture and context, there is more agreement on how to develop leadership skills. Managed mobility (often called job rotation) is the critical lever—moving people to new challenges outside their expertise so they will learn how to lead and gradually develop the authority of leadership as opposed to the authority of expertise.

People who pursue careers in organizations typically start by developing their talents within a particular function or discipline. A capable person will move up through supervisory and managerial responsibilities, developing knowledge and skills in people management, goal setting, planning, and budgeting. There are various transitions to be mastered during this upward path, notably the transition from being an individual contributor to being a people manager.[31] If the company feels that someone has leadership potential, it should put that person in a position where she or he has to learn to lead. Moving to another function or across borders to another culture removes prior experience and expertise, placing people in challenging positions where they have to learn integrative leadership skills of setting direction and aligning people, while focusing on strategic development. The box "The Route to the Top" tells the story of a leader who became chief executive of one of the world's most well-known corporations.

The Route to the Top

The most important tool for leadership development is not self-assessment techniques, or MBA programs, or any other form of training. It is managed mobility—having to learn how to deliver results through people who have greater expertise than oneself.

The example of a senior executive in a major multinational corporation emphasizes this point. When we interviewed him in the mid-1980s, he was president of an important subsidiary in Asia and had an excellent record of leadership success, and deep skills in the management of human resources. He told us,

What led me to this position? It is quite simple. I was trained as a geologist and spent the first seven years of my career trying to discover oil. One day when I was heading an exploration assignment, they called me to the headquarters and told me that they wanted me to take over the responsibility for a troubled department of 40 maintenance engineers on the other side of the world. Geology is the noble elite, and maintenance engineering is somewhere between here and hell in the value system. I didn't want the job—in fact my first thought was that they were punishing me for some mistake I had made—and I told them that I knew nothing about maintenance engineering. "We're not sending you there to learn about engineering," they said. "We are sending you there to learn about leadership."

With a lot of doubts, I took the job, and I was there for just over four years. And I learned practically everything I know about management and leadership in that job—all I've done since is refine what I picked up there. Mind you, it was the most stressful job I've ever had—it nearly cost me my marriage! Fortunately, they sent me on a management training program during the first three months, and that helped me to understand what was happening and how to adjust—otherwise I might not have survived. Afterward I returned into a more senior position in oil exploration, but I'd completely changed as a result of that experience with the maintenance engineers.

In the late 1990s, this man became CEO of one of the largest multinational corporations in the world.

Functional mobility entails moving outside one's area of expertise. Another type of mobility is geographic. Both types foster situational skills—the ability to handle context. Early studies sponsored by Shell provided suggestive evidence that mobility fosters the "helicopter" ability to see the context and big picture and yet zoom in on the details.[32] Today there is emerging research evidence that in-depth multicultural experience builds genuinely new perspectives and enhances creativity—an effect that is not achieved through international business tourism. Multicultural experience is positively related to creative performance (learning from insights, idea generation, and remote association) as well the ability to exploit unconventional knowledge and creative ideas.[33]

A simple logic guided the management of mobility in many leading multinational organizations in the past. Candidates for top positions should have experience in the home country, an established market abroad, and an emerging market. They should have a turnaround management project providing change management experience, as well as experience in a headquarters staff role. They should have experience in multiple business areas within the firm. However, if potential was identified when someone was in his or her late 20s, and if that person were to move successfully into senior management no later than his or her mid-40s, this implied less than two years in each position. The consequence, as we will discuss later, was that people developed skills in starting things but not in deep execution and change management.

Today, firms are more selective in the way they frame the necessary development experiences. Take InBev, the largest beer company in the world since its acquisition of the US firm Anheuser-Busch in 2008. In its leadership principles, InBev explicitly states that the type of challenges people experience are more significant than the function in which they experience them. InBev sees the best development experiences as coming from the following categories of roles:

- Challenging people roles, where leaders acquire experience in supervising and developing large numbers of people.
- Challenging assignments outside an individual's expertise.

- Challenging commercial roles: Customer-facing experience is regarded as essential for developing brand-related competences.
- Challenging expertise roles: Each individual should have a functional area of expertise to fall back on in case of need.

Leadership and managing change are almost two sides of the same coin, so it is not surprising that most successful leaders look back on experiences of managing change as particularly valuable. These typically involve taking responsibility for managing a business turnaround, start-up, or strategic shift. The most valuable experiences for global executives are those involving responsibility for change in a global, or at least regional, business. Most of the challenges that Immelt was assigned at GE involved leading change in global businesses.

Learning How to Work in Split Egg Ways

As we have shown throughout this book, many tasks in today's multidimensional transnational firm require the capacity to take horizontal leadership initiatives while assuming responsibility for results in one's own job. Examples of horizontal initiatives range from lateral steering groups, formed to standardize an organizational process, to innovation groups, put together to explore how a new technology can be adapted to different markets; from functional teams engaged in post-merger integration to teams used to plan other complex change projects.

Therefore, in addition to having a challenging operational job, an important tool of leadership development is cross-boundary project assignments—what we call working in split egg ways (see the box and split egg diagram on page 210 in Chapter 5). According to a recent survey of 12,000 business leaders around the world, special projects within the job that allow cross-functional exposure, the honing of project management skills, and fostering business acumen were at the top of the list of tools for effective leadership development.[34]

When working in split egg roles, conceptual differences between management and leadership start breaking down. The individual is expected to be both an effective manager (doing things right in the operational role) and an effective leader (doing the right things in the project role). The former involves operational performance management; the latter requires initiative, guided by the long-term strategic priorities of the firm. Let us summarize some of the important skills to be learned from split egg assignments:

- **Exercising leadership without authority.** As we have already pointed out in several previous chapters, much of the work as a leader in the multidimensional firm requires exercising influence laterally on people in other parts of the corporation, without having any formal authority over them. These skills become more and more important as managers move up the organization, and involvement in top-of-the-egg initiatives fosters such skills.
- **People management skills.** How do you free up 20 or 30 percent of your time for project initiatives when you are also responsible for delivering on tough operational targets? Having good people to whom you can delegate becomes a matter of personal survival. Managers in split egg roles learn to

pay rigorous attention to staffing—getting the right people into the right places—as well as negotiating performance objectives and coaching subordinates. In short, managers learn that one of their most important tasks is the management of people.

- **Team skills.** Various team skills are vital in the multidimensional organization—building trust and respect, managing conflict and contention, negotiating clear goals on complex and ambiguous tasks, learning to take time out to build relationships, balancing the internal focus on team cohesion with the external focus on managing stakeholders.[35] Working on split egg type projects fosters the learning of these and related teamwork skills.

- **Distance working and virtual team skills.** Much of the work on cross-boundary projects will by necessity be done virtually. The skills that are developed include knowing how to blend face-to-face and virtual communication effectively, building a rhythm in distributed work, and preventing obstacles from becoming self-fulfilling problems.[36]

- **Dualistic thinking and global mindset.** Working in split egg or matrix ways builds a dualistic sense of responsibility for both short- *and* long-term results; for performance or exploitation *and* innovation or exploration; for local *and* regional or global results. Split egg working is one of the key ways of developing a strategic global mindset in the most talented and high-potential managers in a firm.

One can safely argue that no one in a transnational organization should move into a position of leadership responsibility without proven ability in cross-boundary teamwork—which also means accountability for getting results.

People Risk Management

The flip side to the argument that people develop most through challenge is that the bigger the challenge, the greater the risk of making mistakes. When making intransitive moves, like the first move abroad or outside their area of expertise, people will naturally rely on skills and know-how they acquired in the past. So they will make mistakes and become overstressed, which can sometimes lead to a vicious circle of making more mistakes. This risk could be minimized by checking up and close supervision—but that would take away the challenge. So what is needed is people risk management, the second element of development, referring to support in the shape of different forms of coaching, mentoring, feedback, assessment, and training.

Training as Risk Management

From the firm's perspective, the aim of training is to minimize the risk of costly mistakes. This implies that training has to be *synchronous,* closely linked to the challenge of the new assignment or project. All too often, training takes place when people are available, even though this may be the worst time from the value-added perspective. Training that is not linked to current experience largely goes in one ear and out the other. Shell, GE, IBM, and Standard Chartered try to supply the necessary training just in time.

These "promote-and-then-develop" practices are changing the training scene—courses are shorter and inscriptions happen at shorter notice. They are designed and delivered by flexible outside contractors as modular programs that fit around the new job. At IMD and INSEAD, we track closely the percentage of people on general management programs who are there in the context of a change to a new job, and the figure is typically around 55 percent—even after leaving aside those who are participating because of a change in strategy in their firms.

Synchronous training may also give people the courage to take measured risk. When a person moves into a new job, he or she often has a sense of what should be done, but there are usually obstacles—a boss who will not back the change, peers who are hostile. Timely training or coaching can boost an individual's confidence to tackle these obstacles. Or consider assessment—a positive challenge for one person can be a difficult experience for another. Consequently, assessment centers are widely used to validate judgments about potential and to ensure that individuals have a good sense of their own strengths and weaknesses.

Leadership training is big business. The annual expenditures in the United States alone are estimated at more than US$45 billion.[37] But even well-designed training has its own risk. Many firms fear that trained and educated employees can easily be poached. Indeed, some economists recommend caution in investing in generalized skills training and executive development programs, because these increase an individual's market value, ability to negotiate a higher salary, and likelihood of being attracted by other firms. But the consequence of this logic may be declining attention to development and spiraling turnover across a whole market, with detrimental long-range consequences.[38] By way of contrast, research in the insurance industry shows that investment in general-purpose skills may have a beneficial firm-specific effect by reinforcing employee commitment to the firm.[39] There is a balancing act to be managed here—training increases commitment but also may increase an individual's market value.

Action Learning

Action learning is an explicit attempt to couple work on an important strategic challenge, typically a team project, with tailored support, training, and coaching for the team.[40] There is usually a double aim—to tackle some important cross-boundary challenges and to develop the global leadership skills of high-potential individuals. Action learning differs from split egg team projects in that learning, rather than the quality of task delivery, is the prime aim, though there is a real task challenge. Action learning projects will usually report to sponsors in senior management.

Currently, a majority of company-specific training programs, whether run in-company or outsourced to a business school, involve some degree of action learning. This requires training providers to have sophisticated skills in program design, blending classroom and action learning methods, and be able to support action learning with other pedagogical methods for individual leadership development such as 360° assessment and group coaching.

The exchange and confrontation of different perspectives in action learning are intended to develop an individual's understanding of the dilemmas of transnational management. Indeed, there is evidence that action learning is holistic. It develops second-order learning skills and the ability to frame problems in their context, and it satisfies the principle of requisite variety—the complexity of the learning process should reflect the complexity of the outside environment, in this case the global–local environment of the firm.[41]

Can people change their way of thinking over a short period, say, six months? Research indicates that it is possible.[42] At GE, a typical project-based program oriented to global leadership lasts only about four weeks—a team might be asked, for example, to review the firm's investment strategy in Vietnam. But the stakes and tensions within teams are high—the unspoken perception is that the credibility and future career prospects of team members depend greatly on the quality of the final output. Failure to arrive at a recommendation is not an option. The success of action learning also depends on careful selection of participants and the personal commitment of top management to mentoring and coaching.

Nokia is one of many companies that use action learning to combine leadership and corporate development. For example, an action learning team may be set up to explore the convergence of mobile telephony, consumer electronics, and the Internet, with the active sponsorship of the CEO or a member of top management. This project may lead to resourcing decisions affecting sales personnel, decisions on the pay level needed to attract top sales talent, and training plans. At the same time, the project will be used to develop the competencies of its high-potential members, with coaching and training support provided by the corporate HR development function.

Coaching and Mentoring

One of the most important sources of development is relationships with other people—bosses who play coaching roles, mentors, the positive and negative role models of good and bad bosses, and sometimes external coaches.[43] Coaching typically refers to the activities of an external professional who assists an individual or team in professional and personal development in a nondirective way, sometimes in connection with a formal training program. With the right coach, it is potentially a good way of providing just-in-time risk management.

Coaching originated in the United States, though as an indication of its scope, a recent survey reported that 6 out of 10 British organizations use coaching as part of leadership development with either outsiders or insider coaches.[44] Some companies use retired executives as coaches and mentors for leaders who are on accelerated development programs, but the training, certification, and selection of good coaches remains a problem. The experience of leading business schools is that the competence of good professional coaches comes from a combination of management experience, training in psychological processes, personal insight, and other-centeredness.

The term *coaching* also describes a particular supervisory style that facilitates risk management. Take GE as an example of a company known for its emphasis on supervisory coaching. The performance culture of GE drives this approach, where all managers confront highly challenging stretch goals. It makes sense for the boss to adopt a coaching stance: "How can I help you to achieve those impossible stretch targets? What can I do to support you, and are there any obstacles that I can help remove from your path? Because if you achieve those impossible targets, I the boss will achieve my impossible targets too."

Mentoring is sometimes grouped with coaching, although it is conceptually distinct. In mentoring, an experienced leader or professional is paired with a high-potential person in a longer-term reciprocal relationship. It is practiced widely and informally in professional service firms in the transition to the role of partner. However, it can be difficult to organize formal mentoring relationships, partly because of the personal and emotional nature of such relationships and partly because the mentor's contribution may not be visible. Professional organizations can encourage and reward mentoring by asking middle-level associates to identify mentors. This information is then publicized to highlight the contribution of those who are playing this important developmental role.

Mentoring and "buddying" systems can take myriad shapes and forms.[45] Companies in highly competitive sectors needing close links between technological and commercial skills sometime buddy up a high-potential duo for mutual development reasons (see the box "Two-in-the-box Assignments").

For their mutual benefit, Cisco hooks up Cisco veterans with managers from Jordan, Saudi Arabia, South Africa, and elsewhere who are on a talent acceleration

Two-in-the-Box Assignments

Competitive advantage in many industries increasingly depends on coupling technical capabilities with market-facing customer knowledge. While some coordination can be provided by structural mechanisms such as cross-boundary steering groups, tight coupling in leadership roles can be fostered by what Intel calls "two-in-the-box" assignments. These are development assignments where the responsibility for managing a significant project is attributed jointly to two people, one with a strong technical background who may be on a career ladder to a senior technology management position, and the other with a strong commercial or business background who is on a high-potential managerial ladder.[46] The shared responsibility is intended to encourage, indeed oblige, close interaction and joint learning between two different strategic perspectives.

The idea of two-in-the-box originated at Intel, where the three founders were struck by the complementarity of their strengths. Today, numerous firms in hypercompetitive environments relying on technical and commercial skills use such development assignments, among them Apple, Sun Microsystems, Dell, Cisco, and Lockheed. Goldman Sachs is an investment banking firm that practices two-in-the-box staffing at all levels up to the top, with shared responsibility between a market-oriented banker and a more analytic-oriented finance professional.

program based out of Bangalore.[47] Another multinational we know pairs up key sales managers in local countries with R&D managers at the headquarters, each acting as a host to the other. The relationship provides local sales managers with insights into the technical pipeline, and allows R&D managers to scope and test out opportunities for these technologies in the field. IBM has long used shadowing (watching experienced managers at work and sharing their day-by-day tasks) as a way of grooming talented individuals. A survey of how 25 multinationals go about developing local leadership also shows widespread use of mentoring, with nearly two-thirds assigned a mentor (ideally a more senior local person rather than an expatriate).[48] Having a local mentor contributes significantly to expatriate success and knowledge sharing.[49]

Feedback

Providing timely, constructive, all-around feedback is one of the most useful facets of people risk management. Comprehensive, 360° feedback systems have long been standard practice in many firms, typically linked to development but sometimes gradually incorporated into performance management practices. In the past it was argued that such feedback systems were culturally bound and would not function in, for example, an Asian setting. But our experience and research findings suggest that 360° approaches do work well there, as long as they are undertaken in a highly professional way and with strict adherence to the principles of anonymity.[50]

Nevertheless, cultural issues concerning feedback are important, and we discuss these further in the next chapter in the context of performance appraisal. One of Welch's most important contributions to GE was to normalize direct, candid, rapid feedback, legitimizing the open discussion of development needs. But these norms may translate poorly to cultures where feedback is more indirect.

Learning Agility and Leadership Potential

Individuals vary in their ability to handle big challenges and to learn from their experiences. Some people seek out feedback proactively, consult with others, and in effect organize their own coaching; others do not, preferring to do what has worked well for them before. As the box "How Fast Do You Learn?" outlines, learning agility is an important element of leadership potential, and in some companies it is *the* most important factor.

Self-efficacy and resilience are additional traits associated with leadership potential. Self-efficacy has been shown to be particularly important for leading change.[51]

MANAGING LEADERSHIP DEVELOPMENT TOP-DOWN

How should the transnational corporation manage leadership development, following the principles of assigning challenging tasks while providing the necessary people risk management? The traditional approach is top-down, managed from the center, in contrast to an open-market approach, which we explore in the next section.

How Fast Do You Learn?

People's learning speeds vary.[52] One study of 838 managers in six multinational corporations explored the individual characteristics that distinguished successful or high-potential global leaders from solid performers who lacked leadership potential.[A] Eleven characteristics differentiated the two groups, and factor analysis showed that there were two different underlying dimensions, as shown in the following table. The first dimension, encompassing characteristics like the courage to take risks, captures the willingness to assume challenge. The second dimension, with characteristics like seeking out feedback and learning from mistakes as well as criticism, expresses learning agility.

Eleven Characteristics Distinguishing High-Potential Leaders from Solid Performers in Six International Corporations

Factor 1: (Willingness to take on challenge)
- Seeks opportunities to learn.
- Is committed to make a difference.
- Has the courage to take risks.

Factor 2: (Learning agility)
- Adapts to cultural differences.
- Is insightful; sees things from new angles.
- Seeks and uses feedback.
- Learns from mistakes.
- Is open to criticism.

Other Characteristics
- Acts with integrity.
- Seeks broad business knowledge.
- Brings out the best in people.

Source: Adapted from G. Spreitzer, M.W. McCall, and J. Mahoney, "Early Identification of International Leadership Potential: Dimensions, Measurement, and Validation," *Journal of Applied Psychology* 82, no. 1 (February 1997), pp. 6–29.

The importance of learning agility for leadership development has long been recognized, both by corporations and in more academic studies. For example, a study in the early 1980s of 90 prominent leaders in fields from the arts to business singled out personal learning agility as the quality most required for leadership;[53] and it has been described as a meta-competence for managers.[54] India's leading IT firm, Infosys, recruits professionals at entry level principally for "learnability." When Infosys was smaller, it could be choosy in selecting on the basis of technical skills, but not once it became a leading player recruiting thousands of professionals each year in a software process arena where the rate of change is rapid. Learnability is defined as consistent ability in deriving generic knowledge from specific instances. Potential leaders are tested for how quickly they can learn new concepts and then apply them to unfamiliar situations.[55]

[A]Three companies were European multinationals, one American, and one Australian. The ratings were undertaken by the bosses of the 838 subjects. See Spreitzer, McCall, and Mahoney (1997); McCall (1998).

There are good reasons for a centralized, or at least tightly coordinated, global approach to managing leadership development. This is a critical item on the strategic HRM agenda of multinational firms and tends to be the focus of attention of the senior corporate HR officer, along with the CEO. Much depends on the priority given to this issue by the CEO and other top managers.

Indeed, we know of major corporations, like Honda, who did not have a corporate HR function until a relatively late stage in their history, when it was created to manage global leadership development. The company's founder, Soichiro Honda, believed that people management and marketing were so important that he did not wish to compromise line management's responsibility by functionalizing them. But Honda found out that it had to make an exception for leadership development. Without a dedicated organization, functions and countries took local perspectives with too short a time horizon; leadership development took place within silos and without the necessary mobility. Similarly, as the French retail giant Carrefour expanded into Latin America and Asia, it was obliged to create a corporate HR function to provide a global focus on leadership development.

The arguments for building rather than buying talent, as discussed in Chapter 7, are most clear at middle and senior management levels. In 2007, one consulting firm calculated that it cost a company in the United States 50 times as much to recruit a middle manager earning $100,000 from the outside as the average annual cost of training and developing such a person.[56] And a worldwide IBM study concluded that firms make a clear return on their investment on internal management development for middle managers, showing significantly higher profits per full-time employee than competitors who did not develop internally (which was not the case for investments in lower-level professionals).[57]

Identifying and Assessing Potential

While the measures vary from one firm to another, the most common way of defining potential is in terms of suitability for promotion over a period of time, typically five years. Schlumberger identifies roughly 10 percent of its engineers as high potential in this way, although others in the same industry focus on ultimate potential, in other words estimating the level that people are expected to reach at the height of their careers. In firms like Microsoft, potential is equated with high current performance.

Once the decision on how to define talent is made, how should the process work? We will take the multinational model of internal selection[58] as the starting point for our discussion. Local companies recruit and develop professionals for functional jobs, and individuals from within these ranks are subsequently identified as high potential using assessment centers, local nominations, exceptional salary reviews, and other mechanisms. One recent survey found that 60 percent of large corporations used this approach, asking local companies to identify talent that can be moved into corporate development programs.[59]

If a true portfolio approach is to be employed, the development and career of these high-potential individuals should be managed by the corporation, not by the business or country. GE and other firms are explicit about this—those individuals become what many multinationals call, formally or informally, corporate property.

The idea of corporate property makes sense only if the talent is subject to rigorous corporate attention. Most organizations will review their high-potential individuals as part of an annual or periodic organizational review, known at GE as Session C,[60] outlined in Table 8–4. Session C is not an event; it is a continuous process spread throughout the year. This starts with performance reviews within the businesses, leading to talent reviews that are first bottom-up in the businesses and then top-down with the CEO, continuing with a corporate summary of the emerging issues and their implications, and concluding with formal assessment of follow-up actions at corporate, business, and individual levels.

At the heart of such a review is typically an assessment on two or more dimensions, often in the shape of what is known as nine-box assessment.[61] Figure 8–2 shows the framework used by the pharmaceutical giant Novartis.

Evaluations of performance are collected, representing one dimension of the framework. The performance of individuals is sorted into three (sometimes four or five) classifications, according to a rough bell curve. At GE, this is the well-known "vitality curve" that differentiates between the top 20 percent, the highly valued 70 percent in the middle, and the bottom 10 percent. A key challenge in multinational firms is ensuring that the evaluation of performance is undertaken on a globally consistent basis.[62]

The definition of the second dimension (which we summarize as potential) varies from firm to firm. At Novartis, potential is gauged by whether someone demonstrates the key values and behaviors that the company looks for in its future leaders. At GE, potential is a combination of suitability for promotion and values, as expressed by the way someone behaves (for example, paying attention to the development of other leaders and maintaining high ethical standards).

This review process should not only focus on the individuals in the top right-hand box of Figure 8–2, who are strong on both dimensions. Attention to

TABLE 8–4. The Session C Process at GE

December	January	April–May	May	August
Within Businesses	**Within Businesses**	**CEO Discussion**	**Session C Wrap-Up**	**Midyear Reviews**
Prepare for EMS[A]	*Bottom-up*	*One day at business unit*	*Corporate overview*	*Review actions*
• Assess current state. • Ensure all actions completed.	• Organizational assessment. • Individual performance. • Career planning.	• Smaller group and then . . . • Larger group discussion.	• Decisions. • Issues. • Replacement planning.	• Assess changes since January. • Assess gaps.

[A]EMS is GE's performance measurement framework.

FIGURE 8–2. "Nine-Box" Assessment of Performance and Potential: An Example from Novartis

Performance
  objectives

	Partially met expectations	Fully met expectations	Exceeded expectations
Exceeded expectations	Superior results/ unsatisfactory behavior	Superior results/ good behavior	Exceptional performer and recognized as role model
Fully met expectations	Good results/ unsatisfactory behavior	Strong performer (fully acceptable level of performance)	Superior behavior/ good results
Partially met expectations	Unsatisfactory performer	Good behavior/ unsatisfactory results	Superior behavior/ unsatisfactory results

               Partially met   Fully met   Exceeded   **Values/**
               expectations   expectations   expectations   **behaviors**

Source: G. Stahl.

people in all the four corner boxes adds potential value. Retention and development plans need to be developed for high performers who are not currently seen as having leadership potential, for they may be critical to the current performance of the firm. Deep questions need to be asked about those who are high potential but underperforming. Are they misfits? Are they being constrained by difficult bosses? And most companies want to identify the underperforming people with low potential—to turn them around or to turn them out.

Dilemmas in Identifying and Assessing Potential

There are several difficult issues in the process of identifying and assessing leadership talent, and deciding who should get the most challenging assignments. We focus on those that are particularly important in the multinational environment.

When to Identify Potential

A lot of career politics are associated with getting visibility early in the eyes of top management so that one will be given the challenging jobs that count. However, there are real dilemmas associated with the age when potential should be identified—early or late?

Japanese companies have historically identified potential at the time of graduate recruitment, leading to an extended developmental trial period. This makes sense in a culture where individuals pursue lifelong careers in the same firm. But in Anglo-Saxon countries other firms are likely to poach high potentials away, especially if the enterprise has a reputation for selection and development. This happened to P&G in the 1980s and early 1990s, when it developed a reputation as a top-notch incubator, feeding the management ranks of competitors in the fast-moving consumer products industry. Japanese firms can maintain this approach because it is still virtually impossible for Western firms to lure away top Japanese leadership talent.

Alternatively, one could argue for late identification of talent, by which time experience and track record enable one to make good judgments of potential. But this strategy is similarly flawed, since there is insufficient time for high-payoff developmental actions. This was shown by a natural experiment that occurred at Exxon some years ago. Many Exxon executives started their careers at one of the two refinery breeding grounds in the United States. However, senior management consistently came from one of them, Baton Rouge. Why? Ultimately they found only one explanatory difference—at Baton Rouge, leadership potential was identified at age 27–28, whereas at the other refinery the target age was in the early 30s. The implications were clear. Imagine two candidates for a senior leadership job, both in their early 40s. One of them has 14 years of challenging international and multifunctional experience, while the other has only 8. All else being equal, who will be chosen?

If talented international staff are identified much later than those in the home country, their leadership prospects will be compromised. Indeed, this may be another factor explaining why GE has been less successful in developing high-potential leaders from its Asian operations. Talented individuals in the United States were spotted much earlier than their counterparts in Asia—Immelt came to the attention of Welch when he was 27—but until recently GE had no regional corporate offices outside the US that could take on the task of identifying and developing regional talent.

Transparency about Judgments of Potential

Once a judgment is made about who has potential, there is often a dilemma concerning the degree of transparency there should be about the decision. There are two fears about openness: First, good performers who were not identified as having high potential are likely to lose motivation and leave; and second, false expectations about advancement might be raised on the part of those identified as having potential.

The former is unavoidable, endemic to any "quota" process, and one can argue that keeping people in the dark about their career progress in the hope that they will stay in the firm would be shortsighted, at least—if not plainly unethical. As for the second fear, if one accepts that people develop through challenge, then one consequence of being identified as high potential is stretch. It is both difficult and ill advised to hide this, though most companies choose to announce it with a certain amount of discretion.[63]

With this concern in mind, some companies respond by encouraging self-nomination instead of top-down identification. Commonwealth Edison in the US allows people to nominate themselves as high potentials, submitting a list of peers and superiors who will be asked to provide references, similar to the process of tenure review in the academic world. Tatweer, a Dubai group with interests ranging from health care to energy and tourism, goes even further. Employees must apply for a high-potential program, going through a challenging process of assessment and reviews with outside consultants, and they are then expected to continue to perform at a high level in their current jobs while they participate in the program. Those who are not truly motivated and capable will simply shy away.[64]

The risk associated with transparency can be minimized by ensuring that judgments of potential are reviewed regularly. Those who are not yet identified as high potential have an incentive to work themselves into the designated talent pool; while those that are labeled as high potential realize that they need to continue to prove themselves to progress in their career. The quality of these periodic reviews is one of the most important aspects of talent management.

Who Should Be Accountable?

A major challenge for multinational corporations, especially those coming from a heritage of local responsiveness, is how to get the local company to pay attention to talent development at early career stages. In a tightly run, cost-conscious local operation, there may not be much room for high-potential people with advanced degrees and high expectations but no hands-on experience. Furthermore, operationally oriented local HR managers may be ill equipped to cope with the challenges of recruiting, developing, and retaining such individuals. And in some cultures, senior management may be reluctant to recruit young people who want to go beyond the job by exercising initiative.

An additional obstacle for talent identification in an international firm is the natural tendency of subsidiaries to hide their best people—the more one praises an indispensable individual, the more likely it is that the person will be moved elsewhere under the umbrella of corporate leadership development. Indeed, a survey of HR executives from multinational firms singled out this problem as one of the major challenges in talent management.[65] Consequently, CEOs like P&G's A. G. Laffley grow firm, indeed passionate, about the importance of releasing talent, since talent development is a corporate value on a par with financial performance.[66] Hiding talent is an act of corporate disloyalty.

In the past one might have expected loyal expatriates, representing the corporate interest, to combat the silo tendency; but in many markets the senior ranks are increasingly local. Therefore nurturing local talent often becomes a key responsibility of regional management or of an experienced local HR manager who works with subsidiaries across the region. Schlumberger navigates this issue by reengineering the whole process. In countries where local management is operationally focused and strongly technical in orientation, the corporate or regional HR function recruits high-potential individuals, who are then placed in entry-level functional jobs in a third country with a reputation as a talent incubator. When these recruits have successfully mastered the core operational roles, they are repatriated to their home countries for the next step as engineering or service managers—ready to move again as they progress through the organization.

Ensuring Quality Dialogue in Global Talent Reviews

In many firms, talent reviews are part of the business planning process. A typical format is a one-day review of each business unit, with the morning devoted to strategy and business plans, and the afternoon focusing on talent, HR policy, and communications. This is the format of the core of GE's Session C process.

The talent reviews, guided by a nine-box or similar framework, lead to some form of differentiation of individuals on performance, potential, and/or behavioral fit with values. However, the purpose of differentiation is not just to place people's names in boxes, but to ensure that an open dialogue takes place about performance, assessment, and development implications. The important thing is the quality of the information and the dialogue about the individuals under review. Welch was particularly proud of bringing candid, down-to-earth, and well-prepared dialogue into the Session C review. In contrast, we have seen multinational firms where similar reviews are nothing more than formal rituals performed by a quasi-representative committee of stakeholders defending their favorite candidates.

One problem is that these reviews are often biased against managers who are far away from the home country. An individual seen by locals as a strong contributor with high potential may be given only token consideration by the people with power at head office. Consciously or unconsciously, they do not trust local input and ratings and give at best a formal stamp of approval to the person. Moreover, there is an inevitable halo effect—people who look like the evaluators are judged as having higher potential.[67] Local units learn that their views are not taken into account, so they start taking the process lightly or even playing games—the makings of a self-fulfilling prophecy. The consequence will often be that the best local employees will look for opportunities outside the firm—at which point the head office says, "Why bother to invest in them, as they will leave in any case?" To minimize such risks, companies may follow the example of GE and make sure that their senior executives get to know local talent.

Without candid discussion, the inevitable bias in favor of home country nationals who are well networked into the center will prevail. In one major European multinational, which prides itself on its quality of leadership development, a challenging stepping-stone position opened up in the central office, with specifications of high potential and international experience. A home country national with a top educational background and two years of staff experience in another European country was given the job over a South African woman with a degree from a local university who had operational responsibility for 45 countries and an outstanding performance record—nominally because, since she had always worked out of Cape Town, she did not have the international experience required by the job description.

That someone who may be less qualified gets such an opening is not the most important consequence of such decisions—people's qualifications can often be debated. The important consequence is the loss of credibility of the review and appointment-making process in the eyes of managers (and future leaders) around the world. The process is seen as biased and unfairly loaded, and it gradually becomes a time-consuming formality that adds little real value, undermining the credibility of the HR function in a wider sense. Candid dialogue among line executives and professional preparation by both line and HR is at the heart of the talent mindset.[68]

The Danger of Excessive Focus on Identification

It is worth reemphasizing that the point of formally identifying and reviewing people with leadership potential is to ensure what we term "unnatural acts"— value-added actions that would not happen unless attention has been paid to fair assessment of potential. An example of an unnatural act would be ensuring that local nationals who may not have an impressive education but who demonstrate high potential come to the attention of senior management and are provided with special coaching to accompany a challenging project that would not otherwise have been assigned to them. If individuals who have been identified as high potentials are not given the most challenging jobs, any work on identification and review will have been a waste of resources.

In this respect, we find that there is an excessive focus on identification and assessment of potential, at the expense of development action, in many firms. This is partly because the identification side of leadership development demands work that can be undertaken by the HR function, whereas little on the development side can be undertaken without the commitment of the business— apart from sending someone to a training program.

This has several implications. First, senior line managers in the business or functional units must take ownership of leadership identification and reviews. The HR function has to undertake important groundwork, but it is the attention of line managers and those at the top of the organization that counts.[69] P&G's Laffley, cited above, comments, "I spend a third to half of my time on leadership development. . . . Nothing I do will have a more enduring impact on P&G's long-term success than helping to develop other leaders."[70]

Second, companies should be selective, even conservative, in their judgments about who is high potential. Undertaking rigorous Session C–type reviews—with action planning and follow-up—is time-consuming and not worth doing unless it is done well. If the focus is too broad, it will dilute the attention given to it by line managers. One survey of 25 multinationals concluded that no more than 5 percent of the local workforce should be considered high potential, and that the more successful organizations tended to have small talent pools that they reviewed regularly.[71]

Challenges in Developing Potential

As we discussed in the previous section, development means challenging people and taking risks on them. Here we discuss some of the related issues, pitfalls, and dilemmas that multinationals often face when developing identified potential. A general problem underlying these issues is the difficulty of optimizing both short-term performance and long-term development of leaders—in graphic terms, the bottom and top of the split egg we discussed earlier.

Balancing Demand-Driven and Learning-Driven Assignments

When planning appointments, there are often real trade-offs between immediate performance, which argues for appointing a manager with the skills and experience required, and learning and development, which will mean nominating a high-potential individual who will learn from the experience. This is similar to the distinction between demand- and learning-driven expatriation that we made in Chapter 4. One of the roles of the HR function should be to voice these trade-offs so they can be managed objectively.

When a key position opens up in a unit, there will typically be a local functional candidate with many years of experience, a loyal and low-risk person who is sure to perform solidly. And there may be another candidate from the regional talent pool, an outsider to local operations, who has less experience but who might bring new ideas and extraordinary results as well as developing into a higher-level executive. Who should get the position? There are no standard answers, though the preference of local management is usually clear: Unless there is a countervailing force in the shape of a strong regional HR manager who has the backing of senior line management, the conclusion is foregone. And paradoxically the longer-term outcome is that local managers will continue to complain that senior leadership remains dominated by expatriates. Multinational leadership development has been rightly described as guerilla warfare.[72]

An example of conservatively demand-driven staffing is found in the way some international pharmaceutical firms choose project managers. These are critical roles, coordinating the development of a new drug through its different phases and interfacing between research, clinical, and commercial functions, as well as with external drug approval authorities. Faced with the choice between Fred with 10 years of experience and high-potential Heinrich with none, the firm chooses Fred because of the stakes involved. Next time around, an even more experienced Fred is chosen over Maria . . . and so on. Immediate success is chosen instead of taking a risk and investing in the development of new people—and the problem shows up later, when Fred leaves for a competitor or retires.

Companies often find it particularly difficult to find positions abroad for learning-driven development. Headquarters may have the clout and legitimacy to find such assignments for people from the home country—after all, there is typically a tradition of expatriation of home country high potentials. But although everyone may accept that China is a key future market, it is another matter to find developmental jobs for Chinese high potentials in the home country or nearby. ABB deals with this through norms of swapping—if you want to send someone abroad, you have to be prepared to take in someone from outside. 3M has a general principle that the country managing director should not be a local person, thereby ensuring opportunities for geographic mobility at senior levels. Unilever used to have a practice of ensuring that there should be one or more expatriates on all local management teams—and not necessarily from the mother countries of the United Kingdom and Holland.

Focusing on A Positions as well as A Players

A great deal of sustainable competitive advantage comes from strong organizational capabilities that are hard for others to imitate. This means that companies should make sure that future leaders acquire experience in domains regarded as key capabilities. Development discussions should not focus excessively on individuals—the so-called A players—without considering the A positions, jobs that are critical to the competitive advantage of the firm as well as for the development of skills future leaders will need.[73]

Since one of P&G's core capabilities focuses on trusted brands, virtually all high-potential managers will move through a P&L position on a brand team, the plum jobs in that organization. In GE, these A-jobs focus on business development as well as M&A management, and the company earmarks positions that are linked to strategic capabilities as corporate property.

In tightly networked multinationals such as Nestle, Shell, and Unilever, the key jobs are a series of different types of positions across which high-potential individuals will be moved to develop the generalist perspective and skills that are seen as necessary for senior leadership positions. In effect, these career paths accentuate the development of firm-specific skills: mastering networks, understanding the complex value chain, as well as confronting specific business and organizational challenges.[74] But the flip side of this firm specificity is that these individuals have fewer options at the same level of responsibility outside. Functional expertise travels well from firm to firm, but firm-specific generalist experience may have limited market value.

The implication is that firms should be particularly thorough about the selection of people for such generalist paths. We have seen individuals in their mid-40s scrambling to rebuild a marketable functional profile so they can move elsewhere when it became clear that their future in the company was limited.

The Dangers of Excessive Mobility

Mobility is an integral part of leadership development, and lack of mobility is a disqualifier in many firms. But there is significant danger of taking learning and mobility to extremes. We disagree with the authors of the McKinsey talent war studies who suggest that ". . . after two or three years the learning curve in any position tends to flatten out, and capable people start to chafe. . . . One company's line executive held 18 positions in 24 years, and though not everyone can or should move so quickly, companies tend to leave executives in jobs much too long."[75] Too much mobility will compromise the ability to manage change—there is little that can be executed deeply in 18–24 months, especially at middle and senior management. After all, it is not strategy and plans that count but the quality of their execution. This is the reason why we talk of mobility, avoiding the commonly used term "job rotation."

In some companies, especially in emerging markets where there are many career opportunities, rapidity of movement becomes a quasi-indicator of potential. This creates a zigzag management pattern where newly appointed leaders of local units seek out initiatives that respond to the strategic intentions of senior management. But just when the initiatives are taking hold, the individual is promoted. If the successor is cut from the same cloth, he or she will take the unit off on a different initiative, since there are few rewards for implementing changes started by someone else. The consequence is that local organizations go through periodic campaigns—cost cutting, customer orientation, time-to-market, and so forth—but never develop deep capabilities in any of these domains.

It is worth noting that the average time in a job during the career span of CEOs of *Fortune* 100 companies is four years (slightly less than 20 years ago, when it was 4.3 years).[76] This means that they may have been in some jobs for 18 months but in others, where they learned and demonstrated deep skills in execution, for six years or more.

We find that companies often have a simplistic attitude toward excessive mobility. "Yes, we agree that we are rotating our high potentials too fast, and that execution and deep change management are suffering as a consequence. So let's try to get them to stay in a job for three years rather than two." That does not capture the key learning point—that it is important to link tenure to responsibility and accountability. If someone is not responsible for results, a six-month stint may be well justified. But if that person is responsible, the time horizon for implementing proposed changes should be explicitly linked to tenure in the job. If a strategic change in a particular business will take five years to implement in real depth, the question should be "Are you prepared to stay in this job for five years or more? Otherwise don't bring us plans that you are going to start but not carry through."

Developing Emotional Competence

Many firms, particularly in emerging markets and circumstances of rapid growth, are understandably concerned with accelerating the development of leadership competencies. This means frequent mobility, along with careful and creative people risk management. However, there is a danger that such individuals will reach senior positions without having known tough challenges, often called "hardship experiences," which are connected with the emotional side of leadership development.

The role of emotional competence in leadership has been highlighted and popularized in recent decades.[77] Emotional competence—essentially learning to handle one's own feelings—is learned through hardship experiences, business failures and mistakes, or the experience of bouncing back from emotional traumas—in summary by building emotional resilience to deal with situations that fall outside one's comfort zone. While the risks of challenge must be managed, the real risk of failure must remain—another delicate duality.

Kets de Vries has studied what happens when individuals with poor emotional competence ultimately move into the leadership post for which they have been groomed.[78] For the first time, they have to live with the consequences of the initiatives that they start—they are now accountable for whatever happens during implementation. They sometimes experience doubt and loss of confidence and self-efficacy for the first time in their lives. Their prior experience has never equipped them to cope with failure. They react differently. Some fall apart in humiliating ways. The dark side of others' personalities comes to the fore—the decisive leader who becomes a tyrannical autocrat, the cautious individual who becomes obsessive about detail. Or an arrogance untempered by the humility that personal hardship teaches leads them into open display of superiority and self-importance and a complete lack of trust in others.

From Succession Plans to Talent Pools

The process of reviews and planning development assignments is known as succession planning in some companies, leading ultimately to a fixed plan to fill positions as they become vacant. Succession planning is widely practiced in Europe, but less so in the United States except at the most senior levels; while in Asia succession planning has mostly been used at operational levels because of the severe talent shortages that companies experienced during the boom years.[79]

However, succession planning has come under attack for being excessively mechanical. In reality, the decision about who gets the job is all too often made through informal discussion without consulting the succession plan, which is sometimes viewed by line managers as little more than a ritual of the HR function.[80] Indeed, in flat organizational hierarchies, the decision to indicate person X as a likely successor for position Y may be somewhat arbitrary. Also, the requirements for a role may change after the original plan was agreed, or a new CEO may have different criteria for leadership appointments.[81] When only 60 percent of the moves occur as planned, this may spill over into skepticism about the whole process of leadership development. In fact, in the US a majority of companies have abandoned all pretensions at succession planning.[82]

Succession planning may still be viable in slower-moving, predictable work environments, but in many firms it is complemented by talent pool management.[83] The local function or business unit is expected to engage in succession or replacement planning in its own interest, while the region or corporate level maintains a talent pool of high-potential managers. When a position falls empty because of departure, growth, or vacancy in the internal labor market, the local unit will propose its own candidate, while corporate will consult the talent pool (sometimes called an acceleration pool) to see if there is a suitable individual who would benefit from the role and contribute to it. This leads to a review of who is the most appropriate candidate.

It is then a short conceptual step to consider opening up the talent pool to all candidates, not just those on the regional or corporate list, taking advantage of possibilities of Web-based technologies to create an internal job market.

MANAGING DEVELOPMENT BOTTOM-UP: OPEN JOB MARKETS

Until recently, leadership development has largely been managed top-down, which means that the organization takes the prime responsibility for managing the careers of its strategic talent.[84] For nonstrategic staff, such as (in most firms) the sales force, clerical personnel, and technicians, external recruitment has come to prevail, increasingly complemented by intranet-based open job re-sourcing (internal labor markets). What is happening now in some multina-tional firms is that bottom-up staffing through open job markets is spreading up the hierarchy to professionals and management.

This shift is driven by the prospect of being able to deploy talented people and ideas across borders far more effectively, rapidly, and cheaply than with conventional top-down methods. But there are major obstacles in the pathway to realizing these benefits. One significant adjustment is a deep shift from a tradi-tional focus on managing development to an emerging approach based on help-ing people to help themselves—albeit with the best interests of the enterprise in mind. Another is the challenge to conventional leadership views of control.

One strength of internal labor markets is that the firm has better informa-tion about its internal candidates than those from outside. Job posting for blue-collar and lower-level professional positions is a long-standing practice, going back to the early post-WWII years. There were often restrictions on internal mar-kets—the direct supervisor had to sign off on the move of an employee, and one could not apply for a posted job unless one had spent a certain number of years in the position, to prevent job hopping by poor performers. However, executive, management, and professional jobs were always managed top-down.

In the 1980s, a small number of firms started to broaden internal job posting to professional and middle managerial positions, using bulletin boards and company newsletters. With the development of intranets, electronic job posting expanded in the mid-1990s. The talent war for professionals in the years before the 2001 crisis spurred the spread of internal job markets, especially in the electronics and software industries, including established companies like IBM. As discussed in the previous chapter, these companies decided to extend their internal job mar-kets to all professional and many managerial employees, reasoning that if talented people were looking for jobs on the Internet, it was better to offer them alternative jobs internally. By 2005, most major firms in the United States had introduced such electronic job markets, and only half required internal candidates to have the per-mission of their boss before applying for another internal position.[85]

Some companies began to experiment with e-based systems for talent man-agement while simultaneously globalizing their HR processes. This is a massive and very challenging investment, involving the standardization of performance management, potential assessment, recruitment, selection, and other HR practices, as discussed in Chapter 14. But once standardized talent management processes were in place across the globe, these companies were able to tap quickly into the best available resources for a position across geographic boundaries rather than be-ing constrained by the local talent market—something that had not previously been possible at such low cost. At global hospitality company Starwood Hotels, for example, objective setting, performance appraisal, annual 360° feedback linked to potential assessment, and potential reviews are all undertaken on intranet systems, following criteria that are common across the world and complemented by face-to-face discussion. All positions up to the level of regional manager are posted on the intranet, leading to open applications. As a consequence, there is considerable mobility of staff—a hotel in Dubai or Milan might have a Russian room manager, an Indian banquets manager, and an Italian running the kitchen.

Global companies such as Schlumberger, with skilled engineers and technicians spread around the world, realized that it was cumbersome and expensive to try to organize talent search processes in a traditional top-down way. It was better to develop market-based online processes to do the job. Therefore, open job resourcing continues to spread upward into the managerial ranks of the multinational firm, though rarely if ever to the most senior levels. All positions at Hewlett-Packard, except for the top 100, are available on the internal open market system, as they are at Microsoft. At Shell, positions up to the top 250 have been posted internally since 2002.

Making Self-Management Work

Although there is a substantial body of research by labor economists on internal labor markets with respect to employees with generic skills,[86] there has been little research so far on the spread of open job resourcing systems as applied to managerial employees with skills that are more company-specific. Adoption of open resourcing varies from one country to another, with growing acceptance in most developed countries outside Japan, where large companies with lifetime employment practices still favor careful top-down career management. But there are big differences in patterns from one country to another, even within Europe. Careers in organizations tend to be stable in Sweden, Italy, and Germany, with strong top-down influence, whereas there is more mobility in former socialist countries like Hungary and the Czech Republic, as well as in the United Kingdom and Denmark (also in the United States).[87] In the family-oriented firms of Mexico and Latin America, superiors are reluctant to give up control over their subordinates.

The expansion of internal job markets tends to flow with growth and ebb with recession. In times of growth, with tight talent markets, there is more acceptance of the need for internal markets, while the top-down approach prevails in times of slow growth or recession. But there is little doubt that as Generation Z, raised in the Facebook self-help era of social networking, moves into higher echelons, and as e-based processes spread progressively, so open job markets will become more widely applicable to managers and professionals.

One of the deeper implications, which firms are only now beginning to confront, is that the responsibility for career development is shifting from the company to the individual, as outlined in the box "You Are Responsible for Your Own Career!" This mantra is now widely accepted, although its implications have not yet been worked through. Some sociologists and labor economists believe that it may lead to new types of inequality in the workplace—fragmented, patchwork careers for the majority and outstanding prospects for the talented minority.[88]

To help themselves, the younger generations have turned to social networking, facilitated by Internet applications such as MySpace and Facebook. A growing

You Are Responsible for Your Own Career!

In the mid-1990s, some scholars suggested that the pace of change was such that the "career" could best be seen as a social invention that thrived and died with the 20th century,[89] even though the systematic study of careers in organizations had started only 20 years before. Leaving Japan aside, the talent war led to big increases in mobility between firms.

What is clear is that the onus for career management has shifted progressively from the organization to the individual. If the boundaries within and between organizations are becoming more fluid, the same is true of careers—they are also becoming boundaryless.[90] Careers still exist, in the sense of a sequence of steps, but they are not limited to a single organization, function, or conventional path. Boundaryless careers are individualized—some individuals have distinctive careers based on unique sets of skills that are highly valued by the market, but others follow unstable and fragmented career paths.

DeFillippi and Arthur suggest that these boundaryless careers require three sets of personal competencies—knowing how, knowing who, and knowing why.[91] *Knowing how* is the set of skills people build up, often by moving from one firm to another. *Knowing who* is the network of relationships that allows people to transition into new opportunities. Individuals might have invaluable skills, but if they do not have the appropriate contacts, then it is difficult to find new work environments that value these skills. But *knowing why* is perhaps the most interesting implication of the boundaryless career. Whereas career structures in the past provided people with a clear sense of social identity ("I am a manager with IBM," "I am an accountant," "I am a general manager"), the personal challenge for many people today is forging a sense of professional identity out of their portfolio of experiences and skills.[92] How do you respond when your young daughter asks you, "Mommy, what do you do when you are away from home?"

The responsibility of individuals for their careers means that new processes facilitating self-management must be put in place. The search side of self-management is well developed in most countries, in the shape of Internet recruitment, executive search, and indeed expanding internal job markets. However, it lags when it comes to helping people to help themselves.

From the corporate perspective, self-management requires a higher degree of transparency about strategic and business information, equipping people with the necessary information to make sound choices for themselves while matching the needs of the organization. This is a condition that is far from reality in the majority of organizations.

number of multinational firms now provide access to company-specific social networking applications at work, sometimes linked to communities of practice or functional communities, allowing managers and professionals to tap into knowledge networks that are often spread across the world. BT Global has developed "I Click," a platform through which employees can share contact information and details about skills, hobbies, and assignments, search for internal career opportunities, and network to find solutions to professional problems. Schlumberger and other firms allow their professionals to develop their own biographies, which have grown into "blue pages" on the intranet, where individuals can market their talents and skills across boundaries in creative ways. Thus, in parallel with open job markets, we are seeing the development of support systems based on social networking that allow individuals to sell their own abilities bottom-up.[93]

These developments are part of a profound change in control.[94] With top-down management, companies can decide who is invited to meetings and who is involved in decision making. But with open networking the company loses this direct control, since individuals are free to organize their own virtual meetings and to consult with whomever they want. Alignment of people through shared values and a shared identity becomes vital. Firms that have tried to control their internal Facebook-type applications have failed, and organizations are now learning to trust people more. For leading multinationals such as IBM, BT, and Nestlé—all of whom, it should be emphasized, have a high degree of cohesion—internal social networking applications have proved to be largely self-policing and self-maintaining, helping to reinforce a "sticky" sense of belonging, in part because they allow permeability between professional and personal life.

When one has no direct control, the challenge is how to ensure that self-help is in the best interests of the organization. One of the limits of open job market systems, from the leadership development perspective, is that they do not provide incentives for the "unnatural acts" that are the hallmark of successful leadership development in multinational corporations. Without top-down prodding, and the assurance of support and coaching, people may not be willing to risk moving across functions and countries—certainly not to highly challenging assignments with a degree of potential hardship. We saw this at Apple, when the company introduced one of the first open job markets for managers and professionals back in the mid-1980s. Paradoxically, it reinforced already strong functional silos rather than solving emerging needs for cross-functional and cross-geographic leadership. There were many candidates willing to move to sales and marketing roles in plum locations in the US and Europe, but not to less obvious but strongly needed technical interface roles and more difficult markets.[95]

Some companies are tackling these challenges head on. IBM has a globally integrated organization, where (in the words of CEO Sam Palmisano) "work flows to the places where it will be done best—that is, most efficiently with the highest quality." To achieve this, IBM wants to facilitate the mobility of people and ideas across global, functional, and unit boundaries. Consequently, its people strategy is to use open-market mechanisms to free up the flow of ideas, people, and innovation. The strategy is to allow work to move to those who have innovative ideas that inspire others; to allow skilled professionals and managers to move easily to where they see the opportunities within the firm; and help talented individuals to market themselves and their ideas across borders within the enterprise.

Here IBM is capitalizing on major investments that it has made in self-help, e-based HR technology as well as in standardized global HR processes. IBM staff have for many years used the intranet for personnel information—expense accounts, information on what is acceptable, holiday requests, recommended courses that fit their needs, pension information, as well as performance appraisal. In 2007, IBM created a platform that provides self-help in learning, networking, mentoring, career track management, and other elements of traditional top-down career management. The firm has also completely changed its formerly secretive attitude about its work strategy to one of internal transparency (see the box "Self-Help at IBM").

Cisco's internal job market is built around a "jobs can find you" principle, according to which people are expected to look continuously for job openings that correspond to their aspirations. On the company side, Cisco carefully plans the competencies and roles needed to implement its short- and medium-term strategy. These openings and the underlying strategy are made transparent through the intranet, and people worldwide can apply for openings that most closely match their aspirations.[96]

Self-Help at IBM

IBM uses electronic technology to help people help themselves across boundaries—within the spirit of creating a globally integrated enterprise. One side of this people strategy involves reinforcing common values and attachment to IBM, using intranet communication and notably "values jams." The other side focuses on a sophisticated worldwide self-help platform.

- Two sections of the IBM platform focus on *personalized learning assistance* (assessing personal learning needs, mapping out areas where experiential or seminar-based learning is necessary, and providing information on where to go for that support); and mentoring/social networking (who can provide help, who can act as a learning buddy, how one can go about sharing one's knowledge, how one can tap into peer groups or communities of practice spread across the globe).
- Another section focuses on *expertise management* (how people can assess their skill and competence gaps; what they can do about closing gaps; and what are current

and future "hot skills"—domains where there is likely to be strong demand).
- A section called "My development" addresses the *requirements of the current job role*, allowing individuals to manage better their development within the context of their existing positions. This is the entry point into another section on *career tracks*. Career tracks address issues of upward career progression; jobs within IBM are clustered into nearly 500 different career tracks (each person is on at least one track) with explicit transition points and links. All career tracks have sponsoring executives with global responsibilities as well as resources, and identified subject matter experts.
- A sixth section of the platform is *blue pages*, which allow talented individuals to market themselves with personalized biographies and blog-type commentaries.

Guiding this platform and closely aligned with it is information on the current and future strategic plans of the IBM business units, as well as the firm's workforce management strategy.

As the IBM and Cisco examples illustrate, we may be seeing the emergence of global internal job markets that allow firms to deploy internal know-how and skills across borders in a low-cost way that was not previously possible. With the required changes in thinking, particularly around control, and with the necessary investments in global standardization, this transformation may be slow. However, new firms are rapidly appearing, built from the outset on globalized people management systems and self-help social networking technology. To the extent that this develops new sources of competitive advantage, as we suspect, the pace of change may be unexpectedly rapid.

But the world of global open job resourcing and social networking does not replace top-down management—it complements it. The nurturing of key capabilities, including growing future senior leaders through what we call unnatural acts, will continue to require the top-down approach. We witnessed one major multinational that initially abandoned its well-honed traditional top-down management development processes when it put global open job resourcing into place, creating substantial confusion at the time. Recently the company has been learning how to mix effectively its top-down and bottom-up approaches to global talent management.

HOW LEADERSHIP DEVELOPMENT SUPPORTS GLOBAL COORDINATION

One of the reasons why top-down leadership development will persist for the foreseeable future is that leadership development is a powerful vehicle for global coordination. Let us take a simple example to illustrate this. A company wants to have deep expertise in its customer-facing commercial functions and in its global operations discipline, which embraces manufacturing and logistics. But the company also needs tight coordination between the commercial and operations domains.

In the past that coordination was provided by the structure, with decisions referred up reporting lines to top management. But that process was too slow and bureaucratic. So the company started to build lateral coordination mechanisms: joint boards and steering groups covering both disciplines. How can they go further? Explicit career pathing for high-potential leaders is one good way. The company spells out that no one will get onto the management team in the commercial function without proving himself or herself in at least one position at a middle level for a reasonable period of time in operations—and vice versa.

What are the consequences? First, the mobility this implies develops a better quality of leadership than the company has known in the past, since managers are obliged to develop their leadership skills via cross-functional moves. Second, it ensures that the leaders at the top have broad perspectives, the "matrix-in-the-mind" that comes from assuming the responsibility for results in another discipline. Third, it builds relationships between key people in the two disciplines, with the trust that will allow them to work through inevitable differences in functional interest. And fourth, this changes the culture of the enterprise. Ambitious young professionals who want to move into leadership positions quickly learn that it is vital to be professionally competent in one's base discipline but also important to build friendships and collaboration with other functions.

Honda has used this mechanism to steer senior leadership development. Soichiro Honda always wanted R&D to be the driver at the Honda Motor Corporation, so the CEO of the company was always the former head of R&D. This explicit path ensures tight coordination and the breaking down of silos. If the head of R&D does not engage in tight coordination with other functions, then he will inherit the problems created in the next position.

The following story ("Developing a French Executive for a US Multinational") illustrates how a transnational enterprise can use leadership development to enhance its capabilities in global coordination. Without Wilson's foresight in planning his succession early, and his determination to ensure that his foreign candidates would have the necessary challenging assignments, the company would never have managed to build such coordination capabilities—the matrix in the mind of its key leaders.

Developing a French Executive for a US Multinational

Let us take a more subtle example to illustrate how a transnational enterprise can use leadership development to improve global coordination.

A US corporation had a geographic structure in which countries were responsible for marketing a technology-based product. The company had dominated the industry worldwide, but now that industry was becoming more complex and segmented owing to a new technology that it had helped to pioneer, attracting new entrants as well as established players. To master the new realities, the company decided to to reorganize its operations on worldwide business lines.

It made its best people heads of the new global product divisions. There was only one problem—with two exceptions, none of them had working experience outside the United States; and many of them had never ventured far from the East Coast headquarters. Their experience had not equipped them with broad perspectives.

David Wilson,[A] who today is CEO of the corporation, noted at the time, "What that effectively did was to neuter the strength in country operations that we had painstakingly built up for 30 years." Determined to do their best, the US product line managers drove decisions through the organization. The most capable local managers in Germany, Japan, and elsewhere often quit in frustration at the blindness of decisions emanating from the East Coast of the US that ignored the realities of their specific markets.

A few years later, Wilson was appointed regional vice president for Europe to repair the damage (with earlier responsibilities in Latin America, Wilson had been one of the two product managers with prior international experience). He told us at the time that his number one priority was to find and develop a European successor, who would be the first non-American to occupy the role: "I'll be in this job for four years—none of my predecessors ever stayed for more than two. I have one year to find the potential candidates. And then I have to use my influence to secure product line jobs for them at the headquarters. They have to hone their skills, develop their connections, and prove their credibility over there." It was not easy to secure product line jobs—the stepping-stone jobs that all the ambitious stars in the United States were jockeying for—for his European candidates. Wilson had five carefully groomed Europeans, and they were offered planning jobs, deputy roles, and staff positions—all of which Wilson refused. He succeeded in securing only three stepping-stone positions for his people.

When Wilson returned to the United States after his assignment, a Frenchman—a man, like Wilson, with a global mindset—took over his position, having credibly shown that a European could successfully run a global product group at headquarters. One can visualize the coordination capability developed by this action. The Europeans were delighted at having one of their own in the top role, while the Americans trusted a highly effective impatriate. The Frenchman was capable of thinking locally and acting globally. On some initiatives, his response was "Go ahead, here's the budget." On others, he would pause and say, "They've got three years of experience with this at the center—go and draw on their know-how first and maybe set up a global steering team."

[A]Name disguised.

For both top-down and bottom-up leadership and management, one of the biggest obstacles in the path to internationalization is the performance management system. While there are strong arguments for doing things the local way in some domains of HRM, when it comes to performance management, it is an absolute priority that performance standards should be the same in all regions of the world. If high performance means one thing in one region and something different in another, obstacles to mobility, as well as to the transfer of knowledge and best practice, are created. And the dialogue between these different regions will be full of misunderstanding and conflict. Therefore, if leadership development is one of the pillars of HRM in multinational firms, performance management is another. In the next chapter, we explore the challenges of global performance management.

TAKEAWAYS

1. Global leadership development emerges from executive surveys and research as the top priority for international HRM, including multinational corporations in emerging countries.
2. There are three different authority orientations—hierarchical, expertise, and leadership—and national cultures differ on these. While the concept of leadership is culturally anchored, there are some attributes that leaders have in common, such as fairness, vision or sense of direction, and attention to building a team.

3. There is no universal list of global leadership competencies because leadership is intransitive, meaning that the best performer at one level is not necessarily the best performer at the next. This is particularly true for multinational firms.

4. Leaders develop above all through challenging opportunities and assignments. Interfunctional and geographic mobility is essential, complemented by split egg–type cross-boundary projects or initiatives.

5. People risk management—coaching, feedback, training, and mentoring in different shapes and forms—has to go hand in hand with challenge. By combining challenge and risk management creatively, firms can obtain short-term performance and develop competencies for the long term.

6. Learning ability has long been seen as an important element of leadership potential, namely the ability to learn fast and well from challenging experiences.

7. At the heart of the traditional top-down approach to leadership development are rigorous reviews of talent in different parts of the firm, typically based on the assessment of performance, potential, and/or respect for key values. Frank, candid dialogue, with provision for preparation and follow-through, is vital.

8. There are several key issues and dilemmas in leadership assessment and development. Should potential be identified early or late, and how transparent should one be about the judgments made? How can we overcome the tendency of units to hide their best people? How can we avoid excessive mobility?

9. Many firms complement top-down leadership development with bottom-up open job resourcing, built on e-technology and globally standardized HR processes. Despite challenges to traditional concepts of control, this can facilitate rapid deployment of talent across borders.

10. Leadership development is a powerful tool for ensuring coordination in the transnational firm.

NOTES

1. Bartlett and McLean, 2003; Pucik and Lief, 2007.
2. "Follow the Leader," *Industry Week*, November 18, 1996, p. 16.
3. Bartlett and McLean, 2003.
4. Four out of the 18 GE corporate officers in March 2009 were women. See www.ge.com/company/leadership/executives.html.
5. An annual award conducted by the Hay Group with *Chief Executive Review*, based on polling peers, academics, and experts. Only 31 percent of the 790 firms reviewed in 2007 were US-based. GE won the award as best company for leaders in 2006 and 2007. P&G and 3M have also won this award in recent years. See www.chiefexecutive.net/articles/.
6. E. F. Kratz, "Get Me a CEO from GE!" *Fortune*, May 16, 2005.

7. Research has shown this to be the case. Even in international firms that pay scant corporate attention to HRM, leadership development is invariably an area of top management concern (Scullion and Starkey, 2000).

8. Gregersen, Morrison, and Black, 1998; Black, Gregersen, and Morrison, 1999. See also Ready and Conger (2007).

9. IBM, 2008, "Unlocking the DNA of the adaptable Workforce: The Global Human Capital Study" (www.ibm.com/cy/pdfs/HR_Study_2008.pdf). Similar results were found in a DDI survey of 13,700 leaders and HR professionals around the world in 2008: "Global Leadership Forecast 2008/2009: Overcoming the Shortfalls in Developing Leaders," by A. Howard and R. Wellins (www.ddiworld.com/leadershipforecast/). When the dot.com growth bubble ended in 2001, the Ciscos of the new technology era realized that they faced tougher competition and did not have the leadership depth to meet the challenges, and so internal leadership development became a priority (Chatman, O'Reilly, and Chang, 2005).

10. Ready, Hill, and Conger, 2008.

11. M. Joerss, and H. Zhang, "A Pioneer in Chinese Globalization: An Interview with CIMC's President," *McKinsey Quarterly Online Journal*, 2008, www.mckinseyquarterly.com.

12. IBM, 2008, "Unlocking the DNA of the Adaptable Workforce: The Global Human Capital Study" (www.ibm.com/cy/pdfs/HR_Study_2008.pdf); DDI, 2008, "Global Leadership Forecast 2008/2009: Overcoming the Shortfalls in Developing Leaders," by A. Howard and R. Wellins (www.ddiworld.com/leadershipforecast/).

13. DDI, 2008, "Global Leadership Forecast 2008/2009: Overcoming the Shortfalls in Developing Leaders," by A. Howard and R. Wellins (www.ddiworld.com/leadershipforecast/).

14. Hill, 1992.

15. Evans, 1974; 1992.

16. Laurent, personal communication, including the data presented in the figure shown in the box "Cultural Differences in Authority and Leadership." See also Laurent (1983).

17. House et al., 2004.

18. Derailment factors are behavioral factors or qualities associated with career failure, as opposed to being important for career success. See McCall, Lombardo, and Morrison (1988).

19. The term "setting direction" is used by Kotter (1988), while Bennis and Nanus (1985) call it "management of attention," and McCall, Lombardo, and Morrison (1988) use the phrase "setting and implementing agendas."

20. Kotter, 1982.

21. Maruca, 1994, p. 142.

22. For some reviews of this literature, see McCall and Hollenbeck (2002); Caligiuri (2006a); Mendenhall (2006); and Mendenhall et al. (2008).

23. Hollenbeck and McCall, 2001.

24. Charan, Drotter, and Noel, 2001.

25. Bartlett and Ghoshal, 1997; Ghoshal and Bartlett, 1998.

26. Charan, Drotter, and Noel, 2001; Ibarra, Snook, and Ramo, 2008.

27. See McCall and Hollenbeck (2002). The 101 executives in the study held positions such as CEO, executive vice president, managing director, country manager, business unit manager, and controller. There were 46 Europeans, 18 Asians, 10 from the US and Canada, 8 South Americans, 6 from the Middle East and Africa, and 4 from Australia and New Zealand. The interviews focused on key events in their own development.

28. McCall, 1998. Research from the Center for Creative Leadership showed that work experiences with peers and superiors, especially challenging assignments that stretched an individual's abilities, were the most importance source of development and learning for executives (McCall, Lombardo, and Morrison, 1988).

29. Evans, 1974, 1992.

30. Discussion with one of the authors at a 2006 conference.

31. Charam, Drotter, and Noel, 2001. See Hill (1992) for an analysis of the transition from individual contributor to manager.

32. Muller, 1970. See other studies in the journal *Advances in Global Leadership*.

33. Leung et al., 2008; and work by Maddux and colleagues in process.

34. DDI, 2008, "Global Leadership Forecast 2008/2009: Overcoming the Shortfalls in Developing Leaders," by A. Howard and R. Wellins (www.ddiworld.com/leadershipforecast/).

35. These team skills, necessary for lateral coordination, were discussed in Chapter 5.

36. See the discussion in Chapter 5 in the section "Building Cross-Border Teams."

37. DDI, 2008, "Global Leadership Forecast 2008/2009: Overcoming the Shortfalls in Developing Leaders," by A. Howard and R. Wellins (www.ddiworld.com/leadershipforecast/).

38. Cappelli, 2008.

39. Galunic and Andersen, 2000. In any case, almost all training is general, in that it would be useful to some alternative employers at least.

40. Action learning was reportedly disseminated first by Revens (1980). See also Conger and Benjamin (1999).

41. Morgan and Ramirez, 1983; Ramirez, 1983; see also the theory of experiential learning developed by David Kolb and his colleagues (Kolb, 1984). See Raelin (1999) for a review of action learning. It should be noted that in a high-context society such as Japan, learning processes are mostly project-oriented or experiential—there is little emphasis beyond school and university on Western-style didactic learning (Nonaka and Takeuchi, 1995).

42. Arora et al., 2004.

43. McCall and Hollenbeck, 2002.

44. "Learning and Development: Annual Survey Report 2008," CIPD, United Kingdom (www.cipd.co.uk/NR/rdonlyres/3A3AD4D6-F818-4231-863B-4848CE383B46/0/learningdevelopmentsurvey.pdf).

45. See Higgins and Kram (2001) for a review of mentoring from a wider network perspective.

46. For further analysis see Alvarez and Svejenova (2005). The research of Belbin (1981) on eight complementary team roles provides an underlying rationale.

47. "Gamechanger," *BusinessWeek*, March 12, 2009.

48. Eddy, Hall, and Robinson, 2006.

49. Carraher, Sullivan, and Crocitto, 2008.

50. Lepsinger and Lucia, 1997.

51. See Judge et al., 1999.

52. Spreitzer, McCall, and Mahoney, 1997; McCall, 1998; McCall and Hollenbeck, 2002; Hollenbeck and McCall 2001. See also Lombardo and Eichinger (2000).

53. Bennis and Nanus, 1985.

54. Briscoe and Hall, 1999.

55. Agrawal and Kets de Vries, 2006.

56. "It's 2008: Do You Know Where Your Talent Is? Why Acquisition and Retention Strategies Don't Work," Deloitte, www.deloitte.com/dtt/cda/doc/content/UK_Consulting_TalenMgtResearchReport.pdf.

57. IBM, 2005, "The Capability Within: The Global Human Capital Study" (www.ibm.com/services/us/bcs/html/2005_human_cap_mgt_gen.html). As reported in Chapter 7, this return on investment was not found for operational staff (core employees who do not have firm-specific skills).

58. Described in Chapter 7.

59. "Leadership 2012," research report, Corporate University Xchange, Harrisburg PA, 2007; cited by Cappelli (2008, p.145).

60. The origins of the process title, Session C, apparently go far back into GE's strategic and business planning processes. Originally this included sessions A and B, but these have long since been abandoned.

61. When each of the two dimensions on the grid is divided into three categories, this results in a nine-box diagram, hence the name. The Novartis framework in Figure 8–2 is an example.

62. The importance of undertaking globally consistent performance evaluations is discussed in Chapter 9.

63. Japanese corporations that recruit high potentials from universities make regular assessment of performance and potential but are secretive about this during the trial period of seven to eight years. Conversely, during this trial period no actions are taken on the basis of that potential judgment, recognizing that it takes time to come to a reliable judgment of potential.

64. The Commonwealth Edison and Tatweer examples are taken from Cappelli (2008, pp. 197–9).

65. Guthridge, Komm, and Lawson, 2008.

66. "Best Companies for Leaders," November 2005, www.chiefexecutive.net.

67. Mäkelä, Björkman, and Ehrnrooth (Forthcoming).

68. See Chapter 7.

69. See, for example, the McKinsey survey reported by Guthridge, Komm, and Lawson (2008). As indicated earlier, one major challenge confirmed by this survey was the silo problem of hiding good people; the other was lack of commitment by top management and the line to the assessment and development of top talent.

70. "Best Companies for Leaders," November 2005, www.chiefexecutive.net.

71. Eddy, Hall, and Robinson, 2006.

72. McCall, 1998. Cappelli rightly points out that great value in talent management comes from spotting "hidden" local talent and nurturing its development, rather than developing more obvious talent that is already clearly labeled by degrees and qualifications and therefore is more likely to leave the firm for opportunities elsewhere. See Cappelli (2008, pp. 190–5).

73. Huselid, Beatty, and Becker, 2005.

74. The idea of firm-specific leadership skills has been developed further by Ulrich and Smallwood (2007) using the concept of building a leadership brand. They regard about 60–70 percent of leadership skills as generic (vision, the ability to deliver results, interpersonal skills, etc.) and 30–40 percent as specific to the industry and the capabilities of the firm.

75. Michaels, Handfield-Jones, and Axelrod, 2001.

76. Cappelli and Hamori, 2005.

77. See Goleman (1995), building on the pioneering work of Howard Gardner on multiple intelligences. See also Goleman, Boyatzis, and McKee (2002b).
78. Kets de Vries, 1989; McCall, 1998. For a more practical treatment see Dottlich, Noel, and Walker (2004) and the work on so-called "crucible experiences" by Thomas and Bennis (2008).
79. DDI, 2008, "Global Leadership Forecast 2008/2009: Overcoming the Shortfalls in Developing Leaders," by A. Howard and R. Wellins (www.ddiworld.com/leadershipforecast/).
80. As described in Chapter 4, page 142–3.
81. As reported by Cappelli (2008), Citibank had some of the most sophisticated leadership development programs in place until Sandy Weill took over as CEO in 1998. He saw little value in these processes, notably succession planning, preferring to make appointments on the basis of financial performance in the job and company loyalty.
82. Cappelli, 2008.
83. See Chapter 7 for a discussion of talent pools.
84. At very senior levels, particularly in public Anglo-Saxon firms, appointments are often mediated by executive search firms.
85. Reported by Cappelli (2008).
86. See the discussion of internal labor markets in Chapter 7.
87. Mills and Blossfeld, 2008. The concept of the patchwork career implies unstable, fragmented, and precarious employment, where organizations have abandoned responsibility for career management and individuals do not have the capabilities to do anything else but hunt for the next job.
88. Blossfeld, Mills, and Bernardi, 2008.
89. Cappelli, 1999.
90. For a full account of the concept of the boundaryless career and its implications, see Arthur and Rousseau (1996). The parallel concept of the protean career is outlined in Hall (1996).
91. DeFillippi and Arthur, 1996.
92. See Ibarra (2003).
93. Li and Bernoff, 2008; Fraser and Dutta, 2008.
94. This change in control as a result of information and communications technology has long been anticipated (Zuboff, 1984). For a current analysis, see Fraser and Dutta (2008).
95. Evans and Wittenberg, 1986.
96. The Cisco principle is outlined in Doz and Kosonen (2008).

CHAPTER 9

Global Performance Management

Haier: An Emerging Chinese Multinational

One spring day in early 1985, anyone visiting the facilities of Qingdao Refrigerator General Factory, a home appliance manufacturer in the northeastern Chinese city of Qingdao, would have been forgiven for thinking that company CEO Zhang Ruimin had taken leave of his senses. Just a few months after taking the helm of this virtually bankrupt company, at the age of 35, this former city official gathered all factory personnel in the factory courtyard. There, they watched a group of coworkers take sledgehammers to implement an order from their young CEO: "Destroy all refrigerators that have been found to be defective in even a minor way." Zhang had a clear message: The company would no longer produce substandard products. Instead, a high quality of products and services would become the foundation of its global brand.[1]

By 2008, Zhang had turned the small loss-making refrigerator factory into a group of more than 240 subsidiaries, 30 design centers, plants, and companies, employing over 50,000 workers. Haier (as the company is known today) was the world's fourth-largest maker of large kitchen appliances with US$16.2 billion in revenues and a 6.3 percent global share with a particularly strong position in washing machines (#2) and refrigerators (#3). The company's products were sold in 160 countries, in 12 of the 15 top European retailers, and in all of the top 10 retail chains in North America.

A guiding principle of Haier's management system is OEC: Overall, Every, Control and Clear. "Overall" means that all performance dimensions have to be considered. "Every" refers to everyone, everyday, and everything. "Control and clear" refers to Haier's end-of-work procedure each day, which states that employees must finish all tasks planned for that day before leaving work—they are responsible for managing their own workload and reporting to their supervisor.

To support OEC, Haier uses a variety of performance management and motivational tools. For example, a key aspect of Haier's performance management is the system used for performance evaluations and promotions—and demotions—based on the concept of a racetrack. All employees can compete in work-related "races" such as job openings and promotions, but winners have to keep racing—and winning—to defend a title. There is no such thing as a permanent promotion. In keeping with this philosophy, every employee in the Haier Group is subject to frequent and transparent performance appraisals—going against the traditional Chinese culture in which "face" is extremely important.

However, accountability is not shared equally. According to Haier's 80:20 principle, superiors are responsible for 80 percent of results (good or bad)—subordinates for 20 percent. Each manager's performance is reviewed weekly. The criteria for the evaluation involve both achieving quantifiable goals and the degree of innovation and process improvement. At the end of the month, managers receive a performance grade of A, B, or C. The results of this evaluation are announced at a meeting for middle and upper-level managers on the eighth day of each month. Those judged as being ready to move to a higher position are transferred into the Haier talent pool. Selections for the talent pool are made every quarter. There is no philosophy of "once you're in, you're in" at Haier.

Managers' performance rankings are openly displayed at the entrance to the company cafeteria, with a green or red arrow indicating whether their score has gone up or down that month. This practice has been in place for over 20 years. Promotions and demotions are also published in the company's internal newspaper.

Haier has a formal policy for managing employees who do not meet set expectations. The consequence of continued performance in the bottom 10 percent after three negative reviews (either quarterly or annually), despite remedial training, is dismissal. The flip side of this approach is the emphasis on recognizing and rewarding successes and creativity. If an employee develops or improves a product, or suggests an efficient new procedure, the innovation carries the employee's name, and a notice to this effect is prominently displayed.

Another important feature of Haier's HR system is a close connection between performance measurements and compensation. The company provides each employee with a "P&L book," which is updated daily and breaks down and quantifies the financial outcome of the employee's efforts. The bottom line is directly linked to the salary received by the employee. In Haier's language, employees do not receive salaries but their share of profits.

Haier is one of the first Chinese manufacturers to have established manufacturing bases overseas. An interesting question is whether the management practices that seem to have earned the company such success in China are transferable to other cultures as it continues its international expansion. For example, how would American or European employees respond to Haier's approach to managing performance? And if Haier chooses not to apply its performance management approach abroad, will this constrain its ability to coordinate global activities?

OVERVIEW

Haier is a good example of a company with well-defined performance management. Building on the Haier case, we will examine in detail the performance management cycle, first clarifying what global performance management is and why it is important, then focusing on specific challenges in building a robust global performance management system. We will examine both the "upstream" side of this process, which focuses on determining the strategic and operational goals that should be the fundamental drivers of business performance—exploring the tensions embedded in the process, and its "downstream" side, which includes individual and team performance appraisal, feedback, performance evaluation linked to talent management processes, and rewards.

This discussion leads to the conclusion that commitment to rigorous performance management is more important than the sophistication of the methodology. With this in mind, we will then turn to the role that performance management can play in supporting global coordination. We will consider two aspects of global coordination where performance management may have a particularly strong influence. First, we will discuss how performance management may impact various mechanisms for lateral steering, among others global account management. Second, more broadly, we will examine factors influencing performance management in global teams.

In the third part of the chapter we build on our previous discussion of expatriates, exploring core issues concerning managing the performance of employees on international assignments. We address some of the factors that can make the performance appraisal of expatriates different from that of other employees in a multinational firm. We will also review different approaches to managing expatriate compensation, an issue of growing interest to many firms with increasing populations of employees on cross-border assignments.

We conclude this chapter by discussing three questions critical to the implementation of global performance management. The first question concerns the perennial tension between the competing interests of a global approach versus those of local adaptation. The second concerns the ownership of the performance management system; it is essential that this process belongs to the line, not to the HR function. The third question concerns the linkage of performance with business strategy—how can performance management systems contribute to building distinctive capabilities?

THE GLOBAL PERFORMANCE MANAGEMENT CYCLE

The concept of performance management is still in much of the human resource management literature associated that the practices of some well-known Anglo-Saxon firms. But as the Haier example illustrates, in a competitive world, performance management is a process that has no boundaries.[2] In order to become (and remain) a high-performing global organization, it is essential to have an effective, simple, robust, and consistent set of tools and processes to manage performance and to motivate employees to act in alignment with the strategy and values of the company.

What Is Global Performance Management?

We define performance management as a process that links the strategies, objectives, and capabilities of the firm to unit, team, and individual goals and actions, involving periodic appraisal and evaluation, and with reward and development activities that are in turn linked to the outcome of the appraisals. Performance management includes three successive elements:

1. The specification of what is desired performance, involving setting objectives and goals at all levels.
2. The review and evaluation of performance, including feedback and plans for any corrective action.
3. Linking the results of the evaluation to financial rewards and to development activities.

An essential characteristic of the performance management process is the consistency and tight link across the three elements—simple in principle, but potentially difficult in practice, since the three phases of performance management are all too often disconnected.

Designing and implementing an effective performance management may be one of the most complex issues facing organizations operating across borders because global dimensions of performance management further complicate an already difficult-to-master process, as we will see below. For these reasons, leading-edge firms often view their performance management process as a genuine source of competitive advantage and are secretive about their approach. As one global HR vice president commented, "We would no more show our performance appraisal form to a bunch of outsiders than Cola-Cola would let you come in and look over the secret formula for Coke."[3]

Why Is Global Performance Management Important?

In a multinational firm, the performance management process should provide alignment between corporate, business, geographic, and functional objectives. It supports a company's global people strategy, providing input to all functional HR processes, from recruiting and staffing to development and compensation, and linking these clearly to corporate and business aims.

Except for executives at the highest levels, strategies are typically rather abstract for employees. Increasing shareholder value, decreasing time to market, enhancing customer orientation—what do such strategies mean for the behavior of people around the world? In this respect, performance management helps employees to focus on what they have to do, recognizes and rewards them for doing so, and makes clear the consequences of poor performance and behavior. Good performance management processes should provide first, clarity about people's roles, objectives, and contribution to the business, thereby allowing greater autonomy; second, regular feedback on performance so that there is effective learning; and third, ongoing coaching and career development. It should make visible what performance is expected and what rewards (monetary and nonmonetary) this will bring to the employee.

Attention to performance management is also a vital step in building horizontal coordination in the multinational firm. We worked with a successful European corporation that had grown internationally through acquisitions and had, until recently, a multidomestic strategic approach. Country business managers focused on delivering local operating results, while top management's attitude was, "We don't want them worrying about global strategy—it will just distract them from their local targets." But now this company's business was moving rapidly in a new direction. Some customers were buying products across borders, and others wanted global service. Business decisions were becoming more complex, involving global–local trade-offs. Top management was beginning to recognize that managers in individual countries had to become more aligned with the company's overall strategic direction and that achieving this without a common approach to performance management might be impossible. The company realized that it may have to reconsider its performance management system, moving toward a global approach that would support the necessary coordination at lower levels. But this was made more difficult by the fact that cross-border activities were not universal—a lot of business was still strictly local-for-local, as in the past.

However, it should not be forgotten that the goal of collaboration is not collaboration itself, but results. In a multinational corporation, what stimulates the creation of value is the combination of constructive competition, guided by clear goals, metrics, and the other elements of performance management, together with collaborative teamwork.[4]

For a multinational company, perhaps the most important question to ask is whether it should adopt one single global performance management process, differentiate the process by business or region, or allow each local company to develop its own particular process. Historically, multidomestic firms were more local in their approach to performance management; meganational corporations preferred a strong global orientation. However, across the board, the overall trend has for many years been toward more globally integrated, or at least loosely aligned, performance management systems. Among all HR practices, performance management (with the exception of the reward element) tends to be the most globally standardized.[5]

But the extent to which one can generalize about standardization depends on the phase of the performance management process. Let us therefore break the process of performance management down into some of its elements, starting "upstream" with the planning and objective-setting cycle, and then moving "downstream" toward appraisal and evaluation, rewards, and development activities.[6]

The "Upstream" Side of Performance Management

The focus of the upstream side of performance management is on setting global objectives. The first step in the performance management process is determining the strategic and operational goals that should be the fundamental drivers of business performance.

Goal setting is one of the most influential paradigms in the business management field. Hundreds of experiments and research with thousands of people on all continents have demonstrated that clear and challenging goals boost performance. As Locke and Latham note in a review of four decades of goal-setting research, "So long as a person is committed to the goal, has the requisite ability to attain it, and does not have conflicting goals, there is a positive linear relationship between goal difficulty and task performance."[7]

Multinational firms can use many different approaches to set objectives (long-term strategic focus versus short-term financial focus, detailed planning versus entrepreneurial decision making), each with their own embedded paradoxes and limitations.[8] The details of these different processes are beyond the scope of this book, but the specific approach chosen by the multinational in the upstream stage of performance management should be aligned with its global strategy and its organizational structure. Companies organized as differentiated networks may therefore approach performance management differently than those that are configured as a front–back organization.

However, with the increase of cross-border activities, the issue for most companies engaged in international business is not if they should set global objectives. The issue is their scope and how to go about setting these objectives in a way that mobilizes the organizational energy in the desired direction and contributes to the coordination and cohesion of the firm. As Hansen noted in his summary of several decades of research on collaboration in organizations, the most fundamental lever for collaboration and teamwork is unity around a concrete goal that clearly places competition on the outside.[9]

There are several challenges with respect to goal setting in any global performance management system that we will discuss. The first is to ensure that employees around the world interpret the outcome of the goal-setting process in a similar way. The second challenge is to make sure that this understanding is translated into relevant and clear performance objectives with tangible measurements. The process of setting objectives is essentially a commitment-building process, and the third challenge is how to create such commitment. A final challenge is how to deal with the numerous tensions related to the structure and content of the performance objectives and measures.

Developing a Shared Meaning of Objectives

The first priority in the upstream phase of performance management is making sure that employees worldwide share an understanding of what the goals actually mean. Different interpretations of a goal, and equally important, different readings of the consequences of not achieving the objective, can cause a great deal of confusion. In some firms a goal is a promise that must be respected, and so great care will be devoted to planning that goal. In others, a goal is a stretch aspiration that most people will fail to achieve. In yet other firms, the norm is "no surprises" so that goals are constantly moving targets. This is aggravated by differences in cultural heritage, both organizational and national. The box "When Is a Goal a Goal?" presents two contrasting examples.

Maersk and GE (both corporations that have been successful over a long period of time) have very different approaches to performance management, to planning goals, and to their review and consequences. It is not that one conception of a goal is right and the other is wrong—in both cases, there are trade-offs. It is more a question of whether the business units and countries across the world are playing the same game with the same rules. Playing by different rules creates intense frustration that spills over negatively into many other areas of cross-border collaboration.

There are also cultural differences in underlying assumptions about the meaning of goals that affect performance management. For example, school systems in different countries socialize people to think about goals in different ways. Americans are brought up in the belief that the top A grade is achievable. In contrast, French schoolchildren are evaluated on a 20-point scale, where a 15 represents an unusual distinction and an 18 is virtually unprecedented. Time horizon plays a role. The Japanese and Koreans are more likely to accept an

When Is a Goal a Goal?

At A.P. Møller-Maersk, a Danish *Fortune* Global 500 firm in the container transport and shipping industry, the meaning of a goal or target is very clear throughout the company's worldwide operations. A goal, once agreed and accepted, is a promise to deliver. This means exercising what the owner of the company calls "constant care"—debating and reviewing thoroughly with all parties any commitment that one will make since it is precisely that—a commitment. As the owner says, "Your word is your bond"—and everyone knows that he means it. Not meeting a commitment will have serious consequences, maybe dismissal.

In contrast, at GE—another company known for its approach to performance management—the concept of a goal is different but equally clearly defined: It is a stretch target that the majority of people will fail to meet. As GE's annual report notes, "GE business leaders do not walk around all year regretting the albatross of an impossible number they hung around their necks. At the end of the year, the business is measured not on whether it hit the stretch target, but on how well it did against the prior year, given the circumstances. Performance is measured against the world as it turned out to be: how well a business anticipated change and dealt with it, rather than against some 'plan' or internal number negotiated a year earlier."[10]

GE views most goals as stretch targets, and it handsomely rewards those that hit these targets. At the same time, as at Maersk, certain essential targets must not be missed, and these are specified since it is important to avoid setting stretch goals in areas where meeting a particular performance level is critical.[11]

ambitious goal 10 years in the future that represents an aspiration, whereas most Westerners prefer a more tangible and achievable time scope.

More convergence is to be expected since technology is changing the process of performance management, including appraisal and development, bringing about an increase in timeliness and transparency of the goal-setting process. Some companies, like the global hospitality company Starwood Hotels, have long had goals posted on their intranet for consultation by peers and subordinates. Accenture has developed a Facebook-style program where employees post two to three weekly goals that can be viewed by fellow staff members, along with a couple of objectives for each quarter.[12]

Deciding on Measurement Scorecards

What gets measured gets attention. This old idea is no less valid when it comes to implementing processes of global coordination. In our research with managers operating in global businesses, we have consistently seen gaps between the desired and actual levels of collaboration and coordination. Why is the level of coordination low? This is partly because mechanisms such as teamwork and knowledge sharing are missing, but even more fundamentally because the performance management measures and outcomes do not encourage managers to do what they personally believe should be done. When measurements change, so do behaviors. In the HR arena in particular, attention needs to be given to what cannot be easily measured—see the box "Getting Clarity on Unmeasurables."

There are at least two strong arguments for using a common and consistent system of measurement scorecards throughout the multinational firm, including at least some cross-border performance measures:

- Global scorecards reinforce a global mindset among employees by making the nature of the global business visible and tangible for managers and employees in the company.
- Joint performance objectives encourage dispersed units to collaborate, thereby reducing the conflicts that often exist across organizational boundaries, such as between sales/service units and global product groups.

Getting Clarity on Unmeasurables

Some goals are difficult to measure, notably in the people development area. Take for example talent development. Goals such as "ensure that the top 5 percent of the professional workforce have clear development plans" may be too general and too undifferentiated to be useful. How can one get clarity around objectives that are not easy to measure?

Asking people to develop action plans and then reviewing those plans is one way of doing this. "Develop an action plan within one month for the development of the top 5 percent of the professional workforce, and review this with your boss and the regional head of HR." That plan is much more concrete, and specific goals can be set on the basis of the review.

Also, well-designed cross-border measurement scorecards help to decentralize responsibility. Without such metrics, clear accountability is impossible, and relationships between the corporate and unit levels are likely to oscillate between unhealthy extremes of laissez-faire management-by-exception and detailed bureaucratic control over decision making that dampens local initiative.

The existence of transparent and clear metrics allows decentralized initiatives and facilitates constructive debate between corporate and subsidiary levels. The aim is both to help local managers to identify and diagnose problems and to allow top management to monitor that performance. The purpose is to help rather than interfere: "What's the problem? What are you doing to fix it? And how can we help?" And one of the ways of helping is to suggest to local managers that they go and talk with higher-performing units.

BP uses peer groups of business unit managers to add punch to the goal-setting process. The managers of each business unit enter into an annual performance contract with top management and are then free to deliver the results in whatever way they wish. But the "peer assist" process requires managers to get their plans, including investment plans, approved by their peers before finalizing the performance contract with top management. "The peers must be satisfied that you are carrying your fair share of the heavy water buckets," said BP's deputy chief executive. "The old issue of sandbagging management is gone. The challenge now comes from peers, not from management."[13] Half of the unit manager's bonus depends on the performance of the unit, and the other half depends on the performance of the peer group. The three top-performing business units in a peer group have also been made responsible for improving the performance of the bottom three.

Focused measurements linked to core business strategies can be powerful in ensuring coordination. Early on in its international expansion, Motorola faced the challenge of cracking the Japanese market with its semiconductor and telecommunication products. Several previous initiatives had failed. But this time it not only changed its product offering and marketing strategy but also modified the performance appraisal criteria for scores of managers worldwide. The change was very simple. One open-ended sentence was added to the list of appraisal criteria: "What have you done to support Motorola's Japan strategy?" Within weeks, phones started ringing in the company's Tokyo office, with colleagues worldwide inquiring how they could help—with information, knowledge, technical resources, and even people on short-term assignments.

Thus, a common approach to performance metrics needs to be shared across the globe. Many multinationals have established clear guidelines for setting individual goals throughout the corporation, such as Nokia's "SMART" goals: Specific, Measurable, Agreed, Realistic, and Timely. To ensure focus, Starwood limits goals to five—the so-called Big Five, consisting of three financial targets and two qualitative objectives. And to stimulate cross-border learning within companies, the emphasis has to be not only on "what" has been accomplished but also on "how" it was achieved.

Advances in information technology allow real-time measurement worldwide. State-of-the-art IT infrastructure enables global firms like Cisco to close the books on a daily basis. In some companies this may create a fear of "big brother," but if properly used, it can enable self-monitoring and autonomous corrective action at the front line.

Building Commitment

Strategic planning processes used by many firms in the past typically involved a small group of senior executives and planners working on the numbers, leading to strategic objectives that were understood by only a handful of people—without any communication of the logic behind the numbers to the rest of the organization.[14] Consequently, there was little commitment, so implementation of these objectives was often ineffective. Therefore many companies today put a great deal of effort into making sure that not only the goals, but also the strategic logic behind the goals, are well understood by the whole organization.

For example, a Nordic multinational firm decided to confront the problem of traditionally slow implementation of a worldwide reorganization. The HR group prepared advice on how subsidiaries should communicate this to their staff. The executive committee also announced that a special bonus would be paid to business unit managers in six months, based on the results of random interviews with subsidiary staff about their understanding of the purpose behind the reorganization.

Money talks even in Scandinavia, but probably the best way of translating information into understanding reasonably fast, and then into commitment, is dialogue. A critical task in the planning cycle is therefore creating opportunities for such dialogue to occur. Examples are interlocking "conferences" that bring together hundreds of key executives, with intensive preparation to ensure two-way discussion; training programs to introduce a common language for reviewing, say, strategic marketing; workshops that bring together heads of businesses for a week of intensive confrontation on issues that have been suppressed; "workout"-type processes; BP's "peer assist" process mentioned earlier; and fishbowl meetings where local management teams present their plans to top management while other teams sit in on the review.[15]

Building commitment to goals is as important at the individual level as at the unit level. As noted, there is a wealth of research showing that goal setting improves employee performance since individuals are more committed to meeting the goals that they themselves have decided upon.[16] But does this hold true across cultures? There are certainly cultural differences in the roles that subordinates tend to play in the goal-setting process. In cultures characterized by large power distance, the superior commonly decides on the objectives. For instance, one study of performance management in Western multinationals in China concluded that the objectives were set by superiors more often than in their home countries.[17] Nonetheless, even in China, two-way communication about employee objectives helps produce stronger goal commitment, and involvement in goal setting has indeed been found to have positive performance implications across settings and cultures.[18]

Tensions in Performance Management "Upstream"

In the process of deciding on the structure and content of their global scorecards, companies must strive to balance several tensions embedded in this process:

- The mix of financial versus nonfinancial targets.
- Short-term versus longterm goals.
- Unit-level versus corporate-level objectives.
- Incremental versus breakthrough initiatives.
- Standardized measures versus localization of objectives.

There are no "once-and-for-all" or "best practice" answers for resolving these tensions; they simply require continuous attention from senior management as well as HR as the global organization and its environment evolves.

FINANCIAL VERSUS NONFINANCIAL TARGETS. The limitations of using only financial objectives as measures of performance are now well understood, and the trade-offs between various financial measures and their impact on corporate performance are also reasonably well mapped.[19] More difficult, and more critical, is deciding what nonfinancial targets need to be included in the global scorecards, how they should be measured, and what their weight in the overall evaluation should be.

Against this background, the balanced scorecard approach (see the box "Balanced Scorecard") has a particular appeal—provided that it is simple and focused—since it forces recognition of and debate on the dualities that underlie performance.[20]

While financial indicators may have the virtue of simplicity, the balanced approach is more aligned to a world of paradoxes and dilemmas. However, the dilemmas of performance management do not disappear with the balanced scorecard—they just become more explicit for managers.

Balanced Scorecard

The concept of the balanced scorecard was developed by Kaplan and Norton.[21] They observe that financial measures report on the outcomes but do not reflect how the organization manages the drivers of future performance. Therefore, instead of a narrow focus on financial results, they propose looking at the strategy to create value from four different perspectives:

1. **Financial.** The strategy for growth, profitability, and risk viewed from the perspective of the shareholder.

2. **Customer.** The strategy for creating value and differentiation from the perspective of the customer.

3. **Internal business processes.** The strategic priorities for various business processes that create customer and shareholder satisfaction.

4. **Learning and growth.** The priorities for creating a climate that supports organizational change, innovation, and growth.

Kaplan and Norton do not specifically address human resources, except as internal business processes. Perhaps this omission is due to difficulties in measuring human resources.[22] Whatever the reason, the omission of a critical component of performance management is considered by some as a major problem and limitation of the balanced scorecard approach.[23] Some firms have dealt with this by including human resources issues in the learning and growth dimension of their scorecards.

Becker, Huselid, and Ulrich bridged this gap by introducing the concept of the *HR scorecard* focused on measuring the contribution of the HR function to multiple objectives, such as financial, (internal) customers, operations, and HR strategy.[24] The workforce scorecard measures workforce mindset and culture, workforce competencies, leadership, and workforce behavior, all leading to workforce success in achieving the strategic objectives of the business.[25]

SHORT-TERM VERSUS LONG-TERM GOALS. While short-term goals rightly emphasize business deliverables, the measurement scorecard should counterbalance this by adding longer-term objectives. Cutting costs for short-term survival by laying off employees in a time of crisis, for example, may be painful, but the real challenge is cutting costs without jeopardizing the long-term future of the company. Many of the long-term issues may focus explicitly on people-related dimensions, and it is the responsibility of HR managers to ensure that such considerations are taken into account even in difficult times. The HR function in many corporations is often excessively reactive, carried away by growth aims in good times and slashing headcount in difficult periods.[26]

This tension does not surface only in times of crisis. In most firms, long-term and short-term planning are tackled sequentially. Strategic planning is an initial step that leads to operational planning and budget decisions. From then onward, the strategic goals exist only in the distant background. When operational goals in a subsidiary far from headquarters are translated into individual objectives, the connection with corporate strategic objectives is typically vague at best. Targets that are inherently long-term, such as talent development, tend to get pushed out in the process.

UNIT-LEVEL VERSUS CORPORATE-LEVEL OBJECTIVES. There are good reasons to establish challenging but achievable goals for which the unit in question can really be held responsible, motivating managers to work hard to reach them. However, as we have already pointed out, a narrow focus on the individual units may lead to behavior that is suboptimal for the global organization as a whole.[27] Most multinationals therefore establish both local and global (sometimes also regional) objectives for their foreign units. The mix and weight of objectives can change from year to year, as warranted by corporate priorities.

INCREMENTAL VERSUS BREAKTHROUGH INITIATIVES. The performance management process tends to focus on incremental rather than breakthrough change. There has been valid criticism that most global measurement systems have a build-in bias toward optimization, replication, and predictability.[28] They tend to drive out disruptive learning—responding to new and unfamiliar knowledge may have long-run benefits, but it typically involves short-term adjustment costs and losses due to experimentation. Therefore, there might be a need to include long-term "breakthrough" objectives to complement the traditional short-term focus of operational goals.

Some firms have moved to parallel goal-setting processes where operational objectives are separated from the long-term goals—with active top management involvement and focus on the latter. At GE, long-term companywide stretch targets are included in the global scorecard, such as a step increase in operating margins, a decrease in inventory turnover, Six-Sigma quality targets, and not least leadership development objectives. These are reported to the shareholders in the annual report. Other companies, such as Intel, have similarly broadened the conception of performance management to complement the cycle of operational planning with strategic actions oriented toward long-term breakthroughs.[29]

STANDARDIZED MEASURES VERSUS LOCALIZATION OF OBJECTIVES. Multinational firms are rarely, if ever, faced with the same competitive position, the same economic situation, and similar institutional contexts in every corner of the world. Marriott and Citibank use worldwide customer satisfaction measures, but individual units can hardly be expected to achieve precisely the same scores.[30] Therefore, even the most globally standardized performance measures should reflect the differences as they are cascaded down to the local level. However, the logic behind differences often gets "lost in translation." For example, it is natural in a time of economic recession to mobilize the whole organization worldwide to cut costs by setting specific cost reduction targets. Yet it is counterproductive if this is expressed as a ban on adding headcount, particularly in business units that have an opportunity to increase profitability though growth.

It is also important to recognize that the structure of the measurement scorecard is different from the actual goals. Specific goals vary from one business to another and from one subsidiary to the next, and different units of the organization will have different strategic priorities—thus different performance indicators within the scorecard should be given different weights. As an outcome of the "upstream" performance management process, local goals must reflect local competitive realities; otherwise the next stage of the process—appraisal and evaluation—is doomed to run into problems.

The box "Obstacles to Global Collaboration" illustrates the consequences of using performance measures that encourage local suboptimization.

The "Downstream" Side of Performance Management

The "downstream" side of the performance management process consists of individual and team performance appraisal, feedback, and rewards, as well as performance evaluations linked to talent management.

Performance appraisal serves multiple functions—communication of organizational objectives, working out tensions in boss–subordinate relationships, providing information for self-improvement, guiding training and career

Obstacles to Global Collaboration

In order to increase focus and eliminate wasteful internal competition, a European engineering company—in which each business unit was evaluated strictly on the basis of its own P&L—allocated responsibility for the US market for power transmission to its US subsidiary. At the same time, responsibility for development and production of a specialized component gear was consolidated in Switzerland in order to gain sufficient economies of scale in a relatively small global market.

In the process of collaborating on a project in the United States, the Swiss engineers developed a close relationship with a US customer—who then wanted to use the Swiss-made equipment on another project in the United Kingdom. However, since the final contract for delivery in the UK involved a US customer, both the US and UK subsidiaries had to be brought in on the deal. With each claiming its share of the potential profits, participation in the project became financially unattractive to the Swiss.

Source: Adapted from Y. Doz, J. Santos, and P. Williamson, *From Global to Metanational: How Companies Win in the Knowledge Economy* (Boston, MA: Harvard Business School Press, 2001).

development, preparing evaluations that link to talent assessments, providing the basis for pay decisions, and building evidence to justify dismissals—many of which are in conflict with each other. Most US and European firms conduct yearly performance appraisals for all employees, but the appraisal cycle at Cisco takes place every six months, and many other high-tech companies such as Intel and TI have instituted similar policies.[31] There is an ever-expanding range of appraisal practices—some reflecting the latest managerial fad, while others leave a lasting impact on the way companies throughout the world approach this complex process. But any appraisal is rife with challenges, as experienced practitioners know and as HRM textbooks show.[32]

There is no shortage of evidence that performance appraisal may have unintended negative consequences. The father of the Total Quality Management movement, Edward Deming, argued forcefully that appraisal is so dysfunctional that performance improvement efforts should be focused on system improvement—getting at the root problems—rather than on symptoms that appraisal at best raises.[33] Other critics of the process may not go so far, but it is obvious that what is appropriate for one situation is often inappropriate for another. This is true in a domestic company, and even more so in the case of a multinational.

A big part of the challenge of getting it right is again that of global/local differentiation. The trend has been toward more globally integrated performance management practices, also downstream. We would argue that although multinational firms need a global template for the appraisal process, local business units may need some leeway to adapt that template to their circumstances. What is crucial is buy-in among senior management in the subsidiaries on how it should be executed in practice.

It is common to hear local objections and doubts: "Our culture is different, our labor laws are special, performance differentiation is not feasible, our operations are not mature enough." Some of these obstacles may be real, but in our experience many objections reflect the unwillingness to take on probably the most difficult part of any manager's role—to provide timely, fair, and constructive performance feedback. The fact is that most managers, irrespective of culture, find managing performance—especially formal appraisal—to be difficult, time-consuming, and uncomfortable.

Fitting Performance Appraisal with the Local Cultural and Institutional Environment

The concept of performance appraisal practiced today in many multinationals was developed in a Western context (mainly by US-based firms), and an argument can be made that it might not always suit the context of other cultures. There are myriad cultural obstacles to Anglo-American-style performance appraisal, many of them well described in the management literature,[34] ranging from the relationship between the employee and the organization and the nature of the manager–subordinate relationship to feedback and preferences about outcomes.[35]

For example, the manager–subordinate relationship is conceived differently in different cultures. In many cultures, the idea of a two-way dialogue in which the subordinate should be free to challenge the perception of the boss goes strongly against the heritage of power distance.[36] In collectively oriented cultures, behaviors that demonstrate loyalty and cooperative spirit may be just as important as the ability to achieve sales targets, unlike the situation in most Western firms.

Also, it is often argued that one legacy of the Maoist years, reinforced by the strong authority of the boss in the traditional Chinese culture, is that Chinese employees often avoid initiative for fear of being punished. Some Asian cultures do not share the sense of internal control of the Anglo-Saxons—how should a Western executive react when an Indian colleague inexplicably puts off a decision, perhaps having read a horoscope indicating that this would be an unfortunate time to make a choice?

However, there is no need to travel to the Orient to see global performance management constrained by the cultural and institutional context.[37] As late as the mid-1990s, German academic reviews of HR practices made no mention of appraisal practices or performance management.[38] Studies in the collaborative (as opposed to the calculative) culture of Denmark show that performance management was introduced step-by-step over a 20 year period.[39] Attempts to introduce performance management systems in the 1980s were resisted—people did not want to be measured. But in this collaborative culture where dialogue is the norm, performance feedback discussions started to become practice. Then gradually it became clear that these discussions would be improved if everyone agreed in advance on expectations—and so objective setting became accepted. And then why not link all of this to pay? This has been a recent development.[40]

This may be a healthier situation than in many US firms where performance appraisal is often driven more by fear of possible legal sanctions in case of employee complaints than by a genuine commitment to open and far-reaching dialogue.

Still, as we have learned from the example of Haier, making assumptions about a company's performance management based on the cultural or institutional context in which it operates may be misleading. When a company considers performance management as one of the factors supporting its competitive advantage, these constraints may be seen as secondary. One large Scandinavian firm introduced new performance management concepts—learned from its US subsidiary—into the home organization with the intention of overcoming the limitation of the parent country culture.[41] And as one of Haier's HR executives commented to us, "We don't want Haier to be an average Chinese company, so why should we follow what an average Chinese employee may like to believe in?"[42]

Frequently, culture is confused with status quo. Thirty-five years ago, it was predicted that management-by-objectives (MBO) would never take root in France because of the prevailing concept of authority, the avoidance of face-to-face conflict, and the negative connotations of control in that culture.[43] Yet only a decade later by the late 1980s, a survey of 220 large French companies reported that over 85 percent had a policy of fixing objectives for managers and conducting annual performance appraisal reviews.[44] Similarly, leading firms in Italy and Germany have been rushing in the last 15 years to introduce performance management approaches built around objectives and appraisal as an element connected with greater decentralization of accountability. In Japan, where performance evaluations were traditional practice but conducted in secret without formal feedback to the employee,[45] face-to-face performance interviews are now a standard part of managerial routine.

Evidence is emerging that with increasing attention to performance management as a factor driving organizational effectiveness, and despite cultural differences, there are signs of considerable convergence among multinational companies toward perceived best practices in performance management.[46] At least in the private sector, even domestic firms in Western and other countries are moving closer together in their approaches.[47]

Still, customizing the global performance management process to suit the local environment requires the multinational firm to consider the following issues carefully:

- To what extent can the firm implement practices that are at odds with the local institutional and cultural context? Being different may be difficult but acceptable, yet complying with local laws is essential. In Germany, for example, all information pertaining to appraisals is open to employees.
- What can be learned from other firms—not just other worldwide firms but also successful locally owned companies—whose performance management diverges from common local practices? If they can do it, why not others?

- How far is it possible to go in adapting locally without breaking consistency within a global organization? Without global performance management in place, many other global people strategies will be difficult to implement.

There is no simple answer to any of these questions, and one size definitely does not fit all. At the same time, commitment to implementing a rigorous appraisal and feedback process is more important than the sophistication of the methodology.

Providing Feedback

One element of performance management that often creates controversy with respect to cultural context is feedback, given different ways of confronting conflict in different cultures. While the discomfort that surrounds critical feedback is more or less universal, leading to many of the problems with appraisal, it may be particularly acute in certain cultures. A comparative study of performance appraisal practices in the three Chinese cultures of Hong Kong, Singapore, and Taiwan showed a common preference for group-oriented appraisal rather than individual assessment (though otherwise there were significant differences on most other dimensions of appraisal).[48]

However, despite the many cultural and institutional differences, there is evidence that Anglo-American-style appraisal feedback is spreading across the world, even in Japan—at least in multinational firms.[49] In China, where foreign companies were often told that direct feedback is nearly impossible to implement because of potential loss of "face," some firms are learning from Haier and breaking the mold. Similarly, as we have discussed, firms in continental Europe have gradually introduced performance management approaches built around objectives and appraisal as an element connected with greater decentralization of accountability. Multiple-rater appraisals are gaining popularity, particularly for developmental purposes, as outlined in the box "360° Feedback in Multinational Firms." In addition, advances in Internet technology make the global deployment of such systems increasingly easier to implement.

The way in which feedback is provided in the average local unit is, however, likely to vary from one culture to another. Asian cultures tend to deal with sensitive issues, such as negative performance feedback, in subtle and indirect ways; the idea of constructive confrontation is an alien concept for many Chinese and Japanese, though one should not generalize. While it is probably true that most Chinese employees resent direct negative feedback, there are always others who view the Haier-like "racehorse" environment as superior to the traditional emphasis on educational credentials and personal connections.

There is one practice concerning performance management that definitely applies across cultures—it is absolutely vital to train supervisors and managers in how to conduct appraisals. Virtually all multinationals with successful performance management processes have realized this, and performance appraisal training is today mandatory in many leading firms.[50] Such training stresses the

360° Feedback in Multinational Firms

Over the past 20 years, many firms around the world have developed feedback systems to provide managers with direct input on their strengths and weaknesses as leaders. As the pace of change has continued to accelerate, these tools have helped to formalize and speed up the natural, informal feedback processes of the past. Many different approaches have developed, but they all share one thing in common—individuals' own assessments of their behavioral skills are contrasted with the assessments of their bosses, their peers, and their direct reports. These assessments help managers to see the differences between the perceptions they have of themselves and those that others have of them. The results are used to help create appropriate development plans.

360° leadership assessments can be used for both development and evaluation. While there may be some overlap in these two aims, there are some important differences. Organizations that use 360° feedback for evaluation and appraisal often encounter problems in getting honest feedback. Participants will tend to select respondents whom they think will provide positive feedback if they think that it will be used to evaluate them. Managers whose bonuses depend on their 360° results will tend to think about their bonuses first and their development later. For this reason, many firms try to introduce such approaches by using the

results for development purposes, trying to keep 360° feedback separate from the performance appraisal process. As organizations acquire experience with 360° feedback systems, with greater acceptance of the process, they are better able to juggle the competing goals of evaluation and appraisal.

Attitudes toward the process of giving and receiving feedback can vary across nations, as discussed. In general, countries with high power distance and a dislike of conflict will be the most resistant to 360° feedback. But there are also many differences that occur at the firm level rather than the national level. Individual firms have their own values about power distance and managing conflict and may resist attempts at feedback. When a leadership 360° system is introduced into any organization for the first time, it is normal to have skepticism until the system becomes accepted and individuals become more comfortable with giving and receiving feedback.

Sources: M.A. Peiperl, "Getting 360-Degree Feedback Right," *Harvard Business Review*, January 2001, pp. 142–7; J. Ghorparde, "Managing Five Paradoxes of 360-Degree Feedback," *Academy of Management Executive* 14, no. 1 (2000), pp. 140–50; A.S. DeNisi and A.N. Kluger, "Feedback Effectiveness: Can 360-Degree Appraisals Be Improved?" *Academy of Management Executive* 14, no. 1 (2000), pp. 129–39. For more information, see www.denisonculture.com.

importance of well-prepared periodic appraisal discussions as well as ongoing coaching as ways to improve a person's performance.

Performance Evaluation: Linking Appraisal to Outcomes

The next component of the performance management cycle is the link between appraisal and development outcomes such as learning opportunities and individual development plans, the inclusion (or exclusion) of the person from corporate talent pools, and promotion/mobility decisions. Again, context matters. For example, a study of Chinese employee reactions to Western objective-setting and appraisal systems showed that while the processes of negotiating expectations and of performance feedback were often key for Western staff, it was the link between performance and career development that was most appreciated by the Chinese.[51]

One output of the appraisal is the formal performance evaluation of the employee, which typically feeds into the talent management and leadership development processes (described in the previous two chapters). Performance evaluation involves differentiation—typically employee performance is rated on an A–B–C scale; or on an A to E scale, where A is outstanding and E is unsatisfactory; or on an implicit Z curve (where for every person above the average there must be another person below).

While companies such as Schlumberger, Novartis, and Microsoft will acknowledge the need to vary appraisal and feedback processes according to culture, they are insistent on strict global consistency of formal performance evaluations. Every effort must be made to ensure that these evaluations are consistent and comparable across businesses and geographic units. If these performance evaluations are not comparable, then barriers to mobility and the transfer of knowledge are created. Other units are likely to dismiss transferees or learning opportunities by saying that "they only look good because they evaluate performance easily in that unit."

An important issue that arises from evaluation is how to deal with low performers. Leading firms, in particular the US-based multinationals, are redefining the standards in performance evaluation, getting tough in the process and opening up new controversy. Their aim is not only to reward the best but also to systematically weed out those who are underperforming relative to their peers—so Microsoft annually screens out about 5 percent of its workforce.

A visible champion of tough performance standards is GE's former CEO Jack Welch. GE's worldwide review of performance and potential focuses primarily on rewarding, retaining, and developing the top 10 percent of "A players" and quickly removing the "C players" in the bottom 10 percent. In a speech to Japanese industrialists, which one of the authors attended, Welch's remarks on leadership were frequently interrupted by applause, but his advice on how to deal with "C players" was met with stony silence.

One of the justifications for seemingly tough practices in firing low performers is that it may be better to force people out, so that they have the opportunity to restart their careers without the handicapping disadvantage of a bad reputation. A reputation as a low performer is often a self-fulfilling prophecy—see the box "The Set-Up-to-Fail Syndrome." People acquire poor reputations, they are passed from one department in the firm to another, and their performance and self-confidence continue to suffer. In these situations, as argued by Welch, early action may be better not only for the company but also for the individual.[52] A growing number of multinational firms identify low performers using quota systems but then allow up to 18 months to turn the individual either around or out.

The Set-Up-to-Fail Syndrome

The set-up-to-fail syndrome can develop whenever managers start to view certain subordinates as lower performers. Often, these implicit judgments occur early on in the boss–subordinate relationship—within a matter of weeks rather than months and based on initial impressions of attitude or potential. They can have a lasting impact on the performance and development of the subordinates concerned.[53]

What the boss thinks of as a "supporting" style often comes across to the perceived lower performer (PLP) as overly controlling. Typically, they do not receive the same resources, information, and opportunities as their colleagues who are viewed as more capable, making it difficult to prove the boss wrong. Their motivation is hit by the boss's close monitoring. Feeling micromanaged and underappreciated, PLPs may lose confidence in themselves and in their boss, and they often disconnect from their jobs.

Within a surprisingly short time, the PLPs may therefore start demonstrating the very attitudes and underperformance that the boss had anticipated, which means the boss has no reason to question his or her own role in the process. In fact, the self-fulfilling process becomes self-reinforcing as the boss adopts a more intense "remedial" approach.

Managers need to be mindful of the set-up-to-fail syndrome when working with subordinates from other cultures since there may be differences in views on what constitutes effective subordinate behavior. What the subordinate in a certain culture views as deference to the superior may be seen by the expatriate boss as a lack of initiative, triggering a negative cycle of interactions.

Circumstances today favor the spread of the syndrome—increasing bottom-line pressures for results creating hard-driving bosses; wider spans of control so that bosses have less time for each individual subordinate; and the increased prevalence of A–B–C quota systems of performance evaluation.

Challenges in Global Compensation

Historically, compensation policy was typically the most local area of performance management, although often within a broad global structure, such as some version of the Hay system of job classification. In fact, multinational firms have for many years exploited local differences by moving manufacturing and other functions from high-cost to low-cost countries. The one problematic and highly complex area was compensation for international staff (mostly home country expatriates) who moved from country to country. Today, this is changing and companies are considering how to harmonize the compensation of their employees across their worldwide operations.

The basis for a global approach to compensation is a common compensation and reward *philosophy*. Such a common philosophy and at least some commonality in compensation, benefits, and rewards across units are needed to create a common employee value proposition. This can mean, for instance, that the firm has a global policy concerning the average compensation level compared to the local market (that is, the company aims to compensate its employees at a certain percentile) and that common criteria are used to determine rewards. Benefits and actual levels of total compensation for most employees may still differ across countries.

However, it is increasingly difficult to uphold differences in compensation among employees from different geographical units. The examples described in the box "How Should the Bonus Be Paid?" show that what is global and what is local are far from easy to determine.

What guidelines can we get from research? An academic review by Bloom and Milkovich points out the evidence that the design and implementation of reward systems—from pay-for-performance to team-based pay, from stock

---

How Should the Bonus Be Paid?

An American software company operates development centers in California and Bangalore, India, where the programmers are paid in line with local market rates. A critical project that involved extensive coordination between the two locations required a radical redesign, with a deadline that could be met only through extraordinary effort. The company decided to offer a significant bonus to all the programmers involved as long as the redesign was undertaken in time. But how should be this bonus be distributed? In proportion to base pay, taking into account the income gap between the United States and India? Equally among the two groups? Or in proportion to the individual contribution to the success of the project, irrespective of work location?

Consider also the dilemma facing GIC in Singapore, the government fund management firm charged with investing the country's financial reserves on world markets. In the past, it recruited local professionals to fill fund management and analyst jobs, paying them according to local civil service standards. As GIC expanded overseas, it hired talented non-Singaporean staff—again paid locally, but often more than their counterparts at the head office. Today the top foreign staff members are being transferred to Singapore on a permanent basis—and how should they

be paid? The salaries of their peers in foreign-owned financial institutions in Singapore reflect global market conditions—paying less would violate external market equity, making it impossible to retain the best. But if foreign hires are paid at global rates, this will create internal inequity with their Singaporean colleagues. So why not treat all professionals as "globals"? That is possible, but it would then create external inequity with respect to other government employees.

Similarly, top managers at one of Norway's largest international corporations did not worry if a few Americans earned more than them because the Norwegian state would take most of any increment in taxes. But when a large number of middle-level professionals around the world were earning significantly more than the head of a global business at home, it created a disturbing sense of inequity, leading them to advocate a worldwide review of compensation practices. While the members of management teams of subsidiaries are today typically part of a common corporate system of performance-based reward management, many companies wonder if variable compensation, skill-based reward practices, and risk-based compensation such as stock options should not be generalized across local operations.

options to executive compensation—are highly dependent on context.[54] There are national legal constraints (for exampl, it is difficult to pay on a piece-rate basis in Germany or not to pay for overtime in Japan), and differences in taxation systems often argue for local differentiation. But national culture is only one element of context. Variations in norms and values within cultures are just as important as variations across cultures.[55] Consequently, there is considerable variance in compensation practices across firms, industries, and sectors within most nations.

For example, the approach to reward management at Lincoln Electric (combining pure piece-rate compensation and generous bonuses with norms of total transparency to create a strong culture of self-reliance) is fundamental to the success of that firm. Such an enterprise might be obliged to consider extremely carefully the location of its operations. It might avoid countries where institutional barriers render its reward system nonviable, and it should pay meticulous attention to the selection of people (as Japanese firms have done when establishing operations in the United States). In other firms, compensation practices may be less strategic and consequently more of an issue for local management.

In either case, global reward decisions are full of difficult questions. One such question is how rewards should be tied to the balance of global versus local results. There are convincing arguments that compensation should be linked only to outcomes that the employee can influence.[56] This would mean that linking pay directly or indirectly to global results would benefit only a select few in the organization. Others assert the opposite, pointing to the evidence that firm performance improves when the individual rewards at all levels are at least partially tied to broader objectives.[57] And, of course, in some country or industry environments it is accepted that employees may share some of the unit- or firm-level risk, whereas elsewhere such choices may be constrained by custom or regulation.

One cannot consider rewards separately from the other elements of performance management or from the wider context of recruitment and socialization. The Lincoln and Haier examples lead us to emphasize that it is the internal consistency of practices and norms that is powerful—even though consistency creates its own constraints.

SUPPORTING GLOBAL COORDINATION

Unless both upstream and downstream elements of performance management are aligned to reward broader dimensions of performance beyond one's job or immediate business unit, it is unlikely that we will see strong collaborative behavior or support for wider global corporate initiatives. From this perspective, the performance management process is an indispensable part of global coordination.

We will consider two aspects of global coordination where performance management may have a particularly strong influence. First, we will discuss how performance management may impact various mechanisms for lateral steering, among others global account management. Second, we will examine factors influencing performance management in global teams.

Enabling Lateral Steering

There are several imperatives worth repeating that are essential for performance management to successfully support horizontal coordination:

- The underlying approach to measuring performance, what is valued in the organization and how it is measured, has to be global in order to make the various mechanisms of horizontal coordination work in a synchronized manner. The internal consistency and coherence of practices and norms create an environment for lateral coordination.
- Having a global scorecard does not mean that everyone must have the same priorities. But it is important that the inevitable tensions regarding conflicting priorities be explicitly recognized, and that there be clear guidelines concerning the process and the principles on how these should be handled. In ABB, the customer must come first, the corporation second (including the business area and/or country), and the profit center third.
- The third imperative is to recognize the conflict between individual job responsibility and accountability and the demands for lateral coordination and cross-boundary teamwork (the operational and project roles in the "split egg"). Therefore, global teamwork usually requires top management sponsorship, explicitly recognizing the benefits and contributions of global collaborative behavior.

The difficulties in managing performance are likely to be most acute when individuals who are not performing well in their own jobs or whose business units are underperforming are asked to work on cross-border projects, coming under unreasonable pressure to improve their own individual performance *and* to work on lateral coordination teams. If key coordinating roles are staffed by managers who are still settling into new jobs or who have mediocre reputations, this will compromise the success of the global effort. Only people with credibility can successfully manage the inevitable tension between conflicting but legitimate priorities that naturally emerge in any global business.

These lateral project roles typically demand leadership initiative, and they complement job mobility as a way of developing global leadership competencies.[58] A good guideline is *to pay* for job performance but *to promote* for global leadership initiative in split egg project roles. This ensures that the senior ranks of leadership are drawn from a talent pool with a proven global mindset and an excellent track record in working across borders. Without recognition and incentive, it may be difficult to attract high potentials into positions requiring lateral accountability.

Project-oriented global professional services firms like McKinsey and Accenture are in the forefront when it comes to applying performance management that facilitates cross-boundary coordination activities. There, senior partners spend up to a quarter of their time on evaluating managers and partners, collecting the 360° views of clients, research and back-office departments, managers, and subordinates about the contribution of partners and managers.[59]

In Chapter 6 we discussed the vital role of three elements of social architecture in supporting horizontal coordination. However, global social networks, shared values, and global mindset are unlikely to be effective without continuous reinforcement through both subtle and explicit recognition and rewards. This imperative is now recognized by many leading multinationals, irrespective of national origin. The now popular expression "boundaryless behavior" was coined by Jack Welch, who during his years at the helm of GE was very explicit about his determination to break down the silos and foster cross-border collaboration.[60] Today, IBM based in the United States, Toyota based in Japan, Nokia based in Finland, Cemex based in Mexico, Infosys based in India, and Haier based in China have all included in their performance management systems explicit measures intended to support global collaboration. See Table 9–1 for an example drawn from a leading multinational consulting firm.

However, as was noted earlier, cross-border collaboration does not and should not eliminate constructive competition inside the organization. Competition as such is not destructive, though it can quickly become so when measures and rewards are solely focused on individual outcomes.

Many years ago, one of us had the privilege to discuss this issue with Soichiro Honda, the founder of the automotive company bearing his name. Honda himself was famous for his love of racing and fierce competitiveness. He was asked, "Excuse me, Honda-san, but isn't there a contradiction between your emphasis on competition and the core Japanese value of *wa* [harmony]?" Honda pondered the question for a few seconds and then answered, "No, there is no contradiction. Collaboration inside a company is a must. And if I help you more than you help me, then I win."

Performance Management for Global Accounts

A number of these dilemmas are seen when the deployment of lateral coordinating elements is impacted by the performance management philosophy of the multinational firm. Global account management (GAM) is probably the most typical example.

TABLE 9–1. Appraising Global Collaboration at Bain

- Client contributions: What have you done to build our relationship with customers or clients?
- People development: What have you done to recruit and develop the talent for future partners?
- Knowledge contribution: What have you done to increase the intellectual capital of the firm?
- Reputation building: What have you done to enhance the reputation of the firm?
- One-firm behavior: What have you done to build relationships within the firm?

Source: J.R. Galbraith, Designing Matrix Organizations That Actually Work (San Francisco: Jossey-Bass, 2009).

The GAM unit is usually embedded in the global sales organization, an area where tight links between individual performance (usually expressed in terms of sales targets) and short-term financial rewards are generally accepted, even in companies that do not believe in pay-for-performance as a source of employee motivation. However, results in the global account arena come almost by definition from team effort. So if ABB in Germany sells a piece of equipment to a Volkswagen factory in China, who should get the credit for the sale? The sales manager in China, the sales manager in Germany, or the global account manager for Volkswagen sitting in Switzerland?

Most companies resolve this problem by double/triple counting, giving the credit to all involved based on some pre-agreed formula (ideally not too complex!) or on general guidelines for appraising the individual sales effort. They argue that extra effort spent on perfecting the internal allocation of profits would not create much value for the customer, and it might send the wrong message to the employees about what is important.[61]

However, how to work out the bonus formula is probably the simplest issue to resolve. More difficult is figuring out how to motivate global account managers to interface with the customer not only from the point of view of the short-term sale cycle, but also taking into account the long-term relationship with the customer—in effect acting as customer representatives inside the organization.[62] And a related challenge is how to motivate people outside the sales organization to offer customer support. Collecting and disseminating customer feedback on a regular basis, with quick follow-up action, is the starting point for orienting the performance management process in this direction.

If global accounts represent a high proportion of sales, from a compensation perspective this probably means moving at least partially away from the bonus-heavy incentive structure common in many sales organizations, toward fixed salary and a relatively small bonus geared to longer-term targets such as revenue growth. But this also supports the arguments that employees working on global accounts must be essentially self-motivated, and that performance management processes must be anchored in outcomes other than money—individual competence development, career advancement, opportunities to work in an international environment, building relationships with other good people.[63]

Appraising and Rewarding Teamwork

The insights of Soichiro Honda on competition in teams are relevant for global teamwork. Effective team appraisal should not only reward good team players and discourage behaviors that are not conducive to global team effectiveness,[64] but also provide data on differences in performance among the team members.

Performance Appraisal Criteria for Team Members

There seems to be broad agreement that beyond task-specific criteria, the appraisal of team members should include items that are oriented to the team process, such as collaborative problem solving, support of other team members, and effective conflict resolution. With respect to the latter item, since preferred styles of conflict resolution may differ across cultures, what should be rated is resolving conflicts (with implied sensitivity to cultural differences) rather than adherence to a particular approach.

The use of objective criteria to evaluate individual contribution enhances the fairness of the process. A major challenge for many managers of global virtual teams is their inability to physically observe the contribution of their employees. Therefore, it is important to evaluate team members on what they actually do and accomplish rather than what they appear, from a distance, to be doing. When managers have objective data at their disposal, contamination of evaluations by perceptual or cultural biases is also less likely.

Sabre, a US-based multinational offering products and solutions to the travel industry worldwide, has built a comprehensive performance review system using actual customer satisfaction ratings as part of a balanced scorecard measure of global team effectiveness. Sabre managers access individual contributions to the team results by monitoring electronic communications and by systematically collecting data from peers and direct reports.[65]

But how objective are peer ratings collected across different cultures? Some researchers have suggested that team members from collectivist cultures may give more generous evaluations of their fellow team members than team members from more individualistic cultures.[66] Others have proposed that members from highly assertive cultures might be more likely to provide negative feedback than those in less assertive cultures.[67]

The perceptions of the fairness of team appraisal may also vary across global team members. In particular, US studies have shown that employees are concerned about the fairness of team-based performance appraisals, as they may not have the opportunity to rebut or challenge the ratings. However, there is also evidence on the biases in the performance evaluation process of virtual teams.[68]

How to Improve Global Team Appraisals

How can companies enhance the effectiveness of the appraisal of global teams? The typical recommendations from both researchers and practitioners are similar to those one would give for any generic appraisal:

- Include process criteria and a multidimensional mixture of objective and subjective ratings.
- Enhance the fairness of global peer evaluations by training all raters and using job-relevant rating scales.
- Make managers (and team members) accountable for their ability and willingness to provide ratings that differentiate between low and high performance.

Emphasis on process-related criteria may help to tackle the difficult choice between rewarding team members for their individual contributions or the team accomplishments. It may seem obvious to reward team members based on the output of the team, but research evidence is contradictory; in virtual settings,

TABLE 9–2. Rewarding Global Teams: Some Observations from Research

- Team-based reward strategies require stability of group membership.
- Some cultures may prefer rewards based on individual performance, although there is no conclusive evidence on how this translates into work settings.
- It is not only about money; independently of cultural differences, recognition and career opportunities are often as motivating as financial rewards.
- Involvement of team members in designing the reward structure may help foster its future effectiveness.
- High task interdependence increases the valence of team rewards relative to individual-based rewards.
- In project-based global teams, objective setting, the focus of appraisals, and the rewards should be tailored to the stage of the project.

team-based pay seems to lead to high performance as often as it contributes to social loafing.[69] And even with the best of intentions, the priorities of the daily job usually prevail over the more distant team targets.

Given the difficulty in aligning individual and team-based rewards, it is not surprising that some observers see inadequate reward and recognition practices as the single most important factor behind failures of global teams.[70] In this respect, linking positive team behaviors with individual financial rewards may be one way of giving team members incentives to support team performance.

While research on performance appraisal in global teams is still in its infancy, some conclusions seem to be holding reasonably well, as indicated in Table 9–2.

In most circumstances, full-time global teams where the cross-border linkages are important and regular, such as global key account teams, should be rewarded on the basis of team performance, not on the performance of the individual members. If the extent of cross-border linkage is only moderate, financial incentives are less important, as global teams provide many intrinsic rewards: learning challenges, increased visibility, and opportunities to build personal social capital. However, one of the best ways of appraising and rewarding individuals is through the talent review process—indeed cross-boundary projects are an integral tool of leadership development.[71]

PERFORMANCE MANAGEMENT OF INTERNATIONAL EMPLOYEES

Probably no other group of employees in a multinational firm has a bigger impact on global coordination than expatriates—home or third country nationals on international assignments. Therefore, the performance management of international employees—from senior managers to trainees in development positions—is of critical importance, leading us to look at this part of the performance management system in greater detail.

Appraising Performance of International Staff

As we have discussed, conducting performance appraisals in a multinational firm is rarely easy, but the difficulties are compounded with respect to international staff. We will focus on two key issues: What criteria and standards should be used; and who should conduct the performance evaluation?[72]

What Standards and Criteria to Use?

Multinationals around the world use fairly similar criteria in evaluating the performance of their subsidiaries, though the specific targets and standards will obviously be different.[73] However, when it comes to the performance evaluation process of expatriates, there are greater differences. Some companies keep expatriates in the parent country pool for appraisal purposes; some treat expatriates as they would a local employee in the same job.

Many environmental factors such as exchange rate fluctuations, local borrowing costs, and differences in the tax regime have an impact on the performance of the subsidiary, which in turn will affect the performance evaluation of expatriates occupying senior management positions in these subsidiaries. Defining performance in multinational firms is a complex issue, going well beyond matters of accounting, and the way in which performance is measured can have a major impact on how expatriates act. In most situations, objective (measurable) performance criteria (global or local) will have to be supplemented with subjective and contextual ones.[74]

Another critical tension that impacts performance criteria for international staff is the difference in the time horizon of expatriates and locals—short-term success in the job versus accountability for the long-term performance of the business unit. Indeed, short-term focus is one of the most frequent criticisms leveled at expatriate managers by their local subordinates.[75] Rightly or wrongly, expatriates are often perceived as caring about results only within the time frame of their expected assignments.

Who Should Conduct the Evaluation?

A frequent complaint about international staff appraisal is that many expatriates are evaluated mainly by superiors or HR managers in the home office, who may not have much international experience.[76] One global expatriate survey suggested that about 50 percent of the expatriates were monitored and evaluated at least in part by executives in their home countries.[77] Are such raters truly capable of making a correct evaluation? It certainly seems fair to suggest that only those who can observe them in action can have a solid opinion about their developmental needs. Knowing that performance is being judged only at the head office may also induce the expatriates to spend more effort in managing the center rather than the business. On the other hand, it should be said that if the performance of the international employees is evaluated only in the host country, there is a risk that the global perspective will be neglected. One is led to conclude that some form of 360° appraisal is advisable.

The extent to which local managers have an input into the performance appraisal of expatriates is a good indication of the degree to which the company is following a meaningful localization strategy. Yet such inputs do not eliminate the risk of perverse results. In one major multinational, local members of staff politely praised even overtly incompetent expatriates. They knew that if they said anything negative, they would be saddled with the individual for a longer period of time!

One of the challenges in performance appraisal is that people from different cultures often misinterpret one another's behavior.[78] Parent and local managers may also have different perceptions of the priority of different performance criteria and how the expatriate role should be carried out. The use of multiple raters, located both in the host country and in the parent organization, is likely to produce the most valid evaluations.[79]

Does One System Fit All?

Most companies use globally standardized procedures and forms for appraising the performance of expatriates.[80] However, the criteria used to evaluate the performance of the expatriate should reflect the purpose of the assignment—be it corporate agency, problem solving, building experience, or competence development.[81] For example, as we illustrate in the box "Managing Performance of International Staff at Nokia," one of the lessons from Nokia's global expansion is that performance objectives for international staff should be differentiated in the sense that expatriates who occupy different roles should be measured on different criteria.[82]

One of the important decisions a multinational company has to make with respect to the performance management of its international staff is therefore to determine whether such a system should cover all types of expatriate assignments,

Managing Performance of International Staff at Nokia

Nokia[83] has extensive experience with international assignments. Managing expatriate performance is critical to the success of the firm's global business.

Over the years, Nokia has developed a comprehensive global performance management program that includes goal setting, performance appraisal and feedback, continuous training and development, and performance-related compensation. This performance management system is implemented worldwide, but for the purpose of the actual assessment the company's expatriate population has been broadly classified into five groups based on

the nature of their job assignments: (1) senior managers, (2) middle managers, (3) business development, (4) project engineers and specialists, and (5) R&D professionals.

All these categories share some common practices. For example, all expatriates participate in goal setting so they know what is expected of them; they all receive specific feedback on how well they are performing; and they learn about the opportunities to develop new competencies in order to meet present and future job requirements. However, the various expatriate groups are treated differently with respect to how their performance is managed. These differences focus on

- How performance goals are set, who sets them, and what types of goals are set.
- How performance is evaluated and who is responsible for conducting the evaluation.
- What kind of training and development opportunities are available to the expatriates.
- How close the linkage is between performance and the expatriate's pay.

For example, expatriates in senior manager positions are usually appraised by executives from the home office, and their appraisal is likely to have a longer-term focus, with respect both to the current roles abroad and to career and developmental implications. Expatriates in the middle manager group are typically appraised by locally based executives, with the appraisal and incentives linked more to local, relatively short-term goals.

Performance goals and incentives for expatriates in business development and customer project assignments are more tied to the specific nature of their tasks than the earlier two categories—focusing on start-up objectives for the former, and meeting deadlines for network operations is common in the latter.

Source: M. Tahvanainen, "Expatriate Performance Management: The Case of Nokia Telecommunications," *Human Resource Management,* 39, no. 2/3 (Summer/Fall) 2000, pp. 267–75.

or if each category should be treated separately. Our recommendation, similar to the system introduced by Nokia, is the latter approach. In our view, a tight alignment between the purpose of the assignment and the objectives to be evaluated is a necessary foundation for linking the appraisal to rewards—if the upstream of the performance management process does not fit, the downstream will fail as well. However, few multinationals at this time have adopted such a differentiated approach, which indeed involves tackling additional complexity.

Compensation of International Staff

Surveys often show that the cost of expatriation is a major concern of international firms.[84] This is not surprising as the total cost burden for the company is estimated at two to four times an expatriate's salary, depending on the location of the assignment.

The field of international compensation is more the domain of compensation specialists and consultants than of academic research.[85] Over the years, international companies and consulting firms have developed elaborate systems to account for cost-of-living differences between countries, to respond to variations in tax regimes, or to provide incentives for employees to work in so-called hardship areas. Developing an effective international compensation system is a task that goes far beyond technical analysis and is in fact linked closely to the company's internationalization strategy.

The Evolution of International Compensation Strategies

Historically, an expatriate pay package was usually the result of individual negotiations. Since foreign assignments were not considered particularly desirable from the point of view of career progression, financial incentives such as relocation premiums were common. The result was generally high and continuously escalating expatriate compensation costs, accompanied by corresponding difficulties in repatriation after the completion of the assignment.

With the increasing number of expatriates, the ad hoc negotiation-driven approach outlived its usefulness. The next generation of compensation plans attempted to provide at least a common base—usually the home or host country salary, whichever was highest—reducing the size of the negotiated component.[86] However, as the number of international employees continued to grow, so did the need to move away from location-specific approaches to more generic across-the-board compensation schemes.

Today, a number of generic methodologies have emerged (see Table 9–3).[87] The determination of what kind of specific international compensation plan to select is influenced primarily by three sets of considerations:

- Cost efficiency—making sure that the plan delivers the intended benefits in the most cost-effective manner (including tax consequences).[88]
- Equity issues—making sure that the plan is equitable irrespective of the assignment location or nationality of the expatriate.
- Ease of system maintenance—making sure that the plan is relatively transparent and easy to administer.

TABLE 9–3. A Summary of International Compensation Systems

	For Whom Most Appropriate	Advantages	Disadvantages
Negotiation	• Special situations. • Organizations with few expatriates.	• Conceptually simple.	• Breaks down with increasing numbers of expatriates.
Localization	• Permanent transfers and long-term assignments. • Entry-level expatriates.	• Simple to administer. • Equity with local nationals.	• Expatriates usually come from different economic conditions than local nationals. • Usually requires negotiated supplements.
Headquarters-Based Balance Sheet	• Many nationalities of expatriates working together for extended periods.	• No nationality discrimination. • Simple administration.	• High compensation costs. • Difficult to repatriate TCNs[A].
Home Country–Based Balance Sheet	• Several nationalities of expatriates on out-and-back-home assignments.	• Low compensation costs. • Simple to repatriate TCNs[A].	• Discrimination by nationality. • Highly complex administration.

Modified Home Country–Based Balance Sheet	• Many expatriates of many nationalities on project assignments.	• Moderate compensation costs. • Moderately simple administration.	• Lack of conceptual purity.
Lump-sum Approaches	• Consistently short assignments (less than three years), followed by repatriation.	• Resembles domestic compensation practices. • Does not intrude on expatriate finances.	• Exchange rate variation makes unworkable for all except very short assignments.
International Pay Structures	• Senior executives of all nationalities.	• Tax- and cost-effective. • Expatriates and local nationals may be on the same compensation plan.	• Inhibits mobility for lower levels of expatriates. • Lack of consistency among locations.
Cafeteria Approaches	• Senior executives.	• Tax- and cost-effective.	• To be effective, options needed for each country. • Difficult to use with lower levels of expatriates.
Regional Plans	• Large numbers of expatriates who are mobile with region(s).	• Less costly than global uniformity. • Can be tailored to regional requirements.	• Multiple plans to administer. • Discrimination between regionalists and globalists.
Multiple Programs	• Many expatriates on different types of assignments.	• Can tailor compensation programs to different types of expatriates. • Possible lower compensation costs.	• Difficulty of establishing and maintaining categories. • Discrimination by category. • Highly complex administration.

[A]TCN = Third country nationals, as discussed in Chapter 4.
Source: C. Reynolds, *Guide to Global Compensation and Benefits* (San Diego: Harcourt, 2001).

We will examine in more detail the costs and benefits of one method that is commonly used by North American and European firms—the balance sheet approach—and we will also review some of the emerging trends in international compensation.[89]

Balance Sheet Approach

The term "balance sheet" refers to any compensation system that is designed to enable expatriates to maintain a standard of living roughly equivalent to the standard of living in their own country, irrespective of the location of their assignment.

FIGURE 9–1. Balance Sheet Approach to International Compensation

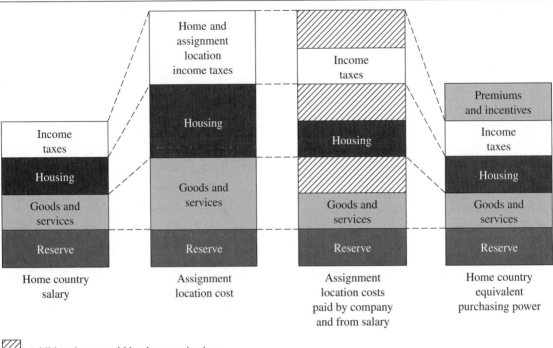

Additional costs paid by the organization

Home country salary is divided proportionately into several components based on norms (see Figure 9–1). A typical breakdown is goods and services, housing, taxes, and a reserve. Home and host country expenses for each component are compared and the expatriate is compensated for the increased cost.

The balance sheet approach is popular, as it is seen as maintaining in a reasonably cost-effective manner the purchasing power of the expatriate, thus eliminating most of the direct financial obstacles to mobility. In reality, given that many expatriates complain about reduced compensation upon repatriation,[90] this methodology tends to overcompensate—but probably less so than most alternatives.

While the balance sheet methodology is simple in concept, it is complex to implement. For example, what is the definition of the home country for the purpose of the balance sheet calculations? When expatriates all come from the same country or economic region, work abroad for a single two-to-three-year assignment, and then are expected to return to their home country, there is no ambiguity. But if expatriates in the same foreign location come from different countries with substantially different costs of living, the result may be unacceptably wide discrepancies in compensation. If the company uses the headquarters location as "home," then expatriates from countries with lower compensation standards will be difficult to repatriate. Some companies use a modified approach where the real home is the base for goods and services while headquarters standards are applied to housing (the most visible component of compensation) (see Figure 9–1).

While the balance sheet approach is a well-accepted methodology, it has further limits. It encourages people to import their lifestyles, thereby creating barriers between expatriates and locals, especially in countries with lower purchasing power. It also eliminates any incentives for expatriates to moderate their spending patterns as they learn to navigate in the new environment. Further, since a sizable part of compensation and lifestyle is guaranteed, it is difficult to establish a clear connection between results and rewards.

Alternatives to the Balance Sheet Approach

Increased heterogeneity of international staff may require a "global" compensation package in which national origin or home has no impact, at least for senior executives. Consider the case of the vice president of a US-based firm, leading a global business unit located in Tokyo. If this person comes from the United States or Europe, it is taken for granted that housing arrangements will reflect the lifestyle back home. If the successor happens to be Japanese (for example, just returning from a senior assignment at headquarters), does this mean that no housing allowance should be paid?

Some version of a cafeteria approach is becoming increasingly more appealing. A weakness of the balance sheet approach is its reliance on norms tailored to the "average" expatriate. Again, the increased heterogeneity of the international staff is creating havoc with this assumption. For example, the balance sheet approach does not work well for those expatriates whose spouses suspend their own careers. For some expatriates, support for their children's education may top the list of essential benefits, while for others it may be long-term care for parents left behind. The cafeteria approach to benefits, pricing such benefits and permitting choice within a limit, is often essential.

For short-term assignments, it may be more convenient to provide simple lump-sum payments to cover the additional expenses and let the expatriates manage their finances the way they see fit. This avoids unnecessary entitlements or intruding too much into private financial circumstances such as tax status.

In some firms, the vast majority of international assignments are confined to a specific region (e.g., the EU or ASEAN). In that case, it may be advisable to tailor the policy to the conditions within that region rather than apply a worldwide policy. Again, differences in treatment of "regional" and "global" expatriates have to be carefully monitored. When employees with similar management responsibility receive dramatically different compensation (usually housing allowance is the biggest differentiator), morale and commitment are bound to suffer. A typical case would be pay inequity among regional office staff composed of multiple nationalities—often with at least three different pay packages: local, regional, and global.

Trends and Challenges in International Compensation

The fact that so many are unhappy with the state of international staff compensation is certainly not caused by a lack of available methodologies. The problem is that most pay methodologies make universal assumptions about where expatriates come from, their roles, and where they are going. However, the population of international employees is increasingly diverse, and no single system can provide satisfactory solutions to the multiple demands of international assignments.

As we have argued, the motives for cross-border transfers vary from one category to another. If a firm's international staff consists of several categories, then compensation packages should arguably be tailored to the specific needs of each group. For example, the financial services group HSBC has four different categories of expatriates (international managers, who are globally mobile senior executives who are moved from one location to another; secondees; "contract executives"; and short-term assignees, mostly technical staff), each with different compensation and benefits packages.[91]

In some firms, this may lead to a unified global compensation plan for the senior executives irrespective of their location, a balance sheet approach for managers and professionals transferred across borders, and essentially local pay packages for entry-level and junior assignees. Alternatively, the company may have one system for career expatriates and another for those on short assignments.

Consequently, when it comes to the choice of compensation strategy for international staff, the starting point is to clarify two key questions:

1. What categories of international staff should the company have?
2. Should all categories of expatriates be paid using the same method?

The answers to these questions will depend on the evolution of the internationalization strategy, the HRM philosophy, and the composition of the international staff population. It is also important to bear in mind that compensation is only one of the factors that determine an employee's desire to accept an international assignment. Nonfinancial rewards, such as learning opportunities and expectations of future career gains, are also important motivators.

One of the growing challenges in the area of international compensation is how to pay TCNs—the fastest-growing segment of the expatriate population. While it may seem logical that pay should be based on home country levels, adjusted for a cost-of-living differential (plus housing and similar allowances), TCNs do not necessarily identify with their home country. And when the differences in living standards between the home country and country of assignment are large, problems are bound to arise—often compounded by misapplication of the traditional expatriate compensation logic.

Today, TCN expatriates have become an increasingly heterogeneous group posing new challenges for the management of international assignments. High-potential TCNs have many alternative opportunities. As for all expatriates, there is no single best formula for TCN expatriate compensation. The purpose of the assignment, its duration, the expected work location after its completion (many TCNs do not return home, continuing to the next international assignment)—all impact the choice of compensation scheme. Any compensation formula that relegates TCNs to the status of second-class "cheap labor" will cause serious damage to morale inside the organization.

The issue of pay equity between international staff and local employees (and across various national groups within international staff) is emerging in importance. While the principle that employees should not be paid less when moving to a different location is well accepted, there are limits. When the cost of an expatriate middle manager equals the cost of 20 locals, it may be hard to convince local employees of the importance of keeping operating costs down.[92]

A related challenge is the compensation of "returnees"—employees returning to their home country on an assignment, usually as expatriates with a foreign passport. When a Chinese-born manager returns to China (usually after acquiring a Western MBA) with a compensation package that is superior to his or her former local peers, she will face considerable resentment from colleagues who feel they have lost out twice—first, because they could not study abroad themselves, and second, because they are being bossed by someone who is getting much better pay and who they believe may not be any better than themselves.

The home country bias of international compensation plans may also be a handicap for international staff from low cost countries. As pointed out by a Malaysian marketing director, "When expatriates come to us, they end up living in bigger houses than at home. When I was offered a job in New York, I moved from a large bungalow with three helpers to a small flat in Manhattan—and my wife had to interrupt her career to take care of the family." There are no simple and easy solutions to this and other problems of pay inequity—other than a radical shift in total compensation philosophy away from country of origin to job content.

Given the complexity of expatriate pay, it is not surprising that in many multinationals—such as NokiaSiemens Networks—it has become common for international assignees to sign local contracts. The traditional, generous expatriate contracts are increasingly confined to only a select part of the international staff.

IMPLEMENTING GLOBAL PERFORMANCE MANAGEMENT

Performance management is an indispensable part of global coordination, and there is an ever-expanding range of practices—some reflecting the latest management fads, others leaving a lasting impact on how companies around the world approach this complex process. What is appropriate for one situation may be inappropriate for another, and probably no other element of people strategy generates as many debates and controversies as performance management.[93] We have summarized the ideas discussed in the chapter in Table 9–4, showing best practices in global performance management.

TABLE 9–4. Best Practices in Global Performance Management

Design principles
- Coherent—aligned to global strategy, vision, and values.
- Simple and easy to use in multiple languages.
- Flexible to reflect changes in the nature of the business.
- For everyone, not only for high performers.

Processes
- Line accountability/ownership.
- Globally consistent, but reflecting local differences.
- Focus on dialogue, not the process or the form.
- Senior management commitment.

Measures
- Explicit link to global and local business goals.
- Not only what, also how.
- Customer feedback incorporated.
- Support for collaborative behavior.

Outcomes
- Understanding what needs to be delivered.
- Key inputs to guide global mobility and development.
- Link to tangible rewards.
- Commitment to action.

Fundamentals
- Fair and transparent.
- Motivational—creates energy.
- Remains constant, not changed all the time.
- Should not be another bland system—differentiate!

When it comes to implementing global performance management, three overarching issues frame the implementation process:

1. How to make sure that it is the line function and not the HR function that "owns" the implementation of any performance management system?
2. How can companies resolve the perennial tension between the competing interests of a global approach versus local adaptation?
3. How can performance management systems contribute to building distinctive capabilities?

Who "Owns" Performance Management?

Although the general idea of performance management is now widely accepted by multinational firms across the world, its implementation invariably runs into problems unless there is commitment from the top down on the part of line management—including local management teams.

Why is the commitment from the top so critical? Although HR usually provides the administrative and coaching support, the responsibility for making the process work lies with the line management, starting at the top of the organization. If senior managers are seen as visibly taking the time to engage in managing performance, including its developmental aspects, others will follow. For example, the attention that senior bankers pay to appraisal at Goldman Sachs is legendary in the finance industry: collecting 360° views, data, and opinions from around the world, feeding them back and working them through, carefully balancing judgments on individual achievement and teamwork. Tremendous care is also given to the design and administration of the bank's compensation system, which must balance rewards for individual achievement and support for the team.

In other words, performance management is a time-consuming and difficult task—in any culture—especially when it involves giving some employees honest feedback on less than stellar performance, justified by solid facts. This requires regular performance monitoring to collect those data—and then a lot of coaching to help the employee improve. So how can global organizations motivate their managers across the world to devote their most limited resource—their own time—to this difficult process? The answer is—through performance management!

What happens to managers who are doing a good job of performance management? And to those doing a bad job? If the answer is that there are no consequences and no differences in how those managers themselves are evaluated, then any performance management system is likely to fail.

Global Approach versus Local Adaptation

Many multinational firms have come to the conclusion that they should strive for a globally consistent approach to performance management, but the path to successful implementation is far from straightforward.

As discussed, the arguments vary with the elements of performance management. There is little doubt that the upstream setting of strategic objectives should be globalized, as is invariably the case. The template for the objective-setting process should be global, and there is a worldwide trend, even at lower levels of management and among professionals, toward objective-based management as opposed to an activity-based approach built around job descriptions. Performance appraisal is the area in which there are the strongest arguments for a mix of global and local approaches, while many multinational firms are coming to the conclusion that performance evaluation should be rigorously global. The situation regarding compensation varies from one company to another.

In addition to institutional/legal constraints on what is feasible, there are infinite variations in approaches to performance management, depending on corporate and national culture, industry, and even levels within the global organization. However, the higher the position of the employee, the greater the likelihood that a global approach will be applied. The strategic orientation of the multinational firm also has an impact on the form of performance management and its ease of implementation. For a meganational firm, introducing global performance management is easier than a similar move by a multidomestic enterprise, where the very concept of a "single" performance management process runs counter to the entrenched culture, norms, and behaviors.

As multinational companies adopt business strategies that pay more attention to the balance between global and local dimensions, their performance management approach usually follows. For example, in the early stages of Nokia's internationalization, profit and loss were measured only at a worldwide level, while local subsidiaries—run mostly by Finnish expatriates—operated on the basis of budgets with only cost and sales targets. Business results for local entities may have been reported for fiscal reasons, but local profitability figures were arbitrary owing to transfer pricing and cross-border cost allocations. When Nokia, in line with its strategy of moving toward a more transnational perspective, started to adopt a performance management system that would emphasize both local responsibility for financial results and alignment with global strategy, it required a fundamental overhaul of its approach to performance management, including the underlying IT and control infrastructure.

Creating Differentiation

Traditionally, debates around performance management systems in multinationals were about fitting them into the local context, usually the environment of the local affiliate. We will conclude this chapter by pointing to the opposite challenge. The deeper issue is not how to fit, but how to build distinctive capabilities—how to differentiate—the last point in Table 9–4.

In Chapter 2 we identified differentiation as one of the guiding principles for HRM in multinational firms, and performance management is one area of HRM where differentiation can indeed have a large impact. Lincoln Electric is an example of a successful corporation that is strongly differentiated from its competitors by its approach to performance management. However, when such companies go abroad, they typically have a dilemma, as Lincoln did; their approach to performance management may not fit with the local context. Does this mean that there is no benefit for a multinational firm from differentiation in its human resource management practices?

A recent review of global performance management commented on the need to align it with the local context as follows: "The notion of 'sharing' rewards or credits for an accomplishment is as foreign a notion in individualistic countries, as say, an 'employee of the month' award would be in collectivistic countries like Japan, China, or Malaysia."[94] This makes intuitive sense—or does it?

Let us return to Haier. Today, one of the most coveted performance-related awards in the company is the "employee of the month" for young employees with less than five years' tenure in the firm. However, this award is not only a plaque on the wall. When employees are selected for the award, their parents are invited to Qingdao for a dinner with Mr. Zhang, today one of the most widely recognized CEOs in China. At the dinner, Mr. Zhang presents the parents with a personal letter thanking them for bringing up such an outstanding child—now a great contributor to Haier's future. The next day, the company PR machinery ensures that the letter and the picture of the parents with the CEO is reprinted in the hometown newspapers.

Is it motivational? It is! Does this mean that the researchers cited earlier were incorrect? Probably not. On average, employees in collectivist societies may indeed not care much about generic "employee of the month" awards. However, the award as deployed by Haier is not generic. Haier has found a way of making this individualistic reward into something distinctively Chinese, in a manner that differentiates Haier from any other company in China—and probably the world. The way Haier rewards its employees of the month reflects the context of contemporary China, with its one-child policy, as well as leveraging the reputation of the firm as a leading Chinese multinational. It is effective because in essence it is very Chinese, but at the same time because it is not in any sense typical. It differentiates.

The lesson from Haier is that differentiation through performance management is neither a question of ignoring culture nor one of "fitting with culture." Rather it means understanding, respecting, and reflecting culture at a much deeper level than broad generalizations about individualism and collectivism. Transnational firms need to be deeply sensitive to local cultural contexts not because they should emulate local practices, but because this knowledge can show them how to differentiate. What is important is to learn how to operate in the context of the local environment while maintaining distinctiveness. As discussed earlier, this may mean paying close attention to selection or socialization. Or, as with the Haier "employee of the month" scheme, it may involve tailoring a practice so that it is meaningful and powerful in the local context.

When a firm is creative in the way it locally adapts its management practices, rather than simply following what is done in the home country or emulating what local firms do, that may inspire other subsidiaries to be similarly innovative. Haier's subsidiary in the United States, for example, has to think through its employee award schemes. Should it copy the practice carried out in China? Probably not, because there is no Mr. Zhang in the US. Should there be a traditional US-style plaque on the wall and column on the company Web site? Are there other firms in the United States that have distinctive and successful ways of rewarding outstanding employees? Is there some other creative way in which the US subsidiary can differentiate itself and reinforce its competitive advantage while remaining true to the spirit of the Haier way?

Performance management is often viewed in mechanical terms as following either global or local practices, rather than as innovating to build distinctive sources of competitive advantage. As we have mentioned, no one wins by doing what everyone else is doing. Despite the weight of a process that in many multinationals is the most centralized of HRM processes, we see in the tension between the global and the local many opportunities for differentiation—as long as one tunes into what "local" means with creative sensitivity. In the future, we expect to see more multinational firms that foster continuous horizontal and bottom-up knowledge sharing and learning (not copying) around performance management practices within the enterprise.

TAKEAWAYS

1. The performance management process is an indispensable part of global coordination.
2. Performance management includes three successive elements: the specification of what is desired performance, involving setting goals and objectives (upstream); the review and evaluation of performance, including feedback; and linking the evaluation results to financial rewards and development (downstream).
3. The essential component of the performance management process is the consistency and tight link across the three elements—simple in principle, but potentially complex in practice, since the three phases of performance management are all too often disconnected.
4. There is little doubt that the upstream setting of strategic objectives should be globalized. Performance appraisal is the area in which there are the strongest arguments for a mix of global and local approaches.
5. There are at least two strong arguments for using a common and consistent system of measurement scorecards throughout the multinational firm. Global scorecards reinforce a global mindset among employees, and joint performance objectives encourage dispersed units to collaborate.
6. Problems in managing performance are likely to be most acute when individuals who are not performing well or whose business units are underperforming are asked to work on cross-border projects, coming under pressure to improve their own performance and *at the same time* work on global teams.
7. Most companies use globally standardized procedures and forms for appraising the performance of expatriates. However, the criteria used to evaluate the performance of the expatriate should reflect the purpose of the assignment.
8. Most global pay methods make universal assumptions about where expatriates come from, their roles, and where they are going. However, the population of international employees is increasingly diverse, and no single system can provide satisfactory solutions to the multiple demands of international assignments.
9. Differentiation through performance management is neither a question of ignoring culture nor one of "fitting with culture." Multinationals need to

be deeply sensitive to local cultural contexts not because they should emulate local practices, but because this knowledge can show them how to differentiate.

10. Commitment to rigorous performance management is more important than the sophistication of the methodology.

NOTES

1. Pucik, Xin, and Everatt, 2003.
2. Note that one should avoid associating performance management with a particular culture, as in some popular characterizations. We know of many well-established Anglo-Saxon firms for whom the performance management ideas discussed here are as alien as for the Chinese state-owned enterprises in the era before the period of economic reforms.
3. As reported by Grote (2000), a survey of best practices in performance management ran into problems when many clearly model companies declined to take part.
4. This combination of competition and cooperation is called coevolution. Eisenhardt and Galunic (2000) argue that coevolution is the key to realizing internal synergies in multidimensional organizations, allowing business teams to quickly identify and execute collaborative opportunities.
5. Björkman et al., 2008.
6. It may be noted that Vance (2006) in his discussion of global performance management uses the terms "upstream" and "downstream" with a different meaning than we do.
7. Locke and Latham, 2006. See also Locke and Latham (1990). Goal-setting theory is not without its critics, however. Ordonez et al. (2009) argue that one should be aware of the side effects of goal setting in the shape of neglect of non-goal domains, inhibited learning, reduced intrinsic motivation, and a rise in unethical behavior.
8. Goold and Campbell, 1987.
9. Hansen, 2009.
10. Quoted from the GE 1994 Annual Report.
11. Stretch goals have a dual purpose—they promote organizational effectiveness and personal growth. Although these purposes are not mutually exclusive, organizations usually employ stretch goals for one reason or the other. See Kerr and Landauer (2004).
12. "Job Review in 140 Keystrokes," *BusinessWeek*, March 23 and 30, 2009.
13. The BP Peer Assist process is described by Ghoshal and Gratton (2002), and the quotation from BP's deputy chief executive is taken from this article.
14. Mintzberg, 1994.
15. Building on his experience as head of planning for Royal Dutch/Shell, De Geus (1988) argues that planning should be considered as companywide learning rather than an analytic process—one of mobilizing people and building commitment to action in the lower reaches of the organization.
16. Locke and Latham, 1990; 2006.
17. Lindholm, 1998.
18. Latham, 2004.
19. Becker, Huselid, and Ulrich, 2001; Huselid, Becker and Beatty, 2005.
20. There is empirical evidence that business analysts assess long-term performance in terms of top management's balanced attention to financial, employee, and customer stakeholders (Kotter and Heskett, 1992).

21. Kaplan and Norton, 1996, 2001.
22. Kaplan and Norton, 1996, pp. 144–5.
23. Flamholtz, 2005.
24. Becker, Huselid, and Ulrich, 2001.
25. Huselid, Becker, and Beatty, 2005, p.70.
26. This point is discussed in a box on "Managing the Sweet and the Sour" in Chapter 11, when discussing change management. See page 450.
27. One of the frequent criticisms of MBO-type processes is that they place too much emphasis on individual objectives (often to facilitate the determination of individual rewards) at the expense of collective commitment to a broader business strategy.
28. Doz, Santos, and Williamson, 2001, pp. 98–9; Goss, Pascale, and Athos, 1993.
29. Burgelman and Grove, 2007.
30. Vance, 2006.
31. In some Japanese firms, performance appraisal for younger employees may take place several times during the year—but without direct feedback. See Pucik, 1989.
32. Cascio, 2006; Varma, Budhwar, and DeNisi, 2008.
33. Deming, 2000.
34. Schneider and Barsoux, 2003.
35. See Schneider and Barsoux (2003) and Cascio (2006). To give one specific empirical study as an example, Vance et al. (1992) found significant differences in managerial style across the United States, Indonesia, Malaysia, and Thailand, which hampers the transferability of appraisal practices across borders. See also Hofstede (1999).
36. Hofstede, 2001.
37. See Claus and Briscoe (2008) for a review of research on performance management in multinationals.
38. Sparrow and Hiltrop, 1994, p. 557.
39. Gooderham, Nordhaug, and Ringdal (1999) show that some European firms and countries have a hard calculative approach to HRM while others have a more collaborative approach.
40. By 2000, nearly one-third of all Danish organizations were offering bonuses to managers. The source for this section on Danish practice is discussions with Professor Henrik Holt Larsen at Copenhagen Business School.
41. Lunnan et al., 2005.
42. See Shen (2004) for an analysis of performance management in Chinese corporations.
43. A frequently cited study is that of Trepo (1973), which Hofstede, Trompenaars, and other culturalists frequently use as an example.
44. Reported by Sparrow and Hiltrop (1994).
45. Pucik, 1984.
46. Faulkner, Pitkethly, and Child, 2002; Shadur, Rodwell, and Bamber, 1995; Harzing and Pudelko, 2007.
47. Shadur, Rodwell, and Bamber, 1995.
48. Paik and Stage, 1996. For example, Hong Kong managers disliked participative appraisal practices, whereas the Taiwanese accepted close supervision more than those in Singapore or Hong Kong.
49. Claus and Briscoe, 2008.
50. Cascio, 2006.
51. Lindholm, 1998.
52. Welch, 2005, p. 45.

53. Manzoni and Barsoux, 2007.
54. Bloom and Milkovich, 1999. See also Bloom, Milkovich, and Mitra (2003) and Festing, Eidems, and Royer (2007).
55. Pucik, 1997.
56. Expectancy theory argues that there should be a tight linkage between (1) the efforts made by the employee (or team/unit), (2) how the performance of the person is measured, and (3) rewards associated with good performance.
57. Milkovich and Newman, 2005.
58. See the discussion of mobility and action learning in Chapter 8.
59. Ghoshal, 1991.
60. Ashkenas et al., 1995.
61. Galbraith, 2000, p. 219.
62. To give this long-term perspective, many firms want global account managers to be willing to stay in their jobs for a long period of time, seven to eight years or more. IBM, for example, also makes a big investment in training global account managers who need strong general management skills to manage the network of relationships with the firm and that of the client firm. These positions often suit the requirements of high potential managers who want some stability in their private lives for family reasons.
63. Birkinshaw and DiStefano, 2004.
64. Gibson and Kirkman, 1999.
65. Kirkman et al., 2002.
66. Kirkman and Den Hartog, 2004.
67. House et al., 2004.
68. Research shows that differences in demographic factors such as race and gender can lower performance ratings for team members who are different from the team leader. See Kirkman and Den Hartog (2004, p. 251).
69. Social loafing effects have been found in a variety of countries. See Kirkman and Den Hartog (2004, p. 252)a nd Thompson (2000).
70. Kirkman and Den Hartog, 2004.
71. The talent review process and the role of such teams in leadership development are discussed in Chapter 8.
72. While the topic may be highly relevant, data and empirical evidence concerning these issues are still scarce. In contrast to the extensive literature on expatriate selection and development, the research domain of international performance management (e.g., criteria, processes, and outcomes) is quite unexplored. A recent review article identified only 11 empirical studies on this topic over a 20-year period (Claus and Briscoe, 2008).
73. Borkowski, 1999.
74. Dowling and Welch, 2005.
75. The perception of expatriates as "short-termers" is so common that it may block any effort to drive long-term change. Advice that is often given to expatriates who are assigned to manage a change project is "Never reveal when you are going home!"
76. According to Gregersen, Black, and Hite (1995), only 11 percent of US HR managers involved in planning international assignments have international experience themselves.
77. Brookfield Global Relocation Services (2009), Global Relocation Trends 2009 Survey Report (www.brookfieldgrs.com). Also, one study of 99 Finnish companies operating internationally reported that in 79 percent of the firms the performance appraisal of expatriates was conducted by the superior located in Finland (Tahvanainen, 2000),

while a more recent study of 301 Finnish expatriates found that a supervisor in the host country was the most typical evaluator (Suutari and Tahvanainen, 2002).

78. Stening, Everett, and Longton, 1981; Torbiörn, 1985.
79. Gregersen, Hite, and Black, 1996.
80. Gregersen, Hite, and Black, 1996; Shi, Chiang, and Kim, 2005.
81. See Chapter 4.
82. Tahvanainen, 2000.
83. The box describes the expatriate performance management system in what now is Nokia Siemens Networks.
84. Reynolds, 1995.
85. Suutari and Tornikoski's (2001) study of Finnish expatriates is one of the very few exceptions. There is also a stream of research on the compensation disparity between expatriates and host country employees from a justice perspective (see for example Chen, Choi, and Chi, 2002).
86. The idea is that expatriates never receive less than they would be paid at home.
87. For a comprehensive review of international compensation methodologies, see Reynolds (1995; 2001, Chapters 4 and 5).
88. For a summary of tax strategies for international compensation, see Orchant (2001).
89. A survey conducted in 2006 found 80 percent of the firms to apply a balance sheet approach ("2006 Worldwide Survey of International Assignment Policies and Practices," ORC, New York, 2007).
90. Black et al., 1999, p.180.
91. "Traveling More Lightly," *The Economist*, June 24, 2006, pp. 99–101.
92. As we will discuss in Chapter 12, this matter is of particular relevance in the case of joint ventures and alliances.
93. In a recent review of relevant research, Cascio (2006, p. 193) also concluded that the field of global performance management is "largely unchartered."
94. Kirkman and Den Hartog, 2004, p. 253.

CHAPTER 10

Managing Knowledge and Innovation across Borders

Driving Global Innovation at Procter & Gamble

Procter & Gamble (P&G) was founded in Cincinnati in 1837. Initially, the company produced soap and candles, but the firm eventually diversified into a range of different consumer goods. An important reason for P&G's growth and success in the decades after World War II was its ability to create innovations, like the industry's first cavity-prevention toothpaste Crest, the heavy-duty synthetic detergent Tide, and the two-in-one shampoo product Pert Plus.

P&G had established its first overseas marketing and manufacturing unit through an acquisition in the United Kingdom in 1930, and it proceeded to expand rapidly abroad after the war. The company originally based its R&D activities in the United States, but since the mid-1980s, P&G has built up a worldwide R&D network, with research hubs in the US, Europe, Japan, and Latin America.[1] However, while the company continued to develop innovative new products in the 1990s, by the turn of the century profits were lackluster, the stock was underperforming,[2] and P&G was facing decreasing returns on its investments in R&D.[3] Of the new product introductions, only a minority returned the development costs.[4]

The company knew that many of the best innovations came when combining ideas from different parts of the corporation. It also had some positive experiences when acquiring new products from outside the firm. The problem was that such connections occurred all too seldom. In 2000, the new CEO, A.G. Lafley, set out to change radically the way the company went about innovation. He set a goal that 50 percent of new products should stem from ideas acquired from outside the company. Lafley thought that this would require a change in "the company's attitude from resistance to innovations 'not invented here' to enthusiasm for those 'proudly found elsewhere.' And we needed to change how we defined, and perceived, our R&D organization—from 7,500 people inside to 7,500 plus 1.5 million outside, with a permeable boundary between them."[5]

The new model that P&G developed was called "Connect + Develop." The goal was to tap into knowledge and ideas outside the company, from entrepreneurs, university labs, individual researchers, its business partners, and even from its competitors. An additional aim was to improve the sharing of knowledge and ideas within the company. P&G appointed 70 senior technology entrepreneurs to work in six regional Connect + Develop hubs, focusing on finding products and technologies that were specialties of their regions. The firm further developed 21 global communities of practice—networks of scientists working in the different business areas.[6]

A strong focus was placed on understanding better the company's customers. Once a year the company created a top-10 consumer needs list for each of the business units. The needs were then developed into science problems to be solved and written up in technology briefs that were communicated throughout the company. P&G also implemented new IT solutions supporting the innovation process. These included an intranet with "ask me" features that some 10,000 employees could use to post questions concerning technologies, products, and processes as well as a secure IT platform to share the technology briefs with the company's suppliers. Finally, the company helped create several firms that operated open networks, typically Web-based, connecting scientists, companies, universities, and government labs.[7]

The Connect + Develop model has been a resounding success. A case in point was the development of a new Pringle potato chip printed with words and pictures. Somebody had come up with the idea in a brainstorming session, but it was not clear how it could be done technically. In the past, P&G would have launched an internal R&D project, but for the printed Pringle it developed a technology brief that was communicated throughout the corporation and its external networks. This led to a small bakery in Bologna, run by a university professor who had invented a method that could be adapted to fit the purpose. The new product, Pringles Prints, was launched in 2004. In less than a year and at fraction of what it otherwise would have cost, P&G had developed a double-digit growth business.

In under 10 years, P&G's innovation success rate (the percentage of new products that return the investments made in them) has more than doubled. The number of new products originated from outside the firm has risen to 35 percent, while R&D spending has been reduced from 4.5 percent of sales in the late 1990s to 2.8 percent in 2007.[8]

Implementing the new model for capturing knowledge across borders has not been easy, requiring a change in the social architecture of the firm. First of all, processes had to be developed to enable Connect + Develop. The functional silos between R&D, marketing research, manufacturing, and other functions had to go, as well as the barriers that had existed between the different business units. Heavy emphasis was placed on building lateral social networks by transferring people across business, functional, and geographical lines. These networks were important throughout the whole process—from the initial idea, through product development and creation of a prototype, to eventual global commercialization—also helping the transfer of best practices across the business areas.[9]

OVERVIEW

As we have seen, P&G has gone through three phases in managing knowledge and innovation. From a time when virtually all its core capabilities were focused in the United States, P&G shifted to coordinating R&D activities that had been built up worldwide. Today, the firm is renowned for effectively tapping into external sources of ideas, transferring and combining these to create new products within the firm (often in collaboration with external partners), which are then introduced across markets for rapid commercialization.

Other multinationals, such as P&G's Swiss competitor Nestlé, have historically been more multidomestic, but Nestlé too has been working hard to increase knowledge transfer among its international subsidiaries, moving toward more globally coordinated innovation processes. Although their trajectories have been different, both companies currently face similar challenges: how to make sure that the knowledge residing in their dispersed operations can be acquired, assimilated, and used productively in other parts of the organization; and how to make sure that they use external as well as internal sources to develop new products. In recent years, a new open innovation model has emerged, whereby multinationals work much more closely with outsiders while at the same time building a high level of cross-boundary collaboration within the firm.

Scholars and business leaders agree that innovativeness and effective sharing of knowledge are important for company performance.[10] While the focus in our introductory P&G story was on the development of new products, the concern with the management of knowledge and innovation is relevant for every part of the corporation. All functions struggle with the issue of how to share knowledge across units and how to innovate in manufacturing processes, in offering services more efficiently and effectively, and in ways of managing the corporation.[11]

In this chapter we describe how to manage knowledge and innovation in the multinational. We first discuss how to facilitate knowledge sharing across geographically dispersed units, which depends on cross-unit social networks, organizational values of collaboration and support, and global mindsets among employees. We also discuss structural mechanisms and a range of HR practices that enhance knowledge sharing. We use experience of international professional service firms to illustrate how different approaches to knowledge sharing are associated with different HRM orientations.

We then explore how multinationals can access and retain external knowledge from different parts of the world. Knowledge acquisition requires investment in external scanning on a global scale; the development of partnerships with customers, research labs, and other organizations; and an ability to use the open market to identify complementary knowledge and interesting ideas. Again, people management and social capital play an important role in this endeavor.

In a global business environment, with shorter product life cycles and competitors that quickly imitate successful innovations, maintaining a competitive advantage requires the ability to innovate continuously.[12] Knowledge acquisition from outside the firm, sharing of knowledge with other organizational units and members, and the recombination of new and existing stocks of knowledge are integral parts of the process leading to corporate innovations. In the final part of this chapter we examine how international firms can manage the whole innovation process—from initial ideas, via the development stage, to worldwide commercialization of the final product or process innovation—and the ways in which HRM can contribute.

SHARING KNOWLEDGE IN THE MULTINATIONAL

The importance of interunit knowledge sharing is now generally well accepted[13]— P&G is only one example. One of GE's five "timeless principles" is the belief that "the ultimate sustainable competitive advantage lies in the ability to learn, to transfer that learning across components, and to act on it quickly."[14] This drove GE to create a boundaryless company by delayering, destroying silos, purging the not-invented-here syndrome, and attempting to create an organization that sees change as an opportunity rather than a threat.

In today's world of sophisticated worldwide markets and increasingly competent affiliates, the focus is shifting from the home country organization (transferring knowledge and new products from the parent organization abroad) to the ability to generate knowledge from local units, transferring this to the parent and other parts of the corporation. Indeed, Kogut and Zander argue that a primary rationale for the existence of multinational firms is their ability to transfer and exploit knowledge more effectively and efficiently than market mechanisms.[15]

Two kinds of knowledge are important to multinational firms. Explicit, or codified, knowledge is knowledge that individuals and organizations know that they have—objective, formal, systematic, incorporated in texts and manuals, and relatively easy to pass on to others.[16] Virtually all knowledge stored in IT-based databases and systems is explicit. In contrast, tacit knowledge is personal, context specific, and hard to formalize and communicate. Individuals may not even be conscious of the tacit knowledge they possess. Tacit knowledge often underlies complex skills, but it is built on the intuitive feel acquired through years of experience and is hard to put into words.

In the past, successful internationalization typically depended on the ability of the multinational firm to transfer superior tacit knowledge residing in the home country organization to its overseas affiliates. Expatriates played key roles in this transfer. In spite of the technological advances over the last few decades, transfer of personnel and person-to-person interaction are still the main ways in which tacit knowledge can be shared and transferred.

In contrast, the advances in information technology have had a big impact on the ability to transfer explicit knowledge. While written manuals and blueprints have always been important in the transfer of explicit knowledge across units, the development of advanced IT-based systems played a central part in the booming interest in knowledge management in the 1990s. Since tacit and codified knowledge are shared through different channels, from an HRM standpoint, the development and sharing of different types of knowledge should be managed in different ways.

Similar conclusions can be made with respect to the specificity and strategic value of knowledge. Some knowledge is firm-specific, unique to the enterprise, and this should be managed differently from knowledge that is more generic and available to all competitors. Knowledge also varies according to its strategic importance to the enterprise. Snell, Lepak, and Youndt developed a framework (shown in the box "Different Forms of Knowledge and HRM") that emphasizes the need for a differentiated approach to knowledge management from the perspective of HRM.

Factors Influencing Knowledge Sharing

As we mentioned earlier, the ability to create and share knowledge across the different parts of the firm is commonly seen as an important source of competitive advantage. Multinational organizations have the potential to access knowledge across a variety of different geographical, cultural, institutional, and social contexts. Units located in different environments are likely to develop different types of knowledge, and this diversity of knowledge can be a great asset to the multinational if it can be shared effectively across these boundaries. However, facilitating knowledge sharing is a complex task. Knowledge is "sticky,"[17] and its stickiness is reflected in the costs associated with knowledge sharing. To overcome the challenges involved in interunit knowledge sharing, firms need to pay attention to a range of technological, organizational, and people-related issues. Our focus here is on HRM aspects of knowledge sharing, but we also discuss a number of organizational issues.

Consider the following example from a firm with which one of us has been working. This multinational corporation has six factories around the world, manufacturing almost identical products using the same equipment, the same tools, and roughly the same work processes. The factories' yields vary from 77 to 98 percent, but they neither knew the productivity of the other units nor shared information about the production process. The obvious question to ask in this situation is how to make sure that the units share knowledge with each other, improving the productivity of the laggards and perhaps also that of the top performers. The degree to which such knowledge sharing takes place depends on (1) the ability and willingness of the sending unit or source to share knowledge, (2) the motivation and ability of the receiving unit,[18] and (3) the suitability of the mechanisms (channels) used to share the knowledge.

Different Forms of Knowledge and HRM

	Low	**High**
High	IDIOSYNCRATIC KNOWLEDGE	CORE KNOWLEDGE
Low	ANCILLARY KNOWLEDGE	COMPULSORY KNOWLEDGE

Firm specificity/ uniqueness

Strategic value

Core knowledge is both unique to the firm and high in strategic value, such as Walmart's expertise in logistics and inventory control, or Toyota's manufacturing capabilities. This constitutes the firm's current source of competitive advantage, and it must therefore be carefully nurtured by HRM, with emphasis on transferring knowledge and capabilities across units by investing in social capital. The employment mode here is oriented to internal development and providing a high level of job security.

Compulsory knowledge may be generic across the industry and of high strategic importance. It is akin to the notion of "table stakes" in card games, essential for a chance to compete but offering no distinctive competitive advantage. Maintenance of the basics is important since a strike, for example of delivery drivers at UPS or FedEx, may be very costly to a firm. But the approach to HRM is likely to be more market-based, since people with such generic skills can be more easily acquired. Compulsory knowledge can also be obtained through acquisitions.

Idiosyncratic knowledge refers to know-how that is unique to the firm, though not necessarily of clear current strategic value. The likelihood that tomorrow's core knowledge may come from this pool drives the HRM approach. General R&D and investment in slack resources are ways of generating idiosyncratic knowledge. The employment mode is often oriented toward partnership alliances to spread the risks.

Ancillary knowledge, which is low on both strategic value and uniqueness, is increasingly likely to be outsourced or automated—examples are administrative activities, such as payroll and accounting. There is no value in investing in building either human or social capital.

Source: Adapted from S.A. Snell, D.P. Lepak, and M.A. Youndt, "Managing the Architecture of Intellectual Capital: Implications for Strategic Human Resource Management." In *Research in Personnel and Human Resources Management: Strategic Human Resource Management in the 21st Century*, eds. P. Wright, L.D. Dyer, J.W. Boudreau, and G. Milkovich (Greenwich, CT: JAI Press, 1999).

Sender Unit Ability and Willingness

The measure of a unit's ability to share knowledge with others can be labeled its "pedagogical ability."[19] With respect to explicit knowledge, pedagogical ability is shown in the source unit's proficiency in codifying knowledge in manuals, reports, and physical systems that are available to other parts of the corporation. However, sharing tacit knowledge is more difficult, and the ability to do so is therefore more crucial for successful sharing to take place. As pointed out, it almost always requires interpersonal, often face-to-face, interaction. Good language and communication skills and a good understanding of cross-cultural factors are some of the ingredients of the pedagogical ability needed to share knowledge across borders.

For knowledge sharing to take place, the source of the knowledge must be willing to share it. In the example at the beginning of this section, the manufacturing units were unwilling to share information about their productivity with others, and even less interested in teaching others how to improve their operations, owing to strong competition between plants. Since the headquarters executives were critically reviewing the structure of the company's international network of manufacturing units, the plants were competing for resources, even survival. Why help others learn something that was a key advantage for their own unit? The subsidiary managers were mostly evaluated on their own unit's performance, strengthening their internal focus and decreasing their willingness to collaborate. Thus, as we will explain, the example shows how interunit knowledge sharing is influenced by the performance management system of the firm and the compensation and rewards that go with it.[20]

Social status and reputation play important roles in shaping the context for knowledge sharing. People gain status when they are perceived as knowledgeable, and sharing knowledge with others is a good way to enhance their reputation. People who are given credit for having shared knowledge are more likely to do so again in the future.[21] This mechanism operates at both an interunit level (does the other unit acknowledge the knowledge source?) and a corporate level (does top management recognize those who share knowledge?). Are there strong social networks within the multinational where reputations are built and people learn not only what the useful sources of knowledge are but also who is willing to engage in problem solving?

Norms of reciprocity are also important. Units and individuals are more willing to invest in sharing their knowledge with others if they trust them to reciprocate these favors in the future. Teaching others requires considerable effort, and in the absence of strong social relationships between the parties, the decision to engage in knowledge sharing is usually based on some calculation of whether or not it is worth the time and money.[22] A higher level of trust is therefore associated with more knowledge sharing, as is the existence of a strong organizational culture, where knowledge sharing is an important shared value.

Receiver Unit Ability and Willingness

Not surprisingly, research has shown that the ability of the receiver to absorb new knowledge is a strong predictor of the extent to which the unit receives knowledge.[23] Absorptive capacity is largely an outcome of the existing stock of knowledge—people who know a lot can learn more than people who know only a little.

Leonard-Barton suggests that one can distinguish between four different levels in the absorptive capacity of a foreign subsidiary, ranging from the capacity (1) to operate assembly or turnkey equipment, (2) to adapt and localize components, (3) to redesign products, to (4) to design products independently.[24] The higher the subsidiary's capacity, the more likely the unit will be able to receive tacit knowledge and put it to productive use by combining this new knowledge with its existing know-how. Developing a high level of capacity to absorb knowledge takes time. For example, according to Leonard-Barton, it took Hewlett-Packard's Singapore unit 20 years to reach level III, and Fuji-Xerox (a joint venture company of Xerox in Japan) 10 years, even when building on a more advanced local knowledge infrastructure. It took HP Singapore almost 30 years to reach level IV.[25] Naturally, a subsidiary may have a higher level of absorptive capacity in some areas than in others, and the ability to profit from the knowledge of others will therefore vary from one domain to the other.

There are paradoxes around absorptive capacity. When two units are similar, it is much easier to understand and absorb knowledge from the other; knowledge sharing is facilitated. Conversely, similar units have less to learn from each other. The more their knowledge overlaps, the less there is to be gained from investment in knowledge sharing.

Absorptive capacity is more than just the ability of a unit to recognize the value of new information, to assimilate it, and to apply it to commercial ends.[26] It also includes the capacity to unlearn, to challenge existing ways of doing things. Generally speaking, the more satisfied people are with current practices and results, the less willing they are to seek out and absorb new knowledge. And even if people realize that they are facing a problem that needs to be tackled, inward-looking units with strong internal social networks may not actively search for relevant knowledge held by other parts of the corporation.

Lack of motivation on the part of many units to learn from others is well documented. There is a natural psychological tendency to inflate the perceived quality of one's own knowledge while deflating that of others. The not-invented-here syndrome has been described in a number of case studies, and is particularly strong if a unit is financially successful and has a long proud history.

Also, the value of the knowledge in question for the receiving unit is rarely clear. When the source unit is perceived as knowledgeable, others will be more interested in learning from it.[27] In the absence of reliable information about the quality of other units' knowledge, people tend to look most to well-performing subsidiaries and those located in the most advanced markets.[28] There is also an understandable tendency to select similar units—those that follow a similar strategy and share common organizational characteristics—as those one can learn most from.[29] However, it is not only the potential usefulness of the knowledge that is difficult to assess; the efforts and costs associated with accessing and assimilating this knowledge in the receiver unit are also unclear. Therefore, the likely return on investment associated with knowledge acquisition and sharing is difficult to estimate.[30]

Ways to Share Knowledge

Explicit and tacit knowledge need to be shared in different ways. Explicit knowledge is the easiest to access and acquire, and also to share within international firms. To the extent that tacit knowledge can be codified, it can be shared through databases, manuals, and blueprints. The consultancy firm Accenture has made big investments in the development of a global knowledge management system consisting of several thousand databases. The system is managed and promoted by 500 knowledge managers around the globe. Consultants are expected to enter information about their projects into the system, where it can be accessed by other members of the organization. One study reported that it was common for an Accenture consultant to access more than 10 different databases daily.[31]

However, most employees—just like a typical academic—are notoriously bad at entering useful knowledge into databases, and not all tacit knowledge can be made explicit. And even though some knowledge is codified, there is usually a need to combine it with tacit knowledge. We have already discussed some of the ways in which firms can share tacit knowledge. In Chapter 4, we showed that a reason for sending people on assignments abroad is to transfer their expertise, while repatriation and impatriation transfer knowledge about the local scene back to the home country. The close interactions of experienced expatriates with employees in their units offer ample opportunity for sharing tacit knowledge.[32] Short-term personal interactions during visits, international conferences and meetings, and corporate training sessions may fulfill the same function, but they are likely to be most successful for knowledge that is explicit and/or relatively narrow in scope.[33]

In our view, too much emphasis has been placed on the "push" of knowledge transfer and sharing and too little on the "pull" from the receiving unit.[34] As the old saying goes, you can lead a horse to water but you cannot make it drink—unless it wants to. Multinationals can benefit from focusing more on stimulating units to adopt knowledge and practices from other parts of the corporation.

How to Stimulate Knowledge Sharing

Multinational firms can use numerous levers to make knowledge sharing effective, efficient, and fast:

- Improving information about superior performance and knowledge.
- Designing structural mechanisms to share knowledge.
- Building a supportive social architecture.
- Implementing a comprehensive approach to mobility and talent management.
- Reinforcing sharing through performance management and incentive systems.

Improving Information about Superior Performance and Knowledge

One of the most obvious reasons for not drawing on knowledge residing in other parts of the multinational is that people are unaware of its existence. For instance, several units may have encountered similar problems in the manufacturing process but be unaware that one has found a viable solution. An often-heard expression illustrates this common problem: "If we only knew what we know." In fact, much of the interest in knowledge management stems from the problem of locating potentially valuable knowledge in large corporations.

As we have pointed out, units perceived by others to be highly capable are more likely to be sought out as sources of knowledge.[35] However, evaluation of a subsidiary's capabilities has a significant subjective element. Studies have revealed that there are only modest correlations between how managers from headquarters and foreign subsidiaries view the capabilities of overseas units.[36] Therefore, it is important to identify superior practices by measuring appropriate dimensions of unit performance. By making performance data widely available—turning the multinational into a fishbowl where strong performance is showcased—the units can themselves uncover examples of unique and valuable knowledge. For instance, Alfa Laval Agri from Sweden held quarterly meetings for all its subsidiary managers where they were required to present performance data along multiple dimensions. This approach triggered knowledge sharing among the units.[37]

Structural Mechanisms to Share Knowledge

Various structural coordination mechanisms can be used in part or even primarily to stimulate knowledge sharing. For instance, product development committees with members from different geographical units and from different functional areas (notably R&D, manufacturing, and marketing) are put together with the aim of tapping into the different perspectives and pools of experience that the members bring to the committee.[38] Temporary international task forces can serve the same purpose. Multinationals may also appoint individuals to liaise between units—for example as competence managers for a specific functional area or as part of a community of practice.[39]

The Knowledge Management Program (KMP) at the world's largest steel manufacturer ArcelorMittal (formed in 2006 through Mittal Steel's acquisition of Arcelor) illustrates how firms may create horizontal groups or committees to enhance interunit knowledge sharing (see the box "Mittal Steel's Knowledge Management Program"). Mittal Steel developed the program back in the 1990s when it expanded to Eastern Europe. The KMP process facilitated the integration process in the new ArcelorMittal group and helps build peer networks.

Working in split egg roles,[40] where managers and professionals have vertical and horizontal responsibilities, is at the heart of BP's focus on global knowledge management in its oil exploration and production business.[41] With the aim of making the unit more valuable than the sum of its parts, peer groups of business unit heads meet regularly. They are given joint responsibility for capital allocation

Mittal Steel's Knowledge Management Program

Mittal Steel chose 25 activities, including manufacturing, finance, maintenance, purchasing, legal work, and information technology, as a base for its Knowledge Management Program. Each of these had groups of approximately 20 members from different plants. They would meet regularly to benchmark the activities undertaken in the different units and to discuss common problems. For specific problems, the groups would use conference calls and smaller specialized ad hoc meetings. The diversity of the groups was viewed as a particular strength—according to Mittal Steel's chief operating officer: "These countries have some very good technology. The Poles, for instance, have always been good in coke-making, and we have recently had a Romanian manager who was very helpful in sorting out a blast furnace problem in Chicago."

Source: R. Muthu Kumar and S.K. Chaudhuri, "Mittal Steel's Knowledge Management Strategy," Case study no. 305-543-1. ICFAI, India, 2005.

and for setting unit performance goals, complemented by a host of cross-unit networks on shared areas of interest. These "top of the egg" knowledge-sharing activities take up to 20 percent of the manager's time. "The model here is an open market of ideas," says one business unit head. "People develop a sense of where the real expertise lies. Rather than having to deal with the bureaucracy of going through the center, you can just cut across to somebody in Stavanger or Aberdeen or Houston and say, 'I need some help. Can you give me a couple of hours?' And that is expected and encouraged."[42]

The knowledge management groups at ArcelorMittal and BP have many of the features associated with open communities of practice. These communities are characterized by some form of collaboration around a common set of interests. They differ from project teams and committees in that the participants' roles are not defined by the firm. Although the focus of these communities is on internal company issues, they may also broker relationships with outside experts. Communities of practice cannot and should not be fully controlled by the firm, building instead on voluntary participation, although corporate support and guidance are essential.[43] The box "Communities of Practice at Schlumberger" provides another corporate example.

Research on communities of practice offers some guidelines on how to make them successful. First, it is most important to have clearly understood objectives and a leader tasked with making sure that knowledge and best practices are shared and developed further. Second, the quality of interactions should be reinforced with workshops, training, exchange of staff, and an appropriate reward structure, with part-time coordination provided on the corporate budget. A study of less successful communities revealed that they lacked a core group of them; there was little one-to-one interaction between them; members did not

Communities of Practice at Schlumberger

At Schlumberger, a Web-based knowledge management system called Eureka links technical experts in its Oilfield Services business into communities of practice, with members having self-created CVs posted on the site. Such communities, formalized or informal, exist in all units to exchange tips, tricks, and conceptual understanding. Schlumberger had tried several times to organize its technical expertise scattered around the world top-down, but without success. In 1998, the CEO said that if the firm could not organize the professional side of the lives of its engineers, then "let them manage themselves." Seven years later, by 2005, there were 23 self-organized communities ranging from chemistry to rock characterization to well engineering, with 140 special interest subgroups and 11,750 members.

At Schlumberger, these communities are led by elected leaders, and elections are frequently contested. One of the few constraints is that community leaders need the backing of their bosses; they might spend 15–20 percent of their time organizing an annual conference and an occasional workshop, overseeing the Web site, and coordinating subgroups. Each technical expert within Schlumberger has two organizational "homes": the formal, hierarchically sanctioned home that corresponds to a position on the organizational chart; and the Eureka technical community, the informal, horizontally linked network of peers who share common interests, goals, and passions about their work in the corporation. Today's chief executive, Andrew Gould, says that the self-governing feature is crucial to the success of the Eureka communities since technical professionals are motivated by peer review and esteem.[44]

identify with the community; participants had a strong belief in their own competence; and the issues discussed were not illustrated concretely enough for others to understand and visualize them.[45]

Mittal refrained from appointing a "best plant" for others to emulate, believing that all units had something to teach others. In other cases, multinationals have appointed geographically dispersed centers of excellence that, among other matters, are in charge of knowledge sharing. Such centers can be formed in various locations around a small group of individuals recognized for their leading-edge, strategically valuable knowledge. As a center of excellence, they are mandated to make that knowledge available throughout the global organization, enhancing it so that it remains on the cutting edge.[46] In contrast to parent-driven knowledge development, these centers tend to rely more on informal networks, often acting as a hub for knowledge-sharing activities.[47]

Building Supporting Social Architecture

The social relationship between the source and the receiver is another strong determinant of knowledge sharing.[48] All three dimensions of social capital (structural, relational, and cognitive) are important.

The structural dimension refers to the pattern of relationships between people and units in the multinational firm. Without a connection of some kind between two units or individuals, it is virtually impossible to share tacit knowledge. Two units that already have a history of interaction are more likely to be aware of potentially useful knowledge residing in the other unit. Through existing relationships, people may gain important fortuitous insights even if they are not searching for ideas on immediate problems. They have also had opportunities to develop a common knowledge base and learn how to work together.[49] A large number of studies have confirmed that the degree of interunit communication is positively associated with knowledge sharing and innovation.[50]

The cognitive dimension of social capital reflects the extent to which two parties are capable of sharing their understanding. A shared language and specialized vocabulary facilitate the interaction of organizational units and greatly enhance their ability to learn from each other. It has been suggested that the construction of shared narratives—collective stories and myths—in a community can aid the sharing even of largely tacit knowledge.[51]

Trust is at the core of the relational dimension of social capital. When two parties trust each other, they are more likely to share knowledge, in part because they are confident that the other party will reciprocate tomorrow for help they receive today. Organizational units, teams, and individuals that are perceived as trustworthy are likely to be sought out by others to share know-how and experience.[52]

In large multinationals, it is also important to build a context that encourages people from different units to build new social relationships and initiate new collaborative efforts as well as capitalizing on existing networks. Therefore, two other aspects of social architecture—social values, beliefs, and norms as well as global mindset—also influence knowledge sharing in global organizations.

Social norms are important. Knowledge sharing will be encouraged if hoarding knowledge is seen as violating the company's values and if those who transfer know-how to other units are presented as heroes. With such norms, knowledge is more likely to be viewed as a corporate resource to be exploited throughout the organization.[53] An organizational culture where sharing and reciprocity are the norm will also encourage people to share insights and ideas with others, and to volunteer to help look for solutions to problems encountered in other parts of the multinational.

More knowledge sharing is also likely to occur in organizations where employees are encouraged to point out opportunities for improvement, and in firms where nobody fears that saying something negative about their own unit or organization will be detrimental to their career.[54] During the early stages of GE's internationalization, the company set up a series of workshops where executives shared their "global battlefield" experiences—with an explicit focus on where and why they failed. The message was loud and clear. It is OK to try something new and fail, but you'd better learn from the experience and make sure that others don't repeat your mistake.

Global mindset is particularly relevant for knowledge sharing in the firm. People who view diversity and heterogeneity as a source of opportunity are more likely to seek out and adopt knowledge from other parts of the multinational.

Mobility and Talent Management Considerations

The skills and knowledge of people are important because an adequate knowledge base is a prerequisite for absorbing new knowledge from others. Furthermore, those involved must speak a common language well enough to share tacit knowledge. While multinational enterprises from many different countries have adopted English as their corporate language, this has not eliminated the language-related problems in knowledge sharing among geographically dispersed units. A Swedish multinational provides an illustration. Headquarters managers noticed that there was a lack of knowledge sharing between the German subsidiary and its Scandinavian sister units. On investigation, it turned out that the general manager of the German subsidiary was not a confident English speaker and therefore did not participate in the informal discussions with his Scandinavian peers that were intended to lead to exchange of know-how. The appointment of an English-speaking deputy to the German subsidiary solved this problem.[55]

The transfer of personnel is one of the most important levers of knowledge sharing that firms have at their disposal. Typically, the transfer and assimilation of complex tacit knowledge into a new context requires the physical relocation of someone with experience—often an expatriate from headquarters. Impatriates may be expected to play the same role during assignments at headquarters and on their subsequent return to foreign units.

Toyota is a case in point. Over the last three decades Toyota's global strategy has been to gain market share by adding new manufacturing capacity in all its major markets.[56] To ensure flawless quality and performance in every new location, the company taught local employees the Toyota Way—its production and management philosophy of continuous improvement. This essentially tacit knowledge was successfully transferred through extensive use of expatriates.[57]

However, Toyota simply did not have enough expatriates to support the company's rapid global expansion.[58] The company had to become even better and faster in building its operating capabilities abroad. Therefore, in order to speed up the learning process and to reinforce the knowledge transfer mechanism, Toyota created in 2003 a Global Production Center in Toyota City and opened regional branches in 2006 in the United Kingdom, United States, and Thailand.[59] Their purpose is to accelerate the development of local trainers, providing them with a deep knowledge of the Toyota production system so the company does not have to rely only on its experienced—and increasingly expensive—expatriates to train local employees.

The Role of Performance Management and Incentives

The performance management and compensation systems of the firm play significant roles in creating a context for knowledge sharing. Compensation strategies are a frequent obstacle. If individuals perceive that they are rewarded for their "proprietary" expertise and contribution to the firm, sharing knowledge with others will naturally be seen as contrary to their interest.

At Schlumberger, GE, and many other firms, knowledge sharing is part of managers' and engineers' formal performance reviews; most Schlumberger field engineers have objectives relating to best practices, lessons learned, and other aspects of knowledge sharing.[60] Not surprisingly, an incentive system that encourages collaboration and knowledge sharing is more likely to produce this than an evaluation system where the hoarding of knowledge and destructive internal competition are tolerated, if not encouraged.[61] For example, a new logic of performance management systems that is gaining acceptance in many multinationals is that managers and executives should be encouraged to contribute to company performance at least one level above the unit for which they are responsible. A foreign subsidiary manager may receive a bonus based on the regional or even global performance of the division or the corporation as a whole. This encourages knowledge sharing and wider collaboration between organizational units.

Conversely, tying incentives to the performance of a subsidiary relative to its sister units will create a strong disincentive to share information and knowledge. A retail company where the heads of neighboring areas were married to each other constitutes an amusing example of the perverse effects that such reward systems may have. The general managers—husband and wife—failed to share knowledge with each other because their bonuses were tied to the relative performance of the two units![62]

In addition to financial rewards, the career implications of knowledge sharing send strong signals about the kind of behavior that is valued and rewarded in the corporation.

KNOWLEDGE SHARING IN PROFESSIONAL SERVICE FIRMS

Professional service firms (PSFs) are different from capital-intensive or labor-intensive organizations in that they are even more firmly based on the management of knowledge.[63] The PSF sells something intangible—not a product, but a promise or expectation. Professions have long been defined in terms of vocations founded on bodies of knowledge and the application of that knowledge.[64] The starting point was self-regulating liberal professions, such as physicians and lawyers; but with the transition to a more knowledge-based society, we have witnessed phenomenal growth in commercial professional service firms. These cover management, engineering, and technology consultancies; accounting firms (some of which cut across many professional sectors); investment banks, advertising agencies, marketing and PR services, HR services, suppliers of software, systems designers, industrial design, graphics . . . and the list continues to broaden.

The approach to knowledge sharing in PSFs is intimately associated with their internationalization and consequent global reach. The path to transnational development in a professional service firm seems to take a different trajectory from capital- or labor-intensive firms. From consultancies to legal firms to advertising agencies, the questions of whether or not to internationalize, and how fast to grow globally, have been the subject of hot debate for a considerable time. The pros and cons are typically complex.[65] On the one hand, there may be pressures to internationalize in certain sectors such as auditing and advertising to service global clients better. There can be significant economies of scale in back-office costs and expertise that become more important with the development of IT. But on the other hand, clients are sometimes indifferent as to whether or not the PSF is operating on a global scale—what counts is the reputation and quality of the local partner. Internationalization has only recently become a hot issue among law firms. Should they expand abroad, following their clients, or should they simply protect and expand their position at home?[66]

The phrase "one-firm firm" may seem strange to those who are not acquainted with the professional service sector, although its significance is obvious to most people in PSFs. The natural route to internationalization has been the federation of otherwise independent firms; analogous to a limited form of multidomestic organization, the federation captures some advantages (client referrals and some exchange of best practices). But the one-firm firm that tries to act as a single global organization, especially in terms of its management practices, has until recently been the exception rather than the rule.

All PSFs have to figure out how to exploit and explore simultaneously, as they have to create new knowledge from the ongoing services that they provide to clients. This leads to further dilemmas. For example, how can one persuade the best professionals to make their learning available for the benefit of others? How can one persuade clients to pay handsome fees for consultants' learning when it will also be applied elsewhere—often to their competitors? Global management of knowledge is particularly important to the PSF since it has no other assets than its people and their individual and collective know-how. Indeed, PSFs have pioneered many of the developments in this domain.

Three Configurations of Professional Service Firms

There appear to be three different approaches to managing the PSF, each reflected in a different approach to the sharing of know-how across boundaries. These approaches—client-driven, creative problem solving, and solution adaptation—reflect different configurations of strategic focus and management orientation.[67] Each is characterized by a different orientation to HRM (see the box "Configurations in the Professional Service Firm and Their HRM Implications").

Ad-Hoc Management of Knowledge in the Client-Driven PSF

In the first and most traditional configuration, the strategy is client-driven.[68] The firm sells its ability to help particular client groups in specific service areas, such as legal advice, insurance brokerage, or compensation/benefits consulting. This

Configurations in the Professional Service Firm and Their HRM Implications

External Strategic Focus

Internal Resource Orientation		Client relations	Creative problem solving	Adaptation of ready solutions
	Organizationally controlled resources	*Insufficient adaptiveness*	⬇➡	**SOLUTION ADAPTATION**
	Team-based (individual & collective)	➡⬇	**CREATIVE PROBLEM SOLVING**	⬆⬅
	Individually controlled resources	**CLIENT-DRIVEN**	⬅⬆	*Lack of coordination & discipline*

Adapted from B. Løwendahl, *Strategic Management of Professional Service Firms*, 2nd ed. (Copenhagen: Handelshojskolens Forlag, 2005).

This figure suggests that there are three stable configurations of professional service firms (PSFs), based on the fit between external strategic orientation and internal resource orientation. The off-diagonal forms are inherently unstable.

The Client-Driven Configuration

This is the prototypical PSF. The expertise and power in the client-driven firm rest with the individual partner, who may even recommend other firms to the client to maintain credibility. The governance of the firm is individualized—no decisions can be made without the buy-in of client partners. Management and administration are primarily seen as overheads, and the coordination capability of the firm is limited.

The recruitment target in the client-driven firm is the mature professional with deep experience within a particular industry and strong generalist skills. The approach to HRM is highly variable, depending on the client partner. The way you are treated depends on whom you work for. Training is also individualized (some might say erratic), through mentorship with senior client managers, and varies with the skills of these partners. In appraisal, performance criteria focus on client satisfaction, retention, chargeable hours, and the number of follow-on contracts with a given client.

The Creative Problem-Solving Configuration

What this firm sells is a credible promise to help a client solve a specific problem by means of the creative inputs of a team of pro-fessionals. The orientation of HRM will be a careful blend of individualism and teamwork. The creative problem-solving firm will devote priority resources to recruiting talented peo-ple and socializing them into teamwork. After intensive HR marketing and screening of can-didates, the chosen few are interviewed by five or more senior professionals and partners before any offer is made: one negative vote and you do not get the job.

MBA graduates are a perfect target, since they like problem solving, can tolerate ambi-guity, are selected for their achievement and leadership talent, yet have demonstrable team skills. Much of the training will be through personalized mentoring. A promotional sys-tem that is up-or-out, accompanied by gener-ous salary raises for those who move ahead, is quite compatible with this orientation—as long as it is rigorously competence-based, and backed up by thorough and fair feedback/appraisal processes. At McKinsey, the fairness of the counseling-out system means that for-mer McKinsey employees later become their most loyal supporters as captains in their client firms.

The Solution-Adaptation Configuration

Here the firm sells a proven solution, where it has built up in-depth expertise. The growth of the firm comes from codifying and adding to that expertise in the solution area, as well as by expanding its portfolio of solutions.

The approach to HRM is correspondingly different. The recruitment target is the under-graduate student, often with an appropriate technical background. Training programs are highly structured and ongoing throughout the first part of the career, as are appraisal processes and career paths, which may all fol-low global criteria. There is a higher degree of control over the design of systems and proce-dure, including in the HR domain. Accenture and PricewaterhouseCoopers are examples of such organizations.

One cannot identify a single "best way" of managing human resources in a PSF. "Best" in this context means the approach that is most consistent with company strategy and the or-ganizational capabilities that support it.

Source: Adapted from B. Løwendahl, *Strategic Manage-ment of Professional Service Firms*, 2nd ed. (Copenhagen: Copenhagen Business School Press, 2005).

ability is typically anchored in experienced client partners, sometimes called "gray hair," as opposed to "brains" or "procedures."[69] These individual partners, who act as counsel to their clients, hold considerable power. Coordination, when required, is most likely to be managed by price mechanisms. If international expansion is necessary for client reasons, then this is likely to take the form of a federation of partners.

The approach to knowledge management in an international federation of partners is informal and ad hoc. Knowledge sharing takes place only when there are clear synergies or benefits to client-oriented partners, using the basic coor-dination mechanisms of face-to-face relations, project groups, limited know-how transfer, and occasional internal boards. Internal seminars may be used to share know-how on key clients and developments. Projects may be set up to ensure cooperation in service delivery, if necessary. Strategies for attracting and retaining professionals may be developed, with mechanisms for some transfers and cross-assignments. The quality and quantity of knowledge transfer across borders are quite limited.

In recent years, many client-driven PSFs, such as large law firms, have pursued an internationalization strategy as they respond to pressures from their clients to serve them across borders.[70] This has put pressure on the traditional management of these firms, pushing them toward adopting some elements of the solution adaptation approach (see the following section). Global law firms have increased their use of standardized processes for service delivery, global client teams, international communities of practice teams, overseas assignments, and global training programs.[71]

Personalization in the Creative Problem-Solving PSF

In the second consistent configuration, exemplified by McKinsey in consulting or Goldman Sachs in investment banking, the strategy focuses on creative problem solving. The firm helps the client solve a specific problem by means of creative professional inputs—for example, designing an appropriate global structure (McKinsey) or negotiating an acquisition opportunity (Goldman Sachs).

The type of knowledge management used to manage boundaries is called "personalization."[72] Most of the knowledge in a problem-solving PSF is tacit rather than codified, anchored in people's brains. The knowledge management strategy focuses on developing social networks to link people together so that this knowledge can be shared, supported by online tools such as internal Yellow Page directories. Through such networks, the manager of a potential engagement in Australia is able to draw on the experience of a specialist in Germany, obtain the part-time collaboration of someone from San Francisco, and draw on presentation material from New York. The incentive systems must recognize knowledge shared directly with other people; at some such firms partners are evaluated on dimensions that include how much help they provide to colleagues, a dimension that can account for nearly a quarter of annual compensation.[73]

Codification in the Solution-Adaptation PSF

A different but equally consistent configuration is solution adaptation. The company sells a proven solution—in the shape of a business system, audit process, or reengineering project—that can be adapted to the client's particular circumstances. The offering is more like a product than the open promise of the creative problem-solving firm, while still remaining knowledge- or expertise-based.

The growth of the firm comes in part from codifying and adding to its systematic expertise in a solution area, and in part through expansion of its portfolio of solutions. Knowledge management is based on codification rather than personalized social networks. Creative problem-solving projects may be set up to tackle new opportunities; then the resulting know-how is formalized for reuse on other projects. There is substantial investment in the IT infrastructure, focusing on an electronic document system that codifies, stores, and disseminates knowledge and experience. Firm revenues are generated primarily from the economics of reuse rather than the economics of expertise.[74]

Tensions in the International Professional Service Firm

These three configurations of PSFs (client-driven, problem-solving, and solution adaptation) are ideal types.[75] All professional service firms experience tensions between two or more of these configurations. In the creative problem-solving firm, professionals see advantages from global standardization and codification. They may seize such opportunities, splitting off to found their own solution-oriented firms. In the solution-oriented firm, local "rainmakers" with strong client relationships may argue for more power, including discretion over their human resources. Again, they may leave the firm to create their own client-oriented practices, taking disaffected professionals with them.[76]

It is difficult for any PSF to grow and deliver superior performance based on multiple simultaneous strategies. If that growth is international, the management and organizational challenges tax the capacities of the firm excessively. McKinsey experienced the tension between the pulls of codification and personalization during development of its worldwide knowledge management strategy. By the late 1980s McKinsey had invested heavily in a computer-based documentation system, backed up by a new career path of specialist managers. But this never took hold, running counter to the strong mainstream culture. Come promotion time, no one reviewed what documents a person had submitted for incorporation in the database. The focus of attention remained on connections—how people had used their internal networks to develop ideas that make an impact on the client. As a senior McKinsey professional commented,

By the early 1990s, too many people were seeing practice development as the creation of experts and the generation of documents in order to build our reputation. But knowledge is only valuable when it is between the ears of consultants and applied to clients' problems. Because it is less effectively developed through the disciplined work of a few than through the spontaneous interaction of many, we had to change the more structured "discover-codify-disseminate" model to a looser and more inclusive "engage-explore-apply-share" approach. In other words, we shifted our focus from developing knowledge to building individual and team capability.[77]

The challenge for the internationalizing PSF, then, is to maintain consistency as it expands across borders, both in terms of the service delivery model and its approach to the management of human resources. The more rapid the expansion, the more difficult this will be. For example, in the creative problem-solving firm there may be a strong temptation to hire local client-oriented partners who are inexperienced in the company's complex appraisal practices. Often these new partners regard such practices as alien to local customs and do not believe that they merit the attention of a senior professional. Local business schools may not supply the talent required, people who combine strong creative individualism with teamwork, and local partners may not see the justification for investing in socialization and training to make up for what the market fails to supply. The pressure to expand may also lead to ill-advised acquisitions, especially if the technology of M&A integration is not well understood.

KNOWLEDGE ACQUISITION

Historically, firms paid little attention to ways in which they might get access to new external knowledge through their international operations. Today, successful multinational corporations are increasingly those that can exploit the possibility of tapping into new knowledge and ideas from their worldwide networks, and then combine these with knowledge residing in the parent company with the aim of producing new innovations. This was the objective of the Connect + Develop model championed by P&G, which many other firms are now trying to emulate. In this section we discuss different strategies for gaining access to external knowledge as well as how to ensure that knowledge is retained. The next section will focus on the innovation process.

Gaining Access to External Knowledge

The tools that multinationals use to enhance cross-border knowledge sharing, such as building social networks and mobility, are also relevant for external knowledge acquisition.[78] Besides these, multinational firms have at their disposal additional levers to access knowledge from the outside: scanning or tapping into the local knowledge base; partnering or merging with other firms; and what might be called playing the virtual market. Each of these has its own set of HRM implications.

Scanning Global Learning Opportunities

Scanning encompasses the efforts made to gain access to external knowledge through what people read, hear, or experience firsthand. Important observations and innovative ideas can emerge from anywhere in the multinational. An example is Nokia's insight into the potential for mobile phones in emerging markets, cited in Chapter 1. Although such insights often come as a by-product of ongoing operations, investment in scanning infrastructure may enhance the external acquisition of new knowledge—especially if this kind of lateral thinking is encouraged and rewarded.

The establishment of a "listening post" is a fairly inexpensive way to begin. The role of the 70 technology entrepreneurs that P&G appointed to work in the company's regional hubs was to scan their environment for ideas that might be useful for the corporation worldwide. The Taiwanese PC manufacturer Acer established a small design shop in the United States, through which it acquired knowledge and skills in ergonomic design that were fed back to the parent organization.[79] Ericsson created "cyberlabs" in New York and Palo Alto (next to Stanford University in Silicon Valley) whose task was to monitor developments in these markets and build relationships with local companies.[80]

While listening posts can be a useful way to access codified knowledge and help the firm identify potential partners, they are less effective when the target is the acquisition of tacit knowledge. Individual scanners and small units typically lack the clout that is necessary for new ideas to be picked up at corporate headquarters. Many multinationals therefore establish fully fledged units in business centers at the forefront of the developments in their respective industries, such as Silicon Valley (high technology), North Italy (fashion), and the City of London (financial services).[81] These districts contain networks of producers, advanced users, supporting industries, universities, research labs, and a fluid labor market with highly competent individuals. Scanning in centers like these takes place through formal collaboration among organizations, formalized networks like trade associations and professional organizations, and more informal social networks.

In the past, it may have been obvious where the Hollywood or Silicon Valley of a certain industry was located. However, the situation today has become more complex. In many high-tech industries valuable knowledge can be found in numerous locations around the world, among them Austin, Texas; Bangalore, India; Cambridge, England; Sophia Antipolis, France; and Tel Aviv, Israel.[82] Yahoo! is one of many US firms with a significant presence in Bangalore. It established an office there in 2000, and while it still had fewer than 20 employees in 2003, by 2007 the unit had more than 1,000 computer scientists and engineers in the company's largest R&D center outside its main US location, charged with developing new and innovative services with global applications.[83] Cisco has gone so far as to split its corporate headquarters into two—the western-facing headquarters in California and the eastern-facing headquarters in Bangalore.

From an HRM perspective, there are pros and cons associated with establishing a unit in "hot spot" locations. On the one hand, there is an ample supply of people with relevant experience, and the social contacts they provide can be invaluable. However, at the same time there is often fierce competition for talent, escalating salaries, and a risk of losing people to competitors. The winners are firms that are better than others at retaining their star performers, while the losers suffer from attrition. Instead of helping a firm to tap into external knowledge, tight social networks can serve as a conduit for its own proprietary knowledge to flow out! And research has shown that firms that try to constrain their employees, in terms of what they are allowed to talk about with others, are likely to lose. They tend to get a bad reputation, impairing their ability to hire the best people.[84]

Accessing and assimilating complex tacit knowledge requires considerable investment of time and resources. Shiseido from Japan learned this when establishing itself in France to acquire knowledge about designing, manufacturing, and selling scent. After an unsuccessful joint venture with a French company, it formed a wholly owned subsidiary, Beauté Prestige International, to develop and produce fragrances. It also established a high-end beauty parlor in Paris and bought two functioning beauty salons. The company relied initially on expatriates to acquire local knowledge, but this did not work. Eventually, it learned to hire local experts with long-term industry experience, putting them in charge of the French operations. Then, through close observation and the interaction between Japanese expatriates and French employees, Shiseido succeeded in acquiring and transferring desired capabilities.[85]

An important HRM issue when establishing a unit abroad is the company's ability to attract competent personnel at competitive costs. Experienced multinationals like Nokia always carry out in-depth HR analyses before they set up new units. Questions they typically ask include these: Do the local universities produce engineering graduates with the required competence level for an R&D center? Will the influx of other corporations to hot spots like Bangalore or Beijing lead to salary escalation that undermines current cost advantages?

Partnering or Merging

A significant proportion of knowledge acquisition comes about through partnering—that is, deep relationships with other organizations. Partners include suppliers, distributers, competitors, and research organizations. Some alliances and joint ventures with partner organizations are established with the explicit objective of co-creating new knowledge; but much knowledge acquisition takes place in partnerships where the focus is on ongoing manufacturing or distribution. P&G quickly realized the potential of the 50,000 R&D staff in its 15 top suppliers. Several measures were taken to increase the number of joint R&D projects with suppliers, including the development of a secure IT platform used to communicate technology briefs (descriptions of what P&G is looking for) with suppliers, and face-to-face meetings to improve relationships and strengthen the understanding of the other's capabilities. The effect was a clear increase in the number of jointly staffed projects.[86]

One of the challenges in learning alliances and joint ventures is that they may involve firms with competing interests, where parties strive to learn from each other to improve their individual position. The NUMMI joint venture (introduced in Chapter 4) formed between Toyota and GM in California more than two decades ago is a classic example. GM's aim was to learn about lean manufacturing from Toyota, whereas the Japanese firm wanted to learn about the US market and gain experience in establishing and operating a local production unit. Most observers agree that Toyota was the more successful of the two in this "race to learn," to a large extent because its HRM strategy and learning objectives were fully aligned.[87] We will discuss this critical issue in much more depth in Chapter 12.

Outsourcing has become widely used in virtually all industries. However, while most attention has been given to the outsourcing of support activities, like accounting and customer service to India, companies also use contractors for more advanced activities. For instance, over the last few years, original equipment manufacturers (OEMs) in the mobile phone industry have invested in building their own product development capabilities, which they offer to companies like Nokia and Motorola. The development of a new mobile phone can be a complex process, involving an OEM, a specialized R&D company, and several units from the mobile phone company. There are many technical and management challenges in running such projects, but the first step should be developing human relationships needed for the collaboration to run smoothly. Another major task is how to capture the individual learning of the key people involved in such partnerships, and translate it into organizational know-how that can be conveyed to others.

Mergers and acquisitions (M&A) are the ultimate form of partnering. Acquiring and retaining local knowledge are frequent objectives in cross-border M&As, and therefore we will look at this in the context of managing post-merger integration, discussed in Chapter 13.

Playing the Virtual Market

The new technologies of the digital revolution allow us to link individuals and organizations in all parts of the world in ways that were unimaginable before. For example, firms can post a specification of what they are looking for on the Internet, together with information about the reward that will be given to anyone who comes up with a solution. In 1999, the CEO of a troubled Canadian gold mine (an intensely secretive industry) decided to post all the geological data about the mine on the Web, offering half a million dollars' prize money to virtual inspectors. The resulting ideas and gold discoveries catapulted Goldcorp from a $100 million underperformer into a $9 billion juggernaut that is one of the most innovative and profitable mining firms in the industry today.[88] Companies can also issue more general calls for research projects. In 2008, HP's open innovation office announced a call for research proposals. It received more than 450 submissions from 200 universities in 22 countries. Forty-one of those proposals were funded.[89]

P&G has paid considerable attention to the question of how best to use the "market" for knowledge acquisition. Together with other large corporations, P&G has helped create firms specializing in connecting enterprises with technology problems with other companies, universities, labs, and individuals who may be able to offer solutions. These market brokers can help write technology briefs and facilitate the interaction between the corporation with the problem and the organization or individual with the potential solution. Market brokers often have a relatively well-specified scope of activity. P&G works with NineSigma, which connects companies and organizations; InnoCentive, which brokers solutions to more narrowly defined technical problems; and YourEncore, a business that connects retired scientists and engineers with client corporations.[90]

The challenges involved in the use of virtual cross-border teams and international alliances are amplified when playing the virtual market. The professional competencies and interpersonal skills of the people managing these relationships are particularly important—they must be able to swiftly develop trust-based relationships with new partners. They also need to reach a shared understanding of performance expectations and decide how they will work together to reach their objectives. Aligning the reward structure is critical. Without incentives, knowledge will not flow in; but with too many incentives, some talented individuals may decide that playing the market is more rewarding than staying with the firm—which brings us to the problem of retention.

Knowledge Retention

While codified knowledge can be physically stored in databases and reports, tacit knowledge resides in people. When individuals with unique and valuable knowledge walk out the door, the company could be losing part of its competitive advantage. What can the firm can do to discourage core tacit knowledge from taking that walk?

There are three basic knowledge retention strategies. The first, which we have already discussed, is to stimulate knowledge sharing among individuals and units, so that the company is less dependent on a small number of people. An obvious illustration of this is when people with unique knowledge are approaching retirement[91]—but with increasing professional employee turnover in most countries and corporations, knowledge sharing has to be encouraged on a continuous basis.

A second strategy is to try to reduce employee turnover in order to avoid the leaking of proprietary knowledge to competitors. We have discussed various mechanisms for retaining employees earlier in the book. However, knowledge retention should also be a factor when analyzing the effects of involuntary turnover, during periods of recession, or when companies are considering relocating operations.

When the price of oil reached its nadir in the late 1990s, many energy firms responded by curtailing exploration activities and laying off experienced staff. Less than five years later, when prices moved in the opposite direction, they had to buy back the same skills from outside at a much higher cost. In some cases they even had to forgo major opportunities, as they simply did not have a sufficiently experienced workforce to manage the projects.

The third strategy is to invest in making tacit knowledge explicit. The Japanese knowledge management scholar Ikujiro Nonaka calls this "externalization." He suggests that metaphors can help individuals to explain tacit concepts that are otherwise difficult to articulate by conveying intuitive images that people can understand.[92] The explicit knowledge can then be codified and saved in databases and the like, where they can be accessed after the people with the embedded knowledge have left the firm.

The issue of repatriates illustrates all three strategies. Multinationals typically pay too little attention to how the organization can benefit from the knowledge that repatriates have gained abroad. Many returnees are dissatisfied with the career opportunities they are offered and begin looking for jobs elsewhere—numerous studies show that a large percentage of international assignees resign shortly after returning home.[93] Retention management[94] is therefore part of a successful approach to repatriate knowledge sharing. The receiving organization must make sure that repatriates have opportunities to share knowledge by appointing them to positions where they can work with others on issues related to their experience, and by assigning them to relevant projects and committees.[95] In some situations, reports and presentations can be appropriate tools for capturing and sharing insights gained during overseas assignments.[96]

FROM IDEAS TO INNOVATIONS

In the two preceding sections, we have discussed internal knowledge transfer and the acquisition of new knowledge from outside the company. Both activities are crucial for nurturing innovation in the multinational firm, as we saw in the P&G case at the beginning of the chapter. In this final section, we take a holistic perspective on the innovation process. We begin by pointing to the paradoxical nature of innovation management in multinational enterprises, then go on to discuss the location and staffing of R&D centers. We suggest that there are stages in the innovation journey—initiation, development, and implementation or commercialization—that have different organizational and HRM requirements.

Paradoxes in How to Encourage Promising Ideas

While there is little debate about how important it is to identify promising ideas for subsequent development, doing so successfully on a global scale is far from easy. Companies must be able to deal with several paradoxical challenges:

- Promoting unit diversity *and* standardization.
- Encouraging chance encounters *and* providing focus.
- Focusing on the hot spots of the industry *and* looking in surprising places.
- Having a culture of experimentation *and* of stretch performance goals.

Indeed, a quality associated with innovative organizations is called "ambidexterity," namely the ability to handle paradox.[97] Let us examine these four aspects of ambidexterity.

Diversity and Standardization

Multinational firms, by their very nature, are exposed to a wide variety of different contexts. This diversity can be a source of new innovations if ideas with the potential to be exploited elsewhere can be identified and developed further.

However, with the pressures for standardization in most multinationals today, there is a danger that different organizational units may become more alike in terms of their operations. Although this may improve interunit collaboration and facilitate the sharing of knowledge, an unintended consequence is the loss of variety that can be tapped for innovation. This observation builds on Weick's model of evolutionary change, with its parallel to Darwinian evolution. Weick argues that a firm should allow for a maximum of variation—natural, unplanned experimentation in its units—out of which will evolve the innovations that allow the firm to adapt in the future.[98] A certain degree of subsidiary autonomy helps combat the natural tendency of organizations to standardize diversity out of the picture. For this reason, knowledge management officers in corporations like Shell see a close relationship with global diversity initiatives, including recruiting outsiders into senior positions.[99]

Rather than trying to standardize everything, good ideas need to be cross-pollinated across units. People need to learn about the ideas of other units and engage in conversations that may spark new ideas. Strong social networks, structural solutions, and corporatewide communities of practices can help achieve such cross-pollination while simultaneously retaining a reasonable level of subsidiary autonomy.

Encouraging Chance Encounters and Yet Focusing the Search

Innovation sometimes begins with random interpersonal encounters. The weekend meeting in Honolulu is a legitimate way to bring people together in the expectation that an exchange over coffee or dinner will spark an innovative collective project. One study on the R&D activities of 32 multinational companies shows that the most successful R&D managers are those who meet face-to-face with their geographically dispersed people at least twice a year.[100]

However, while some new ideas emerge through fortuitous encounters and more or less by chance, companies such as P&G believe strongly in the value of specifying what they are looking for. Thus, the company produces technology briefs that outline the problem it wants to solve, and these are communicated not only within the corporation but also to its network of partner organizations—and sometimes to the world at large.

Another lesson that can be drawn from P&G and other companies that excel at product innovation is the importance of having a profound understanding of customer needs. Input from dissatisfied users can be the source of new ideas, and many firms would benefit from improving the ways in which they collect consumer complaints and analyze the data. For example, customer complaints for one major Western airline are handled by a call center in India. A key task of the managers at this center, who are experienced airline generalists, is to assimilate the implications for marketing and operations in a monthly report that emphasizes necessary adaptation in processes and new opportunities for customer differentiation.

Where to Look? The Hot Spots or the Unexpected Places?

It is almost a truism that companies need to be present in their industry hot spots, along with the most demanding customers—where they can observe their competitors' latest moves, where the most competent people tend to congregate, and where the most advanced partner organizations can be found.

Firms tend to focus on following their most important business ventures, on monitoring what their existing competitors are doing, and on satisfying their largest customers. This also implies that they learn the most from them, which at the end can make the company myopic. Clayton Christensen has forcefully argued that companies pay too much attention to their "best" customers, resulting in market leaders missing ideas from lower-end customers or new competitors.[101] By focusing only on the largest and strategically most important alliances and acquisitions, firms forgo the potential novel and useful insights that can be gained from businesses that may be less prominent.[102]

New ideas may emerge in surprising places. Consider Allianz, the German insurance company. For many years the company had a subsidiary in Thailand, a country that did not stand out for its innovativeness. However, as we describe in the box "Innovation in Surprising Places: The Case of Ayudhya Allianz C.P.," a new management team managed to develop this subsidiary into a highly innovative unit. Several of the innovations developed in the unit were picked up and developed further in other parts of the corporation.

Innovation in Surprising Places: The Case of Ayudhya Allianz C.P.

Thailand is rarely seen as a hotbed of new ideas. Observers have often noted that the Thai culture is not open to innovation because it is very hierarchical—power, symbols of status, and authority are important. Individual initiative is not expected, which is partly the outcome of a school system that discourages analytical skill and creativity in favor of memorizing and rote learning. Hospitality, politeness, and willingness to compromise are deeply ingrained in the culture.[103] In fact, Thai employees rate the lowest on innovation among Asia-Pacific countries.[104]

Nonetheless, Ayudhya Allianz C.P. Life (AACP), the Thai subsidiary of the Munich-based global financial services company Allianz, transformed itself from an old-style local insurance bureaucracy to one of the innovation leaders in the corporation.

AACP was formed in 2001 through a merger of two existing joint ventures, with Allianz obtaining full management control. However, three years later AACP ran into a deep crisis as a number of problems came to a head—the consequences of volume-driven growth, a portfolio built on unprofitable products, a powerful but out-of-control agency system, unbalanced sales compensation, conflicts in the management team—all of which resulted in significant losses. The expatriate CEO and several key local executives were forced to resign. With a new leadership in place, the company embarked on a dramatic overhaul, with an emphasis on innovation at its core.

Historically, like most companies in Thailand, AACP did not have a strong culture of innovation—there was no chance that an idea would be listened to unless it originated from a very senior executive or from the marketing department. In addition, it was difficult to obtain buy-in from others and to work across the departmental silos, so many good ideas never surfaced. But all of this changed within three short years.

The organizational change initiatives included the traditional levers in an insurance company—reorganizing the agency sales force, restructuring the product portfolio, and repositioning the brand. But they also included people management changes, such as redesigning the work environment, overhauling performance management and incentive systems, and engaging employees in social contribution projects. Some of these initiatives dramatically challenged the way business was done in the Thai insurance industry—open floor seating, no formal dress code, hiring of managers with consumer business experience, the use of cross-functional teams, and so on. AACP's new management saw building a culture of innovation as the key to institutionalizing the necessary changes.

Examples of innovation initiatives included brand building and services.

Brand Building

AACP launched a brand-building campaign to change customers' perceptions, to craft a unique position, and to differentiate AACP from its competitors. Instead of emphasizing the negative side of life insurance—typically associated with sickness, old age, and death—AACP adopted the slogan "For the Rhythm of Your Life" and created an entirely different brand image—optimistic, energetic, friendly, and hip. The slogan not only guided the commercial advertising campaign but also extended to all aspects of internal company communication, from office and entrance decoration to new relaxation zones, and even to some unusual locations. For example, a colorful poster in the men's lavatory, depicting a young man with a musical score, urges, "Release the unhappiness, and the moment of happiness will follow." Within a year, a much stronger brand led to a nearly 40 percent increase in sales.

Services

Two service innovations contributed significantly to the bottom line. With its Prestige Service, a personalized fast track for premium customers, AACP successfully copied the airline industry, where first-class passengers have a different experience of travel than economy-class passengers while receiving essentially the same core product. The Mobile Medical Nurse Service allows potential customers to take out life insurance without having the hassle of going to a hospital for a checkup—one of AACP's nurses will travel to their house or workplace to conduct the examination.

By recognizing and mobilizing the latent creativity of its employees, AACP achieved not only a business turnaround but a fundamental transformation. However, success in the local market is only one part of the story. Many of AACP's practices and approaches to innovation management have also been shared with other Allianz subsidiaries in the context of the company's global innovation initiative. In 2008 AACP was recognized as "the most innovative entity" in the Allianz Group worldwide.

Source: Zalan, T. and V. Pucik (2009). "Ayudhya Allianz C.P.: The i2s initiative." Case study no. IMD-3-1968. IMD, Lausanne.

Experimentation and Stretch

A firm's values are extremely important for its innovativeness. It is crucial to create a culture in which experimentation and entrepreneurship are encouraged, and legitimate mistakes are not frowned upon. The impact of corporate role models is significant. At 3M, a firm renowned for its track record of innovation, virtually all senior line managers have pioneered successful innovations—and also experienced dead ends along the way.

Several companies are famous for their culture of innovativeness. At Google, a "70–20–10 rule" governs the ratio of company investment in its core business, adjacent projects, and new ideas. This principle is extended to the way in which technical staff are expected to divide their time: 70 percent on the main task, 20 percent on related projects, and 10 percent on exploratory projects. The rule sends a strong message to employees that they are expected to think outside the box, coming up with solutions to problems that may not even have been recognized yet.

Stretch goals have a different quality than experimentation, but they may also support the creation of new ideas. An excessively strong belief in the company's current activities and products can be a formidable enemy of innovation as it often produces a culture of complacency, contributing to a focus solely on how to best exploit the current capabilities of the firm.

The Organization and Staffing of R&D Centers

The internal R&D organization forms the backbone for innovation in corporations. A distinction is often made between R&D units that focus primarily on developing new technologies and improving existing ones, and those whose main task is product development. Nokia and Shell both make this distinction. Shell has three central technical centers focusing on innovation and technology development, two in Holland and one in Houston, Texas. The other 10 technical centers focus on product development, marketing support, or specific technical assistance for regional operations, located in places ranging from the United Kingdom, France, and Canada to India, Qatar, and Singapore. Shell has invested in developing a 3D virtual reality suite (built within its Second Life virtual world) to enhance collaboration between units.

Just as the advent of the steamship and the telephone heralded a new era of internationalization, so the digital revolution has contributed to globalization. E-mail, videoconferencing, computerized databases, and electronic forums have eliminated much of the distance that hindered collaboration and interaction in the past. Or have they? Why are key employees at Microsoft located only in the United States and, what is more, concentrated in Microsoft's sprawling campus at Redmond, outside Seattle? Why does Cisco still locate some 15,000 people in lookalike buildings in crowded and expensive San Jose in the heart of Silicon Valley? Why, if distance is dead, do these leading advocates of virtuality still have a high degree of co-location?

The answer is that while the digital revolution may have reduced distance as an obstacle to information transfer, it has done little for the creative recombination of divergent knowledge. Microsoft, Cisco, and other firms know full well that knowledge, not information, is the source of their competitive strength.[105] Sharing tacit knowledge requires personal interaction; innovation is above all a social process. Thus, despite all the technological developments and sophisticated communication tools that now exist, distance is far from dead. Research indicates that while inventors are more linked with other parts of the world through travel and the use of information technology, the clustering of people who work closely together is just as important now as it was in the past.[106]

The importance of close interpersonal collaboration can also be seen within Shell's R&D organization. The company has entered into a partnership with the State Key Laboratory of Coal Conversion in Taiyuan, China. The partnership was prompted by Shell's interest in understanding better the challenges facing China, and by China's interest in Shell's coal expertise. Several projects have been chosen for collaboration, with Shell sponsoring doctoral and postdoctoral research. Chinese researchers are also working in Shell's laboratories in Amsterdam, and Shell staff are working in the Chinese facilities.

But where should a multinational firm establish a particular R&D or product development center? One thesis behind global innovation is that a firm should put the right people where the uncertainties are—where the need for information collection and processing is the greatest.[107] If a company is in an industry where consumer tastes change frequently and are difficult to assess, key people should be located locally, close to the customer. If the firm is in an industry dominated by technological changes that are driven by a "Silicon Valley," the R&D function should be located there.

Most large corporations today carry out extensive R&D activities outside their home countries. A 2008 study by the consultancy Booz & Company revealed that the top 80 US corporate R&D investors spent US$80 billion (out of a total $146 billion) abroad; the top 43 Japanese firms invested $40 billion (out of $72 billion) overseas; and the top 50 European multinationals spent $51 billion (out of $117 billion) outside the European continent. China and India have become favorite destinations for R&D investments in the 21st century, with 83 percent of new R&D sites established in these countries.[108]

These investments have partly been made for cost reasons but also, as we have already pointed out, to gain access to local talent, to learn more from and about these markets, and to leverage that skill and knowledge to drive global innovation. For instance, HP's R&D unit in Bangalore, India, does most of the computer unit's work on user interfaces for keyboards. Because of the multiplicity of languages in India, researchers there are best suited to work on this type of problem.[109] Nokia in turn learned that Indian customers often share a mobile phone, leading them to develop software allowing multiple phone books on the same handset—an idea that was subsequently brought to Western markets.[110] Within Toyota, units have been established in Thailand, India, and China to develop affordable cars for the local markets. China has become a center for Nokia's development of new inexpensive mobile devices and Chinese language applications.

The Booz & Company study concluded that multinational companies with a global approach to R&D performed better than those concentrating their research in the home market.[111]

Stages in the Innovation Journey

Much of this chapter has dealt with how international firms can manage the initiation phase of the innovation process. We have argued that this requires an understanding of the paradoxes relating to ways in which the company can encourage the emergence of new ideas. We have also discussed at length how firms can access new knowledge from external sources and share that knowledge across units. Let us now turn to the development and commercialization phases of the innovation process.

Sometimes the three stages of the innovation journey—initiation, development, and implementation or commercialization—reiterate in cycles. Thus an innovation may go through a cycle of initiation, development, and implementation the departmental level, then a cycle at the subsidiary level, and afterward at the global level. However, in multinationals the trend is toward faster innovation processes with fewer iterations across different hierarchical levels. The important element is speed of response to an innovation opportunity.

The three-stage model of the innovation process corresponds in many ways to how Doz, Santos, and Williamson present the "metanational" corporation

The Metanational

Almost all multinationals have grown from a home country base to which they have a deep-rooted attachment. Doz, Santos, and Williamson argue that we are seeing the emergence of a new type of organization that goes beyond national borders—the metanational corporation. The metanational has broken free of geography and builds competitive advantage by discovering, accessing, and leveraging knowledge from many locations around the world. The world is a global canvas dotted with pockets of technology, market intelligence, and capabilities to be tapped. So a metanational organization entering the Internet-based private banking industry would find its expertise on financial markets in New York, its understanding of private banking customers in Geneva, and its know-how on Internet banking in Sao Paolo (where Bradesco and other Brazilian financial service firms pioneered Internet banking long before others).

Metanationals are often born in the wrong place, which (if they are to be successful) forces them to tap into knowledge elsewhere and to think beyond national boundaries. Nokia (mobile telephony) was born in Finland; Acer (computers) in Taiwan, far from Silicon Valley; STMicroelectronics (semiconductors) has its roots in Italy and France.

Doz, Santos, and Williamson argue that successful international firms like these metanationals in the global knowledge economy must excel in three different capabilities: sensing, mobilization, and operationalization.

Sensing

They must sense new knowledge faster and more effectively than their competitors. This requires the following capabilities:

- *Prospecting capabilities*—the predisposition to prospect for emerging pockets of innovative technology and new market needs. This allows companies to anticipate emerging hotbeds of relevant knowledge ahead of competitors.

- *Accessing capabilities*—the ability to plug into innovative technology and new market needs through networks of relationships with foreign customers, suppliers, distributors, universities, and technical institutes. This provides access to emerging pockets of relevant knowledge.

Mobilization

They must mobilize dispersed knowledge to innovate more creatively than their competitors. This requires the following capabilities:

- *Moving capabilities*—an effective process for setting up "magnets" that can identify and move globally dispersed knowledge so that it can be used for innovative problem solving (for example, projects undertaken to serve global customers or to build global product or service platforms).
- *Melding capabilities*—a capability to meld knowledge about new technologies and

novel customer needs from diverse sources into coherent innovations, overcoming the problems associated with recombining complex knowledge and integrating it into solutions.

Operationalization

They must operationalize innovations more efficiently than their competitors. This requires the following capabilities:

- *Relaying capabilities*—an ability to transfer newly created solutions into the day-to-day operations that underpin the supply chain.
- *Leveraging capabilities*—the capability to leverage innovations across global customer segments or applications and to develop an efficient supply chain through the flexible combination of operational strengths from different sites. These may be established sites in an existing network of operations or sites operated by a partner.

Source: Adapted from Y. Doz, J. Santos, and P. Williamson, *From Global to Metanational* (Boston, MA: Harvard Business School Press, 2001).

that excels in managing knowledge and innovation on a global scale.[112] The box "The Metanational" provides a brief summary of their influential work.

Picking and Supporting Winners

Compared to the idea generation stage, the development stage requires more focus and direction. The enterprise needs to concentrate on spotting and selecting viable innovations among the initial ideas, nurturing them, and then retaining and building on those that are successful. Consequently, firms need to create an environment that supports *both* the divergent processes that induce a healthy proliferation of ideas *and* the convergent processes through which options are narrowed, resources are channeled, and implementation is undertaken.[113]

There is a great deal of hyperbole suggesting that "hierarchy is the antithesis of innovation." But things are not as simple as that. Hierarchical processes are necessary at particular stages in the process of innovation—when projects reach the development stage, corporations need to run a tight ship, with appropriate screening processes to channel sufficient funding to the most promising projects.

Innovation experts argue that the biggest challenge is for firms to make an early decision about which ideas to kill. GE's head of research finds this to be his toughest task: "Like a dog with a bone, people don't want to give them up."[114] In multinational corporations, screening project ideas means maintaining a healthy balance. On the one hand, there is a danger of flooding the organization with too many initiatives of unclear value and doubtful connection with corporate initiatives (a frequent danger in companies with a high degree of local autonomy). On the other hand, there is the danger of killing potentially successful projects because they are perceived as too risky or too far from the current strategy.

Multinationals have experimented with different organizational solutions to the problem of how to convert ideas into products that then can be implemented throughout the firm. Ideas that ultimately become products usually require different inputs and perspectives, and ensuring that this happens is part of the development process. People's minds are filled with innumerable creative ideas, but any revenue-generating innovation (whether it is an incremental improvement, a new product, or a new technology) is the result of the combination of knowledge. This integrative ability is one of the foundations of competitive advantage.

A common problem at the development phase is that the new ideas do not receive enough financial and managerial support to ensure that this combinatory process takes place. The person in charge of a business unit may feel that the project takes too much time and money away from current operational demands. If another project is already under way, the new proposal may face budget constraints as well as resistance from people championing the other project. Several multinationals have therefore set up separate funds to finance promising ideas. The box "Shell's GameChanger" describes the rules under which such units may operate.

In short, Shell's GameChanger scheme aspires to provide a sheltered zone where an idea can be developed, tried, and improved upon. If it is seen to work, it can be commercialized within the Shell organization or become an independent new business.

Many other companies have established mechanisms similar to the GameChanger as a key element of their innovation management. P&G has a four-step model where it reviews ideas at project establishment, continuation, capital investment, and progression to market stages. Each stage has explicit go/no-go criteria.[115] The teams or panels used by Shell, P&G, and others to evaluate project ideas consist of executives and professionals from different functions (R&D, production, marketing, etc.) and are staffed by people with a wide range of competencies and experience, representing units from different parts of the world.

Commercialization

The process of innovation over time can be viewed like an hourglass—initially divergent and global, then convergent and more local (possibly with strong

Shell's Gamechanger

The GameChanger screens early innovation ideas submitted by Shell employees and external sources. The objective is to encourage entrepreneurs to develop their ideas into a product that can be introduced to the marketplace. Specifically, Shell looks for innovative ideas that address a demand or significant problem in the energy industry, with the potential to "change the game." Ideas can range from new oil exploration techniques to improved production tools or new forms of energy. Shell can serve as an "angel investor," and the company regularly invests up to $100,000 in ideas.

The first step in entering the GameChanger process is submission of a short description of the idea on the dedicated Web site. A selection panel formed by a group of full-time Shell professionals with diverse backgrounds in the energy industry assesses all proposals. There are three different steps in the review:

1. **Pre-screening:** If the person submitting the pro-posal is an entrepreneur from outside Shell, a member of the panel will contact the entrepreneur after the initial assessment to allocate a Shell technical counterpart with whom to work. The Shell employee will serve as a "co-proponent" of the idea and help the entrepreneur through the screening process.
2. **Screening panel:** The screening panel consists of any two members of the GameChanger team, who will listen to a presentation of the idea. The panelists consider its merits and decide within 48 hours if the idea has the potential to mature into a GameChanger project. If this is the case, the entrepreneur will be invited to prepare a more detailed presentation for an extended panel.
3. **Extended panel:** The extended panel, consisting of three members of the GameChanger team and at least three non-team experts, reviews a presentation of the proposal and preliminary work plan. The GameChanger panel then decides, in principle within 48 hours, whether to go ahead and fund the development of the idea. If funding is awarded, it usually has a time span of two to three years. At agreed tollgates, progress and continuation are discussed with proponents and panel experts.

The GameChanger panel supports projects deemed to have the potential to have a significant impact on the profitability of a business, or to open up growth opportunities, through to their proof-of-concept stage. If proof-of-concept is reached successfully, there are three potential forward paths:

1. **Proprietary:** The project graduates into Shell's internal R&D funnel or another Shell business.
2. **Licensing:** The idea is licensed to a technology provider other than Shell. This usually happens when complementary capabilities are required to develop and deploy the idea.
3. **Venturing:** A new company might be set up to commercialize the idea.

Source: www.shell.com.

international links and tight control), and finally returning to divergence and a more global focus.

The hourglass metaphor was based on a study of innovations in leading Swedish multinationals. In the exploratory sensing stage, there was a great deal of room for local initiative, tapping into collaborative external networks (universities, conferences), while patterns of communication were a blend of electronic media to exchange scientific or technical information and occasional face-to-face meetings. This changed at the development stage. Work became more internally focused and local, with clear responsibilities assigned to particular units. Communication was more intense and face-to-face, facilitating the sharing of deep tacit knowledge. As the project reached the commercialization stage, the orientation broadened once again—local trials were undertaken, and people were encouraged to participate in appropriate conferences. There was now much wider circulation of information via phone calls, e-mail, and personal visits.[116]

There are many examples of the challenges involved in diffusing innovations within multinational corporations. After P&G's successful launch of its Pampers disposable diapers in Germany, it took the company five years to introduce the product in France, allowing Colgate-Palmolive to enter the market with a similar product that gained dominant market share.[117] The challenge involved in commercializing innovations around the multinational firm are in many ways similar to the challenges associated with knowledge sharing. There can be strong not-invented-here symptoms. Innovation champions with corporate clout and extensive social networks within the corporation can help pave the way for global rollouts of new products and processes.

Probably the main way to facilitate implementation is to make sure that the units that will be crucial for the commercialization are involved in the innovation process at an early stage. This will enhance their psychological ownership of the product, technology, or process that is being developed. It also means that early feedback about the emerging innovation can be obtained from a wider range of sources (such as subsidiaries from different countries and people responsible for production or marketing) at the development phase.

DUALITIES OF EXPLORATION AND EXPLOITATION

The fact is that big, complex global organizations have difficulty with innovation. As Kanter notes, it is like teaching elephants how to dance.[118] The biggest problem is not that multinationals do not know how to be innovative—it is that the properties needed to be innovative are the opposite of those needed to be successful in exploiting what they are doing well today. This is just one of the many paradoxes in the domain of global innovation and knowledge management.

Effective knowledge management is important both to exploit existing capabilities on a global scale and to explore new ideas that can be developed into tomorrow's product and service offerings. While both exploration and exploitation are needed, finding a balance between the two is challenging.[119] Companies easily fall into the trap of focusing too much on one at the expense of the other, one of the many dualities that firms are facing.

We have considered many other dualities in this chapter—combining network modes of operating with structural modes, collaboration versus competition with other companies, and inside versus outside orientation. Let us address two additional paradoxes that we have not yet explicitly mentioned—the transfer paradox and the evaluation paradox. The *transfer paradox* argues that the most valuable knowledge—complex and contextual tacit knowledge—is also the most sticky. Sticky knowledge is expensive and difficult to transfer within the multinational, requiring linking mechanisms that build on face-to-face relationships. The *evaluation paradox* holds that this same tacit know-how is also the most difficult and expensive to evaluate and assess. And there are additional paradoxes. For example, it is clear that external contacts in communities of practice can facilitate new knowledge (the bridging of nonconnected networks by boundary spanners in social capital theory). On the other hand, research also shows that too strong an orientation to external knowledge sources leads people to miss deadlines.[120]

Organizing for innovation means managing the tensions that underlie such dualities. This is a theme running through this chapter, because, as Van de Ven and colleagues noted, ". . . contradiction and nonlinearity may be inherent in most innovative undertakings. As a consequence, the central problem in leading the innovation journey may be ambidexterity, the management of paradox."[121]

The innovation process involves alternating cycles of divergent and convergent behaviors—exploring new directions alternating with focused pursuit of a given direction; building new relationships alternating with execution through established networks;[122] leadership that encourages diversity alternating with focused leadership guided by goals and consensus. Innovation is a type of exploration—there is a trade-off between a focus on exploration and on exploitation, between tomorrow's profits and those of today.

Many studies have described the overarching quality needed for innovation as the ability to operate "on the edge" between order and chaos. Eisenhardt and Brown found that successful firms in highly competitive computer markets emphasize "semistructures" as well as improvisation, combining limited structures (priorities, accountability) with extensive interaction and the freedom to improvise.[123] And these firms constantly link time frames, focusing on both present and future. They do not rely on a single plan or scenario, nor are they merely reactive—they constantly use low-cost probes such as experimental products, alliances, consultation with futurists, and incessant feedback to test how the future is emerging.

Strong, cohesive social ties may promote a climate of trust and cooperation, acting as a defense against opportunism and self-interest. But if the social ties become too strong, the group runs the risk of becoming inward-looking and rigid. Galunic and Eisenhardt put it well when they observe the tensions that highly adaptive organizations have to balance: "modularity and relatedness, competitiveness and cooperation, and order and disorder . . . the simultaneous presence of competing tensions is an important motor of adaptation within organizations in rapidly changing markets."[124]

The management of knowledge and innovation on a global scale is clearly a tough challenge, with numerous HRM implications. Companies need to recruit and select employees bearing in mind the acquisition of valuable external knowledge. They also need to socialize new employees to make sure that this knowledge is shared across units. Training and development should enhance the innovative ability of the firm—as well as the ability of people to deliver on their commitments today. Performance management systems and compensation schemes have to encourage both exploration and exploitation. Firms that can master such human resource management challenges will achieve a competitive advantage that will be difficult to match.

TAKEAWAYS

1. One of the key challenges for multinational firms is striking a balance between exploiting existing competitive strengths and exploring new areas of future growth.
2. The ability of the multinational to share knowledge internally is a crucial source of competitiveness. The degree of knowledge sharing depends on the ability and willingness of the sending unit, the motivation and ability of the receiving unit, and the suitability of the mechanisms (channels) used to share the knowledge.
3. To stimulate worldwide knowledge sharing, it is necessary to provide information about where the knowledge is; to design appropriate structural mechanisms and social architecture to support sharing; and to reinforce the culture of sharing through talent management, performance management, and incentive systems.
4. Three organizational configurations can be found in professional service firms, with corresponding implications for their approach to global knowledge management—client-driven, creative problem solving, and solution adaptation. Each configuration is associated with a different orientation to HRM.
5. Acquiring new knowledge from external sources requires investment in scanning on a global scale; a focus on partnering with customers, research labs, and other organizations; and an ability to use the open virtual market to identify complementary knowledge and promising ideas.
6. The tacit knowledge that is embedded in people can be retained by increasing knowledge sharing, through reduction of employee turnover, and by investments in making tacit knowledge explicit.

7. The process of innovation in a firm can be divided into three stages—initiation, development, and implementation or commercialization.
8. The innovation process over time can be viewed like an hourglass—initially divergent and global, then convergent and more local (possibly with strong international links and tight control), and finally returning to divergence and a more global focus.
9. Linking people is crucial for fostering innovation. This is easiest when they are colocated and have strong social relationships.
10. A striking characteristic of global innovation and knowledge management is the need to manage paradoxes and tensions.

NOTES

1. See www.pg.com/translations/history_pdf/english_history.pdf.
2. "Changing The Game With Innovation," *The New York Times*, May 24, 2008.
3. Huston and Sakkab, 2006.
4. "Changing The Game With Innovation," *The New York Times*, May 24, 2008.
5. Huston and Sakkab, 2006, p. 61.
6. "360-Degree Innovation," *BusinessWeek*, October 11, 2004.
7. Huston and Sakkab, 2006.
8. See www.strategy-business.com/press/freearticle/08304.
9. See www.strategy-business.com/press/freearticle/08304.
10. Cho and Pucik, 2005.
11. See Birkinshaw, Hamel, and Mol (2008) for a discussion about management innovation.
12. Cho and Pucik, 2005.
13. Gupta and Govindarajan, 2000.
14. J.F. Welch, "Timeless Principles," *Executive Excellence*, February 2001, p. 3.
15. Kogut and Zander, 1992; 1993.
16. The distinction between explicit and tacit knowledge was first made by the epistemologist Polanyi (1966) and developed by Nonaka (Nonaka, 1994; Nonaka and Takeuchi, 1995).
17. Szulanski, 1996.
18. See Minbaeva et al. (2003) for a discussion of the importance of paying attention to receiver ability and motivation as integrated elements of subsidiary absorptive capacity. Their study revealed that the use of HR practices was positively associated with both ability and motivation.
19. Minbaeva and Michailova (2004) use the term "disseminative capacity" to refer to the ability and willingness of organizational members to share knowledge.
20. Hansen, Mors, and Løvås, 2005.
21. Cross and Prusak, 2003.
22. Cross and Prusak, 2003. A meta-analysis of 75 studies revealed a significant relationship ($r = 0.19$) between receiver absorptive capacity and knowledge transfer (Van Wijk, Jansen, and Lyles, 2008).
23. Szulanski, 1996. The term "absorptive capacity" (Cohen and Levinthal, 1990) is commonly used in the academic literature to describe the ability of the receiving unit to evaluate, assimilate, and exploit new knowledge from the environment. See Lane, Koka, and Pathak (2006) for a discussion of absorptive capacity.

24. Leonard-Barton, 1995.
25. Leonard-Barton, 1995.
26. Zahra and George, 2002; Lane, Koka, and Pathak, 2006.
27. Szulanski, 1996.
28. The term "halo effect" is used to describe people's tendency to believe that low performers have no ideas of value to others (Gupta, Govindarajan, and Wang, 2008).
29. Darr and Kurtzberg, 2000.
30. Cross and Prusak, 2003.
31. Paik and Choi, 2005.
32. Lazarova and Tarique, 2005.
33. Bonache and Zárraga-Oberty, 2008.
34. Support for this conclusion is summarized in Szulanski (1996).
35. Monteiro, Arvidsson, and Birkinshaw, 2008.
36. Dendrell, Arvidsson, and Zander, 2004.
37. Monteiro, Arvidsson, and Birkinshaw, 2008.
38. See Subramanian and Venkatraman (2001) for a study of how cross-national teams contributed to the global product development capabilities of multinationals.
39. We return to lateral structural mechanisms later in this chapter.
40. See Chapter 5.
41. See Hansen and von Oetinger (2001).
42. Hansen and von Oetinger, 2001.
43. Probst and Borzillo, 2008; Wegner and Snyder, 2000.
44. "Motivating Workers By Giving Them A Vote," *Wall Street Journal Online,* August 25, 2005.
45. Probst and Borzillo, 2008.
46. See Moore and Birkinshaw (1998) for a discussion of centers of excellence in service firms.
47. Three types of center have been identified in global service firms—charismatic (formed around an individual); focused (a small group of experts in a single location, e.g., the McKinsey competence units); and virtual (a larger group of specialists in multiple locations, linked by a database and proprietary tools). The charismatic and focused centers are well equipped to handle tacit knowledge, while the focused and virtual centers can process more firm-specific knowledge than any single individual (Moore and Birkinshaw, 1998).
48. See Van Wijk, Jansen, and Lyles (2008) for a review of the relationship between social capital and knowledge transfer in multinationals. Social capital is also important for external knowledge acquisition and sharing, which we cover later in this chapter.
49. Hansen, Mors, and Løvås, 2005.
50. Tsai and Ghoshal, 1998.
51. Nahapiet and Ghoshal, 1998.
52. Trust was found to be the strongest predictor of interunit knowledge transfer in a recent meta-analysis (Van Wijk, Jansen, and Lyles, 2008).
53. Gupta and Govindarajan, 2008.
54. Currie and Kerrin, 2003.
55. Monteiro, Arvidsson, and Birkinshaw, 2008.
56. Takeuchi, Osono, and Shimizu, 2008.
57. Adler, 1999.
58. Interviews with Toyota President Katsuaki Watanabe, published in Stewart and Raman (2007).

59. http://www.toyota.co.jp/en/ir/library/annual/pdf/2008/ar08_e.pdf.
60. Åbø et al., 2001.
61. Björkman, Barner-Rasmussen, and Li, 2004.
62. Gupta and Govindarajan, 2008.
63. See Løwendahl (2005) for a fine analysis of knowledge management in professional service firms; see also Eccles and Crane (1987) and Maister (1993).
64. Volmer and Mills, 1966.
65. Løwendahl, 2005.
66. See "Lawyers Go Global," *The Economist,* February 26, 2000; Brock, Yaffe, and Dembovsky, 2006; Morgan and Quack, 2005. European law practices have been hotly engaged in acquiring and merging to capture the lucrative market for cross-border deals. Lawyers are painfully turned into executives.
67. These configurations were apparent from the research of Løwendahl (2005) and Maister (1993). See also Doorewaard and Meihuizen (2000) for empirical support in a study of Dutch and German PSFs.
68. Løwendahl, 2005.
69. Maister, 1993.
70. Brock, Yaffe, and Dembovsky, 2006; Morgan and Quack, 2005.
71. Segal-Horn and Dean, 2008.
72. Hansen, Nohria, and Tierney, 1999.
73. See example on appraising global collaboration at Bain & Co. introduced in Chapter 9.
74. Hansen, Nohria, and Tierney, 1999.
75. See Doorewaard and Meihuizen (2000) for a more extended discussion of this point.
76. Løwendahl, 2005.
77. Bartlett, 1996.
78. The meta-analysis conducted by Van Wijk, Jansen, and Lyles (2008) found that company-internal and -external knowledge sharing/transfers were largely influenced by the same mechanisms.
79. Doz, Santos, and Williamson, 2001.
80. Birkinshaw, 2004.
81. Inkpen and Tsang, 2005.
82. Doz, Santos, and Williamson, 2001.
83. Teagarden, Meyer, and Jones, 2008.
84. Fleming and Marx, 2006.
85. Doz, Santos, and Williamson, 2001.
86. Huston and Sakkab, 2006.
87. Adler, 1999.
88. Tapscott and Williams, 2007.
89. B. Jaruzelski, and K. Dehoff, "Beyond Borders: The Global Innovation 1000," 2008. See www.booz.com.
90. Huston and Sakkab, 2006.
91. See DeLong (2004) for an analysis of retaining the knowledge of preretirees.
92. Nonaka, 1994.
93. See Chapter 4.
94. See Chapter 7.
95. See Furuya et al. (2009) for an analysis of factors affecting individual learning during expatriate assignments and the application of their ccompetencies in new assignments following repatriation. Oddou, Osland, and Blakeney (2009) offer a conceptual model of factors influencing repatriate knowledge sharing.

96. Lazarova and Tarique, 2005.

97. Ancona et al., 2001.

98. Weick, 1979.

99. Åbø et al., 2001.

100. Kummerle's research is reported in "Winning In A World Without Boundaries," *Industry Week,* October 20, 1997.

101. Christensen, 1997.

102. Tsang, 2002.

103. Komin, 1990.

104. Watson Wyatt (2005): Human Resource Development and Innovation in Thailand. Available at www.watsonwyatt.com.

105. Thanks to Joe Santos for this observation on Microsoft and Cisco.

106. Fleming and Marx, 2006.

107. Afuah, 1998.

108. B. Jaruzelski, and K. Dehoff, "Beyond Borders: The Global Innovation 1000," 2008. See www.booz.com.

109. Prith Banerjee, Senior VP for Research, HP, quoted by B. Jaruzelski, and K. Dehoff, "Beyond Borders: The Global Innovation 1000," 2008. See www.booz.com.

110. "A Gathering Storm," *Economist,* November 22, 2008, pp. 67–68.

111. B. Jaruzelski, and K. Dehoff, "Beyond Borders: The Global Innovation 1000," 2008. See www.booz.com.

112. Doz, Santos, and Williamson, 2001. See Verbeke and Kenworthy (2008) for a comparison of the metanational and the multidivisional form.

113. Leonard and Sensiper, 1998.

114. "Something New Under The Sun. A Special Report On Innovation," *The Economist,* October 13, 2007, p. 14.

115. See www.pg.com.

116. Lindqvist, Sölvell, and Zander, 2000.

117. Hansen and Birkinshaw, 2007.

118. Kanter, 1989.

119. March, 1991.

120. Teigland, 2000.

121. Van de Ven et al., 1999, p. 12. See also Argote (1999) and Dougherty (1996).

122. See McFadyen and Cannella (2004) for an analysis of how the number and strength of relationships are related to knowledge exchange and creation.

123. Brown and Eisenhardt, 1997, 1998.

124. Galunic and Eisenhardt, 2001.

CHAPTER 11

Facilitating Change in Multinational Organizations

Managing The Tensions of Change at MedPharm

MedPharm is a German subsidiary of a leading US pharmaceutical company that develops and manufactures active pharmaceutical ingredients for the parent company and other customers.[1] Under the leadership of a charismatic founder, MedPharm pioneered the development of new complex drug compounds, but to finance expansion, the German founder sold the firm to the American corporation in the 1980s. Today MedPharm has five production sites around the world, two in the United States, and one each in Germany, Switzerland, and the United Kingdom. Plants were initially largely autonomous, making products not only for the US parent but also for other firms. However, since the mid-1990s, under some pressure from the US, coordination among plants has increased, mainly to exchange know-how about manufacturing methods and quality. The result was effective low-cost operations worldwide, as well as greatly enhanced customer focus.

As its pipeline of blockbuster drugs began to dry up, the parent firm embarked on an aggressive growth strategy involving R&D investment and partnerships, with targets to increase overall capital efficiency by 20 percent. This led the newly promoted general manager of MedPharm, along with his global pharma division boss and the corporate director of corporate planning at the parent headquarters, to initiate a project to explore its future opportunities.

The outcome was a new MedPharm vision—to become the main supplier of chemicals to the parent company. It would involve outsourcing the manufacturing of simple compounds to other partners, including low-cost but technically competent Chinese firms, so that MedPharm could focus on complex, high-value compounds. It would also mean taking the responsibility for managing the relationships with other external suppliers of chemicals, and strengthening R&D collaboration with the US parent firm. Managing all this would require the development of a strong global supply chain management capability.

A team of 50 managers, almost all from the German headquarters and US parent, was set up to detail this strategy, and divided into four working groups, including one focused on the supply chain. These groups presented their recommendations to top management and all managers, including those from the plants and countries, at a three-day working conference in Milan. There was polite resistance from many in the room, including some "heavyweight" plant managers, who saw the new vision as an attack on their autonomy and a progressive takeover by the American parent. However, opponents were firmly told to play ball, and a new global supply chain function was created. Each plant appointed a key manager to this function with the mandate of aligning the existing supply chain process with the yet-to-be-developed global supply chain platform and underlying IT system.

Eighteen months later, planning began for a follow-up conference to take stock of progress. MedPharm results continued to be good, and costs continued to decline. But, in the eyes of the general manager, progress on building the global supply chain had been frustratingly slow. "People simply aren't working as a global leadership team," he said. "The results these last few years have been good, but that is irrelevant. Our managers are not yet used to taking a global perspective in addition to their local responsibilities."

Some of the plant managers and supply chain managers commented that, with conflicting priorities, one had to be realistic about time horizons for the supply chain project—attention had to be paid to shortening cycle times in the factories, to staying ahead of the changing regulatory environment, and above all to guaranteeing security of supplies to customers. After all, MedPharm was able to manage the current supply process in the traditional way. While a justification for the global supply chain platform was the planned growth in new products and compounds, many felt skeptical about this growth, pointing out that only one major new product had been introduced over the last five years. There was an underlying feeling out in the plants that the global supply chain project was part of growing movement toward centralization and bureaucracy that would undermine the entrepreneurial spirit that had always been a key to MedPharm's success. The project was seen as part of a dangerous Americanization of the company that should be resisted.

Some who had witnessed periods of centralization in the past felt that this one too would eventually blow away. They were already used to fighting battles with the parent over capital expenditure—this was just another battle to fight. And with the incessant pressure to cut costs, there were no spare resources and people to invest in the supply chain project—the returns on which, in any case, seemed uncertain and unclear. There had been many meetings about this, but as one director commented, "Consultation is part of our culture, which means that we have too many meetings. But decisions aren't taken in our culture until they are implemented."

Meanwhile, the frustration was growing at the parent headquarters, particularly in the IT and finance functions. From their perspective, MedPharm continued to optimize each site and neglect the whole. The corporate vice presidents were putting pressure on the MedPharm general manager. "I thought we had agreement on the vision, but there's no sense of urgency," commented the corporate vice president for IT. "MedPharm keeps pushing back and putting off the development of the global platform." Others at headquarters hinted jokingly that it might be tempting simply to sell MedPharm to the Chinese—things might be more straightforward if they were dealing with an external supplier.

Given these conflicting pressures, and with the follow-up conference scheduled to convene in 10 weeks, the MedPharm general manager gave his head of strategy and business development and the HR director the task of developing a plan to resolve the stalemate.

OVERVIEW

Agreeing on the need for greater global integration is one thing, but implementing such a decision is another. MedPharm had a clear and well-planned strategy, but local managers far from headquarters were not convinced of the urgency or importance of a global process to manage the supply chain. The MedPharm case shows that the implementation of strategy and business plans is largely a question of managing change, and that one of the biggest HR challenges in multinational firms is supporting effective execution.

This chapter is divided into three sections. In the first part, we take a macro view of the dualistic organizational change process in multinational firms that leads step-by-step over many years to the transnational organization. We look at the dynamics of the change process from two different starting points: (1) the multidomestic organization that needs to move in the direction of more global integration; and (2) the home country–centered meganational that must foster greater local responsiveness and variation. The key challenge in both cases is managing cycles of alternating focus on global efficiency on the one hand, and global coordination on the other, preventing excessive and disruptive swings between one extreme and the other. This involves careful steering between dualities, as our basic framework of the three stages of HRM suggests.[2]

The next part of the chapter considers the challenges of executing and implementing strategies and business plans in the international corporation. Execution depends on both analysis and acceptance of the decision. We concentrate on the latter—how to build acceptance of decisions in a multinational organization where those decisions involve sacrifice, hardship, loss of power, and even loss of jobs. Here we build on a framework for understanding the management of change that has been validated in many organizations across a variety of cultures—procedural justice or fair process. We spell out some of the lessons with the help of a *five E* framework—*engagement, exploration* of options, *explanation* of decisions, setting clear *expectations,* and *evaluation* of outcomes. We conclude this part by discussing those key facets of change management that are particularly important for HR managers in their change partner roles.

The pace of external change is increasing. In the final section of this chapter, we discuss how multinationals can build strategic agility. This requires many of the organizational qualities that we have discussed in this book. The key to the development of the strategic agility that drives rapid and effective change is people management.

THE ARDUOUS ROUTE TO TRANSNATIONAL ORGANIZATION

Although there is little research on the topic, our experience is that the route to a transnational organization takes 10–25 years to travel, regardless of whether the starting point is a multidomestic or a meganational organization.[3] Why does it take so long? Formal structures may change quickly, and processes may take more time. But as we will see, it takes longer to change the skill sets of key people, and even longer to change their mindsets. And this route is rarely a linear path—as we discussed in Chapter 1, it typically involves moving and shifting in different directions.

There are different models of complex change processes—the evolutionary model is one and the punctuated equilibrium model is another.[4] The latter is based on the notion of the importance of fit or coherence in organizations. Put simply, organizations go through cycles of evolution (where tight coherence develops) and revolution (where external change leads to radical reconfiguration of fit). This frames theories of transformational change and has been used to analyze how technological innovation leads to strategic, structural, and organizational revolutions in industries.[5]

But a third *spiral* model of change and development captures better the dynamics of transnational organizational development in a world of dualities. For example, a management team may recognize the importance of developing functional excellence. But it also knows that functional excellence, if taken to extremes, can lead to pathologies—rivalry over resources and slow decision making. At the first sign of such symptoms, attention therefore turns to building cross-functional teamwork . . . but with the awareness that this can lead to lowered functional excellence if taken too far. In spiral development, the priorities shift back and forth between functional orientation and teamwork, between local and global, gradually developing layered capabilities that are difficult to imitate.[6] There is always the danger that the spiral development will become a dysfunctional pendulum with excessive swings—sometimes paralyzing the organization, as we saw earlier in the case of ABB.

Many authorities on change believe that the spiral model, which creates virtuous circles if well managed and vicious circles if the cycles oscillate too far—is a better image of complex change processes than that of transformation or "changing A into B."[7] In Figure 11–1, we show the hypothesized spiral change path as a multidomestic organization gradually moves toward becoming a transnational over an extended period of time, taken as 20 years for illustrative purposes.

FIGURE 11–1. **Hypothesized Spiral Change Path over 20 Years as a Multido-mestic Organization Gradually Moves to Transnational**

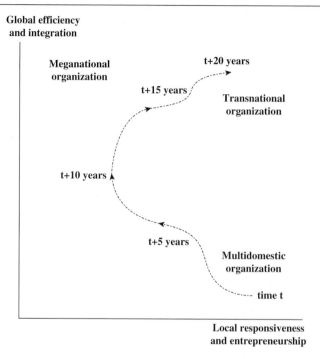

Complex change processes depend on a starting point. In organizational theory, this is known as path dependence—the history of a firm cannot be ignored when assessing the change route it should take. For example, faced with the necessity to respond to a change in basic technology, an enterprise that has been thriving is likely to respond in a different way from an enterprise that is already in a state of crisis.[8]

The context and orientation of change for corporations with a heritage of local responsiveness is quite different from those whose starting point is global integration. Consequently, we will discuss these change paths and dilemmas in "going transnational" separately.

Spiral Evolution of the Multidomestic Organization

Let us start with the change path of an organization that has grown successfully through a multidomestic strategy of local responsiveness. It now finds that competitive forces demand a greater degree of global integration to enable further growth and to ward off low-cost rivals. The consolidation of multiple small-scale manufacturing or engineering facilities around the world may be required to gain economies of scale and to speed up responsiveness to technology change. Greater standardization of processes is needed to lower cost and avoid duplicating initiatives. Slowness in leveraging knowledge across borders means that the firm is losing markets to more nimble competitors, so the traditional silos have to be broken. As with MedPharm, there is a need for a global process to manage a more complex chain of internal and external suppliers across a wider range of products. Time-based competition pushes for strategic integration of development and marketing processes to speed up time to market across the world.

This has been the situation for many firms in industries that historically focused on staying close to local markets, such as those producing consumer goods—Nestlé, Johnson & Johnson, and Colgate are among myriad examples. It is also the case for firms in other industries that grew successfully by replicating core technology in multiple markets, and then found that technologies were changing (Kodak and Philips in the 1980s and 1990s; or, more recently, the music distribution industry following the impact of Internet distribution on compact disk sales).

If a senior executive or the top HR officer of a corporation in this situation were asked for advice on an appropriate change strategy, how should she or he respond? Ghoshal and Bartlett suggest plausibly that there are successful and less successful sequences of steps.[9] Their model of the change process is shown in Figure 11–2. This is based on the simple observation that the performance of

FIGURE 11–2. Change Paths in Moving from Multidomestic Organization to Transnational

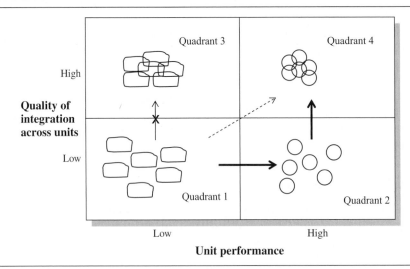

Source: S. Ghoshal and C.A. Bartlett, *Managing across Borders: The Transnational Solution,* 2nd ed. (London: Random House, 1998).

a complex corporation depends on two factors the performance of the individual units (subsidiaries, businesses, countries) and the level of integration and in particular coordination across those units. These are the two axes in Figure 11–2.

Most multidomestic companies face a portfolio of subsidiaries at different starting points, located in different quadrants of the figure, though mostly somewhere in quadrant 1, in a state of satisfactory underperformance. There may be a few strongly performing units that may jealously guard the independence that their results provide (quadrant 2). In the multidomestic firm, there is also a clear lack of linkage, leverage, and coordination across these units.

The direct transformational route to quadrant 4 in Figure 11–2—high unit performance and high integration—may be appealing. But the researchers suggest that this is too ambitious. For example, for over a decade, Philips aggressively pursued synergies and integration, assuming that this would address the underperformance of subsidiaries or divisions—but without much success. The contradictions were too complex, resulting in confusion. It was difficult to integrate operations that were struggling with their own individual performance problems. Ghoshal and Bartlett note that Philips managers concluded skeptically, "Four drunks do not make an effective team."[10] Others have argued cogently that the attempt to pursue synergies does not usually succeed under these circumstances—one of the reasons why "synergy" has become a concept full of disappointment.[11]

Ghoshal and Bartlett argue that a sequenced or spiral process of change is more effective. Global rationalization should be the initial step. GE was an example when it set out to become number one or two in each of its businesses, with clear accountability for results and common performance processes.[12] The focus in rationalization is on performance management, common metrics, and economies of scale. The phase of rationalization is then followed by a focus on integration—breaking down the boundaries between units, fostering the sharing of know-how and cross-boundary projects, as GE did, with its drive to build a "boundaryless" learning organization, and as happened at MedPharm during the last decade. That integration may be facilitated in turn by structural change, with the aggregation of local units into regions (discussed in the next section), which will facilitate further integration. Or, as at MedPharm, attention may focus on introducing a key global process, such as a global supply chain.

Steering to Avoid Organizational Pendulums

The process of change leading to transnational organization is likely to follow alternating phases of attention to unit performance followed by attention to integration and coordination. Nestlé has followed this path—in 2002, top management felt that they could not make further progress toward transnational integration until a common, global, IT-based platform with standardized processes for the enterprise had been created—hence the launch of the GLOBE project.[13] The delicate steering task facing Chris Johnson, the Nestlé VP responsible for GLOBE, was to introduce this global standardization without antagonizing regional and local business managers.

The managers of the most successful units are likely to resist what they see as loss of autonomy, in their eyes a dangerous swing to centralized bureaucracy. Faced with such resistance, corporate leaders are understandably tempted to resort to strong-arm tactics that in turn confirm the worst fears of local managers— the best of whom may be lured away to other opportunities. This may lead to renewed concern about unit performance; so if the change is not managed well, structures and processes oscillate wildly between centralization and decentralization to the point of creating organizational paralysis.

Organizational steering means avoiding disruptive swings of the pendulum. The metaphor of the navigator or helmsman of a yacht, which we introduced in Chapter 2, captures this well—steering close to the wind and then tacking back, taking currents and wind changes into account, to move the boat toward the buoy in a series of smooth curves.[14]

Managers in the field will invariably experience the changes focused on global efficiency as a shift to centralization, bureaucracy, and concentration. Since they have to give up autonomy, and since their roles will change, resistance is inevitable. This is what happened at MedPharm. Senior leadership paid insufficient attention to building the commitment of key MedPharm managers to the introduction of global processes. Although the plant managers were members of the MedPharm executive team, they were certainly not committed to vigorous execution. Change, as we will see later, involves both the head and the heart. The plant managers may have accepted rationally the need for a global supply chain, but emotionally they felt less commitment. As a result, they proceeded with its implementation at a snail's pace.

Local MedPharm managers had many overt reasons for proceeding cautiously, of which the most important was the imperative of guaranteeing supplies to local customers. However, none of the plant managers saw their roles as satisfying today's customers *while simultaneously managing the global change.* The transnational change journey involves this vital but difficult change in mindset, which in turn implies new skills. Instead, they repeated nightmare stories from other companies about the problems of introducing global IT systems and frustrating customers, citing these as a reason for putting off collaboration on the new global IT system (which would indeed cut out most of their local IT departments).

When under pressure, people prefer to exploit the processes they know well rather than venture into the uncertainty of developing new ones. The local MedPharm managers felt they could manage the new product pipeline with existing methods; and they were not convinced that there would be enough new pharmaceutical products to justify the need for the new global supply chain process: "Why waste money when the benefits aren't clear?" A final, more emotional and unspoken argument was that the global supply chain meant that a key function—IT—would be run from the United States. This was viewed as part of a progressive "Americanization" of the company that would undermine its proud German roots. Stories of American IT managers who had never set foot outside their home states, and had no understanding of European needs, fueled this resistance.

The consequence of the slow progress in building the global supply chain was the increasing frustration of the American parent—"We had agreement and now they are dragging their heels." There was discussion about bringing in the heavy guns of top management and either taking over the running of MedPharm or using the threat of selling it off to a third party. As the MedPharm experience shows, the failure to manage understandable local resistance leads to a risk of overreaction toward centralization. A self-fulfilling prophecy can be set in motion; when the headquarters takes over, the best locals will leave, leading to a vacuum that reinforces central control, since it is unlikely that local successors will have been prepared.

When a pendulum swings too far one way, the natural reaction is to correct it by swinging it as far in the opposite direction. Instead of oscillations between central influence and local initiative, there will be swings between centralization and decentralization (terms that any smart organization will take pains to avoid). A good illustration of this is the story of Coca-Cola in the box "When the Pendulum Swings from Local to Global . . . and Back."

When the Pendulum Swings from Local to Global . . . and Back

A striking case of the consequences of taking successive strategies to extremes is Coca-Cola, which expanded successfully through a multidomestic approach under Robert Woodruff from the 1920s until the early 1980s.[15] During this period, more than a thousand local operations around the world were independently managed and supported by Coca-Cola headquarters. Robert Goizueta's strategy from 1981 until his death in 1997 was the opposite, seeking out economies of scale and transferring the American taste for soft drinks to the rest of the world. Overturning the company's multidomestic legacy, he imposed an unprecedented degree of centralization and standardization, led from the headquarters in Atlanta.

By the early 1990s, surveys showed that Coca-Cola, now run as a well-oiled meganational, was the undisputed model for a globalized organization. However, problems with overcentralization were beginning to appear even before Goizueta's successor, Douglas Ivester, took over in 1997. Shortly afterward, a sag in the world economy hit Coca-Cola's expansion, major markets took a nosedive, regulators in Europe resisted the company's attempts to buy new brands, and slow responsiveness to contamination problems in France and Belgium had a negative effect on the company's image. In two years, its stock evaluation declined by US$70 billion from its peak.

The board fired Ivester and brought in Douglas Daft, who decided to take the organization back to the local roots of its past. "Think local, act local" was the motto as 6,000 layoffs were ordered, mostly at the Atlanta headquarters. Local executives were delighted but ill equipped to deal with the sudden strategic reversal. Local advertising campaigns, often poorly conceived, sprung up around the world, and costs increased faster than sales volume.

Daft was obliged to step down, and a retired Coke executive, Neville Isdell, was brought back to run the company in May 2004. His publicly expressed views were that his predecessors had "swung the pendulum too far over." Since then, Isdell has been trying to strike a balance between reinforcing head office capabilities while supporting more variation and innovation at regional and country levels, particularly in big and highly competitive markets like India and China.

Regionalization

With effective steering between local autonomy and global integration, this spiral change path may lead to what we described in Chapter 5 as the differentiated network organization. Lead countries emerge as centers of excellence in specific businesses, taking the responsibility for each business's global coordination. While some economies of scale may be built globally, it is more practical to find others at a regional level.

It has been argued by Rugman that most of the world's major corporations are in fact regionally oriented rather than global in their scope, and that Friedman's portrayal of the "flat world" of globalization is a distortion of reality.[16] Breaking the world into a triad of North America, Europe, and Asia, most of the production and sales of *Fortune* 500 companies are overwhelmingly in their home regions. Competition takes place principally within these regions rather than across the globe.[17] Rugman's argument is that the concept of "transnational" applies to only a small percentage of firms, the vast proportion of multinationals being predominantly focused on a region or even a country.

Indeed, the path to transnational development for multidomestic firms often involves grouping small units into regions to improve coordination.[18] These regions are typically formed on the basis of geographic proximity (which corresponds broadly to other forms of proximity—cultural, administrative, and economic).[19] The regional headquarters usually assumes two roles.[20] The first is *strategy development and implementation*, closely linked to the worldwide headquarters and involving budgeting and control, scouting or local business development, intelligence gathering, signaling regional commitment to internal and external stakeholders, and ensuring the attention of the global headquarters. The second role is providing *coordination and common administrative services*, more closely linked to local operations. This may involve managing lateral interfaces, pooling resources to take advantage of regional economies of scale, local benchmarking, and spreading best practices. In the HR arena, the regional staff often assume responsibility for leadership development.

The managerial approach to the region will vary with the structure and degree of transnational development. As Lasserre and Schütte show, the regional headquarters can manage its relationship with the national units in three different ways—vertically, virtually, and horizontally.[21] The relationship in the *vertical* model is hierarchical, with local managers reporting to the regional leaders. This facilitates rapid decision making and deployment of resources across the region, which may be advantageous in certain industries, but at the risk of loss of local initiative and entrepreneurship. A second model is that of a *virtual* regional headquarters, without a physical center or staff, relying on key local managers who assume regional as well as local roles. GE had a virtual regional structure like this in Europe and Asia for many years, and it can work well if there is a strong worldwide corporate culture along with local managers who can perform well in the face of considerable role ambiguity. A third model is *horizontal,* similar to the virtual model but with a physical regional staff managing lateral projects and coordination zones where it can add value. This allows local managers to retain clear accountability but moderates their individualism. The horizontal coordination may be weak (merely exchanging information), moderate (through a focused committee), or strong (involving joint decision making via a council).

Changes in Managerial Roles

In a multidomestic organization like MedPharm, a key role is that of the country manager, who often has full general management responsibility within the bounds of targets and a strategy negotiated with headquarters. However, the country manager's role changes with transnational development. The general management responsibility disappears, and it is replaced by more complex coordination demands that require sophisticated leadership skills rather than simply the ability to exercise authority. Specific role requirements vary. Sometimes the dimension of resource coordination (of people and local suppliers) remains. Sometimes ambassadorship toward local authorities and key external stakeholders is critical, as well as certain legal responsibilities to represent the organization locally. If the move is to a front–back organization, the role may shift to front-end customer responsibility, with the country manager essentially becoming the local sales and marketing manager. When these shifts toward transnational organization started to occur in the 1980s, there was a widespread view that the country manager's role was no longer necessary. But today companies recognize that this role can be important—at least in large markets like China and India—although it now involves more complex skills.[22] Reality has become more differentiated—not every country needs a country manager.

In the multidomestic firm, the career structure for local managers is relatively transitive—people become bigger kings or queens as they move up in general management. But the leadership career structure in transnational firms is much more intransitive—the role of a country or regional manager requires quite different skills than those of a local business unit manager. For example, new competencies are needed in coordinating without authority and in structuring important but ambiguous strategic tasks. Although there is little research on the topic, some corporations believe that you cannot teach old country managers new tricks, and the more successful they are, the more likely they are to resist; so new people must be brought in.

A multidomestic industrial corporation we worked with decided to strengthen international coordination by adding a virtual dimension to regional committees. The roles of European country managers were matrixed so that they would have horizontal P&L accountability across Europe for a lead product, while retaining vertical responsibility for all products within their countries. A careful assessment led senior management to believe that managers who had been in their country roles for three years or less would adapt with appropriate training and coaching, while those who had been country kings or queens for more than five years would certainly resist. The change strategy was to put pressure on the latter group for two years while preparing potential successors. Two years later, five of the seven managers in this group were indeed replaced.

We remember a discussion with an Asian country manager in another multinational corporation that had just changed to a front–back organization.[23] This change meant that his role had shifted from being the P&L boss to becoming in effect a local sales and marketing manager. Our man experienced the change as a demeaning demotion rather than an opportunity to develop new coordination and leadership skills. "Is this change permanent?" he asked. "Or is it just one of those temporary organizational fads that will blow away?" Having been convinced that the change was real and permanent, he became one of a small minority of local managers in the firm who set out to adapt and develop new skills. Four years later, he was promoted to corporate vice president, heading up all front-end marketing operations across Southeast Asia.

Encouraging Subsidiary Initiative in the Meganational

Let us turn now to the different change path of the organization that has successfully grown through a meganational strategy of global integration. The home culture dominates the company. The capabilities are located in the parent country. Take as an example Intel, a typical meganational run worldwide out of its headquarters in California's Silicon Valley. Until a few years ago, competing on economies of scale and scope in R&D and manufacturing, Intel had a policy called "Copy Exactly," which discouraged experimentation at individual factories. Engineers and technicians would painstakingly clone proven Intel manufacturing techniques from one plant to the next—down to the color of workers' gloves, wall paint, and other features that would seem to have no bearing on efficiency.[24]

Today, the impact of competitive forces means that a higher degree of local initiative is necessary for further growth, as many previously meganational companies have experienced over the last 15 years. Markets around the world, to which simple and standardized goods were once exported, became more sophisticated, coming under attack from innovative local competitors. R&D, with its complex interdependencies between disciplines and functions, could no longer be located solely in the headquarters country. Strategic innovations originate less and less frequently at the center and more often in some lead market elsewhere. So lead countries need their own R&D, and the relevant locations for R&D departments may vary from one business area to another.

As multinational firms become increasingly dependent on local entrepreneurship, the process of encouraging local initiative involves careful steering to avoid costly swings of the pendulum. If local units are suddenly given the unconstrained right to do things in a local way and for local benefit only, as happened at Coca-Cola, wasteful excesses can be expected. The right to exercise initiative has to be earned.

A study of 28 subsidiaries of multinational corporations in Ireland attempted to map out the stages through which subsidiaries gradually evolve to become full-fledged strategic centers that assume worldwide responsibility for a business within a multinational.[25] Foreign affiliates went through eight stages following start-up. Their challenge in the early stages focused on fulfilling the subsidiary mandate in a superior way. This allowed the subsidiary to take initiatives—a product development opportunity, or an opportunity to expand into a third market of marginal concern to the parent. If these projects were successful, the subsidiary gradually assumed greater strategic importance in the eyes of the parent. In time, some units became strategic centers and ultimately the worldwide apex for a business. What is critical in this spiral path is the ability of the subsidiary to take developmental initiative at the same time as it defends its credibility through solid performance on its core mandate.[26]

Transferring Capabilities

Most multinational corporations have developed their international operations from the basis of a strong home country organization. Organizational capabilities were first developed in the parent country and only then gradually transferred abroad. It took P&G almost 100 years to make its first foreign direct investment and Toyota three decades to establish its first manufacturing unit outside Japan.

Capabilities are complex bundles of skills, attitudes, and processes,[27] and they can be most carefully nurtured in the parent country. P&G had its research labs in the US; Toyota's production capabilities were all located in Japan; and Hewlett-Packard's product development capabilities were centered in Silicon Valley. The box on "How Singapore Became HP's Global Center of Competence for Printers" describes some of the HRM challenges associated with the transfer of capabilities to foreign units. These challenges are still relevant today, as more and more multinationals relocate their manufacturing operations to low-cost countries and transfer R&D capabilities to emerging markets.

Organizational capabilities are difficult to transfer because of their complexity—a capability is a firm-specific, interwoven configuration of skills, in which it is impossible to separate the HR elements from the technical or managerial elements. As a former director of research for IBM put it, "It is hard to transfer the full complexity of a technology. . . . If the receptor knows very little, he can do very little with even a simple idea, because he cannot generate the mass of detail that is required to put it into execution. On the other hand, if he knows a great deal and is capable of generating the necessary details, then from just a few sentences or pieces of technology he will fill in all the rest."[28] Transfer is not a simple technical matter, since it involves learning and adapting knowledge to a new context.[29]

How Singapore Became HP's Global Center of Competence for Printers

A unit that started as an assembly outpost for HP in Singapore in the early 1970s ultimately took over global responsibility for HP's computer printers. The story of how this happened illustrates the gradual transfer of organizational capabilities from the home country headquarters to a subsidiary.[30] Let us outline the HRM challenges at each of four different stages.

Stage 1

HP-Singapore began as the start-up phase of assembly operations, when there was maximum dependence on the home country. The HRM challenges were those of the first stage, building foundations[31]—skills training and retention management, managerial and supervisory development, inculcation of basic organizational values, such as maintenance norms, integrity, and safety.

Stage 2

By achieving high productivity at low cost, the Singapore subsidiary earned an extension of its mandate to cover adaptation of the product to local markets, leading to full-scale manufacturing. Now the HRM challenges shifted to the development of local suppliers' competencies and performance management. Greater discipline had to be instilled in areas such as quality management, responsibility, cooperation, and weeding out poor performers—also at supplier firms.

Stage 3

After mastering the entire manufacturing process, the subsidiary began to seek the right to redesign systems (printers) for other Asian markets, such as Japan. Successful passage through this critical stage depends on local development of complex managerial and technical capacities through advanced education of locals (at universities in the parent country), projects, sharing best practices, and personnel transfers. Unless the growing sense of local autonomy and initiative is matched with a high degree of normative integration (selection and development based on shared values), it is not certain that this stage will be successful. Indeed, HP-Singapore experienced various setbacks at this stage, which forced the parent company to question local competencies, although one can argue that failure is a necessary element of such learning.[32]

Stage 4

The Singapore subsidiary now assumed full responsibility for product design, becoming a global center of competence with peer relationships between parent and subsidiary. In the transition to this stage, HR attention should be focused on global projects that transfer competencies in reverse (from the subsidiary to the headquarters), developing matrix roles and responsibilities, facilitating employee mobility, and building social capital across boundaries. Multinationals tend to be much more skilled at transferring capabilities out from the center; the challenge is to transfer them back from the affiliates into the center.

The HP case illustrates how a subsidiary may build up its capabilities over time and eventually achieve important worldwide roles in the corporation as a whole. These lead subsidiaries are expected to coordinate their activities with those of other parts of the multinational and to share their knowledge, although, given the challenges of global knowledge management discussed in the previous chapter, less sharing may take place between foreign units than is perceived by the headquarters.[33]

Managing Increasing Organizational Complexity

During the 1990s, ABB was probably the most bold and celebrated model for how to move from a centrally controlled organization to a transnational model. Local responsiveness was embodied in a structure of 5,000 business units; to manage integration, these business units reported into a matrix of product lines and geographic regions, as well as a central project management function. The idea was to capture the advantages of economies of scale along with local entrepreneurship. But this proved excessively complex, beyond the capacities of ABB's managers, and it was held together for a decade only by the skill and dedication of its architect, Percy Barnevik. His attempt at structuring complexity did not turn out to be the model for the future.

Ghemawat suggests that one strategy is to try to reduce and structure the complexity of high local variation so that global coordination is manageable.[34] One way of reducing complexity is to *manage product focus*. Some products fit well across the world, with little need for variation, while others require a high degree of local adaptation. This argues for moving to an organization based on business or product lines, so that each business can vary the local–global balance accordingly. Another way of structuring complexity is to *organize by geography*, on regional lines, so that variation can be managed within regions, like Southeast Asia, which have some common market and cultural characteristics.

Toyota had only one production base, Japan, for its first 50 years in the automobile business. Driven by exploding sales in the United States, overseas production increased from less than 5 percent in 1985 to almost 30 percent a decade later, reaching 46 percent by 2007. This led to the evolution of Toyota's regional organizations and a growing commitment to building strong regional capabilities. Globalization continued with attempts to share fixed costs by sharing common platforms. Today, some plants have almost global mandates: for example, manual transmissions made at a plant in Asia will not only be shipped to assembly sites in the region but also to Toyota facilities in other parts of the world.

Another strategy for managing complexity is to *externalize areas that require strong local adaptation* through alliances that enable the firm to tap into local knowledge and skills, or through local franchising or outsourcing. For example, Western pharmaceutical companies in China have typically outsourced sales and marketing of nonstrategic products in China to third-party companies that have specific know-how in the Chinese pharmaceutical distribution system. The challenge here is how to stay close to the market, since what is nonstrategic today may be critically important tomorrow.

A further strategy is to try to *reduce the cost of responsiveness* by mass customization, enabled by flexible but efficient plants that can supply products adapted to different markets at low cost. The use of global platforms at Toyota and other auto manufacturers are an example of this, with platforms (such as the transmission system) being made at a small number for sites, but with final assembly taking place at many other local plants. Supply chain coordination becomes a core capability.

In order to steer the organization through continuous change and increasing complexity, as the firm moves from meganational to transnational, it will inevitably also need to invest in developing leaders—at many levels—who have the mindset and skills to cope with these challenges.

Developing New Leadership Competencies

The simple and clear-cut structure of the globally oriented meganational is powerful, especially for the people in positions of responsibility at the headquarters. Driven by the deep—and erroneous—assumption that one size fits all, the strength of the centralized meganational is economies of scale that are indeed likely to be highly visible in the important home market.[35] Adding greater local responsiveness and consequent variation, with more complex differentiated structures, requires a change in leadership skill and thinking—a much stronger global mindset, among both headquarter managers and those out in the field. We have written about the implications for global leadership throughout this book,[36] and we summarize some of them here.

VALUING DIVERSITY. One of the broadest implications is that leaders have to learn to value diversity rather than suppress it. As Hewlett-Packard's former CEO, Carly Fiorina, put it, "We need to recognize the value in diversity. Not everyone must be the same. To build great teams, we need to encourage differences. As a nation, industry, and company, we must start valuing differences. . . . This isn't just the business issue *du jour*—it's a strategic business imperative."[37]

COMPETENCIES OF LOCAL MANAGERS. Local recruitment needs to favor initiative. In the past, this was a major concern in some regions of the world, such as China, Japan, and Russia, where the political regime or the culture discouraged initiative. Japanese enterprises are particularly handicapped, since their leadership development practices do not foster individual initiative—entrepreneurial locals are unlikely to tolerate the rigorous but slow process of socialization in Japanese firms.[38] Senior managers in local subsidiaries in particular need to be selected and groomed for their qualities of entrepreneurship. Their roles should focus on creating and pursuing opportunities, attracting scarce skills and resources, and managing continuous improvement.

NETWORKING. Local managers with an entrepreneurial orientation should be encouraged to build relationships across the wider organization by, for example, involving them in important cross-border projects. There are three main reasons for this: first, to defend local initiatives against undue interference;

second, to be able to draw on corporate resources and support; and third, to ensure that successful initiatives are leveraged by the corporation rather than leading to local fiefdoms.[39]

INTERNATIONAL MOBILITY. A delicate balance needs to be maintained with respect to international mobility. International experience develops networks and global mindset, but excessive mobility among senior local managers may be detrimental to entrepreneurship.[40] One study found that a key factor in raising the ambition of the subsidiary was the tenure of the general manager; high performers had been with their subsidiaries for an average of 12 years, with over six years as general manager.[41] On the other hand, this creates new tensions. The development pipeline through subsidiaries becomes blocked, and after too many years in a post, career and renewal prospects for local general managers may be limited.

COMPETENCIES OF BUSINESS AREA AND REGIONAL MANAGERS. While entrepreneurship is required on the part of local managers, a different set of skills is needed by more senior business area, country, or regional managers. They become strategic coaches. One of their most important roles is maintaining a delicate balance between control and freedom—prioritizing short-term operational results while allowing sufficient budgetary and resource freedom to pursue new ideas and opportunities. In the transnational firm, progression through the hierarchy becomes less predictable (more intransitive)—the best local entrepreneur will probably not be the best business area coach.[42]

Organize One Way, Manage the Other Way

As discussed, the change path to transnational organization, from either a multidomestic or a meganational starting point, involves steering between contradictions while avoiding swings of the pendulum. This is captured neatly by the idea of organizing one way but managing the other way.

Indeed, steering between contradictions means that if the focus of reorganization is on introducing global standardization, management should make sure that local entrepreneurs do not become so frustrated that they leave, because their initiatives will be needed in the future. A good way of doing this is to make sure that projects such as Nestlé's GLOBE[43] are headed by leaders with subsidiary experience and credibility in the eyes of local managers. Conversely, when a company gives rein to local initiatives, its attention should be focused on avoiding the risk of reinventing the wheel and ensuring that such initiatives are taken in a disciplined way.

As successful firms in cyclical industries have learned, there are analogous lessons for people and human resource management. As the box "Managing the Sweet and the Sour" outlines, companies have to anticipate the bad times ahead in the growth periods and, if they can, invest during the bad times for the boom period that lies ahead.

Managing the Sweet and the Sour

In the past, many HR managers tended to be reactive. The focus in times of growth was exclusively on immediate challenges such as finding and retaining talent, no matter what the cost. Then attention would swing to layoffs and rationalization in the downturn. There was rarely a tendency to organize one way but manage the other way.

But HR managers are learning to anticipate the sour during sweet times, and vice versa.[44] Even in the best of the times, leading firms such as GE, Microsoft, and Novartis pay as much attention to managing underperformance as they do to developing top talent.

And companies are becoming increasingly aware that the time to build competitive advantage through people is when the going is tough for the industry or global economy.

A few years ago, in the middle of a boom period, the corporate VP of HR for a well-managed multinational, aware how excessively reactive his function was, took his key managers through an exercise. "Next time there is a crunch, we are not going to swing the pendulum as we've always done in the past. Let's figure out the principles or processes that we in HR will fight to preserve in the rough times that surely lie ahead."

When a downturn comes unexpectedly, as it did for most corporations in 2008 as a consequence of the global financial crisis, HR managers should avoid knee-jerk reactions. Before reaching for the axe to reduce the headcount, they should undertake a thorough cost–benefit analysis on what it will cost to recruit, train, and bring a future replacement up to speed, which can average 50–70 percent of the annual salary for a professional or manager. Alternatives to layoffs, such as offering flexible hours or job sharing, should be explored. When headcount reductions are inevitable, they should be differentiated rather than across the board (another payoff from previous investment in solid performance management and talent assessment). The risk of loss of trust, resistance to future change, and damaged teamwork needs to be minimized so that the organization does not pay a high price in terms of disempowered and distrustful survivors.[45] And rewarding good performers should not be forgotten in sour times—there may not be money for bonuses, but attention and verbal praise count for a lot.

The best time for management and HR to make investments in core processes such as talent management is in sour times, to pave the way for future growth.

IMPLEMENTING AND EXECUTING BUSINESS PLANS THROUGH PEOPLE

MedPharm had a clear plan for change, but it went awry because of people factors. Indeed, strategy implementation has always been at the heart of strategic human resource management. Working with line management, one of the most important roles of HR is managing change and ensuring effective execution—indeed this is the "change partner" task of HR that we described in Chapter 2 and to which we will return later in this chapter.

Challenges of Managing Change

In managing change and the underlying realignment, the most important thing ultimately is thoroughness and speed of *execution*. The world is full of strategies and plans, but financial markets, analysts, and shareholders look first and foremost at the track record of leadership in implementing and executing those plans when they judge the value of an enterprise. Indeed, some studies show that the company's ability to execute corporate strategy is at the top of the list of the intangibles that analysts consider when making their recommendations; second is management credibility—basically, their track record on execution and implementation.[46]

The challenges of managing change are captured well in a simple formula that frames an organizational process for managing change at GE (described in the box "Change Acceleration at GE"):[47]

$$Q \times A = E$$

Q stands for the quality of the business, economic, and analytic reasoning leading to a proposed action plan or solution. Professional managers are well trained to do this, and they can also draw on the experience of internal or external consultants. A signifies acceptance of the change and represents the people side of the process. E stands for the effectiveness of change or execution, which will not be high without a high value of A.

The training and professional work of most managers do little to equip them with skills in building acceptance. Consequently, many people who move up into leadership positions have strong skills and experience in Q, but they are often naïve when it comes to A. And yet this simple formula recognizes that even a superb Q solution will fail if no attention is given to the A side—anything multiplied by zero nets out to zero. A well-thought-out plan—scoring say 7 on a 10-point scale—combined with poor acceptance—say 2 out of 10—leads to 14 percent effectiveness in execution. If more attention is paid to managing A, leading to a score of 6, the involvement of people will probably also increase the quality of the analysis to 8. Now we reach 48 percent effectiveness—more than a threefold improvement because of the multiplier effect.

Global managers typically view managing major change as one of the most significant learning experiences that equips them for leadership.[48] Learning how to build acceptance starts with experience in managing change in one's own local culture, but the challenges in the multinational context have added complexity. The leader steering the MedPharm global supply chain project or the Nestlé GLOBE project has to handle cross-cultural differences as well as barriers of distance. The best way of building acceptance with key stakeholders is through dialogue, and yet when some stakeholders live far away, when there are

Change Acceleration at GE

In the early 1990s, Jack Welch decided that the future was increasingly unpredictable. GE had not anticipated the Gulf War, and it lost considerable money in businesses like aircraft engines because of overcapacity in the years that followed. While some managers argued for better planning, top management drew a different conclusion—GE had to be capable of responding faster to whatever strategic changes it confronted. The HR function was commissioned to develop what became its change acceleration process (CAP), one of the eight corporate capabilities cutting across its businesses.[A]

The guiding formula behind CAP is $Q \times A = E$, and a basic principle is that no change happens without leadership. Leaders must analyze the situation carefully, the plan must be sound, and above all, they must be committed to making the change happen. But before they are given the final go-ahead, they must also hold a CAP workshop to work out a strategy for building acceptance. This workshop convenes the key stakeholders for two to four days—perhaps 30–40 people in a project to build a global supply chain, a global cost reduction effort, or a post-acquisition integration—together with a couple of trained facilitators who are familiar with the issues but outsiders to the business in question.

Using a toolkit of exercises, they work through issues like how to create a shared need, a common understanding of why the change should take place; how to communicate the vision to employees in their terms rather than management's jargon; where the resistance is likely to be greatest and what to do about it; and how to alter the structure in order to empower champions and sideline those who are likely to resist. Much of this methodology is based on well-known principles of change management, and over the years CAP has been used to capture and amplify knowledge on managing change.

The CAP methodology is applied thousands of times every year, and GE has trained more than 20,000 facilitators in the methodology, most of them line managers.

[A]The most well known of these eight processes is Six Sigma, linked to capabilities in quality management.

no existing social relationships, and when they speak the company language less than fluently, there is a temptation to ignore them in planning the change—just as MedPharm's change team of 50 managers excluded the key plant managers.

Gaining Acceptance through Fair Process

Since resistance to change is inevitable, building and managing acceptance are not easy, especially in large multinationals such as MedPharm and its parent corporation. Various frameworks grew out of the organizational development (OD) movement focusing on planned change in the 1970s and 1980s. The most well-known framework for practicing managers is the eight-step model developed by Kotter:[49]

1. Create a sense of urgency.
2. Form a powerful coalition.

3. a vision for change.
4. Communicate the vision.
5. Remove obstacles.
6. Create short-term wins.
7. Build in the change.
8. Anchor the changes in the organizational culture.

These are useful concepts to help in building acceptance, and GE's CAP methodology converts them into a practical toolkit. However, the experience of most managers is that change is rarely linear, neatly following such steps. Sometimes it is coercive, often a spiral process (as we discussed earlier), and more often than not it is emergent rather than planned.[50] Change is path-dependent, contingent on the cultural and organizational context.

We find that a good way of understanding what acceptance means and how to build it is to apply the theory of fair process or procedural justice. Indeed, research has validated this theory across cultures and in multinational organizations.[51]

Managers and organizations usually pay close attention to *distributive justice,* the fairness of outcomes—for example, equity and fairness in resource allocation or compensation systems. Distributive justice is focused on resources and outcomes, but the problem with organizational change is that the outcomes will never benefit everyone. There will always be winners and losers, people or subsidiaries that gain more power and resources while others lose, people or units that have to bite some proverbial bullet, and even some who may lose jobs. *Procedural justice* means paying attention to the perceived fairness of the process by which the company makes decisions, so it is also known as fair process. People may be disappointed with the outcome, but if they respect the way in which it was reached, research shows that they are more likely to retain trust in and commitment to the organization. Conversely, people may be satisfied with an outcome that favors their interests, but if the process of decision making was not fair, they still distrust the organization.

Kim and Mauborgne vividly show the applicability of procedural justice concepts inside the multinational firm.[52] In their empirical study of strategic decision making in international corporations, they found that subsidiary managers who believed their company's decision-making processes to be fair showed a higher level of trust and commitment to their organization. This in turn fostered more active cooperation in implementing decisions, typically improving performance. Conversely, when managers viewed decision-making processes as unfair, they hoarded ideas and dragged their heels when it came to execution.

If we apply this to the MedPharm change, there are going to be winners and losers with the implementation of the new strategy. Local plant managers will have to change their roles. They will have to develop new skills to perform in more complex roles. Many IT staff will lose their jobs. Yet if the change is to be effective, their acceptance is necessary—they must understand this decision, view it as fair, and be supportive of the necessary actions.

The conclusion that emerges from the research of Kim and Mauborgne and others is that people are more likely to trust and cooperate freely with organizational systems—regardless of whether they themselves win or lose by participating—when fair process is observed. Trust is a frequent theme throughout this book—necessary to ensure lateral relationships and to facilitate the transfer of knowledge—and fairness is fundamentally what trust is all about.

Fairness is one of the more essential values in a global organization, whether or not it is formalized in any value statement. One of the reasons why many corporations emphasize fairness is the increasing importance of commitment, as opposed to compliance, as we move to a knowledge economy. As firms become more dependent on talent, the A factor becomes more relevant. Change will always be easier to manage in times of crisis or recession, which legitimizes acceptance of top-down decisions requiring compliance, though organizational change under conditions of crisis is so constrained that it rarely establishes a solid base for sustainable competitive advantage.

Some years ago we took part in the successful crisis turnaround of a Scandinavian bank led by a new CEO who had been brought in to save it. Two years later, the CEO was living with the consequences of his success. Middle management, who had been largely bypassed during the turnaround, took no initiative and looked constantly to the hero CEO for instructions. Anticipating the need for a cross-border merger, he feared that his bank would inevitably be the underdog if it had weak middle management. His new change challenge, much more cultural and intangible in nature, was how to build a strong, empowered, and committed middle management.

The Five E Framework

How does one go about ensuring that a decision will be seen as fair, ensuring the necessary commitment to implementation? How can one steer a change process, from plan to full execution, according to fairness criteria? What are the core elements of procedural justice? These can be summarized with a mnemonic: the five Es.[53]

First of all, people who will be affected by decisions should be *engaged* and asked for their input. This shows respect and increases the chances that the outcome will be seen as fair. Second, options must be *explored* and eliminated if they do not prove to be feasible. Third, once the decision is made, it should be thoroughly *explained*, so people understand and trust the intentions of the decision makers, even if they do not agree with the decision. Fourth, it is important to be clear about *expectations* after the decision is made, translating these into concrete action plans through the performance management system. And appropriate coaching, training, and support need to be provided so that people have the chance to adjust to the new reality. Finally, attention must be paid to *evaluation*, reviewing what worked and what did not, to improve the effectiveness in managing such change processes in the future.

TABLE 11–1. What Does Fair Process Involve?

Engagement
- People want their views to be heard.
- There is a right to refute.
- Communication is sincere and genuine.

Exploration
- Different options are explored . . . and eliminated.

Explanation
- People are informed of the decision.
- Decisions are based on sound facts and reasoning.

Expectations
- Decisions are translated into clear goals, action plans, and behaviors.
- The meaning of a commitment is clear.
- There is appropriate coaching and support.
- Desired behaviors and results are rewarded.

Evaluation
- We learn from our successes and our failures.

These five Es are summarized in Table 11–1. Our discussion highlighting the context of the multinational corporation, focuses on some of the dilemmas involved in working through the five Es.

Engagement

Engagement means involving people in the decisions that affect them by asking for their inputs and allowing them to refute the merits of one another's ideas and assumptions.[54] Basically, this means dialogue during the planning process. Dialogue communicates management's respect for people and their ideas and leads to better analysis and decisions, as well as stronger commitment to implementation.

A central part of engagement is selling the problem to key stakeholders (or creating dissatisfaction with the status quo). To a greater or lesser extent, this will lead to redefining and clarifying the nature of the underlying problem. There is a tendency to define problems in terms of the solutions that one has readily at hand, and engagement minimizes this risk.[55] People will resist actions to confront a problem that they feel has been misperceived and misdiagnosed. A Scandinavian Airlines executive put this well when he said, "People don't resist change; they resist being changed."

The multinational corporation has to cope with cultural differences in engaging people. Frank dialogue, in the form of open confrontation and contention, is acceptable in the United States and quite usual in Israel or Russia. But the "town hall meetings" to put bureaucratic problems on the table that GE favored may be quite unacceptable in Japan, where communication is usually more indirect. Nevertheless, engagement of key staff is far more the norm in Japan than it is in the West, albeit with a distinctively Japanese orientation. The *nemawashi* custom is to gather opinions through one-on-one discussions, traditionally led by a junior high-potential individual (it would be difficult for a Japanese employee to be frank about his or her views if consulted by the boss or a hierarchical superior). It is a process that takes considerable time, leading to slow decision making, although Japanese corporations are renowned for the thoroughness of execution that this creates.

Nokia faced cultural challenges in China, as described in the box on "When the Chinese Won't Engage." In an industry where strategic agility is important, Nokia felt that it had no alternative except to select and train Chinese managers into its organizational culture of open constructive debate.

Not everyone needs to be engaged on all aspects of the strategy, business plan, and implications for execution. It is the *key stakeholders*, whose commitment is needed, who must be engaged. Some of these key actors may be outside the firm (suppliers, unions, government authorities). Many managers assume that the key stakeholders are the people high up in the hierarchy—if they can get the top managers on board, then it is in the bag. But smart top managers may not back a change plan unless they are sure that key people below them are aligned.

When the Chinese Won't Engage

One might expect successful companies in fast-changing and hypercompetitive industries like mobile telecoms and those of Silicon Valley to have cultures with a high level of engagement. Studies confirm this.[56] They practice a high degree of external scanning of markets and technologies, engaging external stakeholders and observers. Open dialogue and constructive debate on the options, across hierarchical and functional levels, is the norm—even for Sony in Japan, where advertisements for salesmen back in the 1960s had the headline "We want salesmen who can argue like an American." The title of one article on the culture of Silicon Valley firms captured this: "Why management teams should have a good fight."[57] Nokia in Finland is no exception, and it regards this climate of constructive debate as essential to its success. Fast exchange of viewpoints and perspectives is a prerequisite for sound, creative, and rapid decision making.

Given the enormous potential of the Chinese market, Nokia established product development labs there. But they found that the Chinese did not respond in the Nokia Way. Chinese engineers and technicians were reluctant to challenge hierarchical superiors, and the no-holds-barred dialogue between functional specialists that worked so well in Helsinki did not catch on. The president of Nokia China told us that this presented the firm with a major dilemma. "Do we go the natural Chinese way and try to adapt the organization around this? Or do we persist in trying to introduce our approach to China, selecting and socializing the Chinese in the Nokia Way?"

Given the nature of their industry, Nokia decided that they had no alternative but to take the latter route.

FIGURE 11–3. A Step-by-Step Strategy for Engagement

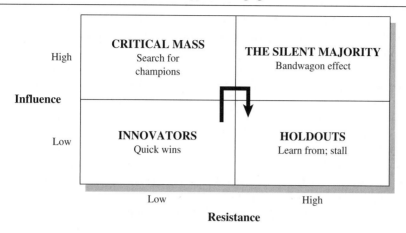

Developing skills in stakeholder assessment is important. Who are the opinion leaders and key experts, the social network leaders and gatekeepers, and the constituencies who could block execution if they are not on board? And what are their interests? In most organizations, there is a sizable group of people called the "silent majority" who appear passive at the beginning of the change process. They will not align themselves with the change or even pay much attention to it until they see others they respect taking the change seriously. Indeed, effective engagement often follows a progressive strategy—Figure 11–3 summarizes a step-by-step strategy for engagement. Some individuals, called innovators or early adopters, will respond quickly, although their influence is not necessarily high. After some initial progress and quick wins, the change team should target influential champions in the critical mass of responsive people. This helps get the interest of the group that in most cases is the largest constituency, the otherwise passive silent majority. Finally, strong resistance from holdouts must be dealt with.

Regional and country HR managers can give good advice about principal stakeholders—because they usually must achieve results without much authority, they may have good mastery of stakeholder analysis and the tactics of engagement.

There are many tools and techniques for engagement, ranging from mass communication via newsletters and intranet to workshops and training.[58] A good nose is needed for sensing the right tool to use at the right time. Without doubt, the most useful tool for engagement is dialogue during face-to-face meetings, which requires a special effort when distance and cultural barriers often mean that the change team finds it difficult to get out of the office to meet distant stakeholders until too late in the change process. This is particularly the case with urgent global projects to improve cost efficiency and rationalization. As at MedPharm, managers misguidedly save on engagement costs and maximize convenience by excluding local managers until the final stages in the planning.[59] Skills of persuasion, influence, and negotiating are also vital.[60]

The traditional levers of engagement are informational or cognitive, oriented toward rational persuasion. However, leaders need to be more alert to emotional levers that appeal to the heart. Cognitive levers may be enough to change the strategic direction in a successful organization, but emotional levers may be needed to overcome organizational stagnation or politicized resistance to change.[61] Past research has focused on the negative emotions associated with change—the feeling of anxiety about the unknown that underlies resistance, as well as excessive emotional attachment to the past.[62] But recent studies of change highlight how the management of positive emotions can play an important role.

As Huy argues, emotions (both positive and negative) are contagious and can either handicap or facilitate the change process.[63] In the early stages of change, expressing sympathy and allowing the opportunity for people to vent their doubts and fears may facilitate what Bridges calls the inevitable stage of "ending," or giving up on the past.[64] Eliciting hope, such as by emphasizing the new career opportunities after an acquisition, can help with collective mobilization. Demonstrably caring for people stimulates attachment, which is vital for retaining talent in an acquired firm. And authenticity in leadership behaviors, such as walk-the-talk transparency, will increase the trust that accompanies a sense of fairness.

Exploration

Exploration of options and the implications of possible actions is an important step in the analysis and planning of change. This process needs to be structured and transparent, if it is to be seen as fair.

Powerful stakeholders, such as unions, may reject management's option, favoring others. Local managers may see quite different options from the headquarters leaders, especially if there is not a strong global mindset in the firm. People may be unwilling to listen to the analysis of the corporate change team unless the team is open-minded about local interests. If feasible alternatives are not explored properly, a stakeholder group may oppose the final decision or implement it only half-heartedly.

The discussion of options can sometimes lead to confusion. Local managers propose a different perspective—and then never hear anything in response from the corporate team until the plan is announced. They are unlikely to consider this fair, accusing headquarters managers of hypocrisy. Options that are open for exploration need to be closed firmly if the analysis shows that they are not feasible.

If the problem has been sold well, an effective way of exploring options is through focused teams that involve key actors. MedPharm took this route, but local managers were neither adequately engaged nor involved in exploring options. In contrast, the story of Canon responding to the challenge of rapidly building an integrated organization in Europe is one successful example (see the box "How Canon Consolidated Its European Organization"), as is the way in which Renault's Carlos Ghosn used a structure of cross-functional teams to explore options in the Nissan turnaround.[65]

How Canon Consolidated Its European Organization

In the 1990s, the consumer and business electronics market in Europe was changing at a rapid pace. There were many forces at work—market entry of low-cost competitors, emergence of cross-border retailing giants with strong bargaining power over suppliers, and Internet sales creating greater pricing transparency, to name just a few. Prices were declining and margins eroding, and the introduction of the euro threatened to exacerbate the problems.

Canon, which had built its presence in Europe through a decentralized infrastructure of 15 semiautonomous and entrepreneurial affiliates, was now poorly positioned to face more integrated competitors like Hewlett-Packard. Various efforts to create a stronger European footprint fizzled out from a lack of support in the operating units.

Realizing the gravity of the competitive situation in 1999, Hajime Tsuruoka, newly appointed president of Canon Europe, decided to consolidate and streamline the organization under a pan-European umbrella to reduce costs, increase profits, and strengthen the Canon brand. The challenge was to obtain buy-in and support for the new operating model from managers and employees in national sales organizations that enjoyed substantial autonomy and stood to lose authority if power shifted to the head office. Tsuruoka was very much aware that consolidation efforts in Europe by some other Japanese companies, including Sony, had failed.

Tsuruoka set up four task forces to make recommendations about how to move forward in specific areas of the business. Team members were selected so that no country or function felt excluded from the planning and decision-making process. In addition, he emphasized the sense of urgency by giving the task forces just two months to come up with their recommendations for a pan-European organization. Simultaneously, in collaboration with a leading European business school, Canon established an executive development program with action-learning projects complementing the task force agenda.

After a year of intensive discussions and detailed planning, the decision was made to transform the fragmented federation of countries into a network of subsidiaries with common platforms and strong lateral coordination along major product lines. Processes in key functions such as IT, logistics, finance, and human resources were to be standardized to gain the required efficiencies, and the sales organization of the consumer business was streamlined and unified to strengthen the brand and market position. Equally important was coordination between previously unconnected units—a variety of functional and customer-oriented cross-border steering groups, pan-European task forces and problem-solving teams, and extensive cross-border transfer of high-potential employees. Nearly all managers appointed to key coordinating roles came from subsidiaries, so the new organization was seen as providing opportunities for career advancement and personal development.

By 2005, with fully restored profitability, Canon Europe became the largest business region in Canon's global family.

Source: V. Pucik and N. Govinder, "Canon Europe: Pan-European Transformation (A), (B) and (C)," case study numbers IMD-3-1074 to 3-1076, IMD, Lausanne, 2007.

Explanation

Once the decision is made, it must be explained to everyone who will be affected and whose commitment is necessary for effective execution. For the process to be fair, people need to understand that a decision has been reached (the time for debate and questioning is over), that it is based on sound reasoning, that their opinions have been considered, and that the decision is in the best interest of the enterprise (even though particular stakeholders may lose out).[66]

Senior leaders in multinational companies are likely to be overfamiliar with the proposed change and the options: it is no longer news to them. Because the rationale behind the decision seems obvious, they are often impatient to move to action. Typically, a meeting to explain the decision to the next level is organized, and managers are told to inform their respective units. A few e-mails are sent out—and the result is that supervisors located three levels below, where behavioral change is needed or where costs will be cut, have never heard the rationale fully explained. Even if employees have access to the information, few understand what it means—dialogue is needed to convert information into understanding. One of the important business support roles of the HR function is to work with line managers to design communication processes that will effectively build understanding at the battlefront of the decision and its rationale.

The Liechtenstein-based tool equipment multinational, Hilti, organized an effective explanation process a few years ago following its decision to implement a major change in global strategy and organization. Information about the change was circulated to staff throughout the world by intranet. Then a meeting lasting two to six hours was organized on a cascade basis for all personnel, right down to the janitors, meeting with the boss's boss and a consultant. The aim of each meeting was to help individuals understand the rationale behind the change, along with what it meant for their part of the organization and for their job in particular. This meeting was followed by another with the immediate superior to work out the implications of the change in terms of targets and action plans—setting clear expectations is the fourth step in fair process management.

Expectations

Setting expectations means translating decisions into clear roles and responsibilities, SMART targets,[67] and action plans, all with clear rewards and sanctions. Desirable (and undesirable) behaviors need to be spelled out. Well-functioning global performance management processes play an important role here.

Fair process does not imply consensus management. At this stage of change, clarity and credibility of performance and behavioral expectations count for most. If expectations and personal consequences (rewards) are clear, and if employees believe, from past experience, that the change will indeed be implemented, even those managers who have dissenting views are likely to accommodate it—especially if they have had the opportunity to voice their views in the planning stage and see that senior leaders are genuinely engaged in keeping them on board.

Organizational change will always require new skills and behaviors from at least some individuals. Most people are understandably anxious about whether they will be able to master new roles. Consequently, there will be a need for appropriate people risk management—training and coaching. We have seen many change processes where the implementation was rocky and sometimes even aborted because the HR function was unprepared to provide this support—because it had not been engaged in the planning process early enough. Advance preparation is essential. New performance metrics have to be set, and it is likely that some individuals will not adjust effectively to their new roles. This will necessitate identifying and preparing a pool of potential successors who can take over from managers who fail to meet expectations after a reasonable period of time.[68] This sort of proactive steering of the implementation process builds the credibility of the organization and its future change capability. Trust in the organization will be strengthened.

Powerful people in key positions, who pay only lip service to the new direction, can represent some of the biggest obstacles to change. If everyone senses that change is unlikely to happen because of their opposition, a self-fulfilling situation of collective wait-and-see will be created. One of the reasons why Jack Welch reinforced leadership development at GE was to accelerate change by having a pool of able leadership candidates ready to replace people who did not fully buy into the need for change. One of the problems with the MedPharm change process was that there was a dominant collective view that the transition to the global supply chain would happen only gradually, sapping the organization's energy and ability to move forward.

Evaluation

The final, often neglected, step in the change process is evaluation or review. As change initiatives occur with increased frequency, a proper evaluation ensures learning about how to improve the change process, and that mistakes will not be repeated. This is another important role for HR.

One of the few multinational firms that takes evaluation seriously is IBM, where there is a long-standing discipline of reviews after every project or change cycle. GE also pays close attention to evaluation, organizing periodic workshops at its Crotonville learning center to diagnose the lessons for the organization from change plans that failed to live up to expectations. Still, we find that most firms at best leave evaluation and learning to the individuals who were involved, while neglecting organizational learning.

Some focused areas of change management, notably acquisitions and alliances, are exceptions to this—a number of multinational firms have a reasonably well-structured approach to learning from the M&A process.[69] The process of managing complex change should ideally be seen as an organizational capability that may require dedicated support for implementation and continuous learning. ABB anchors the responsibility for the management of large global projects, including evaluation and learning, in a corporate-level department.

The Tensions behind Fair Process and the Five Es

The ideal of the multinational enterprise as a smooth harmonious entity, a utopian United Nations, is misguided. Tension lies at the heart of the concept of the transnational firm, and it is a cliché to say that change involves tension. But with continuous change, that tension needs to be built into the firm constructively, generating virtuous spirals of development rather than vicious spirals of decline.

Attention to procedural justice is important. In multinational firms, there will always be decisions and outcomes that go against the vested interests of specific parties—managers, specialists, subsidiaries, and businesses. Change or realignment will always create tensions. How can one be sure that such tensions do not damage human and social capital, leading people to become less satisfied, less committed, less loyal—or even to quit the firm? How can one be sure that these tensions do not undermine the delicate webs of collaborative relationships that are the fabric of the knowledge economy? Paying due attention to fair process and the five Es is vital—and is the reason why a growing number of multinational corporations have fairness as one of their underlying values.

Managers in some regions of the world will point to culture differences and say, for example, that "fairness does not mean the same thing in Asia." It is true that compliance based on respect for traditional authority has been sufficient to run many Asian businesses in the past. But this is changed by the scarcity of talent and the growing importance of commitment. As we mentioned earlier, Japanese corporations have traditionally been rigorous in their respect for fair process, and a growing number of Asian firms, like Siam Cement, Infosys, and Standard Chartered, which see talent as a source of competitive advantage, have fairness as an explicit corporate value.

How did MedPharm decide to tackle the tensions? Top management recognized with hindsight that they had been too focused on the Q and the planning of the supply chain project, with insufficient engagement of the local plant managers and country staff. Efforts to persuade them that there was no other viable option had been inadequate. MedPharm's general manager had asked the head of operations, a leader with high credibility in the organization, together with the HR director to prepare a plan of action, leading to a two-day conference.

The preparation of what turned into a workshop for the top 100 people was a vehicle for intensive face-to-face discussions with all key stakeholders, especially the senior local managers. The focus of both these discussions and the workshop was making sure that everyone understood why it was important to move fast on the global supply chain. A successor was found, with some difficulty, for the most resistant plant manager. The small organizing team, with the general manager, concluded that the biggest challenge was a shortage of experienced global leaders who were at ease managing in split egg ways, and part of the workshop was devoted to discussing the requirements for leaders in a world where silos, territories, and clear general management roles had become dysfunctional. After the workshop, a new program for global leadership development was established, in partnership with the US parent.

The Role of HR in Leading Change

At MedPharm, the head of HR played a key role throughout the change process. However, despite the close relationship between HRM and strategy implementation, there are still relatively few firms where the HR function lives up to the ideal of being a change partner with senior leadership, the task that embodies the second stage in the evolution of HRM.

The organizational development (OD) movement had its roots in Exxon in the 1960s, leading to research and practice that established some basic principles for adaptive management and planned organizational change. Since then, firms such as Shell have institutionalized this role in an OD or organizational effectiveness (OE) function within HR, acting mainly as internal consultants. GE's companywide CAP process was described earlier in the box "Change Acceleration at GE."

The potential contribution of HR to the change process has so many facets that we can provide only a few examples.

PROMOTING CHAMPIONS OF CHANGE. Change rarely happens as intended without committed leadership. This is a fundamental belief at multinational firms that have mastered the art of managing continuous change. Therefore, leaders who can act as champions of change need to be identified, nurtured, and put in appropriate positions. Research points out that some radical organizational change happens simply because a strong leader takes over a unit.[70] Remember that the only way to change fast is to change key people.

CREATING DISSATISFACTION WITH THE STATUS QUO. Change is difficult to manage unless there is an acknowledged need for it. Amplifying dissatisfaction with the status quo through training, two-way meetings, and project groups is an important role for HR, as is ensuring that attention is focused on high-priority problems. In many organizations people are extraordinarily busy, even worried, but they are not focused on the most urgent and important issues.[71]

One of the classic laws of change, which has its roots in the psychology of adaptation, is the inverted U-shaped relationship between change and tension (see Figure 11–4). If tension is low (in other words, if people are happy, contented, apathetic, or complacent because they feel successful), change is unlikely to occur. On the other hand, if the degree of tension is too high, people will react in unpredictable ways to protect their own interests, or they will be paralyzed because they see no possible solutions. Change is best managed with a constructive degree of tension.

FIGURE 11–4. **The Relationship between Change and Tension**

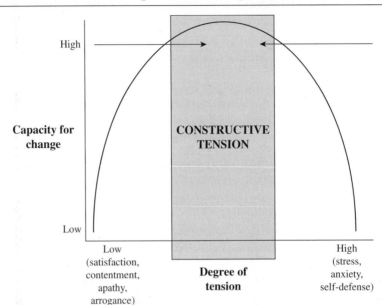

How can one "heat things up," increasing tension while keeping it constructive? There are five interrelated ways where HR support has a role:

1. Through constant scanning, externally (benchmarking, customer contacts, measurement, and competitive analysis) and internally (attitude surveys, management by wandering around, 360° feedback).
2. Through sharing information about substandard performance, threats, and opportunities top-down, in order to counter complacency and mobilize change. The information from scanning should be transparent and shared—cultures that blinker threats and treat information as power hinder this, though it should be added that information sharing has to be balanced with the risk of worrying people unnecessarily and distracting them from their work.
3. Through lateral information sharing (cross-functional or cross-border teamwork, intranet, workshops, data banks).
4. Through mobility (transferring people across boundaries or bringing in new people who see problems with fresh eyes).
5. Through goal setting, accompanied by performance management (appraisal, incentives, and rewards).

   IDENTIFYING KEY STAKEHOLDERS. An important exercise in a CAP workshop at GE involves listing all the key stakeholders by name or unit, including external parties, and identifying where they are positioned on a scale from "actively supportive" to "strongly against." The position where they need to be if the change is to be successful is discussed, and the biggest gaps are explored. What are the interests of these problematic stakeholders? What are the reasons for the gaps? And what are the action implications?

DEVELOPING THE CONFIDENCE OF TOP MANAGEMENT SPONSORS TO COMMUNICATE DIRECTLY WITH EMPLOYEES. Creating an understanding of the need for change and its implications is best undertaken through direct dialogue. Yet it can take courage for senior managers, the sponsors of change, to communicate directly with the workforce, and to engage them in dialogue rather than hiding behind PowerPoint slides. One of the most influential HR vice presidents that we have met viewed one of his key roles as coaching these senior sponsors, building their confidence to engage local stakeholders directly, particularly those local managers in relevant countries abroad who may have quite different perspectives on the change. It is better to consider these perspectives at the planning stage rather than later, when they are undermining the intended change.

DESIGNING PROCESSES TO BUILD COMMITMENT FAST THROUGH FACE-TO-FACE CONFRONTATION OF VIEWS. How does one accelerate the understanding of the need for change in an organization of 100,000 people? Or among employees in a plant located on another continent? One of the important contributions of HR is the design of such engagement and explanation processes—such as the cascade process used by many organizations, or the intensive communication and dialogue in our Hilti example.

It is also important to recognize that what motivates top management is rarely the same as what will motivate middle and lower-level staff. Information needs to be shared in a way that has an impact on the target audience, and senior management is frequently blind to this, needing skilled facilitation.[72] Messages pointing out that "We're performing below industry average—we have to change dramatically to become a top-quartile performer by exploiting our assets better and earning the right to grow" will rarely have much impact on middle managers and supervisors.

VISION BUILDING/AGENDA SETTING. Change is facilitated if the vision or agenda is clear in the minds of change leaders and staff. All too frequently, a change solution (for example, what competitors are doing already) is presented without any clear vision to support it. In these circumstances, it will be difficult to monitor progress. Building a vision for the future may be helped by skilled HR or consultant facilitation. Often simple tools, such as backward visioning or "Future Perfect" (write the story as if seen from the future) can kick-start the process.[73]

HELPING EMPLOYEES TO COPE WITH EMOTIONAL NEEDS AT DIFFERENT STAGES OF THE CHANGE PROCESS. It is important to help individuals cope with the personal transition of major change. Bridges emphasizes the different needs at the three phases of the transition—"endings," where coping with the emotional pain of giving up what is known and appreciated may be important; "neutral zones," where people need dialogue to explore the future state; and "new beginnings," where they need coaching and training to learn new skills and attitudes.[74]

DEALING WITH DIFFERENT TYPES OF PEOPLE DURING IMPLEMENTATION. The ability of people to change depends on their willingness and their capability. Some people are both willing and have the necessary competencies to change, and they may be candidates for positions as champions, typically requiring some restructuring of roles and responsibilities. Training and coaching must be provided for those who are willing but lack the competencies, while those who are neither capable nor willing must be replaced or sidelined. But what about those who are highly capable, indispensable for today's operating results, but who just do not believe in the need to change? Here there are no easy solutions—the role of HR is to assist in working through tailored strategies.

ATTENTION TO SUCCESSION MANAGEMENT. One of the problems in organizational change is making it last.[75] Paradoxically, there is too much change in many firms and not enough continuity. Attention to succession management is one aspect—firms often need successors who will continue the process of implementation rather than taking the unit off in new directions. Changing the culture of the firm is another method of making change last.

ENSURING CONSISTENCY BETWEEN WORDS AND ACTION. One of the biggest factors hindering change is failure to walk the talk. This is rarely deliberate, and one role of HR is to try to build consistency. At an international bank that had invested millions in empowerment, employees knew that there would be dire consequences if a vice president did not have an immediate answer to any question that an executive committee member might ask in the corridor. Until this was pointed out, the executive committee was unaware that the bank's staff was mobilized around keeping their VPs informed of anything and everything just in case they were asked a question—totally inconsistent with empowerment.

It is the classic trap, the folly of hoping for A while rewarding B.[76] The approach of Amgen's CEO, Kevin Sharer, has much to recommend. He asks each of his top 75, "What should I do differently?", sharing his own development needs publicly with them while discussing their behavioral change.[77]

ENSURING THE BALANCE BETWEEN SHORT- AND LONG-TERM PRESSURES. One of the important HRM issues is to ensure that short-term crisis measures do not compromise long-term loyalty when, for example, downsizing. At L'Oréal, the HR function is expected to argue for the long-term view, since this risks being compromised by short-term imperatives.[78]

Overall, we conclude this necessarily incomplete list by noting that Ulrich outlined four roles for HR in the change arena. These roles are the champion who promotes the need for change, the designer who assists in mapping out an effective change process, the facilitator who acts as a coach and catalyst, and the demonstrator who is a role model through consistent behavior.[79]

BUILDING ORGANIZATIONAL AGILITY

In some global industries, major strategic change takes place relatively infrequently, and the pattern is that of the punctuated equilibrium model. This has been true for the car industry as well as defense equipment and cement. An engineer who entered the firm 30 years ago will still deal with the same basic technology as an engineer who starts today. The competitive game shifts periodically, though not continuously. Most change is incremental and operational, and strategy planning may be sufficient to anticipate the infrequent inflection points—though the decline of GM might lead one to question this.

But in other globalized industries, such as information and communications technology, the speed of change is rapid, with frequent inflection points when there are major shifts in technologies and markets.[80] If firms adapt slowly, new competitors—either faster-moving multinationals or nimble entrepreneurial start-ups—can quickly turn yesterday's winners into tomorrow's losers. The disappearance of Digital Equipment, which once dominated the minicomputer scene, is one of many cases in point, along with Nortel in telecom equipment and Compaq in laptops.[81] Moreover, in some of these industries, the change process is highly complex and systemic, and the capacity for change needs to be built into the fabric of the organization. Strategic and organizational agility becomes a survival factor. As multinationals learn to be more agile, speed of responsiveness and change capability are likely to become important competitive success factors in other industries.

Doz and Kosonen have studied various multinational corporations in these industries where success means thriving on continuous waves of change—IBM, Nokia, SAP, Cisco, HP, Accenture.[82] What are the features associated with their strategic agility? Doz and Kosonen single out three:

- A high degree of strategic sensitivity.
- A strong collective commitment.
- Resource flexibility.

Let us discuss each of these briefly, with a focus on the HRM implications.

Developing Strategic Sensitivity

Strategic sensitivity means connectedness—extensive ties with the external environment and a high degree of internal linkage through the social architecture of the firm. This implies maximizing connections with the outside world of customers as well as technology hotbeds like think tanks and universities—constantly scanning for opportunities, threats, market and technological shifts, and innovations. Units need to be established in regions of the world where there are leading developments—as noted earlier, Cisco has split its corporate headquarters into two, the western-facing headquarters in Silicon Valley and the eastern-facing headquarters in

Bangalore, India. Strategic alliances are important tools for scanning and exploring new environments. Think tanks may be established with external partners.

IBM has broadened and refined the intranet jam process that it pioneered to create shared values to innovation jams. An online exchange, connecting 150,000 people for a 72-hour period, including external customers and partners, was first organized in 2006 with the aim of finding ways of moving its latest technologies to market—and this has been repeated since.[83]

All the methods for transferring knowledge internally within the firm, from social networks to people mobility, are part of building strategic agility. Organizational culture is another element, where one might single out the combination of strong ambition (driven by appropriate rewards) along with willingness to experiment and take risks (which implies learning from mistakes rather than punishing them).

But there is one quality that needs to be emphasized above all from the people management point of view: the importance of the quality of internal dialogue. Tapping into external trends, resources and insights, and successful internal experiments are important—but if the quality of internal communication handicaps working through the implications, this will be of little avail. Quality conversations that arouse attention and add value have two characteristics—they are high on either analytic reasoning or emotional authenticity, or both.[84] If internal communication is ritualistic and dehydrated, information is unlikely to be spread and processed effectively. Consequently, a number of multinationals have invested in improving the quality of internal dialogue through training and feedback, though the definition of what may be an effective dialogue will vary from one culture to another.[85]

A related cultural implication is that there need to be norms of transparency around information sharing. Information used to be hoarded as the key to personal power, justified by norms of proprietary secrecy. But in a fast-moving environment, there are few competitive secrets, and those apply mostly to technological specifications. In such industries, competitive value comes far more from agility, speed of responsiveness, and thoroughness in execution than it does from information per se. Twenty years ago, IBM used to be a secretive firm that was reluctant to share information even internally; today there is much more transparency, while reasonable discretion is assured through shared values.

Building Leadership Unity and Collective Commitment

The second key challenge in building organizational agility concerns the capability to build alignment around key decisions. This is well illustrated by studies of high-performing companies in the hypercompetitive environment of Silicon Valley. While there is constant scanning and hot, high-quality internal dialogue, the top leadership knows how to stop the discussion at an appropriate stage, making the necessary strategic decisions, and explaining the rationale clearly.[86] The top team has to be totally united and capable of building "act-with-one-voice" commitment to these decisions aligning the organization around the intended plan of action.

This is not easy in an organization where senior leaders inevitably have different perspectives as well as big egos. But without this capacity for clear, united decision making, corporations are unable to switch from a mode of behavior focused on exploring options to an action mode of execution. In acquisitions, for example, lack of unity among top management is one of the most important obstacles to merger integration, resulting in a long-drawn-out integration process.[87]

This is why the collective sense of accountability, together with individual responsibility for one's own unit or function, are so important in the transnational organization, as we discussed in Chapter 5. It is essential to be able to wear two hats and work comfortably in matrix or split egg roles. Mobility, especially for high-potential individuals, will nurture this sense of collective commitment, as will fair process management—the ability to engage key stakeholders and explore options, and then to explain decisions and set clear expectations.

There is no doubt that it is easier to build collective commitment to an action plan when all key managers are based in the home country headquarters, as they are in a meganational. In a transnational firm, careful attention must be given to manage the five Es, engaging key stakeholders of different cultures in far-flung operations and taking pains to explain decisions when they are made. The travel and communication budgets of such corporations are necessarily high, and it would be dangerous to cut back crudely on such budgets in times of difficulty.

Resource Flexibility

One of the major reasons for the globalization of processes, including HR processes, and for reorganizing common transactions into regional or global shared service centers, is to increase efficiency through resource flexibility. Information processing, expatriate mobility, supply-chain management, payroll, and many other services will no longer be constrained by being fragmented, or under the thumb of local business or geographic managers. Consequently, the organization will respond much more easily and quickly to market or technological changes, and to the need to reorganize, reconfigure, or dissolve particular business units.[88] At Hewlett-Packard, the basic structural unit of the business is the division, and studies even 10 years ago showed that the average life cycle of a division, measured by the length of time before its basic charter was changed, was less than 30 months.[89]

Today, the frontiers of resource flexibility concern people. Finance and information have long been going through a process of global standardization, but talented people are geographically rooted and resistant to being "standardized." The combination of air travel, virtual communication, and cross-boundary project work has greatly facilitated human resource fluidity, and will continue to do so. McKinsey prides itself on allowing any of its managers in any location of the world to tap into the expertise of a leading authority on any issue concerning strategy, structure, or leadership—with two or three phone calls or e-mails. Physical mobility among leaders and technical experts, facilitated by global talent pool management, has greatly increased and is most important, as we have stressed throughout this book.[90] In the future, the expansion of open internal job markets, facilitated by globalized self-help technology, may allow multinational firms to deploy internal know-how and skills across borders in low-cost ways that have not previously been possible.[91]

However, this means that the careers of talented individuals whom the organization wants to retain are no longer controlled by organizational hierarchy. And, agile firms like IBM and Infosys have come to the conclusion that the only way of integrating such people into the organization, and providing them with a sense of belonging as well as guiding their behavior, is through values-based management—normative rather than hierarchical control.[92]

Companies like IBM have put a lot of effort into instilling common values, pioneering new Web 2.0–based ways of engaging people. This emotional integration through shared identity and meaning is important to steer collective action and build vital trust, although a sense of shared identity may be difficult to create from scratch in multidomestic companies that have grown through acquisitions and local entrepreneurship.

Agility Means Riding the Ups and Downs

After the global financial bubble collapsed in the fall of 2008, the world economy faced challenges unparalleled for half a century, with consequences that may reach far into the future. Shared values . . . people mobility . . . high-quality dialogue . . . organizations with a built-in sense of fair process—at a time of recession these may seem out of sync with reality. But one of the characteristics of agile and high-performing organizations is that they pay as much attention to continuity as to driving change.

Most of the largest global financial institutions were heavily impacted by the crisis, but one that weathered it far better than most was Standard Chartered Bank, a British-based multinational drawing 90 percent of its revenues from Asia, Africa, and the Middle East. As the global crisis was starting to bite, its CEO, Peter Sands, commented, "We paid a steep price after former downturns for cutting back on talent. That's not a trap that we will fall into again. The biggest constraint on our future prosperity is not capital or markets but leadership."[93] At the same time, in the middle of the recession, the bank was preparing to launch an internal campaign to reinforce global corporate values of trustworthiness and responsiveness.

TAKEAWAYS

1. One of the biggest HRM challenges in multinational firms is ensuring effective execution of strategy and business plans. Implementation is largely a question of managing change.
2. There are different conceptual models of change—evolutionary, punctuated equilibrium, and spiral. The spiral model appears to capture best the change process leading to transnational organization.
3. Change to become a transnational organization always involves managing tension, notably between global efficiency/integration and local responsiveness/entrepreneurship. It is important to avoid excessive pendulum swings between the two, and the image of steering between dualities captures this.
4. Whether the starting point is a multidomestic or meganational organization, the path to transnational development often involves creating regional structures.
5. One reason transnational development takes so long is the necessity for subtle but vital changes in managerial roles and behaviors. For the multidomestic firm, this requires mastering intransitive leadership development; for the meganational, it implies paying attention to developing global leadership competencies.
6. The effective execution of a strategy or business plan depends on two elements: the quality of analysis or planning, and acceptance of the decision. Managers are usually well versed in the former, but the latter is often neglected, resulting in disappointing execution of plans.
7. The outcomes of decisions made in any change process will never be fair to everybody. In order to build commitment to change and to maintain commitment to the firm, it is important to make sure that the decision-making process is seen as fair.
8. In operational terms, fair process means paying attention to the five Es: engagement, exploration of options, explanation, setting expectations, and evaluation.
9. HR managers in multinational firms have an important role to play in facilitating the change by orchestrating the five Es, helping line managers to recognize the importance of managing emotional as well as rational aspects of change, and by recognizing change champions through talent management.
10. To build organizational agility or change capability, multinational firms need to pay attention to strategic sensitivity (including transparency of information and quality dialogue in processing that information), leadership unity and collective commitment, and resource flexibility.

NOTES

1. MedPharm is a fictitious name. The situation described is accurate, but various details have been changed to hide the company's identity.
2. We introduced a three-stage framework for understanding how HRM adds value in Chapter 2. The first stage of HRM focuses on building foundations; the second stage

involves realignment—the change partner task discussed in the second part of this chapter; and the third stage centers on steering through dualities.

3. Regarding the time horizon for transnational organizational development, an exception is the small number of firms, typically in high-technology sectors, that are multinational from the time of their origins. See also the "metanational" concept, reviewed in Chapter 10.

4. The school of organizational or population ecology is based on *evolutionary assumptions about change* (Hannan and Freeman, 1989). This builds on Weick's influential Darwinian model of change processes (variation–selection–retention) that is outlined in Chapter 10 (Weick, 1979). See also Kimberley and Bouchikhi (1995). By contrast, the organizational development movement that emerged in the 1970s was built on *transformational assumptions about change*, which were elaborated in the punctuated equilibrium view of change (Tushman, Newman, and Romanelli, 1986). See Pettigrew (2000) for a commentary.

5. Tushman and O'Reilly, 1996.

6. Evans and Doz, 1989.

7. Among those who argue for the spiral image of change are Mintzberg and Westley (1992), Hampden-Turner (1990a), Brown and Eisenhardt (1998), and Lewis (2000).

8. Specifically, there is a probability that the latter firm may respond more promptly to the change since it is already, in Lewinian terms, "unfrozen" and in a learning mode.

9. Ghoshal and Bartlett, 1998; Ghoshal and Bartlett, 2000.

10. Ghoshal and Bartlett, 2000.

11. Campbell and Goold, 1998; Goold and Campbell, 1998.

12. BP in the 1990s would be another example, where its Project 90 transformation process was initiated under the driving leadership of Robert Horton, followed by the more participative strategy of David Simon, his successor, followed by successive spirals under Lord Browne.

13. See Chapter 5 for the Nestlé GLOBE story.

14. Hampden-Turner (1990b).

15. The Coca-Cola story is well summarized by Ghemawat (2007).

16. Rugman and Verbeke, 2004, 2008. Friedman's "flat world" argument was discussed in Chapter 1 (Friedman, 2005).

17. Rugman and Verbeke, 2004, 2008.

18. Ghemawat (2007) calls this aggregation.

19. Distance (or proximity in reverse) can be seen as having four dimensions—cultural, administrative, geographic, and economic. See Ghemawat (2007) for details on this CAGE framework.

20. Lasserre and Schütte, 2006; Lasserre, 1996.

21. Lasserre and Schütte, 2006.

22. See Birkinshaw and Hood (1998) and related research by Birkinshaw.

23. Front–back organization is discussed in Chapter 5.

24. "When Intel Says 'Copy Exactly,' It Means It," *China Daily*, May 30, 2006.

25. Delany, 2000.

26. Birkinshaw and Hood, 1998.

27. See the discussion of organizational capabilities in the first section of Chapter 2, using the examples of Lincoln Electric and Southwest Airlines.

28. Cited by Leonard-Barton (1995, p. 215).

29. For empirical evidence on the difficulty in transferring technology, see Zahra, Ireland, and Hitt (2000). See also the discussion of knowledge transfer in Chapter 10.

30. The HP Singapore story is used by Leonard to illustrate the process of transfer of capabilities from the home country abroad (Leonard, 1995; Leonard-Barton and Conner, 1996).
31. This first of the three faces of HRM is described in Chapter 2.
32. Leonard-Barton and Conner, 1996.
33. Gupta, Govindarajan, and Wang, 2008, p. 155.
34. For more detail on the following section, see Ghemawat (2007, Chapter 5).
35. See the discussion in Chapter 4.
36. See in particular Chapters 6 and 8.
37. Extracts from a speech by Fiorina, reported in *Executive Excellence*, January 4, 2001.
38. The management development practices of Japanese firms are discussed in Chapter 7, along with this challenge, seen as the Achilles heel of Japanese management practices in this era of globalization.
39. Birkinshaw and Hood, 2001.
40. As discussed in Chapter 8.
41. Delany, 2000.
42. The issue of increasing intransitivity in leadership development is discussed in Chapter 8.
43. See Chapter 5.
44. See the discussion in Chapter 2 about the lessons of companies in strongly cyclical industries.
45. See Cameron (1994) and that journal issue for research on managing downsizing. See also Mishra, Mishra, and Spreitzer (2009).
46. UAMS and Cap Gemini Ernst and Young, "Measures That Matter," part of presentation "How Intangibles Are Driving Business Performance." (www.uams.be).
47. We do not know the origins of the $Q \times A = E$ formula, which GE adopted. In more academic literature, one finds this way of thinking about change in Beer and Nohria (2000). They use different terminology, calling the Q side "Theory E" (standing for economic reasoning), and the A side "Theory O," meaning organizational reasoning.
48. As discussed in Chapter 8.
49. Kotter, 1996.
50. Mintzberg and Waters, 1985; Mintzberg and Westley, 1992.
51. The concept of procedural justice was first proposed by Thibaut and Walker (1975) in their comparative studies of legal dispute resolution procedures. For reviews of research on procedural justice across cultures, see Pillai, Scandura, and Williams (1999) and Broekner et al. (2000). The interactive relationship between procedural fairness and outcome favorability (or acceptance) is found to be robust and consistent across cultures, though the relationship is stronger in cultures that emphasize people's connectedness to others as opposed to independence from one another (Broekner et al., 2000). For research on the effect of procedural fairness on the acceptance of strategies in the units of multinational corporations, see Kim and Mauborgne (1991, 1998).
52. Kim and Mauborgne, 1991, 1998.
53. Kim and Mauborgne (1997) view three elements as important for a process to be fair—engagement, explanation, and expectation clarity. Van der Heyden has elaborated on this framework, developing appropriate instrumentation, and adding two other elements, namely exploration and evaluation (Van der Heyden and Limberg, 2007; Van der Heyden, Blondel, and Carlock, 2005).

54. Note that the term "engagement" has another meaning among HR practitioners, namely involvement and motivation, as in the use of engagement surveys.
55. Evans, 1994.
56. Eisenhardt and Zbaracki, 1992; Eisenhardt, Kahwajy, and Bourgeois, 1997; Brown and Eisenhardt, 1998; Doz and Kosonen, 2008. See the discussion of strategic agility at the end of this chapter.
57. Eisenhardt, Kahwajy, and Bourgeois, 1997.
58. Beyond face-to-face meetings, the tools of engagement include mass communications (e-mail, newsletters, intranet sites), workshops, training sessions, benchmarking visits, customer or other surveys, rewards and punishments, third-party leverage (arranging for peers to meet key people), upward lobbying, and decrees.
59. Even at times of headcount freezes, it is good practice not to freeze travel budgets on international change projects.
60. Cialdini, 2001; Conger, 1998; Gelfand and Brett, 2004.
61. Doz and Kosonen (2008) elaborate on this hypothesis.
62. Argyris, 1990; Schein, 1996.
63. Huy, 2002, 2005.
64. Bridges, 1980. Huy (2005) discusses the role of positive emotional management in the change process, with a focus on action to express sympathy, hope, fun, attachment, and authenticity.
65. For the Nissan turnaround story, led by Carlos Ghosn, see Huy (2004).
66. An important example of explanation that is discussed in Chapter 13 is the communication about the rationale behind an acquisition, which should take place during the "100 days" following the merger announcement.
67. See the discussion in Chapter 9. The acronym SMART applies to objective setting, where targets should be specific, measurable, achievable or agreed, realistic, and with clear time specifications.
68. These stages in implementation are well mapped out by Beer, Eisenstat, and Spector (1990) as a critical path.
69. See Barkema and Schijven (2008).
70. Doz and Prahalad, 1988.
71. This is the theme of Bruch and Ghoshal (2002) in a study of four multinational organizations.
72. See Aiken and Keller (2009). Zohar (1997) argues that people are motivated by five different forms of impact: on society, on the customer, on the company and its shareholders, on the working team, and on "me" personally. Compelling stories should be designed to create as many of these impacts as possible.
73. See Gratton (2000) for ideas and analysis of how HR can facilitate the development of the vision.
74. Bridges, 1980, 1986.
75. Black and Gregersen (2008) describe the dangers of lack of follow-through in change management at some length. The importance of managing continuity in change is made well in Collins' study *Good to Great*, where he calls this the flywheel effect (see Collins, 2001). See also the discussion in Chapter 8 of the dangers of excessive mobility.
76. Kerr, 1995.
77. Amgen's approach is described by Aiken and Keller (2009).
78. See the discussion of L'Oréal's management philosophy on p. 223.
79. Ulrich, 1997. See also Caldwell (2008).

80. An inflection point is a strategic turning point in the industry, such as a radical change in technology or market. Slow-moving industry leaders often become tomorrow's laggards.

81. Miller (1990) provides many such stories of the Icarus phenomenon.

82. Doz and Kosonen, 2008.

83. The IBM innovation jam is described in Bjelland and Wood (2008). The original intranet jam to create shared values is outlined in our Chapter 6.

84. See Gratton and Ghoshal (2002).

85. For example, one dimension of quality dialogue that varies from one culture to another (as well as situationally) is direct versus indirect communication. Communication in collectivistic cultures is often more indirect, since the desire to be polite and avoid embarrassment overrides the importance of rational truth as defined by individualistic cultures (Smith and Bond, 1999).

86. Eisenhardt, Kahwajy, and Bourgeois, 1997; Brown and Eisenhardt, 1997.

87. See the discussion of this issue in Chapter 13.

88. Doz and Kosonen, 2008.

89. Galunic and Eisenhardt, 2001.

90. See Chapter 8.

91. See the discussion of open job markets in Chapter 8.

92. See Chapter 6 for a discussion of shared values and socialization of talent. The need for a change in concepts of control is discussed in Chapter 8.

93. Speech given by Peter Sands at the Singapore Human Capital Summit, October 2008.

CHAPTER 12

Managing Alliances and Joint Ventures

Rethinking Alliance Strategies at Chemco

In the late 1960s, the US-based chemical company Chemco (name disguised) decided to enter the booming Japanese market. However, Japan's investment policies at the time precluded direct entry. Facing the choice between licensing and a minority joint venture (JV), the company decided to establish a 49/51 percent partnership with a well-known Japanese firm to build a local plant and set up distribution. Chemco would contribute technology in exchange for help in market access. Soon after its launch, the joint venture, led entirely by local managers, became the leader in its industry segment.

Later, the US parent decided to take advantage of the liberalization of the Japanese economy to obtain a majority position in the JV. In their opinion, the JV was becoming "too independent," and they wanted more influence on its future direction. Besides, drawing upon the support functions of the head office could lower costs. After protracted negotiations, the Japanese partner agreed to sell 2 percent of equity to the Americans to give them control, and the board composition was changed accordingly. The JV management was instructed to streamline the product portfolio and to cut costs by integrating several support functions into the global organization. While the local managers never questioned the need for more efficiency, most of the integration projects never really got off the ground. This was officially justified by referring to pressing local customer needs that took up all available resources.

Frustrated by the difficulties in "integrating Japan," the US management decided that additional equity would give it the necessary influence to push through integration plans. After another round of long negotiations, the American parent gained control of 65 percent of the shares. The company was renamed, putting its US partner's name first. A senior vice president of finance (who did not speak Japanese) was dispatched to join the local management team. But despite these changes, the venture continued to be run pretty much as before. While it was profitable, with nearly US$1 billion of sales, margins were well below corporate expectations. As Japanese customers began to migrate to lower-cost sites in other areas of Asia, poor coordination with other affiliates became a serious business problem.

A third generation of US top management decided to address the problem head-on. They retained a consultant to advise them on what to do next. Should they buy even more equity? Send in more expatriates? Or even sell the existing business and start again?

It turned out that the company could not sell the plant in the open market because the surrounding infrastructure belonged to the Japanese parent. In addition, the Japanese partner (located right next door) was the legal employer of the vast majority of employees, including virtually all top managers. Even those recruited well after the JV was established were not employees of the joint venture. They were dispatched to the JV at the discretion of the Japanese partner, and their salaries were determined by their position in the Japanese company hierarchy. All the training, starting with new employee induction, was conducted jointly with employees of the Japanese parent—and they all belonged to the same company union.

All of this was seen as a "good deal" when the JV was originally set up in the 1960s—it meant that there was no need to invest heavily in staff or to worry about HRM issues in an unknown market. But ever since the original agreement was signed several decades ago, each step in the evolution of the relationship had focused only on the financial aspects of control. It was only when the consultant was brought in that HRM and organizational issues were analyzed thoroughly for the first time. So the questions have to be rephrased: Will more equity buy more "respect"? Will more expatriates help the integration? What can be done to change the direction of the joint venture?

OVERVIEW

Alliances are a useful tool for internationalization, but they are also difficult to implement. The example of Chemco illustrates the complexity of alliances and the dangers of ignoring the management and people dimensions of such a strategy. So first, we review the many motives for entering an international alliance and the different organizational forms alliances can take, presenting several perspectives on what constitutes alliance success.

An important dimension of alliances is that they are inherently unstable. We next introduce a framework that helps us to think strategically about alliances and how they may evolve over time. Based on competitive context and knowledge creation requirements, we identify four types of alliances, each with a different set of management and HRM challenges. We illustrate how HR practices and tools can contribute to the long-term success of an alliance strategy.

We then focus on planning and negotiating alliances, paying particular attention to the human resource factors that must be taken into account. Key management roles in the alliance-building process are presented, along with the implications for how managers for these positions are selected and developed.

Once an agreement has been negotiated, it must be implemented, so we next review the people and organizational factors involved, highlighting the HRM agenda in international joint venture management.

The final part of the chapter explores the concept of alliance learning. We first analyze the key obstacles to alliance learning to show the importance of linking HRM to alliance learning objectives. We then describe the human resource processes that can contribute to successful alliance learning, contrasting examples of successful and unsuccessful learning. To conclude, we review the evolutionary perspective on alliances and raise the next-generation challenges facing HRM, as alliances become an organic part of the international operations of many multinationals.

THE WHYS AND WHATS OF ALLIANCES

Joint ventures and other forms of cross-border alliance are important and commonly used tools for international growth. Companies engage in alliances for many reasons.[1] Some are created to cut the cost of entry, others to cut the cost of exit. Some are set up with the objective of leveraging opportunities, others with the aim of acquiring knowledge. Some alliances are focused on economies of scale, other on economies of scope. Understanding *why* a company participates in an international alliance is the first step toward deciding the approach to alliance human resource management.

Alliance Business Drivers

International alliances, usually in the form of joint ventures, began to multiply during the 1960s and 1970s.[2] Their primary objective was to enable firms expanding internationally to secure access to markets where direct presence was not permitted, or where market entry was deemed too costly, too risky, or both. For example, foreign companies targeting the Japanese market, like Chemco, were not allowed to invest independently in Japan until its foreign investment regime was deregulated in the mid-1970s. The only way to enter the booming market early was either to license technology to a local partner or to establish a joint venture. The early flow of foreign direct investment into China in the 1980s and 1990s followed a similar pattern.

Entering a protected market is only one reason why alliances are formed. Even when a wholly owned subsidiary may be feasible, there are many arguments in favor of market entry through partnership with a local firm. Such a partnership can provide knowledge of local business conditions, a desirable location and infrastructure, access to the distribution system, contacts with government, and a supply of experienced labor and management. The need to enter emerging markets rapidly while minimizing risk is another reason. After the collapse of the Berlin wall, alliances minimized the risk of entry into uncharted territories in Eastern and Central Europe.[3] As anticipated in the initial agreements, many local partners have since been bought out. Many foreign investors in China and India are following a similar strategy.[4]

Alliances may support internationalization strategies. For example, while global competition often requires "insider" presence in a number of countries, it is difficult for all but the largest firms to achieve such universal market coverage. In car manufacturing, parts suppliers are expected to follow major car companies as they expand around the world, though it may not be viable to set up independent operations everywhere. "Sharing" the customer with a local partner may be a better idea. Many firms are left with only two choices: either to be acquired or to negotiate alliances with others in a similar position.

Some alliances can remain nonequity contractual agreements for long periods of time. The Airbus consortium was established in 1970 by leading European aerospace firms to compete against the then-dominant US commercial aircraft manufacturers. Risk reduction and economies of scale and scope in R&D and production were the primary drivers behind the push for collaboration.[5] But because the vast majority of Airbus employees were on the payrolls of the partner firms, the organization of the consortium presented major challenges, particularly with respect to managing mobility and coordinating cross-border projects. It was only in 2001 that a separate joint stock company was set up.[6]

In high-technology industries today, international alliances are the norm, not the exception. Most high-tech firms are engaged in scores of technological, manufacturing, and marketing alliances. Their objective is to leverage their current know-how quickly over the broadest possible number of markets and to foster the creation of tomorrow's know-how. The early success of IBM and Toshiba in the emerging laptop computer market was partly a result of their long-term collaboration in designing and manufacturing state-of the-art flat screens. While the two companies never ceased to compete for the final customer, the upstream collaborative efforts allowed them to maximize return on R&D investment and to gain valuable economies of scale in manufacturing. The challenge for both firms was to ensure that capabilities created inside the alliance could be quickly transferred to the parents while maintaining learning parity. This was accomplished by a carefully balanced flow of personnel between the alliance and the two partners.

In short, there are many good reasons for companies to engage in international alliances. Some firms are heavily involved with alliances; others find them tangential to their global strategy. However, most companies will engage in some form of international alliance as they expand abroad. Consequently, it is important to understand the strategic and management issues relating to international alliances and the role of human resources management in alliance success. Indeed the question of what is a successful alliance is often not easy to answer, as we can see in the box "Defining Alliance Success."

Defining Alliance Success

The Chemco case raises the question of what is a successful alliance. This may seem like an obvious question, but it does not have an obvious answer. Does the mere survival of an international alliance indicate success? Is success measured by the return on the funds originally invested? By current profitability and cash/dividend flow? By market share? By transfer of knowledge or creation of new knowledge? Obviously, the choice depends on the specific objective of the alliance, but objectives typically change as the alliance evolves. From this perspective, the only relevant measure of alliance success is the degree to which an international alliance helps the firm to improve its ability to compete.

Contrary to a popular metaphor, an alliance is *not* like a marriage—longer alliances are not necessarily better. Problematic alliances are a drain on management energy and resources, but they often limp on since shutting them down would imply "failure."

For an alliance to be sustainable, it must benefit all partners. Respect for the partner's needs and mutual value creation are prerequisites for a successful relationship. But this does not imply that value creation must be equal or that all alliances should be sustainable for an indefinite period. Most are transitory in nature, reflecting a particular competitive situation at a particular point in time. When the situation changes, so does the need for the alliance. A "win–win" strategy is only a tool to create a healthy alliance; it should not be seen as the goal in itself. The definition of a "win" may change as the company strategy evolves, as will the role that the alliance is expected to perform.

From this perspective, Chemco's alliance in Japan, although growing and profitable, was not as successful as it could have been. This does not mean that the original entry decision was wrong. In fact, in terms of ROI, the deal was the best the company had ever made. But as the company's internationalization strategy evolved, the alliance in Japan did not follow, largely because of inattention to the management and human resource issues involved.

There are ample data showing that many alliances fail to meet expectations and that the cause of the failure is in many cases poor implementation.[7] It has been estimated that fewer than 50 percent of early joint ventures in Japan met the foreign partner's business objectives,[8] and observations of more recent experiences with joint ventures in China suggest a similar pattern.[9] The complexity of managing a business with international partners is a challenge that few firms seem equipped to handle. When alliances break up, HRM issues are often cited as one of the key factors contributing to "irreconcilable differences."[10]

Understanding Alliances

Choosing the right type of alliance for a given strategy is difficult if the strategy is not clear. What is the business objective of the proposed alliance? What is the value added of engaging in a business relationship that will inevitably consume significant resources before yielding results? What form of alliance should a company choose given its objectives, and what are the HRM implications of such a choice?

There are a number of different ways to classify alliances. It is possible to take a functional orientation to identify R&D alliances, manufacturing alliances, or marketing and distribution alliances. Another way to classify alliances is to look at the number of partners involved, from a two-partner agreement to multiple-partner consortia. However, the most common distinction is whether the contractual agreement covering the alliance creates a new jointly owned business unit—usually described as a joint venture (JV)—or whether the collaboration is essentially nonequity based, such as a licensing agreement.

Yoshino and Rangan present a comprehensive classification of alliances (see Figure 12–1) based on the fundamental nature of the contractual relationships between the partners.[11] There are many other classifications, some focusing specifically on HRM issues.[12]

There is a general agreement that, as one moves through the spectrum of alliances from a "simple" marketing agreement with a foreign distributor or OEM manufacturing agreements to stand-alone joint ventures, the management challenges increase, as does the importance of paying attention to human resource management. Much of the discussion in this chapter will therefore focus

---

FIGURE 12–1. Classification of Strategic Alliances

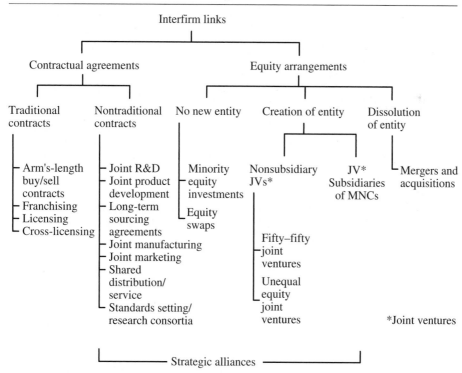

Source: M. Yoshino and U.S. Rangan, *Strategic Alliances: An Entrepreneurial Approach to Globalization* (Cambridge, MA: Harvard Business Press, 1995).

on the role of HRM in the most complex of international alliances—joint ventures between firms based in different countries. However, even among joint ventures, the differences in strategic logic behind their formation may require different HRM strategies and HR tools to be applied.

An Alliance Strategy Framework

As the Chemco case illustrates, an alliance is typically a dynamic phenomenon. The nature of the alliance may change over time, and shifts in the relative bargaining power of the partners and in their expectations about the objectives of the alliance will have corresponding HRM implications.

There are two dimensions of alliances that require careful consideration from an HRM perspective: the strategic intent of the partners, and the expected contribution of the venture to the creation of new organizational capabilities and knowledge. With respect to strategic intent, alliances among firms with competitive strategic interests may require different approaches to HRM than those where interests are complementary. With respect to capability and knowledge creation, while all alliances involve learning, some are actually formed with the main purpose of capability or knowledge creation. The learning aspect of alliances has major implications for the organizational arrangements and thus for the HRM challenges and the roles played by the HR function.

Figure 12–2 shows the four archetypes of alliance strategies based on their strategic and capability/knowledge creation contexts: complementary, learning, resource, and competitive alliances.

A *complementary* alliance is formed when two (or more) partners with complementary strategic aims join forces to exploit their existing resources or capabilities—say, by linking different elements of the value chain—and where

---

FIGURE 12–2. A Strategic Framework for Understanding International Alliances

	Low	High
Competitive	RESOURCE ALLIANCE	COMPETITIVE ALLIANCE
Long-term strategic context		
Complementary	COMPLEMENTARY ALLIANCE	LEARNING ALLIANCE

Opportunities for capability/knowledge creation

capability creation is not a prime objective. A typical complementary alliance is the traditional joint venture where one partner contributes technology and the other facilitates entry into a difficult market. Another example may be when two partners contribute complementary technologies that may lead to a new product stream. In nonequity alliances, this may take the form of a long-term contract, such as between TI and Nokia in the mobile phone chip manufacturing process.

A complementary alliance may evolve into a *learning alliance* if both partners share an interest in enhancing their individual capabilities. This can happen through the exchange of existing knowledge between the partners, or through the development of new knowledge where the partners jointly participate in the same value chain activities. An example of a learning alliance is the Fuji–Xerox joint venture in Japan that will be discussed later in this chapter.[13] Originally set up to facilitate Xerox's penetration of the Japanese market, it then shifted its focus to Asia Pacific and today serves as a critical source of capability development for the Xerox Corporation worldwide. Other alliances may be designed with learning in mind from the outset.[14] Compared to complementary alliances, learning alliances require much more interaction, including shared work and interface management, which creates demand for HR systems and processes that can facilitate effective knowledge creation.

Competitive pressures such as resource constraints, political and business risks, or economies of scale may lead competitors to join forces in a *resource alliance*. Exploration consortia set up to develop and operate oil and gas fields are increasingly common in the energy industry. One company takes the lead but the others share the risk by contributing resources and often staff. For example, BP explored oil deposits off the coast of Vietnam together with Statoil from Norway and the Vietnamese state-owned oil company. Another example would be the sharing of manufacturing facilities in Australia by Nissan and Ford when the Australian government restricted the number of manufacturing sites in the country. Compared to complementary alliances, resource alliances place a greater requirement on HR practices to reduce the frictions that might hamper collaboration.

Finally, there are also learning alliances between partners who are competitors in global markets. One of the best-known examples is NUMMI—the 50/50 joint venture between General Motors and Toyota described in Chapter 4 (page 136).[15] This venture was nominally designed for the joint production of small cars for the North American market, but at the same time, it was intended to serve as a "learning laboratory" for the two competitors. GM gained insights into Toyota's manufacturing system, and Toyota learned how to operate a US-based manufacturing facility. Such partnerships can be described as a *competitive* alliance. Another example is Boeing's long-term collaboration with a consortium of Japanese firms that built segments of Boeing airplanes, while at the same time pursuing a strategy of becoming aircraft designers themselves.[16] This type of alliance, with its emphasis on knowledge creation in a competitive context, is the most complex to manage and requires the highest level of attention to HRM.

None of these types of alliance is "better" than another. Alliances in all four quadrants can enhance a firm's competitive advantage. However, the management challenges associated with each alliance scenario are fundamentally different, and the HRM strategies, processes, and tools should reflect those differences. Problems occur when the company does not know what kind of alliance it has entered or, as in the case of Chemco, when it does not read and respond appropriately to early signals that the nature of the alliance is changing. For example, in a complementary alliance, it might be possible to rely on the local partner to recruit and train the alliance workforce since the loyalty factor may not be an issue—at least in the short term. However, such an approach in a competitive alliance could prove costly in the event of any subsequent conflict between the partners.[17]

In a complementary alliance, it may make sense to set up the venture as a stand-alone entity to promote internal entrepreneurship. In a resource partnership, there are also benefits in creating an entity with clear boundaries so that the competitive strategic context does not inhibit the performance of the alliance—good fences make good neighbors. However, learning alliances should not be constrained by too many fences, as opportunities for knowledge sharing will be greater when the boundaries between the venture and the parent are thin. HR practices in a learning alliance will therefore focus on facilitating the interface between the parent and the venture to increase the speed and quality of information exchange.

In contrast, it is not just fast learning that matters in a competitive alliance but also speed and effectiveness relative to the partner—maintaining learning parity is the key to sustaining such a relationship.[18] The HR approach has to reflect this, for example by integrating measures of the learning outcomes into the performance management process. At the same time, given the competitive context of the alliance, the flow of knowledge has to be monitored, if not restricted—an approach opposite to what is best for a learning alliance.

In all cases, it is important to remember that alliances do not always fit neatly into conceptual boxes. Some partnerships are complementary in some parts of the value chain but competitive in others, and a nuanced approach to HRM may be needed. The critical issue is that the character of most alliances changes over time. Successful complementary alliances will become learning alliances, and learning alliances may turn into competitive alliances as the strategic intent of partners changes over time.[19]

Precisely when a complementary alliance becomes a learning or a competitive alliance is a matter of interpretation. Alliances are typically defined as complementary in the opening public relations statements, but a shift in partnership orientation has to be expected. The anticipation of such shifts needs to be taken into account in formulating the HRM strategy so that the appropriate tools can be used proactively to facilitate such a change. In the Chemco case, the alliance started as complementary, combining the technology of the US partner with the market access capability of the Japanese partner. However, the US partner failed to commit the necessary resources at an early stage to ensure the future integration of the JV into its global network (training, exchange of staff, and so forth).

There were no incentives for the Japanese staff to pay attention to global strategy. They were rewarded solely on local results, and they saw no future for themselves in Chemco's global organization.

One of the few redeeming factors in the Chemco joint venture was that the alliance never migrated into the competitive domain, simply because the Japanese partner had no wish to enter this particular business segment. Had it chosen to do so, there was not much the US partner could have done to protect its market position, as it had little influence over the employees or management in Japan. However, because the partner's position was essentially cooperative, Chemco's top executives and the HR managers did get another opportunity to consider long-term actions to remedy the unsatisfactory situation. We will review later what they did.

Alliance Is a Process, Not a Deal

An alliance is not just a deal between two or more partners; it is a complex process that is full of ambiguities and contradictions. Indeed, companies often learn to manage the contradictions of transnational organization through their alliance experiences. Most alliances either die early or evolve, just like any other business venture. Alliance stability is a contradiction in terms.

There is no best way to structure an alliance. Winning and losing alliances cannot be differentiated by specific configurations of organizing patterns, equity ratios, or reporting relationships.[20] In the case of joint ventures, some argue that 50/50 arrangements work best, since the partners are forced to anticipate each other's interest.[21] Others assert that such arrangements lead to paralysis, for example with respect to staffing and compensation issues, and that it is better when one partner has the power to make a decision when there is deadlock.[22] In fact, both types of ventures appear to generate significant but distinct HRM challenges.[23]

It is not the structure of the deal, but the quality of the management process—in planning, negotiating, and implementing an international business partnership—that makes a difference. However, even here there are variations. In HP and Intel, two high-tech firms with extensive histories of successful alliances, the alliance management process is well defined, highly structured, and institutionalized. On the other hand, Corning, which derives most of its income from alliances, favors a more intuitive and informal approach that reflects the company's culture and mode of decision making. Others use a mix of the two extremes. Whether the approach is formalized or embedded in the company culture, successful alliance players have in common a rigorous and disciplined approach to alliances that includes an appreciation of the HRM contribution.

PLANNING AND NEGOTIATING ALLIANCES

The HR function should be involved early in exploring, planning, and negotiating alliances because a number of key issues relating to control and influence are closely tied to expertise, policies, and practices in human resource management. Unfortunately, HR is often left out at this stage.

Another reason why HR should be involved early is the fact that creating value through superior human resource management can be a source of competitive advantage for the partnership. For example, a partner with proven competence in implementing high-performing work systems, in staffing and recruitment, or in managing innovation through people has additional negotiating leverage. This competence should contribute to the success of the venture—provided that it can be appropriately adapted to its strategic aims and the different cultural and institutional circumstances.

Outstanding HR strengthens bargaining power in the negotiations. A reputation for good HR systems and practices is part of the corporate "brand equity."[24] Well-managed partners are more in demand than poorly managed ones. A company with poor foundations in its own approach to HRM and without proven know-how in aligning HRM with competitive strategy will find itself disadvantaged when it comes to negotiating and implementing alliances.

HRM Issues in Developing an Alliance Strategy

Successful alliances start with a strategy, not with a partner. This may seem an obvious statement, but it is not always followed in practice. Companies, or more precisely their chief executives, sometimes "fall in love." Notwithstanding the importance of personal relationships at the top, it is dangerous to select the partner before the strategic purpose is clarified.

As discussed in the previous section, it is difficult to identify what kind of relationship and what kind of a partner may be appropriate without fully understanding the long-term objectives. Japanese car component manufacturers entered the United States in the late 1980s because they were following their Japanese customers, for instance Toyota and Honda, into the US. These customers expected just-in-time support for their newly transplanted assembly plants, but the component manufacturers knew that they did not have the capability themselves to operate in an alien environment. Given the urgency, the alliance route seemed the most feasible entry strategy, though in the long run they intended to establish an independent presence.

Consequently, human resource considerations played a major role in partner selection.[25] The Japanese firms searched for local partners situated in rural environments, perceived as having harmonious labor environments conducive to Japanese manufacturing methods. They also preferred partners that were family-owned but with no clear succession. This would give them the opportunity to acquire full control with a friendly bid once the US partner decided to retire.

While the HRM issues in an alliance are always framed by the specific strategic and business context, these considerations are sometimes contradictory, requiring careful analysis. For example, when a firm decides to enter an unfamiliar foreign market, the choice of an experienced local partner may seem to be a smart move that overcomes the existing "market knowledge" handicap. Yet, with a strong local partner, there may be less urgency to develop internal market know-how, and investments in knowledge creation may not be a priority. In a complementary alliance, this may not matter. However, if the alliance ever becomes competitive, this may put the foreign partner at a serious disadvantage.

A well-defined alliance management process provides an arena for a full consideration of human resource issues.[26] Early involvement in strategy discussions allows the HR function to understand the business logic of the alliance, highlighting early the issues that may handicap implementation. In addition, important human resource decisions regarding the alliance may need to be made early in the implementation process (such as decisions on negotiation training or selection of an alliance manager).

HR's involvement in alliance strategy is often guided by a plan that is fleshed out as implementation proceeds. A sketch of the issues to be considered is shown in Table 12–1. Given the typical uncertainty surrounding alliance creation, such a plan is only a rough guide. It will become more specific when a

---

TABLE 12–1. The HRM Alliance Strategy Plan

HRM issues that may influence partner selection:
- Desired capabilities that a partner should possess.
- Need for venture HR support from the partner.
- Assessment of HR skills and reputation of potential partners.
- Assessment of the organizational culture of potential partners.
- Exit options.

Venture HR issues that need to be resolved in negotiations:
- Desired negotiation outcomes and possible bargaining trade-offs.
- Management philosophy, notably concerning HRM.
- Staffing: sourcing and criteria.
- Compensation and performance management.
- Who will provide what HR service support.

Specific HRM activities that must be implemented early and resources required:
- Negotiation stage:
  - Negotiation team selection.
  - Negotiation training.
- Start-up stage:
  - Staffing decisions.
  - Alliance management training.

Allocation of responsibility:
- Corporate responsibility.
- Local management team responsibility.
- Partner responsibility.

Measurements to evaluate the quality of HR support:
- Recruitment target.
- Training delivered.
- Skill/knowledge transferred.

---

partner is selected, paving the way for rigorous implementation when the alliance is launched.

Partner Selection

There are two main HRM issues to consider in selecting a partner: the expected contribution of the partner, and how much the HR systems of the partners will interface within the alliance.

The first issue refers to the degree to which the partner's capabilities in human resource management are expected to contribute to the alliance. Will the partner be responsible for staffing the alliance or some of its critical functions? Is the partner expected to provide HR services to the alliance? Does the partner's HR reputation matter? As we will discuss later in this chapter, getting the staffing right is the "make or break" issue for many alliances, and the probability of success can be enhanced by making these questions a part of the selection screen.

The second issue addresses the degree to which the organizational and people processes of the partners will be linked in the course of the alliance, which is likely if one of the strategic aims is learning. Will the alliance be clearly separated from the parents, or will the boundaries be ambiguous? Will there be a lot of mobility between the venture units and the parent companies? Who will evaluate the performance of the venture management and on what criteria?

When the partner is expected to contribute significantly to HR management, or when the venture is unlikely to be autonomous because of interfaces with the parents, it is vital to include the partner's HR philosophy, policies, practices, and culture as a factor in partner selection (see the box "Assessing the Culture and HR Practices of The Potential Partner"). The issue here is not to find a perfect match—a partner who shares the same view on management selection criteria or the role of incentive compensation in the reward package. Rather, the purpose is to identify potential differences and then to determine how these differences might influence the execution of the alliance strategy, whether any differences can be reconciled, and whether there are business risks if the gaps cannot be bridged.

A UK company decided to set up a joint venture in Malaysia to assemble its product for the local market. Soon after the results for the first year were in, the UK managing director proposed performance bonuses that differentiated by nearly 40 percent between managers at the same level of responsibility. A row erupted at the JV board meeting—the local partner objected, as the bonus plan would violate the standards of internal equity among managers and hurt morale. The foreign managing director was puzzled. "You told us that bonuses in your company could be up to 40 percent of the total compensation. That is what I believe our best performers deserve." "Yes," came the answer, "but in our company the bonus percentage is the same for everyone."

Differences in management style and HR practices can, however, sometimes be a powerful argument in favor of an alliance. One of the factors that motivated Toshiba to join forces with General Electric in a Japan-based joint venture was

Assessing the Culture and HR Practices of the Potential Partner

HR policies and practices have a major impact on the culture of the organization, and research has shown that differences in organizational culture may influence alliance success.[27] A cultural audit is therefore an essential part of due diligence—the audit of a potential partner. A number of factors may impact the cultural compatibility between partners, and these should be included in the audit:

- Communication style (degree of formality).
- Hierarchical boundaries (rigid vs. flexible).
- Control mechanism (tight vs. loose).
- Mode of conflict resolution (explicit vs. implicit).
- Compensation philosophy (market position, degree of salary compression).
- Performance management (open vs. hidden).
- Career stratification (gender, race, age, religion, qualifications).

Various maps exist to understand differences in culture. One simple but useful map has been developed by Goffee and Jones, using two dimensions that are well established in sociological and management theory: *sociability* (friendships, emphasis on relationship, networking) and *solidarity* (collective task and goal orientation).[28] They map out four types of cultures: networked (strong on sociability), mercenary (strong on solidarity), fragmented (low on both), and communal (high on both). Each is reflected in different approaches to management and HRM, and each exists in a positive and negative form (for example, the danger for communal cultures is that they become arrogant and inward looking, while mercenary cultures can become ruthless).

It is particularly important is to clarify key operating HR policies and the actual practices:

- How do employees enter the company and what are the selection criteria?
- What are the promotion requirements and timetables?
- Which behaviors are encouraged and which are scorned?
- What are the performance criteria and how much do they matter?
- What are the determinants of salary and how large are the differentials?
- How open is the communication about individual performance?
- How open and transparent is the whole HR system?

This material may not be easily available, but it can be obtained through consultants, a thorough review of press coverage, and local intelligence—and not just leafing through annual reports. Doing the homework eliminates subsequent surprises.

to get an "insider" view of GE's renowned management system. Toshiba's top management actually encouraged GE to introduce many of its systems and practices into the joint venture to see how such practices might be adapted in Japan, and what learning the Japanese parent might gain from the experience.

Selecting Alliance Managers

An alliance manager is typically appointed at corporate level, responsible for planning, negotiating, and implementing alliances. Ideally, this role should be kept separate from the role of venture manager,[29] who is responsible for managing a specific project, business unit, or joint venture within the alliance (see Table 12–2), though obviously not all firms have the resources to do so.

The alliance manager may monitor several existing alliances, supporting business units in identifying opportunities where a partnership could create value. When such opportunities are identified, the alliance manager will take the lead in developing the negotiating strategy and framing the partnership contract. After negotiations are completed and a new alliance formed, they will oversee the evolution of the alliance and the relationship with the partner. This is like managing a portfolio where new ventures get negotiated, added, and monitored.

The alliance manager has a determining impact on the quality of the relationship between the partners and on the ability of a firm to execute its alliance strategy. When selecting alliance managers, it is important to recognize that their role will change from visioning/sponsoring to networking/mediating as

TABLE 12–2. Alliance Manager versus Venture Manager: Roles and Responsibilities[30]

Alliance Manager Roles and Responsibilities
- **Building trust/setting the tone**—unless there is trust and the right chemistry among managers involved in the alliance, it will not go anywhere.
- **Monitoring partner contributions**—how well a firm meets its obligations to an alliance is the most tangible evidence of its commitment.
- **Managing information flow**—drawing the line between information flow that ensures the vitality of the alliance, and unbridled information exchange that could jeopardize competitiveness.
- **Assessing strategic viability/evaluating synergy**—as strategic needs of the firm change over time, what are the implications for the alliance and overall relationship with the partner?
- **Aligning internal relationships**—since an alliance involves many people inside the firm, the alliance manager should mobilize the necessary support across the organization.

Venture Manager Roles and Responsibilities
- **Managing the business**—the venture manager assumes operational responsibility for the success of the venture.
- **Representing venture interest**—the venture manager has to represent without bias the interest of the venture as a business vis-à-vis its parents.
- **Aligning outside resources**—many resources are located outside the venture boundaries in the parent organizations; tapping effectively into those resources is a venture manager's responsibility.
- **Building collaborative culture**—irrespective of the competitive context of the alliance, trust inside the venture is an essential ingredient for success.
- **Developing venture strategy**—successful alliances evolve as any other ongoing business, and this evolution should be guided by solid strategy.

the alliance evolves from initial planning through negotiations, start-up, maturity, and on to eventual decline and dissolution.[31]

Typically, the key requirement for the alliance manager's position is a high degree of personal and professional credibility. Mutual trust is the glue that cements alliance relationships, and without credibility, it is difficult to establish trust. When Motorola established a strategically key semiconductor alliance with Toshiba, it appointed as alliance manager a corporate vice president with a stellar business record. This individual played a central role in developing overall corporate strategy in the sector.[32] The focus of the alliance was to share Motorola's microprocessor know-how with Toshiba in exchange for access to Toshiba's memory technology. The alliance manager's personal credibility and reputation were critical in aligning Motorola's internal resources behind the alliance, and in convincing Toshiba that Motorola's management was determined to make the alliance work.

The job of an alliance manager also requires a high degree of flexibility and adaptability in coping with different national and organizational cultures, management styles, and individual behaviors. As discussed, alliances are by nature unstable and uncertain, so it is difficult to operate under precise rules or to expect that an intended strategy will be followed to the letter. Managers who are not comfortable in working under ambiguity will find it difficult to cope. As one experienced alliance manager put it, "high tolerance for frustration is a must."

In Chapter 5, we indicated that alliance managers are an example of one of the key lateral coordination roles in a multinational firm—much of what alliance managers are required to do involves mobilizing resources across organizational boundaries. They manage laterally in much the same way as a global account manager or an international project leader, but without large budgets or staff, and without direct authority over resource allocation.[33] Instead, the manager has to rely on influencing networks of people inside and outside the firm. As one senior executive in a *Fortune* 500 company put it,

A leader is one who gets people to do what he wants, but who at the same time makes them think that it was all their idea in the first place. An alliance manager also has to work along the same lines. He has no battalions of his own, yet he has to get the job done. He has to get people to buy into his vision of the alliance, make it part of their own job assignment, and actively work to make the alliance a success.[34]

Preparing for Negotiations

Firms need to address HRM issues long before the first encounter between the potential partners. The initial focus is primarily on selecting the negotiating team and facilitating training in handling negotiations.

Selecting the Negotiation Team

Once the long-term strategy of the alliance is in place, its objectives set, and the potential partners established, it helps if the negotiation team is selected quickly. Different types of ventures may require different mixes of entrepreneurial, analytical, and political competencies in the team.[35] The context might also influence the choice of the alliance manager, who in most circumstances should be the core member of the team.

There are different opinions as to whether future venture managers should take part in the negotiations. When venture managers are involved in negotiations they have a vested interest in "getting it right" rather than just "getting the deal," since they will be responsible for implementation. However, when negotiations are protracted (most last longer than anticipated) it is not easy to free up managers who have other responsibilities to participate in negotiations that may fail. An alternative is to assign the responsibility for the venture before the negotiation is completed, but to have another position available in case the negotiations fail.

Training for Negotiations

Alliance negotiations resemble other business negotiations, though they tend to be more complex due to the strategic and cross-cultural issues involved. For team members who lack experience in alliance negotiations, properly structured negotiation training could be a worthwhile investment.

An essential part of such preparation is to help the negotiators to become familiar with the business and cultural context of the partner's country. Given the stakes involved, a number of studies suggest that companies underestimate the need to prepare carefully.[36] Without preparation, it is all too easy to fall back on cultural stereotypes. It is also important to sort out the individual roles in a team, and to review and practice different negotiation scenarios. HR professionals often have strong process facilitation skills, and they may serve as internal consultants in the alliance negotiations. Especially in more complex negotiations, the presence of an experienced facilitator may be beneficial, observing the flow of interactions, interpreting behaviors, and coaching the key actors.

Negotiation Challenges in Joint Venture Formation

When an alliance takes the form of a joint venture, negotiations regarding control and management of the JV should include HR. There are several negotiation challenges where strategy and HRM interact closely. These include issues of

- Equity control versus operational influence.
- Board composition.
- Senior management appointments.
- HR policies for the alliance.

Equity Control versus Operational Influence

The issue of control is often difficult to resolve in joint venture negotiations. Generally, both parties seek to be the majority owner, as this is considered the best way to protect one's long-term interests, particularly in the context of a competitive alliance. However, in the absence of other supporting mechanisms, equity control is no guarantee that the venture will evolve in line with the intended strategy.

Gaining a majority position may provide a tax or financial reporting advantage. However, it is a fallacy to assume that equity control equals management control, as the Chemco case illustrates. A minority equity position, coupled with effective representation on the JV management team and an influence over the flow of know-how, may have more real impact on how the venture operates than a nominal majority exercised from a distance. From an accounting perspective, 51 percent of the shares may entitle the owner to 51 percent of the dividends, but these are often the last piece of the cash pie to be distributed. Internal transfer pricing, purchasing decisions, the cost of services provided by a local partner, and payroll determined by compensation levels all have an impact on cash flow long before any dividends are declared.

In most deals, "the last 2 percent" (going from a 49 percent share to 51 percent) is the most expensive piece of equity. While intangible contributions (the infusion of technical or market know-how, transfer of depreciated assets, brand equity) may substitute for capital in a minority position, a majority position usually requires cash. The important point is that a careful human resource strategy that secures influence can be less costly and more effective than a strategy that focuses on securing equity control.

Acquiring such influence typically starts with the key appointments—the composition of the board and senior management appointments.

Board Composition

Companies often strive for a majority equity position simply to achieve a majority on the board of directors, thus protecting their voting interests in the event of a dispute between partners. In reality, joint venture boards seldom if ever vote. Pushing through a majority vote often constitutes the first step in dissolving an alliance. If the partners have a common interest in maintaining the relationship, disputes are resolved in private, and boards act only to approve such agreements. In addition, the protection of strategic interest can be achieved by other means, such as specific clauses in the agreement or articles of incorporation that stipulate what actions require unanimous or qualified majority consent of the shareholders.

There are advantages in staffing the board primarily to oversee rather than to control. Positions on the board can be used for a variety of other purposes. An appointment to the board can be used to recognize the outstanding contribution of an alliance executive. In many countries, "company director" status is considered the pinnacle of a business career, and such opportunities may serve to increase the morale and retention of senior management. Board appointments can be used to expand linkages to outside business circles and the wider community in the local country, broadening learning and commercial opportunities. A position on the board can also be reserved for an individual who may mediate potential conflicts between the partners.

When setting up the board, there is a natural tendency to appoint alliance champions, people who favored the deal from the outset, who were involved in the negotiations, and who know the partner best. However, it is also useful to appoint at least one "bad cop," who will keep the champions from forgetting that the venture is a business rather than just a relationship—someone a little more skeptical, who sees the potential downfall of various alliance initiatives.[37]

Appointing Senior Management

In most joint ventures, senior managers wield far more strategic and operational control and influence than members of the board.[38] Tasks that determine the venture's success—setting business objectives, interfacing with key customers, monitoring the transfer of knowledge, developing the organization's culture—are all operational responsibilities of the senior managers inside the venture. Moreover, it is always preferable to resolve the inevitable conflicts and differences of opinion at the operational level rather than referring disputes to higher levels of alliance governance.

However, there is a paradox here. The shortage of international managers who can implement a market-entry strategy in an unfamiliar environment is often a motive for choosing a joint venture over a wholly owned subsidiary; yet without a pool of suitable candidates, bargaining about positions is a meaningless exercise. Having such a pool ready requires attention to HR from the very early stage of alliance planning, since it takes time to select and groom potential candidates. It may be preferable to recruit them in the local market and then provide opportunities to be socialized in the parent organization before dispatching them to the JV—again a time-consuming effort. If these HR issues are raised only after the agreement is signed, it may be difficult to find the right candidates in time for the launch. The cost of fixing the problems later grows exponentially with time since misaligned cultures, attitudes, and behaviors are difficult to uproot once embedded.

Note however that executive role expectations may vary from one culture to another. In a 50/50 French–Swedish joint venture located in France, the Swedish company agreed to the appointment of a senior French executive as chairman in exchange for de facto control of the operations. But in the French organization, the chairman was not the honorary figure that the Swedes expected. He was seen as the ultimate decision maker in the venture, while the opinions of the Swedish managers were ignored. Although the venture continued to make strategic sense, the operational frictions generated so much ill will on both sides that it had to be dissolved a few years later.

The leadership and behavioral demands on JV managers are greater than in wholly owned units, and finding suitable managers is not a simple task. Political skills are indispensable, as top JV managers need to use influence to balance partner priorities and overcome conflicts. Cross-cultural sensitivity and flexibility are particularly important when partners come from different cultures and where JV staff represent two or more nationalities. Having a cooperative disposition, a high tolerance for ambiguity, and an internal locus of control are additional personal traits that help international alliance managers to perform well.[39]

In particular, the nomination of the venture general manager can generate intense debate. Who should "own" the JV manager? One can argue that the venture manager must have the goodwill of both parents in order to operate effectively.[40] Installing somebody as venture general manager who represents the interest of only one partner may be counterproductive. And special care is needed when the joint entity is essentially independent of the parents' operations, as in the case of many complementary or resource alliances. There is a fine line between representing the best interests of the venture *and* that of the parent company.

If the venture activities need to be integrated with those of the parent, then an arms-length relationship may not be appropriate. When an insider from one firm seems the logical choice as venture manager—because of his or her knowledge of the business or geographical area—it is important to minimize incentives that show favoritism. It should be clear that the manager's future career depends on the success of the venture. It also helps if alliance managers are seen as its champions—those who believe in the purpose and who work hard to make it succeed; see the box "The Role of Venture Champions."

Identifying alliance champions and recognizing their contribution toward implementing the alliance strategy is a critical driver of its success. Not surprisingly, alliance champions, like alliance skeptics, can be found on both sides of the partnership. Knowing the venture champions on the "other side"—especially those who have sufficient internal credibility to mobilize resources for the benefit of the alliance—is of great value in the negotiations over managerial appointments.

The Role of Venture Champions

An alliance succeeds because managers and employees believe in the promise of the concept and are willing to invest personal effort to make it happen. Alliances without champions do not survive for long because the ambiguity and uncertainty of the relationship impair participants' capacity to deal with the complex issues embedded in most partnerships.

When Whirlpool Corporation established a manufacturing joint venture with Tatramat, the Slovak washing machine maker, Tatramat's former top executive, Martin Ciran, became managing director of the joint venture.[41] The new company later ran into serious financial difficulties that enabled Whirlpool to gain majority control. Yet Ciran retained his position as he was recognized as the key champion of the alliance. His leadership was deemed essential to making the venture a success.

With access to Whirlpool know-how, but under Ciran's leadership, the company was turned around. Today, Whirlpool's Slovak factory—now fully owned—still ranks among its top-performing European subsidiaries.

Human Resource Policies within the Alliance Venture

The need to influence alliance strategy is only one of the arguments for addressing HRM issues early in the alliance formation process. When the success of the alliance depends heavily on people issues, such as competence transfer or reaching new standards in quality and productivity, leaving HRM until later in order to simplify alliance negotiations may handicap the future chances of success.

It is particularly important to pay early attention to HR policies and practices when there are likely to be many complex interfaces between the venture and the alliance parents.[42] In contrast to licensing or supplier–buyer agreements, up-front agreement on HR philosophy and policies may be vital to success in manufacturing joint ventures or shared projects in new product development.

Some researchers advocate a detailed contract clarifying HR policies inside the alliance in order to reduce the uncertainty and conflict over matters of staffing, transfers, promotion, and compensation.[43] However, detailed contracts do not guarantee compliance. Venture synergy comes from shared business interests, not from legal formulations. A clear statement regarding HR principles is in most cases sufficient, without limiting contractually what can or cannot be done.

Sometimes companies take the position "when in Rome, do as the Romans" and delegate all responsibility for human resource matters to the local partner. This makes sense provided the "Roman" organization is a paragon of effectiveness, quality, and customer service. If it does not have solid HR foundations in place, then this attempt to show cultural sensitivity will only result in replicating the dysfunctional aspects of local practice. It is said of many foreign joint ventures in Japan that they represent "museums of Japanese management." They are repositories of obsolete practices that their Japanese parents ditched a long time ago, but that are still presented to the foreign parent as the "Japanese" way of managing people.

IMPLEMENTING ALLIANCES

Once the contract is signed and the partnership becomes operational, a new set of people-related issues appears. How to manage the evolution of the partnership? How to ensure that the knowledge developed inside the alliance is properly shared among the partners? How to keep the partnership objectives aligned with those of the parent?

These issues have two major HRM implications. The first is managing the interface with the parent, which involves influencing the attitudes and behaviors of staff at home who are in contact with the alliance. The second relates to the management of people inside the venture itself.

Managing the Interfaces with the Parent

An important challenge is to manage the interface between the parent organization and the partnership. The objective is to align the internal processes back home so they support rather than hinder external collaboration. Often the organizational units that provide resources to the alliance are not those receiving its outputs. The asymmetry in the perceived costs and benefits of collaboration with the venture may cause internal tensions that undermine willingness to support the partnership. The value of collaboration is sometimes not visible in the hustle and bustle of daily operations, so explicit reinforcements of the message may be required. Ford learned from Motorola's experience, cited earlier, when it entered into broad co-operative agreements in Japan; the question "What have you done to support Ford's alliance strategy?" was featured in the performance evaluations for a large part of the organization.

A rapidly growing US securities firm with global ambitions set up an alliance with a European brokerage to offer its European customers "preferential" access to US financial markets. However, even after the alliance was launched to great fanfare, the operational practices at the New York trading desk did not change. The relatively small orders from Europe did not get the same attention as those from large US institutional clients, reducing profit opportunities for the European partner. The new partner received a similar second-class treatment from other units of the US firm.

Why was this happening? The rigid "meet-the-numbers" reward system in the United States was incompatible with a strategy that did not yield immediate earnings, like the European partnership. No amount of presentations on the benefits of international expansion could make much difference. In Europe, the initial irritation quickly turned to anger and then to suspicions about the true motives of the American partner. Less than two years later the alliance was dissolved. As noted by one of the American HR managers involved, "If this alliance was important for our future, then perhaps it should have been partly my job to create an environment where phone calls from our partners would be returned without delay."

Top Management Role

The company's execution of its alliance strategy places particular demands on top management, who must "walk their talk." The box "The Anniversary Speech" illustrates what happens when top management is not involved.

The Anniversary Speech

A 50/50 joint venture between a Japanese and a US firm celebrated its 25th anniversary. Over time, the JV had evolved from a small marketing start-up to a fully integrated firm with an independent R&D and manufacturing capability that enjoyed a very profitable leadership position in the Japanese market. Given its commercial success, the friction between the two partners in the early days regarding the future direction of the business was replaced by a grudging willingness to continue working together. However, on the American side, executives often voiced concerns that the joint venture operated as if it were a wholly owned affiliate of the Japanese parent, while their influence was being eroded. The loyalty of the workforce was seen as tilted in favor of the local partner.

On the anniversary date, the employees assembled in one of Tokyo's exhibition halls for an afternoon of celebration. The company glee club warmed up with some speeches and songs. Then the 96 year-old former chairman of the Japanese parent, who signed the original deal, was helped onto the stage in his wheelchair to deliver a message of thanks to all employees for bringing his dream to life. His speech was short, owing to his failing health, but it was emotional and made a big impact on the audience. His speech was followed by with a prerecorded video message from the current American CEO who, in three years of tenure, had visited the venture once. He said nothing wrong, but the impersonality of the presentation defeated its purpose. Another skirmish in the loyalty battle was lost.

Capturing the loyalty of the alliance workforce is only one of the human resource tasks that require the support of top management. Internal communication is another; top management plays an indispensable role in ensuring that the reasons for the partnership are well understood inside the firm, especially when it comes to balancing the competitive and collaborative aspects of the alliance. Top management must also work closely with HR on the selection of alliance managers, on resource allocation for learning activities, and on ensuring that reward systems are well aligned with the partnership strategy.

Human Resource Management Issues in Managing the Alliance

Many of the international HRM issues discussed previously in this book are also relevant to international alliances. Here we will examine those that may have the biggest impact on the success of an alliance strategy:

- Staffing of the alliance.
- Mobility between the parent(s) and the venture.
- Competence and capability development.
- Performance management.
- Rewards and recognition.
- Building influence inside the alliance.
- Aligning the social architecture.

However, just as there are no generic alliance strategies, there are few generic blueprints for effective HR policies and practices. Attention to HRM in the alliance depends on the strategic objectives and the position of the alliance in the value chain. The more critical the role of the partnership in creating value, the larger is the need to commit HR resources and support.

Staffing Alliances

Staffing matters! Inappropriate staffing is one of the major causes of alliance failures, and this is typically the most important aspect of HRM in the venture. Perhaps the most important qualification for a potential alliance partner is having sound HR foundations at home. Without that credibility, it may be impossible to establish respect abroad.

Every strategic plan for an alliance should include a review of staffing requirements. Other HR matters, such as training and compensation, have an important impact, but problems in those areas can be addressed—with proper determination—in a relatively short time. Difficulties created by poor staffing, such as correcting the consequences of bad decisions made by people who are not qualified to meet the challenges of managing an alliance, may take years to fix. While the staffing issues will vary from one alliance to another, there are some generic matters to consider:

- What number and skill mix of employees are required?
- Who is responsible for forecasting manpower demands?
- Who will do the recruiting? Each partner individually? Jointly?
- Which positions are to be filled by each parent?
- Which positions are to be filled by expatriates?
- In joint ventures, for whom do the new employees work—for one of the partners, or for the new entity?
- Who decides on new hires? Must there be an agreement among partners?
- How will staffing conflicts be resolved?

In virtually all joint ventures there will be staff from both partners. The box "'Managing' Your Partner's Staffing" addresses the tricky question of how to influence the other company's staffing decisions.

"Managing" Your Partner's Staffing

Asymmetry in the quality of the assignees is often an early signal that a venture is heading for trouble, since it raises questions about the managerial competence or sincerity of the deficient partner. If the partner organization is to provide key operational staff, it is important to find ways of ensuring that they possess the required competencies. This means developing some way to identify the talented people in the partner organization, and understanding the basis by which the partner differentiates between high potentials, solid performers, and low performers.

Inappropriate staffing decisions are common. The partner's management may not understand the skill level required for jobs in the partnership venture, they may overestimate the capability of their internal candidates, or they may simply not have the necessary basic HR capabilities. It is essential to intervene *before* any decisions are taken. Forcing a change once an appointment has been made may be difficult.

The right to be consulted on key appointments is a useful stipulation in a partnership agreement. However, exercising this right requires familiarity with the "rules of the game" in the partner's organization, understanding the internal scorecards, and knowing how careers evolve there, as well as gaining access to the levers of influence. Much of this is tacit knowledge, acquired through extensive informal interaction and built on trust and personal credibility.

Given the importance of staffing, there is a case for formally addressing these issues in the alliance contract, though as noted earlier views are divided since contractual arrangements may be too rigid for evolving staffing needs—mutual agreement on policies may suffice.

One-Way versus Temporary Transfer

When partnerships are formed to create a new business, it is important to consider the costs and benefits of two alternative staffing strategies. One approach is to assign personnel to the JV on a temporary transfer from the partner firm. The other is to staff the JV positions on a "permanent" basis. While it is not unusual to combine the two methods, it is important to consider the conflicting priorities and career aspirations of the two groups of employees. Every position filled—usually at higher cost—by a temporary transferee is an opportunity lost for the permanent staff. If the value of the transferee is not readily apparent, resentment and conflict are not far behind.

There is some evidence that it is better to staff joint ventures with dedicated management teams.[44] If employees are transferred from the parent, they should expect to remain in the venture without a guaranteed ticket back to the parent, so that their future career opportunities are linked entirely to the growth of the new business. In Japan, a country where few JVs survive, several successful joint ventures have at their helm executives who have spent all or most of their careers in the venture. Fuji Xerox, headed for many years by Yotaro Kobayashi, is probably the most notable example of what strong and stable leadership can do for JV performance.

On the other hand, temporary transfers do have merit. They are useful when a venture is evolving rapidly and the required management skills change, when skill gaps cannot be covered internally, or as a tool for organizational learning. Transferees are more likely to remember that their task is not to preserve the alliance at all costs. Indeed, temporary transfers are generally the only way in which the foreign partner can insert its employees into the venture. However, any assignments should be of a reasonable duration since new managers will pass through a learning stage before they can contribute fully to the venture. Frequent churn of key venture managers makes it difficult to establish a shared culture.

The foreign partner may experience greater difficulties than the local partner in convincing first-class employees from the parent firm to transfer to the JV.[45] In such cases, the personal involvement of top management can make a difference. When Procter & Gamble first entered the Chinese market in the 1980s, joint venturing with local partners was the only option. In order to encourage its best candidates to accept these challenging assignments, P&G's top management, including the CEO, took a visible role in candidate selection, acting as a mentor during the assignment and in repatriation. Such leadership commitment to staffing ensured a ready supply of good managers willing to work in China.

A shortage of qualified candidates or cost considerations may persuade foreign partners to limit their representation to a single executive. One person is expected to play the role of corporate ambassador, shadow CEO, chief learning officer, and business developer—quite a challenge! Notably in competitive alliances, this may not be in the best interest of the business.

In most cases, the best strategy is to recruit and develop local talent. When joint ventures are an important part of a company's strategy in a particular market, it may be worthwhile establishing a corporate unit that can serve as a holding company for all operations in the country. Local managers can then be hired by the holding company, and trained and dispatched to joint ventures to represent the interests of the foreign partner, thus lessening the reliance on expensive expatriates with limited local know-how. Many foreign firms investing in joint ventures in China, for example ABB and GE, have chosen this route to develop their local management teams.[46]

Developing Capabilities

The strategic objectives of an alliance often require developing new knowledge, skills, and capabilities, as in the case of learning and competitive alliances. This in turn requires actions to create a learning environment:

- Building understanding among people in the parent company who will be involved directly or indirectly in the partnership.
- Training employees and managers dispatched to the alliance.
- Enhancing collaboration inside the partnership.
- Facilitating integration with the parent firm.

In companies where alliances are critical to the business strategy, alliance training is often used as an integral part of the implementation process. For example, Hewlett-Packard, which is engaged in scores of international partnerships, organizes workshops on a massive scale for managers involved in alliances. The HP alliance management framework, an elaborate knowledge management system focused on alliances, is disseminated using case histories, toolkits, and checklists, as well as comparisons of best practices from other firms.[47]

One of the dilemmas in preparing executives for alliance assignments is that companies may be reluctant to devote resources to alliance management training, or even to select potential venture staff, until the partnership has been agreed on. This is a double bind since there is seldom time for extensive training once an agreement has been reached. Estimates suggest that only one-third of firms involved in alliances offer alliance training.[48] One of the authors has directed alliance management seminars for over 25 years. It is not unusual to see participants subscribing for the course at the last minute, departing for a foreign location virtually as soon as the course ends.[49]

One of the focal areas for management development within the alliance venture itself is in helping the venture team to interact and work effectively with each other and with the parents. This process ideally starts when the alliance is launched, helping employees to get to know each other, and learning about each other's company culture and mode of operations. When Corning creates new alliances, venture staff are briefed on the respective organizational cultures and traditions, corporate values, and venture organization in order to minimize confusion and misunderstanding.[50] Other companies organize team-building workshops, ranging from traditional OD interventions to outdoor experiential learning.[51] It also pays to follow up the "honeymoon training" with periodic workshops, working jointly through specific business and cultural challenges facing the partnership.

In the Chemco case, the US partner realized that it had to modify the structure of functional training workshops it held to improve coordination in Asia Pacific. Previously, these had been limited to wholly owned subsidiaries. Although participants complained about the lack of support from the Japanese, no action could be taken since the Japanese, as part of a JV rather than a wholly owned subsidiary, did not attend. In the new format, Japanese JV employees were invited to take part, and the program was redesigned to take language problems into account and to facilitate dialogue. Participants were now able to identify jointly the obstacles to collaboration, suggest actions to remedy the problems, and commit to new joint business initiatives. The bottom line? Profits from joint projects generated by the first three workshops equaled the annual training budget for the whole region.

A good and relatively inexpensive way to foster the alliance integration process is to open up in-house training to the staff in the alliance unit, and when appropriate to those from the partner. Aside from skill development, this may lead to the creation of personal networks across the alliance boundaries. Real trust cannot be built through contracts—only through human relationships.

Defining Performance

During the planning stage, it is generally not difficult for alliance partners to agree that "performance matters." However, for the operating managers dispatched to the actual JV, it can be much more difficult to agree on what constitutes "performance," how to measure it, and what the consequences of high or low performance should be.[52]

Most fundamentally, the partners may have different objectives for the JV and therefore use different criteria to assess performance. A study of Chinese–German JVs revealed that the Chinese parent organization put much higher value on the acquisition of technology and knowledge, while growth and market share were more important for the German parents.[53] However, disagreements about how to appraise performance are often less obvious.

In an oil exploration joint venture created by British, Norwegian (state-owned), and Vietnamese (government) partners, the parties did not hold the same views about performance management. Yet the split did not cut along East–West cultural lines. British expatriates and locally recruited young Vietnamese managers were in favor of individually focused, achievement-oriented performance criteria with substantial financial benefits for top performers. The Norwegians and the senior representatives of the Vietnamese partner, concerned with equity and harmonious work relations, preferred to give more emphasis to team goals and process implementation, with much less internal differentiation. Although the business principles in the agreement contained a commitment to create a performance-oriented culture, the specifics were never spelled out. The net result was confusion, frustration, conflict, and high turnover—the opposite of what a performance management system is supposed to achieve. It was not that one partner was "right" and the other "wrong"; the real issue was the lack of a common perspective.

Many of the dualities involved in performance management discussed in Chapter 9 can lead to disagreement—short-term versus long-term time horizon, focus on output versus behavior, individual versus group scope, objective versus subjective evaluation, direct versus indirect feedback, and in addition parent versus venture orientation. This last issue—whether managers are evaluated on the performance of the venture or the parent—can become particularly contentious. But an even bigger problem is to align strategic aims. In Chemco's case, as long as the objective of the local management team was only to grow profitably in Japan, the wider strategic aims of the US firm to grow in the region remained neglected.

Many of the tensions around performance management come from three sources: (1) applying homegrown principles inappropriately in a different context; (2) using different standards for parent company and alliance employees; and (3) attempting to combine incompatible approaches.

In a Japanese-controlled JV in the United States, merit increases were linked to performance evaluations, according to local practice. However, the performance feedback process was decidedly "Japanese," indirect and informal. Japanese bosses spent most time with the laggards, hoping that with some encouragement, their performance would improve. On the other hand, they loaded more responsibility on those considered outstanding to signal that they were trusted and were on the way to a bright future in the firm. While these signals might have been correctly interpreted in Japan, several of the top American performers quit, complaining that the merit increases did not reflect the additional responsibilities, that the bosses did not care, and that they did not know where they stood.

Others complained that the Japanese were not honest, since the encouraging words were not matched sufficiently by what they saw on their paychecks.

Strategy matters—in a complementary alliance, a hands-off approach to setting the performance objectives may be appropriate, whereas in a competitive alliance this may be a recipe for disaster. Not surprisingly, resistance to "foreign" ways of managing performance is most pronounced in competitive alliances. This is because managing performance is one of the keys to having an influence inside the venture. The way performance is managed indicates to the alliance staff who is in charge, whose interests have to be taken seriously. Without influence over the performance management process, a partner (especially a distant partner) can expect only nominal control over the direction of the venture. Therefore, performance management issues often become a lightning rod in the latent struggle for influence.

The proper measure of influence is not how much the performance management of the alliance resembles that of the parent, but how it furthers the parent company's strategy. First, this means making sure that the parent's strategic objectives are reflected in the performance targets for the alliance. Second, achieving these targets has to be measured. Third, meeting or failing to meet targets should have consequences.

In Chemco's case, the first and second requirements for effective performance management processes were met once the US partner attained formal majority control and regional targets were included in the annual objectives set for the local management team. However, target setting was merely a ritual since the results had no consequences, positive or negative—and this would remain the case as long as Chemco had no influence over salaries, bonuses, or promotions. This leads us to the reward aspects of performance management.

Aligning Rewards

One of the first actions Chemco took to increase its influence was to negotiate a gradual transfer of all employees in Japan from the payroll of the Japanese parent to JV employee status. The work conditions offered were more favorable, but did not increase the cost as the compensation and benefit system was tailored to the JV workforce. The union and nearly all employees accepted these conditions. As a next step, the management bonus was linked to the achievement of two sets of targets, regional and local, with regional targets being the key objective for senior management. In addition, the variable part of total compensation was increased dramatically, and the company began discussing a stock option scheme. Today, the Japanese partner considers its JV as a "human laboratory" where new HR—novel to the Japanese market—can be tested before being introduced into the parent company.

Of all compensation issues, those relating to variable pay require the most sensitivity and flexibility. Compensation can have a strong impact on strategy implementation because people tend to do what they believe they get rewarded for.[54] But beyond that, people in different countries have very different attitudes to variable pay. This is partly the result of wide differences in accounting standards and tax regimes, for example regarding stock options.[55] There are also different cultural attitudes to issues like uncertainty avoidance and salary differentials. Again, the primary consideration is to align rewards with the alliance strategy rather than to blindly import HR practices because they are successful in the parent firm.[56]

No compensation formula or measurement matrix can overcome a disagreement about strategy. If one partner wants to build market share and the other is interested in cash flow, then developing common performance targets is going to be difficult unless the two partners first agree on priorities. In more complex alliances, building a clear linkage between strategic aims and rewards may not be possible—an additional argument for keeping alliances simple and focused.

Another important compensation issue to consider is the tension between external equity with the parent for expatriates and internal equity for venture staff, frequently leading to asymmetry in earnings among different groups of employees within the alliance. For example, expatriate managers often earn many times more than the income of a typical local JV employee (whose pay in turn may be considerably higher than that of a counterpart in a local firm). The differences in compensation levels may also impact the balance of influence in the alliance since loyalties, not surprisingly, tend to shift toward the higher-paying partner.[57]

These differences, while unavoidable in ventures involving companies from countries with widely different standards of living, may lead to motivational problems and conflict unless the added value of staff who receive superior compensation is visible and appreciated. Disparity in compensation sometimes makes it difficult to persuade the local partner to accept expatriates even when this could be in the best interest of the venture.[58] Local partners may also try to use the disparity to their own advantage. For example, compensation "equality" between foreign expatriates and local managers was often one of the conditions for JV approval by local authorities in China. In reality, the Chinese managers were paid only a fraction of what was stipulated in the contract, while their state-owned employer retained the rest. Foreign partners in Chinese JVs had to bear the expatriation costs of foreign managers while the Chinese partner earned a corresponding profit.

Internal equity issues within the parent firm must also be balanced against the supply and demand for high-quality venture managers. Alliances, in comparison with wholly owned subsidiaries, are difficult to manage. They may be seen as risky since the venture is removed from the politics of getting ahead in the parent company. High performers, who tend to have options, may elect to stay clear of such assignments unless they are sufficiently compensated. On the other hand, corporate cohesion is better facilitated by a degree of consistency in compensation strategy across all affiliates, irrespective of the organizational form.

This paradox cannot be solved simply by recalibrating compensation. To achieve the necessary balance, other components of the HR system have to be aligned as well. The deliberate positioning of alliance assignments as a key element of long-term career progression is a powerful tool for ensuring a supply of requisite talent, as we saw in the case of P&G's staffing strategy for entering China. Influencing and shaping careers provides stronger leverage over expatriate staffing than short-term financial incentives.[59]

Building and Maintaining Influence

One of the best ways to gain allegiance among JV employees is to show commitment to their career development. Shortly after transferring Japanese employees to the JV payroll, Chemco offered some younger staff the possibility of moving to its subsidiaries in Southeast Asia with the assignment of coordinating sales with Japanese customers in the region. The conditions offered were the same as for any other Chemco expatriate. One benefit for Chemco was improved customer service and sales. The other was a dramatic change in how the Japanese staff perceived regional integration. The earlier view that integration was a power game—us versus them—quickly faded. Expatriate perks such as housing were attractive for the young Japanese since they could not afford this at home. But what made the difference was the feeling that career opportunities were now visibly open to all.

Such career development can promote organizational cohesion, though as with any HRM practice, the execution depends on the alliance's strategic context. In competitive alliances, this needs to be carefully considered. The worst outcome is to accept transferees for the sake of the relationship, and then to cut them off from information and influence because they are perceived as untrustworthy. Some transferees will view this as another example of the partner's duplicity and bad intentions.

The form of the alliance also has implications for career development, and again joint ventures pose most of the challenges[60] Employees transferred from the parent to a joint venture can feel left behind, especially if the number of expatriates inside the venture is small. The temporary nature of the assignment only reinforces anxiety about career prospects. Assurances from corporate HR— "Don't worry, we'll take care of you when you come back"—lack credibility in an era of continuous restructuring. The difficulty of managing dual allegiance is one of the arguments in favor of "one-way-transfer" staffing strategies. However, this is often not practical from a staffing perceptive, as we will discuss in the next section, or desirable because of a need to foster knowledge exchange between the venture and the parent.

Visible involvement in career development decisions builds influence. Being an "absentee" parent may be a cost-efficient strategy in the short term, but it can be costly in the long term. In a stand-alone JV, when the initial growth levels off, career development prospects may diminish, and the best and the brightest may leave unless they see the same opportunity to move to increased responsibilities as they would have in a wholly owned subsidiary. If only one of the parents seems to care, then it is likely that commitment and loyalty will shift accordingly.

Developing Shared Culture

In contrast to acquisitions, one has to live with conflicting loyalties in alliances. Whether or not this becomes dysfunctional depends on the type of alliance and the ability of the partners to deal with the contradictions in the alliance relationship. One way to cope is to foster a distinct and shared culture inside the alliance that eases tensions between partners; another is to build strong personal relationships. However, as always, this depends on the business strategies underlying the venture. Alliance independence is not a goal in itself—the purpose of an alliance is to create value for the partners. Instructions to general managers, such as "run this like your own business" when the venture does not have decision-making autonomy, can only create mistrust and cynicism.

A key outcome of a shared culture is trust.[61] Even in a competitive alliance, the partnership will not succeed without trust on an operating level. The best way to build trust is to get to know each other. This can be supported by promoting personnel exchanges and by providing visible examples of commitment to common goals.

Another source of cohesion may be a common enemy, as illustrated by the experience of three middle-sized manufacturers of electronic components. American, German, and Japanese respectively, they established a global alliance aimed at combining R&D resources in a market dominated by two giant competitors. Management teams met regularly around the world to coordinate development activities. However, traditional rivalry, parochial departmental interests, and cultural insensitivity slowed down decision making, causing the alliance to miss several critical deadlines and jeopardizing relationships with key customers. On the initiative of one of the HR managers, signs bearing the logos of the two competitors were installed on the walls in the conference rooms. The signs could be made to light up by pushing a button hidden under the conference desk, reminding everyone that the competition did not go away while they wasted time in unproductive arguments. After only a few meetings, it became embarrassing for anyone to get flashed for allowing a parochial agenda to get in the way of common interest. The speed and decision making and quality of implementation improved dramatically.

SUPPORTING ALLIANCE LEARNING

All alliances include some learning aspects, the least of which is how to work effectively with partners.[62] However, some alliances are created with capability development, knowledge creation, and learning as the focal objectives.

In both learning and competitive alliances, effective alliance learning is important not only to prevent the erosion of a firm's market position, but also as a building block for future competitive advantage. In the case of Fuji–Xerox, the venture was started to facilitate Xerox's entry into the Japanese market. In the late 1980s, other Japanese companies such as Canon and Ricoh aggressively attacked Xerox in its home US market with innovative products, competing on price and quality. Initially, Xerox was not able to respond and lost significant market share. However, recognizing that Fuji–Xerox competed successfully against the same players in Japan, the company launched a massive "learning from Japan" campaign aimed at transferring Fuji–Xerox's capabilities back to the US mother firm.[63] Because of this "reverse technology transfer," Xerox was able to stem the market erosion and began to recapture lost share.

The long-term success of Fuji–Xerox illustrates the fact that many strong strategic alliances focus on mutual learning. Indeed, selecting partners who are known to be poor learners so as to guard against capability leaks is shortsighted. Weak learning capability is a sign of poor management, and poorly managed firms make poor partners. Trust between the partners allows them to concentrate on managing the business rather than on monitoring and control, and their mutual learning strengthens their position in markets worldwide.

The learning ability of an organization depends on its ability to transfer and integrate tacit knowledge that is difficult to copy, thereby building organizational capabilities. Since the capabilities typically are embedded in people, HRM is critical to organization learning. This is especially true in international alliances where the learning occurs in a complex context of competition and cultural differences. Many of the difficulties in implementing long-term alliance strategies can be traced to the quality of the learning process and the underlying human resource policies and practices. The ability to learn is even more important in competitive alliances, where asymmetry in learning can result in an uneven distribution of benefits.[64]

One objective of human resource management in international alliances is therefore to complement business strategy by providing a climate that encourages organizational learning, and by installing appropriate tools and processes to guide the process of knowledge creation and sharing.[65] We have already discussed many of these in Chapter 10, but alliances, particularly competitive alliances, bring particular challenges for HRM.

Obstacles to Alliance Learning

The rapid development of competitive capabilities among leading Japanese firms in the second half of the 20th century is often attributed to successful alliance learning. Alliances were used as the main vehicle for inward technology transfer and capability improvement. More recently, many other companies in developing countries in Asia and Latin America have pursued the same strategy with success. By contrast, many of the traditional US and European firms have struggled to kick-start the learning process, and examples of alliance learning like that of Fuji–Xerox are relatively rare. So what are the obstacles? Some are the consequences of ill-conceived strategies, while others stem from poor HRM practices or are a combination of both (see Table 12–3).

TABLE 12–3. Obstacles to Organizational Learning in International Strategic Alliances

HR Activities	HR Practices
Planning	• Strategic intent not communicated. • Short-term and static planning horizon. • Low priority for learning activities. • Lack of involvement by the HR department.
Staffing	• Insufficient lead time for staffing decisions. • Resource-poor staffing strategy. • Low quality of staff assigned to the JV. • Staffing dependence on the partner.
Training and development	• Lack of cross-cultural competence. • One-way transfer of knowledge. • Career structure not conducive to learning. • Poor culture for transfer of learning.
Appraisal and rewards	• Appraisal focused on short-term goals. • No encouragement to learn. • Limited incentives for transfer of know-how. • Rewards not tied to global strategy.
Organizational design and control	• Responsibility for learning not clear. • Fragmentation of the learning process. • Control over the HR function given away. • No insight into partner's HR strategy.

Source: Adapted from V. Pucik, "Strategic Alliances, Organizational Learning, and Competitive Advantage: The HRM Agenda," *Human Resource Management* 27, no. 1 (Spring 1988), pp. 77–93.

Defensive Strategic Intent

One obstacle to alliance learning may arise because many alliances are driven by a defensive strategic intent. Firms perceive partnerships primarily as a way of reducing risk and conserving valuable resources.[66] This built-in defensive posture may make managers reluctant to make the necessary investments in learning, especially if one of the alliance objectives is to minimize the cost of developing new capabilities. Failing to invest in learning will invariably result in the deterioration of a firm's competitive position, leading to an asymmetry in the relationship and eventually to a conflict with the partner. Dissolution of the relationship is then the logical next step. Successful learning alliances are most often driven by a "top-line" orientation where investment in the development of new capabilities is recovered through the growth of business.

A corollary to defensive intent is the belief that preventing the partner from learning (and thus avoiding asymmetry) may be easier and cheaper than investing in one's own learning. A partner committed to learning will always learn, even if this is made difficult by obstacles put in the way. Meanwhile, the customer feels the obstacles. Secrecy and internal walls lead to suboptimal solutions, excessive costs, and delays. In highly competitive markets, companies that hope to build defensive walls around themselves to prevent knowledge "seeping" to the partner often end up losing the customer.

Low Priority for Learning Activities

Decisions on alliance learning strategy are often based on the assumption that the existing balance of contributions to the venture will not change over time. Consider the case of a partnership where one party provides technology and the other secures market access. The executives of the technology firm may believe that the partner will have to rely on their technological leadership for the foreseeable future, so they see few incentives to invest in learning about the market. However, if the other partner gradually closes the technological gap—after all, technology transfer is often a part of the deal—the basis for the alliance becomes problematic. One partner now has both technology *and* market access, so why share the benefits?

One problem here is that many firms do not recognize the importance of developing soft or invisible competencies. Learning often has to be focused on mastering tacit processes underlying product quality, speed of product development, or linkage to key customers. Firms frequently fail to benefit from alliance learning because they do not recognize the benefits of acquiring the "soft" skills.[67]

Learning through alliances may be faster than learning alone, but it still requires investment. The learning strategy may be compromised by a reluctance to commit the necessary financial resources. In many companies, the traditional focus of the business planning process is return on financial assets, while the accumulation of invisible assets is not evaluated directly since a financial value is hard to assign to these outcomes. Activities that cannot be evaluated in financial terms may be seen as less critical, so learning efforts are given only token support.

Inappropriate Staffing

Expatriate staffing is costly, and firms are tempted to reduce alliance costs by limiting the number of expatriate personnel assigned to the foreign venture. As a result, the few expatriates (sometimes only one) are often overwhelmed with routine work, struggling just to get by in an unfamiliar culture. The opportunities for active involvement in new knowledge acquisition—for example through relationships with local customers or interactions with the partner—are minimal. However keen the expatriates may be to learn, operational matters prevent them from doing so.

In Chemco's case, company policy for nearly 20 years was to dispatch only one senior level executive to Japan, occasionally augmented with an experienced engineer bringing knowledge into Japan. In most cases, the expatriates retired after their assignment in Japan, so there was no organizational transfer of learning. When the company decided to refocus its Japan strategy, the total accumulated experience in the Japanese market among the top management team (Japan was at that time the largest overseas market for Chemco), including business trips longer than one week, was less than six months.[68]

The staffing agenda, however, is not just about how many and where, but also about who. If the managers assigned to oversee or manage an alliance are not credible within their own organization and with the partner, learning will be difficult to achieve. Because these are relatively long-term assignments, they clash with the expectations of fast upward mobility and may not be attractive to high-potential managers. The managers who land in this role may not have the influence to cope with the complex give-and-take of a learning relationship. Long-term career planning is often lacking, as is effective repatriation (as in Chemco's case), which may hinder effective exploitation and dissemination of the acquired know-how.

Poor Climate for Knowledge Exchange

A characteristic of alliance learning is that partner interactions often take place in a context of competitive collaboration.[69] Not surprisingly, competition and learning commonly go hand in hand in high-technology industries where fast learning is an imperative of the business model.

In a competitive alliance, transfer of knowledge to a competitor will often generate legitimate concern among staff over what will happen to their jobs and work groups when their unique knowledge is disseminated to others. Principles of equitable exchange, agreed to at the venture board meeting, do not necessarily translate into perceptions of equity at the operational level. Initial obstacles such as lack of focus and unclear priorities can quickly mushroom into widespread resistance to knowledge exchange. When one partner ignores requests for learning support, it may awaken suspicions of duplicity, inviting retaliation. Very soon, the whole atmosphere of partnership is poisoned.

Internal barriers to the acquisition of learning are often just as serious as unfriendly actions by the partner. The learning from the outside threatens the status quo. The typical attitude is defensive: "It's a good idea, but it will never work here." Contrast this with the attitude guiding GE approach to alliances: "Stealing with pride" is a message that made it into the company's annual report.

No Accountability or Rewards for Learning

Some years ago, one of the authors conducted a survey among foreign joint ventures in Japan. One of the questions put to the HR managers was "Who in the parent firm organization is responsible for learning from Japan?" Less than 10 percent identified a person or a function (usually the top representative in Japan), about a third mentioned "nobody," and over half considered the question "not applicable." Since learning is taken more seriously today, the answers might be more positive, but the lack of clear responsibility remains a major obstacle to alliance learning.

Learning targets are unlikely to be taken seriously if there is no account-ability for meeting them. In complex organizations, perceptions of the poten-tial value of learning from an alliance may vary according to the business unit, function, and territory, and the commitment to provide the necessary support will vary accordingly. This can lead to asymmetry, where one unit supplies the people while another unit expects the learning. During the dot.com boom, a European high-tech company entered a number of partnerships with companies in Silicon Valley, with the aim of exploring ways of leveraging its technology in the Internet world. Several young engineers were dispatched to California to work on specific projects as well as to provide feedback to the technology managers in the mother company. Within a few months, the word came back: "If you want to learn about exploiting the Internet, do it yourself. We don't have the time to teach you."

Traditional market-driven reward systems may implicitly encourage the hoarding of critical information, rather than the diffusion of learning. People who have valued knowledge can command higher salaries on the market, so diffusing their knowledge to others (for example by sharing critical alliance con-tacts) may diminish their market value. Being indispensable is the ultimate in "employability."

HRM Foundations for Effective Alliance Learning

A major role for HR is to help create an organizational context in which alliance learning can flourish (see Table 12–4). Importantly, alliance learning is not about collecting binders of data in the alliance "war room." Rather, effective alliance learning is focused on absorbing know-how and developing or broadening capabilities.

In the context of learning and competitive alliances, the need to focus on HRM from an early stage is especially critical. Acquisition of new knowledge and capabilities happens only through people, and if the people strategy is not

TABLE 12–4. Core Principles for Alliance Learning

1. Build learning into the alliance agreement.
2. Communicate the learning intent inside the parent.
3. Assign responsibility for alliance learning.
4. Secure early HR involvement.
5. Maintain HR influence inside the alliance.
6. Staff to learn.
7. Support learning-driven careers, including repatriation.
8. Stimulate learning through training.
9. Reward learning activities.
10. Monitor your partner's learning.

Source: Adapted from V. Pucik, "Strategic Alliances, Organizational Learning, and Competitive Advantage: The HRM Agenda," *Human Resource Management* 27, no. 1 (Spring 1988), pp. 77–93.

aligned with the learning objectives, the chances of this happening are greatly diminished.

Setting the Learning Strategy

One of the first questions to address in developing an alliance learning strategy is the extent to which this issue should be considered in the alliance agreement.

When the alliance is set up as a separate organization, for example as a joint venture, the partnership agreement or operating principles should provide at least broad guidelines on key HR policies and practices that influence learning effectiveness. These may involve issues such as freedom to move people across alliance boundaries as necessary, and determination of their learning roles and responsibilities. Clarifying HR issues that influence learning is especially important if the alliance operates abroad since it is often difficult—and costly—to renegotiate HR policies for the benefit of one of the partners after the venture is launched.

In a learning alliance, the benefits of being clear about learning expectations among partners are self-evident. But what if the learning is to take place in the context of a competitive alliance? Does it make sense to be open about one's learning strategy, or should this remain a closely guarded secret?

The best, but probably hardest, way to deal with the competitive collaboration is to accept and be open about the "race to learn." Hiding the learning agenda increases mistrust and encourages opportunistic behavior. Both parties should be explicit about their learning objectives, put forward strategies to accomplish such learning together with their HRM implications, monitor mutual progress, and discuss with each other any important reservations. If the learning objectives cannot be openly discussed, the merits of the whole alliance may become questionable.[70]

Once the strategy is set, it has to be clearly and consistently communicated across the organization. What is the purpose of the alliance, what are its boundaries, what needs to be learned, and what is the partner expected to gain? Sometimes, companies are reluctant to communicate clearly that the alliance is actually competitive in nature, because of the fear that such communication may set a bad tone for the relationship. In fact, the lack of communication does not change the reality; competition does not disappear because it is not talked about. The result is confusion and disbelief among the employees. Clear and unequivocal rules of engagement are essential.

While aligning HR processes to the learning strategy is vital, the responsibility for managing learning belongs to the line, not to HR or any other staff function. Who is responsible for learning sends a signal about how important this is. In a product development alliance between an American and Japanese high-technology firms, the HR function put itself forward as the champion of alliance learning, one of the explicit objectives for the alliance.[71] Many of the engineers who were expected to participate dismissed the whole activity as another "HR program." As for the Japanese, the role of the American HR "learning manager" remained a mystery throughout.

There are four basic HR areas where line management and the HR function can leverage alliance learning:

1. Selection and staffing.
2. Training and development.
3. Career planning.
4. Performance management.

Staffing to Learn

The focus on learning starts with appropriate staffing, since the quantity and quality of people involved in the learning effort are fundamental to its credibility and success.[72] There is no such thing as free alliance learning. Strategic intent is no substitute for resource commitment.[73] Obviously, justifying the necessary staffing investments requires fixing clear and measurable learning outcomes. And when some of the desired knowledge resides with the partner's employees, as is usually the case, then the partner's commitment to support the alliance with competent staff is also essential.

The most powerful learning often happens in joint alliance teams where employees from both partners work together on solving business issues. Here it is important to consider the difference between traditional in-company teams and alliance teams. A common company culture and above all shared long-term goals facilitate the team process when working in the company. In alliance teams, none of these "glue" factors exist, introducing additional ambiguity and uncertainty into the learning environment. Selection criteria for alliance learning teams need to take into account the ability of employees to cope with this complexity.

Several years ago, a European consumer products company assigned a group of its fast-track employees to work on a team with its Chinese partner in developing strategies for expansion in China. All assignees had a record of successful postings to wholly owned subsidiaries in the region. However, the added difficulties of working with a partner organization required an adjustment in behavior, communication, and leadership style that several of them could not handle. The project team had to be restructured several times, causing delays and disruptions to the new product launch schedule.

Another critical staffing issue concerns the trade-off between staffing for learning and staffing for effective execution. Consider the case of a joint development project between a US and a European telecommunication company. The main idea behind the collaboration was to pool the complementary technical capabilities of the two firms in order to deliver a novel solution to global customers. A second objective was to learn from each other so that both companies could improve their competitive offerings at home. The execution perspective suggests that each partner should field a team in its area of special expertise, which will foster speed and efficiency in executing the business plan. However, if the partners focus only on what they are good at, how will they acquire new skills? In order to learn, additional staff would have to be assigned to join the team, which might hinder progress in getting the job done, not to mention the additional cost that the project would have to bear. Getting this balance right requires a very clear understanding of the strategic objectives behind the alliance.

Learning to Learn

Different types of training and development activities can stimulate a climate conducive to effective alliance learning. Some training is best conducted internally, with attendance limited to the parent firm so that sensitive issues can be openly discussed. Internal training can help employees to understand the importance of the learning aims of the alliance, as well as how to learn through collaboration, and this type of training should take place early on in the alliance life cycle. This is especially important if the alliance is or is likely to become competitive in nature.

When a US high-tech manufacturer decided to set up a joint new product development project with a Japanese partner, one of the first actions was to conduct a series of alliance management workshops for all key employees who would be directly or indirectly involved. The strategic logic of the project, its scope and boundaries, the learning objectives and opportunities, as well as ideas on specific learning processes were presented and discussed in detail. As a result of these discussions, top management decided to redesign the alliance manager role in order to foster clearer accountability for learning and to adjust the resources allocated to specific learning activities.

Since alliance learning is based on relationships with the partner, joint training activities can enhance collaboration by raising both competence and trust. Team building and joint cross-cultural communication training are especially useful to speed up the getting-acquainted process. These can include intensive discussion of organizational values, structures, decision-making patterns, and the like, so that employees understand the context in which they are expected to work together. Communication problems may otherwise be attributed to "cultural differences"—people learn through such workshops that the real problems are often more tangible matters, such as different interpretations of performance expectations and rewards.

Manager Career Paths to Facilitate Learning

The rotation of employees through alliance positions and back to the parent firm facilitates the transfer of knowledge between the venture and the parent.[74] This requires addressing such issues as the harmonization of salaries/benefits to facilitate moving people back and forth. While these issues do not have to be addressed in the text of the partnership agreement, the transfers need to be planned carefully, especially with respect to future career expectations.[75] If the individual knows that the knowledge acquired in the venture will be put to good use on return, this increases her or his motivation to learn during the assignment.[76]

The need for an explicit strategy to transfer and implement acquired knowledge is well illustrated by the case of NUMMI. Only a handful of selected GM managers were assigned to the venture in the early years—apparently in order not to "contaminate" its new culture with old GM practices.[77] After two to three years of working with the Japanese, these managers were converted to the virtues of Toyota's lean manufacturing system, with a good grasp of its workings. They moved back to different GM locations with the mission of implementing the learning from NUMMI within the GM organization. All these efforts ended in failure—not because of inadequate personal learning but because there was never a critical mass of ex-NUMMI staff to make a difference.

Asymmetry in personnel transfers is usually a good indication of asymmetry in learning. While GM shuffled isolated individuals, Toyota trained more than 100 of its personnel on how to collaborate with NUMMI's American workforce. They were then assigned to Toyota's new wholly owned plant in Kentucky to replicate the NUMMI experience. In contrast, it took over a decade for General Motors to leverage properly its own acquired knowledge. An alumni team from the ventures at NUMMI and CAMI (GM's JV with Suzuki Motors) took charge of a decrepit East German car plant in Eisenach, and within three years, they turned it into one of the most advanced car manufacturing facility in Europe.[78] The knowledge that specific individuals had gained about Toyota's manufacturing system resulted in action only when there was a coherent organizational strategy for applying that learning.

Reinforcing Learning through Performance Management

While successful learning from alliances requires champions of knowledge creation—people who believe in the value of learning and who support the necessary investments—this may not be enough. Thus, alliance learning objectives should be translated into specific measures wherever possible, such as quality or productivity improvement, speed of new product development, or customer expansion.

In Motorola's 12-year alliance with Toshiba to design and manufacture advanced semiconductors (a typical competitive alliance), both companies used explicit learning targets. In Motorola's case, these were translated into individual-level objectives linked to rewards. The explicit measurements allowed both firms to mobilize their internal resources to support learning efforts. Externally, the tangible learning outcomes provided a valuable benchmark for assuring learning symmetry during the life of the alliance. It should be noted that the two executive positions considered most important in this alliance were split between the partners but rotated every couple of years. One was the role of venture chief executive, the other that of human resource manager.

The climate for learning is best when alliance performance is satisfactory. When the alliance does not meet its expected targets, it may be more difficult to focus attention on the learning agenda, and necessary investments may be cut.[79] But even a failed alliance can be a source of valuable lessons. During its ambitious drive to internationalize in early 1990s, GE organized a workshop in which executives who had been involved in failed alliances presented their experiences at a company forum. No amount of lectures on alliance strategy can match the impact of a high-level manager explaining how his assumptions about the foreign partner's business culture were wrong, resulting in a loss to GE of $50 million. Why were these managers willing to share their painful experiences? Because sharing experience with others, positive or negative, was part of their performance objectives.

There are also alliances designed solely for the purpose of learning, where the business results are secondary, at least in the short term. However, problems quickly surface if the partners have different priorities in terms of business results versus learning, especially if this issue was not addressed during the formation of the partnership. In the words of a German manager in a Chinese JV, "We pay the tuition and they go to school." Conflicting priorities usually translate into ambiguous performance indicators for managers assigned to the venture, generating tension and disagreements among the executive team.

Successful learning alliances exhibit a bias for action. The best way of learning, sometimes the only way, is to do things together. "Don't just talk about learning and collaboration. Do it!" Such was the advice of a Japanese executive in charge of a highly successful learning alliance in the electronics industry. In this alliance, the approach to stimulating mutual learning was straightforward; focused joint development teams were assigned to specific tasks and then held responsible for achieving results, with the co-leaders being directly accountable to their parents. Those who were unwilling to share their know-how were quickly moved aside; those who were not keen to apply what they had learned did not last much longer. The race to learn lasted three years. With the learning mission accomplished, the alliance was dissolved, and the companies renewed their competition, both of them stronger than they would have been if they had operated alone.

THE EVOLVING ROLE OF ALLIANCES

Just as alliances themselves evolve, so the role of alliances as part of corporate strategy is evolving. One increasingly frequent pattern of alliance development is the emergence of alliance networks, where firms engage in multiple linkages and relationships, often across the whole spectrum of the value chain from R&D and manufacturing all the way to distribution and after-sales service.[80] Originally limited to the high-technology sector, where multiple alliances were used as a protective device against obsolescence and other technology risks, today they can be found in a number of sectors from airlines to fashion to pharmaceuticals. Such networks pose new challenges for HRM.

Managing Network Boundaries

Alliances among carriers in the airline industry are spreading. Such alliances promise the customer a seamless package of air services around the world. Code sharing (where a particular flight is shared by several airlines) is the most visible example. For example, traveling around the world with Star Alliance[81] may involve purchasing a ticket in Asia from Singapore Airlines, flying to Europe via Cape Town with South African Airlines, then on a Lufthansa plane serviced by United to the United States, and completing the final leg of the trip with a Japan-based air carrier. If a service complaint on such a journey were met with the response "Sorry, but those people were not our employees," then customer loyalty would clearly be compromised. So this raises the question of whom the employees work for—their own airline, or also for Star Alliance?

From the time of reservation until the delivery of luggage at the end of the trip, airlines are a people-intensive business. Some argue that people and the service experience they provide are the only differentiator among carriers.[82] Is it possible to deliver a seamless experience without coordinating or perhaps ultimately integrating HR practices, starting from the profile of who will be hired, to the kind of training they receive, and how they will get paid? How can the airlines share best practices? If at least some amount of coordination of airline HR standards is essential, what kind of process is needed to make it happen? Who should lead it, and where is the accountability?

These are new challenges for HR, particularly since historically the approach for airlines has been strongly domestic in orientation. A typical airline today is international only because it flies to foreign locations. Most major airlines outside the United States are national flag carriers, with close relationships to their home government and strong national unions. Even if the respective management teams in an alliance agree on what behaviors are expected from the employees, the implementation of HR policies influencing these behaviors may be restricted by historic, institutional, and cultural factors.

In the case of Star Alliance, the Lufthansa Business School took a lead, perhaps because it had played an important role in transforming a bankrupt national carrier with a civil service mentality into one of the most profitable global leaders in the industry in the 1990s. Participation on its project-oriented programs was broadened to include partner members, with the aim of not just facilitating coordination but also speeding up the internal transfer of learning from one partner to another. Most of the partners bring particular distinctive strengths—Singapore Airlines in customer bonding, United in logistics, Lufthansa itself in maintenance and managing learning. The HRM vision is that the alliance can be used for mutual learning, to convert weaknesses on the part of individual partners into collective strengths.

The HR challenge in airline alliances is an indicator of things to come. As one senior HR executive in a European airline put it, "Anybody who delivers value to my customer is my employee." This is a bold statement, not yet backed up by practice, but with broad implications that go well beyond the airline industry. The density of international alliances is increasing in all sectors as companies engage in a broader variety of relationships across the supply and value chains to the customer. This raises the question of where the boundary of HR's responsibility lies.

Alliances as Journey toward Transnationalism

The ambiguity of boundaries in an alliance and the need to anticipate future shifts is only one of the tensions in this domain. Alliances are full of tensions between competition and collaboration, between global and local interests, between the venture and its parents, between leveraging and developing capabilities. Ambiguity and complexity are the norm. Bearing in mind that the principal challenge in the internationalization process is learning to manage tension, dilemma, and duality, mastering alliance dilemmas and contradictions helps firms to learn to manage transnational pressures.

In conclusion, let us therefore summarize some of the paradoxes and dualities that the multinational firm learns to confront through its experience in managing alliances:

- Learning how to manage differentiation. There is no such thing as "an alliance"—each alliance has different aims and strategic objectives, implying different courses of management and HR action. The parallel for the transnational is that it has to differentiate the roles of its units and subsidiaries, managing them in different ways.
- Learning to balance the fundamental tension between short-term performance and the long-term learning or knowledge creation that comes through collaboration (the exploitation versus exploration duality). As in the Chemco example, being a hands-off parent can be advantageous in the short term but carry a corresponding long-term cost.
- Learning to recognize and deal with trade-offs where a pathology can be created if one extreme is pushed too far. We see many examples in alliances— if either the interests of the venture itself or the interests of the parent are pushed too far, this can make it impossible to achieve the alliance aims. Similarly, the deal itself is critical, though excessive attention to detail can create rigidities (the first Star Alliance document was only one page long).
- Learning that a delicate balance is needed between external equity for expatriates and internal equity for long-term venture staff.
- Learning to take important but "soft" aims such as learning and convert them into "hard" objectives through measurement and accountability.
- Learning to "manage the future in the present"—the strategic aims of tomorrow may be quite different from those of today. Success of the venture must not be confused with the wider strategic aims of the parent.

Individuals involved in alliances face many challenges. They must learn how to manage boundaries, how to deal with ambiguity and conflicting interests, how to mold a culture that balances competing interests, and how to manage the tensions between exploitation (operating results, cash flow, and profit) and exploration (learning). One of the best breeding grounds for transnational managers may be alliance management.

TAKEAWAYS

1. Initially considered only as a means of securing market access, alliances today are an integral part of global strategies in all aspects of the value chain. Using alliances to generate new knowledge is increasingly important.
2. Alliances are mostly transitional entities; therefore, longevity is a poor measure of success. The aim is not to preserve the alliance at all costs but to contribute to the parents' competitive position.
3. There are four types of alliances: complementary, learning, resource, and competitive. Alliances are dynamic, migrating from one strategic orientation to another. Very few alliances remain complementary for long. Alliances among competitors are increasingly frequent, but they are also the most complex.
4. The approach to HRM is largely driven by the strategic objectives of the partnership. This requires a focus on both managing the interfaces with the parent companies as well as managing people inside the alliance itself.
5. The firm's HRM skills and reputation are assets when exploring and negotiating alliances. Do not enter a complex alliance unless both sides of the partnership have a good grasp of HR basics. The greater the expected value from the alliance, the more HR support is required.
6. The failings of an alliance are too easily attributed to cultural differences, when the real culprit may be the lack of attention to HR issues such as appropriate staffing, performance measures, compensation equity, and career management.
7. Equity control is a costly and relatively ineffective form of alliance control, compared to investing in a carefully designed and implemented HRM strategy.
8. Conflicting loyalties, complex relationships, and boundary management issues, coupled with uncertainty and instability, are characteristic of most alliances. Managers assigned to the alliance need high tolerance for ambiguity.
9. Alliance learning is neither automatic nor free—there must be clear learning targets, sufficient investment in people, and a tight alignment of HR practices with learning objectives.
10. Alliances are full of tensions between competition and collaboration, between global and local interests, and between leveraging and developing capabilities. Mastering alliances helps firms to learn to manage transnational pressures.

NOTES

1. Contractor and Lorange (1988, p. 9) identify seven overlapping objectives for the formation of various types of alliances: (1) risk reduction; (2) achievement of economies of scale and/or rationalization; (3) technology exchanges; (4) co-opting or blocking competition; (5) overcoming government-mandated trade or investment barriers; (6) facilitating initial international expansion; and (7) linking the complementary contributions of the partners in a "value chain." See also Kogut (1988).

2. Hergert and Morris, 1988; Gomes-Casseres, 1988.
3. Cyr and Schneider, 1996.
4. Kale and Anand, 2006; Luo, 2001.
5. J. Rossant, "Airbus, Birth of a Giant, " *BusinessWeek*, July 10, 2000.
6. BAE sold its share in Airbus to EADS in 2006, transforming Airbus into a wholly owned subsidiary.
7. Kanter, 1994; Morosini, 1998.
8. Pucik, 1988a.
9. Luo, 2000.
10. Pucik, 1988a; Cascio and Serapio, 1991.
11. Yoshino and Rangan (1995) describe alliances as linkages based on nontraditional contracts that reflect the long-term and unique nature of the relationship between the partners, such as long-term product development collaboration, not just routine buy–sell agreements. They point out that not all relationships between businesses should be considered alliances—although the word "alliance" has become quite fashionable. They also note that not all equity-based alliances need to be joint ventures; partners may simply decide to invest in each other in order to cement the relationship, or one partner may make a unilateral investment in the other partner. Joint ventures can be further classified based on dominant (majority) or non-dominant (50/50) partnerships and where they fit in the organizational structure of the firm (integrated or stand-alone).
12. One of these classifications compares different forms of alliances, from licensing arrangements to manufacturing joint ventures, based on the degree of *interaction* between partners and alliance entity employees. This scale is determined by the level and frequency of interaction, and the number of people interacting (Cascio and Serapio, 1991). The intensity of focus on human resource factors and the involvement of the HR function are expected to mirror the intensity of people interaction.

    Another framework links the HR role with two dimensions of business strategy: the strategic importance of the cooperative venture for the parent organization and the degree of control over own resources by each partner (Lorange, 1996). Alliances fall into four groups: project-based cooperative networks, strings of renegotiated co-operative agreements, ventures with permanently complementary roles, and jointly owned business ventures. Each alliance type requires a different approach to staffing, personnel control, and evaluation.

    Salk and Simonin (2003) offer a multidimensional map of alliances, encompassing their form, mode, cycle, organization, number of partners, and scope.
13. Fuji–Xerox was established in 1962 as a 50:50 partnership of Fuji Photo with Rank Xerox. Rank Xerox was absorbed into Xerox Corporation in 1997. Xerox Corporation transferred its China/Hong Kong operations to Fuji–Xerox in 2000, and Fuji Photo Film Co. raised its stake in the venture to 75 percent in 2001.
14. Inkpen, 2005.
15. O'Reilly, 1998.
16. Moxon, Roehl, and Truitt, 1988.
17. When the Danone and Wahaha alliance in China collapsed, the workforce and managers in the joint ventures overwhelmingly supported the local partner. Danone discovered too late in the game that it had no management capability on the ground to protect its interests (Liu and Liu, 2007).
18. Hamel, Doz, and Prahalad, 1989.

19. When business is profitable and provides advantages for both partners in the market as well as contributing to the creation of new knowledge, an alliance may continue even after the original learning objectives of the partners have been fulfilled. NUMMI is a good example.
20. Janger, 1980.
21. Beamish, 1985.
22. Killing, 1982.
23. Zeira and Shenkar, 1990.
24. Ulrich, 1997.
25. Cole and Deskins, 1988; Kenney and Florida, 1993.
26. Pucik, 1988b; Schuler, 2000.
27. Parkhe, 1991.
28. Goffee and Jones, 1998.
29. Yoshino and Rangan, 1995.
30. Yoshino and Rangan, 1995.
31. Spekman et al., 1998.
32. Yoshino and Rangan, 1995.
33. Yoshino and Rangan, 1995.
34. Cited by Yoshino and Rangan (1995, p. 146).
35. Lorange and Roos, 1990.
36. Weiss, 1994.
37. Killing, 1997.
38. For a review of strategic control and staffing issues in international joint ventures, see Petrovic and Kakabadse (2003).
39. Adobor, 2004.
40. Killing, 1997.
41. Ferencikova and Pucik, 1999.
42. Cascio and Serapio, 1991.
43. Shenkar and Zeira, 1990.
44. Killing, 1982.
45. Tung, 1988.
46. Lasserre, 2008.
47. In the HP framework, workshop materials are organized in a 400-page proprietary manual, supported by an electronic library devoted to alliances. This serves as a repository for the know-how accumulated by HP over time. Internal knowledge management is important for learning from alliance experience and disseminating that know-how, complemented by internal training if the company has the resources to develop this.
48. Findings from Booz Allen's 1997 survey as cited in the Conference Board, 1997, "HR Challenges in Mergers and Acquisitions," *HR Executive Review* 5(2).
49. This is one of the management development areas where Web-based distance learning may create opportunities for greater flexibility—providing access to just-in-time relevant information anywhere, including links to the in-company alliance knowledge base.
50. Conference Board, 1997, "HR Challenges in Mergers and Acquisitions," *HR Executive Review* 5(2).
51. The context of the relationship will determine the most beneficial development applications. However, off-the-shelf cultural training using the traditional "doing business with . . ." approach is probably of limited value—perhaps even dangerous in building stereotypes.

52. See also Chapter 9 where we discussed performance management in general.
53. Mohr, 2006.
54. Kerr, 1995.
55. A common incentive plan (e.g., stock options) could be a logical tool to support synergy among alliance staff. However, among various tax issues that hinder harmonization of compensation across boundaries, incentive plans are probably the area where the differences are the widest. In some countries, such as France, even the initial exercise of stock option rights is a taxable event, which makes awarding options risky and expensive. In addition, even when tax benefits are available, there are differences—for example, which kind of stock option qualifies for tax benefits in the US and in Germany.
56. Geringer and Frayne, 1990.
57. Shenkar and Zeira, 1990.
58. Sometimes, expatriate cost alone makes a difference between profit and loss. In a dispute between P&G and its Vietnamese partner, the local company alleged that the high cost of expatriates, brought in to deal with unanticipated product launch difficulties, caused the JV to incur major losses. The local partner was ultimately faced with the choice of accepting the JV bankruptcy or allowing P&G to gain equity control through a recapitalization that the local partner could not match ("P&G Plays Down Vietnam Venture Problems," Reuters News Service, 1997).
59. Lorange, 1996.
60. Nonequity alliances are generally temporary, and from a legal perspective, have no "direct" employees. Even those who are assigned to the alliance on a full-time basis are typically paid by and report to their own parent. They expect to return to the parent organization, so that there is no confusion about the focus of their careers. Even if a foreign assignment is involved, a disciplined career development process, which ensures mentoring and a periodic dialogue with the employee, is generally sufficient to avoid a sense of isolation.
61. Child and Faulkner, 1998; Parkhe, 1993.
62. Barkema et al., 1997; Westney, 1988.
63. Gomes-Casseres and McQuade, 1992; Kennedy, 1989.
64. Hamel, 1991.
65. Pucik, 1988b.
66. For example, when both partners perceive the partnership as a complementary or resource alliance, the collaboration can be mutually beneficial for a long period of time without much need for new knowledge creation. However, as we discussed earlier in the chapter, the focus of the alliance often shifts as the partnership evolves.
67. Doz and Hamel, 1998; Tsang, 2002.
68. One of Europe's largest banks formed a learning alliance with a major Japanese bank about 20 years ago. The Japanese used this as an opportunity to send hundreds of managers over on two- to six-month learning assignments to Europe, during which time the Europeans got around to sending only two people to learn from the Japanese. By the time the financial services industry started to globalize seriously in the early 1990s and the Europeans awakened to the benefits of the deal, the Japanese had reached their learning objectives and lost interest in maintaining the alliance.
69. Hamel, 1991.
70. Open discussion about learning needs may result in explicit limitations on knowledge exchange. A clear definition of what is in and what is out is preferable to fuzzy learning boundaries, which only encourage illicit behavior detrimental to trust between the partners.

71. Pucik and Van Weering, 2000.

72. Westney, 1988; Schuler, 2000; Cyr, 1995; Cyr and Schneider, 1996.

73. Simonin, 1999.

74. Harrigan, 1988; Pucik, 1988b.

75. Lei, Slocum, and Pitts, 1997.

76. Conversely, if there is a perceived imbalance in career opportunities, employees may either be willing to move to the alliance venture but less willing to return to the parent, or not want to move to the venture in the first place (Inkpen, 1997).

77. Inkpen, 2005; O'Reilly, 1998.

78. Haasen, 1996.

79. As argued by Inkpen (1998), unexploited learning opportunities may in turn lead to perceptions that the performance of the alliance is not satisfactory.

80. Doz and Hamel, 1998.

81. Star Alliance links the operations of 25 airlines, such as United, Lufthansa, and Singapore. The member airlines coordinate schedules, share codes, match frequent flyer programs, and coordinate activities to benefit from lower costs in areas such as plane maintenance, ground service, and purchasing.

82. Pfeffer, 1998.

CHAPTER 13

Forging Cross-Border Mergers and Acquisitions

Integrating Global Acquisitions at Cemex

In September 2004, only a few months after defining its new global governance model and deciding to implement one global operating system, the Mexican building materials company CEMEX announced its intention of acquiring the UK-based Ready Mix Concrete (RMC) group for US$5.8 billion. With this acquisition CEMEX aimed to consolidate its position as one of the top three global players in the industry.[1]

CEMEX was established in 1906 in Monterrey, Mexico. The current CEO, Lorenzo Zambrano, is the grandson of the company's founder and was appointed to his position in 1985 after working his way up through the organization for 18 years. At that time, the company had five plants and 6,500 employees. Zambrano refused to diversify into other businesses, the route favored by many other Latin American industrialists. Instead he focused on the cement and building materials business he knew well and built up his company through a series of carefully considered and implemented acquisitions, first in Mexico and then from 1992 in Spain, Latin America, Philippines, and the United States.

Top management quickly realized that the newly acquired companies were guided by different operating practices, structures, and cultures than CEMEX. Most had been run quite ineffectively, and CEMEX saw an opportunity to create value by implementing new processes and instilling new management behavior. The backbone of this strategy was a global operating platform, labeled the CEMEX Way. The aims of the CEMEX Way were to unify global operations, to promote the sharing of best practices, to streamline and improve the value chain all the way to the final customers, and to allow rapid and simultaneous deployment of strategic initiatives.

In order to enable faster and smoother acquisitions, CEMEX put in place a systematic post-merger integration (PMI) process to promote best practices and learn

525

from previous experiences. Overlapping teams of managers and functional specialists from different countries were sent to each newly acquired company so that knowledge and best practices would be passed to the team responsible for each new acquisition.

The typical PMI has four stages. During the initial planning stage, pre-assessment teams are sent to the newly acquired company to analyze the situation and plan next steps. This is followed by three execution phases. In phase one, also called "the 100-day plan," transition teams work to identify further synergies through a gap analysis covering all business activities. Phase two focuses on implementation, with the expectation that the CEMEX Way will be fully operational by the end of this stage. Phase three is the return to business as usual—at a higher level of operational efficiency.

The RMC acquisition was bigger, covered more countries (22), and included more diverse cultures and languages than anything CEMEX had encountered previously. The PMI office divided the work between functional teams, like "cement operations" and "back-office"; each of these teams was replicated on a country by country basis. In total, 600 people from within CEMEX and over 400 RMC managers were involved in the RMC post-merger integration. The HR integration was by far the most complex part of the process, and CEMEX spent more than six months defining and building a framework that took staffing and country differences into consideration. At the kickoff of the execution phase, Zambrano addressed RMC managers and executives:

You will quickly discover that CEMEX time seems to have fewer minutes in every hour and more hours in every day. We are highly disciplined and dedicated to consistent, high level performance. We believe in continuous innovation. . . . Our goal—and our track record—is to outperform our competitors year in and year out.[2]

The results were impressive. Under its old owners, a large cement plant in Rugby, England, often ran at only 70 percent capacity. Two months after the takeover and the implementation of CEMEX Way it was running at 93 percent.

In October 2006, CEMEX announced an unsolicited offer to purchase the Sydney-based Rinker group, with operations in Australia and the United States. The target company was known to be very well managed. This acquisition was an opportunity to blend the best parts of CEMEX and Rinker to improve overall profitability, rather than to improve operating efficiency, the motive for previous acquisitions. The Rinker deal was sealed at the beginning of 2007.[3] Instead of scrapping what Rinker had, the PMI plan was to start with a thorough evaluation, identify the best practices of both parties, and determine which parts of Rinker's operating system should be incorporated in the CEMEX Way—an example was a waste-burning initiative common to most Rinker plants.

By December 2007, CEMEX had operations on four continents, with 85 plants in more than 50 countries. The only gaps in its global presence were China and India. CEMEX reported net sales of $21.7 billion and a net income of $2.6 billion. The company was also one of the world's leading traders of cement, as it maintained its own shipping fleet and trading relationships with customers in close to 100 nations.

OVERVIEW

We start this chapter by reviewing the merger and acquisition (M&A) phenomenon and discussing the many reasons why cross-border acquisitions and mergers, such as those carried out by CEMEX, are attractive. We present evidence of companies' varying degrees of success in carrying out international M&As and explore the human and cultural factors that contribute to success and failure. We also introduce a framework for understanding the strategic logic behind the merger or acquisition. This will determine the orientation of the integration process and the role that HR plays in it.

In the second section, we discuss due diligence, the planning and preparation work that should be undertaken in order to explore M&A targets before the deal is closed. The assessment of people and cultural factors needs as much attention as the assessment of strategic and financial factors.

The third section focuses on the post-merger integration process, in which the formula for success combines speed with careful attention to HRM and people processes. We analyze key issues, starting with the implications of the so-called merger syndrome. Retention of key talent is an essential condition for success in most acquisitions, and so we review the steps necessary to make it happen. We also discuss how different aspects of the change process, including communication, need to be managed to facilitate the smooth integration of the new subsidiary into the parent firm, with an emphasis on the role of integration managers and transition teams.

Firms that make successful acquisitions recognize that they must capture their learning in order to enhance their ability to execute acquisitions in the future. In this way, M&A capabilities can become an important source of competitive advantage in the global economy. This is the central idea in the concluding section, in which we summarize the chapter through the lens of what General Electric has learned over the years about the complex process of acquiring and integrating other firms.

THE M&A PHENOMENON

What is a merger and what is an acquisition? From a legal point of view, in a *merger* two companies join together and create a new entity. In an *acquisition*, one company acquires sufficient shares to gain control of the other organization. In reality, the transaction labeling depends mainly on the accounting and tax implications of the deal, as well as strategies for public relations and communication. Some mergers are structured as acquisitions, while some acquisitions are framed as mergers. There are actually very few "mergers among equals." After the agreement is signed, most mergers tend to look like acquisitions. We will focus primarily on acquisitions, which represent the large majority of cross-border deals, referring to mergers when appropriate.

Acquisition bids can be classified as friendly or hostile. From the perspective of shareholders or top management, most acquisitions are friendly, although the workforce often does not see it that way—there are clear winners and losers since being acquired is perceived as a symbol of failure, and the buyer organization nearly always has more power during the integration process. Cross-border hostile acquisitions are relatively rare, although when they occur they tend to generate strong emotions and a lot of public interest.

Mergers and acquisitions are popular alternatives to greenfield investments (that is, business units established from scratch) and strategic alliances as vehicles for internationalization. There has been a dramatic growth in mergers and acquisitions in the global marketplace during the last two decades (see Figure 13–1). During this period, the global distribution of M&As has changed. One significant change is that the proportion of cross-border M&As increased from less than 30 percent in the year 2000 to almost half of the total value of global M&As in 2007. Another shift has been toward more M&As carried out within Asia and by Asian firms—in 2007, 18 percent of the value of global M&As were deals carried out by Asian firms.

Even if M&A fever subsides when the global economy cools off—such as after the ended in 2000 and during the global financial crisis in 2008–2009—more deals can be expected in the long run.

The ultimate driver of international M&A activity is the erosion of national boundaries and the increase in global competition. Until the 1980s, international M&As were relatively rare; governments in many countries did not look fondly on foreigners acquiring local assets. Since then, liberalization of foreign direct investment resulting from multilateral trade agreements has greatly accelerated

FIGURE 13–1. Trends in Global Mergers and Acquisitions

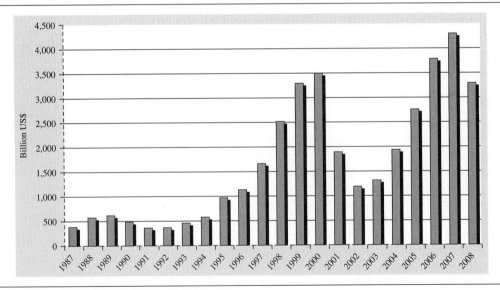

Source: Announced global M&A volumes reported yearly by Thomson Reuter (previously Thomson Financial Inc.).

the M&A phenomenon. And while global megadeals continue to grab the headlines, more and more cross-border acquisition takes place among small and medium-sized firms. Understanding the logic of such strategies for internationalization and their human resource implications and mastering their implementation is becoming one of the competencies required of global managers.

The Drivers of Mergers and Acquisitions

There are a number of reasons why companies pursue cross-border mergers and acquisitions (see the box "The Drivers of International M&As"). Achieving competitive size or increasing market share by adding capacity (like CEMEX), brands, or distribution channels are important reasons behind many cross-border M&As.[4] Larger firms, inspired by Jack Welch's famous GE mantra of "becoming global #1 or #2," aim to gain market power and at the same time deal with overcapacity in many mature industries. Or they pursue large-scale merger or acquisition strategies to leapfrog their competitors—who then try to catch up through their own mergers.

Smaller firms resort to cross-border deals to leverage their niche capabilities in new markets more quickly than they could through organic expansion. For these firms, the primary opportunities for value creation are likely to arise from cross-selling existing products or services and from accessing new markets. M&As are sometimes used instead of in-house R&D. For instance, Cisco from the United States acquired a large number of small and medium-sized high-tech firms mainly to get quick access to new technologies and products; and Nokia bought the US digital map maker Navteq for similar reasons.

The Drivers of International M&AS

International mergers and acquisitions happen for multiple reasons. Some are strategic, some are tactical, and some involve corporate egos.

Market dominance

Banks and insurance companies in Scandinavia are merging across the region to create Nordic financial institutions (Nordea, Danske Bank) in order to gain advantages of market dominance, economies of scale, reduced competition, and channel control.

Geographical expansion

Major global players in the brewing industry (InBev,[5] SAP/Miller, Carlsberg) are using acquisitions to extend geographical reach and global market share.

Leveraging capabilities

Foreign companies (General Electric, Axa) have embarked on large-scale acquisitions in the Japanese financial industry, leveraging their capabilities in new product development, credit risk, and debt management.

Resource acquisition

In the petroleum industry, acquiring existing companies with proven oil reserves could be a more economical way to grow than investing in exploration of new energy sources (BP, Exxon).

Capability acquisition

With market shifts from voice to data transmission, European wireless manufacturers (Nokia, Ericsson) rushed to the United States to acquire small start-ups with competence in emerging data communication technologies.

Executive hubris

There are also cases where—the press release notwithstanding—outside observers see no logic in the move beyond the CEO's desire to run a bigger company.

Most companies launch acquisitions for sound strategic reasons. However, sometimes companies only mimic or match the acquisitions strategies of their principal competitors. And all too often decisions are driven by the general frenzy that can be observed during the waves of mergers that take place at regular intervals (see Figure 13–1).

People issues dominate the management agenda in many of these M&As. In the high-technology sector, in particular, an increasing number of acquisitions are motivated by the need to access talented people and their know-how. The employees may be more valuable than the company's product—price per engineer drives the cost of such deals. In contrast, the strategic drivers in other deals are consolidation and cost cutting. There the focus is on workforce reduction, which in some countries may be as tricky as the retention of Silicon Valley entrepreneurs.

Alliance or Acquisition?

International alliances and M&As are usually alternative strategies,[6] but sometimes an alliance can be a first step toward an acquisition. In countries such as South Korea, where emotional resistance to foreign acquisition may still be strong, gradual entry through a joint venture alliance with a local partner can be an effective strategy. The alliance may also reduce the risk of entry into an unfamiliar territory. If the partnership is successful, the next step may be acquiring the partner's interest or the partner itself. The timing and conditions for this evolution are frequently anticipated in the partnership agreement.[7]

On the other hand, settling for an alliance, rather than making an acquisition, may reduce control over decisions within the venture, including human resources decisions. The consensual governance process in international alliances increases the costs, limiting the possibilities for rationalization.[8] From an HR perspective, the most significant difference between an alliance and an acquisition is that the former limits the degree of leverage over people-related decisions. The freedom to select, promote, and compensate people is such an important management tool that it leads many executives to favor acquisitions. On the other hand, retaining talent may be easier in a partnership, and alliances are often better at preserving entrepreneurship in individual units. In a cross-border context, alliances are easier to align with the local environment.

When making a strategic decision on whether to build an alliance or pursue an acquisition, it is important for human resource considerations to be on the list. These may sometimes be difficult to resolve, as a US start-up discovered when it entered an alliance with a smaller German partner to develop break-through technology jointly. In order to pursue an initial public offering (IPO), the company's investment bankers pushed the two companies to merge to clarify ownership and intellectual property rights. However, a merger would mean loss of independence for the German company, possibly sapping the motivation of its top engineers. In addition, the compensation philosophies of the two firms were radically different, highly leveraged toward stock options in the United States but with more traditional salary structures in Germany—so the employee gains from an IPO would be asymmetrical. In the end, although the deal was eminently sensible from a strategic point of view, it collapsed because the parties were unable to resolve these problems.

Observing the M&A Experience

Given the rapid increase in M&A transactions in all regions of the world, the obvious question is, to what extent have these corporate marriages worked? What factors contribute to the successes? And to what extent do HRM factors account for the failures?

How Successful Are Mergers and Acquisitions?

Extensive research has been conducted on the performance of M&As. Much of the early research was conducted by consulting firms and investment banks, but there is now also a large and still rapidly growing body of academic research on the topic. Several early non-academic studies suggested that only a minority of the deals achieved the promised financial results.[9,10] Recent academic research and consulting reports are more positive, but even there the contribution of M&As to the value of the acquiring firm is *on average* close to zero.[11] In other words, some M&As are successful, some have little effect on the performance of the acquiring firm, and some are disasters for the buyer, and specifically its owners. The sellers virtually always emerge as winners as the buyer typically pays a significant premium for the target.[12] And when the buyer overpays, no amount of post-merger integration skills can bring back the value lost when the deal was signed.

There is some evidence that the success rate of cross-border deals may be higher than for purely domestic transactions.[13] Several reasons have been suggested for this surprising finding. One explanation is that there tend to be greater complementarities between the parties in international acquisitions.[14]

Cross-border acquirers often buy companies in related industries—familiar businesses to which they can add value and, conversely, from which they can gain value. For instance, the acquisition of a foreign competitor can give the buyer access to local markets as well as new products, technologies, and local market knowledge. The target may benefit from the resources and capabilities of the buyer; the increased scale and international experience of the combined organization are additional benefits of such mergers.

Furthermore, it appears that there may be less conflict between the parties in international M&As. Domestic acquisitions of competitors are often accompanied by a history of fierce rivalry that is difficult to overcome. The level of integration tends to be smaller in cross-border than in domestic acquisitions, leading to less tension between employees in the two firms. There is also some evidence that a moderate level of integration in international acquisitions is associated with better performance.[15] Finally, it may be that the more overt cross-cultural dimensions of such deals lead buyers to pay more attention to the softer, less tangible, but critical HRM aspects of M&A management.[16]

Why Do Acquisitions Fail?

M&As, particularly those that reach across borders, are complex and difficult to get right. The business press is full of stories of international mergers and acquisitions that failed to meet the original objectives. Even when the merged firm should apparently enjoy great synergy benefits, one of the major reasons for failure is *difference in vision*. The two sides cannot agree where they want the combined entity to go. For the sake of getting the deal done, these differences are often glossed over. But if firms do not start with a common and specific understanding of where they want to take the new organization, and how they want to get there, the process of integration is likely to be fraught with destructive internal politics.

The acquisition can fail because of *attrition of talent and capabilities*, or because of the *loss of intangible assets*. Customers are not asked for their opinions about the merger and may feel disgruntled about being passed on to another entity. That can lead to an overnight loss of potential value. Relationships with vendors, community, and government can also suffer when the new owner is perceived, rightly or wrongly, to be insensitive to local interests.

An Egon Zehnder study reported that *lack of clarity around systems and processes* in the purchasing company was a major problem in at least a quarter of all acquisitions.[17] This means that firms with a locally responsive orientation will find it more difficult to handle acquisitions than those with tightly integrated approaches.

International M&As can also suffer from underestimating the *high transition and coordination costs* in linking the new entities, due to physical distance, which negate some of the advantages of the potential synergies. Related to these costs is the danger of *synergy gridlock*, when management searches so desperately for ways to deliver the savings originally promised to the stock market that it loses track of the business as costs begin to spiral.

Finally, the failure of international mergers and acquisitions may be linked to the *lack of cultural fit* between the two organizations. It is often said that companies should not entertain deals where a significant cultural mismatch might be a problem. Differences in history, environment, and national culture amplify the difficulties of achieving merger aims.[18] However, the ability to manage the process of cultural integration may be more important than the cultural differences between the parties, as we describe in this chapter.

Underlying all the contributory factors is a phenomenon called *escalating momentum.*[19] Given the stakes involved, one might think that merger assessment is a rational process. In reality, the acquisition process is often described as having a life of its own, where participants feel unable to stop the process or slow the tempo, sometimes leading to closure of the deal under conditions that are unfavorable for the buyer. This is fueled by the secrecy involved, the isolation of decision makers, the need to make decisions under inevitable ambiguity, and the hubris of key executives[20] who simplify the factors behind the decision.

In spite of such difficulties, companies will continue to acquire and merge as they seek to accelerate their international growth. Companies that learn how to manage mergers and acquisitions well enough to overcome these obstacles to success can benefit from significant advantages—and not only because of synergies and scale. They can access needed local resources more quickly. They can be more flexible. And as the know-how of acquiring and integrating new capabilities boosts their confidence, the range of strategic options that can add value may expand significantly.

What Do We Know about Key Success Factors?

The ways in which the two companies *complement* each other are significant to the outcome of an acquisition. There needs to be a clear idea of how the two units can strengthen each other. The board should not approve an acquisition without convincing arguments that the integration of the two organizations will produce surplus value that will offset the premium paid for the target. For example, French automotive component manufacturer Valeo successfully expanded its international reach by buying smaller companies or those with narrow product lines.

What happens before a deal is signed is important. A well-thought-out strategy and thorough due diligence are essential to success, as well as a negotiation team that does not succumb to escalation of commitment during the negotiation process that might lead to paying too much. However, even well-structured and well-negotiated deals have to cope with the complexities of merging organizations across boundaries, and the ability to add value in the merged company depends mostly on what happens after the deal is done. Not surprisingly, high returns go to organizations that execute well the *post-merger integration process.*[21]

Managing integration involves combating the winner–loser syndrome, preparing employees for change, setting up a transition organization, and putting in place the new structure, policies, and practices. Integration is a change process. Companies that have a *good track record in managing change* also tend to be good at managing acquisitions.

Multinationals that have *solid foundations in HR and other functional domains* have an advantage in implementing M&As. Each side may need to teach the other how it goes about business, and this is difficult without firm foundations in functional expertise. A firm like CEMEX or GE can move fast and confidently with its integration strategy when it acquires a company, largely because its own systems and practices are well developed and explicit.

However, probably the best predictor of M&A success is the ability of the acquiring organization to learn from its experience.[22] The ability to learn from past acquisitions, including the mistakes that are inevitably made, is a characteristic that many successful buyers have in common. But experience is not the same as learning. Previous experience may even hurt future M&A performance, if a company believes that its past experiences can be automatically applied to the next case.[23] We will return to discussing how multinationals can build M&A learning capabilities toward the end of this chapter.

A Framework for Thinking about M&As

In successful mergers and acquisitions, partners share the purpose and accept the terms of their relationship. However, in reality, corporate marriages are often based on unattainable assumptions. Therefore, careful and explicit definition of the purpose of the acquisition and the desired end state is the first step in making the new relationship work. People may well resent and resist postmerger change—but they are more likely to adapt if they know the new rules of the game and how these will help them to be successful in the future.

The best approach to integrating the two organizations will depend on the strategic driver behind the acquisition. Each acquisition must be managed in a different way. A simple framework developed by Killing[24] provides a useful overview of different types of acquisition integration (see Figure 13–2).

Stand-Alone

When a cross-border deal is signed, the PR announcement often contains a section noting that the acquired company will keep its independence and cultural autonomy. The aim may be to placate local regulators and/or public opinion; or a major rationale behind the merger may be to get hold of talented management or other soft skills (such as speed of product development) and retain them; or perhaps conformance to the acquiring company rules and systems could be detrimental to the acquired company's competitive advantage.

If stand-alone acquisition is the objective, the key to success is to protect the new subsidiary from unwarranted and disruptive intrusions from the

FIGURE 13–2. Four Types of Acquisition Integration

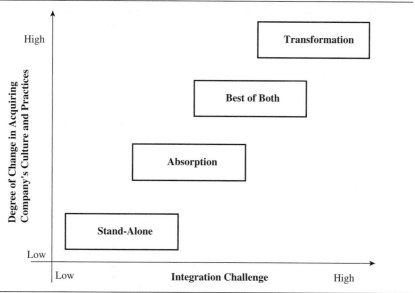

Source: Adapted from J.P. Killing, "Improving Acquisition Integration: Be Clear on What You Intend, and Avoid 'Best of Both' Deals," *Perspectives for Managers,* no. 97, 2003, p. 1.

buyer, though this can be hard to ensure. Even with the best of intentions, there is a danger of creeping assimilation, as the buyer encourages the new unit to adopt its way of working, and to develop systems and processes that match those of the parent organization. Most stand-alone acquisitions do not last.[25]

There is a fundamental question associated with the stand-alone strategy—how can the buyer create value through the acquisition in order to offset the premium that it has paid for the target? A single booster shot of functional knowledge and capabilities soon after the closing is one possible approach to create operational synergies and efficiencies. Or while the business may appear independent to the outside world, at least some functions are merged with the rest of the organization. Normally, however, stand-alone is a temporary phenomenon, lasting until conditions change and the acquired unit can be more fully assimilated into the new parent.

Absorption

This kind of acquisition is fairly straightforward, and it is most common when there are differences in size and sophistication between the two partners in the deal. The acquired company conforms to the acquirer's way of working. Such deals are particularly common when the target company is performing poorly or when market conditions force consolidation.

Most of the synergies may be related to cost cutting, usually on the side of the seller, sometimes from improvements in systems and processes brought in by the acquiring firm. The key to success is to choose the target well, and to move fast to eliminate uncertainty and capture the available benefits.

Yet, in cross-border M&As, companies are sensitive to public perceptions of being a foreign bully. They are often hesitant to declare their objective of absorbing the target, fearing that it may settle the deal. But this can create confusion and mistrust that make the process more difficult. In contrast, GE Capital, the financial services arm of General Electric, offers blunt advice to the management of acquired firms: "If you do not want to change, don't put yourself up for sale." GE makes it very clear that the acquired company must now play by GE's rules, and it provides a framework for doing so. As in the case of CEMEX's acquisition of RMC, absorption does not necessarily mean large-scale firings and layoffs. In fact, 80 percent of identified synergies were realized by changes in processes, repositioning of business operations, and implementation of common management platforms.[26]

A complicating factor in all acquisitions is that there will be parts of the organization where a particular approach to the merger makes sense and others where it does not. Cisco, for example, buys companies for their technology and R&D talent; retention of engineers and scientists in the target is an important objective. Therefore, Cisco has typically fully absorbed the support functions of small innovative start-ups that it acquired for their promising product ideas, while the engineers in charge of developing new products retain much more autonomy. Cisco's approach illustrates that many acquisitions have elements of more than one of the (ideal) acquisition types presented in Figure 13–2.

Best of Both

The intriguing option of best of both is pursued in what is often described as a merger of equals. This holds out the promise of no pain, since in theory it takes the best practices from both sides and integrates them. There are, however, few genuine mergers of equals. The merger of the German car manufacturer Daimler and its US competitor Chrysler in 1998 was presented as a merger of equals. In reality, Daimler was larger, more successful, and clearly the more powerful of the two. Daimler executives soon took over control of the whole merged organization.

The scarcity of examples of best of both attests to its difficulty. Putting together the "best" parts of both sides risks leading to an inconsistent configuration of organizational practices in the two merging units. Another danger is that the integration approach may become too political and time-consuming. Who decides what is "best" and based on what criteria? During the integration process, many decisions are interpreted politically; in the absence of explicit criteria and objective evaluation, the choice of what constitutes best is often viewed as biased. When the Swedish bank Nordbanken and the Finnish bank Merita were combined in a "merger of equals" in the late 1990s, some Finnish employees coined and used the phrase "Best practices are West practices" ("West" meaning "Swedish," as Sweden is located west of Finland).[27]

CEMEX's bid for Rinker could be considered a best-of-both approach, as Rinker's production processes were very advanced in a number of technological areas and geographies. It would be to CEMEX's advantage to leverage this capability within the whole firm. However, without strong mutual respect for the knowledge and skills of each company, this kind of strategy will not work. Saying best of both, without acting accordingly, is likely to backfire as the target employees will view the buyer as untrustworthy.[28]

A key to success is fair process. On the HR side, this may mean hiring a third party to assess the organizational capabilities and practices of personnel in both organizations. The ability to retain people may be a precondition for a best-of-both acquisition, having a balance of management from both firms.

Transformation

In contrast to best-of-both acquisitions, which take existing organizational practices as they come, both companies in a transformation merger hope to use the merger to make a clean break with the past. Merger or acquisition can be the catalyst for doing things differently or reinventing the organization—the way the company is run, the business it is in, or both. When Novartis was created through the merger of two Swiss-based pharmaceutical firms, the proposed management style for the new company reflected the desired transformation: "We will listen more than Sandoz, but decide more quickly than Ciba."

For a long time, the creation of ABB through the merger of Asea and Brown Boveri was considered an archetype of transformational merger, with its successes and failures. More recently, the merger of pharmas Astra and Zeneca into AstraZeneca could be described as a case of transformation through M&A, as is Lenovo's acquisition of IBM's PC business.

This kind of merger is complex and difficult to implement. It requires full commitment, with focus and strong leadership at the top to avoid getting trapped in endless debates while the ongoing business suffers. Speed is essential, with top management in the merging companies using the time period immediately after the merger announcement to carry out major changes. Like the best-of-both strategy, the transformation strategy has a better chance of success if key people from both parties are excited by the vision of the merger leading to a new company with superior capabilities.[29]

Key Human Resource Management Issues

There is no shortage of empirical evidence that attention to "soft" factors or people issues is one of the most critical elements in making an acquisition strategy work. In a pioneering McKinsey study of international M&As in 2000, the four top-ranked factors identified by responding firms as contributing to acquisition success are all people related:

- Retention of key talent (identified by 76 percent of responding firms).
- Effective communication (71 percent).
- Executive retention (67 percent).
- Cultural integration (51 percent).[30]

According to another consulting report, published eight years later, the problems remained the same. Differences in organizational culture (50 percent) and people integration (35 percent) topped the list of M&A challenges—in fact, four of the six top issues were people related.[31] A similar conclusion can be drawn from a Conference Board study of 88 major corporations in the United States and Europe study.[32] At the top of the list of HR concerns in mergers and acquisitions was retention of critical talent, identified as a very important or important factor by 86 percent of respondents. Second on the list was blending cultures, listed by 83 percent, closely followed by retention of key executives (82 percent). Differences in approaches to compensation/benefits were ranked fourth (73 percent). Perhaps surprisingly, impact on workforce size (37 percent), downsizing (35 percent), and redeployment of employees (25 percent) were at the bottom of the list.

It is hard to find an acquisition where people issues do not matter, though the nature of the people challenges vary with the acquisition intent. When the objective is to establish a new geographic presence, managing cross-cultural, language, and communication issues tops the list of priorities. When the aim is to acquire new technology, or to buy market share or capabilities, retaining key technical staff or account managers is the principal challenge. When the objective of the deal is consolidation, dealing effectively with redundancies at all levels is the dominant concern.

Based on these observations, it may seem natural that the HR function should play a significant role in all phases of an acquisition. Yet while this tends to be true during the post-merger integration process, the overall influence of HR during the acquisition process as a whole is patchy. In addition, many companies have neither the functional resources nor the know-how to give the HRM issues the priority they merit.[33]

When Should HR Get Involved?

As discussed, the scope and importance of people issues depend on the type of acquisition—transformational acquisitions demand far more attention to HRM than stand-alone acquisitions—but the HR function can make a substantial contribution at all stages of the acquisition process, as was the case in CEMEX.

However, the reality is often different. HR does not get involved until relatively late in the process. According to a Towers Perrin/SHRM study, HR is fully involved in the M&A planning in less than a third of responding firms.[34] HR involvement is marginally higher during the negotiation stage, but it is only after the deal is signed that 80 percent of firms see HR as fully engaged. It is obviously not easy for HR to ensure the smooth implementation of the deal when it has little or no part in shaping it. US-based companies seem to put more emphasis on early HR involvement than their European counterparts.

One reason for keeping HR out of the room is the secrecy surrounding most acquisitions before the bid or agreement is announced. In many companies, communication about pending acquisitions is treated as strictly confidential, for commercial as well as regulatory reasons, and disseminated on a need-to-know basis. HR is not seen as needy. A determining factor is whether the top HR executive is a member of the senior management team and a full participant in the strategy planning process. HR is unlikely to be involved if is not already perceived as a valuable contributor to business and strategy development.

FROM PLANNING TO CLOSING

The starting point for any merger or acquisition should be the overall strategy of the firm and the organizational capabilities that enable the company to implement the strategy successfully. Even though M&As are often the preferred option for businesses seeking international growth, they should be evaluated as just one of several strategic levers at the disposal of the multinational, with alternatives such as strategic alliances and greenfield investments sometimes making more strategic sense. For example, in some situations it may be better to hire a small team with the desired capabilities rather than to acquire an entire firm.[35]

A typical cross-border acquisition starts with the development of the acquisition strategy and the selection of a target. An integral part of the selection process is the evaluation of the feasibility of the acquisition—due diligence. This examination moves to center stage when formal negotiations begin with the target (or when a hostile takeover bid is launched). If the negotiations or takeover are successful, the transaction proceeds to closing, as long as the conclusion of the due diligence investigation is positive.

Some multinationals have a special acquisition unit that is involved in the planning and execution of every transaction.[36] Much of what is done during the planning and negotiation stage requires specialized and often highly technical, financial, and legal expertise. However, such units should not work in isolation from the managers who will have the responsibility for implementing the strategy and/or managing the acquisition. In some firms, such as GE, the future business leader and the designated HR manager are part of the acquisition team from the very beginning.

Planning Acquisitions: The HRM Perspective

The due diligence process should cover all the important HRM considerations, including cultural assessment and a human capital audit. Cultural compatibility or incompatibility is relevant in many domestic acquisitions, and this is probably the most talked-about factor when acquisitions take place across borders. We will come back to this issue in the next section.

Another important component of acquisition planning is making sure that the company has the appropriate leadership team in place. When Renault considered acquiring a 37 percent stake in Nissan, a big factor in the decision-making process was the confidence that it had a team of seasoned managers who could be dispatched to Japan to guide the restructuring efforts. In the words of Renault's Chairman Louis Schweitzer, "If I didn't have Mr Ghosn [sent by Renault to Tokyo to become president of Nissan], I would not have done the deal with Nissan. That means I sent him in because I had absolute confidence in his ability."[37]

In international acquisitions, the approach toward human resources cannot be separated from the cultural and social context. Often the company may not have any expertise in the particular country or geographical area, so early planning on how to mobilize the necessary resources to guide the firm through unfamiliar territory is important. At this early stage it is also important to provide the necessary orientation to the members of the due diligence team, who are likely to be selected for their analytical and technical skills, rather than for their familiarity with the culture and environment of the target firm. In CEMEX, more than 300 people received training on what to look for in the RMC environment and cultures in which they would be operating.

Some HRM issues have a direct bearing on the selection of targets. How can a buyer get a quick reading on the quality of human assets and characteristics of the organizational culture before committing resources to full-scale due diligence? HR can serve as a valuable resource and a sounding board here, provided it has the capacity to obtain and analyze the information. No one can expect HR to have all the information readily available, but in the words of a GE HR manager who participated in planning a number of acquisitions, "Even if you know the industry, each acquisition is different: different culture, legal framework, management team in place. We are at the table not because we have all the answers, but we certainly know the questions that we have to ask."

Even at the planning stage it is important to figure out broadly how success will be measured and how to learn from the pending acquisition experience. As the saying goes, "Success has many fathers, but failure is an orphan." It is not easy to discover what went wrong after the fact, and valuable insights are often lost if they are not recorded in real time. In large multinationals, the responsibility for capturing the learning usually rests with a specialized M&A unit, but in smaller firms this responsibility is often assigned to HR.

The Due Diligence Process

Getting the strategy right depends very much on doing the homework. Good planning is not possible without good data. There are two aspects to due diligence in an acquisition. The first is to clarify the legal, financial, and business picture. The infrastructure for obtaining this kind of information is well developed, as are the analytic methodologies. The second aspect, equally important but sometimes neglected, is learning about the "soft" factors influencing the fit between the two organizations, such as the culture and the people practices in the target organization.

The Art of Being Truly Diligent

In cross-border acquisitions, the due diligence team must be sensitive to the fact that attitudes toward acquisition due diligence vary from country to country.[38] Under Anglo-Saxon practice, lawyers and their clients expect comprehensive due diligence before the acquisition is completed. In other countries, due diligence may be interpreted as intrusive at best, or as a sign of mistrust or bad intentions on the buyer's part. Getting information about the people side of the business, such as the quality of the management team, requires particular care.

A due diligence team from a US company and their consultant visited a senior Japanese banker in his office to solicit opinions about an external candidate to be installed as the CEO of their new acquisition. Since the banker did not express any reservations, the team felt confident about their selection. At the conclusion of the cordial meeting, the banker invited the team members to dinner that evening. This was politely declined, as it conflicted with the time reserved for a videoconference with headquarters, but the consultant (always eager for good sushi) decided to accept the invitation. During the dinner, the banker presented a list of reasons why the choice was wrong. Why didn't he tell the visitors directly? "But I did." replied the banker. "Why would I otherwise invite them to dinner?"

A list of topics covered by HR due diligence can easily run to several pages, especially if the buyer comes from North America (see Figure 13–3 for the broad categories of issues to investigate). As time is short, it is important to start with key priorities rather than becoming lost in technical details. Some items are checked to protect the company against potential financial exposure, such as pension plan liabilities. Others reflect the strategic intent of the acquisition, such as talent identification, employee rights to technology, trade secrets, and confidentiality.

Where does this information come from? At an early stage, HR due diligence is part of building the overall acquisition roadmap. Former employees, industry experts, consultants, executive search firms, and customers who know the company are usually the best sources of information. Cultivating some of these sources on a longer-term basis helps to mediate the constraints of confidentiality. Some of these data may be in the public domain, and Web-based

FIGURE 13–3. Human Resources Due Diligence Checklist

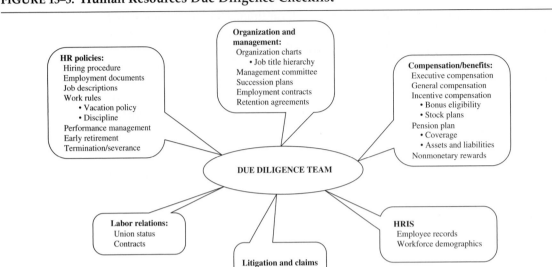

search engines can speed up finding information. Once the agreement to close the deal is reached, HR records and interviews with managers in the target company can be used to supplement and verify the assessment.

The transparency and accessibility of this information vary from country to country. Companies often bemoan lack of information when in fact the real issue is lack of familiarity with local sources. Information about HR policies is relatively easy to obtain; the problem is the amount available. For example, acquiring a firm in the United States may involve reviewing over 20 categories of benefit plans and policies, going back six years to understand all the potential tax liabilities.[39] However, HR due diligence is not just about collecting reams of data to avoid potential financial landmines or to prepare for harmonizing the policies and practices quickly after the deal, important though these tasks are. It is more important to understand how the HR system impacts the values, norms, and behaviors of the company to be acquired.

It is not easy to do this well, even in domestic acquisitions. Less than a third of US HR professionals consider that HR was effective in the due diligence phase of acquisitions.[40] The process of collecting "soft" due diligence data assumes friendly relations between the parties. Often companies believe that this kind of information is not available abroad, especially during the initial planning stage, when secrecy and confidentiality are important. Of course, access to information is especially constrained in the case of a hostile acquisition. However, it is not usually information that is lacking, but discipline and rigor in collecting and analyzing data. Two methodologies can be especially useful here: the human capital audit and culture assessment.

The Human Capital Audit

There are two dimensions to the human capital audit. One dimension is preventive, focused on liabilities like pension plan obligations, outstanding grievances, employee litigation, or other employment-related constraints that may impact the acquisition—for example, the cost of anticipated restructuring. It also includes comparing the compensation policies, benefits, and labor contracts of both firms.

The other dimension focuses on talent identification, and is probably more critical to the success of the acquisition in the long run. Talent identification has a number of important facets: ensuring that the target company has the talent necessary to execute the post-acquisition strategy of the combined units; identifying which individuals are key to sustaining the value of the deal; and assessing any potential weaknesses in the management cadre. It is also important to understand the motivation and incentive structure, and to highlight any differences that may impact retention.

Here are some examples of questions to consider:

- What unique competencies do the employees have?
- How does the quality of the target's talent compare to the buyer's?
- What are the social relationships between people in the organization and how important is social capital to performance?
- What is the background of the management team?
- What will happen if some members of the management team leave?
- What is the compensation philosophy?
- How much pay is at risk at various levels of the firm?

Getting access to talent data may take some effort, and many companies ignore the talent question in the early stages of the M&A process. They do not take the time to define the types of competencies embedded in people who will be critical to the success of the deal, relying instead on financial performance data as a proxy. However, without early assessment, companies may acquire targets with weaker competencies or talent than anticipated and a high likelihood of executive departure. Early assessment helps to pinpoint the potential risk factors so the acquiring company can develop strategies to address them as early as possible. Moreover, this will speed up decisions about who should stay and who should go.[41]

An important component of the human capital audit is the development of action plans to retain key talent (we will revisit this issue again in the next section). These measures must typically be implemented immediately after the deal is concluded. For example, employee stock option plans may provide for option grants to be fully vested when there is a "change of control," such as after an acquisition.[42] Many valuable contributors would therefore have no incentive to stay. In such cases, the retention of key employees must be considered a deal breaker to be incorporated in the acquisition agreement.[43] The additional costs associated with retaining people, for example retention bonuses as well as investment in training and development, must be included in the up-front financial estimates.[44]

At the same time, the audit may uncover significant weaknesses that call for replacement candidates, external local hires, or expatriates ready to step in immediately after the deal is closed. Without advance planning, this may not be possible. And with each replacement there is a potential termination, which again has to be carefully prepared, based on local rules and practice.

Cultural Due Diligence

The issue of cultural assessment is critical in mergers and acquisitions. In 2008, 670 executives from multinationals from around the world participated in a survey of cross-border M&As and identified organizational cultural differences as the most significant issue in recent M&As.[45] Despite this, culture assessment is generally not given much priority *before* the deal is done. In one survey of European executives actively involved in mergers and acquisitions, assessment of cultural fit came close to the bottom of the list.[46] It is therefore not surprising that culture clashes often are a source of difficulties *after* the deal is done.

How to Assess the Culture of the Target Firm

The purpose of cultural assessment is to evaluate factors that may influence organizational fit, to understand the future cultural dynamics as the two organizations merge, and to plan how the cultural issues should be addressed if the deal goes forward. Cultural assessment can be formal or informal, based on a variety of potential sources, such as market intelligence, external data, surveys, and interviews. It is important to have at least a rudimentary framework that helps to organize the issues and draw the proper conclusions.[47]

Some assessment questions should look at the leadership of the company to be acquired and its view of the business environment, as well as its attitude toward competition, customers, and change:

- What are its core beliefs about what it takes to win?
- What drives business strategy? Tradition, or innovation and change?
- Is the company long- or short-term oriented?
- How much risk is the company prepared to accept?
- What is its approach to external partners—competition or collaboration?
- Who are the important stakeholders in the organization?

Other questions examine broader leadership attitudes and how the company manages internal systems:

- Is the company result-oriented or process-oriented?
- Where is the power? Concentrated at the top, in certain functions, or diffused?
- How are decisions made? By consensus, consultation, or authority?
- How does the company manage information? Is the flow of information wide or narrow?

- What makes an employee valuable? Values, skills, or getting results?
- Is the culture oriented to teamwork, individual performance, or both?

Some companies use cultural assessment as an input into a stop/go decision about an acquisition. For example, Cisco avoids buying companies with cultures that are substantially different from its own, recognizing that it would be difficult to retain key staff. On the other hand, GE Capital is less concerned with retention and is more aggressive in its approach—cultural assessment is also a "must" but mainly as a tool to plan integration. It is impossible to say that one approach is better than the other, but both companies are clear about what is important and how they want to get there.

Cultural assessment is not just a question of assessing the other company's culture; it is also a matter of both having a clear culture oneself and understanding it. The "know thyself" adage applies equally well to companies as it does to people. The criteria used in cultural assessment of the target will to a great extent reflect the cultural attributes of the buyer.

The challenge of cultural assessment is to approach it with an appropriate perspective. Where some see cultural obstacles, others may simply observe poor management. "It was like two drunks trying to hold each other up," commented the *Wall Street Journal* on one case of a spectacular cross-border merger fiasco attributed to cultural misunderstandings.

When Do Cultural Differences Matter?

Conventional wisdom suggests that companies should avoid any deal where cultural differences might be a problem. This is rooted in the assumption that cultural differences are largely unmanageable and will undermine the success of a deal. However, the empirical evidence suggests that the fear of cultural differences may be exaggerated. For example, results from a recent study of 800 cross-border acquisitions suggest that cross-border acquisitions may perform better in the long run if the acquirer and the target come from countries that are culturally more disparate.[48]

The research on this topic offers two important conclusions. First, it is important to distinguish between impacts of differences in organizational versus national culture. Second, the nature of the deal matters.[49] For example, in a related acquisition that needs higher levels of business integration, cultural differences can create tensions that make integration more difficult. However, these differences are more likely to be due to differences in organizational than national culture. In addition, organizational culture differences were actually found to be positively associated with post-acquisition performance in M&As that required lower integration, probably due to increased opportunities for mutual learning.[50]

In today's global business environment, where strategic imperatives drive many potential M&A deals forward, companies no longer have the luxury of avoiding potential deals on the grounds of cultural issues. The proper response to cultural differences between buyer and target is not to avoid deals where there is a risk of culture clash but to manage and mitigate the risks. This requires disaggregating imprecisely defined cultural issues into discrete, manageable elements. Most of these are connected to the management of people.

Closing the Deal

Until the agreement to acquire is signed (or a hostile tender offer is announced), much of the vital HR involvement in the acquisition process will go on behind the scenes. Immediately after the deal is signed the scope of the HR agenda expands rapidly. Companies often wait until closing before considering HRM issues because the period between the signature of the agreement and implementation can be anywhere from several months to a year, depending on the need to obtain shareholder and regulatory approval. This time should not be wasted.[51]

Pre-closing Action Plans

The first priority is to complete the due diligence, now with full access to data. The extent and conditions of access to managers and employees are often a part of the M&A agreement. This is a sensitive period, and the first impressions of the new foreign owners may last for a long time. For example, when interviewing, opinions should be solicited from everyone, not just those who can speak the new owners' language. In many countries, union consent is desirable, if not essential, if the transaction is to go ahead. As in all labor relations, honest and open communication with union representatives is most effective.

All of this highlights one of the challenges for HR, namely rapidly acquiring and internalizing new cross-cultural competence, and familiarity with the legal and social context. HR, line, and staff managers involved in cross-border acquisitions have to be able to learn fast. Of course, if the company is already present in the country, the task is much easier. However, most companies require at least some reliance on outside resources, such as local consultants. Assessing and contracting outside resources will require time, so forward planning is essential.

Indeed, the people you hire to work on your behalf may tell local employees a great deal about your intentions and capabilities. In situations where the two organizations have been fierce competitors, the target may see the use of outside consultants to carry out employee assessment as more neutral than sending in the buyer's managers to do it. However, even when using consultants, the buyer would be well advised to invest in enhancing its local knowledge up-front, as the following example illustrates.

A European pharmaceutical firm made a friendly offer to buy one of its large but struggling Japanese distributors. To facilitate the transaction, the company retained a local HR consulting group that, unknown to the Europeans, had a reputation for a confrontational approach to post-merger restructuring. The result: Those Japanese employees who could headed for the door, while the rest set up a union with the aim of blocking the acquisition. Faced with unexpected resistance, the buyer withdrew the offer.

As discussed before, the acquiring company needs to have the key components of the HR implementation blueprint in place by the time the acquisition is ready to close. This includes the organizational structure and reporting relationships, the composition of the new team, the timeline for action on specific HR issues, and so on. The local context influences which acquisition strategy will be most feasible, as well as the desired state of the new organization.

The final element of pre-closing activity is the selection of the integration manager and the transition team who will be charged with the responsibility for combining the two organizations. If the team includes expatriates, which is often the case, they may need to have at least rudimentary cross-cultural orientation and coaching, as they had in CEMEX, since most of them are selected for technical and functional expertise.

THE POST-MERGER INTEGRATION PROCESS

The course of action leading up to closing the deal lays the foundation for next steps, but most of the actual creation (or destruction) of shareholder value happens during the post-merger integration phase. Successful acquirers understand well the challenges awaiting the firm as it embarks on the integration journey.

The M&A Integration Agenda

The change in ownership triggers changes in the target and its leadership. Now is the time to put a new organization in place, appoint new leadership, make sure that key talent is retained—and manage the *merger syndrome*. It is critical to be able to turn the uncertainty associated with most M&As into recognized opportunities for employees to become involved in creating value in the new organization.

Recognizing and Managing the Merger Syndrome

Announcing a merger may be fun—for the top management that clinched the deal. It attracts lots of publicity, and senior management can enjoy their moment in the spotlight. But lower down the ranks in the acquired organization, reactions will be different; a merger often comes as a bolt from the blue, regardless of whether the bid is friendly or hostile. However well the merger has been planned and prepared, the so-called merger syndrome always has to be tackled. At a basic level, this simply reflects the fact that any process of change is stressful.

Those whose company is taken over invariably feel like losers. Reactions to this feeling follow much the same pattern as the shock experienced during bereavement.[52] The initial responses of disbelief and denial are followed by shock, colored by overreaction ("We're going to lose our jobs") or underreaction ("It won't change anything"). This may lead to anger, then attempts to bargain or dig in heels, followed ultimately by acceptance. Acceptance may take a form that will characterize the mood of the firm for long after—fatalism, bitterness, wistful regret, or (ideally) proactive behavior. To some degree, the merger syndrome is unavoidable, because it reflects the process of human adaptation. This means that it must be managed carefully.

There may be a parallel cycle in the acquiring company, in which the initial reaction is often one of victory ("We did it!" "We'll show them how it's done!"). Attitudes toward the "losers" are often condescending, which will only worsen PMI problems. Managers in functional departments and in the subsidiaries of the acquiring firm may have fantasies of expanding their power and scope of responsibility. A sense of rush and urgency takes over, leading to confusion and growing doubt about whether this really is a victory. Increasing command and control and a growing war-room mentality also create an unhealthy climate for integration.

As in CEMEX, people often talk about "the first 100 days" of a merger and how this period sets the tone for the longer task of integration. In a merger, as in any change process, there will typically be some costs. These are measured in lost productivity through distraction (less focus on the here-and-now due to worries or speculation about the future), upheaval created by departures (some talented people always jump ship and other people may be asked to leave), and drop in employee morale. It has been estimated that nearly two-thirds of companies lose market share during the quarter following a merger.[53] Whether these negative consequences of change are moderate and transitory, or whether they are debilitating for the integration process, depends on how these first 100 days are managed. The stress that accompanies change can be made constructive, or it can be allowed to become dysfunctional.

During the early stages of the acquisition, it is the responsibility of HR to ensure a sharp focus on people and leadership issues, making sure that the transitional organization and teams are in place on day one, fully prepared to deal with the complexities of a cross-cultural deal. The next step is staffing—who will stay and who will go? The evaluation of talent that was initiated before closing the deal continues, but it is not easy to assess people quickly in a foreign setting; most HR professionals find it difficult to trust their experience outside their own cultural milieu.[54] And finally, what kind of policies and practices should be introduced in the acquired firm? Human resource management provides a subtle control mechanism by which a parent company can influence its acquisition, so the choice of HR approach is intrinsically linked with the overall strategy for integration.

Creating Inspiration and Involvement

Marks and Mirvis suggest that acquirers need to pay attention to the four Is—insight, information, inspiration, and involvement—to manage the stress and uncertainty of the first 100 days (see the box "The Four Is").

The Four Is

Insight means helping employees to acknowledge that change will be stressful. Pretending that nothing will be different or that there will be no stress only increases tension, undermining the credibility of the acquirer. With hindsight, most executives say that they should have paid more attention to employee concerns in the period immediately after the merger announcement. Workshops for employees where they can voice their anxieties and concerns, and learn about how the integration process will unfold, can help them to tackle integration challenges in a constructive way, reassured that their own feelings have been taken into account.

One cannot do enough to satisfy employees' thirst for *information* in the weeks after the merger—and, in the case of major acquisitions, this includes staff in the acquiring company. The rumor mill about alien owners takes over, amplifying and distorting events, aggravating stress, and distracting people from their day-to-day work. To manage the merger syndrome, a communications campaign needs to be set up, including road shows with visiting executives, e-mail bulletins, telephone hotlines, and careful press announcements.

Inspiration means starting to build positive expectations for the future at the earliest stage. The business plan for the future of the two companies may take time to elaborate, but inspiring (yet realistic) statements can pave the way and lift morale as long as they are genuinely realistic. One of Cisco's principles is to make sure that there are quick, visible wins to counteract despair and anger. These range from the immediate installation of symbolic free beverage machines and access to a sophisticated intranet system, to increased sales as the acquired firm's products get the advantage of broader distribution.

Finally, *involvement* implies the face-to-face contact that is most effective in breaking down feelings of them and us, winners and losers. As in any change process, the more people are involved in direct and personal ways, the more they will understand the rationale for the merger and feel committed to its successful implementation. The use of integration teams, discussed later, is obviously a major tool. However, joint orientation sessions and the opportunity to exchange ideas with functional counterparts will also help.

Source: M.L. Marks and P.H. Mirvis, *Joining Forces: Making One Plus One Equal Three in Mergers, Acquisitions, and Alliances* (San Francisco: Jossey-Bass, 1998).

Separated by language and distance, the merger syndrome is more difficult to combat in a cross-border acquisition, yet just as important. Cisco trained its local HR managers (and other members of local acquisition teams) in countries like China and Korea in its approach to managing the four Is, involving them in the integration process of acquisitions in the United States. As a result, they felt quite comfortable in managing the 100-day integration when acquiring companies back home, including making necessary adaptations.

Managing Post-Merger Integration

The pressure of additional work created by the need to manage integration, on top of everyone's day job, can be formidable. If you add to this the risk of intercultural misunderstanding, the natural tendency to resist change, and the shortage of qualified management talent, you have a recipe for an overstressed, underperforming workplace. Unsurprisingly, the difficulties surrounding the integration process are frequently blamed when acquisition performance falls short of expectations.

As all acquisitions require some degree of integration (even stand-alone deals generally require the integration of financial reporting systems), it is important to tailor integration to the purpose of the acquisition and the characteristics of the companies involved. The integration process requires engaged leadership and often a dedicated integration manager working with a transition team. In most cases, moving with speed is an advantage. A critical part of the process is focusing on the areas where the acquisition can create new value, while maintaining the ongoing business.

Leading the Integration Process

The signing of the deal is often followed by the appointment of new leadership. For most companies, assembling a new leadership team for an international acquisition is not an easy step. Who should head the acquired organization? Ideally, it should be someone familiar with both sides in the deal—for example, a local executive already in a leadership position with the buyer or another foreign company—but these executives are usually in short supply.

As we pointed out earlier, strong and committed leadership is the foundation for the successful execution of integration initiatives—and for successful change management in general. In our research, lack of clear vision and the leadership style of top management consistently topped the list of factors contributing to acquisitions that failed to deliver the expected value. Three competencies are seen as fundamental to the effectiveness of the top leadership: a credible new vision, a sense of urgency, and effective communication.[55] In interviews for a study of M&As in Japan, respondents indicated again and again that creating a sense of urgency around implementing the vision and maintaining momentum in driving change are the keys to success.[56] The ability to articulate vision must be accompanied by soliciting feedback and engaging in two-way communication.

Close collaboration and a sense of trust among the top leaders of the merged organizations can also influence employees' attitudes toward the merger positively, though trust between the respective CEOs is not enough. Shared vision is important, but it is only the first step in the process of implementation. We have seen cases where close personal relationships and trust at the top created dangerous complacency, underestimating the operational obstacles facing the merger. Signals indicating that not all is well are ignored and hard decisions are postponed because pointing out difficulties is seen as rocking the boat.

Finally, another critical factor is getting leadership selection right at the outset. Instability in the top management team seems to be correlated with the likelihood of failed integration. The Daimler merger with Chrysler, which saw three teams of top executives during the first two years after acquisition, is one example of how disruptive leadership discontinuity can be. When Vodafone bought J-Phone—a Tokyo-based mobile telecom company—the top position at J-Phone was occupied by four executives in three years. Although the business strategy remained nominally the same, expectations changed as the company moved from expatriate to local leadership and back again, leading to confusion and instability within the organization. Differences in leadership and communication style between each generation of executives only aggravated tensions already existing in the organization. At the end of three years, the company—by now deeply in the red—was sold to a local competitor Softbank, which brought it back to profitability within six months.

The Role of the Integration Manager

The integration of the acquired company with the new parent is a delicate and complicated process. Who should be responsible for making it happen? After closing the deal, and while the new management team is not fully in place, the due diligence team disbands or goes on to another deal, taking its deep knowledge of the acquired company with it. To avoid a vacuum, companies are increasingly turning to dedicated integration managers, supported by transition teams, to guide the process immediately after the deal is concluded.

Integration managers are transition specialists. Their role is to make sure that timelines are followed and that key decisions are made according to the agreed schedule, while removing bottlenecks and making sure that speed of integration is maintained. They help to engineer the short-term successes that are essential to create positive energy around the merger. They should also champion norms and behaviors consistent with new standards, communicate key messages across the new organization, and identify new value-adding opportunities.[57]

An important aspect of the job is helping the acquired company to understand how the new owner operates and what it can offer in terms of capabilities. The integration manager can help the firm take advantage of the owner's resources, forge social connections, and help with essential but intangible issues, such as interpreting a new language and way of doing things. This is important because, outside the acquisition team, few people will be familiar with the target's capabilities.

The integration manager is the information gatekeeper between the two sides, protecting the acquired business from the eager embrace of an owner who could unintentionally undermine what makes the business work. A major source of frustration in many deals is not so much what the parent wants the newly acquired unit to do, but what it wants to know. New information requirements must be submitted in a very specific format, and reports can be embedded in incomprehensible jargon—indeed, corporate HR is often the guilty party here. When Nokia acquires small high-tech venture companies, one of the rules is that all requests for information from the parent go to the integration manager, who decides whether and how the unit should comply with the request.

What combination of skills does the integration manager need? First of all, deep knowledge of the parent company—where to get information, whom to talk to, how the informal system works. Flexible leadership style is another requirement; the integration manager must be tough about deadlines, yet a good listener, and able to relate to people at different levels in the organization. Other traits that go with this role are comfort with ambiguity, emotional and cultural intelligence, and the willingness to take risks.[58] These jobs are often stepping-stones into business leadership roles.

The Responsibilities of the Transition Team

In most acquisitions, integration teams and task forces support the integration manager. Since many of these teams are expected to start work on the first day after the acquisition deal is closed, the identification of potential members should be part of the due diligence process. HR professionals are often key members of the team because many of the team's activities will have implications for human resource policies and practices.

The specific charter of the transition teams depends on the integration approaches we discussed earlier (stand-alone, absorption, best of both, and transformation). As in the CEMEX case, the key priorities (such as business synergies-where results can be achieved quickly) should be identified early in the integration planning process. Prioritization is critical. Too many task forces slow things down, creating coordination problems, conflict, and confusion. In the ill-fated Daimler-Chrysler merger, the complexity of a transition structure involving over a hundred different projects was one of the reasons why its integration process rapidly came to a standstill.[59] Integration projects should focus on those with high potential savings at low risk, leaving those with greater risk or lower benefits until later. As one experienced M&A manager stated, "We only attack things that will bring benefits to the business. We do not integrate just for the sake of integrating."

Another task of the transition team is to spell out the logic of the new business model and translate it into operational targets. This is important in international acquisitions, where big-picture statements from the corporate center may mean little in a different and far-off national and business context. The transition team can also serve as a role model for how the new organization should act. By facilitating personnel exchanges, the transition team can help both sides to develop a better understanding of each other's capabilities.

Who should be appointed to the transition team? Mixing of line responsibility with transition task force roles may mean that neither is done well. On the other hand, integration teams should not be staffed by second-tier managers. So the best staffing approach may be to appoint up-and-coming managers, leaving the daily business under the original leadership until the new organization can be put in place.

It is important that the transition team has authority. Customers do not like to wait until the team reaches consensus. One of the factors undermining Daimler's (partial) acquisition of Mitsubishi Motors was that local Japanese employees perceived the mostly German integration managers as transients and ignored many of their decisions. Where did this attitude come from? The locals were keenly aware that the team was not empowered to make independent decisions—most had to be approved in Stuttgart—so there was no need to take them seriously.[60]

As CEMEX and other successful acquirers have learned, integration teams are most effective when members come from both the target and acquiring companies. Another example is Air France/KLM, where mixed integration teams were credited for making the integration more successful than other airline mergers.[61] People who are suited for a transition team usually have a mix of functional and interpersonal competencies (including cross-cultural skills), backed up by strong analytic skills. Having an ability to accept responsibility without full authority and being effective in mobilizing resources across organizational boundaries are especially important. Consequently, as we pointed out in Chapter 8, these roles provide good development opportunities for those with high potential.

Moving with Speed

When companies are asked what they learned from their past M&A experiences, they often say, "We should have moved faster; we should have done in nine months what it took us a year to do." GE Capital, for example, has cut the 100-day process back to 60–75 days because it learned how to move faster and developed the tools to do so. Speed is essential. If a company is taking two to three years to integrate, insufficient attention is being paid to what really counts—the customers. According to GE,

Decisions about management structure, key roles, reporting relationships, layoffs, restructuring, and other career-affecting aspects of the integration should be made, announced, and implemented as soon as possible after the deal is signed, within days if possible. Creeping changes, uncertainty, and anxiety that last for months are debilitating and immediately start to drain value from an acquisition.[62]

A survey of European acquisitions of US high-technology firms in Silicon Valley reported that speed was one of the key drivers of successful integration—but also one of the most problematic.[63] The understanding of European acquirers (usually large, established companies with entrenched routines and procedures) of "fast" was very different from Silicon Valley norms. This created confusion, frustration, and ultimately the loss of market opportunities.

Restructuring is often an essential step toward establishing the necessary synergies. Restructuring should not be confused with integrating, but the rule is similar—it should be done *early, fast, and only once.* One problem jeopardizing the success of many acquisitions, motivated by good intentions, has been a tendency to restructure slowly to avoid excessively painful human change. But while time is spent helping people to adjust and not upsetting the old culture, competitors come along and take away the business.

In a study of M&As in Japan, a Japanese HR executive with extensive M&A experience with foreign firms in Japan was unambiguous in her assessment. "When you're changing something, you must do it all in one go, as quickly as possible. It becomes much harder to make small changes later on, when you would have to renegotiate every small detail. If you don't compromise at first, it will be better in the long run."[64]

Sometime, foreign acquirers' fear of cultural backlash slows down the process. At another foreign-owned financial company in Japan, the implementation of several elements of performance-based global HR policies was suspended for two years to give employees a chance to adapt. In retrospect, the company's Japanese CEO thinks this may have been overcautious. "I think perhaps the grace period could have been a bit shorter. Some people got too comfortable for their own good. I think I may have been a bit too lenient because foreign companies are always criticized for being too harsh, for being vultures."[65]

The other dimension of speed is the focus on delivering quick, visible wins, such as new sales generated through a joint effort, or improvements based on shared practices. It is important to take time to celebrate each success and to communicate the accomplishments to the whole organization. A quick win can motivate target employees because it offers tangible proof that the merger or acquisition was a step in the right direction, and shows that their efforts are appreciated.

Yet speed can also have unintended consequences. Bad decisions made under pressure might be avoided if time is spent on a judicious review of the issues. Conversely, good decisions meet resistance when no time is made to explain the new business logic. Again, the optimal speed depends on the strategic intent behind the acquisition and the desired end state for the culture of the new organization.[66] An absorption strategy generally requires more urgency than a best-of-both approach. When the objective of the acquisition is to acquire knowledge and capabilities, the pace of change must be particularly carefully calibrated to minimize the risk of alienating talent, as we will discuss later. Also, it has been argued that successful cross-border acquirers from emerging economies, whose aim is to obtain competencies and technology essential to their global strategies, do not see quick integration as a top priority.[67]

Research also shows differences in the speed of the integration process according to the national origins of the acquiring firm. Japanese and Northern European acquirers tend to move cautiously, conscious of the potential cultural conflicts.[68] This works well if the approach is one of best of both, but it may exacerbate the stress of the 100 days when expected decisions are not forthcoming.

Beyond the 100 days

Maintaining momentum in the integration process is another challenge. The 100 days are only the first stage in the integration process. But even if the early stages are successful, energy typically starts to flag after eight months to a year.

Integration fatigue begins to settle in. As we discussed in Chapter 11, one of the biggest challenges in managing change is maintaining continuity in change.

The pressure remains high since most key individuals have their regular jobs to do while they handle the integration effort. One study points to several dangers at this stage.[69] Divisions in the executive team may begin showing up, slowing down the process. Executives who went along with the fast-paced 100 days, but who were not deeply committed to the vision and ambitions of the process, may now start backtracking just as drive and unity at the top are needed to maintain the pace of change. So changes in the executive team may be required, as well as reconfirming and reinforcing the ambition with the new team. This is also a stage when replacements may be needed for other managers who are failing to measure up to the integration challenge, often by competent people from the outside who do not have affiliations with either of the companies.

To maintain momentum at this stage, HR efforts need to focus on coaching and training people in new behaviors, as well as redesigning measurement, appraisal, and reward systems that will anchor the new culture. If efforts earlier in the integration process focused on "what," at this second stage attention to "how," and to overcoming practical obstacles to change, is needed.

People Challenges of Post-Merger Integration

Post-merger integration is a change process. Companies without the experience in managing the people side of organizational change should be particularly wary about tackling complex acquisitions. Time and time again, top management falls into the classic change trap of focusing on its content (the financials, the restructuring plans for the functions) and not on its process. All the lessons of change management apply to post-merger integration—the need for communication, the need to establish a vision for the future, the need to restructure to remove resistance and empower champions, and management of the learning process by measuring progress against milestones.[70]

Several people challenges impacting the integration process merit particular attention—communication, retaining talent, and managing cultural change.

Communication

Communication is always a vital part of any process of change, but it is critical in cross-border acquisitions, where cultural differences may intensify tensions due to misunderstandings and distance. Furthermore, there are two additional objectives, particularly relevant to mergers, which have to be taken into account in the design of the communication process. One aim of communication is to alleviate the anxiety and stress that accompany every acquisition; another is to provide feedback to top management about the progress of integration and any potential roadblocks.

The need for flawless communication starts on the day the deal is announced. Top management has to express clearly the rationale for the acquisition, the synergies sought, and the degree of integration required.[71] It should also clarify the intended organization. Although the transition teams can work out the details, the message to shareholders and the public has to be consistent with the message to employees in both the target and acquiring company.

This happens far less often than it should. In the survey of European acquisitions in Silicon Valley cited earlier, every single acquired unit reported lack of clarity about its role in the combined organization.[72] The issues that most employees are anxious about are not addressed. What is the intended end state or vision behind the new organization? Will one side dominate? Will it be the best of both, or will a transformation be attempted? Consistent and coherent communication helps to build morale and reassure those unsettled by the changes.

Lack of clarity and consistency from top management can have disastrous consequences. In the failed Deutsche–Dresdner banking merger, mixed signals from the leadership about the future of the combined organization's investment banking operations created opposition in both camps, ultimately forcing the cancellation of a deal that looked promising on paper.[73] The collapse of the deal hit share prices, and the Dresdner CEO was forced to resign. Because of the high rate of defections during the confused weeks after the initial merger announcement, Dresdner Bank was left substantially weakened, forcing it to accept a less favorable offer from another financial institution several years later.

It is imperative, as we discussed earlier in this chapter, to communicate a clear vision of how the acquisition or merger will create value. A company can talk as much as it wants about synergy, but unless employees understand the logic behind it, there is a danger they will see the deal only as a manifestation of the CEO's ego. A well-articulated communication campaign conveys to the workforce that the leadership has a clear vision of where to take the acquisition.[74]

Being open and honest about difficult issues is a must. The hard truth may not go down well, but the consequences are easier to handle than the alienation and mistrust that stem from lack of candor. BP–Amoco is an example of playing it straight. BP took over Amoco with the clear aim of accessing its oil reserves. Since BP felt that the fields could be more productively exploited under its management, the model for the new company's organization and culture was unambiguous. In words of a BP executive, "It is non-negotiable for us. We have developed a structure and systems that have worked for us, and we are anxious to apply them to a larger company." If you were a manager in Amoco with 25 years' experience, you might not have been happy about this. But at least you knew how things stood. You could either go along with being absorbed into the BP way of working, or you could leave.

Effective communication during the integration is a two-way process, from the company to the employees, and also from the employees back to top management. Irrespective of the chosen road to integration, it is important to monitor progress in order to surface hidden issues and concerns that may create conflict in the new organization. This is particularly important in cross-border deals where misinterpretations can quickly poison the atmosphere and create confusion. The ability to react when false rumors spread is essential. Today it is possible to use the intranet to receive feedback on how people in the acquired company feel about the integration process so that something can be done before unhappy staff members walk away.

Retaining Talent

Many acquired businesses lose key employees soon after a merger—a major contributing factor to the failure of acquisitions. Research evidence from US acquisitions indicates that the probability of executives leaving increases significantly when their firm is acquired by a foreign multinational. About 75 percent of the firms' top management leaves by the fifth year, with a majority departing during the first two years.[75]

Given these statistics, it is not surprising that when the Chinese company Lenovo acquired IBM's PC division, the board of Lenovo's controlling shareholder allowed the company to proceed with the deal if, and only if, it could retain IBM's senior executives to manage the merged enterprise.[76] But the talent that Lenovo wanted was not limited to senior executives. When the deal closed, the company offered a job to every IBM employee worldwide, with no obligation to relocate or accept a pay cut.

When insufficient attention is paid to retaining talent, and especially if staff cuts are expected, employees often leave—and the best will exit first. After a deal is announced, and well before the actual closing, headhunters inevitably move in to pick off any promising managers who are unsure about their career opportunities with the new and distant owner. For employees confronted with the uncertainties of a new organization, a firm job offer from another company looks attractive. Retention of key employees is therefore crucial to achieving acquisition goals in both short-term integration tasks and long-term business performance—the key principles are outlined in the box "Five Principles of Talent Retention in M&As."

The first step is to know exactly who the talented people are and why they are essential to the new organization, including those at lower levels in the acquired firm. Obtaining this information is not easy. The typical top-down cascading talent identification process often yields flawed results, since local managers may be protective of their people and unable to be objective about what they offer to the new organization. One of the biggest obstacles in international acquisitions is the difference in performance measures and standards. Even if standards are comparable, many companies are not aware of where their talent is; in one study only 16 percent of surveyed executives believed that their employers could identify their high performers.[77]

The initial talent map needs to be refined quickly, through feedback from direct superiors, peers and subordinates, past performance reviews, personal interviews, formal skill assessments, and direct evaluation of performance during the integration period. While multiple sources of assessment are desirable, the quest for precision may slow down the process too much, increasing uncertainty

Five Principles of Talent Retention in M&As

Find out where your talent is

It is critical to know exactly who the talented people are, and why they are essential to the new organization. The starting point for talent identification is the talent map developed during the due diligence stage.

Attitude matters

In M&As, talent is not only about technical and managerial skills; it is also about attitude and willingness to change. Such talent may be found in unexpected places—perhaps even among employees who may not have been properly recognized in the old organization.

Fast and open two-way communication

Frank conversations about expectations and opportunities help quickly unearth employees' concerns and anxieties so they can be addressed.

Articulate career opportunities

Financial compensation is important, but so are career opportunities. High-potential employees are used to senior-level attention to their careers. They will be more likely to stay if they see opportunities for themselves in the combined firm.

Measure and reward retention

Without retention data, companies have no way of measuring the success of their talent management efforts, and no way of holding managers accountable—and rewarding them—for success in post-merger retention of talent.

and the risk of defection. Since the pace of integration may not allow a comprehensive assessment of all individuals, the focus should be on those most critical to the success of the acquisition.[78]

Fast and open communication is another element of success in retaining talent. Cisco's integration team holds small group sessions with all acquired employees on day one to discuss expectations and answer questions. Often, members of the integration team were themselves brought into Cisco through previous acquisitions. They understand what the newly merged employees are going through, so their messages are invested with additional credibility. GE Capital uses GE's change acceleration process (CAP) methodology to clarify expectations and reveal possible concerns and anxieties so they can be addressed swiftly.[79]

A complementary building block for talent retention is providing inducements for employees to stay. Companies often offer stock options, retention bonuses, or other incentives to employees who stay through the integration or until a specific merger-related project is completed.[80] An important consideration is to highlight the differences between short-term business needs (retention incentives for employees who are not expected to be employed after the completion of the integration process) and long-term talent requirements.

For the second group, even most elaborate financial incentives cannot substitute for a one-on-one relationship with executives in the acquiring firm. Senior management involvement is critical to successful retention. High-potential employees in most companies are used to senior-level attention. Without the same treatment from the acquiring company, they question their future and are more likely to depart. Distance may be an obstacle, but it cannot be used as an excuse. Meetings and informal sessions in the early days of the acquisition, if not before the closing, can go a long way toward building the foundations for long-term relationships. When BP–Amoco acquired Arco, another international oil major, it quickly organized Key Talent Workshops—two-day events in which senior BP executives networked with Arco's high-potential employees.[81]

Talent retention efforts should not stop after the first 100 days of integration. Junior employees may find the initial impact of the acquisition positive, offering them opportunities for responsibility and higher pay (especially if their seniors leave en masse). But many of them leave later because they are not integrated into the leadership development of the new parent company.[82] This may have negative consequences for the company's ability to execute future deals, since its track record in retaining talent will affect its credibility and reputation for managing mergers.

While the link between the retention of talent and acquisition success is widely recognized, it does not necessarily translate into support for specific HR initiatives. For example, in a survey of top executives in the United States, Asia, and South America, 76 percent of respondents indicated that talent retention was the most critical element of integration success. But only 8 percent put human resource management as their top priority during integration.[83] Part of the problem is the lack of clear measures for talent retention. Without retention data, companies have no way of gauging the success of their talent management efforts, and no way of holding managers accountable for success in retention.

Many firms have recognized this issue. They not only measure employee turnover, but they also define the retention of key talent as one of the key performance indicators for integration managers and other executives involved in the integration process.

Building the New Culture

The new organization will have a culture, whether by default or design, that may be marked by enduring conflict or may imply acceptance of shared destiny. The process of building a new culture can take a long time; sometimes hankering after the old ways can drag on for a decade, as it did after the merger between Ciba and Geigy (until it merged with Sandoz into Novartis). In most cases, this does not help the company move forward.

This is the main reason why companies with strong and successful cultures, like GE and BP, impose their culture onto the company they acquire, as BP did when it bought Amoco. Indeed, they see their success as originating from their culture and the practices built on it. However, as acknowledged by

CEMEX, while the directions and expectations are clear, there is an understanding that full cultural integration will take longer than changing the operating system.

The focus on creating—or reinforcing—a performance culture seems to be a unifying theme in most successful acquisitions. Rather than spending a lot of time on assessing pre-merger identities and cultures, the emphasis should be on the new strategy for the merged firm, the organizational capabilities required to implement that strategy successfully, and the values, behavior, and organizational practices that are crucial for the future performance of the merged entity. Recent research suggests that an explicit *performance contract* should be at the core of the performance culture of the merging units, confirming "a set of mutual understandings of how to run the business, such as: how to manage processes, how to deal with customers and business partners, how to make and follow up decisions."[84]

Post-merger cultural change is difficult to manage without continuous reinforcement of the organizational values and norms that guide practice and behavior. To build the new culture of ABB after the merger of Asea and Brown Boveri in the late 1980s, Percy Barnevik spent three months with the new senior management team defining a policy bible to guide the new organization. This was a manual of "soft" principles, such as speed in decision making ("Better to be quick and roughly right than slow and completely right") and methods of conflict management ("You can only kick a conflict upstairs once for arbitration"), as well as "hard" practices, such as the performance measurement system that would apply across all units of the newly merged enterprise.

Values and behavioral norms have to be translated into action, guiding the process of culture building or cultural assimilation after an acquisition. Take the French company AXA as an example of the latter. In the space of a decade, AXA grew via acquisitions from being a local player in the French insurance industry to becoming a top global financial services institution. It makes no pretensions that its acquisitions are mergers of equals, acting quickly to AXA-ize the cultures of the firms it acquires.

Managers from companies brought into AXA have commented that one of AXA's most helpful assimilation tools is the company's 360° feedback process. The AXA values are encoded in this instrument, and to accelerate the process of cultural integration all managers and professionals in the acquired company go through 360° workshops. For most of the managers, this is the first time that they will have been exposed to such a multifaceted assessment, and they find the rigor of the approach reinforces the credibility of AXA as a highly professional organization. It makes the desired culture and values concrete, identifies personal needs for improvement, and leads to follow-up coaching in the AXA way.

New culture can take hold fast when it is seen as beneficial to the employees. A study of three cross-border acquisitions in Korea—one with rapid major change toward more performance-oriented HRM, one with slow major change in the same direction, and one with little change from the traditional Korean system—showed that employees in the first two cases were significantly more satisfied with the change, because it was clear to them that change was necessary to remain competitive and keep their jobs.[85]

M&A AS ORGANIZATIONAL CAPABILITY

For many companies, implementing mergers and acquisitions is still a formidable challenge. The complexity of cross-border deals, due to cultural and physical distance, makes implementation even more difficult. Yet there is little doubt that companies that master the art of international acquisitions will gain significant market advantage, although organic growth may have greater long-term advantage. Some firms, such as CEMEX, GE, and SABMiller, view organizational capabilities in making international acquisitions as one of the supporting pillars of their business strategies.[86] They understand that the ability to execute acquisitions is crucial for the future, and that the intangible human aspects of an acquisition are just as important as its financial dimensions.

Learning from Acquisitions

As we have already pointed out, M&A experience does not automatically translate into successful organizational learning. Much of the problem of learning stems from the complexity of M&As. Mergers and acquisitions are never identical, and firms need to disentangle what works in specific situations and make sure that this knowledge is made available for later M&As. The more different the acquisitions the multinational undertakes, the more difficult it is for the company to gain from previous M&A experience. At the same time, as the CEMEX case illustrates well, when learning is built into the acquisition process, different experiences may enhance the quality of learning—and future execution.

We will focus here on two issues: how to measure M&A success and how multinationals can enhance their learning about M&As.

Measuring M&A Success

An important part of M&A learning is feedback on the organization's progress in reaching the integration goals. Rigorous measurement is essential as most international acquisitions are too complex to be able to rely on anecdotes and impressions.

Measures stimulate management to take early corrective action and to establish benchmarks for future acquisitions—without measurement, especially on the intangible people dimension, learning may not take place.

There is no shortage of measures that can be used to assess the progress of the integration process on the HRM side. Some of these measures focus on key organizational priorities, while others reflect the functional agenda of the HR department:

- **Integration goals:** Reorganization and restructuring targets in terms of schedule and cost, including breakdowns for specific business units or geographical areas.

- **Integration of key HR systems:** Tracking integration objectives in combining systems for human resource information (HRIS), compensation, talent development, and performance management according to established time frames and budgets.
- **Retention of talent:** Retention of acquired talent, retention rates for specific business units and functions, and cost-effectiveness indicators such as retention/replacement expenses.
- **Best practices:** Shared and adopted practices compared across organizational units, including estimation of the impact on revenues, cost, or other performance indicators such as customer satisfaction.
- **Employee feedback data:** These include attitude surveys and data from exit interviews.

In the long term, the only valid measure of acquisition success is the satisfied customer. Does the acquisition establish customer value? Does it make sense from the customer's point of view? If it does not, there is not much chance for long-term growth. When short-term synergies are exhausted, deals that fail to create customer value have little chance of being sustained. Strong focus on the customer can also help generate the energy to push through the necessary changes. This cuts down on internal politics that divert management attention away from the business. And bear in mind that creating customer value occurs only *after* the deal is done, which makes post-merger integration a critical success factor.

Building Learning Capability

One issue to consider is whether it is better to have many individuals involved in acquisitions in order to gain and share wide experience, or to rely on a team of experts. Some companies establish a special acquisition unit that is involved in every transaction. Obviously, this creates a desirable pool of expertise. On the other hand, acquisition competence is increasingly seen as an indispensable generalist skill—having experience with an acquisition is a ticket that should be punched by all high-potential employees. This approach is adopted by GE, and because HR is one of the functions with a guaranteed seat at any GE acquisitions, smart young employees seek out HR jobs to have a shot at joining the acquisition team.

In either case, managers who have developed extensive experience in international acquisition should be viewed as valuable resources for the organization. Part of HR's responsibility is to ensure that it knows who and where they are, so they can be mobilized quickly when required. From the employees' point of view, participation in a cross-border acquisition team is a good way to put to use skills accumulated during past international assignments. There is a significant overlap in the behavioral competencies required by expatriates and integration team members; both roles demand emotional maturity, cultural empathy, tolerance for ambiguity, and skills in interpersonal communication.

In order to learn from experience, it is important to build the appropriate organizational memory. This requires learning to be documented to capture lessons learned; and for this, someone must have the responsibility for facilitating the collection of information and making it available—a role that is performed by the HR manager assigned to the transition team in many successful acquisitions. But gaining a place on the transition team means doing your homework—being proactive is a prerequisite if HR professionals are to be involved.[87]

Research evidence shows that the more companies invest in reflecting on their experiences and in codifying their learning in M&A due diligence and integration manuals, the better they perform.[88] The development of tools helps facilitate and speed up the cross-border acquisition process, from due diligence to integration. There is a qualitative difference in the approach to learning here. Acquisition "best practice" books present scenarios and suggest roadmaps for managers to follow. In contrast, acquisition toolkits provide managers with lists of issues and questions to be addressed at each stage in the acquisition, broad guidelines on what to consider, simple and concise instruments, and sources of advice inside and outside the firm. In repetitive acquisitions, the best practice approach may be sufficient, although most international acquisitions are one of a kind. In all cases, a feedback loop recording what worked, what did not, and what can be added, is essential.

It is useful to keep in mind that effective learning and a solid track record in implementing acquisitions can sometimes have unintended consequences. Being confident that missing skills can always be brought in may stifle in-house innovation and experimentation. For example, it has been reported that acquisitions have negative effects on both R&D intensity (a measure of R&D inputs) and patent intensity (a measure of R&D outputs). Other evidence shows that firms making acquisitions introduce fewer new products into the marketplace.[89] A similar logic may apply to entering new markets via cross-border acquisitions. Firms with successful M&A experience may choose to enter quickly through an acquisition, although the slower greenfield investment path may give the company more leverage over people-related issues such as organizational culture and workforce composition.

From Learning to Action

We conclude this chapter by outlining GE Capital's approach to acquisitions (see Figure 13–4), which illustrates well the importance of human resource management in implementing acquisitions. The figure captures the key elements of its proprietary acquisition process, which, although developed originally within the United States, has been applied successfully in scores of international transactions. This detailed process provides guidance on what needs to be done, highlights the key organizational issues and decision points, and provides the methodology and resources. It is documented on paper and online, but as the company accumulates more experience, it is continuously updated and fine-tuned. However, perhaps the most critical feature is that it allows the people involved in the process to find the right answers for themselves. All deals are different, so flexibility in arriving at solutions is important.

FIGURE 13–4. The Wheel of Fortune at General Electric

Source: R.N. Ashkenas, L.J. DeMonaco, and S.C Francis, "Making the Deal Real: How GE Capital Integrates Acquisitions," *Harvard Business Review*, January–February 1998, p. 167.

The merger implementation process starts well before the deal is out in the open, setting the framework for integration. It begins with an assessment of the target's culture to identify any potential cultural barriers to the success of the acquisition. As a part of due diligence, the strengths and weaknesses of the business leaders are assessed so that it is clear who will stay and who may need to be replaced before the closing of the deal. The integration manager is selected and proceeds to assemble the transition team. When the deal is signed, the communication strategy is ready to go into action on the first day.

The integration manager and the transition teams, now expanded to include employees from the target firm, work together to formulate a specific integration plan. Key processes, including human resources, are aligned. Through workshops and other communication tools, the new employees are oriented to the acquiring firm's way of doing business. The involvement and visibility of senior management are critical, as is accountability for specific integration tasks. This is also the stage when, if necessary, painful decisions on terminations are made, quickly but fairly, so that the new organization can move forward.

As integration proceeds, various process tools and techniques are used to accelerate integration and to deal with any resistance to change. The transition team helps to identify opportunities to demonstrate success, and these projects are given high priority. Short-term international exchanges are particularly motivating at this stage. While the integration is managed tightly, there are regular learning reviews to allow for adjustment, taking into account feedback from employees.

The process of integration is not over in 100 days. To assimilate the new employees into the parent firm, the development of common tools, practices, and processes continues. Corporate education and long-term management exchanges are two sets of tools that help diffuse the shared culture. In acquisitions, learning never stops. Auditing the whole integration process and incorporating any learning into the core blueprint completes the cycle—so that the next acquisition can be done even faster and better.

TAKEAWAYS

1. Most merger or acquisition failures are linked to problems in post-merger integration. Cultural and people issues consistently rank as two of the main difficulties. Do not underestimate the importance of cross-cultural differences; but on the other hand, do not confuse culture and poor management.

2. Companies that have solid foundations in HRM and a good track record in managing change also tend to be good at managing acquisitions.

3. There are different strategic logics between mergers—stand-alone, absorption, best of both, and transformational. Each strategic logic has different implications for the nature of the post-merger integration process. Think about the end state before you start.

4. HR should be involved early in acquisition planning, since the "soft" aspects of the due diligence process, such as culture and people practices in the organization to be acquired, are just as important as financial analysis. This allows the firm to address the cultural and human issues in the early stages of the acquisition.

5. Even the best deals have to acknowledge the complexities of merging organizations across boundaries. The ability to add value in the merged company depends mostly on what happens after the deal is done.

6. The integration process starts with the creation of a vision and strategy for the combined organization. Clarity in communication about the strategy is an essential foundation for success.

7. Many M&As fail because of the loss of key talent, so retention is a key priority. This effort should begin during the due diligence process, so retention plans can be put in place from the start. Longer-term retention requires senior management commitment to building personal relationships with the acquired talent.

8. It is important to move with speed. Key decisions about management structure, senior appointments, and anything related to people's careers should be made as soon as possible. Uncertainty and anxiety after the acquisition drain energy from the business.

9. Several steps in post-merger integration are known to foster success: appointing an integration manager to speed up the process; measuring M&A outcomes and assigning accountability; securing and celebrating quick wins.

10. Some firms view competence in making international acquisitions as one of their core capabilities. For them, the ability to learn from past acquisitions, including the mistakes that are inevitably made, is a major source of competitive advantage.

NOTES

1. The CEMEX material in this chapter draws mainly on the IMD case of Marchand and Leger (2008).
2. Marchand and Leger, 2008.
3. In order to reduce debt, CEMEX sold Rinker in 2009.
4. According to a 1997 Conference Board study ("HR Challenges In Mergers And Acquisitions," *HR Executive Review* 5, no. 2), the major reasons for M&A were "to achieve competitive size" (61 percent of responding firms) and to gain market share (57 percent).
5. After the acquisition of Anheuser-Busch in 2008, InBev renamed itself Anheuser-Busch InBev in November of the same year.
6. See Dyer, Kale, and Singh (2004) for a discussion of whether to choose an alliance or an acquisition.
7. For example, Whirlpool's alliance agreement with Tatramat stipulated terms under which Whirlpool could acquire full control of the venture (Ferencikova and Pucik, 1999).
8. Garette and Dussauge, 2000.
9. Most of these and similar studies looked at the financial outcomes of M&A transactions. There are other stakeholders in the acquisition process, including employees, local communities, and customers.
10. "The Case Against Mergers," *The Economist*, January 1997, pp. 4–7; A.T. Kearney, 1999, "Corporate marriage: Blight or bliss—a monograph on post-merger integration"; KPMG, 1999, "Mergers and acquisitions: A global research report—unlocking shareholder value."

11. King et al., 2004. According to a 2006 KPMG study ("The Morning After"), 31 percent of deals created value, 26 percent reduced value. Dobbs, Goedhart, and Suonio (2006) reported a similar positive trend.

12. The premium is the acquisition price minus the stock exchange value of the target before the deal is announced. The premium tends to vary from a few percent to more than 50 percent.

13. Bleeke et al., 1993; KPMG, 1999, "Mergers And Acquisitions: A Global Research Report—Unlocking Shareholder Value"; Larsson and Finkelstein, 1999; Bertrand and Zitouna, 2008.

14. Morosini, Shane, and Singh, 1998; Vermeulen and Barkema, 2001; Björkman, Stahl, and Vaara, 2007.

15. Slangen, 2006.

16. Morosini, Shane, and Singh, 1998; Björkman, Stahl, and Vaara, 2007.

17. This Egon Zehnder study is outlined by Marks and Mirvis (1998).

18. Stahl and Voigt, 2008.

19. Jemison and Sitkin, 1986.

20. Duhaime and Schwenk, 1985.

21. A.T. Kearney, 1999, "Corporate Marriage: Blight Or Bliss—A Monograph On Post-Merger Integration."

22. Zollo and Singh, 2004.

23. Barkema and Schijven, 2008.

24. Killing, 2003a. Haspeslagh and Jemison (1991) offer a well-known alternative framework for examining different types of M&A integration.

25. Killing, 2003a.

26. See Marchand and Leger (2008).

27. Vaara, Tienari, and Björkman, 2003. See also Vaara (2003) for a discussion of how cross-border integration issues can easily become politicized.

28. Killing, 2003a.

29. Killing, 2003a.

30. Kay and Shelton (2000). A study published by Towers Perrin and SHRM Foundation (Schmidt, 2002) reported similar results.

31. Marsh, Mercer, and Kroll, 2008, "M&A Beyond Borders: Opportunities And Risks," p. 46 (www.mercer.com).

32. Conference Board, 1997, "HR Challenges In Mergers And Acquisitions," *HR Executive Review* 5(2).

33. KPMG, 1999, "Mergers And Acquisitions: A Global Research Report—Unlocking Shareholder Value," p. 15.

34. Schmidt, 2002. Similar conclusions were presented in a 1997 Conference Board study ("HR Challenges In Mergers And Acquisitions," *HR Executive Review* 5, no. 2).

35. See Groysberg and Abrahams (2006) for a discussion of so-called *lift outs*. Hiring a whole team from competitors is most common in professional service industries.

36. Hitt, Harrision, and Ireland, 2001, p. 111.

37. "Renault Steers Forward," *Wall Street Journal Europe*, February 15, 2001, p. 31.

38. Chu, 1996.

39. Johnson and Rich, 2000.

40. Schmidt, 2002.

41. See also Harding and Rouse (2007).

42. In a typical share option plan, options grants are vested over a period of time, often a three-year period. When options are vested, employees have the full right to acquire and sell the underlying shares.

43. In knowledge-intensive acquisitions, it is particularly important to protect the value of the deal from the competitive implications of employee defection. We will discuss specific post-merger retention strategies later, but during due diligence it essential to clarify who has the rights to technology and know-how and who are the key contributors that should be contractually obliged to remain. When trade secrets and confidential information are important assets of the company to be acquired, it is wise to tie the closing to no-competition, no-disclosure agreements with key employees. However, there are large differences in how employment laws in different countries approach these issues.

44. For more on integration of knowledge-intensive acquisitions based on an analysis of how Swedish multinationals integrated foreign R&D units with the aim of enhancing knowledge sharing, see Bresman, Birkinshaw, and Nobel (1999).

45. Marsh, Mercer, and Kroll, 2008, "M&A Beyond Borders: Opportunities And Risks," (www.mercer.com).

46. Angwin, 2001.

47. One frequently used assessment tool is the Denison Culture Survey developed by our colleague Dan Denison of IMD (Denison, Cho, and Young, 2000). For an example of an internally developed instrument, see "Merging Cultures Evaluation Index" (MCEI), described in Marks and Mirvis (1998, pp. 65–6).

48. Chakrabarti, Gupta-Mukherjee, and Jayaraman, 2009.

49. Stahl and Voigt, 2008.

50. Stahl and Voigt, 2008.

51. Because of these delays, not all acquisition agreements go through. Some collapse because of drastic changes in market conditions between announcement and closing; for others regulatory hurdles may prove to be insurmountable; and there are those where parties simply change their minds and find a way to get out of the deal. Meanwhile, of course, people at all levels of the organization speculate about their future in the new organization, some with great expectations, others with fear. It is important that such contingencies be considered in the HR plan, in particular as they pertain to retention of talent.

52. Marks and Mirvis, 1986.

53. Harding and Rouse, 2007.

54. Therefore, many companies are turning to outside vendors to assure the fairness and objectivity of this process.

55. Sitkin and Pablo, 2005; Fubini, Price and Zollo, 2006.

56. Pucik, 2008.

57. Ashkenas, DeMonaco, and Francis 1998; Ashkenas and Francis, 2000.

58. Ashkenas and Francis, 2000.

59. For contrasting interpretations of the Daimler-Chrysler post-merger integration, see Morosini (2004) and Vlasic and Stertz (2000).

60. Froese and Goeritz, 2007.

61. Del Canho and Engelfrit, 2008.

62. Ashkenas, DeMonaco, and Francis, 1998.

63. Inkpen, Sundaram, and Rockwood, 2000.

64. Pucik, 2008.

65. Pucik, 2008.

66. Homburg and Bucerius, 2006.

67. Kumar, 2009.

68. Child, Faulkner, and Pitkethly, 2001; PA Consulting, 2001, "Realising The Value Of Acquisitions: A Comparative Study Of European Post-Acquisition Integration Practices."

69. Haspeslagh, 2000.

70. Some of these principles of change management are reviewed in Chapters 2 and 11.

71. According to research conducted by Krug and Hegerty (2001), the decision of top managers in an acquired company to stay rather than leave following acquisition is positively associated with their positive perceptions of the merger announcement.

72. Inkpen, Sundaram, and Rockwood, 2000.

73. "Torch That Sent A Deal Down In Flames," *Financial Times*, April 12, 2000, p. 22.

74. Marks and Mirvis, 1998, p. 74.

75. Krug and Hegerty, 1997.

76. Harding and Rouse, 2007.

77. Michaels, Handfield-Jones, and Axelrod, 2001.

78. Corporate Leadership Council, 2000, "M&A Talent Management: Identification And Retention Of Key Talent During Mergers And Acquisitions," p. 37.

79. GE's change acceleration process (CAP) methodology is discussed in Chapter 11.

80. Retention bonus guidelines provide desirable consistency, specifying eligibility, amount, performance criteria, etc. Their effect depends, however, on employees' expectations as well as on labor and tax legislation in the countries involved.

81. Corporate Leadership Council, 2000.

82. Krug and Hegerty, 2001.

83. Watson Waytt, 1999, "Watson Wyatt Worldwide's 1998/99 Mergers & Acquisitions Survey," p. 66.

84. Fubini, Price, and Zollo, 2007.

85. Froese, Pak, and Chong, 2008.

86. Hitt, Harrison, and Ireland, 2001.

87. When Citibank top management announced its intention to grow in Europe through acquisitions, senior HR leaders in the region quickly organized an intensive M&A workshop to prepare their key staff for the challenges ahead. Several weeks after the workshop, the bank announced a major deal in Poland—and the local HR manager was ready to participate fully in the acquisition team.

88. Zollo and Singh, 2004; Fubini, Price, and Zollo, 2007.

89. Hitt et al., 1991.

CHAPTER 14

Transforming the Global Human Resource Role

HR Responses to Globalization

Let us introduce this chapter with a number of vignettes that capture the way in which the global role of the HR function is changing:

- At one of our seminars, John Hofmeister was engaged in a question-and-answer discussion with HR executives. John is an ex-GE HR professional who was at the time the head of the human resource function for Royal Dutch/Shell. One of the participants asked him, "What will be the task of the HR leader in the future?" Without hesitation, he responded, "Managing tension and contradiction." There was a thoughtful silence in the seminar room.

- The chief executive of a well-known corporation that has recently undertaken a major international acquisition presented six core platforms on which the group could compete in this era of intense global competition. The last of these competitive platforms specifically focused on people processes: "We need to be a global benchmark for HR." In many ways, the HR executives in the audience could not have hoped for more—a chief executive publicly endorsing the role of HR and willing to invest in it. But this raises a difficult question—how to respond?

- Many of the GE divisions provide HR services to their external customers. For example, GE Power Systems "sells" organizational change technology together with its turbines to state-owned utilities, directly involving the client CEO. Is this the way of the future for leading corporations? What does this mean for HR roles and responsibilities?

- International HR remains a sensitive area in which there is potential for clashes between the HR function and line management. One leading European transnational has introduced global processes in every area—except for HR.

The corporate HR vice president ceded to the pressures from all over the world—"It's just too political. Despite the strong rationale, it takes away much of the discretionary power of regional, country, and business area bosses."

- The HR director of a multinational entertainment company commented on his role as follows: "The CEO knows I will tell him if there's an issue. If he doesn't like what I say, I remind him that it's what he pays me for. He knows I have no baggage and my loyalty to the company is unquestioned—I have to be the thought leader on organizational development, talent management, and executing change. I'm also the closest confidante of the CEO."[1]

OVERVIEW

This chapter focuses on the way globalization is changing human resource management roles, notably those of the HR function and HR professionals. We begin by examining the unique features of the HR function in transnational firms as described in the previous chapters, summarizing the HRM implications of internationalization; the contribution of HR processes to cross-border coordination; and HR's role in managing complex change, strategic alliances, and mergers and acquisitions. From there we go on to discuss how to organize the global HR function, examining separately the different roles of the HR function outlined in Chapter 2: HRM process and content development, highlighting the role of network leadership; the impact of IT on HR service delivery; and the business support role.

In the subsequent section, we examine the boundaries of the HR function, discussing the responsibilities of local, regional, and global HR units; the extent to which the HR function should work with external business partners; and the reciprocal responsibilities of line management and the function for HRM. Subsequently, we address the development of the competencies of the global HR function in general and HR professionals in particular.

We then return to an important task for the HR function, and people management more generally: tension management. Given the contradictions that the transnational enterprise faces, this theme has run throughout the book. One example we examine is the tension between the need to establish a competitive culture while, at the same time, safeguarding the sustainability of the organization. We argue that HR has to be a proactive function, fighting for the long-term perspective. We provide various examples of what this long-term perspective implies, emphasizing the capacity to anticipate future developments.

In the final section of this chapter, we briefly address broader social issues. Although increased market competition and globalization have brought immense advantages to many parts of the world, enabling millions to escape poverty, there are worrying signs that there may be a backlash against free trade and movement of capital if more attention is not paid to those who have been left behind. We discuss the implications of such wider social issues for HR. We conclude the book by asking where HRM is heading in this era of tension and contradiction.

WHAT IS UNIQUE ABOUT THE GLOBAL HR FUNCTION?

What are the distinctive characteristics of the transnational corporation, and what are their HRM implications? Much of the book has focused on these issues, and we will summarize here what this means for the HR function.

Chapters 3 and 4 examined the global strategies of multinationals. The local responsiveness strategy (Chapter 3) reflects the need to adapt to the local markets as well as to the cultural, institutional, and social environments in which the multinational corporation operates. Managing people successfully in a multidomestic firm requires sensitivity to the local context, actively embracing and drawing on multiple sources of diversity, and resisting the temptation to roll out global policies and practices that may not be appropriate to local conditions. Country HR managers need, on the one hand, to demonstrate to headquarters that locally appropriate ways of managing people lead to superior business results, while on the other hand serving as "translators" of desired global policies so that they fit with local realities.

A global integration strategy (Chapter 4) means that decisions are made from a global rather than a local perspective. Expatriates play important roles in achieving global integration by acting as corporate agents who enable control and knowledge transfer. Indeed, until recently the domain of international HRM was often synonymous with the management of expatriates. Even today, expatriation remains an important task for the function, often requiring the expertise of specialists, although its purpose has broadened to include enhancing individual competencies and organizational capabilities. Key issues today for the global HR function are to develop and maintain global HR processes and tools to support integration, while ensuring consistent delivery of HR services worldwide with the highest degree of quality and efficiency.

Coordination becomes a new imperative in transnational organizations that attempt to meet both global and local needs. The structural coordination mechanisms examined in Chapter 5 include multidimensional structures, cross-boundary teams, cross-boundary roles and steering groups, and virtual teams. Senior leaders, together with many managers in various coordination roles, have vertical responsibility and shared accountability for strategy implementation across intra-organizational boundaries. The need to enhance lateral coordination capabilities brings many new challenges for the HR function: how to select and develop managers for lateral coordination roles requiring leadership without authority; how to make sure that global teams are staffed with the right people from different parts of the organization; how to evaluate the performance of individuals who work in split egg roles.

The coordination mechanisms of social capital, shared values, and global mindset discussed in Chapter 6 help ensure that employees working in dispersed units act in accordance with corporate objectives. The HR professional who takes on the social architect role will facilitate the development of cross-boundary social capital and global mindset through cross-border assignments, international training programs, and the support of corporatewide virtual communities of practice. Technology and new software are extending the realm of social architecture in the multinational; the interface between the IT and the HR functions is becoming more important.

Three chapters (7 to 9) dealt with key processes in international human resource management: recruitment and selection, development, and performance management (including compensation). These processes are traditionally "owned" by the HR function, though the commitment of senior line management to support implementation is an imperative. Many multinational firms have followed a trend toward building integrated global HR tools and processes while maintaining some flexibility for local responsiveness in implementation. In particular, the need for a comprehensive perspective on global talent management—including making sure that talented employees from any part of the corporation get suitable career development opportunities—is an important reason for establishing an HR organization with a global mandate.

A superior ability to globally access, share, and recombine knowledge is a hallmark of leading multinationals, and HRM is an integral part of the management of knowledge and innovation in the international firm (see Chapter 10). For the HR function, this means, among other tasks, taking a lead in designing cross-border structural mechanisms to capture and share knowledge, such as global committees, task forces, or communities of practice; building an appropriate social architecture to facilitate knowledge-building networks; and developing supportive performance management and incentive systems.

Chapter 11 addressed one of the most salient and yet neglected areas of international human resource management—how to plan and implement large, complex change. Regardless of whether they have global or local positions, HR managers who act as change partners require an extensive knowledge of the people-related dimensions of organizational change, supporting line management in navigating the dualities facing the transnational enterprise. Similar organizational challenges confront multinational firms as they expand globally through international alliances (Chapter 12) and cross-border mergers and acquisitions (Chapter 13)—with HR professionals playing major roles in planning the strategy as well as during implementation.

How companies handle these and other HRM challenges will have a significant impact on their ability to compete in global markets. While the HR function cannot, and in most cases should not be solely responsible for tackling these issues, it is expected to make important contributions since people management is an essential part of enterprise globalization.

However, despite the opportunities to add value in the globalization process, HR in many companies is still not perceived as a full partner in building the necessary capabilities. Sometimes it is even viewed as an obstacle, slowing down the process through bureaucratic, central procedures.[2] Ethnocentric and parochial HR systems and policies, inherited from the past, focused on the parent company and projected onto the rest of the world, are all too often a barrier to the implementation of effective global organizational processes. Still, this is changing fast, and the HR function is increasingly expected to take a worldwide perspective on how to configure its activities. Furthermore, the expectations go beyond the basics of handling traditional functional processes of recruitment, selection, training, compensation, and the like. Of equal importance is how HR succeeds in influencing the way in which top executives and line managers leverage people management tools when tackling the strategic challenges of international business.

ORGANIZING GLOBAL HUMAN RESOURCES

In this section, we discuss the organization of the HR function; the subsequent section examines how to develop its capabilities to meet the needs of the transnational organization.

In Chapter 2, we proposed that the HR function has to fulfill three roles: HRM process and content development, HR service delivery, and business support. Similar roles have been recommended by other HR scholars,[3] and they correspond to the way in which many multinationals organize their HR function.[4] The way in which HR is organized is significant because it specifies what gets attention—which HRM issues will be focused on, measured, and followed up.[5] The division of what was earlier an integrated function into three distinct organizational areas also leads to the necessity of coordination between them.

HRM Process and Content Development

HRM process and content development (the "functional expert" role as some call it)[6] has for many decades been a core task of professional HR departments, though globalization has meant new challenges for this role. The successful organization of HRM process and content development is a more complex task for the transnational corporation than for multidomestic firms or home country centered meganationals. The local responsiveness–global integration tensions discussed in previous chapters are at the center of this challenge:

- How to achieve a balance between globally coordinated systems and processes involving some measure of standardization *and* sensitivity to local needs.
- How to identify and diffuse innovative local HR practices that can be of use in other parts of the global organization.
- How to make sure that the HR practices implemented in different parts of the corporation support the achievement of business objectives.

Professional knowledge of state-of-the-art HRM is a necessary point of departure. However, as we have pointed out, the implementation of the latest "best HR practices" can have a negative impact on the competitiveness of the firm unless they are tightly aligned with the reality of the business, and are consistent with practices in other HR domains. The involvement of line managers is also essential.

Several structures—usually found in various combinations—are used to organize this role within the global HR function. The traditional solution is to have *functional experts at headquarters* with global responsibility for developing policies, processes, and tools. The advantages of colocating the expert team at corporate headquarters are deep specialization and face-to-face collaboration among the global functions, enabling internal alignment and consistency. However, there is considerable risk that solutions created by centrally placed experts remain home country oriented unless augmented with input from other parts of the organization.

Centers of expertise, often known as centers of excellence, distributed across the global organization are another solution. Proctor & Gamble has organized its HR function into 10 areas of dispersed expertise, among them recruitment, compensation, learning and development, diversity management, and employee relations. This structure allows the firm to achieve economies of knowledge and skills in its HR function. One of the challenges with this structure is to ensure consistency across HR practices.

A variation of the centers of expertise concept involves using split egg or matrix roles rather than full-time jobs. For example, a firm may have an outstanding expert in recruitment processes located in the German subsidiary. Germany is no longer growing as rapidly as in the past. Rather than losing that expertise, why not leverage it across Europe by appointing the person to head up a European expertise center for recruitment? The individual has a budget for this top-of-the-egg activity, builds a virtual team of inside and outside resources, while still continuing with the bottom-of-the-egg responsibilities for recruitment in Germany.

There are many areas of HR that can be organized in a split egg fashion, anything from diversity management to employee attitude surveys, from organizational change advice to communications design, from work safety to communities of practice associated with global knowledge management. These are all areas where local commitment and adaptation are needed, where coordination has benefits, but where it is questionable whether the firm needs to have experts at the corporate center.

Many multinationals use global *functional committees*, regardless of whether they have a centralized HR function or a structure of more dispersed centers of expertise. There may also be more informal HR *communities of practice* where participation is voluntary—people participate because they feel that the sharing of knowledge and expertise adds value. These communities also build social capital that the participants can draw upon in their daily work.

Irrespective of the structural solution selected, the basic mechanism for going about developing corporate HR processes and tools is usually the *cross-boundary project group.*[7] Such teams often include members from the businesses and lead countries, line as well as HR managers and experts. The inclusion of line managers helps to ensure the business relevance of the processes and tools that are being put in place, facilitating their implementation among line managers and in subsidiaries. To the extent that members of the project group have a true global mindset, the team can be kept small and manageable.

The use of cross-boundary project groups to develop global HR policies, processes, and tools reflects a deeper reality in transnational organizations—regardless of how roles are organized, HR managers at worldwide or regional headquarters cannot do the complex work by themselves. They might have been able to in the early stages of internationalization when the necessary expertise was located at the center. However, nowadays that expertise is most likely located around the world in different centers and subsidiaries. Also, building commitment and local buy-in is as important as the quality of the solution.

This does not mean that there is no need for central expertise.[8] However, the coordination needs of the transnational change the nature of the parent's role. The center can no longer be a repository for expertise or a centralized hub where experts tell those in the field what to do. Those at the center must draw upon the expertise out in the subsidiaries, from both the HR function and the line, carefully bringing together the key stakeholders. A different set of skills is needed at the center, which we call *network leadership.*

Network leadership involves the following abilities:

1. **An awareness of leading-edge trends and developments:** The network leader, is typically either a functional staff manager or a headquarters coordinator. Such a leader, free from routine operational work, is expected to be at the cutting edge of developments in the respective functional areas. In practice, what this means is that the staff manager must be well networked, both internally and externally, to be aware of relevant trends.
2. **The ability to mobilize the appropriate resources:** When the network leader senses that a development area is timely, he or she needs to be able to bring together the appropriate people in the form of a project group—those with skills and experience together with key managers from lead application units. This means that the parent leader needs to have a high degree of clout and credibility with units around the world, as well as fine skills in stakeholder analysis. When needed, this also means bringing in outside resources such as consultants and experts, funded by corporate budgets.
3. **A sense of timing and context:** Lastly, the network leader needs an acute sense of timing, and this is perhaps the quality that is most often lacking. If subsidiaries are besieged by short-term operational imperatives, nothing undermines credibility more than having the focus of key people in the subsidiary distracted by a long-term corporate or regional initiative, however important it may be. Over the years, we have witnessed many well-reasoned

initiatives by senior steering groups or corporate staff that have backfired because of a poor sense of timing.

As with other senior line managers in the transnational who share accountability for coordination, the skills of network leadership require the ability to exercise strong leadership without authority.

HR Service Delivery

The key output of the HR service delivery role is regular transactional operations connected with HRM, carried out at low cost and with a satisfactory service level. The HR department has been under considerable pressure over the last 15 years to cut costs as well as improve effectiveness. The typical diagnosis was that the weight of important but nonstrategic transactional tasks was driving out time and attention for value-added activities focusing on HR content or business support. The application of IT to human resource issues, known as e-HR, has opened up new possibilities for standardized service delivery, leading to a response with three connected prongs:

1. The automation of transactional processes allows *self-help*, shifting the work to the users of e-HR tools.
2. Services can be offered by HR *service centers*, often with regional or even global scope.
3. Appropriate HR transactional tasks can be *outsourced*.

It is IT that has opened up the potential for transformation of the traditional administrative HR practices, leading to deployment of e-enabled HR processes that are standardized across a region, or indeed the world. Before IT made these new ways of managing transactional tasks possible, this work was performed by large administrative staffs, and duplicated in country after country.

Examples of transactions that are especially suitable for e-HR are payroll processing; responding to standard employee questions about pensions, benefits, employment rules, and holidays; basic generic training; and occupational health.[9] However, e-HR can support a much wider portfolio of HR practices, many of which are more transformational than transactional, including recruitment and selection, training (e-learning), performance management (objective setting, feedback, and appraisal), talent management and succession planning, and real-time employee surveys. Providers of enterprise resource planning (ERP) systems have developed e-HR modules and systems that span a variety of HR practices, and a large majority of the leading multinationals use such systems, provided for example by SAP and PeopleSoft (owned by Oracle).

E-HR has reinforced the trend to standardize HR practices across worldwide operations (though standardization has many other advantages—facilitating control, reducing duplication, increasing flexibility, aiding mobility and knowledge sharing).[10] As HR processes become regional or global, this has also accelerated the pressure to adopt a common corporate language (typically English, even in firms with headquarters in continental Europe). Further, the use of an integrated HR software package leads to more transparency, as well as the possibility of increased central control over a range of HRM decisions and activities. For example, when data about all new employees must be entered into the global system, the freedom for individual units to hire people in the face of corporate hiring restrictions is curtailed.

The existence of standardized data on operations across the world has in turn fueled the rebirth of manpower planning, today known as workforce planning, allowing corporate management to forecast gaps in supply and demand for talent across the world. With the emergence of new statistical methods for data analysis, data mining by corporate headquarters is leading to greater rigor in the quality of analysis of HRM factors, providing senior HR executives with better information to guide their planning dialogues with senior line management. However, until now, these changes in technology have been perceived as enabling cost saving and standardization rather than driving a transformational change that may in time appear as the significant legacy.

Regardless of the solutions that are chosen for service delivery—typically some combination of self-help, shared service centers, and outsourcing—it is crucial to pay close attention to the process of change, building understanding and acceptance for the new behaviors required by employees. Older employees and managers who were not brought up in the Internet world may still prefer to ask their HR officer. So it is important to involve the service users in the design of HR service solutions, following up with objective measures and subjective evaluations of user satisfaction.

Self-Help

Employees can get the answers online to many of the important but routine questions that they may have about policies, pay, and benefits, and they can also take care of routine transactions themselves. For example, the process of learning and training can be standardized using information technology. If a person needs basic training such as negotiation skills or quality management, then he or she can access a corporate Web site that provides information on certified external courses as well as the names and evaluations of recent attendees. IBM has invested heavily in e-learning technology on generic issues such as the development of basic managerial skills so that staff throughout the world can learn on an anywhere–anytime basis instead of requesting authorization to attend a training seminar. This is guided by a five-step learning model, beginning with basic reading and information, proceeding upward to e-courses, then followed by computer-assisted dialogue sessions and ultimately a face-to-face workshop with certification that is organized locally. As individuals take more responsibility for managing their own careers, e-HR can facilitate mentoring, coaching, career track management, and cross-border mobility.[11]

Typically, self-help service delivery is hierarchically organized. Routine transactional matters are automated in such a way as to allow employees to access information on the intranet. Simple issues needing human response are often be managed by a call center, probably located in a low-cost country (such as India, Costa Rica, or one of the countries in Central or Eastern Europe) or by professionals in a service center.[12] Issues that are not routine—those that require judgment or a decision—are referred to HR professionals or supervisors. Questions of policy or practice are addressed by those responsible for HRM process and content delivery.

The introduction of self-help based on e-HR can translate into significant cost savings in the short term as long as it does not lead employees and/or their superiors to spend unproductive time dealing with issues that would have been resolved faster and more cheaply by local HR professionals. Still, there is a tension between short-term and potential long-term impact. Although e-HR investments may lead to efficiency gains, primarily through reduced HR head count, the gains may be illusory since many activities are simply loaded on managers and employees, and more resources are spent on IT.[13]

Some executives in high-growth emerging markets like Asia and Latin America have raised concerns that the "global solution" increases their costs without visible benefits. In this respect, most major firms accept that the underlying investment to deploy e-HR and self-help is high and cannot be justified solely by the short-term returns. Yet the potential long-term opportunities (such as facilitating knowledge transfer and the rapid deployment of people across boundaries) are so significant that these investments are likely to grow.

All in all, effective implementation of self-help and its underlying e-HR tools requires acceptance across users located in different contexts, who will have to adopt a self-help attitude for a comprehensive transition to e-HR to take hold.[14] As we note later, the pace of change has been uneven across the globe— most rapid in North America and slowest in Asia where electronic systems, until recently, were less common. While it is likely that the speed of change will continue to be influenced by cultural and institutional factors we foresee that e-enabled HR will spread across the globe.[15]

Shared Service Centers

Some firms, such as Cisco, have long organized all their HR activities in global service centers, which began to gain popularity in the 1990s together with the emergence of e-HR. Such centers promised economies of scale and a higher level of specialization since a range of activities could be moved to a joint location— see Table 14–1.

Many multinationals began by establishing HR service centers at the country level; others created them for geographical areas. For instance, IBM established an HR service center for its European operations in Portsmouth in the United Kingdom, processing 252,000 phone calls and 71,000 e-mails annually. Most of the

TABLE 14–1. Potential Benefits of HR Shared Service Centers

- Cost savings through scale advantages.
- Allows "one-stop" solutions for the users.
- Improves international learning and sharing of best practices.
- More consistent HR service across units.
- Deeper functional specialization among HR professionals.
- Greater transparency and follow-up of costs and service levels.
- Allows other parts of the global HR function to focus more on business support and process and content development.

Source: Partly based on F.L. Cooke, "Modeling an HR Shared Services Center: Experience of an MNC in the United Kingdom," *Human Resource Management* 45:2 (2006).

questions were routine in nature.[16] A 2007 survey of UK organizations revealed that two-thirds of companies with more than 5,000 employees had created an HR service center.[17]

Such service centers can cover a range of HR processes, often including the responsibility for the e-HR processes that underlie the self-help functions. The service center will respond to the nonroutine inquiries that people cannot answer using the intranet.

Shared service centers appear to have led to lowered costs, reducing the duplication that existed in HR functions organized on a multidomestic basis.[18] However, there are also widespread reports of user dissatisfaction.[19] Employees complain about the loss of face-to-face contact that helps in the discussion of personal and confidential issues, and managers feel that they now have to carry out HR work for which they are not trained.[20] Therefore, the focus today is on improving end-user satisfaction rather than further reducing service costs.[21]

Some multinationals have taken an additional step by consolidating several support functions. Ten years ago P&G decided to establish a single global business services unit consisting of HR, finance and accounting, facilities management, and (later) IT. The aim was to achieve synergies by integrating the different functions into one organization, thereby facilitating better workflow management across what previously were different functional silos. The company built three service centers, one in Costa Rica, one in the Philippines, and one in the United Kingdom. Later, P&G decided to outsource some of the activities viewed as nonstrategic—IBM was awarded a long-term contract to provide services such as HR data management, payroll processing, compensation and benefits planning and administration, and expatriate and relocation services. Although P&G report some positive effects from its consolidation of the global support functions,[22] time will show whether this will become a new trend.

Outsourcing HR

Outsourcing of selected HR practices has been taking place for many decades—firms have relied on executive search and recruitment firms for parts of the hiring and selection process, and on business schools for help in developing and delivering management training. The outsourcing of larger parts of the HR function gained momentum around the turn of the century. Today, a number of large multinationals like BP, Kraft Foods, and P&G have all signed long-term HR outsourcing contracts.

Outsourcing is most often driven by the HR function itself, under pressure to cut head count and aspiring to become more "strategic" by getting rid of transactional HR activities. Scale advantages and the specialized knowledge in e-HR and shared service centers on the part of the service providers are important reasons for the increase of HR outsourcing, and it may be attractive to start-ups and relatively small firms as it allows them to access some of the scale advantages that only large organizations can afford. Further, the service providers may have deeper specialized professional knowledge and be able to draw on their experience from working with a range of corporate clients.

Surveys suggest that the main objective when outsourcing HR activities is a reduction in HR service delivery costs. Freeing up time for more strategic HRM is another important objective, as is obtaining technologically advanced solutions. Most commonly, firms have outsourced certain HR practices while retaining in-house those viewed as strategically important for competitiveness.[23]

One study based primarily on US and European experience suggests that it is reasonable to expect at least a 20 percent reduction in HR administrative costs as a result of outsourcing,[24] though several studies indicate that HR outsourcing deals have failed to live up to the high initial expectations.[25] Many companies report that they spend more time than expected on managing the outsourcing process. A study on user experiences concluded, "Improvements in areas such as cost, productivity (especially of line managers), service quality, timeliness, and accuracy were all marginal."[26] There are, however, clear differences in how satisfied users are with different services. A 2008 study revealed that managers were most satisfied with the HR self-service tools offered by their outsourcing partners, and least satisfied with staffing and recruitment as well as learning and training administration.[27]

More importantly, in a number of firms, HR managers have discovered that when core processes are fully outsourced, they may end up short on the capabilities necessary to play a significant business support role (more about this later). As a result, some firms have brought several of the previously outsourced HR services back inside, particularly in the area of recruitment.[28]

Implementing an HR Service Delivery Model

One issue that multinationals have to deal with is that the factors impacting HR service delivery (and indeed what is often called the wider process of HR transformation) vary significantly from one region of the world to another. Whereas the pressure to reduce corporate costs is strong in North America, the focus on growth in emerging markets like Asia has meant that cost has been only a distant preoccupation for senior local management. Another motivation for the change in the United States and increasingly in parts of Western Europe is to free up HR time for business support roles; but in most of Asia, the concept of the HR function playing a "business partner" role is at best a novel and somewhat alien notion that is far from the reality of an HR function focused on highly operational tasks such as recruitment in the face of an acute talent war.

The implementation of an HR service delivery model in the US is facilitated by the fact that the country has one language, a single legal system, a long history of devolving people management responsibility to the line, and tightly organized professional HR networks for the exchange of experience. Europe is much more varied, with big differences between one country and another—the notion of self-help in the people management area is even more deeply rooted in Nordic countries, such as Denmark and Finland, than in the United States, but is meeting resistance in Latin Europe, where the HR function is still expected to provide full support. Asia is even more varied, with radically different languages and legal systems, no history of devolution to line managers, and an absence of networks for exchanging ideas and experiences. Consequently, multinational firms have tended to proceed step-by-step with the process of HR transformation—moving boldly in North America, with increasing speed in Europe, but cautiously in Asia.

Doing a great job in terms of HR service delivery is not likely to translate into any sustainable competitive advantage for the firm, although companies that do it poorly will certainly suffer. The importance of efficient, high-quality HR services must not be underestimated in the search for what may seem like more prestigious and high-profile roles for the HR department.

Self-help, shared service centers, and HR outsourcing are complementary and are often used in parallel. Companies should carefully analyze the role that each delivery mechanism should play before the final choice. Changing strategy in midstream is painful—and costly. The box "HR Service Delivery at Shell" describes the experience of one multinational organization.

Business Support

By business support, we mean the activities of HR professionals and managers who work directly with line and top managers on HRM issues. These roles are generalist in nature, requiring competence across different functional areas of HR as well as a close understanding of the specific business. The HR professionals occupying this role support business unit management teams, and they are often members of these teams. One of the questions of matrix balance concerns reporting lines. Typically they report to the line boss (the CEO, division or regional vice president, business unit head, or subsidiary general manager, depending on the level in the organization), with a dotted-line relationship to the corporate, divisional, or regional HR department.

One part of this "HR in the business" role is to contribute to discussions about the people aspects of strategy and organizational capabilities. Strategies are implemented through people, and a key responsibility of this HR generalist is to remind the management team of the opportunities as well as the limitations

HR Service Delivery at Shell

In the late 1990s, Shell initiated a significant organizational restructuring, which saw the launch of its "Global Organization" vision—a desire to increase global integration with fewer lines of business, standardized core processes, and greater coordination. There were three key objectives for HR: greater functional expertise in how HR serves its businesses, greater standardization of HR processes, and the creation of a single global HR system.

This led to the creation of Shell People Services (SPS), launched in 2001. The vision behind SPS was that it should provide direct support to employees and enable them to manage all their basic HR needs on a self-service basis. Six SPS service centers were set up in Houston (the largest to serve the Unites States), London, The Hague in the Netherlands, Kuala Lumpur, Melbourne, and Wellington. This involved the standardization of HR processes, built on a corporatewide, integrated HR software suite (in this case SAP HR). Throughout the world, the language became English.

The move to SPS was aimed at realizing significant cost savings through standardization, lower system maintenance and upgrading, and fewer HR staff. It involved a major change in the role of local HR country managers—they were fewer in number but they would have to play more value-added roles. There was little outsourcing to avoid the risk of higher costs and loss of organizational learning. Nevertheless, the implementation costs were higher than expected in this mammoth project, piloted initially in Malaysia.

SPS plans its work around service agreements that are negotiated with the businesses at market rates. It is governed by Shell's HR Council, with quarterly performance reviews. The major services covered by SPS include the recruitment of all professional-level employees, learning and training, expatriation, internal consulting services, and compensation and benefits. Shell has other shared service centers to cover finance and customer services.

that the existing pool of human resources constitutes for alternative business strategies. As the HR director at one high-tech multinational put it, "Of course we're there to ensure that people issues are thought through. But we should also offer a more long-term and conceptual viewpoint that's our particular contribution." In addition, one of the many support tasks of these HR generalists is to work with functional HR specialists to make sure that HR practices are in place to build the intended organizational capabilities. Another particularly important role is paying attention to the change management implications. As discussed in Chapter 11, management teams often focus disproportionately on the strategy, plan, or solution (the quality of analysis) at the expense of the necessary change process (building acceptance).

Besides strategy and change, HR professionals working within the line organization are likely to get involved with a variety of other people issues. Among their most common tasks is to participate in the evaluation of candidates for key positions, and to undertake the groundwork for periodic talent reviews. HR managers may work closely with management on specific change projects such as organizational redesign. But there is also a need to be involved in more mundane "how to" HRM issues, and business support managers are often called upon to help resolve employee concerns of various kinds. They should become linking pins between business units and the centrally located functional expertise centers as well as with the service delivery centers.

Since the 1990s, HR managers and professionals have been strongly encouraged to adopt a role as *strategic partners,*[29] *business partners,*[30] or *strategic players.*[31] A survey of 1,188 practitioners revealed that 56 percent aspired to become strategic business partners, although only 33 percent stated that they performed the role at the time of the research.[32] Another study of more than 700 UK organizations reported that 81 percent had restructured the HR function; by far the most important reason for the reorganization was to enable the function to become more "strategic."[33]

Indeed, the business support role is easier if HR managers and professionals have "a seat at the table" when strategy discussions take place—something that is not always the case. The extent to which the HR function lives up to the calls for it to play an active business support or even strategic partner role varies considerably, and Table 14–2 contrasts the responses of line and HR managers in 46 organizations across the world. Line managers are clearly more critical about the HR function than are HR managers themselves!

For the multinational, there is a risk that HR business support managers and professionals working in business units and foreign subsidiaries gradually "go native." This is problematic if it means that they become so focused on their own units that they fail to understand the importance of balancing local considerations

TABLE 14–2. Line and HR Manager Views about the HR Function

Statement	HR Managers[A]	Line Managers[A]
HR is an administrative department, not a strategic department.	51	60
HR doesn't provide enough support to line managers.	43	58
HR relies too much on best practices— some of which are inappropriate—when designing systems.	30	38
HR is not held accountable for success or failure of talent management initiatives.	36	64
Talent management is viewed as the responsibility of HR.	58	36
HR lacks authority/respect to influence the way people are managed.	38	47
HR lacks capabilities to develop talent strategies aligned with business objectives.	25	58

[A]Percentage of interviewees who agree with the statement.
Source: M. Guthridge, A.B. Komm, and E. Lawson, "Making Talent a Strategic Priority," *McKinsey Quarterly*, no. 1, 2008, pp. 49–59.

with the overall need of the global organization. Additionally, they may become so detached from the corporate functional specialists and the professional HR community in general that they gradually fall behind in terms of functional knowledge.

WHERE ARE THE BOUNDARIES OF HR?

So far, we have discussed the changing roles and tasks of the HR function. However, how should these tasks and roles be organized in the multinational firm? And with increasing reliance on external partners to deliver value to the final customer, what are the boundaries of HR's responsibility? Moreover, what is the boundary between the responsibility of line management for people processes and that of the HR function?

Three specific issues concerning the boundaries of the HR function are of particular importance:

- How should responsibilities be distributed between local, regional, and global HR units?
- To what extent should the HR function work with external business partners?
- How should the responsibility for HRM be divided between the HR function and line managers?

The Responsibilities of Local, Regional, and Global Units

In the past, the organization of HR activities in the multinational was approached on a simple binary scale—what should be centralized (global) and what should be decentralized (local)? This started to get more complex when a middle ground came into the picture—what should be coordinated and what should be carried out at a regional rather than a local or global level? Today we recognize that there are a variety of delivery mechanisms for HR activities—outsourced activities, tasks that are best undertaken by local businesses or countries, activities that should be managed by global or regional service centers and those that could best be run by centers of expertise, tasks that should be carried out by the corporate center, and complex activities that merit the attention of international committees or cross-border project groups. This is shown in Figure 14–1, where the two dimensions that guide the organization of HR activities are respectively the requirements of global integration, and differentiation by business or geography.

We have argued that the most strategic function of HRM in most firms, and notably in the multinational corporation, is management development for key positions and of those with the potential to occupy such roles.[34] Indeed, one study showed that firms that do not exercise tight central control over strategic talent face acute shortages of international managers, which handicaps the implementation of their global strategies.[35] This means that management, leadership, or talent development (whatever name is used by the firm) will be

---

FIGURE 14–1. Organization of HR in the Transnational Firm

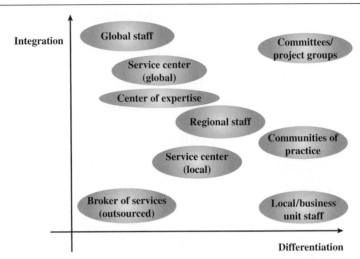

tightly integrated at the center, even in multidomestic companies. Local HR business support managers should have a strong dotted-line reporting relationship with global HR within their business, and sometimes a regional structure with a focus on talent management may be required. This is often the case in Asia, where the roles of local HR managers can be so operational that they do not have the professional know-how or network influence to get involved in leadership development.

Aside from this, what should be globally integrated through corporate HR staff depends on the strategy and the structure of the firm. For example, if the strategy for growth is based on international acquisitions, then managing acquisitions will be part of integrated corporate HR responsibility, as it is at Cisco. Some years ago, AT&T moved its top HR officer into a position heading up corporate acquisitions and ventures for this very reason. Whatever is deemed to be a corporate capability should be reflected in the structure of corporate responsibilities. Building a boundaryless organization has been a desired capability at GE, and so this is steered by the chief learning officer (CLO), who also heads up its Crotonville management development center. The CLO is responsible for managing the process of collecting, certifying, and transferring best practice know-how across the complex matrix of GE businesses.[36]

Some HR matters require a high degree of differentiation according to the country or business. Here the locus of decision making and action should lie with the local unit. In most companies, the recruitment and technical training of the operational workforce fall into this category. Owing to the country specificity of union relations, this tends to be true of collective bargaining—although that matter can come into question when there are regional trends such as EU social regulation or union pressure for cross-border negotiation of collective agreements.

The structure of the multinational will obviously influence the distribution of HR responsibilities. In locally responsive companies, most HR matters aside from senior leadership development will be decentralized to the local units, perhaps with some loose coordination—unless there are clear grounds for arguing otherwise. But many multinationals are shifting toward more global HR integration, where the situation is the reverse—local subsidiaries must adapt to central policies and guidelines, facilitated by parent company expatriates in key positions. However, with the pursuit of HR cost reduction, there is a risk that companies may reduce local HR staffing beyond a reasonable limit so that local units overwhelmed by operational tasks will lose their ability—and desire—to engage with headquarters on its global standardization and centralization of HR delivery, leading to suboptimal people management solutions.

It may be fairly clear how to handle activities that are at the extremes—high on either integration or on differentiation but not on the other dimension. But what about the many activities in the middle zone, when some measure of both global integration and differentiated solution by country or business unit is needed? Here, regional HR staff, regionally organized service centers, and centers of expertise may be useful ways to cope with activities requiring moderate integration and regional differentiation.[37] For example, some corporations that are structured around product lines have a regional structure in emerging markets such as Southeast Asia. In developed Western markets, the businesses have all the necessary HR experience and expertise, but this may not be the case for business units in Thailand or Argentina for example. There, an overlay of regional HR managers provides guidance and expertise to local management teams on recruitment, resourcing, development, expatriation, and the like.

Where Is the External Boundary of HR's Responsibilities?

Most competent HR professionals see themselves as customer-focused—but their customers are all internal to the firm. A provocative question for HR professionals is to ask how they add value to the external customer—"Justify your existence in terms of your added value, not to your *internal* customers, but to your *external* customers!" A focus solely on satisfying internal customers leads easily to a bits-and-pieces approach to HRM, rather than one that really contributes to the competitiveness of the firm.

GE managers have a response to that question. They use GE's mastery of HR foundations as a way of building relationships with its external customers: "If the customers are so impressed by our internal processes that they can learn from them, they'll stick with us as loyal purchasers of our products." So the HR function at GE acts as an adviser or external consultant to client firms on HR and management practices. United Technologies (UT) is another corporation with impressive HR practices. Some time ago we helped Pratt & Whitney, a company within the UT Group, to organize a conference on HRM for its potential clients in China, the regional airlines and the Chinese civil aviation authority. It achieved what technical partnerships and marketing strategy had not been able to pull off—attracting the participation of most of the airline presidents and party secretaries, who spent the evenings networking with Pratt & Whitney's top executives. And both Ericsson and Nokia have organized high-profile management training programs for customers as well as government organizations in China.

We find some outstanding HR executives who have had a prior career in marketing, and some who have joint responsibilities in a subsidiary for a client-facing marketing role as well as their HR position. Another external interface is working with suppliers on HRM issues that help them improve their effectiveness and, in some countries, their compliance with ethical standards and regulations. It is generally accepted today that multinationals have to take some responsibility for how their suppliers conduct their business. Failure to ensure that suppliers follow local labor laws and abide by international labor standards may cost the firm dearly in terms of international reputation. Many multinationals have therefore specified health, safety, environmental, and other labor standards that their suppliers have to follow, and compliance teams are responsible for making certain that the firms abide by these standards. An increasing number of multinational corporations are also hiring auditing firms to do supplier audits to ensure that the suppliers follow, among other matters, employee relations agreements.

The box "H&M Participates in the Fair Labor Association" describes how the Swedish clothing retailer H&M has worked with the Fair Labor Association (FLA) in China, joining the ranks of other participating companies such as Adidas, Nike, and Nordstrom.

H&M Participates in the Fair Labor Association

In 2006, H&M became a member of the Fair Labor Association (FLA), a coalition of companies, universities, and NGOs dedicated to protecting workers' rights and improving working conditions. Participation in the FLA involves a commitment to implementing the FLA's Workplace Code of Conduct, along with monitoring and remediation. The FLA's accreditation process requires a company's compliance program to undergo performance reviews over a two- to three-year period, including an audit of the company's internal monitoring protocols, training programs, and auditing systems. Companies must also submit to independent monitoring of their supplier facilities (FLA makes unannounced visits to some of H&M's suppliers' factories in China), develop corrective action plans for any problems found, and subject those plans to verification inspections.

Participating companies that have been accredited commit to continued implementation and independent monitoring, with reviews every three years for reaccreditation. The FLA publishes the results of the independent audits in a yearly report.

Source: http://www.hm.com/us/corporateresponsibility/ independentmonitoring__independentmonitoring.nhtml.

The Responsibility for HRM—Line Managers or HR?

Who is responsible for human resource management issues in the corporation—line management or the HR function? While the HR function obviously has a role in providing expertise and focused attention, the simple answer is that for HRM to be successful, *general managers at different levels* must be involved, and they must at least feel a shared responsibility.[38] First, general and top managers are responsible for preparing and implementing the strategy of the firm: human resources constrain strategy and its execution to such a degree, they would be foolish to delegate such matters to the HR function.[39] People factors are so constraining that general managers are obliged to get involved—indeed, they should typically be the drivers of talent management processes, as well as modeling performance management practices with their own behavior. Second, it is difficult to implement any policies and practices in a firm without at least some measure of involvement and visible support by line management. Third, the line managers who carry responsibility for the results can best make many of the operational decisions around people management—including recruitment and the selection of new employees, training and development decisions for their subordinates, and the management of the performance of employees in their units.

The broader question of *devolvement* of responsibility for HRM beyond general and top management to line managers throughout the organization is one that is more open.

The idea that people management is the prime responsibility of line managers, with the personnel function playing a support role, was already the theme of a 1970 best-selling book—*Every Employee a Manager*—based on the experience of Texas Instruments and other firms.[40] However, in other companies, questions of recruitment, promotion, talent development, performance evaluation, and the like are regarded as so strategically important that the HR function reports tightly to the CEO or general manager, with a low degree of devolvement to other line managers. The HR function often plays a policing role, or "guarded strategist" as it has been called, and we see this in some Chinese, French, and Scandinavian firms.[41]

The devolvement of responsibility to line managers for HRM issues has been studied for many years by HR scholars. Several rounds of surveys have shown that the degree of devolvement has steadily increased.[42] However, there remain clear differences across countries in how far the trend toward devolvement has proceeded. According to the latest European survey, Finland and Denmark have the highest level of devolvement, followed by the Netherlands and Norway. There is the least degree of devolvement in France, Italy, Ireland, and Spain.[43]

Research suggests that the devolution of HR activities to line managers has a positive impact on the image of the function.[44] Not surprisingly, firms where HR strategies and policies are decided upon and implemented by HR professionals sitting in ivory towers, detached from the business realities of line managers, are less likely to have an HR function that is seen to contribute significantly to the business results. However, the trend toward devolvement is not without problems:

- Line managers may not want the increased responsibility for HRM.
- Managers may not have time to deal with this role properly.
- They may not have the ability and up-to-date functional knowledge to handle HRM issues effectively.
- The views of some line managers may be limited by their own units' interests rather than reflecting a broad organizational and long-term perspective on people management issues.[45]

One of the reasons why attention to leadership development is so important is that managers who have worked outside their initial area of functional expertise, and who have received appropriate training and coaching, are more likely to view the management of people as a prime element of their leadership responsibility.[46] Inspiring and helping line managers to carry out successfully their responsibility for people management issues across borders is among the competencies that HR professionals need in today's corporations.

DEVELOPING THE CAPABILITIES OF THE HR FUNCTION

The expanding global scope of the HR function imposes new staffing and skills requirements. What are the competencies needed by HR professionals and managers today and in the future, and how can multinationals develop these competencies? For the last 15 years, this question has received more and more attention.

HR Competencies

A number of competence frameworks for people working in the HR function have been developed. An influential model developed by Ulrich and his coauthors distinguished between "knowledge of business," "functional expertise," and "management of change," reflecting the growing conviction of many that HR involves more than just professional functional know-how.[47] A more recent competence framework proposed by Ulrich and Brockbank suggests that the necessary competencies cluster around six roles:[48]

- Credible activist (taking a credible position on issues).
- Culture and change steward (shaping the culture and facilitating change).
- Talent manager/organization designer.
- Strategy architect (engaging customers and sustaining strategic agility).
- Business ally (articulating the value proposition and interpreting social context).
- Operational executor (daily HR administration and policy).

Other general competence frameworks—generally anchored in a performance-based view of competencies[49]—have also been presented, often containing a large number of individual skills, knowledge areas, and personal characteristics.[50]

General frameworks can provide a useful starting point for assessing the competence needs of the global HR function as some issues—such as business understanding, general functional knowledge, and a global mindset— are likely to be useful for all professionals and managers working in the HR function of global organizations. For instance, it is crucial for functional specialists developing new HR tools and content to understand how to translate the business needs of the firms into appropriate HR processes. HR people in business support roles must be able to provide insightful advice on most functional aspects of people management. And a global mindset helps the head of HR service centers deal with the local–regional–global tensions involved in HR service delivery.

However, for those in senior HR leadership positions, focusing only on performance-based competencies may have limited value. These leadership roles also require strong strategy-based competencies. Strategies need to be translated into behaviors through bold talent management and culture change actions, and the implementation of a new strategy requires many of the HR change facilitation skills that were outlined in Chapter 11. To make new strategies come alive, HR leaders should ideally be coaching line managers in how to walk their own talk. Indeed, given the growing importance of values-based leadership in many multinational corporations such as IBM and Infosys, which see values as the binding glue for a talented workforce, the role of HR leadership in helping top management to make explicit their values and act in accordance is likely to become more important in the future.

In addition, the competencies of local HR managers will vary significantly according to the strategic orientation of the multinational firm in question. In multidomestic firms, the skill requirements will tend to mirror the local norms and the demands of the general manager. However, this often means that local HR managers in multidomestic firms are ill equipped to meet the talent management demands that the corporate headquarters may like them to assume. If the multidomestic firm is to move toward becoming a transnational, this may require the creation of a strong regional infrastructure supporting development of future leaders.[51]

As a meganational corporation moves in a transnational direction, one of the most challenging international HR roles is that of local or regional HR managers. This requires a combination of strong networking, negotiation, and conflict management skill. When a decision comes from headquarters concerning a head count reduction or a new reorganization, the local HR person is responsible for facilitating its implementation locally. However, there are likely to be local obstacles of which headquarters has no understanding—local legal constraints, local competitive circumstances, the resistance of some key regional stakeholders. Without having any particular authority, the local HR manager has to negotiate an acceptable plan, working through his or her network of contacts locally, in other comparable countries, at headquarters, in the line as well as the HR function—and also drawing upon advice from peers in other local multinationals.

Local and regional HR manager positions are invaluable opportunities for the development of network leadership competencies, as described earlier in this chapter. Then, when people skilled in network leadership move into key HR roles at the corporate center, this will further facilitate consolidation of global mindset in the whole organization— leading to an appropriate steering of global talent and performance management processes.

There are also important differences in the competence requirements associated with the different roles played by the HR function.[52] Deep functional knowledge is the natural basis for the *HRM process and content development* role. This means being well connected to professional networks consisting of academics, consultants, and colleagues both within and beyond the own company. Given the lack of formal authority in this role, the ability to engage in network leadership is a prerequisite for doing a good job in this domain.

Managers in charge of *HR service delivery* are typically evaluated on cost and service quality measures, and they require a combination of two different skill sets. On the one hand, they need "factory management" and process competencies, and on the other hand, they require a high degree of sophistication in HR process and content to manage the exceptions to the standard service norms and identify those that raise questions of policy. Additionally, in the multinational enterprise, the ability to handle tensions is part of any senior service delivery job. There are likely to be tensions between standardization and scale advantages on the one hand, and demands for local responsiveness and individual treatment of internal customers (individuals and business units) on the other.

The *business support* role has attracted the most attention when it comes to the competence requirements for HR, at least in Western multinationals. There is general agreement that the business support role requires a generalist HR competence profile and a profound business understanding. As the "HR manager in the line," the role of credible activist involves advising senior managers about issues closely related to the core capabilities of the firm, placing an emphasis on the influence of the person occupying this role, and the ability to function as a sparring partner.[53]

Table 14–3 provides some advice from experienced business support executives on what is important in order to play this sparring partner role. Building strong personal relationships with line management is even more important than in the other HR roles in order to influence HRM decision making and day-to-day activities in the line organization. Having work experience outside HR adds the greatest value to this role since it provides an understanding of internal customers' perspectives as well as credibility with line management. According to a UK study, 83 percent of the HR directors of large corporations had experience outside HR, notably in sales or operations.[54]

TABLE 14–3. Some Advice from Experienced Business Support Executives on Playing the Role of "Trusted Adviser" to Senior Line Executives

- Become a *Deep generalist.*
- *Listen deeply*—then argue and act.
- On people issues, always make the *business case.*
- *Think and talk straight*—but respect confidences and show deference.
- *Go out on a limb*—but admit mistakes.

Source: Adapted from B. Gandossy and A. Sobel, "Trusted Adviser," *Human Resource Executive*, October 20, 2002.

Personal credibility, global mindset, business acumen, and, as we argue below, international and cross-functional experience are arguably vital for those who advance to the *HR director* level in large multinationals. The résumés of HR directors in some multinational corporations are a testimony to this. For example, Hallstein Mörck (a Norwegian by nationality who has worked in a number of countries) was recruited to the HR director position at Nokia from a senior line position at HP, where at one point of his career he was also responsible for the regional HR function.

Developing HR Managers for the Transnational Firm

There are two fundamental ways to develop the capabilities of the HR function in the multinational firm: first, developing existing HR professionals and second, transferring persons from other functions.

Competence Development

The obstacles to globalization of the HR function are partly individual in nature—transnational development requires changes in roles, competencies, and career structures. One of the paradoxes is that while HR has a vital role to play in enterprise globalization, which is often openly espoused by those in central HR positions, the reality is that many HR managers and professionals at headquarters have little if any international experience. In fact, of all functions, HR tends to have the least foreign experience. Worse still, because they take a plane from time to time to visit the subsidiaries abroad, managers may *think* that they have a truly international perspective. We joke that there is only one thing more dangerous than the executive who has never been to India—the executive who spent two weeks in India and who is now an Indian expert! Sometimes the corporate HR executive who takes an occasional plane trip around the world suffers from a delusion that he or she has the answer to all the subsidiary problems.

A similar challenge exists at the local level. While multinational companies make sure that their future line executives have varied international experience, this does not always apply to their high potential local HR managers, who may not be exposed to many cross-border opportunities. In addition, local

HR managers often have highly operational roles focused on recruitment and training, without the skills to play strategic roles in long-term development. Therefore, in companies such as Schlumberger, talent development and other strategic tasks requiring coordination skills are the responsibility of high-potential HR staff working in regional HR roles who thereby acquire international experience.

A high degree of *mobility* is essential. Many of the HR professionals who are promoted to top corporate positions within the function do so after having gone through a zigzag pathway. Their careers may contain moves both within and, increasingly, outside the function, with participation in global, cross-functional projects as an additional developmental activity. The advantages of mobility are straightforward and have been summarized by an HR director as follows: "[My work] as a general business manager . . . improved my understanding and credibility with line managers. It also broadened my skills giving me better all round understanding of a business."[55]

A subtle but powerful tool, *mentoring relationships*, is increasingly complementing developmental vehicles such as mobility.[56] Many firms pair up HR and line people, headquarters and field people, and HR and IT people. At Cisco, HR staff members have a business mentor—they prepare their personal development plans with this partner, typically someone in sales (the same applies to sales and engineering, establishing key linkages). *Shadowing* is a related developmental mechanism used by some firms, where junior HR professionals are assigned as "shadows" to line managers working on important international projects. This allows them to get involved in international business activities, to learn the ropes, and to figure out how HR can add value to such projects.

HR professionals often get valuable exposure in *formal training programs*.[57] Many corporations are training their middle and senior HR managers in strategic and business knowledge and skills. Such programs will never develop a "business leader," but they can foster the confidence to question line management and to play a more active role as a sparring partner or credible activist. Action learning assignments for cross-national teams of HR professionals with different functional roles are a natural part of HR competence development programs in multinationals. Although there are many advantages to organizing separate programs for the HR function (these can be tailor-made to the needs of the function and used to develop global HR practices through action learning assignments), individual HR professionals can also benefit greatly from participating in regional or global cross-functional management development.

Of course, not everyone working in HR will be able to develop the competencies required for new roles. The following quote from an HR director describes what may happen:

We've been raising business partners from the basics up . . . encouraging them to becoming strong business influencers. The move is from that of "helper" to cutting edge, transformational roles. We started four years ago, and took out half of 50 generalists. We worked on a dozen but only three made it to the end of the assessment and development. It was a painful process.[58]

Internal Transfers

How do you get high-potential individuals to request a transfer into the HR function? HR professionals often receive lower salaries than do their colleagues in other functions, and the HR function is sometimes seen as a dead end, a less interesting career move. Furthermore, it appears that many line and HR managers alike believe that the caliber of people in the HR function is not on par with that of other corporate functions.

If one accepts that mobility (both cross-functional and international) is the most important tool for leadership development,[59] then HR should be on the map of functions through which high-potential individuals will move. Many companies accept this in principle—"It would be great to give our high potentials experience in an HR staff role." However, companies where this is common practice, like Singapore Airlines and Mars, are the exception rather than the rule.

Our experience is that companies are tackling the wrong end of the problem. Rather than trying to attract talented line managers who have a gift for people management *into* the HR function, they should instead tackle the problem of exit routes *out of* the HR function. In many firms, HR has a reputation for being a one-way path—once you are in it, you will never get out of the function. Unfortunately, this perception has sometimes been reinforced by a practice of using senior HR positions as a parking ground for loyal executives whose careers in general management did not work out for one reason or another.

One will never attract good people into HR unless there are clear routes out of that domain. The issue is of considerable importance to the multinational firm. HR does not control price, costs, quality, or flexibility—the parameters that directly impact business results.[60] The right for a place at the executive committee table has to be earned. HR leaders can have a tremendously positive influence on profitable growth, but only if they are superbly competent. This is unlikely to be the situation unless the function can attract the very best talent—by allowing this talent also to move out of HR into top line management roles.

One additional issue is worth mention. Companies occasionally appoint non-HR professionals directly to senior positions in HR, even as head of the function. Such appointments usually indicate that top management perceives there to be a lack of business understanding within the HR function. However, this brings about the danger that the evils of one extreme—excessive professionalism where the means become the end—are replaced by equal evils of another extreme—reinventing the wheel, trying to score quick wins, failing to understand the powerful principles of coherence and consistency—ultimately undermining of the credibility of the HR function itself. Ultimately, a non-professional—lacking solid functional HR expertise—will again be replaced by an HR expert charged with restoring professional depth.[61] This can become another destructive pendulum, so rotation of line managers through HR needs to be supplemented with deep HR professionalism in the rest of the function.

GLOBAL CHALLENGES WORTH STANDING UP FOR

The HR function has often been considered as an implementer, focusing on the operational role in the bottom of our split egg concept. But what are the "top of the egg" projects or issues that HR should stand up for? In our view, the HR function will never be considered a vital contributor to organizational success unless it constructively fights for perspectives that safeguard both the competitive and the long-term interests of the enterprise. We would like to illustrate what is required by looking outside of the traditional HR domain at four issues worth fighting for:

- Building a competitive culture.
- Standing for organizational sustainability.
- Fighting for the long-term perspective.
- Taking into account the social implications of globalization.

Building a Competitive Culture

The primary purpose of HRM is to ensure competitiveness of the organization. It is the success of the enterprise in the market, not lofty statements on people as "our most important assets", that secures financial and career opportunities for the employees. Therefore, focus on competitive performance and the development of competitive culture must be at the foundation of all HRM activities.

No One Remembers Number Two

One Japanese company that has always maintained its competitiveness is Honda. Honda had to fight for its existence from its early days. The Japanese government, which felt that there were too many auto producers, did not support Honda's entry into the car business. One factor that helped Honda to survive and prosper was its highly competitive culture.

During the early 1990s, the company was not doing well in its home market. One of the hot debates inside the firm was over whether it should continue Formula 1 racing. This was not a technical issue but one about the approach to management development. Honda had always used Formula 1 racing to mold the attitudes of future executives, putting fast trackers on the team supporting the racing specialists.

One thing you learn in Formula 1 racing is that the only thing that counts is to be number one. Nobody cares who number two is. You do not come to the race saying that my strategic objective is to be a strong number two. You might end up number two or number four, but there will be another race. You must figure out what went wrong and try again. So you learn.

The second thing with Formula 1 is teamwork. You can have a brilliant driver, a superb mechanic, and a great engineer, but the only way to win is if you put the whole thing together right. It is a powerful message. What counts is not just you as an individual but also how you work as a team.

Third, you learn that you had better be on time. If your car is late on the starting line, then you have no chance of winning. There are no excuses. The same is true for quality. If on the 23rd lap the transmission catches fire, you cannot say that it is the fault of the supplier. You end up as a footnote, a car that dropped out of the race.

Honda saw Formula 1 racing as teaching an even more fundamental principle. Once the race starts, there is nothing a manager can do to influence the result. Once the race has started, giving instructions over the walkie-talkie will only mess things up. The only thing that you can do is go to the grandstand, observe what happens, and go back after the race to tell people what went well and what went not so well—and help them to win next time round.

The debate at Honda over whether to keep Formula 1 was heated. Some Honda executives felt that the messages conveyed were too one-sided, getting managers to pay less attention to auto manufacturing basics such as energy efficiency and emission standards. The debate was not so much over costs but over the signals that one sends to the organization. Honda eventually decided to get out of Formula 1 (though it has since returned and left again), but it still pays strong attention to making sure that the idea of competition is well understood within the global enterprise.

Guiding Values and Philosophy

The fact that there was hot debate over whether Honda's Formula 1 racing was giving the right signals is not an indication of unhealthy corporate politics— quite the contrary. When circumstances change, there must be such debate over what norms and values should guide behavior. Senior executives and high-potential managers in particular must internalize the new values.

Highly competitive cultures typically have explicit values, indeed often an explicit philosophy like the Toyota Way or the Lincoln Electric value system. The reason this is desirable, perhaps vital, is to guide consistency—it is the coherence and consistency between the practices that creates a competitive culture, not the practices themselves. Many firms try to increase their competitive culture by introducing more transparency of measurement and performance-based rewards. However, they find that this has only a token effect on the underlying culture. A coherent set of practices, down to the little details such as how the janitor is treated and whether free beverage machines are installed, needs to be guided by a well-thought-out and clearly understood management philosophy. The intense discussion at Honda and the decade-long reconsideration of the tenets of the HP Way reflect a process of internalizing a modification in guiding values that will pay off in a new but consistent configuration of practices.[62] A firm that decrees new practices or new values at a single weekend conference for key staff is unlikely to enjoy any competitive benefits.

Moreover, the translation of value systems into competitive cultures typically will involve working through conflicts and dualistic tensions, just as Honda's Formula 1 training captures tensions over when managers should be hands-on and when they should be hands-off. Another tension to be anchored in the culture through the careful design of HR practices is that between competition (in the shape of individual accountability and comparison) and teamwork.[63]

Organizational Sustainability

In May 1996, five climbers, members of two international climbing expeditions, including two of the best-known Himalayan expedition leaders at the time, perished on the descent from the summit of Mount Everest. The unfolding tragedy was captured in several best-selling books and films, including cases taught in business schools around the world.[64]

A number of incidents—many seemingly irrelevant when they occurred—contributed to the fatal outcome. However, one factor seemed to play a decisive role. Until the very last day of the climb, all team members were reminded by their leader about the cardinal rule of the Mount Everest ascent: "If you are not at the top at 2 pm, you turn back and come down." Without such a definite rule in place, there was a danger that in pursuit of their lifelong dream, climbers would endanger themselves and their teammates and miss a window to descend safely during daylight. Yet on the fateful day, only a handful of climbers from the two teams turned back below summit at the predetermined hour. The rest continued to climb towards the top—including the two leaders who did not turn the teams around. When a fierce storm unexpectedly hit the top of the mountain, many of the climbers were caught unprepared, completely exhausted, too high up to come down safely. At this altitude, most people cannot survive the night.

When we discuss this case in corporate leadership programs, the blame for breaking the rules and the tragic end of the expedition is quickly put squarely on the leaders. They did not walk the talk, they broke the rule they themselves set, so they are responsible for their own deaths and those of several others. But why did so many others follow the leaders beyond the point of no return?

Clearly, some continued to climb because they trusted the judgment of their leaders. After all, they wanted to reach the top, and the concern that they would have to turn back close to the summit was always on their mind. When there was no order to turn back, they did not object.

Yet there were those who knew better—several experienced guides and local Sherpas. They knew very well that by continuing the climb they were putting their own lives at risk and that by not questioning the wrong decision by the leaders, they were risking the survival of the whole team. But they all maintained silence.

Following the disasters, some of them were asked why they went along with what they knew was a bad decision. The answers were chilling:

- "I was number three in the team. It was not my job to make the decision."
- "I looked at X, and he said nothing, so I decided to stay quiet."
- "If I questioned my boss, I would not be hired again."

All these would perhaps be reasonable answers in the context of a large bureaucratic organization facing an unpopular truth, but this was a life-and-death situation at the top of the highest mountain in the world—yet people did not speak up even when their own lives were at risk. The simple fact is that challenging how things are done in an organization, even if its survival is at stake, is a very difficult task.

Unfortunately, there is no shortage of companies that were caught up in the storm and lost their way. Some survived (Ahold, Siemens, Shell), but other disappeared (Enron, Worldcom)—and thousands lost their jobs. The "2 pm" rules these companies broke were diverse, but two factors in all these cases were in common: (1) Scores of people were aware that the rules were being broken, and (2) virtually no one spoke up until it was too late. If no one speaks up, the very existence of the organization—its sustainability—can be at risk. Justifiably, society has less and less tolerance for those who break the rules.[65]

Preserving organizational sustainability is an emerging HR domain. In ABB, which has a heavy exposure to markets in some emerging countries where corruption is still rife, the new rule of accountability for living up to the corporate governance rule is simple. Full compliance is the general manager's responsibility—and that of HR. If things are done the wrong way, for whatever reason, either the HR head knows and chooses to remain silent, and there will be consequences, or he or she does not know—but should—which is equally unacceptable. The logic is harsh but simple—if the organization had a climate of openness, someone would have spoken up—and now HR is responsible.

Fighting for the Long-Term Perspective

Building a healthy sustainable organization requires a long-term perspective. However, while everyone acknowledges the importance of a long-term perspective, all the pressures foster a short-term orientation. Quarterly reports driven by accountability to shareholders are becoming the norm, even in Japan and Germany with their traditionally longer-term horizons. Ideas of long-term employment and careers are increasingly incompatible with the immediate pressure to be flexible and responsive. Not least of all, the future has become quite unpredictable, leading to the demise of long-term planning.

Yet HR must stand for the long-term perspective. Investments in human and social capital take time to yield rewards. Those rewards are rich in providing competitive advantage precisely because it will take others a long time to catch up. We confess to being worried when we see HR executives ceding to the pressures of our times, saying that the bottom line is the only thing that counts. Sure, HR managers must demonstrate a high quality of operational professionalism and keep an eye on efficiency. However, at a time when the long-term perspective is often compromised, HR wins its credibility both by being highly professional in its day-by-day role *and* by acting as the guardian of the long term. As we argued earlier, HR leaders need to keep future growth in mind when everyone else is taking the axe in the pits of recession—and keep the future downturn in mind when people are scrambling to exploit immediate growth opportunities.

Acting as the guardian of the long term does not mean cumbersome planning systems in which abstract future strategies are translated into present implications on the drawing boards of planners. It means catalyzing and persuading senior managers to think through their values and formalize them. Yes, a business can survive well in the short term without values. But it is questionable whether the powerful coherence of all the elements of organization that provide sustainable competitive advantage can be achieved without the strong thread that is provided by a value system.

If layoffs are necessary for the survival of the firm, then acting as a guardian of the long term means fighting to ensure that these layoffs will be undertaken in a humane and socially responsible manner and by making sure that the capabilities that are necessary for future competitiveness are retained. Certainly, a firm will survive in the short term if layoff notices are sent by mass e-mail to people who have dedicated their lives to the organization. Yet it is questionable if such a firm will thrive in the future when it has undermined all vestiges of loyalty and trust.

Acting as a guardian means fighting to ensure that the person who gets a key job in a local subsidiary is not always the best available (or best connected) local employee but sometimes an individual from another subsidiary who may benefit from an international experience. A subsidiary may do quite well in the short term by focusing on developing its own people, but it is doubtful if the multinational can prosper unless its future leaders have adopted the global mindset that can only be developed by international experience.

What this means is that the HRM role, whether it is exercised by the line manager or the HR professional, is to put the long-term consequences on the table for debate. HR has little decision power, but it has an obligation to get dilemmas, dualities, and tensions out on the table for discussion. Sometimes the outcome will favor the short term, sometimes the long term. This is not simply acting as the social conscience of the firm; it is constructively fighting to ensure that due attention is given to the opposite position that others in the organization may be neglecting.

What does this mean in practice? The future may be unpredictable, and this rules out conventional long-term planning. But if one accepts that there is a pattern that leads from the present to the future, then *anticipation* is the quality that is desperately needed. There appears to be such a pattern or rhythm to life and to organizations. This rhythm is defined by the tension between dualities—the underlying theme of our chapter on managing change, and indeed behind this book. It is seen in the phenomena of paradox, in pendulum swings, and in the pathologies that occur when people or organizations take something positive to an extreme.

Often, what determines who gets to the top in a firm is the ability to anticipate. When the firm is focused on decentralization, the person who ultimately gets ahead is frequently the one who anticipates that the pendulum will one day swing to integration. When the pendulum does begin to swing, the board will say, "There's an individual who was foresighted." The same is likely to apply to HR in multinational firms. There, leaders must learn to anticipate the need for greater international coordination when they have structures that are built around local entrepreneurship, or vice versa, anticipating the need for local entrepreneurship when their structures focus on global integration. They must learn to organize one way but manage the other way. They must learn to build the future into the present.

The Social Implications of Globalization

One of the coauthors was invited by the ILO (the International Labor Office in Geneva that is part of the UN family) to chair a panel of distinguished business leaders discussing the theme of "human resource–based competitive strategies." The panel discussed the talent war that was raging, the importance of localization, and the challenges of leadership and innovation that Western and Japanese companies face in the struggle to be globally competitive. When the panel shared these observations in the plenary session, there was a strong reaction from the representatives of the third world, who constituted a good part of the audience. "What incredibly elitist ideas! In your discussions of talent, in your attempts to localize management in China and Indonesia, you are focusing on 2 percent, maybe 5 percent of the world's population. The other 95 percent are not worried about talent. They are just worried about keeping their jobs and having enough food for their family to survive."

There is a great deal of truth to the argument. Acceleration of globalization and the triumph of markets since 1989 have brought immense economic benefits to the world's population, including many of the poor. Some countries in Asia, such as Singapore and Korea, have gone in 50 years from third-world to first-world status. The purchasing power of the average citizen in China has more than quadrupled since the early 1990s. Thriving middle classes have emerged in previously poor countries with a profound impact on economic and social development.[67] And there has been increasing business attention to those at "the bottom of the pyramid," with the beginnings of some profound change in thinking about the poor.[68] Yet the majority of the world's population still falls into the category of being far below what we would regard as subsistence level of existence. Entire regions such as many parts of Africa suffer from deeper and seemingly intractable economic deprivation, fueling social conflict, political instability, and what appears to be a growing number of countries and regions that are viewed as ungovernable.

Economic progress is a relative matter. The protest against globalization could be safely dismissed if one could show that the world's income distribution has also become more equal in the past few decades. Combined with the increase in absolute standards of living, this would be powerful proof for the all-around virtues of globalization. Unfortunately, the evidence does not clearly support this view.[69]

Although there are big statistical problems in measuring global inequality and trends in income distribution,[70] studies show that global inequality has not become smaller.[71] While there has been an undeniable trickle-down effect to growing middle classes, it appears that net differences between rich and poor within many countries, notably between rural and urban China and India but also within Western countries,[72] have been widening. Technological change and uncontrolled financial liberalization have led to a disproportionately rapid increase in income at the extreme rich end of the populations, while the income of the extreme poor has changed little. The verdict is still out on the impact of the economic turbulence in 2008-2009, but it may only exacerbate this trend.[73]

So the rich are getting richer—globalization allows a top performer to capitalize on his or her talents throughout the entire globe rather than just in a single region or country. The concept of talent has a corrosive face to it, as Malcolm Gladwell commented: The new talent mind-set orthodoxy becomes a justification for self-serving behaviors,[74] while others struggle in a patchwork world without careers or any assurance of jobs.[75] The gaps are widening, and new forms of inequality are appearing. Why should we be concerned?

In our view, globalization and free markets have brought with them immense benefits. Most leading sociologists, developmental economists, psychologists, and social commentators are supporters of globalization and free market competition. They are aware of the benefits that these have brought to the human race and to them in particular. However, many are consciously or unconsciously aware of the dynamics of duality. Some emphasize the need to be conscientious about helping the poor regardless of inequality; others feel that inequality is the principal challenge.[76] The poor peasants in rural China can watch the well-off middle class in Shanghai on their new television screens. The poor in slums of Latin America or South Africa are only a stone's throw away from the rich. And those who lost their jobs in the global recession brought on by unscrupulous financial wizardry can read in the press about how now-retired wizards are enjoying their gains. In either case, if the benefits of economic growth are not shared more equally and if more is not done to eliminate poverty, we risk undermining what we have won. The global age that we have created is precarious.

History shows that the dynamics of duality and contradiction lead to backlashes that undermine what is virtuous. The historian Arnold Toynbee argued that this was the basic pattern underlying the rise and fall of civilizations.[77] Societies would take their success formula to the extreme, leading to an unraveling of civilizations such as the Roman Empire or the Spanish Empire of the middle ages. Too much of a good thing is bad, as another concerned commentator, Charles Handy, emphasizes.[78] Excesses and backlashes have historically undermined the virtues of what led to civilization or growth or success in the first place, leading to historic dark ages of confusion and social floundering. Three current issues increase the risk of such a backlash:

- The first issue is the increasing concern about the impact of economic growth on the sustainability of the economic system, from depletion of energy and food sources, to pollution and global warming. One of the premises of globalization is that economic growth is good—when the wisdom of pursuing economic growth is questioned, so is globalization.

- The second issue is the credibility of free markets and the global financial system—both underpinning globalization. Indeed, in the long term, markets are self-regulating; speculative bubbles will not last forever. However, are the risks shared equally? When the penalty for excess is pushed on the weakest, there are inevitable calls for more restrictions and regulations—not only on the flows of capital, but also on flows of trade. Yet without free trade, globalization will wither.
- The third issue focuses on the political context of globalization. The United States is viewed around the world as the strongest proponent of globalization, at least in terms of the direction desired for the world economy. However, the excesses of American foreign policies after 9/11 created distrust in many parts of the world community, which will take time to heal. When globalization is perceived, rightly or wrongly, as delivering benefits in an unequal manner, the first question to ask is, In whose interest?

Handy's major critique is that capitalism and globalization lack a human face. Shareholder value makes no one feel proud, spiraling expectations lead to disenchantment, the pursuit of another dollar provides no meaning to life once the basics of maintenance are assured. He points out that even Keynes noted that capitalism was such a soulless philosophy that it was unlikely to be attractive unless it was remarkably successful. Handy's concerns are shared by a constituency of leading business figures, including Bill Gates and George Soros.

Why should such matters be of importance to HRM and the HR function? After all, the HR function cannot do anything about such complex issues. Yet if HR takes a passive stance, it condemns itself at best to pedestrian irrelevance, at worst to be sanctioned by history as a guardian of the status quo. At a minimum, HR professionals need to be cognizant of the vital social debates that will shape the course of our lives in the future. Better still, at least those working the field of international HR need to be proactive partners in this debate. Ideally, HR should be a vital catalyst in building *socially responsible competitive cultures*—businesses that create sustainable economic value for all stakeholders. HRM cannot "solve" this oxymoron, but it can influence it in powerful ways.

The potential backlash against globalization is most likely to be unleashed on the multinational enterprises that are both the principal agents and beneficiaries of this process—the elephants that mate with other elephants, as Handy calls them.[79] These elephants are so necessary to us since they transfer technology, take ideas from throughout the world and develop them, and provide jobs and livelihoods to billions of people. "How can I be confident that these elephants will continue to do good in the world?" asks Handy. His answer is that this depends entirely on the moral values of the people—the *mahouts*—who are riding the elephants.

The media and world opinion will increasingly hold business leaders accountable for the actions of their corporations. They must grapple on the one hand with the pressures of increasing shareholder value—pressures that come from us, the well-off citizens, since we have invested our future pensions in their success. However, they must also be equally concerned with the still widespread poverty in the world around us, the fragility of the ecosystem, and the potential consequences of increasing inequality.

Therefore, faced with the delicate questions of balance in maintaining and exploiting a global economy, the leaders of tomorrow need to combine business pragmatism with global vision, social and environmental conscience with economic realism, and awareness of the imperatives of the present with awareness of how the future must be shaped—for the benefit of all of us. It is not the task of HR to resolve the world's dilemmas. However, HR policies and practices from leadership development to performance management shape, consciously or unconsciously, the orientations and value systems of those entrusted with responsibility to address the challenge.

HRM AS TENSION MANAGEMENT

Contradiction is the defining characteristic of the transnational enterprise. As we have moved into this global era, an era that may be lasting or short-lived, so we have moved into a world of visible paradox, contradiction, and duality—and the tensions that these create. These tensions can lead us to frustration, vicious circles, and decline, or they can inspire us with vitality and purpose. It is not profit or human fulfillment or innovation that are the dependent variables that we seek to understand, but the tensions that are created by the interplay between these parameters of life.

The global era that we live in is fragile, of very recent origin. It is imbued by tensions that we must learn to recognize and work through. Remember that it is for the second time in a hundred years now that we are on the threshold of a global world. The first time was in the "golden age" of the early 20th century that ended with the destructive tensions leading to World War I and the 30 years of turmoil that followed.

Some of the tensions relating to HRM that we have debated in this book underlie the principles shown in the box "Guidelines for Global Leadership in the 21st Century." A duality is embedded in each of these guidelines, with the tension between its opposite poles. For example, the duality between exploration and exploitation is embedded in the idea that "to innovate you need slack, diversity, flexible budgets, and lots of experimentation . . . and to make profits from your innovations you need discipline, targets, and deadlines." The global–local duality is embedded in others, and the reader will find short-term/long-term, change–continuity, accountability–teamwork, and other dualities. One can clearly see that if anything positive is taken to an extreme, then it risks creating a pathology. Armed with surveys and statistical tools, researchers in the future will undoubtedly unravel the dimensions of these dualities and the tensions they create.[80]

If we accept that we live in a world of dynamic tensions, then this brings deeper challenges to our ways of thinking. As managers, people of action, we

Guidelines for Global Leadership in the 21st Century

Understand cultural stereotypes	. . . but don't use them in practice.
Be sensitive to local culture and context	. . . but make sure that a person's passport is of no importance.
Make sure that responsibilities and accountabilities are clear	. . . and then focus on building teamwork where it will add value.
Organize one way (for example a globally integrated structure)	. . . but manage the other way (to encourage local entrepreneurship).
Benchmark against others, copy practices, network externally to learn	. . . but never forget that superior performance comes only from being different.
Foster constructive debate about your options and alternatives	. . . so that you will have no debate when it comes to action.
To innovate you need slack, diversity, flexible budgets, and lots of experimentation	. . . and to make profits from your innovations you need discipline, targets, and deadlines.
The more valuable the know-how that you have in one part of the firm	. . . the more you are going to have to invest to transfer and exploit it to other parts of the firm.
Tackle "sour" processes like global rationalization and layoffs today	. . . with the awareness that you will need teamwork, commitment, and loyalty tomorrow.
Be prepared to cannibalize what makes you a leader today	. . . in order to have a chance of being a leader tomorrow.
Nurture your capabilities by fine-tuning the coherence that lies behind them	. . . but don't forget that these strengths can be your biggest liabilities.
Develop your people by giving them more challenge than they think they can handle	. . . and train them, coach them, and guide them so they won't make big mistakes.
Organizational values and management philosophy provide the consistency underlying great organizational cultures	. . . and they can lead to cloning, kill the lifeblood of innovation, and lead to the weakness of strong cultures.
Build face-to-face relationships well	. . . so that you can use e-technology to bridge the distance.
Make sure that your future leaders have business line experience	. . . in order to function effectively in key country or regional leadership roles.
Work hard as a professional in your operational job	. . . in order to find a maximum of time for your project role.
Matrix everything	. . . except the structure.
Embrace market competition	. . . but with human values in mind.
Invent locally	. . . and act globally.

are trained to think in terms of coming up with solutions. However, there are no "solutions" to tensions. The dualities that underlie them cannot be resolved once and for all. Early researchers on duality and tension rightly used the metaphor of the seesaw.[81] The manager, and particularly the leader, stands with two feet on either side of the fulcrum of the seesaw. The seesaw can never be balanced—the notion of balance or stable equilibrium is a poor image. The seesaw is in constant motion, moving from one side to the other, and the role of the leader is to anticipate and counteract with movement in the other direction. The result of good leadership can be a harmonious and enjoyable game of fluid movement that is enjoyed by all—or it can be a bitter struggle that leads all participants to opt out of the game. We have used the related image of the sailor, the navigator, whose task it is to anticipate the winds ahead.

Because there is no solution that the leader can provide, the nature of the game is different from in the past. It is a game that cannot be played unless all of the key participants understand the nature of seesaw processes. This is what we mean by "global mindset"—understanding the nature of this global seesaw. And one of the questions for human resource management is how to foster a widespread global mindset. That is the one of the aims behind this book.

Where is human resource management heading in the era of globalization? The notion of people as resources was born in the minds of scholars and social observers earlier last century as a result of these seesaw dynamics. Attention at the time was focused on natural and financial resources. People were treated by economists as "labor," a "factor" of production. There was a seesaw reaction against this—shouldn't people be treated as a resource on a par with other factors generating wealth? What about "human" resources? And then this was adopted by the world of practice to umbrella a host of developments and initiatives that were wider than the technical concerns of personnel management. The HR function was born in the early 1970s.

Today, almost 50 years later, the phrase *human resource management* is on everyone's lips. No one can deny its fundamental importance, and a vast literature on HRM has been produced. But this brings new challenges. Is HRM a line responsibility, ultimately of top general management, or a functional role? Should the HR function focus on the vital but ever-changing foundations or basics, or should it also be concerned with the bigger issues, such as those discussed above—coping with the tensions of a global society?

It is not just practicing managers that have different views. Academic scholars are divided. When we organized a workshop on the shape of international human resource management, convening the top scholars from both sides of the Atlantic, they were split in their views. One-half argued forcefully that research should focus on the challenging basics of HRM, while the other half suggested equally forcefully that the field of HRM should be a central player in the big strategic and social debates that will determine the future of our world.

Our own stance in this debate is quite predictable for those who have read through our book until this closing section. It is not a question of either/or—HR's role is to face up to *both* of these. One cannot be met without the other, just as the top part of our split egg role (the project role) needs the bottom half of the egg (the operational role). People have to learn to work in split egg ways—and that includes those in the HR function. Unless they have the big picture of dualistic tensions in mind through their work on broader organizational and societal projects, HR managers will always be followers rather than leaders in the vital task of realigning the constantly changing basics of HRM. And unless they are focused on the tangible practices of operational human resource management, they will be out of a job.

What is our scenario for the future of HRM? Whither HRM? There are many different scenarios. At the corporate level, the convergence between IT, planning, learning and knowledge management, and HR—and the tensions between these functions—may well lead in the near future to the emergence of new functional labels that relegate the HR function to the history books. Alternatively, the HR function may play a spearheading role in the management of tensions. The future, as an interplay between these different forces, is unpredictable.

We ourselves are strong advocates of the role that HRM in general and the HR function in particular can play in this era of tension and paradox. But we are reminded of the words of Georges Doriot. The late General Doriot was one of those remarkable sages. He was French-born but a US citizen, quartermaster general for the American armed forces during World War II, a legendary professor of production management at Harvard Business School, one of the first venture capitalists in the United States, and a cofounder of one of Europe's leading business schools. Like most sages, Doriot was careful with his words, and his advice was usually to be heeded. We remember vividly a discussion with him at a time when HRM was in the process of becoming very fashionable. "Watch out," he said. "The term 'human resource management' is important but ephemeral. Don't get hung up on the label. People are *not* resources, they are people."

TAKEAWAYS

1. HR functional managers with a responsibility for HRM process and content development in multinationals have to know how to work through network leadership. This requires awareness of trends, the ability to mobilize the appropriate resources, and a good sense of timing.
2. IT in the shape of e-HR has changed the way in which HR delivers its basic services, allowing standardized, low-cost services through a combination of self-help, shared service centers, and outsourcing. Most firms are still struggling to achieve effective and efficient global HR service delivery, with different paces of development in different regions of the world.
3. The HR business support role covers a range of different activities, from having influence on strategic decision making to facilitating change, but it also may include tasks that are quite operational. Caution: Line managers are usually more critical about the quality of support provided than the HR function itself.
4. Increasingly, the responsibilities of the global HR function go beyond the formal boundaries of the firm. HR needs to be able to answer the question

"What's the HR value added to the external customer?" and work closely with both downstream and upstream business partners.

5. There are three reasons why senior line management must drive HR—with support of the function: First, HR factors like talent supply greatly constrain strategy; second, their support is essential for implementation of HR practices; and third, they make many of the operational decisions.

6. Certain competencies—such as business understanding, general functional knowledge, and a global mindset—are likely to be useful for all professionals and managers working in HR. Senior HR leaders need to demonstrate strategically based competencies, and increasingly values-based leadership.

7. Many corporate HR managers lack deep international experience, which can be dangerous. The HR function needs to attract good people, which means providing clear exit routes out of the function.

8. Faced with many important operational tasks, HR leaders need to keep an eye on the "top of the egg" issues. Some of these are worth keeping constantly in mind—indeed worth fighting for: maintaining a competitive culture while protecting organizational sustainability, proactively fighting for the long-term perspective, as well as taking care of the basics.

9. Globalization and market competition have brought immense benefits to the world's population, including many of the poor. Yet HR has to be aware that the continued presence of widespread poverty, combined with the widening global inequalities between rich and poor, mean that there is a risk of a backlash that would jeopardize further progress.

10. HR cannot provide solutions to complex global problems, but it has a social responsibility to ensure that future leaders are sensitive to such challenges and equipped to respond to them. This is one of the many instances of the role of HRM in tension management.

NOTES

1. Lambert, 2009, p. 47.
2. Pucik, 2003.
3. Lawler, Boudreau, and Mohrman, 2006; Caldwell, 2008; Ulrich, Younger, and Brockbank, 2008; Wright, 2008. See Chapter 2 for the earlier discussion of our three roles.
4. Kates, 2006; Lambert, 2009.
5. Caldwell and Storey, 2007.
6. Ulrich and Brockbank, 2005.
7. For a more extended discussion of cross-boundary project groups, see Chapter 5.
8. Some firms have probably gone too far in eliminating headquarters staff, especially in HR, which may result in weakening of support for global coordination. See McGovern (1997) for a discussion of the dangers of excessive devolvement to line managers of HR responsibilities.
9. Information systems for the internal use of the HR function are commonly referred to as *HRIS* (Human Resource Information System).

10. See the discussion of standardization in Chapter 4.
11. See the discussion of e-HR applied to bottom-up internal labor markets in Chapter 8, with an example of new approaches to self-management that IBM has developed.
12. One of the HR challenges for firms with regional or global call centers is to recruit people who can serve employees in their native language. For instance, how can one find Danish-, Finnish-, and Dutch-speaking individuals for an HR service center located in Bulgaria?
13. Strohmeier, 2007.
14. Ruta (2005) provides a theory-based description of the implementation of the @HP Employee Portal.
15. See the discussion in Sparrow, Brewster, and Harris (2004), who also refer to studies arguing that culture rather than technology is determining the pace of progress. See also DeFidelto and Salter (2001).
16. Sparrow, Brewster, and Harris, 2004.
17. Reilly, Tamkin, and Broughton, 2007.
18. Caldwell and Storey, 2007; Caldwell, 2008.
19. Sparrow, Brewster, and Harris, 2004; Cooke, 2006.
20. Cooke, 2006.
21. SharedExpertise and Hewitt (2007) HR Shared Service Centers 2007. Available at http://www.hroaeurope.com/file/3991/hr-shared-service-centres-2007-into-the-next-generation.html.
22. The P&G case is described in Bloch and Lempres (2008).
23. Towers Perrin, 2005, "HR Outsourcing: New Realities, New Expectations"; Towers Perrin, 2008, "Staying Ahead of Change: Evolving Realities and Expectations in HR Outsourcing." Both available at http://www.towersperrin.com.
24. Lawler et al., 2004.
25. Lambert, 2009.
26. Towers Perrin, 2008, p. 3.
27. Towers Perrin, 2008.
28. Our source for the observation on reintegrating previously outsourced activities is discussions with senior executives from different outsourcing providers.
29. Ulrich, 1997.
30. Barney and Wright, 1998.
31. Ulrich and Beatty, 2001.
32. Caldwell and Storey, 2007.
33. CIPD, 2007, "The Changing HR Function. Survey Report September 2007." Available at http://www.cipd.co.uk.
34. See Chapter 8.
35. Scullion and Starkey, 2000.
36. Hodgetts, 1996.
37. See Schütte (1998) and De Konig, Verdin, and Williamson (1997) for a discussion of the merits of regional structures.
38. Baron and Kreps, 1999.
39. Baron and Krebs, 1999.
40. Scott Myers, 1970.
41. The "guarded strategist" role of HR was described by Brewster and Larsen (1992), where HR factors are viewed as highly strategic but with low belief in devolvement. In an empirical European study, they found this particularly in Norway and France, which matches our observations.

42. See Larsen and Brewster (2003) for the results of a European survey and Kulik and Bainbridge (2006) for findings on Australian firms.
43. Larsen and Brewster, 2003.
44. Kulik and Perry, 2008.
45. Larsen and Brewster, 2003.
46. As discussed in Chapter 8.
47. Ulrich et al., 1995.
48. Ulrich et al., 2008. They view the Credible Activist role as the most important predictor of performance in an HR role, followed by the Cultural Steward role.
49. See the discussion of three approaches to competence management in Chapter 7—performance -based, strategy-based, and values-based.
50. See, for example, Lambert (2009).
51. See the discussion of the change process leading to transnational management in Chapter 11.
52. Caldwell, 2008.
53. Wright, 2008.
54. See "Power to the People Managers," *Financial Times*, October 31, 2005, p. 8. We suspect that the percentage of HR directors with experience outside HR is lower than 83 percent in most other countries.
55. Kelly and Gennard, 2000. We stressed in Chapter 8 the important role of mobility in developing a strong leadership orientation.
56. A lot of research on mentoring was undertaken in the early 1980s. See Kram (1985) for a review. For a practitioner's overview of a related matter, namely coaching, see Goldsmith, Lyons, and Freas (2000).
57. See Ulrich and Brockbank (2005) for a more comprehensive list of principles that can be used when developing HR functional training programs.
58. Lambert, 2009, p. 122.
59. The role of mobility in leadership development is discussed in Chapter 8.
60. Leaving volatility or flexibility out of the picture, an economist would point out that profitable growth (the aim of most business organizations aside from enterprises such as some family businesses and Chinese entrepreneurial firms) boils down to a simple formula: (Price − Cost) × Quality.
61. Lambert, 2009.
62. The original HP Way was well adapted to its instruments business but ill suited to the computer world that Hewlett-Packard was forced into when instruments became computerized. The struggle to adapt the HP Way is described in Beer and Rogers (1995).
63. As mentioned in Chapter 9, the tension between competition and teamwork is at the heart of coevolutionary theories of international organization (see, for example, Eisenhardt and Galunic, 2000).
64. Roberto and Carioggia, 2002.
65. The fundamental purpose of the sustainable organization is to meet the need of the present without compromising the future—thus earning the "license to operate" from society. A sustainable organization lives by its principles and values and pays attention to its economic, ecological, and ethical performance.
66. We refer here to Cappelli's reasoning around talent management (Cappelli, 2008), as discussed in Chapters 7 and 8.
67. See "Burgeoning Bourgeoisie: A Special Report on the New Middle Classes in Emerging Markets," *The Economist*, February 14, 2009.

68. See Prahalad, (2004).

69. For these data and assessments, see R. Wade, "Global Inequality: Winners And Losers," *The Economist*, April 28, 2001.

70. For example, should income be measured using purchasing power parity (PPP or the purchasing power over comparable bundles of goods) or actual exchange rates? The latter typically accentuates that gap.

71. B. Milanovic, "Global Income Inequality: What It Is And Why It Matters," World Bank Policy Research Working Paper 3865, 2006. Available at http://www-wds.worldbank.org/servlet/WDSContentServer/WDSP/IB/2006/03/02/000016406_20060302153355/Rendered/PDF/wps3865.pdf.

72. OECD, 2008, "Are We Growing Unequal? New Evidence On Changes In Poverty And Incomes Over The Past 20 Years." Available at http://www.oecd.org/dataoecd/48/56/41494435.pdf. See also "Spare a dime? A special report on the rich," *The Economist*, April 4, 2009.

73. "Spare A Dime? A Special Report On The Rich." *The Economist*, April 4, 2009

74. Gladwell, M., "The Talent Myth," *New Yorker*, July 22, 2002.

75. As discussed in Chapter 8; see Blossfeld, Mills, and Bernardi (2008).

76. See the lead article on "Does Inequality Matter?" *The Economist*, June 16, 2001, pp. 11–12.

77. Toynbee, 1946.

78. Handy, 1998.

79. Handy, 1998.

80. As Evans and Génadry (1998) point out, the analysis of dualistic tensions poses considerable challenges for data analysis. Conventional statistical methods are based on bipolar measurement scales where one end represents the low point and the other the high point and assume a Gaussian normal distribution of data points. However, in tension analysis both ends of the scale are "low points" whereas the healthy point is the midpoint of the scale—for example, when a person recognizes that both "local" and "global" perspectives are equally valid (sometimes one must prevail, sometimes the other). Tension itself is easy to measure; tension is simply the variance. If the tension is high, the variance in views will be high; if the tension is low, then the variance will be low. On the other hand, the interpretation of tension scores measured on dualistic scales is more problematic (see Evans and Génadry, 1998).

81. Hedberg, Nystrom, and Starbuck, 1976.

Bibliography

Åbø, E., L. Chipperfield, C. Mottershead, J. Old, R. Prieto, J. Stemke, and R.G. Smith (2001). "Managing knowledge management." *Oilfield Review* 13 (Spring): 166–83.

Abrahamson, E., and G. Fairchild (1999). "Management fashion: Lifecycles, triggers, and collective learning processes." *Administrative Science Quarterly* 44(3): 708–40.

Adler, N.J. (1981). "Re-entry: Managing cross-cultural transition." *Group and Organization Studies* 6(3): 341–56.

_____ (1984). "Women in international management: Where are they?" *California Management Review* 26(4): 78–89.

_____ (1986). "Do MBAs want international careers?" *International Journal of Intercultural Relations* 10(3): 277–99.

_____ (1987). "Pacific Basin manager: A Gaijin, not a woman." *Human Resource Management* 26(2): 169–91.

_____ (1991). *International dimensions of organizational behavior.* Boston, MA: Kent.

Adler, N.J., and S. Bartholomew (1992). "Managing globally competent people." *Academy of Management Executive* 6(3): 52–65.

Adler, P.S. (1993). "The learning bureaucracy: New United Motor Manufacturing, Inc." *Research in Organizational Behavior* 15: 111–94.

_____ (1999). "Hybridization: Human resource management at two Toyota transplants." In *Remade in America: Transplanting and transforming Japanese management systems,* eds. J.K. Liker, W.M. Fruin, and P.S. Adler. New York: Oxford University Press.

Adler, P.S., and S.-W. Kwon (2002). "Social capital: Prospects for a new concept." *Academy of Management Review* 27(1): 17–40.

Adobor, H. (2004). "Selecting management talent for joint ventures: A suggested framework." *Human Resource Management Review* 14(2): 161–78.

Afuah, A. (1998). *Innovation management: Strategies, implementation, and profits.* New York: Oxford University Press.

Agrawal, A., and M. Kets de Vries (2006). "The moral compass: Values-based leadership at Infosys." Case study no. 09/2006-5391. INSEAD, Fontainebleau.

Aiken, C., and S. Keller (2009). "The irrational side of change management." *McKinsey Quarterly* 2: 101–9.

Albert, S., and D.A. Whetten (1985). "Organisational identity." In *Research in Organisational behaviour*, eds. L.L. Cummings and B.M. Staw. Greenwich, CT: JAI Press.

Allen, D., and S. Alvarez (1998). "Empowering expatriates and organizations to improve repatriation effectiveness." *Human Resource Planning* 21(4): 29–39.

Allen, N.J., and J.P. Meyer (1990). "The measurement and antecedents of affective, continuance and normative commitment to the organization." *Journal of Occupational Psychology* 63(1): 1–18.

Almond, P., T. Edwards, and I. Clark (2003). "Multinationals and changing business systems in Europe: Toward the "Shareholder Value" model?" *Industrial Relations Journal* 34(5): 430–45.

Altman Y., and S. Shortland (2008). "Women and international assignments: Taking stock—a 25-year review." *Human Resource Management* 47(2): 199–216.

Alvarez, J.L., and S. Svejenova (2005). *Sharing executive power: Roles and relationships at the top.* Cambridge: Cambridge University Press.

Alvesson, M., and H. Willmott (2002). "Identity regulation as organizational control: Producing the appropriate individual." *Journal of Management Studies* 39(5): 619–44.

Amason, A.C. (1996). "Distinguishing the effects of functional and dysfunctional conflict on strategic decision making: Resolving a paradox for top management teams." *Academy of Management Journal* 39(1): 123–48.

Amason, A.C., K.R. Thompson, W.A. Hochwarter, and A.W. Harrison (1995). "Conflict: An important dimension in successful management teams." *Organizational Dynamics* (Autumn): 20–35.

Ancona, D., and H. Bresman. (2007). *X-teams: How to build teams that lead, innovate, and succeed.* Boston, MA: Harvard Business School Press.

Ancona, D., and D.F. Caldwell (1992). "Bridging the boundary: External activity and performance in organizational teams." *Administrative Science Quarterly* 37(4): 634–65.

Ancona, D., P. Goodman, B. Lawrence, and M. Tushman (2001). "Time: A new research lens." *Academy of Management Review* 26(4): 645–563.

Angwin, D. (2001). "Mergers and acquisitions across European borders: National perspectives on preacquisition due diligence and the use of professional advisers." *Journal of World Business* 36(1): 32–57.

Argote, L. (1999). *Organizational learning: Creating, retaining and transferring knowledge.* Boston, MA: Kluwer.

Argyris, C. (1967). "Today's problems with tomorrow's organizations." *Journal of Management Studies* 4(1): 31–55.

———— (1990). *Overcoming organizational defenses.* Boston, MA: Allyn and Bacon.

Arora, A., A. Jaju, A.G. Kefalas, and T. Perenich (2004). "An exploratory analysis of global managerial mindsets: A case of US textile and apparel industry." *Journal of International Management* 10(3): 393–411.

Arthur, W., and W. Bennet (1995). "The international assignee: The relative importance of factors perceived to contribute to success." *Personnel Psychology* 48(1): 99–113.

Ashby, W.R. (1956). *An introduction to cybernetics.* New York: Wiley.

Ashforth, B.E., S.H. Harrison, and K.G. Corley (2008). "Identification in organizations: An examination of four fundamental questions." *Journal of Management* 34(3): 325–74.

Ashkenas, R.N., L.J. DeMonaco, and S.C. Francis (1998). "Making the deal real: How GE Capital integrates acquisitions." *Harvard Business Review* (January–February): 165–78.

Ashkenas, R.N., and S.C. Francis (2000). "Integration managers: Special leaders for special times." *Harvard Business Review* (November–December): 108–16.

Ashkenas, R.N., D. Ulrich, T. Jick, and S. Kerr (1995). *The boundaryless organization: Breaking the chains of organizational structure.* San Francisco: Jossey-Bass.

Bacon, N. (1999). "The realities of human resource management?" *Human Relations* 52(9): 1179–87.

Bae, J., S. Chen, and J. Lawler (1998). "Variation in human resource management in Asian countries: MNC home-country and host-country effects." *International Journal of Human Resource Management* 9(4): 653–70.

Baker, J.C., and J.M. Ivancevich (1971). "The assignment of American executives abroad: Systematic, haphazard or chaotic?" *California Management Review* 13(3): 39–44.

Baker, W. (1994). *Networking smart: How to build relationships for personal and organizational success.* New York: McGraw-Hill.

Barham, K., and C. Heimer (1998). *ABB: The dancing giant.* London: Financial Times/Pitman.

Baritz, L. (1960). *The servants of power: A history of the use of social science in American industry.* Middletown, CT: Wesleyan University Press.

Barkema, H.G., J.H. Bell, and J.M. Pennings (1996). "Foreign entry, cultural barriers, and learning." *Strategic Management Journal* 17(2): 151–66.

Barkema, H.G., and M. Schijven (2008). "How do firms learn to make acquisitions? A review of past research and an agenda for the future." *Journal of Management* 34(3): 594–634.

Barkema, H.G., O. Shenkar, F. Vermeulen, and J.H.J. Bell (1997). "Working abroad, working with others: How firms learn to operate international joint ventures." *Academy of Management Journal* 40(2): 426–42.

Barley, S.R., and G. Kunda (1992). "Design and devotion: Surges of rational and normative ideologies of control in managerial discourse." *Administrative Science Quarterly* 37(3): 363–99.

Barner-Rasmussen, W., and I. Björkman (2006). "Language fluency, socialization and inter-unit relationships in Chinese and Finnish subsidiaries." *Management and Organization Review* 3(1): 105–28.

Barney, J. (1991). "Firm resources and sustained competitive advantage." *Journal of Management* 17(1): 99–120.

Barney, J., and P.W. Wright (1998). "On becoming a strategic partner: The role of human resources in gaining competitive advantage." *Human Resource Management* 37(1): 31–46.

Baron, J.N., M.D. Burton, and M.T. Hannan (1996). "The road taken: Origins and evolution of employment systems in emerging companies." *Industrial and Corporate Change* 5(2): 239–75.

Baron, J.N., and D.M. Kreps (1999). *Strategic human resources: Frameworks for general managers.* New York: Wiley.

Bartlett, C.A. (1996). "McKinsey & Company: Managing knowledge and learning." Case study no. 9-396-357. Harvard Business School, Boston.

Bartlett, C.A., and A.N. McLean (2003). "GE's talent machine: The making of a CEO." Case study no. 12128659. Harvard Business School, Boston.

Bartlett, C.A., and J. O'Connell (1998). "Lincoln Electric: Venturing abroad." Case study no. 398095. Harvard Business School, Boston.

Bartlett, C.A., and S. Ghoshal (1989). *Managing across borders : The transnational solution.* Cambridge, MA: Harvard Business School Press.

_____ (1990). "Matrix management: Not a structure, a frame of mind." *Harvard Business Review* (July–August): 138–45.

_____ (1992). "What is a global manager?" *Harvard Business Review* (September–October): 124–32.

_____ (1997). "The myth of the generic manager: New personal competencies for new management roles." *California Management Review* 40(1): 92–116.

_____ (1998). *Managing across borders: The transnational solution*, 2nd ed. Boston, MA: Harvard Business School Press.

_____ (2000). "Going global: Lessons from late movers." *Harvard Business Review* (March–April): 133–42.

Bartlett, C.A., S. Ghoshal, and J. Birkinshaw (2003). *Transnational management*, 4th ed. New York: McGraw-Hill.

Bartlett, C.A., and H. Yoshihara (1988). "New challenges for Japanese multinationals: Is organization adaptation their Achilles' heel?" *Human Resource Management* 27(1): 19–43.

Bartolomé, F., and P.A.L. Evans (1980). "Must success cost so much?" *Harvard Business Review* (March–April): 137–49.

Bass, B.M., and R.M. Stogdill (1990). *Handbook of leadership: Theory, research and managerial applications*. New York: Free Press.

Bauer, T., H. Bonin, L. Goette, and U. Sunde (2007). "Real and nominal wage rigidities and the rate of inflation: Evidence from West German micro data." *The Economic Journal* 117(524): F508–29.

Bauer, T. N., E.W. Morrison, and R.R. Callister (1998). "Organizational socialization: A review and directions for future research." *Research in Personnel and Human Resources Management* 16: 149–214.

Beamish, P.W. (1985). "The characteristics of joint ventures in developed and developing countries." *Journal of World Business* 20(3): 13–19.

Beamish, P.W., and N.C. Lupton (2009). "Managing joint ventures." *Academy of Management Perspectives* 23(2): 75–94.

Becker, B., and B. Gerhart (1996). "The impact of human resource management on organizational performance." *Academy of Management Journal* 39(4): 779–801.

Becker, B.E., M.A. Huselid, and D. Ulrich (2001). *The HR scorecard: Linking people, strategy and performance*. Boston, MA: Harvard Business School Press.

Becker, B.E., M.A. Huselid, P.S. Pickus, and M.F. Spratt (1997). "Human resources as a source of shareholder value: Research and recommendations." In *Tomorrow's HR management*, eds. D. Ulrich, M.R. Losey, and G. Lake. New York: Wiley.

Beer, M., R. Eisenstat, and B. Spector (1990). *The critical path to corporate renewal*. Boston: Harvard Business School Press.

Beer, M., and N. Nohria (2000). "Cracking the code of change." *Harvard Business Review* (May–June): 133–41.

Beer, M., and G.C. Rogers (1995). "Human resources at Hewlett-Packard (A) (B)." Case study no. 9-495-051. Harvard Business School, Boston.

Beer, M., B. Spector, P.R.Lawrence, D.Quinn Mills, and R.E. Walton (1984). *Managing human assets*. New York: Free Press.

Behfar, K.J., R.S. Peterson, E.A Mannix, and W.M.K. Trochim (2008). "Critical role of conflict resolution in teams: A close look at the links between conflict type, conflict management strategies, and team outcomes." *Journal of Applied Psychology*: 93(1), 170–88.

Belbin, R.M. (1981). *Management teams: Why they succeed or fail*. London: Heinemann.

Bennis, W., and B. Nanus (1985). *Leaders: The strategies for taking charge*. New York: Harper & Row.

Benson, J., M. Yuasa, and P. Debroux (2007). "The prospect for gender diversity in Japanese employment." *International Journal of Human Resource Management* 18(5): 890–907.

Berg, N.A., and N.D. Fast (1983). "Lincoln Electric Co." Case study no. 376028. Harvard Business School, Boston.

Bertrand, O., and H. Zitouna (2008). "Domestic versus cross-border acquisitions: Which impact on the target firms' performance?" *Applied Economics* 40(17): 2221–38.

Bettenhausen, K. (1991). "Five years of groups research: What we have learned and what needs to be addressed." *Journal of Management* 17(2): 345–81.

Beyer, D. (2006). "Fixing the talent problem." *Oil & Gas Financial Journal* 3(9).

Bhaskar-Shrinivas, P., D.A. Harrison, M.A. Shaffer, and D.M. Luk (2005). "Input-based and time-based models of international adjustment: Meta-analytic evidence and theoretical extentions." *Academy of Management Journal* 48(2): 257–81.

Birkinshaw, J. (1999). "Acquiring intellect: Managing the integration of knowledge-intensive acquisitions." *Business Horizons* (May–June): 33–40.

_____. (2004). "External sourcing of knowledge in the international firm." In *The Blackwell handbook of global management: A guide to managing complexity*, eds. H.W. Lane, M.L. Maznevski, M.E. Mendenhall, and J. McNett. Oxford: Blackwell Publishing.

Birkinshaw, J., J. Bessant, and R. Delbridge (2007). "Finding, forming, and preforming: Creating networks for discontinuous networks." *California Managament Review* 49(3): 67–84.

Birkinshaw, J., and J. DiStefano (2004). "Global account management: New structures, new tasks." In *The Blackwell handbook of global management: A guide to managing complexity*, eds. H.W. Lane, M.L. Maznevski, M.E. Mendenhall, and J. McNett. Oxford: Blackwell Publishing.

Birkinshaw, J., and C.B. Gibson (2004). "The antecedents, consequences, and mediating role of organizational ambidexterity." *Academy of Management Journal* 47(2): 209–26.

Birkinshaw, J., G. Hamel, and M.J. Mol (2008). "Management innovation." *Academy of Management Review* 33(4): 825–45.

Birkinshaw, J., and N. Hood (1998). "Multinational subsidiary evolution: Capability and charter change in foreign-owned subsidiary companies." *Academy of Management Review* 23(4): 773–95.

_____ (2001). "Unleash innovation in foreign subsidiaries." *Harvard Business Review* (March): 131–7.

Bjelland, O.M., and R.C. Wood (2008). "An inside view of IBM's innovation jam." *MIT Sloan Management Review* 50(1): 32–40.

Björk, S. (1998). *IKEA: Ingvar Kamprad og hans imperium*. Copenhagen: Børsen.

Björkman, I., W. Barner-Rasmussen., and L. Li. (2004). "Managing knowledge transfer in MNCs: The impact of headquarters control mechanisms." *Journal of International Business Studies* 35(5): 443–55.

Björkman, I., P. Budhwar, A. Smale, and J. Sumelius (2008). "Human resource management in foreign-owned subsidiaries: China versus India." *International Journal of Human Resource Management* 19(5): 964–78.

Björkman, I., and C.D. Galunic (1999). "Lincoln Electric in China." Case study no. 09/1999-4850. INSEAD, Fontainebleau.

Björkman, I., and M. Gertsen (1993). "Selecting and training Scandinavian expatriates: Determinants of corporate practice." *Scandinavian Journal of Management* 9(2): 145–64.

Björkman, I., and J.E. Lervik (2007). "Transferring HR practices within multinational corporations." *Human Resource Management Journal* 17(4): 320–35.

Björkman, I., and Y. Lu (1999). "The management of human resources in Chinese–Western joint ventures." *Journal of World Business* 34(3): 306–24.

_____ (2001). "Institutionalization and bargaining power explanations of HRM practices in international joint ventures: The case of Chinese–Western joint ventures." *Organization Studies* 22(3): 491–512.

Björkman, I., G.K. Stahl, and E. Vaara (2007). "Cultural differences and capability transfer in cross-border acquisitions: The mediating roles of capability complementarity, absorptive capacity, and social integration." *Journal of International Business Studies* 38(4): 658–72.

Black, J.S. (1988). "Work role transitions: A study of American expatriate managers in Japan." *Journal of International Business Studies* 19(2): 277–94.

Black, J.S., and H.B. Gregersen (1991a). "When Yankee comes home: Factors related to expatriate and spouse repatriation adjustment." *Journal of International Business Studies* 22(4): 671–94.

_____ (1991b). "The other half of the picture: Antecedents of spouse cross-cultural adjustment." *Journal of International Business Studies* 22(3): 461–77.

_____ (1991c). "Antecedents to cross-cultural adjustment for expatriates in Pacific Rim assignments." *Human Relations* 44(5): 497–515.

_____ (1999). "The right way to manage expats." *Harvard Business Review* (March–April): 52–63.

_____ (2008). *It starts with one: Changing individuals changes organizations.* Upper Saddle River, NJ: Wharton School Publishing.

Black, J.S., H.B. Gregersen, and M.E. Mendenhall (1992). *Global assignments: Successfully expatriating and repatriating international managers.* San Francisco: Jossey-Bass.

Black, J.S., H.B. Gregersen, M.E. Mendenhall, and L.K. Stroh (1999). *Globalizing people through international assignments.* Reading, MA: Addison-Wesley.

Black, J.S., H.B. Gregersen, and A. Morrison (1999). *Global explorers: The next generation of leaders.* London: Routledge.

Black, J.S., M. Mendenhall, and G. Oddou (1991). "Toward a comprehensive model of international adjustment: An integration of multiple theoretical perspectives." *The Academy of Management Review* 16(2): 291–317.

Black, J.S., and G.K. Stephens (1989). "The influence of the spouse on American expatriate adjustment in overseas assignments." *Journal of Management* 15(4): 529–44.

Blackburn, R., S. Furst, and B. Rosen (2003). "Building a winning virtual team: KSAs, selection, training, and evaluation." In *Virtual teams that work: Creating conditions for virtual team effectiveness,* eds. C.B. Gibson and S.G. Cohen. San Francisco: Jossey-Bass.

Blazejewski, S. (2006): "Transferring value-infused organizational practices in multinational companies." In *Global, national and local practices in multinational companies,* eds. M. Geppert and M. Mayer. Hampshire, UK: Palgrave Macmillan, 63–104.

Bleeke J., D. Ernst, J. Isono, and D.D. Weinberg (1993). "Succeeding at cross-border mergers and acquisitions." In *Collaborating to compete: Using strategic alliances and acquisitions in the global marketplace,* eds. J. Bleeke and D. Ernst. New York: Wiley.

Bloch, M., and E.C. Lempres (2008). "From internal service provider to strategic partner: An interview with the head of Global Business Services at P&G." *McKinsey Quarterly* 3: 49–59.

Bloom, M., and G.T. Milkovich (1999). "A SHRM perspective on international compensation and reward systems." In *Strategic human resources management: Research in personnel and human resources management,* eds. P.M. Wright, L.D. Dyer, J.W. Boudreau, and G.T. Milkovich. Stamford, CT: JAI Press.

Bloom, M., G.T. Milkovich, and A. Mitra (2003). "International compensation: Learning from how managers respond to variations in local host context." *International Journal of Human Resource Management* 14(8): 1350–67.

Blossfeld, H.-P., M. Mills, and F. Bernardi (2008). *Globalization, uncertainty and men's careers: An international comparison.* Northhampton, MA: Edward Elgar.

Boam, R., and P. Sparrow (1992). *Designing and achieving competency: A competency-based approach to developing people and organizations.* London: McGraw-Hill.

Bonache, J., and J. Cervino (1997). "Global integration without expatriates." *Human Resource Management Journal* 7(3): 89–100.

Bonache, J., and C. Zárraga-Oberty (2008). "Determinants of the success of international assignees as knowledge tranferors: A theoretical framework." *International Journal of Human Resource Management* 19(1): 1–18.

Borkowski, S.C. (1999). "International managerial performance evaluation: A five country comparison." *Journal of International Business Studies* 30(3): 533–55.

Boselie, P., G. Dietz, and C. Boon (2005). "Commonalities and contradictions in HRM and performance research." *Human Resource Management Journal* 15(3): 67–94.

Bouchikhi, H., and J. Kimberly (2008). "Leadership challenges in the age of identity." *Management Today* 24(3): 16–21.

Boudreau, J.W., and P.M. Ramstad (2007). *The new science of human capital.* Boston: Harvard Business School Press.

Bowen, D.E., and C. Ostroff (2004). "Understanding HRM–firm performance linkages: The role of the 'strength' of the HRM system." *Academy of Management Review* 29(2): 203–21.

Boxall, P. (1996). "The strategic HRM debate and the resource-based view of the firm." *Human Resource Management Journal* 6(3): 59–75.

Boxall, P., and J. Purcell (2003). "Strategy and human resource management." *Industrial & Labor Relations Review* 57(1): 145–6.

Boxall, P., J. Purcell, and P. Wright, eds. (2007). *The Oxford handbook of human resource management.* New York: Oxford University Press.

Boyatzis, R., A. McKee, and D. Goleman (2002). "Reawakening your passion for work." *Harvard Business Review* (April): 86–94.

Branham, L. (2005). *The 7 hidden reasons employees leave: How to recognize the subtle signs and react before it's too late.* New York: AMACOM.

Braun W.H., and M. Warner (2002). "Strategic human resource management in Western multinationals in China." *Personnel Review* 31(5): 553–79.

Breaugh, J.A. (1992). *Recruitment: Science & practice.* Boston, MA: PWS-Kent.

Bresman, H., J.M. Birkinshaw, and R. Nobel. (1999). "Knowledge transfer in acquisitions." *Journal of International Business Studies* 30(4): 439–62.

Brett, J.M., and L.K. Stroh (1995). "Willingness to relocate internationally." *Human Resource Management* 34(3): 405–24.

Brewster, C. (1991). *The management of expatriates.* London: Kogan Page.

_____ (1995). "Towards a 'European' model of human resource management." *Journal of International Business Studies* 26(1): 1–21.

_____. (2006). "Comparing HRM across countries." In *Handbook of research in international resource management*, eds. G.K. Stahl and I. Björkman. Cheltenham, UK: Edward Elgar.

_____ (2007). "Comparative HRM: European views and perspectives." *International Journal of Human Resource Management* 18(5): 769–87.

Brewster, C., and A. Hegewisch, eds. (1994). *Policy and practice in European human resource management: The Price Waterhouse Cranfield Survey.* London: Routledge.

Brewster, C., and H. H. Larsen (1992). "Human resource management in Europe: Evidence from ten countries." *International Journal of Human Resource Management* 3(3): 409–34.

Brewster, C., W. Mayrhofer, and M. Morley (2004). *Human resource management in Europe: Evidence of convergence.* Boston, MA: Butterworth-Heinemann.

Brewster, C., and H. Scullion (1997). "A review and agenda for expatriate HRM." *Human Resource Management Journal* 7(3): 32–41.

Brewster C., P. Sparrow, and G. Vernon (2007). *International human resource management,* 2nd ed. London: Chartered Institute of Personnel and Development.

Bridges, W. (1980). *Making sense of life's transitions.* New York: Addison-Wesley.

_____ (1986). "Managing organizational transitions." *Organizational Dynamics* 15(1): 24–33.

Briscoe, J.P., and D.T. Hall (1999). "Grooming and picking leaders using competency frameworks: Do they work?" *Organizational Dynamics* 28(2): 37–51.

Brock, D., M.T. Yaffe, and M. Dembovsky (2006). "The global law firm: An initial study of strategy and performance." *International Journal of Business and Economics* 5(2): 161–72.

Broeckx, P.V., and R. Hooijberg (2007). "Nestlé on the move: Evolving human resources approaches from company success." In *Being there even when you are not: Leading through strategy, structures, and systems,* eds. R. Hooijberg, J. Hunt, J. Antonakis, K. Boal, and N. Lane. Amsterdam: Elsevier.

Broekner, J., Y. Chen, E.A. Mannix, K. Leung, D.P. Skarlicki (2000). "Culture and procedural fairness: When the effects of what you do depend on how you do it." *Administrative Science Quarterly* 45(1): 138–59.

Brown, S.L., and K. Eisenhardt (1997). "The art of continuous change: Linking complexity theory and time-paced evolution in relentlessly shifting organizations." *Administrative Science Quarterly* 42(1): 1–34.

_____ (1998). *Competing on the edge: Strategy as structured chaos.* Boston, MA: Harvard Business School Press.

Bruch, H., and S. Ghoshal (2002). "Beware the busy manager." *Harvard Business Review* (February): 62–9.

Bryan, L.L. (2004). "Making a market in knowledge." *McKinsey Quarterly* 3: 100–1.

Bryan, L.L., E. Matson, and L.M. Weiss (2007). "Harnessing the power of informal employee networks." *McKinsey Quarterly* 4: 82–6.

Burgelman, R.A., and A.S. Grove (2007). "Let chaos reign, then reign in chaos—repeatedly: Managing strategic dynamic for corporate longevity." *Strategic Management Journal* 28(10): 965–79.

Burt, R.S. (1987). "Social contagion and innovation: Cohesion versus structural equivalence." *American Journal of Sociology* 92 (May): 1287–335.

_____ (1992). *Structural holes: The social structure of competition.* Cambridge, MA: Harvard University Press.

Burt, R.S., R.M. Hogarth, and C. Michaud (2000). "The social capital of French and American managers." *Organization Science* 11(2): 123–47.

Caldwell, R. (2008). "HR business partner competency models: Re-contextualising effectiveness." *Human Resource Management Journal* 18(3): 275–94.

Caldwell, R., and J. Storey (2007). "The HR function: Integration or fragmentation?" In *Human resource management: A critical text,* ed. J. Storey, 3rd ed. London: Thomson.

Caligiuri, P.M. (2006a). "Developing global leaders." *Human Resource Management Review* 16(2): 219–28.

_____ (2006b). "Performance measurement in a cross-national context." In *Performance measurement: Current perspectives and future challenges*, eds. W. Bennet, D. Woehr, and C. Lance. New Jersey: Laurence Erlbaum Associates.

Caligiuri, P.M., and R.L. Tung (1999). "Comparing the success of male and female expatriates from a US-based multinational company." *International Journal of Human Resource Management* 10(5): 763–82.

Cameron, K. (1994). "Strategies for successful organizational downsizing." *Human Resource Management* 33(2): 189–211.

Campbell, A., and M. Goold (1998). *Synergy: Why links between business units often fail and how to make them work*. Oxford: Capstone.

Canney Davison, S., and K. Ward (1999). *Leading international teams*. New York: McGraw-Hill.

Cappelli, P. (2008). *Talent on demand: Managing talent in an age of uncertainty*. Boston, MA: Harvard Business School Press.

Cappelli, P., and M. Hamori (2005). "The new road to the top." *Harvard Business Review* (January): 25–32.

Carlos, A.M., and S. Nicholas (1988). "Giants of an earlier capitalism: The chartered trading companies as modern multinationals." *Business History Review* 62 (Autumn): 398–419.

Carraher, S.M., S.E. Sullivan, and M.M. Crocitto (2008). "Mentoring across global boundaries: An empirical examination of home- and host-country mentors on expatriate career outcomes." *Journal of International Business Studies* 39(8): 1310–26.

Cascio, W.F. (2000). *Costing human resources: The financial impact of behavior in organizations*. Cincinnati, OH: South-Western College Publishing.

_____ (2006). Global performance management systems. In *Handbook of Research in International Human Resource Management*, eds. G.K. Stahl, and I. Björkman. Cheltenham, UK: Edward Elgar.

Cascio, W.F., and M.G. Serapio, Jr. (1991). "Human resources systems in an international alliance: The undoing of a done deal?" *Organizational Dynamics* 19(3): 63–74.

Cerdin, J.-L., and J.-M. Peretti (2000). "Les déterminants de l'adaptation des cadres français expatriés." *Revue Française de Gestion* 129 (July–August): 58–66.

Chakrabarti, R., S. Gupta-Mukherjee, and N. Jayaraman (2009). "Mars–Venus marriages: Culture and cross-border M&A." *Journal of International Business Studies* 40(2): 216–35.

Chambers, E.G., M. Foulon, H. Handfield-Jones, S.M. Hankin, and E.G. Michaels III (1998). "The war for talent." *McKinsey Quarterly* 3: 44–57.

Chandler, A.D. (1962). *Strategy and structure*. Cambridge, MA: MIT Press.

_____ (1977). *The visible hand*. Cambridge, MA: Harvard University Press.

_____ (1986). "The evolution of modern global competition." In *Competition in global industries*, ed. M. Porter, Cambridge, MA: Harvard University Press.

_____ (1990). *Scale and scope: The dynamics of industrial capitalism*. Cambridge, MA: Harvard University Press.

Chang, E., and M.S. Taylor (1999). "Control in multinational corporations (MNCs): The case of Korean manufacturing subsidiaries." *Journal of Management* 25(4): 541–65.

Charan, R., S. Drotter, and J. Noel (2001). *The leadership pipeline: How to build the leadership powered company*. Boston, MA: Harvard Business School Press.

Chatman, J.A. (1991). "Matching people and organizations: Selection and socialization in public accounting firms." *Administrative Science Quarterly* 36(3): 459–84.

Chatman, J., and S.E. Cha (2003). "Leading by leveraging culture." *California Management Review* 45(4): 20–34.

Chatman, J., C. O'Reilly, and V. Chang (2005). "Cisco Systems: Developing a human capital strategy." *California Management Review* 47(2): 137–67.

Chaudhuri S., and B. Tabrizi (1999). "Capturing the real value in high-tech acquisitions." *Harvard Business Review* (September–October): 123–30.

Chen, C., J. Choi, and S.-C. Chi (2002). "Making justice sense of local–expatriate compensation disparity: Mitigation by local referents, ideological explanations, and interpersonal sensitivity in China–foreign joint ventures." *Academy of Management Journal* 45(4): 807–17.

Cheung, C., and G. Yong (2006). "Job referral in China: The advantage of strong ties." *Human Relations* 59(6): 847–72.

Child, J. (1969). *British management thought: A critical analysis.* London: Allen & Unwin.

_____ (2000). "Theorizing about organization cross-nationally." In *Advances in international comparative management,* vol. 13., eds. J.L.C. Cheng and R.B. Peterson. Stamford, CT: JAI Press.

Child, J., and D. Faulkner (1998). *Strategies of cooperation: Managing alliances, networks, and joint ventures.* New York: Oxford University Press.

Child, J., D. Faulkner, and R. Pitkethly (2001). *The management of international acquisitions.* Oxford: Oxford University Press.

Child, J., D. Faulkner, and S.B. Tallman (2005). *Cooperative strategy: Managing alliances, networks, and joint ventures.* Oxford: Oxford University Press.

Child, J., and G. Möllering (2003). "Contextual confidence and active trust development in the Chinese business environment." *Organization Science* 14(1): 69–80.

Child, J., and Y. Yan (1998). "National and transnational effects in international business: Indications from Sino–foreign joint ventures." Working paper 31/98. Judge Institute of Management Studies, Cambridge.

Cho, H.-J., and V. Pucik. (2005). "Relationship between innovativeness, quality, growth, profitability, and market value." *Strategic Management Journal* 26(3): 555–75.

Christensen, C.M. (1997). *The innovator's dilemma: When new technologies cause great firms to fail.* Boston, MA: Harvard Business School Press.

Chu, W. (1996). "The human side of examining a foreign target." *Mergers and Acquisitions* 30(4): 35–9.

Chung, L.H., P.T. Gibbons, and H.P. Schoch (2006). "The management of information and managers in subsidiaries of multinational corporations." *British Journal of Management* 17(2): 153–65.

Chusmir, L.H., and N.T. Frontczak (1990). "International management opportunities for women: Women and men paint different pictures." *International Journal of Management* 7(3): 295–301.

Cialdini, R.B. (2001). *Influence: Science and practice,* 4th ed. Boston, MA: Allyn & Bacon.

Ciceri, H. (2007). "Transnational firms and cultural diversity." In *The Oxford handbook of human resource management,* eds. P. Boxall, J. Purcell, and P. Wright. New York: Oxford University Press.

Clark, T., and G. Mallory (1996). "The cultural relativity of human resource management: Is there a universal model?" In *European human resource management,* ed. T. Clark. Oxford: Blackwell.

Claus, L., and D. Briscoe (2008). "Employee performance management across borders: A review of relevant academic literature." *International Journal of Management Reviews* 10(2): 175–96.

Coase, R.H. (1937). "The nature of the firm." *Economica* 4 (November): 386–405.

Coens, T., and M. Jenkins (2000). *Abolishing performance appraisals: Why they backfire and what to do instead.* San Francisco: Berrett-Koehler.

Coff, R.W., D.C. Coff, and R. Eastvold (2006). "The knowledge-leveraging paradox: How to achieve scale without making knowledge imitable." *Academy of Management Review* 31(2): 452–65.

Cohen, J. (1992). "Foreign advisors and capacity building: The case of Kenya." *Public Administration & Development* 12(5): 493–510.

Cohen, W., and D. Levinthal (1990). "Absorptive capacity: A new perspective on learning and innovation." *Administrative Science Quarterly* 35(1): 128–52.

Cole, R.E., and D.R. Deskins, Jr. (1988). "Racial factors in site location and employment patterns of Japanese auto firms in America." *California Management Review* 31(1): 9–22.

Collings, D.G., H. Scullion, and M.J. Morley (2007). "Changing patterns of global staffing in the multinational enterprise: Challenges to the conventional expatriate assignment and emerging alternatives." *Journal of World Business* 42(2): 198–213.

Collins, J.C. (2001). *Good to great: Why some companies make the leap . . . and others don't.* New York: HarperBusiness.

Collins, J.C., and J.I. Porras (1994). *Built to last.* New York: HarperBusiness.

Combs, J., Y. Liu, A. Hall, and D. Ketchen (2006). "How much do high-performance work practices matter? A meta-analysis of their effects on organizational performance." *Personnel Psychology* 59(3): 501–28.

Conger, J.A. (1998). "The necessary art of persuasion." *Harvard Business Review* (May–June): 84–95.

Conger, J.A., and B. Benjamin (1999). *Building leaders: How successful companies develop the next generation.* San Francisco: Jossey-Bass.

Conger, J.A., and B. Fishel (2007). "Accelerating leadership performance at the top: Lessons from the Bank of America's executive on-boarding process." *Human Resource Management Review* 17(4): 442–54.

Contractor, F.J., and P. Lorange (1988). "Why should firms cooperate? The strategy and economics basis for cooperative ventures." In *Cooperative strategies in international business,* eds. F.J. Contractor and P. Lorange. Lexington, MA: Lexington Books.

Cook, M. (1999). *Personnel selection: Adding value through people.* Chichester, UK: Wiley.

Cooke, F.L. (2006). "Modeling an HR shared services center: Experience of an MNC in the United Kingdom." *Human Resource Management* 45(2): 211–28.

Crichton, A. (1968). *Personnel management in context.* London: B.T. Batsford.

Cross, R., and L. Prusak (2003). "The political economy of knowledge markets in organizations." In *The Blackwell handbook of organizational learning and knowledge management,* eds. M. Easterby-Smith and M. Lyles. Malden, MA: Blackwell.

Currie, G., and M. Kerrin (2003). "Human resource management and knowledge management: Enhancing knowledge sharing in a pharmaceutical company." *International Journal of Human Resource Management* 14(6): 1027–45.

Cyr, D.J. (1995). *The human resource challenge of international joint ventures.* Westport, CT: Quorum Books.

Cyr, D.J., and S.C. Schneider (1996). "Implications for learning: Human resource management in East–West joint ventures." *Organization Studies* 17(2): 207–26.

Darr, E.D., and T.R. Kurtzberg (2000). "An investigation of partner similarity dimensions on knowledge transfer." *Organizational Behavior and Human Decision Processes* 82(1): 28–44.

Davidson Frame, J. (1987). *Managing projects in organizations.* San Francisco: Jossey-Bass.

Davis, S.M., and P.R. Lawrence (1977). *Matrix.* Reading, MA: Addison-Wesley.

De Cieri, H., and P.J. Dowling (1999). "Strategic human resource management in multinational enterprises: Theoretical and empirical developments." In *Strategic human resources management in the twenty-first century*, eds. P.M. Wright, L. Dyer, J.W. Boudreau, and G.T. Milkovich. Stamford, CT: JAI Press.

De Geus, A.P. (1988). "Planning as learning." *Harvard Business Review* (March–April): 70–4.

De Konig, A., P. Verdin, and P. Williamson (1997). "So you want to integrate Europe: How do you manage the process?" *European Management Journal* 15(6): 252–65.

De Meyer, A. (1991). "Tech talk: How managers are stimulating global R&D communication." *MIT Sloan Management Review* 32(3): 49–66.

Del Canho, D., and J. Engelfriet (2008). "Flying higher together." *Business Strategy Review* 19(1): 34–7.

DeFidelto, C., and I. Slater (2001). "Web-based HR in an international setting." In *Web-based human resources: The technologies that are transforming HR*, ed. A.J. Walker. London: McGraw-Hill.

Delany, E. (2000). "Strategic development of the multinational subsidiary through subsidiary initiative-taking." *Long Range Planning* 33(2): 220–44.

DeLong, D. (2004). *Lost knowledge: Confronting the threat of an aging workforce*. Oxford: Oxford University Press.

Deming, W.E. (2000). *Out of the crisis*. Cambridge, MA: MIT Press.

Dendrell, J., N. Arvidsson and U. Zander. (2004). "Managing knowledge in the dark: An empirical study of the reliability of capability evaluation." *Management Science* 50(11): 1491–503.

Denison, D. (1996). "What is the difference between organization culture and organization climate? A native's point of view on a decade of paradigm wars." *Academy of Management Review* 21(3): 619–54.

Denison D., H.-J. Cho, and J. Young (2000). "Diagnosing organizational cultures: Validating a model and method." Working paper 2000-9. IMD, Lausanne.

Derr, B.C., and G.R. Oddou (1991). "Are U.S. multinationals adequately preparing future American leaders for global competition?" *International Journal of Human Resource Management* 2(2): 227–44.

Dess, G.G., and J.D. Shaw (2001). "Voluntary turnover, social capital, and organizational performance." *Academy of Management Review* 26(3): 446–56.

Dickmann, M., N. Doherty, T. Mills, and C. Brewster (2008). "Why do they go? Individual and corporate perspectives on the factors influencing an international assignment." *International Journal of Human Resource Management* 19(4): 731–51.

Dickmann, M., and H. Harris (2005). "Developing career capital for global careers: The role of international assignments." *Journal of World Business* 40(4): 399–408.

Dierickx, I., and K. Cool (1989). "Asset stock accumulation and competitive advantage." *Management Science* 35(12): 1504–11.

DiMaggio, P.J., and W.W. Powell (1983). "The iron cage revisited: Institutional isomorphism and collective rationality." *American Sociological Review* 48 (April): 147–60.

Dobbs, R., M. Goedhart, and H. Suonio (2006). "Are companies getting better at M&A?" *McKinsey Quarterly* (December): www.mckinseyquarterly.com/ (online only).

Dodd, D., and K. Favaro (2007). *The three tensions: Winning the struggle to perform without compromise*. New York: Wiley.

Doh, J.P., S.A. Stumpf, W. Tymon, and M. Haid (2008). "How to manage talent in fast-moving labor markets: Some findings from India." Working paper. Villanova School of Business, Villanova, PA.

Donaldson, L. (1995). *American anti-management theories of organization: A critique of paradigm proliferation*. Cambridge: Cambridge University Press.

Donnelly, T., D. Morris, and T. Donnelly (2005). "Renault–Nissan: A marriage of necessity." *European Business Review* 17(5): 428–40.

Doorewaard, H., and H.E. Meihuizen (2000). "Strategic performance options in professional service organisations." *Human Resource Management Journal* 10(2): 39–57.

Doornik, K., and J. Roberts (2001). "Nokia Corporation: Innovation and efficiency in a high-growth global firm." Case study no. S-IB 23. Graduate School of Business, Stanford University.

Dore, R. (1973). *British factory, Japanese factory: The origins of national diversity in industrial relations.* Berkeley, CA: University of California Press.

Dottlich, D.L., J.L. Noel, and N. Walker (2004). *Leadership passages: The personal and professional transitions that make or break a leader.* San Francisco: Jossey-Bass.

Dougherty, D. (1996). "Organizing for innovation." In *Handbook of organization studies,* eds. S.R. Clegg, C. Hardy, and W.R. Nord. London and Thousand Oaks, CA: Sage.

Dowling, P.J., and R.S. Schuler (1990). *International dimensions of human resource management.* Boston, MA: PWS-Kent.

Dowling, P.J., and D.E. Welch (2005). *International human resource management: Managing people in a multinational context,* 4th ed. Mason, OH: Thomson South-Western College Publishing.

Doz, Y., C.A. Bartlett, and C.K. Prahalad (1981). "Global competitive pressures and host country demands." *California Management Review* 23(3): 63–74.

Doz, Y., and G. Hamel (1998). *Alliance advantage: The art of creating value through partnering.* Boston, MA: Harvard Business School Press.

Doz, Y., and M. Kosonen (2008). *Fast strategy: How strategic agility will help you stay ahead of the game.* Harlow, UK: Wharton School Publishing; New York: Wharton School Publishing/Pearson Education.

Doz, Y., and C.K. Prahalad (1984). "Patterns of strategic control within multinational corporations." *Journal of International Business Studies* 15(2): 55–72.

_____ (1986). "Controlled variety: A challenge for human resource management in the MNC." *Human Resource Management* 25(1): 55–71.

_____ (1988). "A process model of strategic redirection in large complex firms: The case of multinational corporations." In *The management of strategic change,* ed. A.M. Pettigrew. Oxford: Basil Blackwell.

Doz, Y., J. Santos, and P. Williamson (2001). *From global to metanational: How companies win in the knowledge economy.* Boston, MA: Harvard Business School Press.

Drucker, P. (1996). "Foreword." In *The leader of the future,* eds. F. Hesselbein, M. Goldsmith, and R. Beckhard. San Francisco: Jossey-Bass.

Duarte, D.L., and N.T. Snyder (2006). *Mastering virtual teams,* 2nd ed. San Francisco: Jossey-Bass.

Duhaime, I.M., and C.R. Schwenk (1985). "Conjectures on cognitive simplification in acquisition and divestment decision making." *Academy of Management Review* 10(2): 287–95.

Duncan, G.J. (1976). "Earnings functions and nonpecuniary benefits." *Journal of Human Resources* 11(4): 462–83.

Dunning, J.H. (1988). *Explaining international production.* London: Unwin Hyman.

Dyer, J.H., H.B. Gregersen, and C.M. Christensen, (2008). "Entrepreneur behaviors, opportunity recognition, and the origins of innovative ventures." *Strategic Entrepreneurship Journal* 2(4): 317–38.

Dyer, J.H., P. Kale, and H. Singh (2004). "When to ally and when to acquire." *Harvard Business Review* (July–August): 108–15.

Easterby-Smith, M., and M.A. Lyles (2003). "The political economy of knowledge markets in organizations." In *The Blackwell handbook of organizational learning and knowledge management*, eds. M. Easterby-Smith and M.A. Lyles. Malden, MA: Blackwell.

Eccles, R.G., and D.B. Crane (1987). *Doing deals: Investment banks at work.* Boston, MA: Harvard Business School Press.

Eddy, J., S. Hall, and S. Robinson (2006). "How global organizations develop local talent." *McKinsey Quarterly* 3: 6–8.

Edström, A., and J.R. Galbraith (1977). "Transfer of managers as a coordination and control strategy in multinational organizations." *Administrative Science Quarterly* 22(2): 248–63.

Egan, M.L., and M. Bendick, Jr. (2003). "Workforce diversity initiatives of U.S. multinational corporations in Europe." *Thunderbird International Business Review* 45(6): 701–27.

Egelhoff, W.G. (1988). "Strategy and structure in multinational corporations: A revision of the Stopford and Wells model." *Strategic Management Journal* 9(1): 1–14.

Eisenhardt, K.M., and D.C. Galunic (2000). "Coevolving: At last, a way to make synergies work." *Harvard Business Review* (January–February): 91–101.

Eisenhardt, K.M., J.L. Kahwajy, and L.J. Bourgeois (1997). "How management teams can have a good fight." *Harvard Business Review* (July–August): 77–85.

Eisenhardt, K.M., and M. Zbaracki (1992). "Strategic decision making." *Strategic Management Journal* 13 (Winter Special Issue): 17–37.

Ellis, F. (2000). *Rural livelihoods and diversity in developing countries.* Oxford and New York: Oxford University Press.

Erickson, T.J., and L. Gratton (2007). "What it means to work here." *Harvard Business Review* (March): 104–14.

Evans, P.A.L. (1974). "The price of success: Accommodation to conflicting needs in managerial careers." Unpublished doctoral dissertation. Alfred P. Sloan School of Management, MIT, Boston.

_____ (1992). "Developing leaders and managing development." *European Journal of Management* 10(1): 1–9.

_____ (1994). "The paradoxes of a world where solutions are looking for problems." *EFMD Forum* 94(3): 67–74.

Evans, P.A.L., and F. Bartolomé (1979). *Must success cost so much?* London: Grant McIntyre; New York: Basic Books.

Evans, P.A.L., and Y. Doz (1989). "The dualistic organization." In *Human resource management in international firms: Change, globalization, innovation*, eds. P.A.L. Evans, Y. Doz, and A. Laurent. London: Macmillan.

_____ (1992). "Dualities: A paradigm for human resource and organizational development in complex multinationals." In *Globalizing management: Creating and leading the competitive organization*, eds. V. Pucik, N.M. Tichy, and C.K. Barnett. New York: Wiley.

Evans, P.A.L., and M. Engsbye (2003). "Danmark og danskerne foran den globale udfordring." In *Den Globale Udfordring*, eds. P.A.L. Evans, V. Pucik, J.-L. Barsoux, and M. Engsbye. Copenhagen: JP-Boeger.

Evans, P.A.L., and N. Génadry (1998). "A duality-based prospective for strategic human resource management." In *Research in personnel and human resources management, Supplement 4: Strategic human resources management in the twenty-first century*, eds. L.D. Dyer, P.M. Wright, J.W. Boudreau, and G.T. Milkovich. Stamford, CT: JAI Press.

Evans, P.A.L., and P. Lorange (1989). "The two logics behind human resource management." In *Human resource management in international firms: Change, globalization, innovation*, eds. P.A.L. Evans, Y. Doz, and A. Laurent. London: Macmillan.

Evans, P.A.L., and A. Wittenberg (1986). "Apple Computers Europe." INSEAD case series, Fontainebleau. Reprinted in *Transnational management: Text, cases, and readings in cross-border management*, eds. C.A. Bartlett and S. Ghoshal. Homewood, IL: Irwin, 1992.

Farndale, E., and J. Paauwe (2007). "Uncovering competitive and institutional drivers of HRM practices in multinational corporations." *Human Resource Management Journal* 17(4): 355–75.

Farrell, D., M. Laboissière, and J. Rosenfeld (2006). "Sizing the merging global labor market: Rational behavior from both companies and countries can help it work more efficiently." *Academy of Management Perspectives* 20(4): 23–34.

Faulkner, D., R. Pitkethly, and J. Child (2002). "International mergers and acquisitions in the UK 1985–94: A comparison of national HRM practices." *International Journal of Human Resource Management* 13(1): 106–22.

Feldman, D.C., and M.C. Bolino (1999). "The impact of on-site mentoring on expatriate socialization: A structural equation modelling approach." *International Journal of Human Resource Management* 10(1): 54–71.

Ferencikova, S., and V. Pucik (1999). "Whirlpool Corporation: Entering Slovakia." Case study no. IMD-3-0796. IMD, Lausanne.

Fernandez J.A., and L. Underwood (2006). *CEO voices of experience from 20 international business leaders*. Singapore: Wiley.

Ferner, A., P. Almond, I. Clark, T. Colling, T. Edwards, L. Holden, and M. Muller-Camen (2004). "The dynamics of central control and subsidiary autonomy in the management of human resources: Case study evidence from US MNCs in the UK." *Organization Studies* 25(3): 363–91.

Ferner, A., P. Almond, and T. Colling (2005). "Institutional theory and the cross-national transfer of employment policy: The case of 'workforce diversity' in US multinationals." *Journal of International Business Studies* 36(3): 304–21.

Ferner, A., and J. Quintanilla (1998). "Multinationals, national business systems and HRM: The enduring influence of national identity or a process of 'Anglo-Saxonization.'" *International Journal of Human Resource Management* 9(4): 710–31.

Festing, M., J. Eidems, and S. Royer (2007). "Strategic issues and local constraints in transnational compensation strategies: An analysis of cultural, institutional and political influences." *European Management Journal* 25(2): 118–31.

Fey, C.F. and P.W. Beamish (2001). "The importance of organizational climate similarity between parent firms and the JV: The case of IJVs in Russia." *Organization Studies* 22(5): 853–82.

Fey, C., P. Engström, and I. Björkman (1999). "Doing business in Russia: Effective human resource management practices for foreign firms in Russia." *Organizational Dynamics* 28(2): 69–80.

Fine, C.H. (1998). *Clockspeed: Winning industry control in the age of temporary advantage.* Reading, MA: Perseus Books.

Fiol, C.M. (2002). "Capitalizing on paradox: The role of language in transforming organizational identities." *Organization Science* 13(6): 653–66.

Flamholtz, E.G. (2005). "Human resource accounting, human capital management, and the bottom line." In *The Future of Human Resource Management*, eds. M. Losey, S. Meisinger, and D. Ulrich. Hoboken, NJ: Wiley.

Flannery, T.P., D.A. Hofrichter, and P.E. Platten (1996). *People, performance, and pay: Dynamic compensation for changing organizations.* New York: Free Press.

Fleming, M., and M. Marx (2006). "Managing creativity in small worlds." *California Management Review* 48(4): 6–27.

Fombrun, C., N.M. Tichy, and M.A. Devanna (1984). *Strategic human resource management.* New York: Wiley.

Ford, R., and W. Randolph (1992). "Cross-functional structures: A review and integration of matrix organization and project management." *Journal of Management* 18(2): 267–94.

Forster, N. (1997). "The persistent myth of high expatriate failure rates: A reappraisal." *International Journal of Human Resource Management* 3(4): 414–34.

Francis, I., V. Pucik, K. Xin, and L. Shengjun (2004). "Michelin China." Case study no. CC-403-021. China Europe International Business School (CEIBS), Shanghai.

Fraser, M., and S. Dutta (2008). *Throwing sheep in the boardroom: How online social networking will transform your life, work and world.* San Francisco: Jossey-Bass.

Friedman, T.L. (2005). *The world is flat: A brief history of the twenty-first century.* New York: Farrar, Straus and Giroux.

Friedmann, J. (2007). "The wealth of cities: Towards an assets-based development of newly urbanizing regions." *Development and Change* 38(6): 987–98.

Froese, F.J., and L.G. Goeritz (2007). "Integration management of Western acquisitions in Japan." *Journal of Asian Business & Management* 6(1): 95–114.

Froese, F.J., Y.S. Pak, and L.C. Chong (2008). "Managing the human side of cross-border acquisitions in South Korea." *Journal of World Business* 43(1): 97–108.

Frost, T.S., J.M. Birkinshaw, and P.C. Ensign (2002). "Centers of excellence in multinational corporations." *Strategic Management Journal* 23(11): 997–1018.

Fryxell, G.E., J. Butler, and A. Choi (2004). "Successful localization programs in China: An important element in strategy implementation." *Journal of World Business* 39(3): 268–82.

Fubini, D., C. Price, and M. Zollo (2006). *Mergers: Leadership, performance and corporate health.* New York: Palgrave Macmillan.

Furuya, N., M.J. Stevens, A. Bird, G. Oddou, and M. Mendenhall (2009). "Managing the learning and transfer of global management competence: Antecedents and outcomes of Japanese repatriation effectiveness." *Journal of International Business Studies* 40(2): 200–15.

Gabor, A. (1990). *The man who discovered quality.* New York: Times Books.

Galbraith, J.R. (1977). *Organization design.* Reading, MA: Addison-Wesley.

_____ (2000). *Designing the global corporation.* San Francisco: Jossey-Bass.

_____ (2002). "Organizing to deliver solutions." *Organizational Dynamics* 31(2): 194–207.

_____ (2009) *Designing matrix organizations that actually work.* San Francisco: Jossey-Bass.

Galbraith, J.R., and D.A. Nathanson (1979). "The role of organizational structure and process in strategy implementation." In *Strategic management,* eds. D.E. Schendel and C.W. Hofer. Boston, MA: Little Brown.

Galunic, C.D., and E. Andersen (2000). "From security to mobility: Generalized investments in human capital and commitment." *Organization Science* 11(1): 1–20.

Galunic, C.D., and K.M. Eisenhardt (2001). "Architectural innovation and modular corporate forms." *Academy of Management Journal* 44(6): 1229–50.

Galunic, C.D., and S. Rodan (1998). "Resource recombinations in the firm: Knowledge structures and the potential for Schumpeterian innovation." *Strategic Management Journal* 19(12): 1193–1201.

Garette B., and P. Dussauge (2000). "Alliances versus acquisitions: Choosing the right option." *European Management Journal* 18(1): 63–9.

Gelfand, M., and J.M. Brett (2004). *The handbook of negotiation and culture.* Stanford, CA: Stanford University Press.

George, C.S. (1968). *The history of management thought.* Englewood Cliffs, NJ: Prentice Hall.

Gerhart, B., and M. Fang (2005). "National culture and human resource management assumptions and evidence." *International Journal of Human Resource Management* 16(6): 971–86.

Geringer, M. J., and C.A. Frayne (1990). "Human resource management and international joint venture control: A parent company perspective." *Management International Review* 30 (Special Issue): 103–20.

Gerstner, L.V. (2002). *Who says elephants can't dance? Inside IBM's historic turnaround.* New York: HarperBusiness.

Ghemawat, P. (2007). *Redefining global strategy: Crossing borders in a world where differences still matter.* Boston, MA: Harvard Business School Press.

Ghoshal, S. (1991). "Andersen Consulting (Europe): Entering the business of business integration." Case series. INSEAD, Fontainebleau.

Ghoshal, S., and C.A. Bartlett (1997). *The individualized corporation.* New York: HarperBusiness.

_____ (1998). *Managing across borders: The transnational solution,* 2nd ed. London: Random House.

_____ (2000). "Rebuilding behavioral context: A blueprint for corporate renewal." In *Breaking the code of change,* eds. M. Beer and N. Nohria. Boston, MA: Harvard Business School Press.

Ghoshal, S., and L. Gratton (2002). "Integrating the enterprise." *MIT Sloan Management Review* 44(1): 31–8.

Ghoshal, S., and N. Nohria (1987). "Multinational corporations as differentiated networks." Working paper no. 87/13. INSEAD, Fontainebleau.

Gibson, C.B., and B.L. Kirkman (1999). "Our past, present, and future in teams: The role of human resource professionals in managing team performance." In *Evolving practices in human resource management: Responding to the changing world of work,* eds. A.I. Kraut and A.K. Korman. San Francisco: Jossey-Bass.

Gilbert, J.A., and J.M. Ivancevich (2000). "Valuing diversity: A tale of two organizations." *Academy of Management Executive* 14(1): 93–105.

Gittell, J.H. (2000). "Paradox of coordination and control." *California Management Review* 42(3): 101–17.

Gluesing, J.G., and C.B. Gibson (2004). "Designing and forming global teams." In *The Blackwell handbook of global management: A guide to managing complexity,* eds. H.W. Lane, M.L. Maznevski, M.E. Mendenhall, and J. McNett. Oxford: Blackwell Publishing.

Goffee, R., and G. Jones (1998). *The character of a corporation: How your company's culture can make or break your business.* New York: HarperBusiness.

Golden, K.A., and V. Ramanujam (1985). "Between a dream and a nightmare: On the integration of human resource management and strategic business planning processes." *Human Resource Managment* 24(4): 429–52.

Goldsmith, M., L. Lyons, and A. Freas (2000). *Coaching for leadership.* San Francisco: Jossey-Bass/Pfeiffer.

Goleman, D. (1995). *Emotional intelligence.* London: Bloomsbury.

Goleman, D., R. Boyatzis, and A. McKee (2002a). "The emotional reality of teams." *Journal of Organizational Excellence* 21(2): 55–65.

_____ (2002b). *Primal leadership: Learning to lead with emotional intelligence.* Boston, MA: Harvard Business School Press.

Gomes-Casseres, B. (1988). "Joint venture cycles: The evolution of ownership strategies of U.S. MNEs, 1945–75." In *Cooperative strategies in international business,* eds. F.J. Contractor and P. Lorange. Lexington, MA: Lexington Books.

Gomes-Casseres, B., and K. McQuade (1992). "Xerox and Fuji Xerox." Case study no. 391156. Harvard Business School, Boston.

González, S.M., and D.V. Tacorante (2004). "A new approach to the best practices debate: Are best practices applied to all employees in the same way?" *International Journal of Human Resource Management* 15(1): 56–75.

Goodall, K., and M. Warner (1997). "The evolving image of HRM in the Chinese workplace: Comparing Sino–foreign joint ventures and state-owned enterprises in Beijing and Shanghai." Paper presented at the LVMH Conference, February 7–8. INSEAD, Fontainebleau.

Gooderham, P.N., O. Nordhaug, and K. Ringdal (1999). "Institutional and rational determinants of organizational practices: Human resource management in European firms." *Administrative Science Quarterly* 44(3): 507–31.

Goold, M., and A. Campbell (1987). *Strategies and styles: The role of the centre in managing diversified corporations.* Oxford: Basil Blackwell.

_____ (1998). "Desperately seeking synergy." *Harvard Business Review* (September-October): 131–43.

Goss, T., R. Pascale, and A. Athos (1993). "The reinvention roller coaster: Risking the present for a powerful future." *Harvard Business Review* (November–December): 97–108.

Granovetter, M. (1973). "The strength of weak ties." *American Journal of Sociology* 78(6): 1360–80.

Grant, R.M. (1996). "Toward a knowledge-based theory of the firm." *Strategic Management Journal* 17 (Winter Special Issue): 109–22.

Gratton, L. (2000). *Living strategy: Putting people at the heart of corporate purpose.* London: Financial Times Prentice Hall.

Gratton, L., V. Hope-Hailey, P. Stiles, and C. Truss (1999a). *Strategic human resource management.* London : Oxford University Press.

_____ (1999b). "Linking individual performance to business strategy: The people process model." *Human Resource Management* 38(1): 17–31.

Gratton, L., and S. Ghoshal (2002). "Improving the quality of conversations." *Organizational Dynamics* 31(3): 209–24.

_____ (2003). "Managing personal human capital: New ethos for the 'volunteer' employee." *European Management Journal* 21(1): 1–10.

Gregersen, H.B., and J.S. Black (1992). "Antecedents to commitment to a parent company and a foreign operation." *Academy of Management Journal* 35(1): 65–90.

_____ (1995). "Keeping high performers after international assignments: A key to global executive development." *Journal of International Management* 1(1): 3–31.

Gregersen, H.B., J.S. Black, and J.M. Hite (1995). "Expatriate performance appraisal: Principles, practices, and challenges." In *Expatriate management: New ideas for international business,* ed. J. Selmer. Westport, CT: Quorum Books.

Gregersen, H.B., J.M. Hite, and J.S. Black (1996). "Expatriate performance appraisal in U.S. multinational firms." *Journal of International Business Studies* 27(4): 711–38.

Gregersen, H.B., A.J. Morrison, and S. Black (1998). "Developing leaders for the global frontier." *MIT Sloan Management Review* 40(1): 2–32.

Greiner, L.E. (1972). "Evolution and revolution as organizations grow." *Harvard Business Review* (July–August): 37–46.

Greller, M., and D.M. Rousseau (1994). "Guest editors' overview: Psychological contracts and human resource practices." *Human Resource Management* 33(3): 383–4.

Griffeth, R.W., P.W. Hom, and S. Gaertner (2000). "A meta-analysis of antecedents and correlates of employee turnover: Update, moderator tests, and research implications for the next millennium." *Journal of Management* 26(3): 463–8.

Grote, D. (2000). "The secrets of performance appraisal: Best practices from the masters." *Across the Board* (May): 14–20.

Groysberg, B., and R. Abrahams (2006). "Lift outs: How to acquire a high-functioning team." *Harvard Business Review* (December): 133–40.

Guest, D.E. (1990). "Human resource management and the American dream." *Journal of Management Studies* 27(4): 377–97.

Guest, D.E., and N. Conway (2002). "Communicating the psychological contract: An employer perspective." *Human Resource Management Journal* 12(2): 22–38.

Guest, D.E., J. Michie, N. Conway, and M. Sheenan (2003). "Human resource management and corporate performance in the UK." *British Journal of Industrial Relations* 41(2): 291–314.

Gupta, A.K., and V. Govindarajan (2000). "Knowledge flows within multinational corporations." *Strategic Management Journal* 21(4): 473–96.

Gupta, A.K., V. Govindarajan, and H. Wang (2008). *The quest for global dominance*. San Francisco: Jossey-Bass.

Guthridge, M., A.B. Komm, and E. Lawson (2008). "Making talent a strategic priority." *McKinsey Quarterly* 1: 49–59.

Guthrie, J.P. (2001). "High-involvement work practices, turnover, and productivity: Evidence from New Zealand." *Academy of Management Journal* 44(1): 180–90.

Haasen, A. (1996). "Opel Eisenach GmbH: Creating a high-productivity workplace." *Organizational Dynamics* 24(4): 80–5.

Hailey, J. (1993). "Localisation and expatriation: The continuing role of expatriates in developing countries." Working paper 18/93. Cranfield School of Management, UK.

_____ (1996). "The expatriate myth: Cross-cultural perceptions of expatriate managers." *The International Executive* 38(2): 255–71.

Hailey, J., and W. Harry (2008). "Localization: A strategic response to globalization." In *International human resource management: A European perspective*, eds. M. Dickmann, C. Brewster, and P. Sparrow. London: Routledge.

Hall, E.T., and M.R. Hall (1990). *Understanding cultural differences: Germans, French, and Americans*. Yarmouth, ME: Intercultural Press.

Hamel, G. (1991). "Competition for competence and inter-partner learning within international strategic alliances." *Strategic Management Journal* 12 (Summer Special Issue): 83–103.

Hamel, G., Y. Doz, and C.K. Prahalad (1989). "Collaborate with your competitors—and win." *Harvard Business Review* (January-February): 133–9.

Hamel, G., and C.K. Prahalad (1994). *Competing for the future*. Boston, MA: Harvard Business School Press.

Hamilton, S., and J. Zhang (2008). "Danone & Wahaha: A bitter-sweet partnership." Case study no. IMD-3-1949. IMD, Lausanne.

Hampden-Turner, C. (1990a). *Charting the corporate mind: From dilemma to strategy*. Oxford: Basil Blackwell.

_____ (1990b). *Corporate culture: From vicious circles to virtuous circles*. London: Hutchinson/Economist Books.

Hampden-Turner, C., and F. Trompenaars (1993). *The seven cultures of capitalism.* New York: Currency Doubleday.

_____ (2000). *Building cross-cultural competence.* New Haven: Yale University Press.

Handfield-Jones, H. (2000). "How executives grow." *McKinsey Quarterly* 1: 117–23.

Handy, C. (1998). *The hungry spirit: Beyond capitalism—a quest for purpose in the modern world.* London: Arrow Books.

Hannan, M.T., and J. Freeman (1989). *Organizational ecology.* Cambridge, MA: Harvard University Press.

Hansen, M.T. (2009). *Collaboration: How leaders avoid the traps, create unity, and reap big results.* Boston, MA: Harvard Business School Press.

Hansen, M.T., and J. Birkinshaw (2007). "The innovation value chain." *Harvard Business Review* (June): 121–30.

Hansen, M.T., M.L. Mors, and B. Løås (2005). "Knowledge sharing in organizations: Multiple networks, multiple phases." *Academy of Management Journal* 48(5): 776–93.

Hansen, M.T., N. Nohria, and T. Tierney (1999). "What's your strategy for managing knowledge?" *Harvard Business Review* (March–April): 106–16.

Hansen, M.T., and B. von Oetinger (2001). "Introducing T-shaped managers: Knowledge management's next generation." *Harvard Business Review* (March): 107–16.

Harding, D., and Rouse, T. (2007). "Human due diligence." *Harvard Business Review* (April): 124–31.

Harrigan, K. (1988). "Strategic alliances and partner asymmetries." *Management International Review* 28 (Special Issue): 53–72.

Harris, H. (1999). "Women in international management: Why are they not selected?" In *International HRM: Contemporary issues in Europe*, eds. C. Brewster and H. Harris. London: Routledge.

Harris, H., and C. Brewster (1999). "An integrative framework for pre-departure preparation." In *International HRM: Contemporary issues in Europe*, eds. C. Brewster and H. Harris. London: Routledge.

Hart, S.L., and R.E. Quinn (1993). "Roles executives play: CEOs, behavioral complexity, and firm performance." *Human Relations* 46(5): 543–74.

Harvey, M. (1997). "Dual-career expatriates: Expectations, adjustment and satisfaction with international relocation." *Journal of International Business Studies* 28(3): 627–58.

Harvey, M., C. Speier, and M.M. Novicevic (1999). "The role of inpatriates in a globalization strategy and challenges associated with the inpatriation process." *Human Resource Planning* 22(1): 38–50.

Harzing, A.-W. (1995). "The persistent myth of high expatriate failure rates." *International Journal of Human Resource Management* 6(2): 457–74.

_____ (1999). *Managing the multinationals: An international study of control mechanisms.* Cheltenham, UK: Edward Elgar.

_____ (2001). "Of bears, bumble-bees, and spiders: The role of expatriates in controlling foreign subsidiaries." *Journal of World Business* 36(4): 366–79.

Harzing, A.-W., and M. Pudelko (2007). "HRM practices in subsidiaries of US, Japanese and German MNCs: Country-of-origin, localization or dominance effect?" *Human Resource Management* 46(4): 535–59.

Haslberger, A., and C. Brewster (2009) "Capital gains: Expatriate adjustment and the psychological contract in international careers." *Human Resource Management*, 48(3): 379–97.

Haspeslagh, P. (2000). "Maintaining momentum in mergers." *European Business Forum* (Winter) 4: 53–6.

Haspeslagh, P.C., and D.B. Jemison (1991). *Managing acquisitions: Creating value through corporate renewal*. New York: Free Press.

Hastings, D.F. (1999). "Lincoln Electric's harsh lessons from international expansion." *Harvard Business Review* (May–June): 162–78.

Hatch, M.J. (1993). "The dynamics of organizational culture." *Academy of Management Review* 18(4): 657–93.

Hauschild, P.R. (1993). "Interorganizational imitation: The impact of interlocks on corporate acquisition activity." *Administrative Science Quarterly* 38(4): 564–92.

Hays, R.D. (1974). "Expatriate selection: Insuring success and avoiding failure." *Journal of International Business Studies* 5(1): 25–37.

Hearn, J., B. Metcalfe, and R. Piekkari (2006). "Gender and international human resource management." In *Handbook of research in international human resource management*, eds. G.K. Stahl and I. Björkman. Cheltenham, UK: Edward Elgar.

Hedberg, B.L.T. (1981). "How organizations learn and unlearn." In *Handbook of organizational design*, eds. P.C. Nystrom and W.H. Starbuck. London: Oxford University Press.

Hedberg, B.L.T., P.C. Nystrom, and W.H. Starbuck (1976). "Camping on seesaws: Prescriptions for a self-designing organization." *Administrative Science Quarterly* 21(1): 41–65.

Hedlund, G. (1986). "The hypermodern MNC: A heterarchy?" *Human Resource Management* (Spring): 9–35.

Hedlund, G., and J. Ridderstraale (1995). "International development projects: Key to competitiveness, impossible, or mismanaged?" *International Studies of Management and Organization* 25(1/2): 158–84.

Held, D., A. McGrew, D. Goldblatt, and J. Perraton (1999). *Global transformations: Politics, economics, and culture*. Cambridge: Polity Press.

Heenan, D.A., and W. Bennis (1999). *Co-leaders: The power of great partnerships*. New York: Wiley.

Heifetz, R.A. (1994). *Leadership without easy answers*. Cambridge, MA: Belknap Press of Harvard University Press.

Hennart, J.-F. (1991). "Control in multinational firms: The role of price and hierarchy." *Management International Review* 31 (Special Issue): 71–96.

Hergert, M., and D. Morris (1988). "Trends in international collaborative agreements." In *Cooperative strategies in international business*, eds. F.J. Contractor and P. Lorange. Lexington, MA: Lexington Books.

Hieronimus, F., K. Schaefer, and J. Schroder (2005). "Using brand to attract talent." *McKinsey Quarterly* 3: 12–14.

Higgins, M.C., and K.E. Kram (2001). "Reconceptualizing mentoring at work: A developmental network perspective." *Academy of Management Review* 26(2): 264–88.

Hill, L.A. (1992). *Becoming a manager: Mastery of a new identity*. Boston, MA: Harvard Business School Press.

Hinds, P., and D. Bailey (2003). "Out of sight, out of sync: Understanding conflict in distributed teams." *Organization Science* 14(6): 615–32.

Hitt, M.A., J.J. Harrison, and R.D. Ireland (2001). *Mergers & acquisitions: A guide to creating value for stakeholders*. New York: Oxford University Press.

Hitt, M.A., R.E. Hoskisson, R.D. Ireland, and J.J. Harrison (1991). "Are acquisitions a poison pill for innovation?" *Academy of Management Executive* 5(4): 22–34.

Hodgetts, R. M. (1996). "A conversation with Steve Kerr." *Organizational Dynamics* 24(2): 68–79.

Hofstede, G. (1980). "Motivation, leadership and organization: Do American theories apply abroad?" *Organizational Dynamics* 9(1): 42–63.

_____ (1991). *Cultures and organizations: Software of the mind*. London: McGraw-Hill.

_____ (1999). "Problems remain, but theories will change: The universal and the specific in 21st century global management." *Organizational Dynamics* 28(1): 34–44.

_____ (2001). *Culture's consequences. Comparing values, behaviors, institutions, and organizations across nations*, 2nd ed. Beverly Hills and London: Sage.

Hollenbeck, G.P., and M.W. McCall (2001). "What makes a successful global executive?" *Business Strategy Review* 12(4): 49–56.

Homburg, C., and M. Bucerius (2006). "Is speed of integration really a success factor of mergers and acquisitions? An analysis of the role of internal and external relatedness." *Strategic Management Journal* 27(4): 347–67.

House, R., P.J. Hanges, M. Javidan, P.W. Dorfman, and V. Gupta (2004). *Culture, leadership and organizations: The GLOBE study of 62 societies*. Thousand Oaks, CA: Sage.

House, R., P.J. Hanges, A. Quintanilla, P.W. Dorfman, M.W. Dickson, M. Javidan et al. (1999). "Culture, leadership, and organizational practices." In *Advances in global leadership*, ed. W.H. Mobley. Greenwich, CT: JAI Press.

Hsieh, T., J. Lavoie, and R.A.P. Samek (1999). "Are you taking your expatriate talent seriously?" *McKinsey Quarterly* 3: 71–83.

Human Resource Management International Digest (2007). "Employees come first at high-flying Southwest Airlines: Model contrasts with the Ryanair approach to low-cost aviation." 15(4): 5–7.

Hunt, J., and P. Boxall (1998). "Are top human resource specialists strategic partners? Self perceptions of a corporate elite." *International Journal of Human Resource Management* 9(5): 767–81.

Huselid, M. (1995). "The impact of human resource management practices on turnover, productivity, and corporate financial performance." *Academy of Management Journal* 38(3): 635–72.

Huselid, M.A., R.W. Beatty, and B.E. Becker (2005). "'A' players or 'A' positions?" *Harvard Business Review* (December): 110–17.

Huselid, M.A., B.E. Becker, and R.W. Beatty (2005). *The workforce scorecard: Managing human capital to execute strategy*. Boston, MA: Harvard Business School Press.

Huselid, M., S.E. Jackson, and R.S. Schuler (1997). "Technical and strategic human resource management effectiveness as determinants of firm performance." *Academy of Management Journal* 40(1): 171–88.

Huston L., and N. Sakkab (2006). "Connect and develop: Inside Procter & Gamble's new model for innovation." *Harvard Business Review* (March): 58–66.

Huy, Q.N. (2002). "Emotional balancing of organizational continuity and radical change: The contribution of middle managers." *Administrative Science Quarterly* 47(1): 31–69.

_____ (2004). "Building emotional capital for strategic renewal: Nissan (1999–2002)." Case study. INSEAD, Fontainebleau.

_____ (2005). "An emotion-based view of strategic renewal." *Advances in Strategic Management* 22: 3–37.

Ibarra, H. (1992). "Structural alignments, individual strategies, and managerial action: Elements toward a network theory of getting things done." In *Networks and organizations*, eds. N. Nohria and R.G. Eccles. Boston: Harvard Business School Press.

_____ (2000). "Making partner: A mentor's guide to the psychological journey." *Harvard Business Review* (March–April): 146–55.

Ibarra, H., and M. Hunter (2007). "How leaders create and use networks." *Harvard Business Review* (January): 40–7.

Ibarra, H., S. Snook, and L.G. Ramo (2008). "Identity change in transition to leadership roles." Working papers, no. 32. INSEAD, Fontainebleau.

Iles, P. (2007). "Employee resourcing and talent management." In *Human resource management: A critical text*, ed. J. Storey, 3rd ed. London: Thomson Learning.

Imai, M. (1986). *Kaizen: The key to Japan's competitive success*. New York: Random House.

Ingham, J. (2007). *Strategic human capital management: Creating value through people.* Oxford: Butterworth-Heinemann.

Inkpen, A.C. (1997). "An examination of knowledge management in international joint venture." In *Cooperative strategies: North American perspectives*, eds. P.W. Beamish and J.P. Killing. San Francisco: New Lexington Press.

_____ (1998). "Learning and knowledge acquisition through international strategic alliances." *Academy of Management Executive* 12(4): 69–80.

_____ (2005). "Learning through alliances: General Motors and NUMMI." *California Management Review* 47(4): 114–36.

Inkpen, A.C., A.K. Sundaram, and K. Rockwood (2000). "Cross-border acquisitions of U.S. technology assets." *California Management Review* 42(3): 50–71.

Inkpen, A.C., and E.W.K. Tsang (2005). "Social capital, networks, and knowledge transfer." *Academy of Management Review* 30(1): 146–65.

Jackson, S.E., and R. Schuler (1999). *Managing human resources*. Cincinnati, OH: South-Western College Publishing.

Jacoby, S.M. (1985). *Employing bureaucracy: Managers, unions and the transformation of work in American industry, 1900–1945*. New York: Columbia University Press.

Janger, A.H. (1980). *Organization of international joint ventures*. New York: Conference Board.

Jarvenpaa, S.L., K. Knoll, and D.E. Leidner (1998). "Is anybody out there? Antecedents of trust in global virtual teams." *Journal of Management Information Systems* 14(4): 29–64.

Jarvenpaa, S.L., and D.E. Leidner (1999). "Communication and trust in global virtual teams." *Organization Science* 10(6): 791–815.

Jay, A. (1967). *Management and Machiavelli: An inquiry into the politics of corporate life.* New York: Holt, Rinehart and Winston.

Jemison, D.B., and S.B. Sitkin (1986). "Corporate acquisitions: A process perspective." *Academy of Management Review* 11(1): 145–63.

Jin, Z., R. Mason, and P. Yim (1998). "Bridging US–China cross-cultural differences using internet and groupware technologies." Paper presented at the 7th International Association for Management of Technology Annual Conference, February, Orlando, FL.

Johansen, R., D. Sibbet, R. Mittman, P. Saffo, and S. Benson (1991). *Leading business teams: How teams can use technology and group process tools to enhance performance.* Reading, MA: Addison-Wesley.

Johanson, J., and J.E. Vahlne (1977). "The internationalization process of the firm: A model of knowledge development and increasing foreign market commitment." *Journal of International Business Studies* 8(1): 23–32.

Johanson, J., and F. Wiedersheim-Paul (1975). "The internationalization of the firm: Four Swedish cases." *Journal of Management Studies* 12(3): 305–23.

Johnson, G., K. Scholes, and R. Whittington (2005). *Exploring corporate strategy: Text & cases*, 7th ed. Harlow, UK: FT Prentice-Hall.

Johnson, J.P., T. Lenartowicz, and S. Apud (2006). "Cross-cultural competence in international business: Toward a definition and a model." *Journal of International Business Studies* 37(4): 525–43.

Johnson, L., and J. Rich (2000). "Dealing with employee benefit issues in mergers and acquisitions." *SHRM's Legal Report* (March–April). Arlington, VA: Society for Human Resource Management.

Jones, C. (1996). "Careers in project networks: The case of the film industry." In *The boundaryless career: A new principle for a new organizational era*, eds. M.B. Arthur and D.M. Rousseau. New York: Oxford University Press.

Jones, G. (1996). *The evolution of international business*. London: Routledge.

Judge, T.A., C.J. Thoresen, V. Pucik, and T.M. Welbourne (1999). "Managerial coping with organizational change: A dispositional perspective." *Journal of Applied Psychology* 84(1): 107–22.

Kale, P., and J. Anand. (2006). "The decline of emerging economy joint ventures: The case of India." *California Management Review* 48(3): 62–76.

Kamprad, I., and B. Torekull (1999). *Leading by design: The IKEA story*. New York: Harper-Collins.

Kanter, R.M. (1985). *Change masters: Innovation for productivity in the American workplace*. New York: Simon & Schuster.

_____ (1989). *When giants learn to dance: Mastering the challenge of strategy, management, and careers in the 1990s*. New York and Toronto: Simon & Schuster.

_____ (1994). "Collaborative advantage: The art of alliances." *Harvard Business Review* (July–August): 96–108.

_____ (1995). *World class: Thriving locally in the global economy*. New York: Simon & Schuster.

Kaplan, R.S., and D.P. Norton (1996). *Translating strategy into action: The balanced scorecard*. Boston, MA: Harvard Business School Press.

_____ (2008). "Mastering the management system." *Harvard Business Review* (January): 63–7.

Kates, A. (2006). "(Re)Designing the HR organization." *Human Resource Planning* 29(2): 22–30.

Katzenbach, J.R., and D.K. Smith (1993). *The wisdom of teams: Creating the high performance organization*. Boston, MA: Harvard Business School Press.

Kaufman, B. (2007). "The development of HRM in historical and international perspective." In *The Oxford handbook of human resource management*, eds. P. Boxall, J. Purcell, and P. Wright. New York: Oxford University Press.

Kay, I.T., and M. Shelton (2000). "The people problems in mergers." *McKinsey Quarterly* 4: 29–37.

Kelly, J., and J. Gennard (2000). "Getting to the top: Career paths of personnel directors." *Human Resource Management Journal* 10(3): 22–37.

Kennedy, C. (1989). "Xerox charts a new strategic direction." *Long Range Planning* 22(1): 10–17.

Kenney, M., and R. Florida. (1993). *Beyond mass production: The Japanese system and its transfer to the U.S.* New York: Oxford University Press.

Kepes, S., and J.E. Delery (2007). "HRM systems and the problem of internal fit." In *The Oxford handbook of human resource management*, eds. P. Boxall, J. Purcell, and P. Wright. New York: Oxford University Press.

Kerr, S. (1995). "An academic classic: On the folly of rewarding A, while hoping for B." *Academy of Management Executive* 9(1): 7–14.

Kerr, S., and S. Landauer (2004). "Using stretch goals to promote organizational effectiveness and personal growth: General Electric and Goldman Sachs." *Academy of Management Executive* 18(4): 134–8.

Kets de Vries, M.F.R. (1989). "Leaders who self-destruct: The causes and cures." *Organizational Dynamics* 17(4): 5–17.

_____ (1994). "Percy Barnevik and ABB." Case study no. 05/94-4308. INSEAD, Fontainebleau.

Kets de Vries, M.F.R., A. Agrawal, and E. Florent-Treacy (2006). "The moral compass: Values-based leadership at Infosys." Case study no. 806-050-1. INSEAD, Fontainebleau.

Kiesler, S., and J.N. Cummings (2002). "What do we know about proximity and distance in work groups? A legacy of research." In *Distributed work*, eds. P. Hinds and S. Kiesler. Cambridge, MA: MIT Press.

Kilduff, M., and W. Tsai (2003). *Social networks and organizations.* London: Sage.

Killing, J.P. (1982). "How to make a global joint venture work." *Harvard Business Review* (May–June): 120–7.

_____ (1997). "International joint ventures: Managing after the deal is signed." *Perspectives for Managers*, no. 1. Lausanne: IMD.

_____ (2003a). "Improving acquisition integration: Be clear on what you intend, and avoid 'best of both' deals." *Perspectives for Managers*, no. 97. Lausanne: IMD.

_____ (2003b). "Nestlé's Globe Program (A): The early months." Case study no. IMD-3-1336, with video. IMD, Lausanne.

Kim, C., and R. Mauborgne (1991). "Implementing global strategies: The role of procedural justice." *Strategic Management Journal* 12 (Summer Special Issue): 125–43.

_____ (1997). "Fair process: Managing in the knowledge economy." *Harvard Business Review* (July–August): 65–75.

_____ (1998). "Procedural justice, strategic decision making, and the knowledge economy." *Strategic Management Journal* 19(4): 323–38.

Kim, K., J.-H. Park, and J.E. Prescott (2003). "The global integration of business functions: A study of multinational businesses in integrated global industries." *Journal of International Business Studies* 34(4): 327–44.

Kimberly, J.R., and H. Bouchikhi (1995). "The dynamics of organizational development and change: How the past shapes the present and constrains the future." *Organization Science* 6(1): 9–18.

King, D.R., D.R. Dalton, C.M. Daily, and J.G. Covin (2004). "Meta-analyses of post-acquisition performance: Indications of unidentified moderators." *Strategic Management Journal* 25(2): 187–200.

Kirkman B.L., and D.N. den Hartog (2004). "Performance Management in Global Teams" In *The Blackwell handbook of global management: A guide to managing complexity*, eds. H.W. Lane, M.L. Maznevski, M.E. Mendenhall, and J. McNett. Oxford: Blackwell Publishing.

Kirkman, B.L., B. Rosen, C.B. Gibson, P.E. Tesluk, and S.O. McPherson (2002). "Five challenges to virtual team success: Lessons from Sabre, Inc." *Academy of Management Executive* 16(3): 67–79.

Klein, J.A. (2004). *True change: How outsiders on the inside get things done in organizations.* San Francisco: Jossey-Bass.

Kobrin, S.J. (1988). "Expatriate reduction and strategic control in American multinational corporations." *Human Resource Management* 27(1): 63–75.

Koen, C.I. (2004). "The dialectics of globalization: What are the effects for management and organization in Germany and Japan?" *Research in International Business and Finance* 18(2): 173–97.

Kogut, B. (1988). "Joint ventures: Theoretical and empirical perspectives." *Strategic Management Journal* 9(4): 319–32.

Kogut, B., and U. Zander (1992). "Knowledge of the firm, combinative capabilities, and the replication of technology." *Organization Science* 3(3): 383–97.

_____ (1993). "Knowledge of the firm and the evolutionary theory of the multinational corporation." *Journal of International Business Studies* 24(4): 625–45.

Kolb, D.A. (1984). *Experiential learning: Experience as the source of learning and development.* Englewood Cliffs, NJ: Prentice Hall.

Komin, S. (1990). "Psychology of the Thai people: Values and behavioral patterns." Bangkok Research Centre: National Institute of Development Administration (NIDA).

Kopp, R. (1994). "International human resource policies and practices in Japanese, European, and U.S. multinationals." *Human Resource Management* 33(4): 581–99.

Kostova, T. (1999). "Transnational transfer of strategic organizational practices: A contextual perspective." *Academy of Management Review* 24(2): 308–24.

Kostova, T., and K. Roth (2002). "Adoption of an organizational practice by subsidiaries of multinational corporations: Institutional and relational effects." *Academy of Management Journal* 45(1): 215–33.

_____ (2003). "Social capital in multinational corporations and a micro-macro model of its formation." *Academy of Management Review* 28(2): 297–319.

Kotter, J.P. (1982). "What effective general managers really do." *Harvard Business Review* (November–December): 156–67.

_____ (1988). "The leadership factor." *McKinsey Quarterly* (Spring).

_____ (1996). *Leading change.* Boston, MA: Harvard Business School Press.

Kotter, J.P., and J.L. Heskett (1992). *Corporate culture and performance.* New York: Free Press.

Kraatz, M.S. (1998). "Learning by association? Interorganizational networks and adaptation to environmental change." *Academy of Management Journal* 41(6): 621–43.

Kram, K. E. (1985). *Mentoring at work.* Glennview, IL: Scott, Foresman.

Krug, J., and W.H. Hegerty (1997). "Postacquisition turnover among U.S. top management teams: An analysis of the effect of foreign versus domestic acquisition of U.S. targets." *Strategic Management Journal* 18(8): 667–75.

_____ (2001). "Predicting who stays and leaves after an acquisition: A study of top managers in multinational firms." *Strategic Management Journal* 22(2): 185–96.

Kuin, P. (1972). "The magic of multinational management." *Harvard Business Review* (November–December): 89–97.

Kulik, C.T., and T.J. Bainbridge (2006). "HR and the line: The distribution of HR activities in Australian organizations." *Asia Pacific Journal of Human Resources* 44(2): 240–56.

Kulik, C.T., and E.L. Perry (2008). "When less is more: The effect of devolution on HR's strategic role and construed image." *Human Resource Management* 47(3): 541–58.

Kumar, N. (2009). "How emerging giants are rewriting the rules of M&A." *Harvard Business Review* (May): 115–21.

Kuvaas, B. (2008). "An exploration of how the employee–organization relationship affects the linkage between perception of developmental human resource practices and employee outcomes." *Journal of Management Studies* 45(1): 1–25.

Lafley, A.G. (2008). "P&G's innovation culture." *Strategy+Business Magazine* 52(3).

Lambert, A. (2009). "Configuring HR for tomorrow's challenges." London: Corporate Research Forum.

Lane, C. (1989). *Management and labour in Europe: The industrial enterprise in Germany, Britain and France.* Aldershot, UK: Edward Elgar.

Lane, P.J., B.R. Koka, and S. Pathak (2006). "The reification of absorptive capacity: A critical review and rejuvenation of the construct." *Academy of Management Review* 31(4): 833–63.

Larsen, H.H., and C. Brewster (2003). "Line management responsibility for HRM: What is happening in Europe?" *Employee Relations* 25(3): 228–44.

Larsson, R., and S. Finkelstein (1999). "Integrating strategic, organizational, and human resource perspectives on mergers and acquisitions: A case survey of synergy realization." *Organization Science* 10(1): 1–26.

Lasserre, P. (1996). "Regional headquarters: The spearhead for Asia Pacific markets." *Long Range Planning* 29(1): 30–7.

_____ (2008). *Global strategic management*. London: Palgrave Macmillan.

Lasserre, P., and P.S. Ching (1997). "Human resources management in China and the localization challenge." *Journal of Asian Business* 13(4): 75–96.

Lasserre, P., and H. Schütte (2006). *Strategies for Asia Pacific*, 3rd ed. London: Palgrave Macmillan.

Latham, G. (2004). "The motivational benefits of goal setting." *Academy of Management Executive* 18(2): 126–9.

Laurent, A. (1983). "The cultural diversity of Western conceptions of management." *International Studies of Management and Organization* 13(1/2): 75–96.

Law, K., C.-S. Wong, and K.D. Wang (2004). "An empirical test of the model on managing the localization of human resources in the People's Republic of China." *International Journal of Human Resource Management* 15(4/5): 635–48.

Lawler, E.E. (1992). *The ultimate advantage: Creating the high involvement organization*. San Francisco: Jossey-Bass.

_____ (2002). "The folly of forced ranking." *Strategy+Business* 28(3).

_____ (2003). *Treat people right*. San Francisco: Jossey-Bass.

_____ (2008). *Talent: Making people your competitive advantage*. San Francisco: Jossey-Bass.

Lawler, E.E., J.W. Boudreau, and S.A. Mohrman (2006). *Achieving strategic excellence: An assessment of human resource organizations*. Stanford, CA: Stanford University Press.

Lawler, E.E., D. Ulrich, J. Fitz-Enz, and J.C. Madden (2004). *Human resources business process outsourcing: Transforming how HR gets work done*. San Francisco: Jossey-Bass.

Lawrence, P.R., and J.W. Lorsch (1967). *Organization and environment*. Boston, MA: Harvard Division of Research.

Lazarova, M., and I. Tarique (2005). "Knowledge transfer upon repatriation." *Journal of World Business* 40(4): 361–73.

Lazonick, W., and M. O'Sullivan (1996). "Organization, finance, and international competition." *Industrial and Corporate Change* 5(1): 1–49.

Leana, C.R., and H.J. Van Buren III (1999). "Organizational social capital and employment practices." *Academy of Management Review* 24(3): 538–55.

Legge, K. (1995). *Human resource management: Rhetorics and realities*. London: Macmillan.

_____ (1999). "Representing people at work." *Organization* 6(2): 247–64.

Lei, D., J.W. Slocum, Jr., and R. Pitts (1997). "Building cooperative advantage: Managing strategic alliances to promote organizational learning." *Journal of World Business* 32(3): 203–23.

Leidner, D., T.R. Kayworth, and M. Mora-Tavarez (1999). "Leadership effectiveness in global virtual teams." Working paper no. 99/68/TM. INSEAD, Fontainebleau.

Lengnick-Hall, M.L., and C.A. Lengnick-Hall (2003). "HR's role in building relationship networks." *Academy of Management Executive* 17(4): 53–63.

_____ (2006). "International human resource management and social network/social capital theory." In *Handbook of research in international human resource management*, eds. G.K. Stahl and I. Björkman. Cheltenham, UK: Edward Elgar.

Leonard, D. (1995). *Wellsprings of knowledge: Building and sustaining the sources of innovation*. Boston, MA: Harvard Business School Press.

Leonard, D., and S. Sensiper (1998). "The role of tacit knowledge in group innovation." *California Management Review* 40(3): 112–32.

Leonard-Barton, D. (1992). "Core capabilities and core rigidities: A paradox in managing new product development." *Strategic Management Journal* 13 (Summer Special Issue): 111–25.

_____ (1995). *Wellsprings of knowledge: Building and sustaining the sources of innovation*. Boston, MA: Harvard Business School Press.

Leonard-Barton, D., and S. Conner (1996). "Hewlett-Packard: Singapore (A), (B), (C)." Case study nos. 694-035, -036, and -037. Harvard Business School, Boston.

Lepak, D.P., and S.A. Snell (1999). "The human resource architecture: Toward a theory of human capital allocation and development." *Academy of Management Review* 24(1): 31–48.

_____ (2002). "Examining the human resource architecture: The relationships among human capital, employment, and human resource configurations." *Journal of Management* 28(4): 517–43.

_____ (2007). "Employment subsystems and the 'HR architecture'." In *The Oxford handbook of human resource management*, eds. P. Boxall, J. Purcell, and P. Wright. New York: Oxford University Press.

Lepsinger, R., and A.D. Lucia (1997). *The art and science of 360° feedback*. San Francisco: Pfeiffer.

Lervik, J.E.B. (2005). "Managing matters: Transferring organizational practices within multinational companies." Doctoral thesis. Norwegian School of Management, Oslo.

Leung, A.K., W. Maddux, A. Galinsky, and C. Chiu (2008). "Multicultural experience enhances creativity." *American Psychologist* 63(3): 169–81.

Levitt, B., and J.G. March (1988). "Organizational learning." *Annual Review of Sociology* 14: 319–38.

Levy, O., S. Beechler, S. Taylor, and N.A. Boyacigiller (2007). "What we talk about when we talk about 'global mindset': Managerial cognition in multinational corporations." *Journal of International Business Studies* 38(2): 231–58.

Lewis, M. W. (2000). "Exploring paradox: Toward a more comprehensive guide." *Academy of Management Review* 25(4): 760–76.

Lewis, R.E., and R.J. Heckman (2006). "Talent management: A critical review." *Human Resource Management Review* 16(2): 139–54.

Li, C., and J. Bernoff (2008). *Groundswell*. Boston, MA: Harvard Business School Press.

Low, J., and T. Siesfield (1998). *Measures that matter*. Boston, MA: Ernst & Young.

Liker, J.K., and M. Hoseus (2008). *Toyota culture: The heart and soul of the Toyota Way*. New York: McGraw-Hill.

Lindholm, N. (1998). *Performance appraisal in MNC subsidiaries: A study of host country employees in China*. EIASM Workshop on Strategic Human Resource Management, Brussels.

Lindqvist, M., O. Sölvell, and I. Zander (2000). "Technological advantage in the international firm: Local and global perspectives on the innovation process." *Management International Review* 40(1): 95–126.

Littrell, L.N., and E. Salas (2005). "A review of cross-cultural training: Best practices, guidelines, and research needs." *Human Resource Development Review* 4(3): 305–34.

Liu, G., and D. Liu (2007). "Danone and Wahaha: China-style divorce (A) and (B)." Case study nos. 207-021-1 & 207-022-1. China Europe International Business School (CEIBS), Shanghai.

Liu, X., and M.A. Shaffer (2005). "An investigation of expatriate adjustment and performance." *International Journal of Cross Cultural Management* 5(3): 235–54.

Locke, E.A., and G.P. Latham (1990). *A theory of goal setting and task performance.* Englewood Cliffs, NJ: Prentice Hall.

_____ (2006). "New direction in goal-setting theory." *Current Directions in Psychological Science* 15(5): 265–8.

Løwendahl, B. (2005). *Strategic management of professional service firms*, 2nd ed. Copenhagen: Handelshojskolens Forlag.

Lombardo, M., and R.W. Eichinger (2000). "High potentials as high learners." *Human Resource Management* 39(4): 321–9.

Lorange, P. (1996). "A strategic human resource perspective applied to multinational cooperative ventures." *International Studies of Management and Organization* 26(1): 87–103.

Lorange, P., and J. Roos (1990). "Formation of cooperative ventures: Competence mix of the management teams." *Management International Review* 30 (Special Issue): 69–86.

Lorsch, J.W., and T.J. Tierney (2002). "Aligning the stars: How to succeed when professionals drive results." Boston, MA: Harvard Business School Press.

Loveridge, R. (1990). "Footfalls of the future: The emergence of strategic frames and formulae." In *The strategic management of technological innovation*, eds. R. Loveridge and M. Pitt. Chichester, UK: Wiley.

Lowe, K.B., M. Downes, and K.G. Kroeck (1999). "The impact of gender and location on the willingness to accept overseas assignments." *International Journal of Human Resource Management* 10(2): 223–34.

Lu, Y., and I. Björkman (1997). "MNC standardization versus localization: HRM practices in China-Western joint ventures." *International Journal of Human Resource Management* 8(5): 614–28.

Lunnan, R, J.E. Lervik, L.E.M, Traavik, S, Nilsen, R.P. Amdam, and B. Hennestad (2005). "Global transfer of management practice across nations and MNC subcultures." *Academy of Management Executive* 19(2): 77–80.

Luo, Y. (2000). *Partnering with Chinese firms: Lessons for international managers.* Aldershot, UK: Ashgate.

_____ (2001). *Strategy, structure, and performance of MNCs in China.* Westport, CT: Greenwood Publishing Group.

Mabey, C., D. Skinner, and T. Clark, eds. (1998). *Experiencing human resource management.* London: Sage.

MacDuffie, J.P. (1995). "Human resource bundles and manufacturing performance: Organizational logic and flexible production system in the world auto industry." *Industrial and Labor Relations Review* 48: 197–221.

_____ (2007). "HRM and distributed work." *Academy of Management Annals* 1(1): 549–615.

Mael, F., and B.E. Ashforth (1992). "Alumni and their alma mater: A partial test of the reformulated model of organizational identification." *Journal of Organizational Behaviour* 13(2): 103–23.

Maerki, H.U. (2008). "The globally integrated enterprise and its role in global governance." *Corporate Governance* 8(4): 368–73.

Maister, D.H. (1993). *Managing the professional service firm.* New York: Free Press.

Mäkelä, K., I. Björkman, and M. Ehrnrooth (Forthcoming). "How do MNCs establish their talent pools? Influences on individuals' likelihood of being labeled as talent." *Journal of World Business*.

Manning, S., S. Massini, and A.Y. Lewin (2008). "A dynamic perspective on next-generation offshoring: The global sourcing of science and engineering talent." *Academy of Management Perspectives* 22(3): 35–54.

Mannix, E.A., and H. Sondak (2002). *Research on managing groups and teams*, 4th ed. New York: Elsevier Science.

Manzoni, J.-F., and J.-L. Barsoux (2007). *The set-up-to-fail syndrome: How good managers cause great people to fail*, 2nd ed. Boston, MA: Harvard Business School Press.

March, J.G. (1991). "Exploration and exploitation in organizational learning." *Organization Science* 2(1): 71–87.

Marchand, D., and Leger, K. (2008). "Cemex Way to profitable growth: Leveraging post-merger integration and best-practice innovation." Case study no.IMD-3-1884. IMD, Lausanne.

Marks, M.L., and P.H. Mirvis (1986). "The merger syndrome." *Psychology Today* 20(10): 36–42.

_____ (1998). *Joining forces: Making one plus one equal three in mergers, acquisitions, and alliances*. San Francisco: Jossey-Bass.

Marschan-Piekkari, R., D. Welch, and L. Welch (1999). "In the shadow: The impact of language on structure, power and communication in the multinational." *International Business Review* 8(4): 421–40.

Martinez, J.I., and J.C. Jarillo (1989). "The evolution of research on coordination mechanisms in multinational corporations." *Journal of International Business Studies* 20(3): 489–514.

Maruca, R.F. (1994). "The right way to go global: An interview with Whirlpool CEO David Whitlam." *Harvard Business Review* (March–April): 135–45.

Mayer, M., and R. Whittington (1999). "Euro-elites: top British, French and German managers in the 1980s and 1990s." *European Management Journal* 17(4): 403–8.

Maznevski, M., S.C. Davison, and K. Jonsen (2006). "Global virtual team dynamics and effectiveness." In *Handbook of research in international resource management*, eds. G.K. Stahl and I. Björkman. Cheltenham, UK: Edward Elgar.

McCall, M.W. (1998). *High flyers: Developing the next generation of leaders*. Boston, MA: Harvard Business School Press.

McCall, M.W., and G.P. Hollenbeck (2002). *Developing global executives: The lessons of international experience*. Boston, MA: Harvard Business School Press.

McCall, M.W., and M. Lombardo (1990). *Off the track: Why and how successful executives get derailed*. Greensboro, NC: Center for Creative Leadership.

McCall, M.W., M. Lombardo, and A. Morrison (1988). *The lessons of experience: How successful executives develop on the job*. New York: Free Press.

McFadyen, M.A., and A.A. Cannella, Jr. (2004). "Social capital and knowledge creation: When do marginal costs associated with social capital exceed marginal benefits?" *Academy of Management Journal* 47(5): 735–46.

McGovern, P. (1997). "Human resource management on the line?" *Human Resource Management Journal* 7(4): 12–29.

McGregor, D. (1960). *The human side of enterprise*. New York: McGraw-Hill.

McGregor, J. (2005). *One billion customers: Lessons from the front lines of doing business in China*. London: Nicholas Brealey.

Melvin, S., and K. Sylvester (1997). "Shipping out." *China Business Review* (May–June): 30–34.

Mendenhall, M.E. (2006). "The elusive, yet critical challenge of developing global leaders." *European Management Journal* 24(6): 422–9.

_____ (2008). "Leadership and the birth of global leadership." In *Global leadership: Research, practice and development*, eds. M.E. Mendenhall, J.S. Osland, A. Bird, G.R. Oddou, and M.L. Maznevski. London: Routledge.

Mendenhall, M.E., and G. Oddou (1985). "The dimensions of expatriate acculturation: A review." *Academy of Management Review* 10(1): 39–47.

_____ (1986). "Acculturation profiles of expatriate managers: Implications for cross-cultural training programs." *Columbia Journal of World Business* 21(4): 73–9.

Mendenhall, M.E., J.S. Osland, A. Bird, G.R. Oddou, and M.L. Maznevski, eds. (2008). *Global leadership: Research, practice and development*. London: Routledge.

Mendenhall, M.E., and G.K. Stahl (2000). "Expatriate training and development: Where do we go from here?" *Human Resource Management* 39(2/3): 251–65.

Meyer, J., and B. Rowan (1977). "Institutional organizations: Formal structure as myth and ceremony." *American Journal of Sociology* 83(2): 340–63.

Meyer, J.P., D.J. Stanley, L. Herscovitch, and L. Topolnyutsky (2002). "Affective, continuance, and normative commitment to the organization: A meta-analysis of antecedents, correlates, and consequences." *Journal of Vocational Behavior* 61(1): 20–52.

Meyerson, D., K.E. Weick, and R.M. Kramer (1996). "Swift trust and temporary groups." In *Trust in organizations: Frontiers of theory and research*, eds. R.M. Kramer and T.R. Tyler. Thousand Oaks, CA: Sage.

Michaels, E.H., H. Handfield-Jones, and B. Axelrod (2001). *The war for talent*. Boston, MA: Harvard Business School Press.

Micklethwait, J., and A. Woolridge (1996). *The witch doctors: Making sense of the management gurus*. New York: Times Books.

Milkovich, G.T., and J.W. Boudreau (1997). *Human resource management*, 8th ed. Chicago: Irwin/McGraw Hill.

Milkovich, G.T., and J.M. Newman (2005). *Compensation*. New York: McGraw-Hill.

Miller, D. (1990). *The Icarus paradox: How exceptional companies bring about their own downfall*. New York: HarperBusiness.

Mills, D.Q. (1994). *The GEM principle: Six steps to creating a high performance organization*. Essex Junction, VT: Oliver Wight.

Mills, M., and H.-P. Blossfield (2008). "Globalization, patchwork career and the individualization of inequality? A 12-country comparison of men's mid-career job mobility." In *Globalization, uncertainty and men's careers: An international comparison*, eds. H.-P. Blossfeld, M. Mills, and F. Bernadi. Northampton, MA: Edward Elgar.

Minbaeva, D., and S. Michailova (2004). "Knowledge transfer and expatriation practices in MNCs: The role of disseminative capacity." *Employee Relations* 26(6): 663–79.

Minbaeva, D., T. Pedersen, I. Björkman, C. Fey, and H. Park (2003). "MNC knowledge transfer, subsidiary absorptive capacity and knowledge transfer." *Journal of International Business Studies* 34(6): 586–99.

Mintzberg, H. (1979). *The structuring of organizations: A synthesis of the research*. Englewood Cliffs, NJ: Prentice Hall.

_____ (1989). *Mintzberg on management: Inside our strange world of organizations*. New York: Free Press.

_____ (1994). *The rise and fall of strategic planning*. Englewood Cliffs, NJ: Prentice Hall.

Mintzberg, H., and J.A. Waters (1985). "Of strategies, deliberate and emergent." *Strategic Management Journal* 6(3): 257–72.

Mintzberg, H., and F. Westley (1992). "Cycles of organizational change." *Strategic Management Journal* 13 (Winter Special Issue): 39–59.

Mishra, A.K., K.E. Mishra, and G.M. Spreitzer (2009). "Downsizing the company without downsizing morale." *MIT Sloan Management Review* 50(3): 39–44.

Mitroff, I., and H. Linstone (1993). *The unbounded mind: Breaking the chains of traditional business thinking.* Oxford and New York: Oxford University Press.

Mohr, A.T. (2006). "A multiple constituency approach to IJM performance management." *Journal of World Business* 41(3): 247–60.

Mol, S.T., M.P. Born, M.E. Willemsen, and H.T. Van der Molen (2005). "Predicting expatriate job performance for selection purposes: A quantitative review." *Journal of Cross-Cultural Psychology* 36(5): 590–620.

Monteiro, L.F., L. Arvidsson, and J. Birkinshaw (2008). "Knowledge flows within multinational corporations: Explaining subsidiary isolation and its performance implications." *Organization Science* 19(1): 90–109.

Moore, K., and J. Birkinshaw (1998). "Managing knowledge in global service firms: Centers of excellence." *Academy of Management Executive* 12(4): 81–92.

Moore, K., and D. Lewis (1999). *Birth of the multinational.* Copenhagen: Copenhagen Business Press.

Moran, Stahl, and Boyer Inc. (1988). "Status of American female expatriate employees: Survey results." Boulder, CO: Moran, Stahl, and Boyer Inc.

Morehart, K.K. (2001). "How to create an employee referral program that works." *HR Focus* 78(1): 3–5.

Morgan, G. (1986). *Images of organization.* Newbury Park, CA: Sage.

Morgan, G., and S. Quack (2005). "Institutional legacies and firm dynamics: The growth and internationalization of UK and German law firms." *Organization Studies* 26(12): 1765–85.

Morgan, G., and R. Ramirez (1983). "Action learning: A holographic metaphor for guiding social change." *Human Relations* 37(1): 1–28.

Moriguchi, C. (2000). "Implicit contracts, the Great Depression, and institutional change: The evolution of employment relations in US and Japanese manufacturing firms, 1910–1940." Working paper. Harvard Business School, Boston.

Morosini, P. (1998). *Managing cultural differences: Effective strategy and execution across cultures in global corporate alliances.* Oxford and New York: Pergamon.

Morosini, P., S. Shane, and H. Singh. (1998). "National cultural distance and cross-border acquisition performance." *Journal of International Business Studies* 29(1): 137–58.

Morosini, P., and U. Steger (2004). "Global mergers and acquisitions: Why do so many fail? How to make them successful." In *Managing complex mergers*, eds. P. Morosini and U. Steger. London: Financial Times Prentice Hall.

Morris, M.A., and C. Robie (2001). "A meta-analysis of the effects of cross-cultural training on expatriate performance and adjustment." *Journal of Management Development* 20(7): 639–49.

Morrison, M. (2007). "The very model of a modern senior manager." *Harvard Business Review* (January): 27–39.

Moxon, R.W., T.W. Roehl, and J. Truitt (1988). "International cooperative ventures in the commercial aircraft industry: Gains, sure, but what's my share?" In *Cooperative strategies in international business*, eds. F.J. Contractor and P. Lorange. Lexington, MA: Lexington Books.

Muller, H. (1970). "The search for qualities essential to advancement in a large industrial group: An exploratory study." The Hague, Holland: Royal Dutch/Shell publications.

Murtha, T.P., S.A. Lenway, and R.P. Bagozzi (1998). "Global mind-sets and cognitive shift in a complex multinational corporation." *Strategic Management Journal* 19(2): 97–114.

Muthu Kumar, R., and S.K. Chaudhuri (2005). "Mittal Steel's knowledge management strategy." Case study no. 305-543-1. ICFAI, India.

Myloni, B., A.-W. Harzing, and H. Mirza (2004). "Human resource management in Greece: Have the colours of culture faded away?" *International Journal of Cross Cultural Management* 4(1): 59–76.

Nahapiet, J., and S. Ghoshal (1998). "Social capital, intellectual capital, and the organizational advantage." *Academy of Management Review* 23(2): 242–66.

Neves, P., and A. Caetano (2006). "Social exchange processes in organizational change: The roles of trust and control." *Journal of Change Management* 6(4): 351–64.

Nicholson, N. (1984). "A theory of work role transitions." *Administrative Science Quarterly* 29(2): 172–91.

Nishii, L.H., and M.F. Özbilgin (2007). "Global diversity management: Towards a conceptual framework." *International Journal of Human Resource Management* 18(11): 1883–94.

Noe, R., J. Hollenbeck, P.M. Wright, and B. Gerhart (1999). *Human resource management*. New York: McGraw-Hill/Irwin.

Nohria, N. (1992). "Is a network perspective a useful way of studying organizations?" In *Networks and organizations*, eds. N. Nohria and R.G. Eccles. Boston, MA: Harvard Business School Press.

Nohria, N., and S. Ghoshal (1997). *The differentiated network: Organizing multinational corporations for value creation*. San Francisco: Jossey-Bass.

Nonaka, I. (1988a). "Creating organizational order out of chaos: Self-renewal in Japanese firms." *California Management Review* 30(3): 57–73.

_____ (1988b). "Toward middle-up-down management: Accelerating information creation." *MIT Sloan Management Review* 29(3): 9–18.

_____ (1994). "A dynamic theory of organizational knowledge creation." *Organization Science* 5(1): 14–37.

Nonaka, I., and H. Takeuchi (1995). *The knowledge-creating company: How Japanese companies create the dynamics of innovation*. New York: Oxford University Press.

Nummela, N., S. Saarenketo, and K. Puumalainen (2004). "Global mindset: A prerequisite for successful internationalization?" *Canadian Journal of Administrative Sciences* 21(1): 51–64.

O'Connor, E. (1999). "Minding the workers: The meaning of 'human' and 'human relations' in Elton Mayo." *Organization* 6(2): 223–46.

Oddou, G.R. (1991). "Managing your expatriates: What the successful firms do." *Human Resource Planning* 14(4): 301–8.

Oddou, G., J.S. Osland, and R.N. Blakeney (2009). "Repatriating knowledge: Variables influencing the 'transfer' process." *Journal of International Business Studies* 40(2): 181–99.

O'Dell, C., and C.J. Grayson (1998). *If only we knew what we know: The transfer of internal knowledge and best practice*. New York: Free Press.

O'Grady, S., and H.W. Lane (1996). "The psychic distance paradox." *Journal of International Business Studies* 27(2): 309–33.

O'Hara-Devereaux, M., and R. Johansen (1994). *Globalwork: Bridging distance, culture and time*. San Francisco: Jossey-Bass.

Orchant, D. (2001). "Expatriate taxation." In *Guide to global compensation and benefits*, ed. C. Reynolds. San Diego: Harcourt.

Ordonez, L.D., M.E. Schweitzer, A.D. Galinsky, and M.H. Bazerman (2009). "Goals gone wild: The systematic side effects of overprescribing goal setting." *Academy of Management Perspectives.* 23(1): 6–16.

O'Reilly, C.A. (1998). "New united motors manufacturing, Inc. (NUMMI)." Case study. Stanford Graduate School of Business, Stanford.

O'Reilly, C.A., and J. Chatman (1996). "Culture as social control: Corporations, cults, and commitment." In *Research in Organizational Behavior*, eds. B. Staw and L. Cummings. Greenwich, CT: JAI Press.

O'Reilly, C. A., and J. Pfeffer (2000). *Hidden value: How great companies achieve extraordinary results with ordinary people.* Boston, MA: Harvard Business School Press.

O'Reilly, C.A. III., and M.L. Tushman (2004). "The ambidextrous organization." *Harvard Business Review* (April): 74–81.

Orlitzky, M. (2007). "Recruitment strategy." In *The Oxford handbook of human resource management*, eds. P. Boxall, J. Purcell, and P. Wright. New York: Oxford University Press.

Orrù, M. (1997). "The institutional analysis of capitalist economies." In *The economic organization of East Asian capitalism*, eds. M. Orrù, N.W. Biggart, and G.G. Hamilton. Thousand Oaks, CA: Sage.

Osland, J.S., A. Bird, M. Mendenhall, and A. Osland (2006). "Developing global leadership capabilities and global mindset: A review." In *Handbook of research in international human resource management*, eds. G.K. Stahl and I. Björkman. Cheltenham, UK: Edward Elgar.

Osono, E., N. Shimizu, and H. Takeuchi (2008). *Extreme Toyota: Radical contradiction that drives success at the world's best manufacturer.* New York: John Wiley.

O'Toole, J. (1985). *Vanguard management.* New York: Doubleday.

Ouchi, W.G. (1981). *Theory Z: How American business can meet the Japanese challenge.* Reading, MA: Addison-Wesley.

_____ (1989). "The economics of organization." In *Human resource management in international firms: Change, globalization, innovation*, eds. P.A.L. Evans, Y. Doz, and A. Laurent. London: Macmillan.

Oxley, G.M. (1961). "The personnel manager for international operations." *Personnel* 38(6): 52–8.

Paauwe, J. (2004). *HRM and performance: Achieving long-term viability.* Oxford: Oxford University Press.

_____ (2009). "HRM and performance: Achievements, methodological issues and prospects." *Journal of Management Studies* 46(1): 129–42.

Packard, D. (1995). *The HP way: How Bill Hewlett and I built our company.* New York: HarperBusiness.

Paik, Y., and D.Y. Choi (2005). "The shortcomings of a global knowledge management system: The case of Accenture." *Academy of Managent Executive* 19(2): 81–4.

Paik, Y., and C.M. Stage (1996). "The extent of divergence in human resource practice across three Chinese national cultures: Hong Kong, Taiwan and Singapore." *Human Resource Management Journal* 6(2): 20–31.

Palmisano, S.J. (2006). "The globally integrated enterprise." *Foreign Affairs* (May–June) 85: 127–36.

Parkhe, A. (1991). "Interfirm diversity, organizational learning, and longevity in global strategic alliances." *Journal of International Business Studies* 22(4): 579–601.

_____ (1993). "Partner nationality and the structure-performance relationship in strategic alliances." *Organization Science* 4(2): 301–24.

Pauly, L.W., and S. Reich (1997). "National structures and multinational corporate behavior: Enduring differences in the age of globalization." *International Organization* 51(1): 1–30.

Penrose, E. (1959). *The theory of the growth of the firm.* New York: Wiley.

Perlmutter, H.V. (1969). "The tortuous evolution of the multinational corporation." *Columbia Journal of World Business* 4: 9–18.

Peters, T.J., and R.H. Waterman (1982). *In search of excellence.* New York: Harper & Row.

Peterson, M.F., T.K. Peng, and P.B. Smith (1999). "Using expatriate supervisors to promote cross-border management practice transfer: The experience of a Japanese electronics company." In *Remade in America: Transplanting and transforming Japanese management systems,* eds. J.K. Liker, W.M. Fruin, and P.S. Adler. New York: Oxford University Press.

Peterson, R., S. Behfar, and K. Jackson (2003). "The dynamic relationship between performance feedback, trust, and conflict in groups: A longitudinal study." *Organizational Behavior & Human Decision Processes* 92(1): 102–12.

Peterson, R.B. (2003). "The use of expatriates and inpatriates in Central and Eastern Europe since the Wall came down." *Journal of World Business* 38(1): 55–69.

Petrovic, J., and N.K. Kakabadse (2003). "Strategic staffing of international joint ventures: An integrative perspective for future research." *Management Decisions* 41(4): 394–406.

Pettigrew, A.M. (2000). "Linking change processes to outcomes." In *Breaking the code of change,* eds. M. Beer and N. Nohria. Boston, MA: Harvard Business School Press.

Pfeffer, J. (1994). *Competitive advantage through people.* Boston, MA: Harvard Business School Press.

_____ (1998). *The human equation: Building profits by putting people first.* Boston, MA: Harvard Business School Press.

Pfeffer, J., and R.I. Sutton (1999). "Knowing 'what' to do is not enough: Turning knowledge into action." *California Management Review* 42(1): 83–108.

Pieper, R. (1990). *Human resource management: An international comparison.* Berlin and New York: de Gruyter.

Pil, F.K., and J.P. MacDuffie (1999). "What makes transplants thrive: Managing the transfer of 'best practice' at Japanese auto plants in North America." *Journal of World Business* 34(4): 372–91.

Pillai, R., T.A. Scandura, and E. Williams (1999). "Leadership and organizational justice: Similarities and differences across cultures." *Journal of International Business Studies* 30(4): 763–79.

Podsakoff, P. M., S.B. MacKenzie, J.B. Paine, and D.G. Bachrach (2000). "Organizational citizenship behaviors: A critical review of the theoretical and empirical literature and suggestions for future research." *Journal of Management* 26(3): 513–63.

Polanyi, M. (1966). *The tacit dimension.* London: Routledge and Kegan Paul.

Porter, M.E. (1980). *Competitive strategy: Techniques for analyzing industries and competitors.* New York: Viking.

_____ (1986). *Competition in global industries.* Boston, MA.: Harvard Business School Press.

Powell, W.W., and P.J. DiMaggio (1991). *The new institutionalism in organizational analysis.* Chicago: University of Chicago Press.

Prahalad, C.K. (2004). *Fortune at the bottom of the pyramid.* Upper Saddle River, NJ: Wharton School Publishing.

Prahalad, C.K., and Y. Doz (1987). *The multinational mission: Balancing local demands and global vision.* New York: Free Press.

Prahalad, C.K., and K. Lieberthal (1998). "The end of corporate imperialism." *Harvard Business Review* (July–August): 69–79.

Prescott, R.K., W.J. Rothwell, and M. Taylor (1999). "Global HR: Transforming HR into a global powerhouse." *HR Focus* 76(3): 7–8.

Price Waterhouse Change Integration Team (1996). *The paradox principles: How high performance companies manage chaos, complexity, and contradiction to achieve superior results.* Chicago: McGraw-Hill/Irwin.

Probst, G., and S. Borzillo (2008). "Why communities of practice succeed and why they fail." *European Management Journal* 26(5): 335–47.

Pucik, V. (1984). "White-collar human resource management in large Japanese manufacturing firms." *Human Resource Management* 23(3): 257–76.

_____ (1988a). "Strategic alliances with the Japanese: Implications for human resource management." In *Cooperative strategies in international business*, eds. F.J. Contractor and P. Lorange. Lexington, MA: Lexington Books.

_____ (1988b). "Strategic alliances, organizational learning, and competitive advantage: The HRM agenda." *Human Resource Management* 27(1): 77–93.

_____ (1992). "Globalization and human resource management." In *Globalizing management: Creating and leading the competitive organization*, eds. V. Pucik, N.M. Tichy, and C.K. Barnett. New York: Wiley

_____ (1989). "Managerial career progression in large Japanese manufacturing firms." In *Research in personnel and human resources management*, eds. K Rowland and G. Ferris. Greenwich, CT: JAI Press.

_____ (1994). "The challenges of globalization: The strategic role of local managers in Japanese-owned US subsidiaries." In *Japanese multinationals: Strategies and management in the global kaisha*, eds. N. Campbell and F. Burton. London: Routledge.

_____ (1997). "Human resources in the future: An obstacle or a champion of globalization?" *Human Resource Management* 36(1): 163–8.

_____ (2003). "Developing global leaders." In *Organization 21C: Someday all organizations will lead this way*, ed. S. Chowdhury. London: Pearson Education.

_____ (2005). "Global HR as competitive advantage: Are we ready?" In *The future of human resource management*, eds. M. Losey, S. Meisinger, and D. Ulrich. New York: Wiley.

_____ (2006). "Reframing global mindset: From thinking to acting." In *Advances in Global Leadership*, eds. W.H. Mobley and E. Weldon. Oxford: Elsevier.

_____ (2008). "Post-merger integration process in Japanese M&A: The voices from the front-line." In *Advances in mergers and acquisitions*, vol. 7, eds. G.L. Cooper and S. Finkelstein. Bingley, UK: JAI Press.

Pucik, V., S. Fiorella, and E. van Weering (2000). "American Diagnostic Systems." Case study no. IMD-3-0870. IMD, Lausanne.

Pucik, V., and N. Govinder (2007). "Canon Europe: Pan-European Transformation (A), (B) and (C)." Case study nos. IMD-3-1074 to 3-1076. IMD, Lausanne.

Pucik, V., M. Hanada, and G. Fifield (1989). "Management culture and the effectiveness of local executives in Japanese-owned U.S. corporations." Ann Arbor, MI: Egon Zehnder International.

Pucik, V., and N. Hatvany (1981). "An integrated management system: Lessons from the Japanese experience." *Academy of Management Review* 6(3): 469–80.

Pucik, V., and C. Lief (2007). "Leadership at General Electric: A healthy disrespect for history." Case study no. IMD-3-1780. IMD, Lausanne.

Pucik, V., and T. Saba (1998). "Selecting and developing the global versus the expatriate manager: A review of the state-of-the-art." *Human Resource Planning* 21(4): 40–54.

Pucik, V., K. Xin, and D. Everatt (2003). "Managing performance at Haier (A)." Case study no. IMD-3-1332. IMD, Lausanne.

Pudelko, M., and A.-W. Harzing (2007). "How European is management in Europe? An analysis of past, present and future management practices in Europe." *European Journal of International Management* 1(3): 206–24.

Punnett, B.J., and J. Clemens (1999). "Cross-national diversity: Implications for international expansion decisions." *Journal of World Business* 34(2): 128–38.

Quinn, R.E. (1988). *Beyond rational management: Mastering the paradoxes and competing demands of high performance.* San Francisco: Jossey-Bass.

Quinn, R.E., and J. Rohrbaugh (1983). "A spatial model of effectiveness criteria: Towards a competing values approach to organizational analysis." *Management Science* 29(3): 363–77.

Raelin, J.A. (1999). "The design of the action project in work-based learning." *Human Resource Planning* 22(3): 12–28.

Ramirez, R. (1983). "Action learning: A strategic approach for organizations facing turbulent conditions." *Human Relations* 36(8): 725–42.

Rangan, S., and A. Drummond (2004). "Explaining outcomes in competition among foreign multinationals in a focal host market." *Strategic Management Journal* 25(3): 285–93.

Rausch, S., and J. Birkinshaw (2008). "Organizational ambidexterity: Antecedents, outcomes, and moderators." *Journal of Management.* 34(3): 375–409.

Ravasi, D., and M. Schultz (2006). "Responding to organizational identity threats: Exploring the role of organizational culture." *Academy of Management Journal* 49(3): 433–58.

Reade, C. (2001). "Antecedents of organizational identification in multinational corporations: Fostering psychological attachment to the local subsidiary and the global organization." *International Journal of Human Resource Management* 12(8): 1269–91.

Ready, D., and J. Conger (2007). "Make your company a talent factory." *Harvard Business Review* (June): 68–77.

Ready, D., L. Hill, and J. Conger (2008). "Winning the race for talent in emerging markets." *Harvard Business Review* (November): 63–70.

Redding, G. (2001). "The evolution of business systems." Euro-Asia Centre Report no. 72. INSEAD, Fontainebleau and Singapore.

Reich, R.B., and E.D. Mankin (1986). "Joint ventures with Japan give away our future." *Harvard Business Review* (March–April): 78–86.

Reilly, P., P. Tamkin, and A. Broughton (2007). *The changing HR function: Transforming HR?* London: CIPD.

Revens, R.W. (1980). *Action learning: New techniques for management.* London: Blond and Riggs.

Reynolds, C. (1995). *Compensating globally mobile employees.* Scottsdale, AZ: American Compensation Association.

_____ (2001). *Guide to global compensation and benefits.* San Diego: Harcourt.

Rhinesmith, S.H. (1993). *A manager's guide to globalization: Six keys to success in a changing world.* Homewood, IL: ASTD & Business One Irwin.

Rigby, M., R. Smith, and C. Brewster (2004). "Trade unions and democracy: Strategies and perspectives." Manchester: Manchester University Press.

Riketta, M. (2002). "Attitudinal organizational commitment and job performance: A meta-analysis." *Journal of Organizational Behavior* 23(3): 257–66.

Roberto, M.A., and G.M. Carioggia (2002). "Mount Everest—1996." Case study no. 303061. Harvard Business School, Boston.

Rodrigues, S.B., and J. Child (2008). "The development of corporate identity: A political perspective." *Journal of Management Studies* 45(5): 885–911.

Rosenzweig, P. (2006). "The dual logics behind international human resource management: Pressures for global integration and local responsiveness." In *Handbook of research in international human resource management*, eds. G.K. Stahl and I. Björkman. Cheltenham, UK: Edward Elgar.

Rosenzweig, P.M., and N. Nohria (1994). "Influences on human resource management practices in multinational corporations." *Journal of International Business Studies* 25(2): 229–51.

Ross, J.W., and C.M. Beath (2007). "Beyond the business case: New approaches to investment." *MIT Sloan Management Review* 43(2): 51–9.

Rousseau, D.M. (1995). *Psychological contracts in organizations: Understanding written and unwritten agreements*. Thousand Oaks, CA: Sage.

Rousseau, D.M., and S.L. Robinson (1994). "Violating the psychological contract: Not the exception but the norm." *Journal of Organizational Behavior* 15(3): 245–60.

Rudlin, P. (2000). *A history of Mitsubishi Corporation in London: 1915 to present day*. London: Routledge.

Rugman, A., and A. Verbeke (2004). "A perspective on regional and global strategies of multinational enterprises." *Journal of International Business Studies* 35(1): 3–18.

———— (2008). "A regional solution to the strategy and structure of multinationals." *European Management Journal* 26(5): 305–13.

Rumelt, R.P. (1974). *Strategy, structure, and economic performance*. Boston, MA: Harvard University Press.

———— (1996). "The many faces of Honda." *California Management Review* 38(4): 103–11.

Ruta, C.D. (2005). "The application of change management theory to HR portal implementation in subsidiaries of multinational corporations." *Human Resource Management* 44(1): 35–53.

Russo, J.E., and P.J. Schoemaker (2002). *Winning decisions: Getting it right the first time*. New York: Doubleday/Piatkus.

Ryan, A.M., D. Wiechmann, and M. Hemingway (2003). "Designing and implementing global staffing systems: Part II—best practices." *Human Resource Management* 42(1): 85–94.

Sampson, A. (1975). *The seven sisters: The great oil companies and the world they made*. London: Hodder and Stoughton.

Salk, J.E., and B.L. Simonin (2003). "Beyond alliances: Towards a meta-theory of collaborative learning." In *The Blackwell handbook of organizational learning and knowledge management*, eds. M. Easterby-Smith and M.A. Lyles. Malden, MA: Blackwell.

Sanchez, F. (2007). "Principles of global integration." *Industrial Management* (September–October): 8–13.

Santos, J. (2001). "Virtual teams and metanational innovation." Working paper. INSEAD, Fontainebleau.

Schein, E.H. (1985). *Organizational culture and leadership: A dynamic view*. San Francisco: Jossey-Bass.

———— (1996). "Kurt Lewin's change theory in the field and in the classroom: Notes toward a model of managed learning." *Systems Practice* 9(1): 27–47.

Schisgall, O. (1981). *Eyes on tomorrow: The evolution of Procter & Gamble*. New York: Doubleday.

Schlesinger, L.A., and J.L. Heskett (1991). "The service-driven company." *Harvard Business Review* (September–October): 71–81.

Schmidt, J.A., ed. (2002). *Making mergers work*. Alexandria, VA: Towers Perrin and SHRM Foundation.

Schmidt, F.L., and J.E. Hunter (1998). "The validity and utility of selection methods in personnel psychology: Practical and theoretical implications of 85 years of research findings." *Psychological Bulletin* 124(2): 262–72.

Schneider, S.C. (1988). "National vs. corporate culture: Implications for human resource management." *Human Resource Management* 27(2): 231–46.

Schneider, S.C., and J.-L. Barsoux (2003). *Managing across cultures*, 2nd ed. Harlow, UK: Financial Times Prentice Hall.

Schuler, R.S. (2000). "HR issues in international joint ventures and alliances." In *Human resource management: A critical text*, ed. J. Storey. London: International Thomson.

Schütte, H. (1998). "Between headquarters and subsidiaries: The RHQ solution." In *Multinational corporate evolution and subsidiary development*, eds. J. Birkinshaw and N. Hood. London: Macmillan.

Scott, W.R. (2001). *Institutions and organizations*, 2nd ed. Thousands Oaks, CA: Sage Publications.

Scott Myers, M. (1970). *Every employee a manager: More meaningful work through job enrichment*. New York: McGraw-Hill.

Scullion, H. (1994). "Staffing policies and strategic control in British multinationals." *International Studies of Management and Organization* 24(3): 86–104.

_____ (1995). "International human resource management." In *Human resource management: A critical text*, ed. J. Storey. London: Routledge.

Scullion, H., and K. Starkey (2000). "In search of the changing role of the corporate human resource function in the international firm." *International Journal of Human Resource Management* 11(6): 1061–81.

Segal-Horn, S., and A. Dean (2008). "Delivering 'effortless experience' across borders: Managing internal consistency in professional service firms." *Journal of World Business* 44(1): 41–50.

Selmer, J. (2001). "Psycological barriers to adjustment and how they affect coping strategies: Western business expatriates in China." *International Journal of Human Resource Management* 12(2): 151–65.

Selmer, J., and C.T. de Leon (2002). "Parent cultural control of foreign subsidiaries through organizational acculturation: A longitudinal study." *International Journal of Human Resource Management* 13(8): 1147–65.

Shadur, M.A., J.J. Rodwell, and G.I. Bamber (1995). "The adoption of international best practices in a Western culture: East meets West." *International Journal of Human Resource Management* 6(3): 735–57.

Shaffer, M.A., D.A. Harrison, and K.M. Gilley (1999). "Dimensions, determinants, and differences in the expatriate adjustment process." *Journal of International Business Studies* 30(3): 557–81.

Shaw, J.D., J.E. Delery, G. Jenkins, and N. Gupta (1998). "An organization-level analysis of voluntary and involuntary turnover." *Academy of Management Review* 41(5): 511–25.

Shen, J. (2004). "International performance appraisals: Policies, practices and determinants in the case of Chinese multinational companies." *International Journal of Manpower* 25(6): 547–63.

Shenkar, O., and Y. Zeira (1990). "International joint ventures: A tough test for HR." *Personnel* 67(1): 26–31.

Shih, H.-A., Y.-H. Chiang, and I.-S. Kim (2005). "Expatriate performance management from MNEs of different national origins." *International Journal of Manpower* 26(2): 157–76.

Shimada, H., and J.P. MacDuffie (1999). "Industrial relations and 'humanware': Japanese investments in automobile manufacturing in the United States." In *The Japanese enterprise*, ed. S. Beechler. London: Routledge.

Siegel, J.I. (2007). "Lincoln Electric." Case study no. 707-445. Harvard Business School, Boston.

Simon, H. (1996). *Hidden champions: Lessons from 500 of the world's best unknown companies.* Boston, MA: Harvard Business School Press.

Simonin, B.L. (1999). "Ambiguity and process of knowledge transfer in strategic alliances." *Strategic Management Journal* 20(7): 596–623.

Simons, T.L., R. Peterson, and S. Task (2000). "Task conflict and relationship conflict in top management teams: The pivotal role of intragroup trust." *Journal of Applied Psychology* 85(1): 102–11.

Sippola, A., and A. Smale (2007). "The global integration of diversity management: A longitudinal case study." *International Journal of Human Resource Management* 18(11): 1895–1916.

Sisson, K. (1994). "Personnel management: Paradigms, practice and prospects." In *Personnel management*, 2nd ed. Oxford: Blackwell.

Sitkin, S.B., and A.L. Pablo (2005). "The neglected importance of leadership in M&As." In *Mergers and acquisitions: Managing culture and human resources*, eds. G.K. Stahl and M.E. Mendenhall. Stanford, CA: Stanford University Press.

Slangen, A.H.L (2006). "National cultural distance and initial foreign acquisition performance: The moderating effect of integration." *Journal of World Business* 41(2): 161–70.

Smith, P.B., and M.H. Bond (1999). *Social psychology across cultures*, 2nd ed. Boston, MA: Allyn and Bacon.

Snell, S.A. (1999). "Social capital and strategic HRM: It's who you know." *Human Resource Planning* 22(3): 62–5.

Snow, C., R.E. Miles, and H. Coleman (1992). "Managing 21st century network organizations." *Organizational Dynamics* (Winter): 5–20.

Snow, C., S.A. Snell, S.C. Davison, and D.C. Hambrick (1996). "Use transnational teams to globalize your company." *Organizational Dynamics* 24(4): 50–67.

Solomon, C.M. (1998). "Today's global mobility." *Workforce* 3(4): 12–17.

Sonnenfeld, J.A., and M.A. Peiperl (1988). "Staffing policy as a strategic response: A typology of career systems." *Academy of Management Review* 13(4): 588–600.

Sorensen, J.B. (2002). "The strength of corporate culture and the reliability of firm performance." *Administrative Science Quarterly* 47(1): 70–91.

Sparrow, P.R. (1999). "International recruitment, selection and assessment." In *The global HR manager: Creating the seamless organisation*, eds. P. Joynt and B. Morton. London: Institute of Personnel and Development.

_____ (2007). "Globalization of HR at function level: Four UK-based case studies of the international recruitment and selection process." *International Journal of Human Resource Management* 18(5): 845–67.

Sparrow, P.R., and J.-M. Hiltrop (1994). *European human resource management in transition.* New York: Prentice Hall.

Sparrow, P., C. Brewster, and H. Harris (2004). *Globalizing human resource management.* London: Routledge.

Spear, S.J. (2004). "Learning to lead at Toyota." *Harvard Business Review* (May): 78–86.

Spekman, R.E., L. Isabella, T. MacAvoy, and T.M. Forbes III (1998). "Alliance management: A view from the past and a look to the future." *Journal of Management Studies* 35(6): 747–72.

Spreitzer, G.M. (1996). "Social structural characteristics of psychological empowerment." *Academy of Management Journal* 39(2): 483–504.

Spreitzer, G., M.W. McCall, and J. Mahoney (1997). "The early identification of international leadership potential: Dimensions, measurement and validation." *Journal of Applied Psychology* 82(1): 6–29.

Springer, B., and S. Springer (1990). "Human resource management in the US: Celebration of its centenary." In *Human resource management: An international comparison*, ed. R. Piper. Berlin: de Gruyter.

St. John, C.H., S.T. Young, and J.T. Miller (1999). "Coordinating manufacturing and marketing in international firms." *Journal of World Business* 34(2): 109–27.

Staber, U. (2003). "Social capital or strong culture?" *Human Resource Development International* 6(3): 413–20.

Stahl, G.K. (2000). "Between ethnocentrism and assimilation: An exploratory study of the challenges and coping strategies of expatriate managers." Proceedings of the Annual Conference of the Academy of Management, Toronto.

Stahl, G.K., I. Björkman, E. Farndale, S. Morris, J. Paauwe, P. Stiles, J. Trevor, and P. Wright (2007). "Global talent management: How leading multinationals build and sustain their talent pipeline." Working paper no. 2007/34/OB. INSEAD, Fontainebleau.

Stahl, G.K., C.H. Chua, P. Caligiuri, J.-L.E. Cerdin, and M. Taniguchi (2009). "Predictors of turnover intentions in learning-driven and demand-driven international assignments: The role of repatriation concerns, satisfaction with company support, and perceived career advancement opportunities." *Human Resource Management* 48(1): 89–109.

Stahl, G.K., and M.E. Mendenhall, eds. (2005). *Mergers and acquisitions: Managing culture and human resources*. Stanford, CA: Stanford University Press.

Stahl, G.K., E.L. Miller, and R.L. Tung (2002). "Towards the boundaryless career: A closer look at the expatriate career concept and the perceived implications of an international assignment." *Journal of World Business* 37(3): 216–27.

Stahl, G.K., and A. Voigt. (2008). "Do cultural differences matter in mergers and acquisitions? A tentative model and examination." *Organization Science* 19(1): 160–76.

Stalk, J.G. (1988). "Time: The next source of competitive advantage." *Harvard Business Review* (July–August): 41–53.

Steger, U., and C. Kummer (2004). "Challenges of governance structures in international mergers and acquisitions." In *Managing complex mergers*, eds. P. Morosini and U. Steger. London: Financial Times Prentice Hall.

Stening, B.W., J.E. Everett, and P.A. Longton (1981). "Mutual perception of managerial performance and style in multinational subsidiaries." *Journal of Occupational Psychology* 54(4): 255–63.

Stewart, T.A., and A.P. Raman (2007). "Lessons from Toyota's long drive." *Harvard Business Review* (July–August): 74–83.

Stopford, J.M., and L.T. Wells (1972). *Managing the multinational enterprise*. London: Longman.

Stroh, L.K. (1995). "Predicting turnover among repatriates: Can organizations affect retention rates?" *International Journal of Human Resource Management* 6(2): 443–56.

Stroh, L.K., J.S. Black, M.E. Mendenhall, and H. Gregersen (2005). *Global leaders, global assignments: An integration of research and practice*. London: Lawrence Erlbaum.

Stroh, L.K., A. Varma, and S.J. Valy-Durbin (2000). "Why are women left at home: Are they unwilling to go on international assignments?" *Journal of World Business* 35(3): 241–55.

Strohmeier, S. (2007). "Research in e-HRM. Review and implications." *Human Resource Management Review* 17(1): 19–37.

Subramaniam, M., and Venkatraman, N. (2001). "Determinants of transnational new product development capability: Testing the influence of transferring and deploying tacit overseas knowledge." *Strategic Management Journal* 22(4): 359–78.

Sullivan, J.J., and I. Nonaka (1986). "The application of organizational learning theory to Japanese and American management." *Journal of International Business Studies* 17(3): 127–47.

Sumelius, J., I. Björkman, and A. Smale (2008). "The influence of internal and external social networks on HRM capabilities in MNC subsidiaries in China." *International Journal of Human Resource Management* 19(12): 2294–307.

Suutari, V., and C. Brewster (1999). "International assignments across European borders: No problems?" In *International HRM: Contemporary issues in Europe*, eds. C. Brewster and H. Harris. London: Routledge.

_____ (2000). "Making their own way: International experience through self-initiated foreign assignments." *Journal of World Business* 35(4): 417–36.

_____ (2003). "Repatriation: Empirical evidence from a longitudinal study of careers and expectations among Finnish expatriates." *International Journal of Human Resource Management* 14(7): 1132–51.

Suutari, V., and M. Tahvainen (2002). "The antecendents of performance management among Finnish expatriates." *International Journal of Human Resource Management* 13(1): 55–75.

Suutari, V., and C. Tornikoski (2001). "The challenge of expatriate compensation: The sources of satisfaction and dissatisfaction among expatriates." *International Journal of Human Resource Management* 12(3): 389–404.

Szulanski, G. (1996). "Exploring internal stickiness: Impediments to the transfer of best practice within the firm." *Strategic Management Journal* 17 (Winter Special Issue): 27–43.

Tahvanainen, M. (2000). "Expatriate performance management: The case of Nokia Telecommunications." *Human Resource Management*, 39(2/3): 267–76.

Tahvanainen M., D. Welch, and V. Worm (2005). "Implications of short-term international assignments." *European Management Journal* 23(6): 663–73.

Takeuchi, H., and I. Nonaka (1986). "The new product development game." *Harvard Business Review* (January–February): 137–46.

Takeuchi, H., E. Osono, and N. Shimizu (2008). "The contradictions that drive Toyota's success." *Harvard Business Review* (June): 96–104.

Tanure, B., P.A.L. Evans, and V.Pucik (2007). *A gestao de pessoas no Brasil*. Rio de Janeiro: Elsevier.

Tapscott, D., and A.D. Williams (2007). *Wikinomics: How mass collaboration changes everything*. New York: Penguin.

Taylor, F.W. (1911). *Principles of scientific management*. New York: Harper.

Taylor, S. (2007). "Creating social capital in MNCs: The international human resource management challenge." *Human Resource Management Journal* 17(4): 336–54.

Taylor, S., S. Beechler, and N. Napier (1996). "Toward an integrative model of strategic international human resource management." *The Academy of Management Review* 21(4): 959–85.

Taylor, S., and N. Napier (1996). "Working in Japan: Lessons from women expatriates." *MIT Sloan Management Review* 37(3): 76–84.

Tead, O., and H.C. Metcalf (1920). *Personnel administration*. New York: McGraw-Hill.

Teagarden, M.B., J. Meyer, and D. Jones (2008). "Knowledge sharing among high-tech MNCs in China and India: Invisible barriers, best practices, next steps." *Organizational Dynamics* 37(2): 190–202.

Teece, D.J. (1987). *The competitive challenge*. Cambridge, MA: Ballinger.

Teece, D.J., G. Pisano, and A. Shuen (1997). "Dynamic capabilities and strategic management." *Strategic Management Journal* 18(7): 509–33.

Teigland, R. (2000). "Communities of practice in a high-technology firm." *The flexible firm: Capability management in network organizations*, eds. J. Birkinshaw and P. Hagström. New York: Oxford University Press.

Terpstra, D.E., and E.J. Rozell (1993). "The relationship of staffing practices to organizational level measures of performance." *Personnel Psychology* 46(1): 27.

Thibaut, J.W., and L. Walker (1975). *Procedural justice: A psychological analysis*. Hillsdale, NJ: Lawrence Erlbaum.

Thomas, D.A. (2004). "Diversity as strategy." *Harvard Business Review* (September): 98–108.

Thomas, D.C., and M.B. Lazarova (2006). "Expatriate adjustment and performance: A critical review." In *Handbook of research in international human resource management*, eds. G.K. Stahl and I. Björkman. Cheltenham: Edward Elgar.

Thomas, R.J., and W.G. Bennis (2008). *Crucibles of leadership: How to learn from experience to become a great leader*. Boston, MA: Harvard Business School Press.

Thompson, L. (2000). *Making the team: A guide for managers*. Upper Saddle River, NJ: Prentice Hall.

Tichy, N.M., M.I. Brimm, R. Charam, and H. Takeuchi (1992). "Leadership development as a lever for global transformation." In *Globalizing management: Creating and leading the competitive organization*, eds. V. Pucik, N.M. Tichy, and C.K. Barnett. New York: Wiley.

Tichy, N.M., and S. Sherman (1993). *Control your destiny or someone else will*. New York: HarperBusiness.

Timming, A.R. (2007). "European Works Councils and the dark side of managing worker voice." *Human Resource Management Journal* 17(3): 248–64.

Toh, S.M., and A.S. DeNisi (2005). "Host country nationals: The missing key to expatriate success and failure?" *Academy of Management Executive* 19: 132–46.

Torbiörn, I. (1982). *Living abroad: Personal adjustment and personnel policy in the overseas setting*. New York: Wiley.

_____ (1985). "The structure of managerial roles in cross-cultural settings." *International Studies of Management & Organization* 15(1): 52–74.

Torrington, D., and L. Hall (1995). *Human resource management*. London: Prentice Hall.

Toynbee, A. (1946). *A study of history*, vols. 1–6. New York: Oxford University Press.

Trepo, G. (1973). "Management style à la française." *European Business* (Autumn): 71–9.

Trompenaars, F. (1993). *Riding the waves of culture: Understanding cultural diversity in business*. London: Nicholas Brealey.

Tsai, W., and S. Ghoshal (1998). "Social capital and value creation: The role of intrafirm networks." *Academy of Management Journal* 41(4): 464–76.

Tsang, E.W.K. (2002). "Acquiring knowledge by foreign partners from international joint ventures in a transition economy: Learning-by-doing and learning myopia." *Strategic Management Journal* 23(9): 835–54.

Tung, R.L. (1981). "Selection and training of personnel for overseas assignments." *Columbia Journal of World Business* 16(1): 57–71.

_____ (1982). "Selection and training procedures of US, European, and Japanese multinationals." *California Management Review* 25(1): 57–71.

Tung, R.L. (1988). "Career issues in international assignments." *Academy of Management Executive* 2(3): 241–44.

_____ (1995). "Women in a changing global economy." Paper presented at the Tenth Annual Conference of the Society for Industrial and Organizational Psychology, Orlando, FL.

_____ (1997). "Canadian expatriates in Asia-Pacific: An analysis of their attitude toward and experience in international assignments." Paper presented at the meeting of the Society for Industrial and Organizational Psychology, St. Louis, MO.

_____ (2004). "Female expatriates: A model for global leaders." *Organizational Dynamics* 33(3): 243–53.

Tushman, M.L., W.H. Newman, and E. Romanelli (1986). "Convergence and upheaval: Managing the unsteady pace of organizational evolution." *California Management Review* 29(1): 29–44.

Tushman, M.L., and C.A. O'Reilly (1996). "Ambidextrous organizations: Managing evolutionary and revolutionary change." *California Management Review* 38(4): 8–30.

Ulrich, D. (1997). *Human resource champions: The next agenda for adding value and delivering results.* Boston, MA: Harvard Business School Press.

Ulrich, D., and D. Beatty (2001). "From partners to players: Extending the HR playing field." *Human Resource Management* 40(4): 293–307.

Ulrich, D., and W. Brockbank (2005). *The HR value proposition.* Boston, MA: Harvard Business School Press.

Ulrich, D., W. Brockbank, D. Johnson, K. Sandholtz, and J. Younger (2008). *HR competencies: Mastery at the intersection or people and business.* Alexandria, VA: SHRM.

Ulrich, D., W. Brockbank, A. Yeung, and D. Lake (1995). "Human resource competencies: An empirical assessment." *Human Resource Management* 34(4): 473–95.

Ulrich, D., and D.G. Lake (1990). *Organizational capability: Competing from the inside out.* New York: Wiley.

Ulrich, D., M.R. Losey, and G. Lake (1997). *Tomorrow's HR management: 48 thought leaders call for change.* New York: Wiley.

Ulrich, D., and N. Smallwood (2007). *Leadership brand: Developing customer-focused leaders to drive performance and build lasting value.* Boston, MA: Harvard Business School Press.

Ulrich, D., J. Younger, and W.B. Brockbank (2008). "The twenty-first-century HR organization." *Human Resource Management* 47(4): 829–50.

Ulrich, D., J. Zenger, and N. Smallwood (1999). *Results-based leadership.* Boston, MA: Harvard Business School Press.

Vaara, E. (2003). "Post-acquisition integration as sensemaking: Glimpses of ambiguity, confusion, hypocrisy, and politicization." *Journal of Management Studies* 40(4): 859–94.

Vaara, E., J. Tienari, and I. Björkman (2003). "Global capitalism meets national spirit." *Journal of Management Inquiry* 12(4): 377–93.

Van de Ven, A.H., D.E. Polley, R. Garud, and S. Venkataraman (1999). *The innovation journey.* New York: Oxford University Press.

Van der Heyden, L., C. Blondel, and R.S. Carlock (2005). "Fair process: Striving for justice in family business." *Family Business Review* 18(1) 1–22.

Van der Heyden, L., and T. Limberg (2007). "Why fairness matters." *International Commerce Review* 7(2): 93–102.

Van Maanen, J., and E.H. Schein (1979). "Toward a theory of organization socialization." In *Research in organizational behavior*, vol. 1, ed. B. Staw. Greenwich, CT: JAI Press.

Van Veen, K., and I. Marsman (2008). "How international are executive boards of European MNCs? National diversity in 15 European countries." *European Management Journal* 26(3): 188–98.

Van Wijk, R., J. Jansen and M.A. Lyles (2008). "Inter- and intra-organizational knowledge transfer: A meta-analytic review and assessment of its antecedents and consequences." *Journal of Management Studies* 45(4): 830–53.

Vance, C.M. (2006). "Strategic upstream and downstream considerations for effective global performance management." *International Journal of Cross Cultural Management* 6(1): 37–56.

Vance, C.M., S.R. McClaine, D.M. Boje, and D.H. Stage (1992). "An examination of the transferability of traditional performance appraisal principles across cultural boundaries." *Management International Review* 32(4): 313–26.

Varma, A., P.S. Budhwar, and A.S. DeNisi, eds. (2008). *Performance management systems: A global perspective.* London: Routledge.

Vaupel, J.W., and J.P. Curhan (1973). *The world's largest multinational enterprises.* Cambridge, MA: Harvard University Press.

Verbeke, A., and T.P. Kenworthy (2008). "Multidivisional vs. metanational governance of the multinational enterprise." *Journal of International Business Studies* 39(6): 940–56.

Vermeulen, G.A.M., and H.G. Barkema (2001). "Learning through acquisitions." *Academy of Management Journal* 44(3): 457–76.

Vernon, R. (1966). "International investment and international trade in the product cycle." *Quarterly Journal of Economics.* 80: 190–207.

_____ (1977). *Storm over the multinationals: The real issues.* Cambridge, MA: Harvard University Press.

Vernon, R., L.T. Wells, and S. Rangan (1997). *The manager in the international economy.* Englewood Cliffs, NJ: Prentice Hall.

Visser, J. (2006). "Union membership statistics in 24 countries." *Monthly Labour Review* 129(1): 38–49.

Vlasic, B., and B.A. Stertz (2000). *Taken for a ride: How Daimler-Benz drove off with Chrysler.* New York: Wiley.

Volberda, H.W. (1998). *Building the flexible firm: How to remain competitive.* New York: Oxford University Press.

Volmer, H.M., and D.L. Mills (1966). *Professionalization.* Englewood Cliffs, NJ: Prentice Hall.

Vora, D., T. Kostova, and K. Roth (2007). "Roles of subsidiary managers in multinational corporations: The effect of dual organizational identification." *Management International Review* 47(4): 595–620.

Waddington, J. (2003). "What do representatives think of the practices of European Works Councils? Views from six countries." *European Journal of Industrial Relations* 9(3): 303–25.

Walker, J.W. (1980). *Human resource planning.* New York: McGraw-Hill.

Wang, X., and D.Z. Nayir (2006). "How and when is social networking important? Comparing European expatriate adjustment in China and Turkey." *Journal of International Management* 12(4): 449–72.

Waxin, M., A. Roger, and J.L. Chandon (1997). "L'intégration des expatriés dans leur nouveau poste, une analyse contingente et quantitative, le cas des expatriés français en Norvège." In *GRH face à la crise: GRH en crise?*, eds. B. Sire and M. Tremblay. Montreal: Presse HEC.

Wenger, E.C., and W.M. Snyder (2000). "Communities of practice: The organizational frontier." *Harvard Business Review* (January–February): 139–45.

Weick, K.E. (1979). *The social psychology of organizing.* Boston, MA: Addison-Wesley.

Weiss, S. E. (1994). "Negotiating with 'Romans'—Part 1." *Sloan Management Review* 35(2): 51–61.

Welch, D.E., and L.S. Welch (2006). "Commitment for hire? The viability of corporate culture as a MNC control mechanism." *International Business Review* 15(1):14–28.

Welch, D.E., and V. Worm (2006). "International business travellers: Challenge for IHRM." In *Handbook of research in international human resource management*, eds. G.K. Stahl and I. Björkman. Cheltenham, UK: Edward Elgar.

Welch, D.E., V. Worm, and M. Fenwick (2003). "Are virtual international assignments feasible?" *Management International Review* 1 (Special Issue): 95–114.

Welch, J., with S. Welch (2005). *Winning*. London: HarperCollins.

Westney, D.E. (1988). "Domestic foreign learning curves in managing international cooperative strategies." In *Cooperative strategies in international business*, eds. F.J. Contractor and P. Lorange. Lexington, MA: Lexington Books.

Westphal, J.D., R. Gulati, and S.M. Shortell (1997). "Customization or conformity?: An institutional and network perspective on the content and consequences of TQM adoption." *Administrative Science Quarterly* 42(2): 366–94.

Whitley, R.D. (1990). "The societal construction of business systems in East Asia." *Organization Studies* 11(1): 47–74.

_____ (1992). *European business systems: Firms and markets in their national contexts*. London and Beverly Hills: Sage.

_____ (1999). *Alternative systems of capitalism*. New York: Oxford University Press.

Wiechmann, D., A.M. Ryan, and M. Hemingway (2003). "Designing and implementing global staffing systems: Part I—Leaders in global staffing." *Human Resource Management* 42(1): 71–83.

Wilkins, M. (1970). *The emergence of multinational enterprise*. Cambridge, MA: Harvard University Press.

_____ (1988). "European and North American multinationals, 1870–1914: Comparisons and contrasts." *Business History* 30(1): 8–45.

Williamson, O.E. (1975). *Markets and hierarchies: Analysis and antitrust implications*. New York: Free Press.

Winterton, J. (2007). "Training, development, and competence." In *The Oxford handbook of human resource management*, eds. P. Boxall, J. Purcell, and P. Wright. New York: Oxford University Press.

Womack, J.P., D.T. Jones, and D. Roos (1990). *The machine that changed the world*. New York: Rawson Associates.

Wong, C.S., and K. Law (1999). "Managing localization of human resources in the PRC: A practical model." *Journal of World Business* 34(1): 26–40.

Wren, D.A. (1994). *The evolution of management thought*. London: Wiley.

Wright, C. (2008). "Reinventing human resource management: Business partners, internal consultants and the limits to professionalization." *Human Relations* 61(8): 1063–86.

Wright, P.M., and W.R. Boswell (2002). "Desegregating HRM: A review and synthesis of micro and macro human resource management research." *Journal of Management* 28(3): 247–76.

Yamazaki, Y., and D.C. Kayes (2004). "An experiential approach to cross-cultural learning: A review and integration of competencies for successful expatriate adaptation." *Academy of Management Learning and Education* 3(4): 362–79.

Yamin, M., and R.R. Sinkovics (2006). "Online internationalisation, psychic distance reduction and the virtuality trap." *International Business Review* 15(4): 339–60.

Yip, G.S., and A.J.M. Bink (2007). "Managing global accounts." *Harvard Business Review* (September): 103–11.

Yoshihara, H. (1999). "Global operations managed by Japanese." (In Japanese.) Discussion Paper Series No. 108. Research Institute for Economics and Business Administration, Kobe University, Kobe, Japan.

Yoshino, M., and U.S. Rangan (1995). *Strategic alliances: An entrepreneurial approach to globalization.* Cambridge, MA: Harvard Business School Press.

Zaheer, S. (1995). "Overcoming the liability of foreignness." *Academy of Management Journal* 38(2): 341–63.

Zahra, S.A., and G. George (2002). "Absorptive capacity: A review, reconceptualization, and extension." *Academy of Management Review* 27(2): 185–203.

Zahra, S.A., R.D. Ireland, and M.A. Hitt (2000). "International expansion by new venture firms: International diversity, mode of market entry, technological learning, and performance." *Academy of Management Journal* 43(5): 925–50.

Zalan, T., and V. Pucik (2007). "Rebuilding ABB (A)." Case study no. IMD-3-1797. IMD, Lausanne.

Zalan, T. and V. Pucik (2009). "Ayudhya Allianz C.P.: The i2s initiative." Case study no. IMD-3-1968. IMD, Lausanne.

Zbaracki, M.J. (1998). "The rhetoric and reality of total quality management." *Administrative Science Quarterly* 43(3): 602–34.

Zeira, Y., and O. Shenkar (1990). "Interactive and specific parent characteristics: Implications for management and human resources in international joint ventures." *Management International Review* 30 (Special Issue): 7–22.

Zellmer-Bruhn M., and C. Gibson (2006). "Multinational organization context: Implications for team learning and performance." *Academy of Management Journal* 49(3): 501–18.

Zohar, D. (1997). *Rewiring the corporate brain: Using the new science to rethink how we structure and lead organizations.* San Francisco: Berrett-Koehler.

Zollo, M., and H. Singh (2004). "Deliberate learning in corporate acquisitions: Post-acquisition strategies and integration capability in U.S. bank mergers." *Strategic Management Journal* 25(13): 1233–56.

Zollo, M., and S.G. Winter (2002). "Deliberate learning and the evolution of dynamic capabilities." *Organization Science* 13(3): 339–51.

Zuboff, S. (1984). *The age of the smart machine.* New York: Basic Books.

Name Index

n. notes
t. table
f. figure
d. diagram

3M 46, 66, 117, 329
Abacha, Sani 85
ABB 1–3, 14, 24, 26, 49, 60, 94, 180, 194,
    301, 329, 537, 560
Åbø, E.L. 431n, 432n
Abrahams, R. 567n
Abrahamson, E. 122n
Accenture 207, 353, 368, 399, 408
Accumulatoren-Fabrik 7t
Acer 411, 422
Adler, N. 155, 165n, 168n, 169n, 216n,
    251n, 252n, 254n, 430n, 431n
Adobor, H. 522n
Afuah, A. 432n
AGC Group 239
Agilent 214n, 268
Agrawal, A. 254n, 344n
Ahold 116, 599
Adidas 588
Aiken, C. 474n
Airbus Consortium 23, 479
Albert, S. 253n
Alfa Laval Agri 400

Alibaba 82, 119n, 262
All China Federation of Trade Unions
    (ACFTU) 109
Allen, N.J. 79n, 168n
Almond, P.T. 165n, 169n
Alvarez, J.L. 168n, 343n
Alvesson, M. 253n
Amason, A.C. 216n
American Airlines 214n
American Express 591
American Radiator 7t
Amoco 559
Amstel 27
Anand, J. 521n
Ancona, D. 215n, 216n, 432n
Andersen, E. 343n
Angwin, D. 568n
Anheuser Busch InBev 27, 314, 566n
    see also InBev
AP Moller-Maersk 352 see also Maersk
Apple 319
Apud, S. 254n
Aramco 255
ArcelorMittal 400, 401
Arco 559
Argote, L. 432n
Argyris, C. 39n, 474n
Arias, Maria 121n

Arora, A. 254n, 343n
Arthur, W. 166n, 335, 345n
Arthur Anderson 12
Arvidsson, L. 430n
Asea Brown Boveri *see* ABB
Ashforth, B.E. 253n
Ashkenas, R.N 40n, 389n, 568n
Alstom 1
AstraZeneca 537
AT&T 13, 79n
Athos, A.388n
A.T. Kearney 566n, 567n
Audi 234
AXA 560
Axelrod, B. 345n, 569n
Ayudhya Allianz 418-9

Bacon, N. 77n
BAE 122n, 521n
Bagozzi, R.P. 254n
Bailey, D.E. 215n
Bain & Co. 431n
Baker, J.C. 166n,
Baker, W. 214n
Baker Hughes 256
Bamber, G.I. 388n
Bannerjee, Prith 432n
Barham, K. 37n
Baritz, L. 38n
Barkema, H.G. 119n, 474n, 523n,
    567n, 567n
Barley, S.R. 38n
Barner-Rasmussen, W. 252n, 431n
Barnevik, Percy 1, 180, 248, 284,
    447, 560
Barney, J. 45, 77n, 609n
Baron, J.N. 77n, 254n, 297n, 609n
Barsoux, J.L. 120n, 253n,
    388n, 389n
Bartholemew, S. 254n
Bartlett, C.A. 4, 24, 26, 34, 37n, 39n,
    40n, 41n, 75, 77n, 80n, 117, 122n,
    163n, 213n, 214n, 215n, 254n, 298n,
    299n, 309, 310, 341n, 342n, 431n,
    438, 439, 472n
Bartolomé, F. 300n
Bass 27

Bass, B.M. 216n
Bauer, T. 253n
Bayer 7t, 121n
Beamish, P.W. 252n, 522n
Beath C. 77n
Beatty, R.W. 296n, 344n, 387n,
    388n, 609n
Beauté Prestige International 412
Becker B. 63, 77n, 79n, 120n, 258,
    296n, 344n, 357, 387n, 387n,
    388n, 388n, 474n
Behfar, K.J. 215n, 216n
Belbin, R.M. 343n
Bell, J.H. 119n
Bendick, M. 121n
Benetton 106
Benjamin, B. 343n
Bennett, W. 166n
Bennis, W. 342n, 344n
Benson, J. 298n
Berg, N. 77n
Bernardi, F. 345n
Bernhoff, J. 345n
Bertrand, O. 567n
Bettenhausen, K. 215n
Beatty, R. 258, 259t
Beyer, D. 296n
Bhaskar-Shrinivas, P. 166n, 167n, 168n
Bink, A. 191, 215n
Birkinshaw, J. 80n, 191, 214n, 215n,
    389n,
    429n, 430n, 431n, 432n, 472n,
    473n, 568n
Bismarck 106
Bjelland, O. 475n
Björk, S. 252n
Björkman, I. 77n, 120n, 121n, 122n,
    165n, 166n, 252n, 296n, 344n,
    387n, 431n, 567n
Black, J.S. 40n, 147, 149f, 166n, 167n,
    168n, 253n, 254n, 298n, 342n, 389n,
    390n, 474n
Blackburn, R. 215n
Blakeney, R. 431n
Blazejewski, S. 165n
Bleeke, J. 567n
Bloch, M. 609n

Blondel, C. 473n
Bloom, M. 366, 389n
Blossfeld, H.-P. 345n
BMW 234, 273
Boam, R. 298n
Boeing 301, 483
Boliang, Mai 303
Bolino, M. 168n
Bonache, J. 169n, 430n
Bond, M. 475n
Boon, C. 79n
Booz Allen 522n
Borkowski, S. 389n
Borzillo, S. 430n
Boselie, P. 79n
Boston Consulting Group 82
Bouchikhi, H. 253n, 472n
Boudreau, J. 296n, 608n
Bourgeois, L. 474n, 475n
Bowen, D. 77n
Boxall, P. 77n
Boyatzis, R. 345n
Boyer, Inc 168n
BP 300n, 595
BP-Amoco 556, 559
Brabeck, Peter 170
Brahma 27
Branham, L. 300n
Braun, W. 122n
Breaugh, J. 297n
Bresman, H. 215n, 216n, 568n
Brett, J. 167n, 474n
Brewster, C. 78n, 121n, 142,
    164n, 166n, 167n, 169n, 298n,
    609n, 610n
Bridges, W. 474n
Briscoe, J. 298n, 344n, 388n, 389n
Brock, D. 431n
Brockbank, W. 78n, 608n, 610n
Broeckx, Paul 213n
Broekner, J. 473n
Brookfield Global Relocation
    Services 138
Broughton, A. 609n
Brown, S. 252n, 427, 432n, 472n,
    474n, 475n
Bruch, H. 474n

Bryan, L. 252n
BT 69
BT Global 335
Bucerius, M. 569n
Budhwar, P. 388n
Burgelman, R. 388n
Burt, R.S. 113, 122n, 252n
Burton, M. 254n
Business Week 14

Caetano, A. 252n
Caldwell, R. 215n, 474n, 608n,
    609n, 610n
Caligiuri, P. 169n, 342n
Callister, R. 253n
Cameron, K. 473n
CAMI 516
Campbell, A. 164n, 214n, 387n, 472n
Cannella, A. 432n
Canney Davison, S. 215n
Canon 458, 459
Cap Gemini Ernst and Young 473n
Capelli, P. 268, 270, 288, 297n, 299n,
    300n, 343n, 344n, 345n, 610n
Carioggia, G. 610n
Carlock, R. 473n
Carlos, A. 37n
Carraher, A. 343n
Carrefour 322
Cascio, W. 300n, 388n, 390n, 521n, 522n
CEMEX 31, 48, 86, 525-6, 537, 566n
Centerman, Jörgen 2, 180
Cerdin, J.-L. 168n
Cervino, J. 169n
Cha, S. 298n
Chakrabarti, R. 568n
Chambers., John 192
Chandler, A. 18, 38n, 39n
Chandon, J. 166n
Chang, E. 164n, 299n, 342n
Charan, R. 343n, 343n
Chase, Rodney 354
Chatman, J. 252n, 253n, 298n,
    299n, 342n
Chemco 476-7
Chen, S. 122n, 390n
Cheung, C. 297n

Chi, S.-C. 390n
Child, J. 38n, 106, 121n, 122n, 252n, 253n, 388n, 523n, 569n
Ching, P. 120n
Cho, H.-J. 121n, 429n, 568n
Choi, D. 430n
Choi, J. 390n
Chong, L. 569n
Christensen, C. 122n, 432n, 418
Chrysler 536, 551
Chu, W. 567n
Chung, L. 164n
Chusmir, L. 169n
Cialdini, R. 474n
Ciba 559
Ciceri, H. 298n
CIMC 262, 303
Ciran, Martin 495
Cisco 40n,192, 215n, 262, 271, 319, 420, 529, 545
Citibank 14, 345n, 358
Clark, T. 77n, 121n, 165n
Claus, L. 388n, 389n
Clemens, J. 216n
Coase, R. 163n
Coats, J&P 7t
Coca-Cola 84, 119n, 441
Coff, R. 80n
Coffin, Charles 301
Cohen, J. 120n
Cohen, W. 429n
Cole, R. 522n
Coleman, H. 215n
Colgate-Palmolive 280
Colling, T. 165n
Collings, D. 168n
Collins, J. 474n
Colt 6
Combs, J. 79n
Commonwealth Edison 326
Conger, J. 297n, 342n, 343n, 474n
Conner, S. 473n
Continental 271
Contractor 520n
Conway, N. 77n
Cook, M. 298n
Cooke, F. 609n

Coopers & Lybrand 12
Corley, K. 253n
Corning 14, 485, 491, 502
Corus 31
Cramer, R. 215n
Crane, D. 431n
Cranfield 121n
Crawford, L. 169n
Crocitto, M. 343n
Cross, R. 429n, 430n
Cummings, J. 215n
Curhan, J. 38n
Currie, G. 430n
Cyr, D. 521n, 524n

Daft, Douglas 441
Daimler 111, 121n, 536, 551, 553
Danone 86, 521n
Darr, E. 430n
Davidson Frame, J. 215n
Davis, S. 39n
Davison, S. 209, 215n, 216n, 252n
De Cieri, H. 41n
De Geus, A. 387n
De Leon, C. 254n
De Konig, A. 609n
De Meyer, A. 215n
De Vries, M. Kets 254n, 298n, 331, 344n, 345n
Dean, A. 163n, 431n
Debroux, P. 298n
DeFidelto, C. 609n
DeFillippi, R. 335, 345n
De Geus, A. 214n
Dehoff, K. 431n, 432n
Del Canho, D. 568n
Delany, E. 473n
Delery, J. 78n
Dell 250, 319
Deloitte 344n
Deloitte Touche Tohmastu 271
DeLong, D. 431n
Dembovsky, M. 431n
Deming, W. 359, 388n
DeMonaco, L. 568n
Den Hartog, D. 389n, 390n
Dendrell, J. 430n

DeNisi, A. 166n, 168n, 363, 388n
Denison, D. 216n, 252n, 568n
Derr, B. 165n
Deskins, D. 522n
Dess, G. 252n
Deutsche-Dresdner 556
Devanna, M. 39n, 298n
DHL 53
Dickmann, M. 167n, 168n, 169n
Dietz, G. 79n
DiMaggio, P. 121n
Disney 86
DiStefano, J. 191, 215n, 389n
Dobbs, R. 567n
Dodd, D. 80n
Doh, J. 300n
Donaldson, L. 38n
Donnelly, T. 215n
Donner, Frederick G. 11
Doorewaard, H. 431n
Doornik, K. 163n
Dore, R. 253n
Doriot, George 607
Dormann, Jürgen 2
Dottlich, D. 345n
Dougherty, D. 432n
Dow Chemicals 14, 39n
Dowling, P. 41n, 389n
Downes, M. 169n
Doyle, Frank 66
Doz, Y. 24, 40n, 41n, 79n, 80n, 119n,
    163n, 253n, 345n, 359, 388n, 422,
    431n, 432n, 472n, 474n, 475n,
    521n, 523n, 524n
Drotter, S. 342n, 343n
Drummond, A. 119n
Duarte, D. 215n, 216n
Duhaime, I. 567n
Duncan, G. 80n
Dunning, J. 38n
Dussauge, P. 566n
Dutch East India Company 4, 5
Dutta, S. 345n
Dyer, J. 122n, 566n

E.ON 111
EachNet 82, 89

Eastvold, R. 80n
eBay 81-2, 85, 88, 89, 117, 119n, 262
Eccles, R. 431n
Eddy, J. 343n, 344n
Edström, A. 20, 40n, 139, 165n, 238, 254n,
Edwards, P. 165n
Egan, M. 121n
Egelhoff, W. 164n
Ehrnrooth, M. 344n
Eidems, J. 389n
Eisenhardt, K. 252n, 427, 428, 432n,
    472n, 474n, 475n, 610n
Eisenstat, R. 474n
Ellis, F. 252n
Emerson 262, 271
Engelfriet, J. 568n
English East India Company 4, 5
Engström, P. 120n
Enron 599
Ensign, P. 214n
Erickson, T. 252n
Ericsson 25, 26, 227, 412, 588
Ericsson Academy 91
Ericsson, L.M. 7t
Evans, P. 77n, 79n, 80n, 300n, 342n,
    343n, 345n, 472n, 474n, 611n,
Everatt, D. 387n
Everett, J. 390n
Exxon 14, 85, 169n, 288, 300n, 325, 463
ExxonMobil 255

Fair Labor Association (FLA) 588
Fairchild, G. 122n
Fang, M. 121n
Farndale, E. 165n, 166n
Fast, N. 77n
Faulkner, D. 252n, 388n, 523n, 569n
Favaro, K. 80n
Federal Express 28, 274
Feldman, D. 168n
Fenwick, M. 169n
Ferencikova, S. 522n, 566n
Fernandez, J. 120n
Ferner, A. 122n, 165n, 165n
Festing, M. 389n
Fey, C. 120n, 122n, 252n
Fifield, G. 163n

Finkelstein, S. 567n
Fiorina, Carly 214n, 473n
Flamholtz, E. 388n
Flannery, T. 121n
Fleming, M. 431n, 432n
Florida, R. 165n, 522n
Fombrun, C. 18, 39n, 298n
Ford, R. 39n, 25
Foreign Affiliated Managers
    Association (FAMA) 112
Forster, N. 166n
Fox, J. 163n
Francis, I. 215n, 253n, 568n
Fraser, M. 345n
Frayne, C. 523n
Freas, A. 610n
Freeman, J. 472n
Friedman, T. 29, 41n, 443, 472n,
Friedmann, J. 119n
Frost, T. 214n
Froese, F. 568n, 569n
Frontczak, N. 169n
Fubini, D. 568n, 569n
Fuji Photo Film 12
Fuji-Xerox 398, 481, 507, 508, 521n
Furst, S. 215n
Furuya, N. 431n

Gaertner, S. 300n
Galbraith, J. 20, 39n, 40n, 78n, 139,
    163n, 165n, 213n, 214n, 215n,
    238, 254n, 389n
Galunic, C. 77n, 343n, 387n, 428, 432n,
    475n, 610n
Gandossy, B. 593
Gardner, Howard 345n
Garette, B. 566n
Gates, Bill 603
Gazprom 255
GE *see* General Electric
GE Capital 536, 545
GE China 91
Geigy 559
Gelfand, M. 474n
Génadry, N. 80n, 611n
General Electric (GE) 66, 92, 114, 166n,
    247, 263, 272, 301-2, 352, 488

General Motors 11, 136, 137, 516
Gennard, J. 610n
George, C. 37n, 430n
Gerdau 262
Gerhart, B. 120n, 121n
Geringer, M. 523n
Gersten, J. 166n
Ghemawat, P. 34, 41n, 119n, 447,
    472n, 473n
Ghorparde, J. 363
Ghoshal, S. 4, 24, 26, 34, 37n, 39n,
    40n, 41n, 75, 80n, 117, 122n,
    163n, 213n, 214n, 215n, 216n,
    220, 251n, 252n, 253n, 254n, 309,
    310, 342n, 387n, 389n, 430n, 438,
    439, 472n, 475n
Ghosn, Carlos 193, 248, 458, 540
Gibbons, P. 164n
Gibson, C. 80n, 215n, 389n
GIC 366
Gilley, K. 168n
Gittell, J. 214n
Gladwell, M. 611n
GLOBE 97, 104, 440, 449b
Gluesing, J. 215n
GM *see* General Motors
Goedhart, M. 567n
Goeritz, L. 568n
Goffee, R. 522n
Goizueta, Robert 441
Goldcorp 414
Golden, K. 40n
Goldman Sachs 287, 319
Goldsmith, M. 610n
Goleman, G. 345n
Gomes-Casseres, B. 521n, 523n
Gonzáles, S. 78n
Goodall, K. 120n
Gooderham, P. 119n, 388n
Google 85, 86, 87, 119n, 260, 268, 271
Goold, M. 164n, 214n, 387n, 472n
Goss, T. 388n
Gould, Andrew 255, 402
Govindarajan, V. 254n, 429n,
    431n, 473n
Govinder, N. 459

Granovetter, Mark 221, 251n, 297n
Grant, D. 77n
Gratton, L. 69, 79n, 80n, 252n, 387n, 474n, 475n
Gregersen, H. 40n, 122n, 149f, 166n, 167n, 168n, 253n, 342n, 389n, 390n, 474n
Greiner, L. 80n
Greller, M. 39n
Griffeth, R. 300n
Grote, D. 387n
Grove, A. 388n
Groysberg, B. 567n
GSK 70
Guest, D. 77n, 121n
Gupta, A. 254n, 429n, 431n, 473n
Gupta-Mukherjee, S. 568n
Guthridge, M. 296n, 297n, 298n, 344n
Guthrie, J. 79n

H&M 588
Haasen, A. 524n
Haier 48, 103, 262, 346-7, 359, 386
Hailey, J. 120n
Hall, E. 87, 120n, 298n, 343n, 344n
Halliburton 256
Hamel, G. 41n, 429n, 521n, 523n, 524n
Hamori, M. 345n
Hampden-Turner, Charles 74, 80n, 97, 121n, 472n
Hanada, M. 163n
Handfield-Jones, H. 345n, 569n
Handy, Charles 602, 611n
Hannan, M. 254n, 472n
Hansen, M. 216n, 252n, 351, 387n, 429n, 430n, 431n, 432n
Harding, D. 567n, 568n, 569n
Harrigan, K. 524n
Harris, H. 78n, 142, 166n, 167n, 168n, 298n, 609n
Harrison, D. 168n
Harrison, S. 253n,
Harrison, J. 567n, 569n
Harry, W. 120n
Hart, S. 216n
Harvey, M. 167n, 169n

Harzing, A.-W. 120n, 122n, 163n, 164n, 165n, 166n, 169n, 254n, 388n
Haspeslagh, P. 567n, 569n
Hastings, D. 77n
Hatch, M. 253n
Hatvany, N. 40n
Hauschild, P. 122n
Hay Group 100, 341n
Hays, R. 38n, 165n
HCL Technologies 262
Hearn, J. 252n
Heckman, R. 296n
Hedberg, B. 80n, 611n
Hedlund, G. 21, 24, 40n, 215n
Hegerty, W. 569n
Heimer, C. 37n
Heineken 27, 130, 194
Held, D. 40n
Hemingway 297n, 298n
Hennart, J-.F. 164n
Hergert, M. 521n
Heskett, J. 164n, 387n
Hewlett, Bill 284
Hewlett-Packard 69, 104, 185-6, 214n, 268, 398, 469, 485
Hieronimus, F. 298n
Higgins, M. 343n
Hill, L. 297n, 342n, 343n
Hilti 460
Hiltrop, J.-M. 298n, 299n, 388n
Hinda, Soichiro 369
Hinds, P. 215n
Hite, J. 389n, 390n
Hitt, M. 472n, 567n, 569n
Hodgetts, R. 609n
Hofmeister, John 570
Hofstede, Geert 19, 40n, 97, 100, 101, 104, 120n, 121n, 388n
Hogarth, R. 252n
Hollenbeck, J. 311, 342n, 343n
Homburg, C. 569n
Honda 148, 234, 596
Honda, Soichiro 234, 235, 322, 339
Hood, N. 214n, 472n, 473n
Hooijberg, R. 213n
Horn, P. 300n

Horton, Robert 472n
Hoseus 78n, 251n, 253n
House, R. 120n, 216n, 342n, 389n
Howard, A. 342n, 343n
HP *see* Hewlett-Packard
HSBC 157, 380
Hudson's Bay Company 4
Human Resource Planning Society 39n
Hunter, J. 298n
Huselid, M. 63, 79n, 258, 259t, 296n,
      300n, 344n, 357, 387n, 388n
Huston, L. 429n, 431n
Huy, Q. 474n

Ibarra, H. 214n, 342n, 345n
IBM 14, 53, 59, 97, 183, 184, 208, 230,
      231, 342n
IKEA 127, 132, 165n
Iles, P. 296n
IMD 28, 225, 317, 566n
Immelt, Jeff 74, 80n, 284, 302
InBev 27, 262, 314
Infosys 48, 230, 241, 262, 272, 273,
      284, 291, 462
Ingham, J. 296n
Inkpen, A. 431n, 521n, 524n,
      568n, 569n
InnoCentive 414
INSEAD 28, 225, 317
Intel 104, 147, 485
Ireland, R. 472n, 567n, 569n
Isdell, Neville 442
ITT 25
Ivancevich, J. 166n
Ivester, Douglas 441

J. Walter Thompson 12
Jackson, S. 79n, 215n, 300n
Jacoby, S. 38n
Janger, A. 522n
Jansen, J. 429n, 430n, 431n
Jarillo, J. 39n, 163n
Jaruzelski, B. 431n, 432n
Jarvenpaa, S. 215n
Jay, A. 165n
Jayaraman, N. 568n
Jemison, J. 567n

Jin, Z. 215n
Joerss, M. 342n
Johansen, R. 119n, 215n
Johanson, J. 40n
Johnson & Johnson 235, 247, 438
Johnson, L. 253n, 254n, 567n
Johnson, Chris 201, 440
Jones, D. 431n
Jones, D.T. 165n
Jones, G.R. 522n
Jones, G. 37n, 38n
Jonsen, K. 209, 215n, 216n, 252n
J-Phone 551
Judge, T. 343n

Kahwajy, J. 474n, 475n
Kakabadse, A. 522n
Kale, P. 521n, 566n
Kallasvuo, Olli-Pekka 124
Kamprad, Ingvar 235, 236, 253n
Kanter, R. 254n, 432n, 521n
Kao 25
Kaplan, R. 284, 298n, 356, 388n
Kates, A. 608n
Katzenbach, J. 215n
Kaufman, B. 38n
Kay, I. 567n
Kayes, D. 166n
KazMunaiGaz 255
Kelleher, Herb 47
Keller, S. 474n
Kelly, J. 610n
Kennedy, C. 523n
Kenney, M. 165n, 522n
Kenworthy, T. 432n
Kepes, S. 78n
Kerr, S. 474n, 523n
Kerrin, M. 430n
Kiesler, S. 215n
Kilduff, M. 251n
Killing, J.P. 201, 213n, 522n,
      535, 567n
Kim, C. 164n, 473n
Kimberly, J. 253n, 472n
Kindle, Fred 2, 37n, 180
King, D. 567n
Kirkman, B. 389n, 390n

Klein, J. 254n
Kluger, A.N 363
Knoll, K. 215n
Kobayashi, Yotaro 500
Kodak 438
Koen, C. 121n
Kogut, B. 29, 40n, 41n, 394, 429n, 520n
Koka, B. 429n, 430n
Kolb, D. 343n
Komin, S. 432n
Komm, A. 296n, 297n, 298n, 344n
KoneCranes 213n
Kopp, R. 163n
Kosonen, M. 79n, 163n, 345n, 474n, 475n
Kostova, T. 165n, 251n, 252n, 253n
Kotter, J. 342n, 387n, 473n
KPMG 567n
Kraatz, M. 122n
Kraft 174
Kram, K. 343n, 610n
Kratz, E. 341n
Kreps, D. 77n, 297n, 609n
Kroeck, K. 169n
Kroll 567n, 568n
Krug, J. 569n
Kuin, P. 40n, 120n
Kulik, C. 610n
Kumar, N. 569n
Kunda, G. 38n
Kurtzberg, T. 430n
Kuvaas, B. 79n
Kwon, S.-W. 251n, 252n

L'Oréal 223, 224, 294, 466
Labatt 27
Lafarge 86
Laffley, A.G. 80n, 325, 328, 391
Lague, D. 121n
Lambert, A. 608n, 609n, 610n
Lane, C. 121n,
Lane, P. 429n, 430n
Larsen, Henrik Holt 388n, 609n, 610n
Larsson, R. 567n
Lasserre, P. 120n, 442, 472n, 522n
Latham, G. 351, 387n
Laurent, A. 120n, 342n, 97

Law, K. 120n
Lawler, E. 78n, 122n, 213n, 298n, 300n, 608n, 609n
Lawrence, P. 39n, 78n, 163n
Lawson, E. 296n, 297n, 298n, 344n
Lazarova, M. 168n, 430n, 432n
Leana, C. 252n
Leffe 27
Leger, K. 566n, 567n
Legge, K. 39n, 41n, 121n
Lei, D. 524n
Leidner, D. 216n
Lempres, E. 609n
Lenartowicz, T. 254n
Lengnick-Hall, C., 251n, 252n, 297n
Lengnick-Hall, M. 251n, 252n, 297n
Lenovo 262, 537, 254n
Leonard, D. 41n, 432n, 473n
Leonard-Barton, D. 80n, 398, 472n, 473n
Lepak, D. 52, 78n, 79., 296n
Lepsinger, R. 343n
Leung, A. 343n
Lever Brothers 7t
Levinthal, D. 429n
Levy, O. 254n
Lewin, A. 297n
Lewis, D. 37n
Lewis, M. 472n
Lewis, R. 296n
Li, C. 345n, 431n
Liedner, D. 215n
Lief, C. 341n
Liker, J. 78n, 251n, 253n
Lincoln Electric Company 42-3, 46, 48, 103, 116, 367
Lindahl, Göran 2, 180
Lindholm, N. 387n, 388n
Lindqvist, M. 432n
Linstone, H. 80n
Littrell, L. 167n
Liu, D. 521n
Liu, G. 521n
Liu, X. 166n
Locke, E. 351, 387n
Lockheed 319
Lombardo, M. 342n, 343n
Longton, P. 390n

Lorange, P. 79n, 520n, 522n, 523n
Lord Browne 472n
Lorsch, J. 78n, 163n, 216n
Løvås, B. 252n, 429n, 430n
Loveridge, R. 122n
Lowe, K. 169n
Løwendahl, B. 431n
Lu, Y. 120n, 122n
Lucia, A. 343n
Lufthansa 518
Lunnan, R. 388n
Luo, Y. 521n
LVMH 234
Lyles, M. 429n, 430n, 431n, 610n

Ma, Jack 82
Mabey, C. 77n
MacDuffie, J. 165n, 215n
Maddux 343n
Mael, F. 253n
Maerki, H. 214n
Mahoney, J. 343n
Maister, D. 431n
Mäkelä, K. 344n
Maljers, Floris 33
Mallory, G. 121n
Mannesmann 111
Manning, S. 297n
Mannix, E. 215n
Manzoni, J.-F. 389n
March, J. 80n, 432n, 567n, 568n
Marchand, D. 566n, 567n
Mark, Reuben 280
Marks, M. 548, 567n, 568n, 569n
Marks and Spencer 167n, 232
Marriott Hotels 358
Mars 595
Marschan-Piekkari, R. 252n
Marsman, I. 298n
Martinez, J. 39n, 163n
Maruca, R. 342n
Marx, M. 431n, 432n
Mason, R. 215n
Massini, S. 297n
Matson, E. 252n
Matsushita, Konosuke 25, 26, 93, 230, 235

Mauborgne, R. 473n
Mayer, R. 431n
Mayo, Elton 9
Maznevski, M. 209, 216n, 215n, 252n
McCall, M. 311, 342n, 343n, 345n
McDonald's 86, 127, 131, 164-5n
McFadyen, M. 432n
McGregor, Douglas 174, 213n
McKee, A. 345n
McKinsey 12, 78N, 211, 287, 368, 407, 470
McLean, A. 298n, 341n
McLelland, David 342n
McQuade, K. 523n
'MedPharm' 433-5, 439, 440, 462
Meihuizen, H. 431n
Melvin, S. 120n
Mendenhall, M. 149f, 166n, 167n, 168n, 252n, 342n
Mercer 567n, 568n
Merck 169n
Merita 537
Metcalfe, B. 252n
Metcalf, H. 38n
Meyer, J. 79n, 165n
Meyerson, D. 215n
Michaels, E. 345n, 569n
Michailova, S. 429n
Michaud, C. 252n
Michelin 48, 190, 235
Micklethwait, J. 122n
Microsoft 87, 198, 263, 298n, 322, 364, 420
Milanovic, B. 611n
Miles, R. 215n
Milkovich, G. 366, 389n
Miller, D. 168n, 253n, 253n, 475n
Mills, M. 345n, 431n
Minbaeva, D. 429n
Mintzberg, H. 39n, 78n, 163n, 214n, 387n, 472n, 473n
Mirvis, P. 548, 567n, 568n, 569n
Mirza, H. 120n
Mishra, A. 473n
Mitra, A. 389n
Mitroff, I. 80n

Mitsubishi Motors 553
Moberg, Anders 229
Mohr, A. 523n
Mohrman, S. 608n
Mol, S. 167n, 429n
Monster.com 263, 271
Monteiro, L. 430n
Moore, K. 37n, 430n
Morehart, K. 297n
Morgan, G. 41n, 343n, 431n
Moriguchi, C. 38n
Morley, M. 168n
Morosini, P. 521n, 567n, 568n
Morris, M. 167n, 215n, 521n
Morrison, M. 40n, 253n, 298n, 299n,
    342n, 343n
Mors, M. 252n, 429n, 430n
Motorola 70, 91, 271, 354, 491, 497
Moxon, R. 521n
Muller, H. 343n
Murtha, T. 254n
Murthy, Narayan 241
Muscovy Company 4
Myklebust, Egil 64, 295
Myloni, B. 120n

Nahapiet, J. 220, 251n, 430n
Nanus, B. 342n, 344n
Napier, N. 169n
Nathanson, D. 39n
National Cash Register Company 38n
National Civic Federation 10
National Personnel Association 10
Navteq 529
Nayir, D. 166n
NEC 25, 40n
Nestlé 7t, 84, 86, 160, 170-1, 174, 189,
    330, 393, 438
Neves, P. 252n
Newman, W. 389n, 472n
Nicholas, S. 37n
Nicholson, N. 168n
Nike 27, 588
NineSigma 414
Nishii, L. 298n
Nissan 193, 540
Nobel, R. 568n

Noel, J. 342n, 343n, 345n
Nohria, N. 28, 41n, 53, 59, 70, 116, 119n,
    123-4, 120n, 121n, 160, 162, 163n,
    174, 213n, 214n, 215n, 221, 236,
    253n, 269, 272, 422m 431n, 529, 588
Nokia 161, 185, 240, 241, 245, 248, 374
Nokia Siemens Networks 185, 240,
    374, 390
Nonaka, Ikujiro 343n, 415, 429n, 431n
Nooyi, Indra 280
Nordbanken 536
Nordhaug, O. 119n, 388n
Nordstrom 588
Norsk Hydro 64, 79n, 295, 300n
Norton, D. 284, 298n, 356, 388n
Novartis 288, 323, 364, 537, 559
Novicevic, M. 169n
Novo Nordisk 312
Nummela, N. 254n
NUMMI 136
Nystrom, P. 611n, 80n

O'Connell, J. 77n
O'Connor, E. 38n
O'Hara-Deveraux, M. 119n
O'Reilly, C. 80n, 165n, 252n, 253n, 299n,
    342n, 472n, 521n, 524n
Oddou, G. 165n, 166n, 167n, 168n, 431n
Ollila, Jorma 123, 211
Omidyar, Pierre 82
Oracle 577
Orange 185
Orchant, D. 390n
Ordonez, L. 387n
Orlitzky, M. 297n
Orrù, M. 121n
Osland, J. 431n
Osono, E. 251n, 430n
Ostroff, F. 77n
Ouchi, W. 40n
Ovilsen, Mads 312
Owen, Robert 6, 8
Oxley, G. 40n
Özbilgin, M. 298n

P&G *see* Procter & Gamble
Paauwe, J. 79n, 165n

Pablo, A. 568n
Packard, Dave 284, 298n
Paik, Y. 388n, 430n
Pak, Y. 569n
Palmisano, Sam 213n, 214n, 183, 236
Panasonic 25
Park, S. 164n
Parkhe, A. 522n, 523n
Pascale, R. 388n
Pathak, S. 429n, 430n
PayPal 82
Peiperl, M.A. 363; 297n
Peng, T. 165n
Pennings, J. 119n
Penrose, E. 38n, 80n
Peretti, J.M. 168n
Perlmutter, H. 21, 24, 40n, 254n, 298n
Perry, E. 610n
Peters, T. 39n, 213n, 230
Peterson, R. 165n, 169n, 215n, 216n
Petrobras 255
Petrovic, J. 522n
Pettigrew, A. 472n
Pfanner, E. 119n
Pfeffer, J. 165n, 252n, 524n
Pfizer 121n
Pfizer Japan 108
Philips 25, 84, 438, 439
Piekkari, R. 252n
Pieper, R. 121n
Pil, F. 165n
Pillai, R. 473n
Pisano, G. 77n
Pitkethly, R. 388n, 569n
Pitts, R. 524n
Pizza Hut 127
Polanyi, M. 41n
Porter, M. 77n, 215n
Powell, W. 121n
Prahalad, C. 24, 40n, 41n, 119n, 163n,
    253n, 474n, 521n, 611n
Pratt & Whitney 587, 588
Prescott, R. 40n, 164n
Price, C. 568n, 569n
Price Waterhouse 12, 80n, 121n
PriceWaterhouseCoopers 53, 408

Probst, G. 430n
Procter & Gamble 11, 19, 20, 55, 59, 92,
    127, 391-2, 411, 580
Prusak, L. 429n, 430n
Pucik, V. 40n, 77n, 121n, 139, 163n,
    164n, 166n, 168n, 214n, 215n,
    254n, 297n, 299n, 341n, 387n,
    388n, 389n, 429n, 459, 521n,
    522n, 523n, 524n, 566n,
    568n, 608n
Pudelko, M. 122n, 388n
Punnett, B. 216n
Purcell, J. 77n
Puumalainen, K. 254n

Quack, S. 431n
Quinn, R. 72, 80n, 216n
Quintanilla, J. 122n

Raelin, J. 343n
Raman, A. 251n, 430n
Ramanujan, V. 40n
Ramirez, R. 343n
Ramo, L. 342n
Ramstad, P. 296n
Randolph, W. 39n
Rangan, S. 38n, 119n, 481, 521n, 522n
Rank Organisation 12
Rausch, S. 80n
Ravasi, D. 254n
Reade, C. 253n
Ready, D. 297n, 342n
Ready Mix Concrete (RMC) 525
Redding, G. 106, 121n
Reilly, P. 609n
Renault 193, 540
Revens, R. 343n
Reynolds, C. 390n
Rhinesmith, S. 254n
Rich, J. 567n
Ridderstraale, J. 215n
Ringdal, K. 119n, 388n
Rinker Group 526, 537
Ritz-Carlton 250
Roberto, M. 610n
Roberts, J. 163n
Robie, C. 167n

Robinson, S. 343n, 344n
Robinson, S.L. 39n
Rockwood, K. 568n, 569n
Rodrigues, S. 253n
Rodwell, J. 388n
Roehl, T. 521n
Roger, A. 166n
Rohrbaugh, J. 80n
Rolls-Royce 238
Romanelli, E. 472n
Roos, J. 165n, 522n
Rosen, B. 215n
Rosenzweig, P. 41n, 119n, 120n, 121n, 165n
Ross, J. 77n
Rossant, J. 521n
Roth, K. 165n, 251n, 252n, 253n
Rothwell, W. 40n
Rouse, T. 567n, 568n, 569n
Rousseau, D. 39n, 77n, 345n
Rowan, B. 165n
Rowntree 38n
Royal African Company 4
Royal Dutch 7
Royal Dutch/Shell 20, 570, 583
Royer, S. 389n
Rozell, E. 298n
Rudlin, P. 164n
Rugman, A. 443, 472n
Ruta, C. 609n
Ryan, A. 297n, 298n
Ryanair 48

Saarenketo, S. 254n
Saba, T. 166n, 168n, 254n
Sabre 371
Sakkab, N. 429n, 431n
Salas, E. 167n
Sampson, A. 38n
San Miguel 94
Sanchez, F. 214n
Sandoz 559
Sands, Peter 295, 470, 475n
Santos, Jose 198, 215n, 359, 388n, 422, 431n, 432n
Sarin, Arun 280

SAS 293
SC Johnson 438
Scandura, T. 473n
Schaefer, K. 298n
Schein, E. 120n, 253n, 254n, 474n
Schijven, M. 474n, 567n
Schisgall, O. 38n
Schlesinger, L. 164n
Schlumberger Co. 91, 255-6, 262, 263, 265, 269, 273, 279, 322, 364, 402
Schlumberger, Conrad 255
Schlumberger, Marcel 255
Schmidt, F. 298n,
Schmidt, J. 567n
Schneider, S. 100, 120n, 253n, 388n, 521n, 524n
Schoch, H. 164n
Scholes, K. 253n
Schroder, J. 298n
Schuler, R. 79n,300n, 522n, 524n
Schultz, M. 254n
Schütte, H. 122n, 442, 472n, 609n
Schweitzer, Louis 540
Schwenk, C. 567n
Scott, W. 121n
Scullion, H. 166n, 168n, 297n, 342n, 609n
Segal-Horn, S. 163n, 431n
Selmer, J. 254n
Sensiper, S. 432n
Serapio, M. 521n, 522n
Servan-Schreiber, Jean-Jacques 12
Shadur, M. 388n
Shaffer, M. 166n, 168n
Shane, S. 567n
Shaw, J. 252n, 300n
Shell 7, 14, 20, 85, 86, 94, 160, 190, 194, 200, 230, 255, 263, 330, 599
Shelton, M. 567n
Shen, J. 388n
Shenkar, O. 522n, 523n
Sherman, S. 252n
Shimada, H. 165n
Shimizu 251n, 430n
Shing, Li Ka 82
Shiseido 412, 413
Shortland, S. 169n

Shuen, A. 77n
Siam Cement 462
Siegel, J. 77n
Siemens 6, 7t, 27, 123, 599
Simon, David 472n
Simonin, B. 524n
Simons, T. 215n
Singapore Airlines 518, 595
Singer Co. 6, 7t
Singh, H. 566n, 567n, 569n
Sippola, A. 120n
Sisson, K. 254n
Sitkin, S. 567n, 568n
Skinner, D. 77n
Slangen, A. 567n
Slater, I. 609n
Slocum, J. 524n
Smale, A. 120n, 122n
Smallwood, N. 120n, 344n
Smith, D. 215n
Smith, P. 165n, 475n
Snell, S. 52, 78n, 79n, 296n
Snook, S. 342n
Snow, C. 215n, 216n
Snyder, N. 215n, 216n
Sobel, A. 593
Softbank 82, 551
Solomon, C. 166n
Sölvell, O. 432n
Sondak, H. 215n
Sonnenfield, J. 297n
Sony 24, 196
Sorensen, J. 252n, 253n
Soros, George 603
South African Airlines 518
SouthWest Airlines 46, 47, 214n
Sparrow, P. 78n, 166n, 298n, 299n,
    388n, 609n
Spear, S. 253n
Spector, B. 474n
Speier, C. 169n
Spekman, R. 522n
Spreitzer, G. 78n, 343n, 473n
St Gobain 7t
St John, C. 214n
Staber, U. 253n
Stage, C. 388n

Stahl, G. 121n, 166n, 168n, 252n,
    296n, 297n, 298n, 324, 567n,
    567n, 568n
Standard Chartered 295, 300n, 462, 470
Star Alliance 518, 524n
Starbuck, W. 80n, 611n
Starkey, K. 297n, 342n, 609n
Starwood Hotels 333
State Key Laboratory of Coal
    Conversion 421
Stella Artois 27
Stening, B. 390n
Stephens, G. 167n
Stertz, B. 568n
Stewart, T. 251n, 300n, 430n
STMicroelectronics 422
Stogdill, R. 216n
Stopford, J. 38n, 40n, 608n, 609n
Stringer, Howard 280
Stroh, L. 166n, 167n, 168n, 169n, 253n
Strohmeier, S. 609n
Subramanian, M. 430n
Sullivan, J. 343n
Sumelius, J. 122n
Sun Microsystems 319
Sundaram, A. 568n, 569n
Suonio, H. 567n
Suutari, V. 166n, 169n, 390n
Suzuki Motors 516
Svejenova, S. 343n
Sylvester, K. 120n
Szulanski, G. 429n, 429n, 430n

Tacorante, D. 78n
Tahvanainen, M. 169n, 375,
    389n, 390n
Takeuchi, H. 251n, 343n,
    429n, 430n
Tallman, S. 252n
Tamkin, P. 609n
Tanure, B. 77n
Taobao 82, 119n, 262
Tapscott, D. 431n
Tarique, I. 430n, 432n
Task, S. 215n
Tata Consulting 262
Tata Steel 31

Tatramat 495, 566n
Tatweer 325
Taylor, F 8, 38n, 40n, 164n, 169n, 252n,
Tead, O. 38n
Teagarden, M. 431n
Teece, D. 77n
Teigland, R. 432n
Terpstra, D. 298n
Tetrapak 300n
Texas Instruments 589
Thibaut, J. 473n
Thomas, D. 168n, 298n
Thompson, L. 119n, 389n
Tichy, N. 18, 39n, 252n, 298n
Tienari, J. 567n
Tierney, T. 216n, 431n
Toh, S. 166n, 168n
Tom Online 82, 119n
Torbiörn, I. 167n, 390n
Torekull, B. 253n
Tornikowski, C. 390n
Toshiba 491, 516
Towers Perrin 539, 567n, 609n
Toynbee, Arnold 80n, 602, 611n
Toyoda, Sakichi 217
Toyota 22, 46, 48, 55, 100, 136, 137,
    167n, 174, 189, 194, 217-8, 220,
    234, 237, 250, 447
Trepo, G. 388n
Trompenaar, F. 97, 101, 104, 120n, 121n
Truitt, J. 521n
Tsai, W. 251n, 252n, 430n
Tsang, E. 431n, 432n
Tsuruoka, Hajime 459
Tung, R. 38n, 165n, 166n, 167n,
    168n, 169n, 522n
Tushman, M. 80n, 472n

UAMS 473n
Ulrich, D. 38n, 78n, 100, 120n, 344n,
    387n, 388n, 466, 474n, 522n, 590,
    608n, 609n, 610n
Underwood, L. 120n
Unilever 19, 25, 26, 33, 59, 84, 86, 88,
    117, 174, 247, 329, 330
United Autoworkers 136
UPS 53

Vaara, E. 567n
Vahlne, J. 40n
Valeo 533
Valero 272
Valy-Durbin, S. 169n
Van Buren, H. 252n
Van de Ven, A. 432n, 427
Van der Heyden, L. 473n
Van der Veer, Jeroen 248
Van Maanen, J. 253n, 254n
Van Veen, K. 298n
Van Weering, E. 524n
Van Wijk, R. 429n, 430n, 431n
Vance, C. 387n, 388n
Varma, A. 169n, 388n
Vaupel, J. 38n
Venkatraman, N. 430n
Verbeke, A. 432n, 472n
Verdin, P. 609n
Vermeulen, G. 567n
Vernon, R. 38n, 40n, 298n
Vlasic, B. 568n
Vodafone 111, 185, 551
Voigt 567n, 568n
Volkswagen 271
Volmer, H. 431n
Von Oetinger, B. 216n, 430n
Vora, D. 253n

Wade, W. 611n
Wahaha 521n
Walker, J. 39n, 345n, 473n
Wal-Mart 86, 108, 109, 116, 127
Walton, Sam 235
Wang, X. 120n, 166n, 473n
Ward, K. 215n
Warner, M. 120n, 122n
Watanabe, Katsuaki 217, 430n
Waterman, R. 39n, 213n, 230
Waters, J. 473n
Watson Wyatt 432n, 569n
Waxin, M. 166n
Weckström-Nousainen, Sonja 252n
Weick, K. 215n, 417, 432n, 472n
Weill, Sandy 345n
Weiss, S. 252n, 522n

Welch, Jack 66, 114, 169n, 223, 235, 252n, 253n, 254n, 294, 301, 364, 388n, 389n, 429n
Wellins, R. 342n, 343n
Wells, L. 38n, 40n
Western Electric 9
Westley, F. 472n, 473n
Westney, D. 523n, 524n
Westphal, J. 122n
Whetten, D. 253n
Whirlpool Corporation 86, 566n, 495
Whitlam, David 307
Whitley, R. 106, 121n
Whitman, Meg 82
Whittington, R. 253n
Wiechmann, D. 297n, 298n
Wilkins, M. 37n
Williams, A. 431n, 473n
Williamson, O. 163n, 359, 388n, 422, 431n, 432n, 609n
Willmott, H. 253n
Wilson, David 339
Winter, S. 77n
Winterton, J. 298n
Wittenberg, A. 345n
Womack, J. 165n
Wong, C. 120n
Wood, R. 475n
Woodruff, Robert 441
Woolridge, A. 122n
World Bank 104
Worldcom 599
Worm, V. 169n
Wren, D. 37n
Wright, C. 608n, 609n, 610n
Wyman, O. 165n

Xerox 12, 508 *see also* Fuji-Xerox
Xin, K. 387n

Yaffe, M. 431n
Yahoo! 82, 87, 119n, 412
Yahoo! Hot Jobs 263
Yamazaki, Y. 166n
Yan, Y. 122n
Yandex 85, 119n
Yibo, Shao 82
Yim, P. 215n
Yip, G. 191, 215n
Yong, G. 297n
Yoshihara, H. 163n, 299n
Yoshino, M. 481, 521n, 522n
Young, S. 568n
Younger, Y. 608n
YourEncore 414
Yuasa, M. 298n

Zaheer, S. 119n
Zahra, S. 430n, 472n
Zalan, T. 214n
Zambrano, Lorenzo 525
Zander, U. 29, 40n, 41n, 394, 429n, 430n, 432n
Zara 159, 160
Zárraga-Oberty, C. 430n
Zbaracki, M. 122n, 474n
Zehnder, Egon 532, 567n
Zeira, Y. 522n, 522n, 523n
Zenger, J. 120n
Zhang, H. 342n
Zhang, Ruimin 346, 385
Zitouna 567n
Zohar, D. 474n
Zollo, M. 77n, 567n, 568n, 569n
Zuboff, S. 345n

Subject Index

f. figure
d. diagram
n. notes
t. table

360° appraisal 59, 114, 207, 317,
    333, 362, 363
  advisability of 373
  process 560
  systems 320
  Welch's key contribution 320
7-S model 18

Absorption
  strategy 554
  logic of 536
Absorptive capacity 398; paradoxes
    around 398
Accountability
  collective sense of 469
  Nestlé's model 181f
  tenure, linking to 331
Acquisition
  alliance, alternative to 530
  complexity in 536
  definition of 527
  delays, failure through 568n
  failure, reasons 532
  four Is 548–9

HR implementation blueprint 547
integration, different types 535f
knowledge-intensive 568n
launching, reasons 530
learning from 561
planning, HRM perspective 540
process
    GE's Wheel of Fortune 564f
  strategic drivers behind 534
  success factors 533, 534, 538
  target selection and HRM
    issues 540
  tool kits 563
  winners, sellers as 531
  see also Mergers
Action
  learning 317–8
    assignment 226, 594
    cross-cultural, at
    NUMMI 136
    success factors 318
  plans 353
Adaptive organizations,
    characteristics 176
Agency problems 37n
Agenda setting 465
Agility 470
Allegiances, multiple, balancing
    148, 149f

Alliance
  airline industry, in 517–8
    challenge in 518
  assignments, careers and 506
  capabilities, developing 501
    learning environment, creating 501
  character changing over time 484
  champions, identifying 495
  classifying 481
  complexity of 477
  cross-border, drivers 478
  experience, learning from 522n
  evolving role of 517–9
  factors for sustainability 480
  failed 202–3
  good reasons for 479
  growth through 23
  HRM issues in managing 498
  implementing 188, 496–507
    collaborative aspects 498
    loyalty of workforce in 498
    top management role 497
  influence, building 506
  instability, inherent 485
  international, motives for entering 477
  learning
    as focal objectives 507
    bias for action in successful 517
    career paths facilitating 515
    climate for 515
    focus on mutual learning 508
    NUMMI and 515–6
    solely for 517
  learning through 509
  management 516
    core principles 512t
    four HR functions to leverage 514
    HRM foundations and 512
    obstacles to 508–12, 509t
    supporting 507–17
  loyalties, conflicting 507
  management
    breeding ground for managers 519
    framework at HP 501
  managers
    flexibility of role 491
    impact on relationship quality 490

    roles and responsibilities 490t
    seeking 489–90
  managing 476–524
    paradoxes and challenges in 519
    partner's 499
  motivational issues 505
  negotiations, preparing for 491–2
  objectives for formation of 520n
  partner selection in 488
  partner's culture, assessing 489
  performance
    management, dualities in 502, 503
  personnel transfers in 500
  planning and negotiating 485–96
  process, as 485
  purpose, communicating 513
  rewards and 504
    attitudes to variable pay 504
  strategy
    benefits from partner
    differences 488
    business risks 488
    complementary, in 504
    HRM issues in 486–92
    plan 487t
  staffing 499
  strategic, classification 481f
  success, defining in 480
  tensions around 503, 519
  training 492, 501
  transnationalism and 519
  understanding 480–5
  value, purpose to create 507
  venture, HR policies in 496
Ambidexterity 74, 186, 416
  four aspects 416–9
Ambiguity, tolerance for 143, 308
Anti-globalization 22
Antitrust legislation 11
A-players 330
A-positions 330
Appraisal 100
  cycle, Cisco's 359
  differentiation and 364
  evaluation, competing goals with 363
  group-oriented 362
  in Hong Kong's Chinese cultures 362

multiple-rater 207, 362
outcomes, linking to 363
outputs, formal 364
practices, expanding range 359
reward system, and 207
tools 59
training, importance of 362
Apprenticeship system, German 106
Assignments, two in the box 310
Authority, hierarchic nature of 304

Babel team 199
Balanced perspectives 243
Balanced scorecards 356–7
Bandwagon imitation 114
Behavioral competences, overlap
    in M&As 562
Beliefs, shared *see* Values, shared
Benchmarking
    information 113
    international 5
Bonding, internal 221
Bonus
    appraisal criteria for 42
    formula, calculating 370
    payment methods 366
Boundaries, ambiguous 488
Boundary spanning 221
Boundaryless
    behavior 369
    company 394
    organization 23
    organization, CLO and 586
Bretton Woods Agreement 12
BRIC countries 111, 303
Brookfield Global Relocation Trends
    Survey 2009 Report 167n, 168n
Buddying systems, *see* Mentoring
Business
    coordination teams 192
    coordination teams 193
        regional management and 193
    coordinators 189
    lines, differentiation across 78n
    partners 61, 584
    plans, executing through people
        450–66

strategy 44–9
    difficulty of linking with HR 45
support
    role 61, 582–5, 592–3
    advice on 593
Business Process Re-engineering (BPR) 9

CAGE Framework 119n
CAMI 516
Capabilities 28
    building 258
    development 74
    implementing 46–8
    key feature 28
    leveraging 127
    need for 16, 46
    three criteria 46
    Toyota's development of 445
    transferring 445
Capitalism
    a soulless philosophy 603
    Anglo-Saxon 106
    Chinese 107
    European 106
    European Industrial District form
        121n
    forms 107
    Japanese form of 107
    Korean 107
    national varieties of 106
    six configurations of 106
Career development
    alliance form and 506
    responsibility moving to individual 334
Career tracks 337
Cartels 11, 38n
Center of excellence, concept
    of 182, 183, 575
Centralization 75, 130
Chaebol, Korean 107, 111
Challenge
    as starting point 312
    development through 312
Change Acceleration Process (CAP)
    at GE 452
    methodology 453
    GE Capital in acquisitions 558

Change
  agent 78n
  capability 62, 461, 467
  champions of, promoting 463
  continuous, as reality 71
  cynicism about 70
  danger of fixation on 70
  dualistic pattern in 71, 436
  evolutionary assumptions
    about 472n
  HR, role in leading 463–6
  HRM need to anticipate 44
  management, competency
    framework 590
  managing as capability 461
  managing, challenge of 451
  need for, understanding 465
  partner 463
    HR as 69
  path dependency of 453
  planned, eight-step model for
    managers 452
  processes, models of 436
    emotional needs and 465
  process of attention to 578
  spiral models of 436
  success in driving, keys to 550
  tension and 464f
  transnational organization 437f
Chief Learning Officer (CLO) 586
China
  capitalism 107
  CEO leading concerns 297n
  engagement 456
  initiative, cultural avoidance 360
  rewards, non-financial 385
  social capital 228
  standardization in Western-owned
    firms 134t
  values 235
Cloning behavior 530
Coaching 318–20
  expatriates and 146
  management, as new
    approach 186
Coevolution 387n
Cognitive conflict 209

Collaboration, importance
  of 183, 393, 400–5
  long-term, IBM and Toshiba 479
Collective bargaining 10, 108, 109t
  differentiation and 586
Commitment
  building 355
  collective, leadership unity and 468–9
  processes to build 4650
Common knowledge base 222
Common language, importance of 125–6
Common professional interest,
    communities of *see* communities
    of practice
Communication 57t
  advances in 12
  face-to-face and electronic,
    complementarity of 204
  importance in cross-border
    acquisitions 555
  processes, HR function role in 460
  see also Virtual teams
Communism, fall of 22
Communist Revolution 11
Communitarian business system 98t, 107
Communities of practice 29, 225, 402
  HR and 575
Commuter, international 159
Company-of-origin effect 116
Compensation 347
  alternatives to 379
  caféteria approach 379
  complexity 378
  discrepancies in 378
  disparity in 505
  home country bias 381
  international staff and 375
  international, balance sheet approach
    377–9, 378t
  international, summary of 376–7t
  philosophy, common 365
  practices, variations in 366
  returnees and 381
  schemes 376
  strategies
    international, evolution of 375
    choosing 380

Competence
  core, 28
  development 593
  development of 188
  frameworks, reasons for adoption 298n
  HR 590–5
  of local managers 448
  professional and technical, in
    expatriates 143
  Singapore, HP's global center 446
Competency framework 284, 590
  defined 280
  six roles 590
  three approaches 280–5
  too generic 280
Competition, pace of 174
Competitive advantage 33t
  alliances building 484
  erosion of 24
  from leveraging know-how 174
  integration a key 123
  integrative ability key to 424
  new sources in people management
    systems 338
  SouthWest Airlines 47
Competitive collaboration 511
Competitive culture
  building 596
  emerging 23
  Formula 1 and 596
  socially responsible, HR as catalyst
    to build 603
  transition of value systems into 597
Competitive
  perspective 173
  platforms 127
  strategies, for competitive
    advantage 242
  strength, from knowledge 420
Competitiveness, sources of 28, 29
Complexity 3
  learning process reflects 318
  means of reducing 447–8
  trust impact on ability to deal with 221
Conflict
  ability to handle 308
  managing 205

  resolution, social capital as 223
    key features 224t
  see also Contention management
Confrontation rooms 223
Consistency, in HR 50–1, 367, 368
Content development role
  in HR 60, 574–7
Contention management 223
  norms for 224
Continuous improvement 100
  See also Kaizen
Control
  approaches, mix of 5
  coordination and 163–4n
  defined 13–14
  difficulty of distance 4
  mechanisms 35t, 128
  structures 4
  systems 4
  varied national approaches 164n
  vertical 172–9
  see also Coordination
Convergence 114, 361
Coordination 178
  capabilities 3
  capacity 175
  defined 14
  emergence of 173
  hierarchy, importance of 214n
  high degree of 185
  horizontal 172–9
  mechanisms 35t
  three elements to 177
  transnational 173
  see also Control
Core competences 28
Corporate governance, traditional
    model of 172
Corporate HR practices,
    internalization 135
  implementation 135
Corporate property, individuals as 323
Corporate social responsibility
    27, 601–4
Corporate welfarism 10
Corruption, social capital and 230
Country-of-origin effect 116

Cranet project 107, 121n
Creativity, enhanced by multicultural
    experiences 314
Credible activist role 610n
Cross-border
  projects 246
  teams, building 197–203
    disruptive avoidance of conflict 205
    diversity of 205
    four types of 198f
    importance of credibility 202
    relationships build on 202
    working in 204–7
Cross-boundary
  groups 192
  project groups 576
  teams 177
  teamwork, ability in 316
Cross-company teams (CCTs)193
Cross-cultural
  adjustment 147
  competence, challenge for HR in
    acquiring 546
  psychologists 144
  sensitivity 494
  training 146, 160
  understanding 54
Cross-functional teams (CFTs) 193
Cultural
  assessment 540, 544
    framework 544
    challenges of 545
  differences 97
    importance of 545
    national versus organizational 545
  distance 97
  embeddedness 97
  explanations, appeal of 103
  fit 230
    argument 103
    lack of 533
  flexibility 167n
  hypothesis, assumptions
    within 102
  perspective 96–7, 243
    limits 101

practices, GLOBE study 99t
  sensitivity 143, 167n
  stereotypes 104
  steward role 610n
  tensions 97, 98t
Culture
  building new 559
  CEMEX way, the 525
  change, post-merger 560
  clashes in 230
  company's, selection and 275
  costs associated with strong 232
  critical factor for learning 514
  developing shared 507
  IKEA's Way 132
  limitations of parent country,
    overcoming 361
  management
    difficulty of 240
    requirement for 240
  national and organizational 234
  Nokia Way, the 124
  organizational, strengths 231–2
    advantages 232
  shock 147
  social capital across, impact of 227
  status quo and 361
  trust as key outcome 507
  Toyota Way, the 217, 218
  see also Values
Customer-centric, becoming 185

Daihyo torishimariyaku 304
Deal, closing the 546
Decentralization 1, 75
  culture of 171
  handmaidens of 117
  pendulum swing between
    centralization and 441
Demographic changes 260–3;
    in Germany 260, 261f
Deregulation 23
Development
  and training 57t, 58
  experiences, best from roles 314–5
  managing 332–8

Dialogue
  importance in commitment 355
  quality of 468
  safeguarding open 205
Diaspora team 199
Differentiated network, global
    company organized as 181, 183
Differentiation 33t, 51–5, 78n
  benefits of 53
  creating 384
  organizational design and 56
  purpose of 327
Dirigente 304
Discrimination, countering in selection
    process 277
Distance
  dimensions to *see* CAGE Framework
  four dimensions of 472n
Distributed capabilities,
    leveraging 183
Distributive justice 453
Diversity 249
  geocentric orientation 279
  importance of 57
  local adaptations 110
  management 229
    business reasons for 279
    gender targets 278
    programs 110
    selection and 278
  multinational firms and 416
  national, ethnocentric orientation
    and 279
  network perspective 111
  sources of 96
  theoretical perspectives 96
  understanding 96
  valuing 448
Dominance, global through
    efficiency 124
Downsizing 17, 466
Downturn, coping with 450
Dual allegiances, managing 506
Dual citizens 149, 149f
Dual reporting relationships,
  role of 211

Dualities 33t
  balancing 55–6, 249
  exploration and exploitation and 426
  facing international firms 72t
  focus on 71–6
  global mindset and 249
  perspective 75
  risks of challenge and failure 331
  steering between 73–4
  synonyms 72
  tensions 611n
Duality theory 73; pioneer of 74
Duality, dynamics of 436, 437–441, 602
Duality-oriented studies 80n
Due diligence
  checklist 542f
  cultural 544
  process 540, 541–2
  strengths of business leaders 564
Dynamic capabilities 77n

Ease of Doing Business Index
    104, 105t
Economies of scale 127, 442, 444
  alliances encouraging 479
e-HR 336–7, 577–9
  efficiency gains from 579
  functions suitable for 577
  solutions 60
Electronic job markets 333
Elite political approach
  French education system and
    286, 299n
  Ivy League universities and 287
Emotional
  competence, developing 331
    role in leadership 331
  self-control 308
Employee
  groups, differentiation among
    51–5, 52d
  referrals 271
  surveys 239
Employee Value Proposition (EVP),
    building 273–5, 274f
  need for differentiated 274

Employer
  of choice, reputation as 273
  marketing the firm as 55
Employment contracts 5
Employment offices 8
Employment policy 32t
Empowerment 175, 213n
Enabling, as new approach 186
Engagement
  Chinese and 456
  levers of 458
  strategy for 457f
  tools to build 457
  Web 2.0 ways 470
Enterprise Resource Planning (ERP)
    systems 577
  PeopleSoft 577
  SAP 577
Equal opportunity 245; barriers to 246
Equitable access, for talented
    employees, key challenge 245
Escalating momentum 533
Ethnocentric orientation 20
Ethnocentricity, perceptions 128
European Community 12
European organization, Canon's
    consolidation of 459
European Works Council
    Directive 109
Evaluation paradox 427
Evaluation, IBM's approach 461
Evaluation, who conducts 373
Executive search 272
Expatriate
  adjustment, dimensions in 147–8
  assignment preparation 145–6
  assignment refusal 145, 167n
  changing demographics of 154
  commitment, patterns of 148
  coping problems 168n
  corporate agency role 140
  corporate culture, used to
    transfer 238
  cost of 523n
  crucial role of 124
  cycle 142
    tensions in 152–3

differing roles 141
dual career considerations 156
evaluation, globally standardized
    procedures for 374
failure 13, 141, 167n
family considerations and 145, 147
female 154
global integration and 130
hierarchic mechanisms and 131
knowledge transfer, key role in 394
language competency and 147
learning assignments and 156
learning, individual and 431n
management, evolution of 137
myths about 155
performance evaluation of 373
performance management 150
re-entry 150
rewards and 94
selection 94, 142
    tools for 144, 167n
social capital and 227
spouses and 155
success, defining 142, 143
survey 139t
time horizons, different 373
training 146
underperformance 142
understanding the
    phenomenon 138–42
work adjustment, training and 167n
younger 156
Expatriation 12, 90
  alternatives to 158, 158t
  as process not event 142
  assignment duration and 157
  cost of market entry 153
  costs of 13
  demand- and learning-driven 329
  demand-driven 139
  emotional development,
    necessary for 308
  insecurity of 157–8
  international HRM and 137
  learning-driven 139
  mastering 137–52
  motives for 139

policies 20
practices supporting effective
    151–2, 152t
purpose of 139, 140d
repatriation and 157
resistance to 151
Roman Empire and 138
stereotypes 138
third country nationals and 157
traditional model, beyond the 152
virtual 159
Expectancy theory 389n
Experience, generalist, limited
    value of 330
Expertise
    authority of 304
    management 337
Explanation processes 460
Exploitation-exploration
    dilemma 73, 426–8
Exploration 73 *see also* Resource
    development
External
    customer, focus on 188
    knowledge, gaining access to 411
    labor market orientation 268
    recruitment 266
Externalization 415

FaceBook 334
    corporate 222
    platforms 29
Failure of success paradox 74
Fair Labor Association, H&M and 588
Fair process 78n
    acceptance through 452, 453
    benefits of 454
    corporate value, as explicit 462
    critical value 454
    Five E Framework 454
    Five Es 462–3
    success for mergers, key to 537
    tensions 462–3
Feedback 320
    and learning , promoting 207
    from employees in M&As 562
    loop, essential in M&As 563

negative, resented 362
    providing 362
Firm
    as network 173
    resource-based view 45
Fit, achieving 68
Flatteners 29; 10 forces for 30t
Foreign affiliates 445
Foreign Direct Investment (FDI) 5, 8
Foreign firm network effect 116
Foreignness, liability of 83
Formula 1, Honda and 596–7
Four Box Framework 78n
Free agents 148, 149f
Free markets, credibility of 603
Front-back organization 182, 185, 444
Functional
    committees 575
    councils 193
        as vehicle to communicate best
        practice 194
    expertise, competency framework 590
    experts 575
Future leaders, challenge of
    developing 303

Gaishikei 91
Genchi genbutsu 217, 232, 235t
Gender
    discrimination 278–80
    expatriation 154–6
    prejudice 155
General Agreement on Tariff and
    Trades (GATT) 12
Geocentric
    corporation 21
    managers, need for 242
    organization 24
German firms, unusual
    structure 39n, 106
Global account management (GAM) 369
    complexity in 191
    GAM unit, the 370
    implementing 191
    managers 190
    performance management for 369
    three generic approaches 191

Global acquisitions, integrating 525–69
Global branding 127
Global collaboration
　appraising 369t,
　obstacles to 359
Global compensation, challenges in 365
Global competence managers 190
Global convergence effect 116
Global coordination
　serving 127
　structuring 170–216
　supporting 367–8
Global diversity 83
Global employer branding 272–3
Global executives
　development experiences 311t
　source of 312
Global firm, competitive
　　advantage of 250
Global HRM
　organizing 574
　processes, standardized 336
　structural solutions 575
　three organizational areas 574–85
　transforming the role 570–611
　uniqueness of 572
Global inequality 601
Global innovation, driving 391
Global integration 22
　achieving 123–69
　as competitive necessity 126
　business advantages of 126–8
　expatriates, without 158
　IBM facilitating mobility 336
　levers of 128
　limits of 161–2
　logic of 125–37
　strategies, benefits of 124
　tools for 128–30
　traditional industries for 162n
Global knowledge management
　　33t, 391–416
Global leaders, developing 300–345
　insufficient supply of 303
Global leadership 303–11
　change management and 311
　competences 307–8

development, principles of 311–20
failure, main reason 304
guidelines for 604
pyramid 308f; four key 308
Global markets, realities of 175
Global mindset 178, 219, 240–50
　change, implications for 448
　complementary perspectives 242–4
　defined 242
　how to develop 245–9
　HRM fostering 606
　international mobility as
　　development tool for 246
　leaders, developing in 448
　management training and 247
　measuring 244
　measuring scales 244t
　reinforcing 248
　rethinking the paradigm 249
　top management, context from 248
Global multidimensional structures,
　　emerging forms 180–7
Global performance management
　　346–390
　best practices 382t
　competitive advantage, source of 349
　cycle 348–67
　definition 349
　implementing 381–6
　implementing effective,
　　challenge of 349
　importance of 349–50
　local versus global 383
　three elements of 349
　three overarching issues 382
　well-defined, example of 348
Global processes 178; standardized 178
Global project management teams 193
Global scorecards 353
Global service firms, three types of
　　center 430n
Global staffing processes 266
Global standardization 131–7, 577–8, 583
　advantages 133t
　China, degree of in 134
　difficulties from 134
　scale advantages 132

Global supply chain
  capability 434
  slow building 441
Global talent
  management 78n
    new source of 338
  managing 255–300
  reviews 326–8
Global team appraisals, how to
    improve 371
Global teams 172
  challenges, complexities of 209
  failure of 205
  leadership roles in 206
  rewarding 372t
Global teamwork
  challenge of enabling 208
  foundations of 199
  enabling factors 199
  importance of clear goals 200
  implementing 208–11
  see also Cross-border teams
Global transfer policies 161
Globalization 21–31, 33t, 262
  dismissing protest against 601
  lacking a human face 603
  meaning of 22
  opportunities, source of new 22
  paradoxes of 219
  political context of 603
  potential backlash 603
  progressive of talent
    management 262
  questioned 602
  roadmap for managing 24–6
  social implications for 601
Globally integrated enterprise 182
  enablers of 184
GLOBE study 97–99, 104, 120n, 170,
  306–7
Glue factors 514
Goal setting
  challenges around 351
  influential paradigm 351
  peer groups and 354
  process, cultural differences 355
  theory, critics 387n

Goals
  cultural differences in 352
  long-term, short-term versus 357
  Nokia's SMART 354
  Starwood Hotels' Big Five 354
  stretch 420
  stretch targets 352
  time horizons, cultural
    differences 352–3
  unity around, as lever for
    teamwork 351
Going native 149
Grands Écoles 299n
Great Depression 10, 11
Greenfield investment, M&A
  alternative to 528
Group coaching 317
Groupthink 436
Guanxi 228
Guarded strategist 589

Halo effect 327, 430n
Harvard Multinational Enterprise
  Project 14
Head office, localization and 93–6
Headquarters staff, eliminating 608n
Hierarchic
  control 180
    dilemmas of 173
  mechanisms, inability to cope 175
High-performance work systems 63
Holdouts, dealing with 457
Home country nationals, bias
  towards 327
Horizontal coordination 170–216, 369
Host country effect 116
Human and social capital 9, 62
  audit 540, 543
Human Relations 32t
  Movement 10
Human Resource Management (HRM)
  American model of 107
  Anglo-Saxon model 107
  architectures 52
  boundaries of 585
    three specific issues 585
  competences 590

Human Resource
  Management (*continued*)
 core tasks 56
 devolution to line managers 589
 different views 606
 e-enabled 579
 evolution of 3
 employee experiences with 77n
 as field of study 9
 firm approach to 54
 formal training programs and 594
 four roles in change arena 466
 foundations, focus on 66
 function
   alliances, issues in 490
   capability development 590
   centers of expertise 575
   exit routes from 595
   external orientation at GE 587
   generalists, support tasks of 583
   global challenges and 596
   Global, specialization
    within 132
   handicap 67
   least foreign experience in 593
   managers, developing for
    transnational firm 593
   obstacles to globalization 593
   roles, defining 59–61
   views about 584
 global standardization of 132–4
   drivers for 132
 link with multinational strategy 24
 long-term perspective and
    599, 600
 need for current knowledge of 575
 new-found legitimacy 13
 non-HR professionals in 595
 organization, in transnational firm 586f
 orientation, global mindset requiring
    shift in 246
 outsourcing 580–1
 planning 32t
 practice
   contextual influences on 115–6
   core, designing 56–9, 57t
   firm performance and 63

 global implementation as lever 171
 hybrid in subsidiaries 135
 potential for differentiation 55
 structure to ensure
    consistency of 575
Process and Content Development 574
realigning 67
responsibilities, external
    boundaries of 587
responsibility for 589
responsiveness, cultural
    features and 100
role
   dualities, tensions, dilemmas, duty
    to explore 600
   in the business 582
   long-term consequences 600
   strategies, to assist in 466
Roles 59–61, 574–93
scorecard 357
service centers 579
   potential benefit of 580
   language obstacles and 609n
service delivery 577
   at Shell 583
   implementing model 581–2
   international variations in 582
   key output 577
   outsourcing as cost reduction
    in 581
strategy, fundamental pillar of 184
systems, integration in M&As 562
tension management and 604
three guiding principles 50
three stages of 65t
tools, IT-based 132
variety of delivery mechanisms
    for 585
Wheel, key elements 44, 49–64, 49f
Human resources, use of term 38n

Ideas, open market 401
Impatriates, 117
  boundary spanning roles 221
  communications and 160
  global integration and 160–1
  HR policies to support 160

Implementation, importance of
commitment to 355
Inclusiveness, workforce diversity
and 279
Individual values, distribution of 102t
Individualism 98t, 100
Induction programs, formal,
socialization and 237, 277
Industrial betterment 6, 8, 32t
Industrial productivity, US 11
Industrialization
impact of 5
strategies 12
Industry, structural fit and 162n
Inequality, new forms of 602
Inflection point 467, 475n
Information sharing, norms of
transparency around 468
Information transfer, distance as
obstacle to 420
In-groups 229
Initiative, avoided in Chinese
culture 360
Initiatives, incremental versus
breakthrough 357
Innovation
as social process 420
champions, need for 426
diffusing within multinationals 426
groups 315
hierarchy the antithesis of 423
Hourglass metaphor in 426
in surprising places 418
initiatives, examples 419
jam 475n
journey, stages in 422
managing across borders 391–432
organizing for 427
Proctor & Gamble's connect +
develop model 392
Shell's GameChanger 424, 425
Innovativeness 222
Institutional
environment 84
frameworks, differences in US and
European 108
perspective 104–11

theory 106
Integration 78n, 123–169
acquisition, in 547–61
clarity of role of acquired unit 556
communication a two-way process 556
cultural assessment as plan for 545
goals 561
initiatives 550
leading the process 550
local responsiveness and 162
loss of 55
maintaining momentum 554–5
manager
role of 551–2
as transition specialists 551
as information gatekeeper 551
skills needed by 552
mechanisms 128
organizational design and 56
process
auditing 565
post-merger 547–560
post-merger 533
speed key success driver 553
strong normative, at Toyota 284
tailored to purpose of acquisition 550
teams, mixed 553
unintended consequences 554
Integrative leadership orientation 196
Intercultural communications 204
Internal labor markets (ILMs) 266, 333
advantages and disadvantages 267t
integral element of good HRM
system 267
talent management, need for
effective 267
used at Microsoft, Shell, Hewlett
Packard 334
see also Open job markets
Internal resourcing 266, 269
Internal selection, challenges
of 285–289
Internal talent management
elite cohort approach 285, 299n
elite political approach 286
functional approach 287
regional differences 285

Internal transfers 595
International assignments
    as competence development 140
    assignment failure 141
    development opportunities 140
    interpersonal networks from 140
    short-term learning
        assignments 140–1
International compensation, trends
    and challenges to 380–1
International HRM
    a sensitive area 570
    challenges 1–41
    theories 31–4, 32t
International mobility
    building on 246–7, 313, 329, 330
    enhancing global mindset 247t
    limitations development tool for
        global mindsets 246
International transfers,
        managing 142–52
Internationalization 3, 4, 7t
    alliance in support of strategy 479
    alliances useful tool for 477
    first step towards 126
    new models 114
    obstacles to 340
    strategies, HRM influence on 33
    three paths 27
    traditional approaches 3
Internet 30t
    employment, effect on 263
    global trends, effect on 111
    recruitment 271
Internships 271
Interpersonal skills 225, 304,
        308f, 344n
Intracultural variation 118
Intranet jam process, IBM's 468
Intransitivity, leadership 309
Isomorphism 107

Japanese Challenge, the 19
Japanese
    Challenge, the 19
    corporate values 234, 235t
    discrimination 278

management
    business practices 218
    distinctive features 40n
    museums of 496
    subsidiaries with local
        managers 164n
    social capital 229
    strengths 195
    *see also Daihyo torishimariyaku;
        Gaishikei; Genchi genbutsu;
        Jinzai; Kaizen; Wa; Zaibatsu*
    Jinzai 38n
Job
    classification, Hay system 365
    rotation 313, 330–1
    specifications 8
Joint Venture (JV)
    alliance as 481
    board composition 492
    control and influence issues 492
    formation, negotiation
        challenges 492
    managers, demands on 494
    managing 476–524
    senior management, appointing 494
    see also Alliance

Kaizen 100, 217, 235t
Knowledge 28
    ability to receive 397
    ad hoc management in PSFs 406
    acquisition 411–6
        market for 414
        through partnering 413
    economy, shift to 260; importance of
        talent in 260
    exchange, climate for 511
    in HRM, forms of 396
    innovation management, and 179
    management 391–432
        codification basis of 409
        important for exploration
            and exploitation 426
        in PSFs 405–11
        Mittal Steel's program 401
    of business, competency
        framework 590

practices and, expatriates conduit
for 135
push and pull 399
retention 415
three strategies 415
sharing
communities of practice and 401
conditions to enable 397
depends on 395
global mindset relevant for 404
hubs of 402
important levers of 404
in professional service firms
(PSF) 405
inter-unit 394, 397
in the multinational 394–405
repatriating 416
role of performance
management in 404
Social architecture, building
supporting 402
stimulating 399
structural mechanisms
to aid 400
talent management
considerations 404
stickiness, expensive nature of
395, 427
tacit, need for investment 412
transfer
information technology,
impact on 395
repatriation and impatriates
enabling 399
two kinds of 394
value to receiving unit 398
varies according to strategic
importance 395
ways to share 399
Knowledge-based careers, intransitivity
for 310

Labor
industrial relations and 57t
relations 108
unions 87
role of 108

Language, shared, importance of for
culture 236
Lateral coordination 39n, 175, 309, 368
importance of 185
hierarchical control and 172
see also Horizontal coordination
Lateral design, success of 197
Lateral leaders
competences 196t
developing coordination
skills of 197
four domains requiring 188
roles 188
skills 196
Lateral steering
enabling 368
groups 315
people strategies supporting 196–7
tools 187–97
Law of requisite complexity 41n, 211
Leaders, high-potential,
characteristics 321
Leadership, authority of 305
cultural differences 306
hierarchic, needed by networks 186
Leadership, behavioral complexity
theories 216n
Leadership competences, Hay-McBer
study 306
in transnational development 448–9
Leadership development 301–345
focus on 32t
global coordination supported by
338–40
HR agenda, critical item on 322
implications of intransitive
structure for 310
importance in GE 301
managing 320–32
priority in multinationals 302
Leadership effectiveness, cultural
views 307
Leadership initiative, lateral project
roles demanding 368
Leadership intransitivity 302, 309
Leadership, managing change and 315,
451–2, 463, 468

Leadership, national culture and 304
  cross-cultural differences 306
  cultural differences in 304
  different roles 304
Leadership pool, high-potential 264
Leadership potential 285, 313
  traits associated with 320
  see also Potential
Leadership skills 307–8
  firm specific 344n
  integrative 313
Leadership training 317
Leadership, transformation of 186
Lean manufacturing 413
  system, Toyota's 516
Learnability 285
Learning
  agility 320, 321
  alliance 413, 483
    Fuji-Xerox as 483
    in NUMMI joint venture 413
    reaching objectives 523n
  assistance, personalized 337
  capability, building in M&As 562
  codifying in M&As 563
  gap, local and multinational
    firms 112
  internal barriers to 511
  locally, advantages 28
  low priorities and 510
  mutual 508
  objectives, explicit 513
  organizational 508
  parity 484
    in alliances 479
  reviews, IBM projects end with 208
  speeds, varying 321
  strategy, setting the 513
  targets 512
  teams 226
Learning-driven
  assignments 144, 329
  development, finding positions
    for 329
Licensing agreement, alliance as 481
Lifecycle differentiation 275
Listening post 411, 412

Local
  adaptation 265
  differentiation 265
  entrepreneurship 1, 3, 75
  isomorphism 116
  responsiveness 81–122
    business advantages of 85–7
    drivers of 85, 86, 115–7
  talent, attracting 19, 90
    retaining 92
Local to global, swing from 441–2
Local versus global 27
Localization 19, 33t
  as part of corporate mantra 88
  bottlenecks in 93
    negative outcomes of 93
    expatriates and 93–4
  cost of expatriation a driver of 153
  elite cohort approach
    incompatibility 286
  excessive 96
  firms evaluated by degree of 89
  implementing 88–96
  objectives 95
  strategy 94
    sustaining 95
  traps, avoiding 95
Low performers, dealing with 364

M&A
  challenges, culture top of 538
  keys to success 538
  HR involvement 538–9
  see also Mergers; Acquisitions;
    Mergers & acquisitions
Management by objective (MBO)
    361, 388n
Management
  Anglo-Saxonization of 111
  competences, model of 310
  credibility 451
  localization of 83, 90
    barriers to 90–3
    case for localization 89
  practices, effect of WWII on 9
  system, Haier's 346
  thought, pendulum of 8

Managerial Grid 13
Managing
  change, GE formula for 451
  knowledge and innovation, three
    phases 393
  performance, difficulties in 368
Manpower planning 9, 32t, 269
Market, prime control mechanism for
    transactions 162n
Mass-customization 250
Matrix
  frame of mind, as 16
  in the mind 338,339
  management, two dimensions of 16
  organizations 14
  organizations unable to avoid 211
  pressures 75
  reporting lines and balance 582
  roles 575
  roles and responsibilities 212
  see also Split Egg working
  structure 3, 14–16
    difficulties with 15
    as difficult structures 179
  transitional organizational
    form 180
MBAs, recruitment, benefits to social
    networks 226
Measurement
  customer satisfaction 358
  focused 354
  real-time 355
  scorecards 353
  standardized 358
Meganational firm, the 25, 125
  strategy 3, 126
  subsidiary initiative in 444–9
Meister 106
Mentoring 318–20, 610n
  forms of 319
  relationships 594
Merger
  definition of 527
  difficult without articulated
    approaches 66
  implementation process 564
  of equals 536

  syndrome 547
    managing 547–8, 549
  people challenges of 555
  post-, integration process 547–60
  transformation 537
  see also Acquisitions
Mergers and acquisitions
  clear vision of value 556
  cross-border 525–69
  drivers 528, 529–30
  greenfield investment,
    alternative to 528
  integration agenda 547
  key HR issues 537–9
  management competences in 529
  measuring success 561
  phenomenon of 526–39
  speed, importance of 553
  success factors 531
  trends in global 528f
Metanational, the 422
  features of 422–3
Métier, functional sense of 305
Metrics, clear and transparent 354
M-form divisional structure 38n
Mittelstand structure in German
    firms 121n
Mobility
  advantages of 594
  cross-boundary 313
  excessive 70, 330
  facilitators of 263
  functional 314
  geographic 314
  HR professionals, necessity for 594
  increasing individual 262–3
  international 238–9, 449
  obstacles to 340
  simplistic attitude towards 331
Motivation theories 100
Multicultural teams, effectiveness of 209
Multidimensional organizations
  archetypes of 181
  configuring 181t
  implications of 186–7
  structures 172, 177, 179
    factors shaping 181

Multidomestic 25
   firm, transitive career structure 443
   organization, change paths 438f
   organization, spiral evolution of 437
   strategy 3, 85
Multi-focal organization 24
Multinational
   change in, organizations facilitating
      433–475
   company, most important question
      for 350
   emotional conflict in 209
   leadership development 288–9, 329
   mergers & acquisition, one strategic
      lever in 539
   modern, the 11–21
   people management in, challenges 31
   performance management a
      key tool 59
   stages of HRM in 64–76
   structure, trigger for 14
   top-down structure 309
MySpace 334

National business systems 83, 106
Negotiations, alliance like
      business 492
Nemawashi 39n, 16, 455
Network
   boundaries, managing 517
   leadership competences 592
   leadership, abilities involved 576
   peers, dominance of 113
   perspective 112–15
   theory 175
   ties 115
Networking, encouraging 448
Networks 219–30
   company, role of 115
   international, influence of 115
   separate 112
Nine-box assessment of potential 323–3,
      327, 344n
Non-financial rewards 380; distinctively
      Chinese reward 385
Normative control 129
Normative integration 39n

Norms, shared *see* Values, shared
Not invented here 229, 391, 398, 426

Objective setting, approaches to 351
Objective-based management 383
Objectives
   localization 358
   shared meaning 351–3
   unit- versus corporate-level 357
One-best-way thinking 101, 243
One-firm firm 406
OPEN competency framework 299n
Open job markets 332
Open job resourcing, family oriented
      firms and 334
Open-door practices 50
Operations
   competitive advantage from 132
   IKEA
   maintaining global standards in 131
   McDonald's, consistency at 131
Opportunistic behaviour, risks 5
Optimal under-manning in
      project teams 201
Organizational
   accountability of HR 599
   agility, building 467
   capabilities 43, 44–9
      difficult to transfer 445
      expectation for HRM to support 66
      in multinationals 48–9
      M&A as 561–4
   change, levers 418–9
   cohesion, career development
      and 506
   compliance, manager's
      responsibility 599
   culture 9, 32t
      challenges in managing 239
      Toyota's Production System 113
      see also Culture, Values
   Development (OD) 13, 463
      movement 213n
   Effectiveness (OE) 463
   identification 232–3
      dual 233
   identity 253n

outcomes, focus on 62
pendulums, steering to avoid 439
socialization, international
transfers and 238
sustainability 598–9
theory & perspective 175
Orientation programs,
socialization and 237
Out-groups 229
Output control 129, 164n
Outsourcing 413, 577
driven by HR function 581
central HR processes and 61

Particularism 97, 98t
Patchwork career 345n
Pedagogical ability, in knowledge
management 397
Peer
assist process 354, 355
ratings, objectivity of 371
People risk management 312, 316
facilitated by coaching 318–9
just-in-time 318
training as 316
People strategies, alignment
with 2, 181
Perceived lower performer (PLP) 365
Performance
-based approach 280, 281–3, 281t
framework 282t
capabilities needed 439
evaluation
criteria 373
A-B-C quota 365
consistency 323
Novartis' 9-Box Assessment 324
potential associated with 322
Performance appraisal 347
challenges in 374
cultural environment, local and 360
multiple functions 348–9
unintended consequences 359
Performance culture, building 560
Performance management 57t,
58–9, 100, 178
approaches 383–4

Maersk and GE 352
Goldman Sachs and 383
attention to 350
best practice in 361
boundaryless process 348
context, constrained by 360
downstream side of 358–67
global 348–50
HR practice, standardized 350
international employees and
372, 373
metrics, global mindsets and 248
nature of 211
organizational alignment,
establishing 179
ownership 382–3
struggles for influence 504
systems, collaboration in IBM, Nokia,
Infosys, Haier 369
upstream side of 351–8
Performance measures 5, 347
local suboptimization and 358
Performance metrics
common approach 354
new 461
Performance standards,
champion of 364
Personal control 128
Personnel transfers, asymmetry 516
Peter Principle, the 309
Piece-rate systems 47
Pillar jobs 302, 312
Polycentric corporation 21
Portfolio approach 322
Post-merger integration (PMI)
547–60, 555
four stages 526
process 525
Potential
assessing and developing 285–9,
320–1, 322–32
challenges in developing 328
identifying 289, 322, 324
late identification 325
obstacles 325
transparent judgments on 326
Power distance 97, 98, 360

Pre-industrial era 4–5
Priorities, balancing competing,
    need to 244
Privatization 23
Problem solving, confrontational 223
Procedural
    control 129
    justice 453
        concept of 473n
        importance of 462
Process development role in
    HR 60, 574–7
Procurement function, transformation
    of 183, 184
Product
    customization 170
    innovation 417
    life cycles 71
        speed of 73
Professional service firms
    configurations 406, 407
    personalization in 409
    solution adaptation 409
    tensions in 410
Project management
    capability, essential 195
    cross cultural differences 195
    Japanese strengths 195
    teams 194
    Western strengths 195
Project sequencing 194
Prokurists 304
Psychological
    contract 47, 77n
    empowerment 78n
    profiling 144
Psychometric tests 144
Punctuated equilibrium model 436
Pushback, inevitability of 297n

Quality assurance, world-class 127

R&D Centers
    benefits of global approach to 421
    HP in Bangalore 421
    organization and staffing 420
    Shell's organization of 421

Realigning
    change as 68, 251
    constant, risks from 71
    HRM 65, 65t, 79n
    task, two cycles in 69
Reciprocity, norms of 397
Recruitment 257, 269–75
    advertising 272
    agencies 272
    forecasting 269
    psychological testing 10
    relationships 271
    selection and 56, 57t
Regional headquarters 442
Regionalization 442–4
Relationship, with boss, quality 290
Relationships, as asymmetric 175
Repatriates, knowledge from 415
Repatriation 150
Reporting lines, focus on 14
Resource
    alliance 483
    -based view of firm 29, 33t, 45, 73
    flexibility 469
    utilization, efficient 188
Responsibility
    accountability and 180–1, 181f
    decentralizing 60
Responsiveness
    challenge to differentiate 84
    limits of 117–8
    roots of 83–8
Retention
    acquisitions, in 543
    bonds 290
    compensation 290
    high velocity environments and 293
    key employees as deal breaker 543
    management 257, 416
    managers' accountability for at
        IBM 291
    managing 92–3, 289–93
        internal development and 293
        factors in 92–3
    research into 290
    talent data, access to 543
    turnover 290

Returnees 158
  compensation schemes and 381
Rewards 57t
  selection and 276
  system, design of 366
  variable 54
Risk management, see People risk
    management
Role clarity 150

Salary differentials, alliances 505
Scientific management 8, 32t
Second Life, Shell's suite 420
Seesaw, metaphor of 605
Selection
  as two-way process 277
  bias 278
  focus of literature 298n
  importance of 233
  methods, context and 276
    different 276
  socialization process, as first
    step in 277
Selection and assessment 257
  four issues 275
  managing 275–89
  recruitment distinct from 269
Self efficacy 143
Self-help 60, 337, 577, 588
  at IBM 337
  Five-step learning model 578
Self-management 334–8
Sequenced layering 74
Service centers, HR 59, 61, 577,
    579–80, 583
Service delivery 60, 67
Session C 323
  origins 344n
  process at GE 323t, 327
Set-up-to-fail syndrome 364, 365
Shadowing 594
Silo
  functional 392
    reinforced at Apple 336
  tendency 325
Single European Market 23
SMART targets 460

Social architecture 14, 62, 177, 219
  foundation of 177
  knowledge sharing and 403
  shared values, key part 178
Social capital 33t, 219, 402
  advantages 222
  bridging perspective 221
  building and managing 224
  China and 228
  cognitive dimension 403
  corruption and 230
  darker side of 228–30
  defined 220, 251n
  driver, long-term employment 228
  interlinked dimensions 220–1
  Japanese companies and 229
  leveraging 219–30
  management training and 226
  private good 230
Social
  climate 93
  communications 203
  control, organizational culture
    as 231
  engineering, culture management
    seen as 239
  entity, every organization an 219
  loafing 372
  mechanisms 56
  networking 334
    at IBM, BT, Nestlé 336
    BT's I-Click335
    importance of 219
    research 251n
    self-management and 335
  ties, risk of strong 427–8
  understanding, developing 197
Socialization 20
  balance needed in 238
  employee, managing 236–8
  extensive, at NUMMI 136
  process 237
    emphasis on 218
  see Normative control
Societal cultures 83, 106
Sogo shosha 229
Sparring partner, HR role as 69, 592, 594

Spin-offs 213n
Split egg working 303, 315, 328,
    368, 575
  learning how 210
  skills to be learnt from 315
  working methods 209
  see also Matrix roles
Staffing
  challenge 194
  cross-border teams, in 200
  policies, realigning 161
Stakeholder
  assessment, skills in 457
  identifying key 464
Standardization 132–5, 164n, 266,
    577–8, 583
  regional 135
State of the Art (SOTA) Surveys 40n
Status quo, creating dissatisfaction
    with 463
Stealing with pride 511
Steering through dualities 439–42, 449, 64
  Via HRM 65, 65t
Steering groups
  accountability and 192
  lateral 192–6
  size 195
  traps in managing 195
Stereoptyping 104
Strategic
  advantage, breakdown of historic 23
  agility 62, 63, 467–70
    features of 467
    importance of 73
    organizational culture and 468
  capabilities, positions linked to 330
  HRM 18, 32t
    change and 18
  intent, developing 509
  management, key concern of 45
  partner 78n, 584
  perspective 243
  players 584
  sensitivity, developing 467
Strategy
  -based approach 280, 283–4
  HRM and fit 18

implementation 45
  change, about managing 435, 442
  role of people in 45, 435, 450–463
  industry characteristics 27
  performance, link with 79n
Stretch 419–20
  Google's 70–20–20 rule 420
  goals 352, 358, 387n
Structural holes 252n
Structure, decentralized, weakness
    of 170
Subsidiaries
  foreign, institutional pressures
    on 111
  importance of 182
  importance to multinational 173
  role of in differentiated network 182
  types distinguished by strategic
    importance 213n
Succession
  management 466
  pipeline 96, 270, 286, 309
  planning 288, 332
Supplier audits 588
Supply chain
  coordination, core
    competence 434, 448
  fragmented 171
  reasoning in staffing 266, 272,
    288, 599
Sustainability, impact of economic
    growth 602
Sustainable business performance, 63
  HRM and 42, 598–9
Swift trust 203
Synchronous training 316
Synergy
  gridlock 532
  disappointing concept 439
Systems thinking 9, 32t

Talent
  A, B and C positions 259t
  attracting 269
  build or buy 266–8
  corrosive elements 602
  definition 258

developing, key strength 256
development 32t
forecasting supply and demand 270
global pioneers in 262
hiding as act of corporate
    disloyalty 325
identification, in M&As 543, 558
importance of 261
key employees crucial to acquisition
    goals 557
local, benefits from developing 501
pools 190, 264, 332
    management 332
    origins of 297n
    pools, small 328
portfolio approach 258
retention, in M&As 543, 557,
    558t, 562
    inducements to stay 558
    Key Talent Workshops 559
    acquisition success and 559
reviews, 233
    loss of credibility in 327
    periodic, core HR task 583
    Session C at GE 301
search processes 334
spotting hidden local 344n
supply and demand 259–63
Talent management 9
    activities embraced by 264
    competence logics driving 281t
    competences and 280
    consistency. pressure for 257
    defined 257
    e-based systems for 333
    globalized approach and184
    importance of 257–63
    in M&As, five principles 558
    key challenges 263–8
    long and short term in 294
    mindset 264–5, 291
    retention essential to 263
    retention, key element 289
    reviews, importance of 316
    skills, firm-specific 52–3, 263
    transnational 256
    value, barriers to 264

Targets
    financial 356
    Six-Sigma quality 358
    stretch 358 *see also* Stretch
Team
    appraisal, perception of fairness 371
    -based rewards, aligning individual
        with 372
    culture, conflict resolution dependent
        on 206
    members, performance appraisal
        criteria for 370
    -methods, problem-solving 136
    tightly integrated 126
Teamwork
    appraising and rewarding 207, 370
    competence 285
    Formula 1 and 596
Technology transfer, complexity 446
Temporal consistency 51, 71
Tension
    change not always causing 462
    change, managing 433–75
    constructive 464f
    dynamic, a world of 605
    management, HR's role 607
    management, HRM as 604
    resolving 223
T-groups 9
Theory X 40n, 174
Theory Y 40n, 174
Theory Z 40n
Ties 220–1
    Strong 252n
Time horizon 472n
Total quality management
        (TQM) 100, 114
Total Shareholder Returns (TSR) 80n
Trade barriers 11, 84
Training
    aim of 316
    investment, as good 79n
    just-in-time 316
    power of, McDonald's and 164–5n
    promote-and-then-develop 317
Transfer paradox 427
Transferring managers, motives for 20

Transfers, merits of temporary 500
Transformation 436
  drivers of 173
  process, BP's Project 90 472n
Transition team
  management, dualities and 74
  responsibilities of 552
  team, selection of 547
Transnational approach, towards 288
  change journey 436–49
  concept 33t
  development, path for domestic
    firms 442
    adapting competences to 285
    flexibility in governance of 192
    HR organization in 586f
    developing HR managers for 593
  development, path for
    meganational firms 444–49
    intransitive leadership 443
  managers 243
  organization 4
    birth of 24
    change path to 449
    differentiated 174
    route to 436–50
    transitive model
    dysfunctional for 309
  orientation, firms' 26
  pressures 26
  matrix inspired 27
  top management role 27
Transnationalism, alliances and 519
Transport, advances in 12
Treaty of Rome 12
Trust, importance of 183
T-shaped
  concept 216n
  manager 211

Uncertainty avoidance 97, 505
Uncertainty, 4Is to reduce in
  acquisitions 548
Underperformance, focus on 450
Unions
  consent, in acquisitions 546
  differing structure 109

French 105
  membership 10, 108, 109t
Unit identification, corporate versus
  local 232
Universalism 97, 98t
Universalism-particularism
  dimension 101
Unmeasurables 353

Value chain
  analysis 214n
  close control over 125
  links in 127
Value creation, stimulus in
  multinational corporation 350
Value differences between cultures 103
Value systems 84
Values
  as non-negotiable 239
  Asahi Way 239
  Chinese Way 235
  corporations, shaped by CEOs 235
    stories and sagas 236
  Hewlett-Packard Way 239,
    240, 254n, 597
  jamborees 236, 240
  Japanese corporate 235t
  Lincoln Electric System 239, 597
  monitoring adherence 239
  multinational firms and 230
  philosophy, guiding 597
  process of realigning 240
  shared 231, 233–9
  shared, organization culture and 234
  sharing globally 230–40
  stemming from founders 241
  Toyota Way 230, 239, 597
  traditional Japanese 234
  see also Culture
Values-based
  approach 280, 284–5
  leadership 231, 241
Venture champions, role of 495
Virtual team 199
  communication challenges 204
  cultural differences 203
  difficulties of developing 199

supporting high performance in 208
trust, importance of 203
Virtual teamwork 171, 204–8
Virtual world, Shell's 3D suite 420
Vision building 465
Vitality curve 302
Vocabularies, shared 236

Wa, core Japanese value 369
Wage incentive programs 8
Weak ties 251–2n
Welfare
  programs 32t
  secretaries 8, 10

Work system, transplanting 135–7
  Toyota Way, the 136
Workforce scorecard 357
Working practices, Japanese 136, 137
Work-life
  balance 273
  retention and 290
  programs 291
Work-related values 97
  national culture and 97

Zaibatsu 11
Zentralebereiche 16
Zigzag management pattern 330